SERENITY HOUSE

From Addiction to Deliverance

Ursula V. Battle

SERENITY HOUSE: FROM ADDICTION TO DELIVERANCE

Copyright © 2021 by Ursula V. Battle.

For information contact : Ursula V. Battle

http://battlestageplays.com/uvbs-serenity-house-the-novel.html

First Published 2021 by Coal Under Pressure, LLC
109 Ambersweet Way, 280, Davenport, FL 33897
www.coalunderpessure.com

Book and Cover design by Chrita Paulin, Coal Under Pressure
ISBN : 978-0-9913704-5-0 (Hard Cover)
ISBN: 978-0-9763400-7-2 (Paperback)
ISBN: 978-0-9763400-9-6 (Ebook)
Library of Congress Control Number: 2021908960

First Edition: August 2021
10 9 8 7 6 5 4 3 2

Dedication

To my parents John and Vashtied, children Devin, Vashtied, and Asha, friends Hal O. Arnold, Dr. Gregory Wm. Branch, Dr. E. Lee Lassiter, Tracey Stephenson, Dena Wane, Carol Williams, and all of those who support the vision God placed in me to transform lives through writing. This book is also dedicated to all of those who find themselves in the dark chasm of hopelessness and despair. Never stop believing there is light ahead.

Weeping may endure for a night, but joy cometh in the morning. - Psalm 30:5

Acknowledgments

It was in 2015 that Dr. Gregory Wm. Branch asked me to write a stage play about addiction in response to the opioid crisis. To be perfectly honest, I was hesitant to write a piece that would place the ills and heart-wrenching tales of addiction "center stage." However, after significant pushing and prodding by Dr. Branch and Carol Williams, I finally sat down at my computer one morning and began pecking away at the keys. That morning began what would become my six-year journey in completing first, the stage play, "Serenity House: From Addiction to Deliverance," and now the Novel of the same name. I thank Dr. Branch for asking me to write the groundbreaking piece, which has touched so many lives, and now has taken shape in the form of this book. It is my hope this Novel will encourage people all over the world. I lovingly express my gratitude to all of those who have "played a role" in bringing this book to fruition. First, I humbly give praise and honor to God! The Creator of it all! Without Him, I would not be able to type a single letter, let alone write a book.

I acknowledge my parents, John Battle – an entrepreneur who opened Battle's Barber Shop during the late 1960s and cut generations of hair at his shop at the corner of Mount and Mosher Streets in Baltimore – and my mother Vashtied Battle Brown, who taught Special Education in the Baltimore City Public School System for over 40 years. They not only provided me with love and support but taught me that achievement is not handed to you on a platter. You must earn it…and you earn it by hard work and perseverance. Moreover, they taught me to always put forth my very best effort in all that I do. My sincerest thanks to my stepfather Joseph M. Brown, Jr. who not only taught me how to drive and read a map but gave me treasured insight about navigating this course called "life." He also taught me how to check the oil and transmission fluid of my first car…a red, white, and blue 1972 Ford Pinto. That was important because it taught me at an early age to take good care of the things you have been blessed to have. A special thanks to my siblings, Toni, Tyiese, Jonita, William, Joseph, Tracy, William, John, and Shantel, children Devin, Vashtied, and Asha, and my cousin Debra Brown, who has never missed a show. I acknowledge New Hope Baptist Church on Fremont and Dolphins Streets, founded by my grandfather Rev. Dr. William Nelson Stokes and his wife and my grandmother Vashtied Stokes. My spiritual foundation can be traced to New Hope. Even now, I still vividly recall the sermons preached from that pulpit and the resounding Gospel singing accompanied by the sound of the pipe organ, ringing throughout the neighborhood. And I am always grateful to my paternal grandparents Johnny and Jimmie Lee Battle, servants of the Lord who taught me how to grow my own fruits and vegetables. I will never forget my grandfather's grapevine in the back yard on Penhurst Avenue, nor my grandmother's switches which taught us we better mind what she said.

I also thank New Life Fellowship Worship Center and my Pastor Edward Ferguson, along with his wife Helen, for my continued spiritual growth. Pastor Ferguson has allowed me to minister to the downtrodden, tend to the church's garden, and even preach. All these things have allowed me to discover something new about myself. I also owe a debt of gratitude to Walbrook High School, the Broadcasting Institute of Maryland, Coppin State University, and the University of Baltimore. Each of these schools instilled a standard of excellence, and touted professors who would accept nothing less. Several of them along with the legendary *AFRO-American Newspaper* sportswriter Sam Lacy would mark up my academic papers and news articles with red ink. I didn't like the red ink, but it certainly made me a better writer. Eventually, the red ink was replaced with black or blue ink. I knew I had elevated my writing! I am always grateful to the *AFRO-American Newspaper* (The AFRO) for supporting my work and giving me an opportunity. The AFRO hired me as a Staff Reporter in the late 1990s – my first writing job. So many people in my academic, professional, theatrical, and spiritual walks of life have played such integral "roles" in stretching my creativity to newer and greater heights. Though decades have passed since I ran Track & Field for Ed Waters, Garrison Jr. High School, and Walbrook, I thank Coach Larry McCoy and my other trainers. They taught me about endurance, speed, practice, and to never stop running until I cross the finish line!

I also acknowledge my mentor and friend Dr. E. Lee Lassiter, my Journalism instructor at Coppin State University. A journalistic pioneer, Dr. Lassiter has not only been a constant supporter along with his wife Louise but has inculcated so much knowledge in me about the craft of writing. A great wise man, yet so eloquently humble! A heartfelt thanks to Joy Bramble, Dena Wane, and Kathy Reevie of *The Baltimore Times Newspaper* for publicizing my work in the paper and providing me with an outlet to write about the good news of Baltimore and beyond. I also thank Hal O. Arnold and Valerie Hawkins, who have sold tickets and distributed thousands of promo cards all over Baltimore, and Lee Michaels, John Carrington, and Ernestine Jones who continuously promote my work through the airwaves of radio. A special thanks to Patricia Martin and Dena Wane who have provided valuable feedback from the earliest versions of this work all the way up to its completion! I also thank authors Odessa Rose and Stella Adams for sharing their time, insight, and experiences on authoring a book. Well-deserved kudos also goes to Chrita Paulin, the Editor and Publisher of this Novel. Chrita's thoughtful insight and feedback prompted me to go back and revise the entire book…when I thought it was finished! I wanted this book to be exceptional…my best work… so I followed her suggestions…a process which took several more months. I believe what you will read has made all the tedious work worthwhile.

A standing ovation to the cast and crew of the Serenity House production and our other amazing stage plays. A special thanks to cast members Kim Chase, Rose Hamm, Dravon James, Leonard and Yvonne Stepney, and Stage Manager Sandra Meekins. Under directors Dr. Branch, Tracey Stephenson, and Cheryl Pasteur – all of these wonderful people helped to take my scripts from the page to the stage. I thank Ms. Pasteur for seeing something special in my very first script, Ursula V. Battle's "The Teachers' Lounge" – taking me under her wing and directing my very first production. I also thank Brian and Tracey Stephenson. Tracey has been a constant anchor over the years, serving in a multitude of capacities including director, actress, composer, and singer. Brian has fixed props, portrayed the unforgettable 'Deacon Mumbles,' and provided sound, and transportation. Thanks to Al Beads for ensuring we always have water, pizza, and peppermint puffs during rehearsal! I am grateful for the support of Thelma Rogers and Dr. Tammi Rogers. From props to people in the seats, Ms. Rogers and her daughter Tammi have done so much to support my work. I wish I could name everyone that has helped or contributed in some way but cannot – there are simply too many. I thank each and every one of you for the "role" you played – no matter how big or small. I believe God strategically placed each of you in my life, and all of you in some way, have helped bring this book to fruition. Finally, I thank you, the reader who decided to purchase this Novel! You too, are playing a "part" by reading this story of human resilience, transformation, faith, and the miraculous workings of God. It is my prayer that this story inspires you. Get ready to embark on an incredible journey…

~ Ursula V. Battle

Author's Notes

While some of the dialogue in this book may appear as gross misspellings, the author has purposely written the speech this way to depict the manner in which certain characters speak.

Content Warning: *While Spiritual and Scriptural in nature, this book contains raw descriptions of violence, drug use, nudity, profanity, and sexual encounters. Reader discretion is advised.*

FOREWORD

1F and 1G were just a door away from one another. The apartment building on Hoyt Street in Brooklyn, New York where I grew up was in "the projects." My family lived in Apt.1G, Miss Dorothy, and her three children - Michelle, Michael, and MaKai – lived in Apt. 1F.

Ms. Dorothy was a single mom. She was also hooked on heroin and often overdosed. My father was an ambulance driver and when Ms. Dorothy overdosed, her older children, Michelle and Michael, banged on the steel door of our apartment yelling desperately for my father's help. "Mr. Leroy! Mr. Leroy!" they would scream. For them and for Ms. Dorothy, my Dad, the ambulance driver, was the closest and fastest form of intervention.

What Dad lacked in medical degrees and experience, he made up for in his willingness to do what he could to help anyone in trouble. Each time Ms. Dorothy's children pounded on our door, my dad would rush over and help to resuscitate their mother.

Although this was many decades ago, the sound of those children screaming for someone to help their mother still fills my ears. I was a little boy, but I vividly remember the scenario… Ms. Dorothy overdosing…her children banging on our door for help …and my father running towards Apt. 1F.

A few times, I ran behind him. During one such occasion, I saw my father pull Ms. Dorothy out of an ice-filled bathtub, unresponsive…limp…and dying…and Dad doing whatever he could to bring her back from the other side…wherever that side might have been.

These chaotic moments were always scary, terrifying, and trauma-inducing. I can still see the neighbors on our floor. Some sticking their heads out of their doorways. Others rushing into the hallway. A few standing at the door of Apt.1F – all hoping and praying that my father was able to resuscitate Ms. Dorothy again.

During all of this, my father would "radio in" for help, and paramedics would arrive to take Ms. Dorothy to the hospital. Between the efforts of my father, the paramedics, and the hospital, Ms. Dorothy would survive her brush with death. A few hours later she would be discharged and would sometimes come over to thank Dad.

There was always a collective sigh of relief amongst my family, the neighbors, and most notably, Ms. Dorothy's children. However, the cycle would repeat …over and over and over again...until that day arrived when Ms. Dorothy could not be revived. She died of an overdose.

The horror in Apt. 1F was addiction. This silent, unrelenting assassin lurked patiently until it finally claimed Ms. Dorothy's life.

The horror in Apartment 1F is a grim story that has played on society's stage, time and time again. Addiction grabbing ahold of someone…squeezing and strangling until it finally chokes the life out of them. Ms. Dorothy represents the many men, women, and children who have lost their lives to an addiction that ultimately kills them.

It is the story of Apt. 1F and its inhabitants that prompted me to become a physician. A physician, whom like my late father Leroy P. Branch, Sr., will do whatever it takes to save lives.

Ms. Dorothy also represents the "Cynthia's" of the world, a woman I saw lying lifelessly along North Avenue in Baltimore City on Monday, September 11, 2017. That day, we were holding auditions for the stage play production of "Serenity House: From Addiction to Deliverance" the award-winning production upon which this book is based. I use visual and performing arts to transform lives through my role as a Musical and Theatrical Director.

When I saw "Cynthia" lying outside on the pavement that day, I immediately ran to help her just like my father often ran to help Ms. Dorothy. A man named Clyde was at Cynthia's side. Recognizing me, Clyde began shouting, "Please help her, Doc! Please help Cynthia!" His face wearing the same petrified look I saw on the faces of Michelle and Michael when they knocked repeatedly on the door of Apt. 1G for my father to help their mother.

911 was called, but I handed my car keys to an acquaintance and instructed her to grab the NARCAN from my car. Once the paramedics arrived, they continued to work on "Cynthia". Meanwhile, those who gathered around were all hoping and praying that our efforts would resuscitate Cynthia. Their faces and their actions were exactly like the neighbors outside of Apt. 1F back in Brooklyn those many years ago.

Moments after receiving a couple of doses of NARCAN, Cynthia sat up, dazed and disoriented, but alive. Sadly, she did not seem concerned about the fact that she almost died.

With a gratuitous look on his face that reminded me of Ms. Dorothy's children when she was revived, Clyde exclaimed, "Thank you, Doc! Thank you for helping to save Cynthia's life!"

Ursula V. Battle, the writer of the stage play production of "Serenity House: From Addiction to Deliverance" and the author of this book, felt as I did – that the events of that day were not by happenstance. It reaffirmed our belief that God was in the midst.

He birthed a vision in me that day to present a production centered on addiction to show a dying world there is a better way. I knew without a doubt that I was where I needed to be…when I needed to be…just like Dad was for Ms. Dorothy.

For far too many, (like Ms. Dorothy), there comes a time when there are no more rescues; a time when they take their last 'hit.' I never saw Cynthia again, but often wonder if she finally reached that moment. I pray that is not the case.

We went on to premiere the show to sell-out audiences in 2018, dedicating the performances to Cynthia and the hope for her deliverance. The stage play production of "Serenity House: From Addiction to Deliverance," has received rave reviews, and has touched every audience that has come through the doors of Turner Auditorium at Johns Hopkins Hospital to see it.

I am grateful to Johns Hopkins for affording me the opportunity to co-found Unified Voices of Johns Hopkins. This diverse group of gospel singers spread hope, health, and healing through harmony. We have been able to touch countless audiences through our concerts and stage play productions.

Recently, one of the attendees of "Serenity House: From Addiction to Deliverance," whom we will refer to as "Jackie," shared these words with Ursula and me. "I attended that play when I was in Wilson House, a recovery program for women. That play helped me to get clean. It showed me I had to get to the root of my problem, and I did."

Despite 'The Horror of Apartment 1F' and the many stories like it, "Jackie" represents why Ursula and I do what we do, which is to encourage, uplift, and inspire through our productions. "Jackie" represents "Hope" and serves as a living witness – like many others – that addiction can be defeated. Those who have fallen prey to it can overcome.

That is the goal of the stage play production, and that is the goal of this book.

Finally, while the story you are about to read contains a multiplicity of storylines and characters, the central story centers around one family's struggle with addiction. This book is an extension of the production. The goal is to put a face on the countless number of individuals and families who find themselves caught up in the web of addiction. It is our goal that through this work, stories like 'The Horror of Apartment 1F' will have a better ending. Ultimately, we hope this literary work provides encouragement to people all over the world and illustrates that God can open the door to a better life.

Note: Names and identifying details have been changed to protect anonymity.

Dr. Gregory Wm. Branch is the Director of Health and Human Services and Health Officer for Baltimore County. A native of New York City, Dr. Branch graduated Magna Cum Laude and is a member of Alpha Omega Alpha Honor Society from the State University of New York at Buffalo School of Medicine and Biomedical Sciences. He completed his training at the Johns Hopkins Hospital in the William Osler Internal Medicine Residency Program.

Nationally recognized as a Certified Physician Executive, Dr. Branch earned the Masters of Business Administration degree from the University of Baltimore Merrick School Of Business. He is currently on the faculty at the Johns Hopkins School of Medicine and School of Public Health and is an Adjunct Professor in the Department of Epidemiology and Public Health at the University of Maryland, Baltimore. Dr. Branch has practiced medicine for over 30 years. He is internationally recognized as a Fellow of the American College of Physicians, a mark of distinction representing the pinnacle of integrity, professionalism, and scholarship for those who aspire to pursue careers in Internal Medicine.

Humble in his heart, Dr. Branch is the proud father of two sons, Byron (Brittney) and Allen (Jasmine), and the grandfather of four, Braelyn, London, Tatum, and Noah.

CONTENTS

PART ONE

SERENITY HOUSE: FROM ADDICTION TO DELIVERANCE
PROLOGUE

Welcome to United in Victory Tabernacle located in Baltimore, Maryland. Founded by Bishop Al. B. Wright Just, Sr. in 1956, the non-denominational church is a historic staple in Baltimore. Armed with a calling from God to preach the Gospel of Jesus Christ, outstanding oratorical skills, phenomenal singing ability, and a burning desire to uplift the community through civil rights activism, Rev. Just, Sr. started his ministry in a small East Baltimore rowhouse.

Rev. Just, Sr.'s style of 'fire and brimstone' preaching, intertwined with his dynamic singing ability – a talent leading to his nickname, 'The Singing Preacher', and calls for racial equality from the pulpit, drew crowds from all over the city and surrounding areas. People everywhere were talking about the minister who could not only preach a sermon, but sing it, leading to a rapid increase in new members. By 1957, the church relocated to a small warehouse on Riggs Avenue. However, the burgeoning membership rolls of the church called for an even larger location.

The search for a new church home got underway, spearheaded by a search committee assembled by the young pastor who wanted a beautiful house of worship where all were welcome. During a time where segregation was fashionable and Blacks were being lynched, Pastor Just. Sr. believed the church was the place where people could gather and be lifted up through uncertain, oppressive times through God's Word.

An active member of the Baltimore City Branch of the NAACP (National Association for the Advancement of Colored People), and a Civil Rights activist, Rev. Just, Sr. sometimes hosted the organization's meetings at the church, and needed more space to accommodate attendees. He was also a passionate follower of the Rev. Dr. Martin Luther King, Jr. and strongly supported the Civil Rights Movement. Like Dr. King, he was also a graduate of Morehouse College and a member of Alpha Phi Alpha (APA) Fraternity.

In 1955, Rev. Just., Sr., traveled to Dexter Avenue Baptist Church in Atlanta, Georgia to hear Dr. King preach, and heard his sermon entitled, "The Impassable Gulf (The Parable of Dives and Lazarus). The experience would have a profound impact on Rev. Just, Sr. and play an important role in his future ministry and community outreach work. In what would also become a pivotal moment in the young preacher's life, he met Dr. King after his sermon that day, telling him he was not only a civil rights activist, but also a graduate of Morehouse College and a member of Alpha Phi Alpha Fraternity. The two shared a light-hearted conversation about being Frat (Fraternity Brothers) and fellow Morehouse alums. He and Dr. King also talked seriously about Ministry and the Civil Rights Movement.

Following their short, but moving conversation, Dr. King stunned the 20-year-old minister by jotting down his number on a piece of paper and telling him to stay in touch. Rev. Just, Sr. said he would, tucking what would become one of his most prized possessions – Dr. King's phone number written in the preacher's penmanship – in his jacket pocket. After their initial meeting, Rev. Just, Sr. called Dr. King from time to time and traveled to hear him speak whenever his schedule allowed. This included being among the estimated 250,000 people who witnessed the delivery of Dr. King's famous, 'I Have a Dream' Speech, during the March on Washington in 1963. Dr. King's oratorical masterpiece further fueled the youthful pastor's desire to help eradicate racial hatred, provide needed resources to provide stability for people to live more productive lives, and provide a big enough venue to accommodate large numbers of people to hear the Gospel of Jesus Christ.

Rev. Just., Sr. bore all these things in mind in wanting to relocate his growing congregation to the right location, with the ultimate goal of fulfilling the vision of the church's motto: *'Kingdom-building and winning souls for Christ.'* He also wanted a big enough edifice to accommodate large numbers of people, and the structure to be a living memorial in his honor, long after he was gone.

With their pastor's wishes in mind, the search committee meticulously looked for a new location for their growing church. By 1959, their search came to an end. Pastor Just, Sr. learned a Catholic church was moving from its North Avenue location in Baltimore City to Pikesville, Maryland in Baltimore County. Pastor Just, Sr. had driven past the church many times and always marveled at its majestic architecture, but had never been inside. He directed the committee to arrange a tour of the property and report back to him with their findings and recommendations. The committee scheduled a tour of the property and were awe-struck.

The gray Formstone church touted a bell tower and steeple, which could be seen from miles away. The church featured several large stained-glass windows with mosaic designs and the likenesses of Jesus Christ, the Virgin Mary, the psalmist David, Moses holding a tablet with The Ten Commandments, angels, cherubim, and other religious figures.

A towering crucifix hung from the wall behind a specially-crafted, hand-carved wooden altar. Chandeliers were strung from high ceilings with wooden arches. The church was also outfitted with mahogany pews, a balcony, carpet, choir rooms and a sound system. The upper level of the church was home to a parsonage, and the downstairs included bathrooms, a fully-equipped kitchen, a community food pantry, classrooms, and meeting rooms. The lower-level of the church also included a multi-purpose room to feed large gatherings, and to host banquets, plays, lectures, and other events. A rectory for the priests was housed on the grounds along with a convent for nuns. Between the sanctuary and balcony, the church could comfortably seat up to 1000 congregants. The church's architecture also included a grand organ loft outfitted with a massive organ with towering copper pipes.

The search committee could hardly wait to tell the pastor about their tour and the church's beautiful exterior architecture and its breathtaking interior design. They knew he would love the church and all of its grand amenities. They were right. Pastor Just, Sr. personally toured the church and its grounds and was sold. There was no need to look farther. He felt this church was the perfect location for United in Victory and prayed that God would bless them with the property. The Lord answered his prayers, and the church began the process of purchasing the building.

By 1959, the church was ready to march into its new place of worship. For the special occasion, Pastor Just, Sr., invited his famous friend – Dr. King to preach at the church. Dr. King accepted the invitation, speaking at the church one unforgettable 1959 Sunday. His appearance not only further expanded the popularity and respect of Pastor Just., Sr., but the reputation and notoriety of United in Victory, prompting many more to join the church.

Moreover, Dr. King speaking at the church coupled with a membership comprised mostly of low-paid, African Americans in Jim Crow Baltimore, made the accomplishment of moving to the grand location all the more remarkable. The historic occasion was marked with a weeklong calendar of activities kicked-off with Dr. King speaking at the church. Festivities also included Pastor Just., Sr's name being etched on a cornerstone brick, along with the year the church was founded. The brick also read: *Upon this rock I will build my church; and the gates of hell shall not prevail against it* – Matthew 16:18.

United in Victory now had a magnificent, new location along with a large, faithful congregation, which now included several White Catholics who remained from the previous church. Now, Rev. Just., Sr. felt the church needed a musician. A lover of Hymns and Gospel Music, and a talented Baritone singer himself, Rev. Just, Sr. was eager to grow the church's Music Ministry. Throughout its young history, the church would pay various musicians to play for Sunday worship services and special events. However, Pastor Just, Sr. wanted to hire a permanent musician.

He and United in Victory's Board of Trustees immediately began a search for the right musician. The musician had to strike just the right balance of talent, leadership, and innovation. The successful candidate would be charged with playing the massive organ and serving as Director of the church's Mass Choir. Additionally, the successful candidate would be responsible for the establishment of a Youth Choir at United in Victory and orchestrating large concerts.

Rev. Just, Sr. would encourage a friend and 'Frat Brother' from Morehouse College by the name of Malachi Madison to apply for the job. The two met in Pastor Just, Sr's senior year in college. Mr. Madison was a freshman, but the young musician's talents, particularly on the Hammond B3 organ, quickly brought him fame all over the campus. The highly sought-after musician applied for the job at United in Victory and stood tall among the talented pool of applicants.

In 1960, Pastor Just and the Board unanimously chose the talented and handsome Mr. Madison as the church's musician. Consequently, it came with a high price. In accepting his new post, the brash musician first provided the committee with a list of requirements, which included the church purchasing a multi-tiered Hammond B3 electric organ and that it be added to the loft. The committee met his list of expensive requirements, purchasing the costly organ for him to play. Mr. Madison's list also included a private office area with new furniture, access to various areas of the church, a personal driver, and that buttered croissants, fresh strawberries, and water chilled with exactly ten ice cubes and a wedge of lemon be prepared for him every Sunday morning before service. The committee complied at the behest of Pastor Just, Sr., but some privately mumbled their new musician was a 'Premadonna'.

Despite grumblings amidst their inner circle, the Trustee Board all admitted they never heard anyone play a Hammond B3 like Malachi Madison. Nicknamed 'The Adonis of Music' because of his fine looks, Mr. Madison was the musical version of the painter *Rembrandt* on the Hammond B3 – a Master. Under the tutelage of Mr. Madison, the church's Mass Choir quickly became what many considered to be the best in the city.

With Mr. Madison, came a certain *je ne sais quoi*. A showman who was always dressed to the nine, he was highly entertaining, his theatrics on the organ comparable to an actor on a *Broadway* stage. The musician perched high on the organ loft was a grand scene full of pomp and circumstance and was talked about far and wide.

By 1962, Rev. Just, Sr. earned a Doctorate in Theology from Loyola College (now University), and on April 19, 1963, he, and Amanda, had their first and only child, Al B. Wright, Just, Jr. He would groom his namesake to become the church's next leader. The year 1963 was also marked with Dr. Madison earning a Doctorate in Music and being named the church's *Minister of Music*.

As word continued to spread about Dr. Just's thunderous sermons accented by his singing ability, and now, the skillful hands of Dr. Madison chording behind him, worship services and concerts drew standing-room only crowds. United in Victory's harmonious Mass Choir which also had its fair share of monumental singers, only added to the church's infamy. However, many people jammed into the church for the sole purpose of seeing and hearing Dr. Madison play the church's famed Hammond B3. His brilliance, and God-given ability on the organ were simply unmatched.

Dr. Madison helped put United in Victory on the musical map. Under his leadership came the development and establishment of a Youth Choir. The church had many talented children, and they budded under Dr. Madison. Like their older counterparts, the Youth Choir also drew large numbers to the church, whose coffers continued to grow along with its membership. At its height, the church boasted well over 1,000 members.

The riots of 1968 following the death of Dr. King would mark another historic chapter in United in Victory. Pastor Just., Sr. was deeply grieved by the loss of his friend. Despite his mourning and anger over Dr. King's assassination, Rev. Just., Sr., took to the streets to calm tempers and to remind people of the slain Civil Rights leader's message of non-violence. The era also ushered in more Blacks moving to the area as more and more Whites began to move out. Catholics in other areas of the city were also selling their churches and relocating elsewhere – 'White flight' opening a pathway for many Black churches to move into the beautiful structures.

Despite the rioting and looting, and a mass exodus of their counterparts, the White Catholics who became members of United in Victory after the building was sold by their former religious leaders remained at the church. Many were also subjected to backlash, but bravely remained, subsequently playing a vital role in the church's make-up reflecting not only Baptists, but growing to include more Catholics, followed by Episcopalians. This diverse make-up led many to fondly call the church 'United in Victory Tabernacle on the Hill Freewill, Baptist, Catholic and Episcopal Church of God in Christ.'

In 1970, Dr. Just was consecrated as a Bishop. By this time, the church had many Boards and Ministries. He had also established a Community Outreach Ministry. Through the ministry, the church distributed hot meals and groceries through its Food Pantry. The Ministry also oversaw clothing distribution efforts, and even provided monetary assistance to those struggling to pay rent and utility bills. The church's parsonage offered temporary shelter to those who had fallen on hard times.

The Lord continued to bless United in Victory. In 1971, a huge parcel of land next door to the church went up for sale. The church purchased the property and began to discuss plans for their new land. Due to difficulty in finding parking near the church, the congregation overwhelmingly wanted a new parking lot. The aging members wanted the church to open a senior building. Dr. Just decided to give its congregation both.

In 1972, plans began to move forward on the paving of a new parking lot and erecting a senior building on the church's newly acquired property. In 1973, the church broke ground on the land, which was marked with a momentous Groundbreaking Ceremony.

However, in 1973, a peculiar and unfortunate event also took place. Bishop Just's wife Amanda went missing. No one had a clue as to what had happened to Mrs. Just. She seemingly vanished into thin air, her unexplainable disappearance leaving the Bishop to raise their then 10-year-old son Al, Jr. The strange occurrence also caused the church's rumor mill to turn, as members began speculating about what could have happened to their beloved 'First Lady'. As the congregation wondered, and the Bishop mourned, the church continued to chug forward with its capitol plans.

In 1974, the church parking lot was completed. In 1976, construction of the senior building – complete with its own parking lot, was finished. Both were marked with memorable ceremonies. The stately senior building was named 'Bicentennial Towers' in commemoration of 1976 being America's *Bicentennial Year*, the 200th anniversary of the Declaration of Independence. Building upon that theme, the residential facility would celebrate the longevity of seniors and independent living. In 1977, *Bicentennial Towers*, opened for occupancy.

Over the years, other capital projects and renovations at United in Victory have included the rectory being converted into a church house, and the convent receiving upgrades to accommodate the church's nuns.

Between its 'Singing Preacher' – a highly-recognized Bishop, the church's charity, its famous Music Ministry, and the fervent prayers and other works of its leader, elders, evangelists, deacons, and other members of its congregation, the church was fulfilling its vision. Under the spiritual leadership of its pastor and founder Bishop Al B. Wright Just, Sr., United in Victory was revered for its *good works* within and outside its church walls.

In 2009, the younger Just succeeded his then 74-year-old father Bishop Just as the church's pastor. Attributed to his worsening Dementia, the Bishop shouted some obscenities from the pulpit. The memorable event shocked the congregation, and ultimately led to his 46-year-old son becoming the pastor of United in Victory.

The younger Just wanted to build on the great works of his father and was also drawn to outreach. He was troubled by what was happening to the community, painfully watching the surrounding neighborhoods slowly crumble under the weight of poverty, drug trafficking, gangs, violence, and addiction.

To the chagrin of many congregants, Pastor Just, Jr. decided United in Victory needed to take a more active role in combatting addiction. His unwavering position prompted fierce disagreement and murmurings amongst his church members.

From its inception until now, United in Victory's congregation is intricately woven into its historical quilt. Members come with their own distinctive set of traits and personalities. Some are living, while others are deceased. Some joined the church and stayed, while others joined the church and left. Whatever the circumstance, each congregant has contributed their own unique fiber to the church's colorful patchwork.

Welcome to the world of United in Victory Church.

With the church as its marvelous backdrop, a multitude of intriguing characters and eye-popping events comprise the fascinating narrative of United in Victory. Stories of alimony and matrimony, friction and feuds, hymns and mayhem, holiness and haughtiness, malice and miracles, set-ups and cover-ups, sanctity and scandal, The Gospel and gossip, temptation and triumph, sin and salvation, and even murder are all nestled within this church's history. Now, the untold stories are being told.

From the Annals of United in Victory Church, comes the story of ***Serenity House: From Addiction to Deliverance.***

PART ONE

CHAPTER ONE

ADDICTION

Baltimore, Maryland
Thursday, July 30, 1998

Summer of 1998

Michael "Lil Mike" Thomas laid in his bed at his home on Gwynns Falls Parkway with his eyes tightly closed. The eight-year-old could feel the warmth of sun rays beaming through his bedroom window onto his face. He could hear the birds chirping from the trees near his home. The sound of cars and Mass Transit Administration (MTA) buses driving up and down his busy street filled the youngster's ears. Lil' Mike lazily opened his eyes and tilted his neck towards his bedroom window. The bright, clear, blue skies reflected in his big dark-brown eyes. It was a beautiful spring morning in Baltimore City. However, Lil Mike was not receptive to the sights and sounds of a new day. It had been a long night. He had gotten little sleep and was still tired. The piercing cries of his infant sister, Angel Adams, kept him up throughout the night. His mother, Melvina A. Thomas, had also kept him running up and down the steps of their Northwest Baltimore rowhouse to retrieve Angel's baby bottles. Lil' Mike repeated the routine several times throughout the night. It entailed getting out of his warm bed, going downstairs to the kitchen, taking a bottle out of the refrigerator, warming it up in the microwave, and handing it to his mother before trudging back upstairs. Between Angel's constant crying and his mother bellowing out his name to get baby bottles, Lil' Mike barely got a wink of sleep.

"I can't believe it's already morning," he muttered as he yanked his bedcovers over his head.

Just as he drifted back to sleep, came the unnerving sound of Angel crying. Her cries had repeatedly shattered the silence of nighttime. Now daytime, her wailing had once again awakened him. They reminded Lil' Mike of the loud shrill of an unwanted alarm clock. Lil Mike knew what was coming next. He sunk deeper beneath his covers and curled into a fetal position beneath. Then came the inevitable sound of his mother's yell.

"Lil Mike!" she bellowed from the downstairs living room.

"I know, I know," he grumbled under his breath. "Get the baby's bottle."

"Did you hear me Lil' Mike?!"

"Yes ma'am!" he responded as he slid out of his bed. "Coming!"

Lil' Mike rubbed his eyes as he walked over to the calendar taped on his bedroom wall. Since learning how to read a calendar in school, he would mark off each new date.

"Thursday, July 30th, 1998," said Lil' Mike, marking off the date with a black marker. "It's only been about two weeks since mama brought Angel home from the hospital, but all she does is cry. She never stops crying. Mama says storks deliver babies to the hospital. Sometimes, I wish the stork would take Angel back to the hospital."

Angel was born in May. However, she stayed in the hospital for more than two months before being brought home. When Lil' Mike asked his mother why she did not bring Angel home with her from the hospital, she told him Angel was sick. She also told him Angel was born earlier than expected and needed to stay in the hospital.

Lil' Mike couldn't wait for his sister to be brought home. His Aunt Caroline brought the baby to the house for his mother. But Angel coming home wasn't anything like Lil' Mike expected. He had no idea his new sister would cry and fuss so much. Sometimes it seemed like nothing would stop her crying. Lil' Mike likened her crying to his former classmate Darryl Mathias. Darryl would annoy everyone by running his fingernails across the green chalkboards whenever their teacher left the classroom. Lil' Mike and the other students would cover their ears. They hated the cringing sound. Angel's screeching crying reminded Lil' Mike of Darryl's chalkboard antics. Similarly, her cries were just as constant and just as annoying.

Angel was also tiny and frail. His mother always made him feed her. But she was so small, Lil' Mike feared he would mistakenly drop her on the floor. Lil' Mike liked his new role as a big brother. He loved his new sister. But he never thought his mother would depend on him so much to help take care of her.

"Get the baby's bottle, feed the baby, change the baby, watch the baby," he grumbled to himself. "Mama wants me to do everything!"

Before heading downstairs, Lil' Mike picked up his book, *I Rose ABOVE it All* by Ursula V. Battle, from the dresser. Santa Claus left the book for him under the tree last Christmas. For weeks, he had been working hard to learn "I Rose ABOVE it All," one of the book's poems. Lil' Mike knew his mother loved that poem, and he wanted to memorize every word.

Lil' Mike opened the book to the page he had bent. That was his bookmark. Before heading downstairs to help his mother with the baby, he wanted to read over a section of the poem. This was the part he memorized so far. He did his best to concentrate in an effort to drown out Angel's crying. In his mind, Lil' Mike had formulated his own idea as to what each line of the poem meant. As he read Battle's lines aloud, he acted out his own ideologies of them.

"With the arrows of your words, you've shot me again; Piercing a piece of my heart so hard to mend," Lil' Mike exclaimed, gesturing his hands and arms as if he were releasing an arrow from its bow. "You say success is something I'll never taste; Feasting on the sadness that besets my face," he cried, pretending to gobble down food. "You delight in seeing me in my lowest place; Pain and hurt you love to paste!" he cackled hanging his head. "As if life were a piece of paper and you were the glue – taking his glue stick, school scissors, and new composition notebook off a shelf – "Affixing shapes of bitterness in all you do," he bellowed, cutting a triangle, and pasting it onto one of the sheets.

"Soon I'm gonna know the entire poem by heart," he happily exclaimed. "Mama's gonna be so proud of me! Boy, will she be surprised!"

Lil Mike's blissful moment was interrupted by Angel's bawling. Reciting and acting out the poem temporarily took his mind off her cries. But now, her cries seemed unrelenting.

"I wish Angel would shut up," he grumbled.

"Lil' Mike!" his mother screamed. "What's taking you so long to come downstairs?! Don't you hear the baby crying?"

"Coming Mama!" Lil' Mike closed the book and placed it on his bedroom dresser. He headed towards the door, silently fussing about the resumption of the routine that had gone on all night. "Why did Mama and Daddy ask the stork to bring them a baby and make me do all the work?" he wondered scooting down the flight of stairs.

"Angel's bottle is in the microwave," said his mother. "What were you doing?"

"Reading, Mama."

"Well, it damn sure took you long enough to get down here! Now take your ass in the kitchen and get your sister's bottle out of the microwave! Shit! She's about to drive me up the motherfuckin' wall with all this damn cryin!"

"Okay, Mama."

Lil' Mike slid a kitchen chair over to the counter and stepped onto it so he could reach the microwave. He was smaller than many of the kids his age. His mother told him it was because he was born early. After grabbing Angel's bottle out of the microwave, Lil' Mike stepped down from the chair and headed back to the living room.

Lil' Mike's mother always laid sprawled out on the living room couch when she was home. There was a time when his mother would sleep in the upstairs bedroom. Lil' Mike liked that much better. She was closer to his room at night when it was dark. That made him feel safer. But ever since his mother changed, all she wanted to do was lay across that disgusting couch.

Lil' Mike was with his mother when she purchased the couch from a furniture store on Pratt Street. He was about five at the time and remembered the outing well. He helped her pick it out. It was white when she purchased it. Not anymore. The dirt was so consuming the couch took on a permanent brown hue.

"A few more shades, and it'll be black," Lil' Mike thought to himself.

Not only was the couch all dirty, but the cushions were stained with pee. The cushion reeked of urine, and so did his mother. Nowadays, she always seemed to smell bad. That was not always the case, but so many things had changed when it came to Mama.

He recalled the good ole days when Mama took him places all the time. Every Friday, they went to Lexington Market.

"Friday is payday and fish fry day at our house," she always said.

Lil' Mike had fond memories of their outings to Lexington Market. The fish was on display at stalls throughout the busy indoor marketplace. He always felt the fish was staring at him as they laid on the glistening ice chips. Mama stopped at one of the stalls, looked at the fish, checked the prices, used paper towels to pick up the ones she wanted, and dropped the fish onto a large piece of white paper. She always went to the same man. She called him the 'Fish Man". He grabbed the paper holding the fish, plunked it down onto a scale with big numbers that resembled a funny clock that didn't tell time, told her how much was owed, and she paid him.

Lil' Mike loved going to Lexington Market. The sights and sounds were so much fun. He enjoyed watching the non-stop bustling of activity. Men sat high-up in chairs like kings getting their shoes shined. Grown-ups pushed their children around in strollers and toted babies in sacks that hung from their backs. Sometimes, he saw his classmates from school with their parents and Mama ran into people she knew from their neighborhood and church.

A medley of smells, including cotton candy, fried chicken, hot peanuts, pastries, and other delicious aromas filled the air. All kinds of meats, cheeses, cakes, cookies, candies and other foods and sweets were also on full display in glass cases. He saw strange things like pig tails and pig ears in the cases. He even saw entire pig heads. Lil' Mike didn't like those. They looked too scary. Mama looked carefully in the glass meat case until she saw just the right piece of fatback. "I'll take that piece of fatback right there," she said pointing to the red and white-colored meat. He thought fatback was a piece of a person's back. But he just couldn't imagine his mother cooking a part of someone's back. One day he asked her, "What is fatback?" With a chuckle, she said, "Son, fatback is the salt-cured backside of a hog. It's a secret ingredient in some of the best, finger-lickin' Southern cookin' you can put in that belly of yours. But don't tell nobody I told you about fatback being my secret ingredient. That's our little secret."

Mama also made a pit stop at one of the lunch meat places to buy a quarter-pound of hog head cheese and a quarter pound of American cheese. He liked the American cheese, but not the hog head cheese. He tried it once but didn't like the way it tasted. "Ewww," he told her after biting into a piece. "It's too sour." But his mama loved it.

His mother also stopped past the Utz potato chip booth to buy two bags of potato chips. One for him and one for her. She told him that was the best place in Baltimore to get fresh potato chips. His mama also liked to stop by Rheb's Candy to buy pieces of chocolate. She would purchase four for herself and let him pick out any two pieces he wanted.

As his mother made her rounds around the big market, she also grabbed a bag of hot peanuts from Konstant's Peanuts. Those were for his father, Michael "Big Mike" Adams. Daddy really liked those peanuts. But he made such a mess when he ate them. He dropped peanut shells all over the floor, and Mama had to clean them up.

After Mama bought peanuts for Daddy, the two walked over to a place in Lexington Market called Mary Mervis. She ordered and paid for a corned beef sandwich on rye bread with mustard for his Aunt Caroline. Aunt Caroline was his father's sister and really loved those sandwiches.

Their outing continued as they walked towards the back of Lexington Market to get crab cakes from Faidley's Seafood. His mother told him they were for her and Daddy. As they walked towards Faidley's, Lil' Mike watched men and women stand at a counter and slurp down oysters and clams. Bottles of hot sauce sat in front of them on the counter. Some shook hot sauce on their oysters and clams before gulping them down. Others ate them with boiled eggs. Lil' Mike didn't want any clams or oysters. They looked too slimy. Yuck! He thought whenever he saw people eating them. He silently wondered if they were unknowingly swallowing pearls as they gulped them down one after another.

People of all colors shopped and worked at Lexington Market. It was like an adventure. Something new always awaited, and no two trips were ever alike.

Before they left Lexington Market, Mama always bought him a big, pretty, red candy apple. He loved candy apples. However, she wouldn't let him eat his delicious confection until after he ate dinner. In one hand, he held his candy apple, whilst his mother toted a bag full of things she bought from Lexington Market. Lil' Mike could hardly wait to get home and eat the delicious dinner his mother prepared. Then he could gobble down his candy apple.

When they arrived home, Mama turned on the oven and seasoned and battered the fish before she dropped each piece into a hot skillet of Crisco cooking oil. As the fish fried in the sizzling grease, she headed to the cupboard and pulled out a box of Jiffy cornbread mix. She poured the cornbread mix into her favorite mixing bowl and added eggs, milk, a can of creamed corn, a pinch of nutmeg, and other ingredients. She let him stir the batter around and around until all the lumps were gone. Once it was nice and smooth, Mama set the mix on the side. She pulled her big, burnt-looking skillet from a cabinet, put it on the stove, and turned the pilot up high. She removed the fatback she bought from Lexington Market from its package and dropped it into the square cast iron skillet.

"I won't tell anybody about our secret ingredient," he told her.

"You better not," she replied with a smile.

After the fatback naturally made its own grease, Mama poured it off into the awaiting batter. She removed the piece of fatback from the skillet, chopped it into small pieces which she called cracklin, and drizzled them in with the bowl's other ingredients before pouring the mix into the piping hot skillet.

"This is gonna be some good eatin," said Mama as she popped the mix into the now-heated oven.

As the cornbread baked, she opened another can of creamed corn, poured it into a small pot, and added butter, sugar, pepper, and other seasonings. As the creamed corn bubbled on the stove, she made a large pitcher of Kool-Aid and spooned in cupful after cupful of sugar until it was thick like syrup. As she stirred the Kool-Aid, Lil Mike grabbed two Styrofoam cups and placed them on the counter. Once she finished stirring the Kool-Aid, and it was sweet enough to her liking, Mama filled the two cups with the syrupy mix and put them in the freezer to make frozen cups which they ate later. The best part was licking the syrupy top of the frozen cup and then turning it upside down to slurp its juicy bottom.

If it wasn't Kool-Aid she fixed to drink with dinner, it was Sweet Tea. She put a pot of water on the stove, plunked in several Lipton teabags, and boiled them on the stove until they were immersed in hot bubbles. After turning off the pot, Mama spooned in heaping after heaping of sugar, slurping dribbles off the spoon tip as she went along until it tasted sweet enough. She set the tea aside to cool and sometimes added more sugar after it cooled down.

Soon, the delicious smells of fried fish, baked cornbread, and creamed corn filled the whole house. Lil' Mike couldn't wait to eat. And when he did, the taste was worth the wait.

"Mama, this food is soooooo good!" he said.

"Thanks, Lil' Mike," she replied. "And watch out for those fish bones. Mama don't want you to choke."

However, those days were long gone. Mama never went to Lexington Market. Not anymore — because she never cooked anymore. I sure miss Lexington Market, he often thought. Especially those candy apples.

Lil' Mike also missed the good meals she cooked. Since Mama turned into a different person, most of our meals come from the microwave or fast-food restaurants. Nowadays, his mama always cooked packs of Oodles of Noodles. His mother once told him they were cheap and easy to fix. But he was tired of eating Oodles of Noodles all the time. Their refrigerator and cupboards were once full. But now, the cupboards were bare, and the refrigerator was always empty.

Aunt Caroline would make a big fuss about the empty refrigerator when she stopped by the house. He recalled Aunt Caroline asking Mama why there was no food in the house when she received food stamps.

"Did you and Michael sell those food stamps again?!" Aunt Caroline yelled from the kitchen as she opened and closed the refrigerator and cabinets. "You and Michael need to be ashamed of yourselves!"

All his mother would do is nod off on the couch. "Get your coat, nephew!" said Aunt Caroline before taking him to McDonalds to buy him a Happy Meal. He liked those. Especially the French fries and toys. She also bought groceries for the house. But she no longer visited, and he really missed Aunt Caroline.

School was out for summer vacation, but Lil' Mike could hardly wait for the school year to start. He attended Gwynn's Falls Elementary School, where he would start third grade in the fall. He felt the meals at school were much better than the ones he ate at home. At school, the menu changed each day. Some days, the ladies in the cafeteria served pizza. That was his favorite. Other days they served cheeseburgers and French fries. He liked that meal too. They also served Sloppy Joe on buns. That was his least favorite. He didn't like soggy bread. At home meals were always the same. Cold food Mama brought home from fast-food restaurants or Oodles of Noodles. Before she changed, his mama would get up early and cook a good breakfast. Scrambled eggs, bacon, grits, home fries, and homemade pancakes. Yummy! She would put butter on my pancakes and drizzle them with King Syrup.

"Those pancakes were so good. And she always poured me a glass of orange juice too. Mama used to be the best cook in the whole wide world."

After his mother stopped cooking, Lil' Mike started eating breakfast at school. That was the only way he could eat a nice, hot breakfast. But now to eat breakfast, he had to arrive at school early. Before she changed, his mother walked him to school when he was in pre-k, kindergarten, and first grade. During that time, he was never late to school. But halfway through second grade, things changed. A former early riser, she began to sleep late into the morning. After waking his mother up, he pleaded with her to take him to school. After fussing at him for waking her up, she snored back off to sleep. She finally got up, but by the time she walked him to school, he was late. Sometimes, he didn't make it to school at all. Lil' Mike was halfway through second grade and didn't want to fail because he was late or absent too many times.

Lil' Mike loved school and didn't like arriving late and getting a late pass. He especially did not like being marked absent. He also didn't want to miss breakfast. When he was hungry, he sat in class thinking about food. His stomach growled so loudly in class he knew his classmates could hear. This was embarrassing. So, to eat breakfast, be on time, and avoid awakening his mother, Lil' Mike began walking to school. The hot meals were worth the walk.

For a youngster his age, the nine-block walk to school was treacherous and dangerous. Once Lil' Mike left his home, he crossed several side streets until he reached the busy intersection of Gwynns Falls Parkway and Dukeland Street where his school was located. Sometimes, Lil Mike would leave so early that he would arrive before the school's crossing guard. On those days, he would have to cross the busy intersection all alone. Back when she walked him to school, his mother taught him to look both ways when crossing the street. He knew how to cross the street, but crossing this busy street sometimes scared him. He would look both ways and quickly dart across when the cars stopped coming. He was always careful. But one time, he almost got hit by a car.

Despite the scary trek to school, he preferred it this way. Mama looked so bad, that he didn't want the other students to see her walking him to school. He knew they would tease him, and he didn't want to get in any fights. He was not about to allow anybody to joke or crack on Mama.

Lil' Mike stood in the living room entranceway still holding Angel's bottle. He watched as Mama incessantly rocked the crying infant. His mother looked like a madwoman.

"Mama never used to look like this," he thought. Now she looks like this all the time. Her hair was sticking up all over her head. It reminded Lil' Mike of how the characters on the cartoons looked when they got electrocuted or were scared out of their wits.

Once again, Lil' Mike got caught up in the moments of yesteryear. Back when his mama got her hair done at Miss Henrietta's Beauty Salon. He thought about the pink smock Miss Henrietta wore. It was all covered in splotches of hair dye. Her name "Miss Henrietta" was stitched on the front in cursive handwriting.

Miss Henrietta had black hair and brown skin. When she talked, she always put her hands on her hips. Lil' Mike thought she looked and acted a lot like 'Florence' – a maid on a television show called "The Jeffersons". His mother used to watch that show all the time. Lil' Mike hated going to Miss Henrietta's salon with his mama. He would frown his face every time she told him she was going there. He would have to sit and behave for hours and hours. He could judge the wait time based on the number of ladies who were there when they arrived. One, two, three, four, five, six he counted to himself. Sometimes, there would be less. Sometimes, there would be more.

Miss Henrietta and some of the other ladies would always pinch his cheeks and tell him he was cute. Whenever he and his mother walked into her shop, Miss Henrietta would stop whatever she was doing to rush over to him. She would stoop down and tell him how fast he was growing and give him a wet, sloppy kiss. Just like the ladies at church. But at church, their breath smelled like peppermints. But Miss Henrietta's breath smelled like stinky onion pickles and pickled pig feet. Lil' Mike would see them in big jars at the neighborhood corner stores his mama sometimes frequented. Between doing hair, Miss Henrietta would stop and nibble on onion pickles and pickled pig feet and talk about how good they were. They might taste good, Lil' Mike thought to himself, but they make her breath smell bad. Sometimes, with a shop full of customers, she would leave to pick up lunch and sit and eat it while the ladies all waited.

He recalled the sign taped to a glass pane on the shop's front door. It read, "Walk-ins Welcome." His teachers always told him he was an excellent reader. Lil' Mike always hoped that no one paid attention to the sign. More ladies coming in meant they would be there even longer. Every now and then, a "walk-in" lady came through the door. Lil' Mike never saw Miss Henrietta turn away a customer. Miss Henrietta would stop working, walk over to the walk-in lady, and carry on a long conversation. Lil' Mike would exhale. It was going to be another long day at Miss Henrietta's salon.

During the long wait, Lil' Mike took naps. When he awoke, he kept himself busy. He colored and doodled in the activity books his mama told him to bring along. The activity of the salon was also a source of entertainment. It was always buzzing with chatter. The ladies talked non-stop. They discussed all kinds of grown-up things. They talked about their husbands' good jobs. They talked about the new cars their husbands bought for them. They talked about how their husbands and boyfriends were "acting up". They talked about their children and grandchildren. They talked about the sales being offered at the stores. They talked about what was going on in their churches. They talked about their jobs. As Ms. Henrietta washed, permed, curled, styled, dyed, or made their hair straight with a hot comb, she shared her views on the topics of discussion. When Lil' Mike's mother was a good mama, she always told him that cursing and using the "N-Word" was bad. But Miss Henrietta and some of the other grown-ups did both.

Lil' Mike recalled a lady in the salon telling the others about her plight at home. Her husband wanted her to iron all his clothes – including his underwear.

"Now I can understand you ironing your husband's trousers and shirts," Miss Henrietta told the lady while curling her hair. "But I ain't ironing no nigger's drawers!"

All the ladies laughed, while another commented, "Well Henrietta, I guess that's why you ain't got a husband!"

"And it's gonna stay that way if a man expects Henrietta to iron his damn drawers!" said the hairstylist as she stopped curling and put her hands on her hips. "I'll be damned! I use my hands for a lot of things. But one of them won't be ironing no nigger's drawers!"

Once again, the ladies all laughed.

Amidst the chatter and occasional bursts of laughter, the steady hum of hairdryers and the smell of perm filled the air. Lil' Mike hated the smell of perm.

"Phew," he thought. "That perm stuff smells like rotten eggs."

He watched as Miss Henrietta mixed up colors and put them in the ladies' hair. Most of the ladies got black color. Others got brown. Some ladies even got blue. "Why would someone want blue hair?" He wondered.

After putting the color in their hair, Miss Henrietta would slap a plastic bag on their heads and set them under a hairdryer. The plastic bags reminded Lil' Mike of the ones worn by the lunch ladies in the school cafeteria.

Lil' Mike could still recall the smell and sound of Miss Henrietta straightening some of the ladies' hair with a hot comb. The hair grease she put on their hair sizzled and crackled as she ran the hot comb through it. The smell of hot hair and grease filtered through the shop. He once asked Miss Henrietta what that way of making hair straight was called.

"Pressing, Sugar," she responded.

Pressing. That's how Miss Henrietta did his mama's coal, black hair. Then she would curl it nice and pretty.

Miss Henrietta also put in Gheri Curls. Lots of them. It was a popular style and many people had them. But Lil' Mike hated when Miss Henrietta put one of those in. They took such a long time. "I wish Miss Henrietta would hurry up and finish their greasy heads," he thought as he impatiently watched her put them in the heads of both men and women.

During the course of the morning, Miss Henrietta would walk over to the television. No matter what everyone was already watching, she would turn the channel knob to "The Price Is Right". She said that was her favorite show. Then the ladies would guess what they thought was the correct pricing on the show's various games, including the Showcase Showdown. They would comment on how dumb some of the contestants' answers were. As the day wore on, they would watch soap operas and talk about them.

Ladies and sometimes men sat under hairdryers, back at the shampoo bowl, or simply waiting for Miss

Henrietta to get started on their hair. The luckiest person would be the one sitting in Miss Henrietta's black swivel chair getting their hair hot combed, curled, or activator sprayed in his or her Gheri Curl because that person's hair was almost done. The unlucky ones still had a long wait, and Lil' Mike's mama was one of them. All he could do was try to keep himself busy until it was time for his mama to sit in the swivel chair. We're gonna be here forever, Lil' Mike thought as he sighed.

"Mama, why do you and these other ladies have to wait so long just to get your hair fixed?" he once asked his mother during an appointment.

"Because we all want our hair to look good," she replied.

"That's right," Miss Henrietta chimed in as she curled. "And as long as your mama and all these other gals in here got money, they can come all they want."

His mother and the other grown-up ladies all laughed, Lil' Mike shrugging his shoulders. He couldn't understand why they all thought what Miss Henrietta said was so funny. "I wasn't even talking to Miss Henrietta".

Now, Lil' Mike only thought this to himself. He knew better than to ever dare say such a thing out of his mouth. His mama would have smacked his lips clear across the floor. She had taught him good manners. He knew better than to disrespect, question, or talk back to grown-ups. Smart talk would have been grounds for a beating.

Then there was this lady named Miss Brenda who always came into the salon. She was always selling something. All the ladies – including Miss Henrietta - would flock over to her to see what she had inside of the big tote bag she always carried. Miss Brenda sold all kinds of things. Clothes, shoes, jewelry, bottles of aspirin, soap, detergent, jewelry, hair care products…you name it. They called her "Brenda Da Booster." His mother told him they called her that because she was always stealing things from the store and then selling them.

Lil' Mike couldn't understand why anyone would take things from a store without paying for them, so he asked his mother. "Drugs make people do all kinds of things," was his mama's response. "Steal, lie, whatever. Just make sure you never get tangled up in no drugs."

As he looked at his mother sprawled across the sofa he had come to hate, Lil' Mike only wished she had taken her own advice.

His mama stopped going to Miss Henrietta's salon when he was six. That was two years ago. Although he didn't like the long waits, Miss Henrietta made his mama's hair look pretty. Now, it always looked ugly. Lil' Mike used to hate it when his mother went to Miss Henrietta's. Now, he wished she would go back. He felt Miss Henrietta could make his mama look pretty again.

Not only was his mama's hair a mess, but the hair had sprouted beneath her chin and underarms like flowers from seeds. Her underarms used to be nice and smooth. Every morning, she would bathe and put on deodorant, good-smelling perfume, and oils. Now, her underarms were unshaven and smelled all funky.

"Mama never used to look like this," Lil' Mike thought. "And her underarm hair is all nappy. And they stink."

Her underarm hair reminded him of Bobby Jennings, one of his former classmates. He and Bobby had been in the same second-grade class last school year. Bobby's head had small, individual knots of hair, and all the kids teased him. The boys and girls all called Bobby, "Beady Beads". Lil' Mike wondered if Bobby would be in his third-grade class when school started again in September.

His mama also used to go to a nail place down the street from Miss Henrietta's salon. It was called Jackie's Nail Place. Ms. Jackie always made his mama's fingers and toes nice and pretty. Sometimes Miss Jackie painted his mama's nails red, sometimes pink, sometimes purple. The colors reminded him of the Crayola crayons he used in his coloring books. But now, his mama's nails and toes never looked pretty. They were always raggedy and full of dirt. To Lil' Mike, everything seemed to look dirty now. The clothes his mother wore, and their house. Their Gwynns Falls Parkway home used to be sparkly clean. There was a time when it would have been hard to find a piece of lint on the floor. Now, trash, debris, and empty beer bottles were all over the place.

His mama guzzled down tall bottles of Colt 45 malt liquor beer bottles like water. She called them her "forties". Lil' Mike often watched as she tossed the empty bottles down to the floor. Sometimes, she made him pick them up and throw them in the kitchen trash can. One time, he started to taste some before tossing the bottle in the trash. There was still a little beer at the bottom. Lil' Mike thought he would drink it to see why his mother liked it so much. But first, Lil' Mike put the bottle up to his nose. Phew, that beer stuff stinks, he thought before throwing the bottle in the trash can.

There was a time when their living room was full of nice furniture. But now, all that remained was the dirty couch, a wooden coffee table with burn stains and water spots all over it, a few rickety end tables, a small black and white television, and a few lamps whose shades had light bulb burns. White paint was peeling from the walls, and the ceiling had cracks. On days when rain poured from the skies, water dripped in through the soiled ceiling. His mama would make him get pans and set them on the living room floor to catch the drops of falling water.

Angel's white bassinet was also in the living room. His mama had placed it next to the nasty couch. The bassinet was a baby shower gift from his Aunt Caroline. He thought about his aunt all the time. He really missed Aunt Caroline. Before his mother and Aunt Caroline stopped speaking, they were best friends. His mother told him they had been friends for a long time.

"Your Aunt Caroline and I met when she moved to the neighborhood," his mother told him. "We were students at Walbrook High School. That's the big school I pointed out to you one day as we rode through Walbrook Junction. Your Aunt Caroline's family had just moved to Baltimore from Mississippi, and she was a new student at the school. We were both about 16, and sophomores at the time.

"We hit it off right away. Caroline and I had so much in common. That included cooking. She and I both loved to cook. We became best friends. Now your Aunt Caroline mentioned she had an older brother or bruuuuuther. That's how she pronounces brother," his mama said with a laugh.

"I know," Lil Mike responded. "It's so funny."

"Well Lil' Mike, it was a while before I finally got to meet your Aunt Caroline's bruuuuuther," she said imitating his aunt. "But boy when I finally got to meet him, I thought he was the cutest guy in the world. I thought he had the prettiest eyes. And the rest is history."

Then his mother looked at him and said, "Funny thing…your Aunt Caroline didn't want me to date your daddy." Turning away, his mama let out a deep sigh, and uttered under her breath, "Maybe I should have listened." Lil' Mike didn't think his mother realized he had heard what she said. But he did.

Like his father, Aunt Caroline talked much differently than the way people in Baltimore talked. She and his daddy had their own special way of saying words. His mother told him the two talked "country".

Lil' Mike thought Aunt Caroline was the best aunt in the whole, wide world. She would buy him things, take him places, and made him laugh all the time. Aunt Esther - one of the characters on a show his mama would watch called "Sanford and Son" – reminded him of his Aunt Caroline. Not only did the two look alike, but they also acted alike. Aunt Esther always talked about church. So did Aunt Caroline. Aunt Esther wore dresses all the time. So did Aunt Caroline. 'Aunt Esther' squinted her eye. So did Aunt Caroline. 'Aunt Esther' was always shouting and throwing her hands up when she got "happy". Aunt Caroline did that too. "Happy" – that's what they called it in church when people shouted and jumped up and down.

His mother would always tell his Aunt Caroline she "had an old soul to be so young." Aunt Caroline called his mother 'M," the first initial in her name, Melvina. Aunt Caroline said 'M' was a lot easier to say than Melvina. She was the only person who called his mother by her first initial.

"M, you ain't never too young or too old to serve the good Lawd," she always said. Then his Aunt Caroline would get happ, yell "Glory!" and start hollering and shouting like people did in church.

His Aunt Caroline was a missionary and a church usher. Lil' Mike could still recall the white uniform she wore with the gold pin that said "Usher". Her usher uniform was white as snow. So were her shoes, stockings, and the round napkin on her head she called a "doily". She told him she had gone to ushering school.

Aunt Caroline and Uncle Carl would pick him and his mama up from the house and take them to church. They would pull their car in front of the house and blow the horn for them to come outside. Uncle Carl was Aunt Caroline's husband. Uncle Carl would drive, Aunt Caroline sat in the front seat, and he and his mama sat in the back. Angel hadn't been born yet.

During one Sunday morning ride to church, Lil' Mike asked his Aunt Caroline, "What's an Usher?"

Pronouncing usher as "ursher" and tabernacle as "tabanaca" which she always did, Aunt Caroline proudly said, "Nephew, an ursher, is the doorkeeper of God's Tabanaca. Urshers keep folks in line so that the church service moves along with decency and order. No paper on the floor, no talking, no playing, and definitely no chewing gum. In other words, no foolishness. And nephew, all your Aunt Caroline got to do is look at somebody like this," she said turning to look at him and squinting one of her eyes. "They know they better stop whatever foolishness they're doing."

Lil' Mike missed his Aunt Caroline so much. She and Mama used to go shopping together, eat lunch together, and go to the movies together. They would do lots of things together. But all that came to a stop a few weeks ago. Lil Mike remembered the exact date. It was his birthday – July 10, 1998.

Aunt Caroline stopped by the house and picked him up to take him to Chuck E. Cheese for his eighth birthday. Lil' Mike was glad to get out of the house and away from Angel's constant crying. His mother had given her a bottle and changed her stinky, poop-filled Pamper. However, Angel still would not stop crying.

Once he and Aunt Caroline arrived at Chuck E. Cheese, she bought him lots of game tokens, a big pepperoni pizza, and soda. He even danced with Chuck E. Cheese. Lil' Mike had so much fun. He played skee ball, threw mini-basketballs through hoops, and played video games. Before they left, Lil' Mike took the tickets he won to a counter and picked out a prize. He wouldn't have had any fun on his birthday if it had not been for his Aunt Caroline. However, when his aunt took him home later that day, she and his mama got into a big argument. When they got there, Angel was lying in her bassinet – still crying. His mother was pacing the floor. Lil' Mike assumed she was waiting for his father to bring her some crack stuff.

"My Lawd!" Aunt Caroline told his mother, "I ain't never seen a baby holler so much in my life! She was crying when we left, and she's still crying. Look at her over there just a screamin' and a kickin'! I know that's my sweet, little baby niece, but that cat-eyed little baby is a mean, little thang! Mean and on'ry…just like my bruuuuurther!"

"Angel's driving me up the wall," his mother frustratingly replied. "I fed her, I burped her, I picked her up, and I changed her. And she still won't stop crying! I don't know what else to do!"

"Well M, I would help you out to give you a break, but the last time I took that baby to the house, she cried like a banshee! Howled all night like a wolf hollering under a full moon! Carl had to work the next morning and she kept him up all night! He had a fit! Told me I better not bring no chil'ren back to the house to babysit! And oh Lawd, M. You got the baby's soiled diapers in here on the floor! They stink and need to go outside! Lawd, I better use the bathroom before I soil myself."

Lil' Mike watched as his aunt covered her ears to drown out Angel's crying as she headed to the downstairs bathroom. He headed upstairs to play with the things he got from Chuck E. Cheese.

"Lawd have mercy, M!" he heard Aunt Caroline cry from the downstairs bathroom. "When are you going to clean up this nasty house! You never used to keep your bathroom looking like this! It's filthy! This bathroom ain't fit for a dawg!"

Pat! Pat! Pat! Pat! Pat! Pat! It was the sound of his aunt stomping her feet on the bathroom floor.

"M!" shouted Aunt Caroline, using the nickname by which she referred to his mother. 'I'm in here mashin' these roaches with my new shoes from the Hecht Company! You got roaches everywhere! In the kitchen, in the living room, on the walls, and on the ceiling! I got ready to wipe myself, and they were crawling on the toilet paper! I'm jumping in here more than I jump in church!"

"Ahhhhhhhhhh!" screamed Aunt Caroline.

Her scream scared Lil' Mike. He ran downstairs as fast as he could to see what was wrong.

"Lawd have mercy! Help me, Jesus! A mouse just ran over my foot!" Aunt Caroline yelled. "I plead The Blood!" A few seconds later, Aunt Caroline flung the bathroom door open and ran out. "I gotta get outta here! I can't take this! I'm havin' heart pala-patations!" she shouted. "I'll have a heart attack if I stay in this God-forsaken house a minute longer!" she yelled dashing towards her keys and purse. "I pray none of these roaches in here crawled inside my pockabook!" she exclaimed. Aunt Caroline noticed her purse had been opened. "Why is the clasp on my pockabook open?" she asked turning to his mama and giving her the squinted-eye look. "All the roaches in the world ain't strong enough to open a pockabook!" Looking through her purse and rummaging through it, Aunt Caroline bellowed, "Mel-vi-na-A-Tho-mas! You stole my money! Now give me my money back!"

"I didn't steal your money, Caroline!" his mother fired back. "How dare you stand in my house and accuse me of stealing?! You probably ain't have no money in that pocketbook anyway!"

"The Bible says, thou shalt not steal Melvina! I know how much money I had in my pockabook! Forty dollars to be exact!"

"I ain't steal shit from you, Caroline!"

"How dare you cuss me, M?! You never used to use the Devil's vocabulary! Those drugs you and Mike are usin' have changed ya, M!"

"Get the hell outta my house, Caroline!"

"I'm leavin' you, thief, before I do somethin' I will regret! And you had better be glad that I'm saved, sanctified, pressed down, and filled with the Holy Ghost, or I'd cuss ya out right back! I nicknamed you 'M' because it's short for Melvina, but I should have named you 'M' for Moolah because you sure stole mines! I may have not seen you take it, but Gawd sure did!" she shouted.

Lil' Mike watched Aunt Caroline march to the front door. He had never seen her so mad. His Aunt Caroline abruptly stopped, turned around, and looked at him. "I'm so sorry you had to hear your Aunt Caroline and your mama carry on, Lil' Mike!" she said, now turning and rolling her eyes at his mother. "Grown folks talkin' and fussin' should never take place in front of chil'ren! But your mama sittin' over there on that ol' nasty couch, done gone plum crazy!"

"Crazy?!' his mama hissed, stooping down, picking up an empty beer bottle, and jumping up from the couch. "I'll show you crazy! I'll bust you upside your motherfuckin' head!"

Trembling with fear, little Mike cowered in the corner, praying his mama didn't hurt Aunt Caroline.

"You better not think about striking me you spawn of Satan!" yelled Aunt Caroline. "And your mouth is just as filthy as this house!"

"You been talkin' about my damn house since you got here Caroline! I'm not gonna stand here and let you insult me like this in front of Lil' Mike!" she barked, spit flying from her mouth like a mad dog.

Mama is as mad as 'Cujo', Lil' Mike thought, recalling the rabid dog in the movie of the same name.

"Me insult you in front of Lil' Mike?!" Aunt Caroline responded, laughing sarcastically. "Ha! That's a laugh! You of all people! Walkin' around here lookin' like a wild woman with your hair all over your head and smellin' like a wet pig in his own slop!"

"I don't stink!" said Mama, looking at him before turning and asking, "Do I Lil' Mike?" Lil Mike didn't want to lie, nor did he want to anger his mother. Instead of responding, he looked down at his feet.

"I don't know why I asked you anyway!', Mama shouted, now turning to look at Aunt Caroline. "This ain't about me Caroline! This is all about you! And right now, you're tryin' to make me look bad in front of my son! I know damn well I don't stink!"

"I swear fo' God you do stink! You smell worse than a scared skunk in the sticks of Mississippi! I have to spray my car down with Lysol before you get in and after you get out! And you got the nerve to talk about someone insultin' Lil' Mike?! Well, I've got news for you, M! You're an insult to Lil' Mike, my bruuuuuther Michael and yourself!"

"Your brother Mike — pardon me for my pronunciation — I meant to say bruuuuuther as you call him with your country ass self, is the one who got me hooked on the shit in the first place!"

"Oh, so now it's Michael's fault?! I told you not to mess with my bruuuuuther, but you didn't listen! But that's beside the point because neither one of us can change the past! What's done is done! But for the sake of your future, Michael's future, and most of all, them chil'ren's future, you both need to leave them drugs alone!"

"I don't need to hear this right now, Caroline!"

"Well your gonna hear it, M! Both of you need to get yourselves together with your hard-headed selves! And if Michael keeps it up, he's gonna lose that job he just got! Just like you lost yours at the bakery! I have told you over and over again that you need to get into a clinic somewhere to get help with your addiction! It's bad! Real bad!"

"I don't need no help!"

"Yes, you do, M! The fact that you stole my forty dollars outta my pockabook should tell you somethin'!"

"I told you I didn't steal your damn money, Caroline!"

"Oh no?!" asked Aunt Caroline. "Well, who took it then? There ain't but four of us in here. Me, you, Lil' Mike, and Angel, whose over there crying her eyes out in that bassinet! She's probably cryin cause you stole my money! 'Now I know they didn't take my money, and I sure ain't steal my own money, so that leaves you!" she screamed, pointing at Melvina.

"I didn't take your money, Caroline. Why would I take your money?!"

"What else?' asked his aunt. "To buy that Crack you are all strung out on! That's what!"

"I ain't strung out, Caroline! I can stop anytime I'm ready!"

"If you coulda stopped on your own, you would have stopped by now! You can't leave that poison alone to save your life! They talk about Crack all the time on the news! And it's killin' people! And M, I am prayin' you get the help you need before it's too late! You have lost control of everything in your life!"

"I'm still in control, Caroline! I know what I'm doing!"

"No, you don't! Look at you! Look at this house! Your mama is probably turnin' over in her grave! She kept this place so clean you could eat off the floor! She never kept this house lookin' like this! She left it to you free and clear! Paid off in full! All you had to do was take care of it!"

Walking towards Aunt Carolina, Mama screamed, "Shut the fuck up Caroline! Leave my mama out of this!"

"Shut the cuss word up?!" hollered Aunt Caroline.

"You heard what the hell I said!" yelled Mama pushing up her sleeves like he often saw kids do when they were preparing to fight. But Mama was also toting a beer bottle.

My heart is beating a million miles a minute! Lil' Mike thought. Should I run upstairs to my room and hide in the closet?! Should I stay down here in case I need to jump between them?! Should I call 9-1-1 like Mama taught me to do in an emergency?! What should I do?! He started up the steps towards his room.

"I'm about ready to bust you upside your damn head bringing my mother into this!" shouted Mama, prompting Lil' Mike to fly back down the steps.

"Look at you with your heathen self, ready to tussle!" yelled Aunt Caroline. "Listen to me and you listen to me good, M! Ya mouth is filthy! Ya house is filthy! Ya clothes are filthy! And ya chil'ren are filthy! I bet you can't even remember the last time you bathed them kids!"

"Don't you worry about when I washed my children Caroline! Them my kids!"

"And they're my niece and nephew! I'd take them myself if I could!"

"You and what army?!" his mother fired back looking at Lil' Mike and Angel. "Ain't nobody takin' my kids!"

"I hope you don't lose them kids! You need much prayer! Speaking of prayer, you need to let Pastor Payne and the elders pray them demon spuruuuuuuurits of addiction outta ya! You stopped goin' to church with me and Carl after you got hooked on that stuff! But you need to come back!"

"Shut up Caroline!"

"No, M! I'm not shuttin' up! And I know why Angel won't shut up! Cause my poor little ol' niece is a crack baby! That's why she cries all the time! The truth hurts?! Doesn't it?!"

"I ain't got to listen to this shit!" his mama yelled, raising the beer bottle. "Now get the hell outta my house! I ain't tellin' you no more!"

"Don't you worry, M! I'm gittin' out of this dirty house! And you better be glad you didn't threaten me like this before I got saved! If I were a fightin' woman, I would have given you a good, old-fashioned, southern-style ass-whuppin'!' Looking towards the ceiling Aunt Caroline said, "Sorry Lawd, that one slipped out. I repent in the name of Jesus!" Turning to his mother, Aunt Caroline shouted, "Now look at what you have done, M! You made me cuss!"

"So you think you can whip my ass?" Mama shouted. "Well let's just see about that!" His mother took off toward his Aunt Caroline with the raised bottle like a raging bull charging a matador.

He was so scared, his stomach felt full of butterflies. Racing over to his Mama as fast as he could, Lil' Mike jumped in front of her, threw his arms around her waist, and held her with all his might to keep her still. "Mama! No!" he pleaded. "Please don't hit Aunt Caroline!"

"Get thee behind me Satan!" his Aunt Caroline yelled, pointing the big cross hanging from her neck towards Mama.

"Get your ass out of my house Caroline!" said Mama lowering the bottle. "Before you send me to jail!"

"I'm leavin', M! And you ain't ever got to worry about me settin' foot in this ol' dirty, nasty, filthy, stinky, roach and mice-infested house again! Got the nerve to raise a bottle to hit me! Them drugs done turned you into a heathen! And you better pray I don't call CPS on you! Got these chil'ren livin' in this cesspool of sin and filth! You evil sea witch you!"

Aunt Caroline left, slamming the door so hard behind her that a framed photo that hung on the wall fell to the floor and broke. It was the photo that he, his mama, and Angel took at Mondawmin Mall. The three took the photo a few days after Angel came home from the hospital. The frame's glass had shattered into tiny pieces. Shattered. Just like his mama and aunt's friendship.

Walking over to the photograph, Mama shouted, "That Bitch broke my picture!" She picked it up and brushed the glass shards off the photo. "Shit! I cut my damn finger!" she hollered slamming the photo down on the table. "Lil' Mike! Go get the broom and dustpan and clean up that glass!"

"Yes, Mama."

Looking at Angel who was still in the bassinet screaming at the top of her lungs, Mama said, "And after you do that, heat the baby a bottle."

"Yes ma'am," replied Lil' Mike, watching her plop back down on the couch.

"Shut up Angel!" his mother hollered at Angel violently shaking the bassinet. "First Caroline's mouth, and now your mouth! Stop all this damn crying! What the hell is wrong with you?! All you do is cry! Shit!"

Aunt Caroline stopped coming to the house just like she said she would.

"I haven't seen Aunt Caroline since she and Mama had that big argument on my birthday. I hope they make up. I miss Aunt Caroline so much." Although he didn't want to admit it, deep down inside, Lil' Mike felt his mama took Aunt Caroline's money. He saw his mother take something out of her bra before she left the house later that day. He couldn't tell for sure, but it looked like balled-up money.

Lil' Mike thought about when his Sony PlayStation went missing a few months ago. Santa Claus left it under the Christmas tree when he was five years old. His five video games also disappeared. He knew them all by heart. *Crash Bandicoot*, *Gran Turismo*, *Madden NFL 98*, *Cool Boarders*, and *Oddworld: Abe's Oddysee*. He was so distraught. He cried and cried. When he asked his mother about the console and games, she told him she didn't know what happened to the items but promised to replace them.

"Somebody must have broken into the house and took your PlayStation and games Lil' Mike," he recalled her saying. "Don't cry. Mama's gonna get you another gaming system and games."

Weeks went by, and his mother still had not bought him another PlayStation and games. He thought about the day he went over to Lance Williams' house to play. Lance lived a few doors down and the two attended the same school. His friend took him upstairs to his bedroom, and the two plunked down on Lance's bed to watch cartoons and play with Lance's Teenage Mutant Ninja Turtle action figures.

Lil' Mike noticed the Play Station sitting on a table in Lance's room. Scattered next to it was *Crash Bandicoot*, *Gran Turismo*, *Madden NFL 98*, *Cool Boarders*, and *Oddworld: Abe's Odyssey*. "Those are the exact video games I used to have," Lil' Mike thought to himself. "And that PS1 has the exact same scratch marks on the top and side that mines had."

Lil' Mike politely asked Lance where he had gotten the PlayStation and games.

"Miss Melvina sold them to my mama," Lance said matter-of-factly. "She told my mama she bought you a new PlayStation and games, and so she was selling your old console and games."

Lil' Mike jumped up from Lance's bed and ran down the steps towards the front door as fast as he could.

"Come back, Mike! What did I say?! What's wrong?!" cried Lance.

Those were the last words Lil' Mike heard running tearfully out of Lance's house.

Crack. The argument between his mother and Aunt Caroline on his birthday wasn't the first time Lil' Mike heard the word. Some of his classmates said their parents used crack and that it turned them into monsters. His mama wasn't a monster, but she sure looked like a zombie.

Lil' Mike had seen his mama and daddy use the substance many times. He called it 'that crack stuff.' To him, the little things were nothing more than small pebbles. But to them, they were like gold. Especially to his mama. She was always careful not to drop a single speck whenever she took it out of a small, clear bag. He would watch as they put the crack stuff in a weird-shaped pipe, use a flame from his daddy's cigarette lighter to cook it in the pipe and, smoke it.

Lil' Mike hated when his father came around. Not only did he use that crack stuff with his mama, but he was scary. His daddy's breath always smelled like cigarettes, and he had ugly, round, burn marks on his arms and legs. His father told him he would put the same marks on him if he ever disobeyed or told on him. Sometimes, his daddy's threats were silent. He would just look at Lil' Mike with his mean, green eyes and pat the shirt pocket that held his pack of Kool cigarettes. Other times, his daddy would simply look at him and smile as he extinguished a burning hot cigarette in an ashtray.

Lil' Mike couldn't understand why his father was so cold and mean. He never showed any love towards him, his baby sister, or his mama. Why doesn't daddy love us? He often wondered. His daddy worked as a driver, but he rarely brought him anything. His father never played baseball or threw a football with him like the other daddies in the neighborhood did with their sons at Hanlon Park. The park was across the street from Lil' Mike's house. His mother would walk him there. She would take him by the hand and the two crossed their busy street for the short walk. Once they arrived, she would let him play at the park. But like so many things when it came to his mother, that too had stopped.

Sometimes, his father gave his mama money to buy food and other things for him and Angel, but he had a mean way of handing her the money. Instead of putting it in her hand, he would throw the money at his mother. Sometimes, he would throw it on the floor and make her crawl to pick it up. Although his daddy and Aunt Caroline were brother and sister, they were nothing alike. Aunt Caroline was nice. But to Lil' Mike, his father was as mean as the villains he watched in the cartoons.

Another reason Lil' Mike didn't like it when his father came over, was that he and his mother argued. They argued a lot. Especially over that crack stuff. Some days, his mama left to go get it herself. When she didn't go out to buy it, she waited for his daddy to bring it. On those days, she would pace the floor and peek out the windows to see if he was coming up the walkway. She was also jittery and moody. Just the other day, he watched such an episode play out. After walking back and forth for what seemed like hours, his mother plopped down on the couch, twisted open a bottle of beer, and stared at the front door. He listened as his mama used a lot of bad words and fussed and fussed. There was a time she would never use bad words, but now she always used them. She kept fussing and cussing to herself about how long his father was taking to bring that crack stuff.

When his mama finally heard the jingling of his daddy's keys opening the door, she jumped up like a jack-in-the-box. "Did you get it?!" his mother inquired, frantically running up to his father as if he was a famous person like Lil' Mike's favorite basketball player, Michael Jordan of the Chicago Bulls. "I got your durn crack Melvina,' his daddy responded in his Southern drawl. "Ya gonna have to get up off ya ass and git back to work! This shit ain't free!"

"You took a long ass time getting here Big Mike. Now give me my shit!" said his mother grabbing at the crack stuff in his hand like a hungry dog lunging for a steak.

"I ain't got to give you a damn thing Melvina!" his father said backing away from Mama and waving the pebbly-looking crack stuff in her face. "You can kiss my black ass!" He backed up and held the crack stuff up high in the air, his mother reaching for it. He moved it to the left. She jumped to the left. He moved it to the right. She jumped to the right. Lil' Mike knew his daddy was teasing his mama.

He watched his father spit in his mama's face and slap her so hard she fell to the floor. Lil' Mike was afraid, so he left the living room and crept halfway up the stairwell. However, from where Lil' Mike sat, he could still see and hear the scene playing out between his parents.

"Go fetch it!" his father yelled to his mother, who had landed on her hands and knees. Then his daddy tossed the crack stuff across the floor as if he were throwing a bone to a dog. His daddy smiled and shook his head as he watched his mama scramble across the floor like a dog walking on all fours. Like an animal about to attack its prey, Daddy ran over to Mama, got down on the floor behind her, and pulled down both her pants and his. Lil' Mike watched in shock as his father took out his private part and said, "I'm gonna give it to you doggy-style, Bitch!" before ramming it into his mother. Why is Daddy treating Mama so mean? Lil' Mike wondered. Why does Mama allow Daddy to treat her like a dog just for that Crack stuff? Maybe that Crack stuff has her under some kind of magic spell. Lil' Mike did not want to watch his parents anymore. Crying, he crept up the stairs to head to his room. Walking up the stairwell, he heard a loud cry like a dog yelping in pain. That's no dog crying out. That's Mama screaming.

Lil' Mike hated when his father hurt his mother. But he was afraid of his father and felt helpless. He was little in comparison to his daddy's size. I'll be glad when I get big, he thought. Then I can help Mama. That day, Lil' Mike escaped the sounds of his parents' activity downstairs by picking up I Rose ABOVE it all. After closing his door, he opened the book and worked on memorizing more lines.

"You say things to hurt me all the time; To dampen my spirit and poison my mind," Lil' Mike wailed lowering his head. "You seek to implode my confidence and esteem; As if I were a building toppling down from its beams," he sobbed, falling to the floor. "Why do you look at me with malice in your eyes?" Lil' Mike questioned, imitating his father's sharp stares. "Hating that I dance with such soul in my thighs" he mused, swinging his hips. "Why does it bother you that I jaunt with joy?" he asked. "A stride full of confidence you seek to destroy" – pretending to push someone to the ground. "But like the sun climbing towards its horizon, and an eagle soaring high, I too, will rise!" he giggled flapping his arms, while slowly standing to his feet.

He felt the words of this poem were so powerful. When Lil' Mike told his mother how sad he was that Santa Claus only left him a book for Christmas and no toys, she also told him this book could inspire him like no toy ever could. Although he was still hurt and sad about only receiving a book for Christmas, Lil' Mike believed his mother was right. The words of this poem were special. They made Lil' Mike feel like he could win. They made him feel like he could beat anything. They made him feel like he could beat anyone. No matter how difficult. No matter how big. No matter how bad.

One day, I'm gonna stop Daddy, he thought. I'm gonna stop him from hurting me, and I'm gonna stop him from hurting Mama.

"Lil' Mike! How long are you gonna stand over there! Bring me Angel's bottle!"

"Yes ma'am."

Lil' Mike got caught up in his daydreams. The youngster did not realize he had been standing at the living room entrance for several minutes holding Angel's bottle.

"Why are you standing over there staring at me like that?"

"No reason Mama. Just thinking."

"Thinking about what?"

"How things used to be."

"Take it from me, Lil' Mike. Nothin' ever stays the same. Now come on over here and feed your sister. Mama has a run to make. Your noodles are in the microwave."

You always have a run to make, he thought to himself as his mama handed him the crying baby. And I'm sick of Oodles of Noodles. He watched as his mama ran upstairs. A few minutes later, she ran back downstairs. She had changed from her robe into clothes. "I'll be right back Lil' Mike," Mama said before darting out the door.

"Sure you will" he mumbled to himself as he carefully cradled the tiny infant in his arms. She got on his nerves with all her annoying crying, but the last thing he wanted to do was drop Angel. Lil' Mike never sat on the dirty couch to feed Angel. The last time he sat next to his mama on the couch, it made him all itchy. He either took

Angel to his room to feed her, or he sat at the kitchen table. Today, he would sit at the kitchen table and feed Angel as he ate his noodles.

First, he gently laid the crying baby in her bassinet. Then he walked to the kitchen, grabbed a chair, and stood on it so that he could reach the microwave. After grabbing his noodles from the microwave and setting them on the table along with a spoon, he headed back to the living room to get Angel. Then he took her into the kitchen, sat at the table, and fed Angel her bottle. He prepared to eat, but first, he said his Grace. Before she changed, his mama taught him to always say his Grace before eating. "God is great, God is good, let us thank Him for our food, Amen." Lil' Mike looked down at Angel. He couldn't believe it. She stopped crying! Angel sucked her bottle, staring back at him with her tiny, emerald-green eyes. Aunt Caroline said Angel and Daddy had 'cat eyes.' Lil Mike and his mother's eye color was dark brown.

"Mama shouldn't be leaving us in the house all alone like this Angel," Lil' Mike said to the infant as if she understood his plight. He propped her bottle against his chest so that he could free one hand to eat his noodles. A few minutes later, Lil' Mike heard the jingling of keys and footsteps.

"Mama is that you?"

"No, it's me. Is your mama here?"

"No Daddy, she left."

Lil' Mike cradled Angel tightly as their father insidiously made his way over to them. "Go on to bed boy," said his father, pointing towards the upstairs. I hate when Daddy sends me to bed, lamented Lil Mike slowly walking up the stairwell.

Later that afternoon, his mother returned home. His father told her that he was taking Lil' Mike to Mondawmin Mall, the big shopping center near their house. His mother was shocked.

"What?!" she asked. "I don't believe it, Big Mike! You're actually taking Lil' Mike to the store?"

"That's what I said Melvina. I'm taking the boy to the store to get him a toy."

"Well, it's about damn time."

"Shut up Melvina. You need to figure out how you are gonna get some more furniture in this filthy house of yours. You done sold damn near everything you had in here. I can hardly find a place to sit my black ass down."

"Well give me some money to buy some more furniture then!"

"For what?! So you can smoke it up?"

"Shut up before you wake the baby up!"

Lil' Mike looked over at Angel who was fast asleep. When his daddy made him go to bed earlier, he laid her down in the bassinet, crying herself to sleep. He waved goodbye to his mama. Then he and his daddy left out the door and headed to Mondawmin Mall.

Lil Mike and his daddy walked to the corner of Gwynns Falls Parkway and Longwood Street. He looked over at Hanlon Park. It was a crisp fall day and the orange and brown leaves danced as they fell from the trees and landed on the park grounds. He felt like dancing too. Earlier that day, Lil' Mike was so sad and hurt, he cried and cried. But now, he was happy and excited. He couldn't remember the last time his father took him to the store. He watched his father hold out a finger to flag down a 'Hack'. A few minutes later, a man pulled over to the curb and rolled down his car window.

"Where ya goin bro?" the man asked.

His daddy responded, "Mondawmin Mall."

"Okay, get in."

He and his daddy climbed into the back seat of the hack's car. Lil' Mike knew all about Hacks. He and his mama would walk to Mondawmin Mall, and catch a Hack back home. One day, he curiously asked her, "Mama, what's a Hack?"

"They're like cabbies" she explained. "They ride you in their cars and you give them money. You can pay hacks what you want, but with cabbies, you can't do that. Hacks don't have meters in their cars. Cabbies do. And meters mean more money. And the meters in cabbies go up faster than you can blink those cute little eyes of yours. Not only are Hacks cheaper, but they'll even help their riders to load and unload bags in their cars. Most cabbies don't do that.'

Hacks were always lined up outside Mondawmin Mall. Especially in front of the Stop Shop and Save supermarket. "Need a ride?" they always asked. His mama always looked for a Hack by the name of 'Mr. Billy'. He had a big, brown car she liked to ride in that said 'Buick' on the back. When he and his mother were ready to leave the mall, she always looked for Mr. Billy out front. If she didn't see Mr. Billy, she would ride with another hack. But his mama preferred Mr. Billy. She thought he was much friendlier than the other Hacks and way more good-looking. She also thought the gold tooth in his mouth was nice.

Lil' Mike's favorite schoolteacher was Miss Vashtied Battle-Brown. She was really pretty, and always dressed nice. She told him he was really good at remembering things. He could remember Mr. Billy always keeping a cigarette tucked behind his right ear. Mr. Billy is so cool, Lil' Mike thought, whenever he and his mama climbed in the back seat of his car. Mr. Billy had straight, black hair streaked with grey that he kept neatly combed back. His mama would always say, "Mr. Billy got that good Indian hair."

"Mama why isn't my hair like Mr. Billy's hair?," Lil' Mike asked one afternoon during a ride home from Mondawmin Mall.

"Because you got curly hair like your father," his mother replied.

"Son, you could have had Mr. Billy's Indian hair had your mama come along before I met my wife," said the Hack, turning and winking at Mama. "Ain't that right Miss Melvina?"

"I ain't studyin' you, Mr. Billy," she laughed. "You know good and well you are old enough to be my father. As a matter of fact, you worked with my father."

"That's right. Out at good, ole, Bethlehem Steel. A lot of us Black men used to make good money out there at 'The Point' until business slowed down. A lot of people got laid off. I was one of them. That's the reason I'm out here hacking now."

Once Lil' Mike's mother stopped taking him to Mondawmin Mall, the rides in Mr. Billy's car also stopped. The Hack his father flagged down was now turning into Mondawmin's parking lot. Lil Mike looked for Mr. Billy's

Buick in front of the market but didn't see it.

"Drop us off at the entrance on the Metro side," his father instructed the man.

"Sure brother," said the Hack, driving to another mall entrance and then stopping. Big Mike reached into his shirt pocket, pulling out a $1 bill, and handing it to the Hack. "Come on Lil' Mike," said Daddy, climbing out the car, with Lil' Mike following suit.

"Hey brother!" hollered the Hack, staring open-mouthed at the dollar bill. "You only gave me one —"

Before the Hack finished his sentence, his father slammed the car door. Big Mike stuck his middle finger up at the Hack and walked towards the mall door with Lil' Mike in tow. "Green-eyed motherfucker!" the Hack hollered before pulling off so furiously his tires screeched.

Once Lil' Mike and Big Mike were inside Mondawmin Mall, they began making their way to KB Toy Store. Walking past Music Liberated, Lil' Mike heard a familiar song blaring from the record store.

"I don't know all of the song, but I do remember the words 'Back down memory lane," Lil' Mike told his father, recalling a small radio that once sat on the kitchen counter of his home. "Mama used to listen to a radio station all the time called Magic 95.9 and I remember hearing them play that song. You know the name of that song Daddy?"

"Back down memory lane," his father replied.

"Do you know the name of the lady who sings that song Daddy?"

"Minnie Rippatin" said Big Mike referring to singer Minnie Riperton.

"She sure has a pretty voice, huh Daddy?"

"Uh-huh."

For Lil' Mike, 'Back Down Memory Lane' was the perfect melody for reflecting on the good ole days. He and his father walked past Kazin Shoes. Mama used to buy shoes there. He saw Princess Shops, Lexington Lady, Rite Aid, and Charlie Rudos. Mama used to shop at all of those stores. When he and his father walked by Mama Lucia's, Lil' Mike glanced inside the pizzeria. Me and Mama would go there and sit in the booth and eat pizza slices and drink fizzy fountain Coca- Colas.

His last outing to Mondawmin Mall was after Angel came home from the hospital. Mama got me and Angel all dressed up and brought us here so we could all take a picture together, Lil Mike silently recalled. Angel cried and cried and cried. But the photo man made funny faces until Angel finally stopped crying and quickly snapped the photo of me, Mama, and Angel before she started crying again. Before we left the mall, Mama bought a frame, and when we got home, Mama placed our photo in the frame and hung it on the wall. That's the frame that fell and broke after Mama and Aunt Caroline's big argument.

Lil' Mike looked over at the center of the mall. Although it was July, the bells of Christmas rang in his mind. He thought about the mall's Santa Claus. His mama would take him over there to see Santa every Christmas. In all the Christmas storybooks Lil' Mike read, and in all the cartoons he watched, Santa Claus was White. But Mondawmin Mall's Santa Claus was Black. The youngster would climb on the jolly, cotton-bearded man's lap, and tell him all the things he wanted for Christmas. After Lil' Mike finished running down his list in Santa's ear, the plump man nodded, reached into his red, velvet bag, took out a candy cane, and handed it to Lil' Mike.

Afterward, 'Santa's Helper', - a petite, pretty Black lady, would snap his picture with Santa. A print that froze them in time, would slowly begin to emerge from the bottom of the camera. Santa's elves are inside the camera. They drew our picture, and now they are pushing it out, he thought. Santa's Helper set the photo down by the cash register while it developed. Lil' Mike was just tall enough to see the photo develop. He was amazed. With each passing second, images began to form. A few minutes later, there was he and Santa.

"Wow! The elves sure drew a good picture of me and Santa!" he told Santa's Helper.

"Polaroid elves," Santa's Helper responded with a grin, placing the photo in a cardboard-like holiday frame and handing it to his mother.

"Look at my baby and Santa," said his mama gleefully, handing Santa's helper some money.

For Lil' Mike, Christmas was a joyous time back then. Sometimes, Mama would make him cover his eyes while she brought things in the mall. But that was Christmas past. Christmas present was different. For the past two Christmas', his mother had not gone to Mondawmin Mall. Last Christmas was the worst ever, Lil Mike thought, remembering how he woke up Christmas morning and raced down the steps to see what Santa Claus left him under the tree. To his shock and disappointment, the only gift Santa Claus left for him was a book – I Rose ABOVE it all.

Lil' Mike loved reading books. Especially fairy tales. They transported him from the doldrums of what had become his new normal, to beautiful, imaginary worlds. Books took him to castles, rivers, rain forests, amusement parks, islands, and other fun, faraway places. The characters were interesting and fun and kept him company when he was lonely. Mama never used to leave me in the house alone until she started using that Crack stuff, he often thought.

Lil' Mike likened himself to a character in a movie he and his mama once watched. The movie was called Home Alone. He was like 'Kevin McCallister'. But Kevin's mother left him home alone by mistake. But when Lil' Mike's mother left him home alone, it was no mistake. Kevin's life was also a make-belief movie; Lil' Mike's life was real. This was no movie.

With the loss of his Sony Play Station and his mama gone more and more often, Lil' Mike turned to reading books. In his loneliness, the book's characters kept him company. Once his mother brought Angel home from the hospital, she left him alone in the house to tend to his sister. Lil' Mike would balance cradling Angel against his chest with one hand while holding a book in the other. Yet, as much as he enjoyed reading books, Lil' Mike still couldn't believe all Santa left him under the tree was a book. The book Santa left me isn't even new. It's used. Lil' Mike was so hurt and distraught, he hadn't even bothered to open the book, let alone read it. But that all changed a few weeks ago. Still fuming over his one gift, he glanced at the book, which was sitting on a shelf in his bedroom collecting dust. Picking up the book, he decided, "I'm going to tell Mama exactly how I feel about Santa leaving me one dumb book for a Christmas present."

Walking over to his mother who was sitting on the couch, Lil' Mike told her, "Mama, I cried last Christmas more than I ever cried in my whole life. I was a good boy all year long, and all Santa Claus brought me was this lousy book!" he said holding up the book. "I don't understand why Santa is mad at me."

Tears welling in her eyes, his mother said, "Santa Claus ain't mad at you Lil' Mike. He left you something real special. I Rose ABOVE it all was written by a famous Black writer named Ursula V. Battle. Not only is that Santa's favor-right book. But that's my favor-right book too."

"Favorite Mama. That's how you say that word. Favorite."

"You got your way of saying it, and I got mines," said his mother with a smile. "There's a poem in that book called I Rose ABOVE it all. That's my favor-right poem. The words in that poem can give you more power than any toy ever could."

"Really Mama?" he asked.

"Yes, baby," she said. 'Santa knows how much you help me and your baby sister. He knows how much we depend on you. You take good care of us. You are Mama's big boy. Mama's little man of the house. And one day, you're gonna grow up and help a whole lot of people. Just like you help us."

"You think so, Mama?"

"I know so. You're gonna do some amazing things, Lil' Mike. Santa knows how smart you are. He also knows how special you are. That's why he left you such a special book."

That was the day Lil' Mike decided to open the book, I Rose ABOVE it all, and learn his mama's favorite poem by heart and recite it to her. She'll be so surprised, he thought. That'll make Mama really happy. I want my Mama to be happy. Just like she used to be.

Snap! Snap! Snap! The sound of his father's fingers halted Lil' Mike's thoughts.

"Snap out of it boy," said Big Mike. "We're here." Lil' Mike had been so engrossed in his thoughts, that he hadn't noticed that he and his father had reached KB Toy Store.

"Go on and pick out something," his father instructed.

"Okay, Daddy."

A case with video consoles and games caught his eye. "Daddy can I get another PlayStation and some games?!" he asked, excited over the prospect of being able to play video games again.

Perusing the $199.99 price tags on the console and the games, most ranging from $29.99 to $69.99 games, his father said, "Nah, can't buy those right now Lil' Mike. Too expensive. Pick out something else that don't cost so much."

Lil' Mike walked the aisles of the store, a bright red truck catching his eye. "I want that truck right there, Daddy!" said Lil' Mike pointing to a truck sitting high on a top shelf. Standing on his tippy toes, he tried to take the truck off the shelf but was not tall enough to reach it.

"Alright, let's go," said Big Mike picking the truck up from the shelf. He paid for the truck, and they headed back to the house. Once he was home, Lil' Mike ecstatically ran to show the new truck to his mother.

"Mama! Mama! Look at the new truck daddy got for me!" he exclaimed.

"That's nice baby," she muttered from the couch. "It's about damn time your father bought you something."

"At least I did buy the boy something," Big Mike told Melvina, before turning to look at Lil' Mike. "Now remember our little agreement Lil' Mike," his father reminded him. "And if I were you, I'd hide that truck before your Crackhead mama sells it."

"I'm not a damn Crackhead, and don't be calling me that shit in front of Lil' Mike!"

His parents now arguing, Lil' Mike exhaled loudly and trotted up the steps to his room to play with his new truck.

CHAPTER TWO

TROUBLE KNOCKS AT THE DOOR

Baltimore, Maryland
Sat. August 8, 1998

A little over a week passed since Big Mike and Lil' Mike's outing to Mondawmin Mall. Melvina laid sprawled out on the living room couch. Angel was sleeping in her bassinet, and the local news played on the old, black, and white television set. Melvina sleepily opened her eyes and felt the seat of her pants. They were soaking wet.

"Damn, I pissed on myself again," she mumbled to herself. "I thought I had gotten up to use the bathroom. I'll change my clothes later. Right now, I need a blast." Hours earlier, Melvina guzzled down two ice-cold forties of Colt 45 and smoked some Crack with Big Mike. He purchased the forties from a corner liquor store and the Crack from a street dealer. Now, her body was peeing out the malt liquor beer she drank and aching for more Crack. Rolling her eyes at the old, black and white television set, she grumbled, "I couldn't even get five damn dollars for your old ass! Everybody wants fuckin' color now. If it works, what difference does it make?"

A sportscaster's voice excitedly blared from the television, 'The Baltimore Ravens will open the pre-season today against the Chicago Bears, and will play the game at their new football stadium at Camden Yards!'

"Today's just Saturday, August 8th, and they're already talking about football," Melvina remarked. "I'm no football guru, but I know we had a team, lost a team, and now we have a team again and the whole damn city is happy."

Melvina thought about the city's former NFL team, the Baltimore Colts leaving the city back in 1984 under dark, snowy skies. "I still remember seeing those Mayflower trucks on the news sneaking the team out of the city back in 1984. 1984…the same year I was supposed to graduate from Walbrook High School. I was 18, and Earlene was just six."

In 1996, NFL football returned to Baltimore with The Baltimore Ravens (formerly the Cleveland Browns). For

Baltimore, the year represented the beginning of a new football era. For Melvina, 1996 represented the beginning of her addiction to Crack cocaine.

The sportscaster's report about the Ravens' pre-season game kicked off a dizzying blitz of reflections for Melvina. Laying in urine-soaked clothes, she replayed event after event of previous years in her mind, including the city's euphoria of getting another football team after a 12-year NFL hiatus.

"I can still remember how angry Mr. Hawkins was when the Colts left," she recalled, referencing her longtime neighbor Rufus Hawkins. "He was a big Colts fan and when they left the city, he was mad as shit! I can still remember Mr. Hawkins dressed in his mailman's uniform cussing while he was ripping down the Colts flag that used to hang from a pole on his front porch. Now, he has a Ravens flag out there. I have known Mr. Hawkins since I was a little girl, and he always pronounced the name of our city Bawl'more instead of Baltimore. I guess that's just the way he talks. He would call the old team the Bawl'more Colts. Now he calls the city's new team the Bawl'more Ravens."

Melvina dragged herself up from the couch and tiptoed over to the television, careful not to awaken Angel. "I need to turn off the TV before it wakes the baby up. Angel cried all damn night! I don't want to hear her nerve-racking crying today." Just as Melvina flipped off the television, she heard the loud, unsettling sound of her own stomach gurgling. "I already pissed on myself," she grumbled. "I'll be damn if I'm gonna stand here and shit on myself too!" Melvina quickly made her way to the bathroom and plunked down on the toilet seat. "Whew! I just made it!" Looking at the black droppings peppered all over the bathroom floor she said in disdain, "Damn mice! They are leaving their nasty ass shit everywhere!" After finishing her business on the toilet, Melvina washed her hands at the sink, gazing at the boney woman staring back at her from the bathroom's mirrored, medicine cabinet. "I know that I'm you, and you're me," said Melvina pointing to the reflection pointing back at her. "But I don't like either one of us."

Melvina didn't want to admit it but knew the person staring back at her was contrastingly different from the old Melvina A. Thomas. The effects of her Crack using were written all over her body. Standing five foot five, she was never heavy but had lost a massive amount of weight. All her clothes were now far too big. The pants she was wearing at this very moment were not only damp with urine but dirty and would not stay up around her waist. The shirt she had on was stained and falling off her shoulders.

"You've got to get yourself together," she told the reflection staring back at her with eyes that were sunken and encamped within dark circles. "Look at your damn hair. It's all over your head. Henrietta wouldn't believe your hair was looking like this."

Melvina reflected on her and Lil' Mike's walks to Henrietta's Beauty Salon. She would take him by the hand, and they would walk there together.

"Mama, how do you pronounce the name of that street?" he once asked, glancing up at the street sign during one of their walks there.

"Reisterstown Road," she responded. "Now let me hear you say it Lil' Mike."

"Re…re…reis…ters..town. Reisterstown Road, Mama" he replied.

"That's it! Good job Lil' Mike."

Melvina thought about how smart Lil' Mike was, and how well he did in school. His teachers told her his reading and math levels were beyond his grade level. They were all impressed with his ability to memorize what they taught, and he always had good report cards. At that time, Melvina walked him to school, and she talked to his teachers almost every morning. She thought about how mature Lil' Mike was to be just eight. He was well-mannered, walked to school by himself, and helped her with Angel. She didn't know what she would have done without Lil' Mike's help when it came to Angel. Her infant girl was born prematurely and stayed in the hospital for several weeks after she was born. Before Melvina brought the baby home, doctors told her Angel would be fussy and would cry more than 'normal' babies. But nothing they said prepared Melvina for this.

Angel's high-pitched, screaming cry was so irritating and so annoying, Melvina felt like tearing her hair out. Her wailing tore at the very core of her eardrums. Most of the time, Angel seemed inconsolable. Warm bottles, changed diapers, burping, rocking, cradling, and other actions typically welcomed by babies, contrarily did little to stop her from crying.

When Melvina and Lil' Mike picked her up, Angel sometimes squirmed and kicked. Angel seemed to reject the human touch. Melvina likened her baby daughter to an angry cat. She would tighten her tiny fingers and claw at the clothes and faces of anyone who tried to hold her in their arms. She arched her back like a threatened feline and howled like a band of alley cats under dark skies. Angel's striking green eyes only intensified her cattish similarities. Caroline would say Angel had 'cat eyes' like her older brother, Michael. Caroline referred to him as her 'bruuuuuther', while Melvina called him 'Big Mike.' She and Caroline had not spoken since their argument on Lil' Mike's birthday.

"Damn, I miss Caroline," said Melvina, again talking to her reflection in the medicine cabinet as if it would respond.

Melvina was still angry at Caroline for all the things she said during their argument, but Melvina knew Caroline was right. Angel's constant crying was a direct result of being born a crack baby. As she stood looking at herself in the medicine cabinet, Melvina thought about the many times she smoked crack throughout her pregnancy.

After Angel's premature birth on May 7, 1998, the baby remained in the hospital for several weeks intubated and sleeping in an incubator. When it was time for Angel to leave the hospital, she was released to Caroline – not Melvina. Under hospital policy, a drug-addicted baby could not be released into the care of a drug-addicted mother. Caroline kept Angel for one night and rushed her to Melvina the following morning.

"Take this crying baby!" said Caroline handing Angel to Melvina. "I ain't never heard a chile holler like that before in my life. It was terrible. She cried all night. Even after I changed her soiled diapers, gave her warm bottles, and sang sweet lullabies as I rocked her in my arms, she just wouldn't stop crying. Me and Carl ain't get a wink of sleep. If I took this crying baby back to the house, I might as well look for another place to stay and another husband, because I would lose both ."

The experience Caroline shared about Angel's crying was a prelude to what was to come for Melvina. Melvina cringed whenever Angel cried. Her cries were so harrowing, Melvina thought they would drive her to the brink of insanity.

"Shut the fuck up!" Melvina sometimes yelled at the infant. "Stop all that damn crying before I throw you out the damn window!"

Big Mike was of little help. He was madder about having a second baby with Melvina than he was with the first. By the time she was pregnant with Angel, the two would engage in volatile arguments.

"I told you I ain't wont no babies, and here you come tellin' me you pregnant again!" he bellowed after she broke the news to him.

"Fuck you Big Mike!" she screamed back. "It took two of us to make this baby. I didn't get pregnant by myself!"

"You told me you had taken your birth control! I got a mind to cut that baby right out of your stomach you lyin' Bitch!"

"And your ass will be going to jail for a long ass time too!" she threatened. "Remember, you're the one on probation! Not me!"

"You better be glad I'm on probation!" he screamed. "You fuckin' Crackhead!"

Melvina heard whimpering coming from the steps. It was Lil' Mike sitting on the steps crying.

"I didn't know you were on the steps Lil' Mike," she told him. Meanwhile, Big Mike stormed out the house shouting, "You're always babyin' that boy!" before slamming the door behind him. "Lil' Mike, I'm sorry you heard what your father said about not wanting any children. Don't pay him any mind son. I fixed you some Oodles of Noodles, baby. They're in the microwave."

Big Mike carried on badly throughout her pregnancy with Angel. However, he still bought Melvina beer to drink and Crack to smoke. Melvina thought Big Mike would eventually warm up to their green-eyed baby girl. But he only seemed to grow meaner and colder. And Angel's constant crying only made things worse.

"Can't you get that baby to hush up!" he always told her. "All that damn cryin' is getting on my damn nerves! I can't even hear myself think! Shit!"

"Well, the least you can do is hold her!" Melvina shouted. "She's yours too!"

"I ain't holdin' that 'cryin' ass baby! Since you were the one so hellbent on gittin' pregnant again, you hold her!"

Caroline once commented on how much Angel looked like Big Mike and their grandfather. She told Melvina one day she would retrieve a photo from an old family photo album, to show the resemblance. This was surprising to Melvina. Caroline and Big Mike rarely talked about their family, and Melvina had never seen any family photos. Caroline kept her word. One day she brought two photos over to Melvina's house.

"Here's a photo of my grandpa and my grandma," said Caroline. "I brought it over so you could see the resemblance. That crying baby Angel got green eyes just like my bruuuuuther and Grandpa."

"Big Mike looks just like your grandfather," said Melvina, staring at the old black and white photograph of a tall, lanky, light-complexioned, green-eyed man. Then she looked at the woman standing next to him. She was medium-complexioned, had squinty, dark-colored eyes. and a stocky build.

"And everybody says I look like my grandma," said Caroline.

"You sure do," said Melvina now staring at the woman in the old photo.

"They took that photo standing in front of their farmhouse in Mississippi."

Caroline also showed Melvina a photo of her and Big Mike's mother. She was a fair-skinned woman, who also had squinty, dark-colored eyes, and a stocky build.

"This is our mother Annie Mae Adams,". said Caroline.

"Wow," said Melvina. "You look just like your mother and grandmother."

That was the first and only time Melvina ever saw photos of Caroline and Big Mike's family. She hoped giving him children would bring her and Big Mike closer together. But instead, they only grew further apart. A sobering thought punched Melvina in the gut as she looked at the woman in the mirror.

"Caroline was right about her brother, but I love him," Melvina whispered to the reflection staring back at her from the mirrored medicine cabinet. "Damn. I miss Caroline. We've been through so much together."

In thinking about Caroline, Melvina's mind flashed back to the1980s. Vivid images of her late parents Melvin and Margaret Thomas materialized in her mind. Her name 'Melvina' was derived from her father's name – Melvin. Her father died in 1981, while her mother died in 1982.

At the time of her father's death, Melvina was a 15-year-old freshman at Walbrook High School. An alcoholic, he died at age 47. Prior to battling alcoholism, he was a fun, loving father who enjoyed cracking jokes. He took the family to Carlin's Drive-In, Edmondson Drive-In, and Bengies to see movies. On Sundays after church, they ate at Ponderosa and Rustler steakhouses. They sometimes dined at Circle One, atop the Holiday Inn downtown. They drove to Kings Dominion and Busch Gardens. They attended AFRAM, a free annual city festival dedicated to the culture and art of African Americans. She had fond memories of the event, which draws tens of thousands each year. AFRAM was so much fun. Daddy would buy us all kinds of food. I also loved getting my face painted and watching and listening to all the singers and groups perform on stage. I always saw myself one day performing on the AFRAM stage.

However, excursions to AFRAM, and other events like the City Far, stopped after her father lost his job at Bethlehem Steel. Depressed and out of work, he started drinking rum. That's when he changed, Melvina recalled. Every morning, he would drive to one of the neighborhood's cut-rates to get himself a 'shorty'. The shorties grew into half-pints, and the half-pints grew into fifths. He crashed his car and eventually lost his driving privileges after several DWIs (Driving While Intoxicated). Looking back, Melvina couldn't help but think about her mother's stoicism. The more her father slipped into alcoholism, the more he verbally abused her mother. He stayed drunk all the time. In his drunkenness, her father would berate her mother. After a long workday, her mother would come through the door only to be greeted with his slurred, profanity-laced babble. But her mama simply ignored him, and went about her business - cooking, carrying out household chores, and preparing for the next workday. This went on for years until he died of cirrhosis of the liver.

Her mother Margaret cooked and cleaned houses for Jewish families that lived in Park Heights. She had done that as far back as Melvina could remember. At the crack of dawn, her mother got up to feed and dress Earlene while Melvina got ready for school. Then, her mother would walk Earlene to sitter Essie Mae Brown's house before going to work. Mrs. Brown and her husband Ned were neighbors. A retired cook who was known for making delicious pound cakes from 'scratch,' Mrs. Brown had been babysitting Earlene since she was a baby.

But one October day in 1982, her mother returned home after taking Earlene to Mrs. Brown's house. That was strange. Her mother typically caught the bus straight to work after dropping off Earlene. However, on this particular day, her mother came back home. She told Melvina she felt tired and nauseous and was staying home from work. Melvina found this highly unusual. She couldn't recall her mother ever being sick. A stickler for time, her mother was never late for work, let alone miss a day.

"You want me to stay home with you Mama?" Melvina asked.

"No baby," her mother replied. "Mama's just feelin' a little under the weather. That's all. Nothin' that a little rest and some castor oil won't cure."

"Castor oil…ewww…yuck," said Melvina with a grimace, recalling how much she hated the taste of castor oil. Her mother made her drink it every time she had a cold. "Drinking that stuff is just like drinking liquid Vaseline."

"Castor oil might not taste good," said her mother. "But it does miracles to help cure illness. Now you go on to school chile. Mama's gonna be just fine."

Melvina kissed her mother goodbye and made the short walk to Caroline's house. She and Caroline met in the summer of 1982. Caroline came to live with Wilhelmina Simpson, who lived in the neighborhood at the time. After Caroline moved in with Miss Simpson, she and Melvina struck up a friendship. Caroline was a shy, country girl, whose family moved to Baltimore the prior year. Melvina was an introvert who mostly stayed to herself. Neither of them had any close friends. Miss Simpson lived a few doors down from the Thomas home. Before long, Melvina and Caroline became best friends. They were the same age, in the same grade, attended the same school, enjoyed going to church, and took great delight in cooking.

They attended Walbrook High School on Ellamont Street in Walbrook Junction. Miss Simpson enrolled Caroline at the school after she moved in with the elderly lady. Each morning, Melvina and Caroline walked to school together. During the walk, they talked about boys, movies, peer pressure, recipes, and lots of other things. Melvina reflected on one of their conversations about the school's educators.

"Miss Ellis is my favor-right teacher," she told Caroline, referring to the school's popular Business teacher, Melva Ellis.

"That ain't how you say that word," Caroline said. 'It's pronounced 'fav'ret.'

"You ain't pronouncing it right either with your country self," Melvina retorted.

"Yes I am too, honey, with your Bawlamore self," said Caroline.

"It's Hon," said Melvina. "Not honey. But you wouldn't know. "Cause it's a Baltimore thang." She and Caroline both giggled and with their book bags strapped to their bags, headed to Walbrook High.

Walbrook was the source of many fond memories. In addition to Miss Ellis, there was the school's principal, Dr. Samuel R. Billups. A man who balanced stern leadership with tender love for his staff and students. There was the school's Assistant Principal, Mr. Roy Pope. A man who walked the hallways wearing a suit and tennis shoes and toting a baseball bat. All it took was a sharp gaze from Mr. Pope for her and the other students to 'straighten up.' The administrators also included Mrs. Louise Lassiter who always greeted the students with a warm smile and words of encouragement. Lois Scherer a department head in the Guidance Department was a friendly woman who offered advice and urged Melvina to begin to think about life after high school.

There was Genevieve Perry, the Home Economics teacher who taught her and the other students how to sew. It was Ms. Perry's class that heightened Melvina's interest in cooking. The students learned recipes and even brought dishes to school for their classmates to sample. There was Drama teacher Cheryl Pasteur. It was in Miss Pasteur's class that Melvina learned how to act, and performed her first monologue. There was the Art teacher, Reva Lewie, who taught her about painting and palettes. Melvina didn't know she could paint so well until Mrs. Lewie's Art class. The list of Walbrook High School's memorable educators went on and on. Melvina came to the school as a teen mother who was unsure of herself. But the school and her mother boosted her confidence. Both instilled that with hard work and discipline, she could still achieve her goals.

Melvina was scheduled to be among Walbrook's graduating Class of 1984. Their slogan: 'Open the Door, Say No More, We're the Class of '84.'

Melvina couldn't wait for the day when her mother and the school's staff would proudly watch as she was handed her Maryland High School Diploma. In her mind, she visualized that moment many times. However, Graduation Day never came for Melvina.

During their walk to school one sunny, brisk fall morning, Melvina and Caroline made plans to study and do homework together later that afternoon. The two 16-year-olds also discussed walking to a nearby carryout to play their favorite arcade game, Ms. Pac-Man, after they were done. But Melvina was troubled. Her mother staying home from work was still in the back of her mind.

Melvina hoped by the time she returned home her mother would be feeling better. She and Caroline headed to her house after being dismissed from school. The two walked through the front door of Melvina's house and found her mother sprawled out on the living room floor.

"Mama! Mama!" Melvina cried, tearing her book bag from her back, and frantically rushing to her mother's side.

"I'll call 911!" Caroline shouted, running to the phone, and turning its rotary dial.

A short time later, paramedics arrived. They feverishly worked on her mother before rushing her to nearby Provident Hospital. After her mother's arrival, she and Caroline waited for a doctor to give them an update. It seemed like an eternity. A few minutes later, a somber-faced doctor delivered the devastating news. Her mother had passed. The last thing Melvina remembered was screaming and then everything going black. She had fainted.

In reflecting, Melvina thought about how Caroline helped her get through the devastating loss of her mother. Caroline was a Godsend. After her mother passed, a steady flow of friends, neighbors, and church members came by to offer their condolences and bring food. Those visits tapered off until they stopped altogether. But Caroline remained by her side.

Melvina's mother was only 46 when she died of a massive heart attack. Melvina recalled her mother as being a kind, God-fearing, nurturing woman who worked long days to take care of her family. While her mother never complained, she had also taken years of verbal abuse doled out by Melvina's alcoholic father. Looking back, Melvina felt stress, bottled-up emotions, poor diet, and rare doctor visits may have played a part in her mother's early demise. Her mother always took care of everyone else and placed her own health at the bottom of the totem pole. This was indicative of many Black women Melvina had come to know. After Melvina gave birth to Earlene at age 12, her mother paid the sitter, brought pampers, formula, clothes, and babysat whenever she could. Her mother helped her with Earlene up until the day she died. Ever since she could remember, her mother carried a heavy load. Melvina secretly struggled with feelings of guilt around her mother's death.

At 16-years-old, Melvina was an emancipated minor and an orphan simultaneously. And her mother was no longer around to help with four-year-old Earlene. With her mother gone, Melvina was forced to grow up fast. Her mother left behind a $20,000 life insurance policy. The money more than covered her final expenses and left Melvina with a large sum of money. Melvina deposited the funds at Maryland National Bank's Mondawmin Mall branch for safekeeping. It was just under $15,000. Melvina planned to save the money for Earlene's college education, her own tuition should she decide to further her education and emergency purposes.

An only child, Melvina also inherited her parents' house. The house was paid off, but Melvina knew she still needed a steady income. Utility and other household bills would have to be paid, and Earlene still needed things. Melvina decided it was best if she dropped out of school and find a job. It was a difficult decision. Caroline tried everything to convince Melvina to stay in school, but Melvina's mind was made up. She dropped out of high school in her sophomore year and began looking for employment. She was hired by Ty Moonie owner of Ty's Bakery. Melvina loved working at the small Monroe Street bakeshop. Miss Moonie taught her a variety of new skills such as how to use large, commercial baking pans, how to bake in a commercial oven, and how to place bread, buns, and other goods on a commercial baking cooling rack.

Miss Moonie was a petite 41-year-old who wore her sandy brown hair pulled up in a neat bun, her distinct hairline coming together in a V-shape at the center of her forehead known as a 'Widow's Peak.' The self-made entrepreneur trained Melvina on how to operate a cash register and placing orders for flour, sugar, nonpareil sprinkles, and other supplies. The customers were friendly and working there afforded Melvina the opportunity to earn money while doing something she enjoyed, to learn a plethora of skills, and meet new people. The smell of fresh-baked bread filled the shop and the store's glass display cases were full of cupcakes, pastries, and Bundt, 7-Up, Pound, and other cakes she helped to create and bake. She mixed the artistry of Mrs. Lewie's Art class, with the baking skills she acquired in Miss Perry's Home Ec. class, with her love for cooking. She delighted in doodling designs atop cakes and cupcakes. "My little masterpieces," she said on many occasions, gazing inside the cases at the edible works of art.

Sometimes she caught the bus to work, and other times she walked. For years, Melvina watched her mother go to work. Her mother went to work in all kinds of weather – hot, cold, sunshine, snow, and rain. Her father did the same until he started drinking. Both parents were sticklers when it came to being punctual and going to work. Melvina brought the same work ethic to Ty's Bakery. Home and school had proven to be wonderful prerequisites for the work world.

Melvina also helped Caroline get a job at the bakery. After Caroline was interviewed by Miss Moonie, she was hired. Caroline worked at Ty's part-time, attending school during the day, and working in the evenings and Saturdays. Melvina worked every other Sunday. However, Caroline never worked on Sundays.

"That's the Lawd's day," Caroline always said. "I ain't workin' for nobody on Sunday. Even God rested on the seventh day."

"You sure are an old-time Saint to be so young," Melvina told Caroline.

"You ain't never too young to be on fire for Gawd," said Caroline.

Caroline was able to save up enough money to attend Easy Method Driving School. She completed driving school, got her Learner's Permit, and ultimately went to the MVA (Motor Vehicle Administration) at Mondawmin and passed the Driver's Test. Miss Simpson owned a white Oldsmobile and occasionally allowed Caroline to drive to church. Some Sundays, Melvina would get a glimpse of them heading to church as she stood at her screen door. Caroline would see Melvina and toot the horn.

"I'm gonna enroll in driving school and get my Driver's License too," Melvina thought, waving at Caroline and Miss Simpson as they drove by. I'm just gonna wait until Earlene gets a little older.

In 1984, Caroline graduated from Walbrook. Melvina attended the Commencement Ceremony to support Caroline. The graduation was held on the school's infield on a sunny June morning. But attending the graduation was difficult for Melvina. She was happy for Caroline, but deep down inside, she was a little 'jealous' of her best friend, decked out in her graduation regalia along with the other graduates. I should be graduating too, she thought, watching Caroline and other members of the graduating class being handed their diplomas. But ain't no use in being sore about it. I'll get back in school. Or maybe I'll enroll in a G.E.D. program. I'm just 18 and I still have my whole life in front of me. I've got plenty of time.

By 1986, Melvina was drifting into an abyss of loneliness. There was her six-year-old daughter Earlene, but Melvina missed the time she was accustomed to spending with her best friend, Caroline. Caroline was now 'going steady' with Carl Howard. The two began dating as students at Walbrook High School, and like Caroline, Carl was deeply religious. Melvina thought Carl was a good match for her best friend. The two shared a great love for the Lord. He was quiet and reserved, but Caroline disclosed to Melvina that he could sometimes be a 'little cranky.' She also told Melvina that Carl told her he never wanted to have any children.

"Why?" Melvina asked.

"He ain't say why," Caroline replied. "But it don't bother me, 'cause I can't give him none anyway." My bruuuuuther feels the same way, but he don't mind fornicatin' and shackin' up."

Melvina chalked Caroline's statement up to the fact that her best friend was still a virgin and would not sleep with a man until after marriage.

Caroline matriculated to business school after completing her studies at Walbrook. Caroline attended business school by day and worked at the bakery by night. Melvina worked at the bakery during the day, and her afternoons were spent helping Earlene with homework and cooking dinner. The best friends crammed in time together before Caroline headed to work. They ate at Double T Diner on Baltimore National Pike and went shopping. Sometimes Mrs. Brown babysat Earlene, and other times the youngster went with them.

However, the time Caroline and Melvina spent together was quickly diminishing. While Caroline remained a faithful friend, she was devoting more time to Carl. Not only did Melvina miss spending time with Caroline, but she was still mourning the loss of her parents. Her closest relatives lived in Durham, North Carolina, so there was no family in close proximity she could visit or with whom to spend time. I feel all alone, she thought. A 20-year-old single parent with the weight of the world on my shoulders trying to survive and do everything by myself. And now I feel like even Caroline is deserting me.

Nevertheless, growing up in the church, Melvina knew she could find solace and comfort in a place of worship. Her parents were devout Christians who had been members of New Hope Baptist Church, founded by the Rev. Dr. William Nelson Stokes, a dynamic preacher known all over the city. Her parents were lifelong members of the church, located on Fremont Avenue and Dolphin Street.

Melvina's father was an ordained deacon at New Hope but stopped attending church altogether after drinking got ahold of him. Her mother was a deaconess and missionary and attended the church up until the time she died. Melvina had not been back to the church since her mother's funeral. As far back as Melvina could remember, her parents took her to New Hope, where she sang on the church's choirs dating back to childhood. As much as she missed the worship experience and singing at New Hope, she couldn't bring herself to attend without either of her parents. Melvina shared this sentiment with Caroline, who told her church would help her through the grieving process.

"And not only that," said Caroline. "But M, you are an anointed singer. God blessed those lungs of yours in a mighty way! And if I didn't know any better, I'd swear that voice of yours belonged to Mahalia Jackson or Aretha Franklin! Keep sangin' for the good Lawd! Using that beautiful voice of yours will not only bless others, but it will bless you too!"

What have I got to sing about? Nothing. I don't want to sing right now…not even for the Lord. The way I feel, I may not ever sing again.

One Sunday morning, feeling depressed and lonely, Melvina was crying on tear-soaked pillows when she heard a knock at the front door. She wasn't expecting anyone and thought, I don't feel like being bothered with nobody. I'm gonna lay right here in this bed.

Knock! Knock! Knock! Knock! Knock! The persistent knocks prompted Melvina to slowly drag herself out of bed and walk to the door. She peered out the peephole to see who was knocking. It was Caroline. Melvina unlocked the door and headed back upstairs. She, laid in a fetal position on her bed and cried and cried. Caroline opened the door and went up to her room, sat next to her, trying her best to hold and console her dear friend.

"I know how you feel losing your mama and all," said Caroline.

"You have no idea what it feels like," said Melvina. "You didn't lose your mama."

"That's where you're wrong," replied Caroline. "I lost my mama too."

That April 6, 1986 morning, Melvina listened to Caroline's shocking story of what happened to her mother.

"That's terrible and so sad,' said Melvina. "I am so sorry Caroline. I'm speechless."

"Like I said, I know how you feel M. After my mama passed last year, the sorrow was so great, it felt as if it was eating away at my very soul. And I had already been through some other traumatic things in my life I wouldn't dare repeat. I really didn't want to go on. I felt like the rug of life had been pulled out from under me. I didn't see it coming, and I went down hard. But Gawd gave me the strength to get back up. And I ain't gonna lie…it's still hard accepting what happened to my mama…especially the way she died. But M, there's a certain inner peace that only comes from the good Lawd. He can give you the strength to get you through M, just like He is doing for me. He is the Great Comforter. And I'm reminded of the grace and goodness of Gawd ev'ry Sunday I go to church. The worship experience is a beautiful thang, M. I already drove Miss Simpson to church. Now I've come back to get you.'

Melvina and Caroline slowly rocked one another and shared a long, tearful hug. Caroline wiped the tears from her eyes. Caroline helped her to get dressed. Caroline brushed her hair. Caroline dressed Earlene. Caroline cooked breakfast for her and Earlene. Afterward, they headed out the door and Caroline drove to United in Victory Tabernacle, where she and Miss Simpson were members. The grand church was located on North Avenue and was pastored and founded by Bishop Wright Just, Sr. a well-known Baltimore preacher and Civil Rights activist. "Dr. Martin Luther King, Jr. once preached at United in Victory," said Caroline. "People are still talking about that."

Melvina's first visit to the church with Caroline was memorable. She went up for prayer during Altar Call, and her downtrodden spirit was immediately lifted with feelings of hope and renewed faith. Listening to the choir under the direction of the church's famous musician Dr. Malachi Madison was also inspiring. I have never heard anyone play a Hammond B3 organ like that! she thought. And my Lawd, that is a good-lookin' man!

Hearing the choir also reminded her of how much she missed singing. She possessed remarkable singing ability but had not sang since she stopped going to church. Bishop Just preached a sermon entitled, 'God Will Bring You Through', singing parts of the sermon. It feels like he is preaching to me, she thought. I am so glad I came to church with Caroline. This sermon is just what I need to hear. And my Lawd can that Pastor sing! I see why Caroline calls him The Singing Preacher! She said he sounded like Marvin Winans, but he reminds me of Rev. James Cleveland.'

Melvina enjoyed the service so much, she and Earlene attended with Caroline and Miss Simpson every Sunday she didn't have to work. On Sunday, June 8, 1986, a little over two months after Caroline first took her to United in Victory, Melvina joined the church. She also joined the church's Mass Choir. Melvina's beautiful Gospel-seeded voice led Dr. Madison, to select her as its lead singer.

"What a magnificent voice you have Sister Thomas," Dr. Madison told her. "I am astonished at your ability to sing highly complex vocal runs and your range is simply amazing. The manner in which you can hold notes for considerable amounts of time is remarkable. No matter or how low or how high, you can belt out even the most difficult of song verses with relative ease. You are a masterful mix of power and eloquence. You, my dear, are fabulous!"

Dr. Madison also held the position of Minister of Music and was even more impressed with Earlene, who was a member of the Youth Choir. "Earlene boasts the same talents as you do," Dr. Madison expressed to Melvina. "She has a plethora of talents…and at such a young age! I am thoroughly impressed with both of you, and I am not impressed easily. I believe Earlene has so much talent at age eight that she could be the next Whitney Houston! I would like to work with her personally to further broaden her already-impressive range."

Humbled by how highly Dr. Madison thought of their singing, particularly her daughter's, Melvina agreed to allow Dr. Madison to work with Earlene one-on-one. Under his personal tutelage, Earlene's singing became all the more dynamic. Like Melvina, Earlene led the choir on nearly every song. Melvina and Earlene were an integral part of both choirs, which brought the choir even more popularity and acclaim. Sometimes Dr. Madison would bring mother and daughter together to lead a song, which brought many a crowd to their feet during church service and concerts. They also performed with several famed groups including the prestigious and highly-touted Unified Voices of Johns Hopkins choir founded by Dr. Gregory Wm. Branch.

Caroline and Carl married in 1989, and Melvina was Maid of Honor in her best friend's wedding. The former Caroline Adams was now Caroline Howard. Caroline had also completed her studies at the business school. After Caroline married Carl, she moved out of Miss Simpson's house. The 23-year-old newlyweds purchased a rowhouse on Norfolk Avenue in Northwest Baltimore. Carl had a cousin by the name of Dartha Battle who worked at the Circuit Court for Baltimore City. Melvina did not know Ms. Battle personally. However, her brother John Battle owned a barbershop on N. Mount Street in Sandtown/Winchester and was Lil' Mike's barber. Ms. Battle was the first African American to integrate what was once known as Circuit Court Number One. After the consolidation of the Baltimore City courts, she was appointed Manager of the Civil Division. Her office assisted many notable people, including Civil Rights Attorney Mrs. Juanita Jackson Mitchell.

Ms. Battle tenaciously worked her way up the ranks, to the Criminal Division of Circuit Court, owning the distinction of being the first African American and female to oversee it. As head of the court's Criminal Division, Ms. Battle wielded authority to be able to hire other African Americans. Impressed with Caroline, Ms. Battle told her about a clerical job opening at the courthouse. Caroline applied for the position and was hired. She gave notice to the bakery she would be resigning to accept a new job. After Caroline married Carl, she left United in Victory Tabernacle to join his church — New Life Fellowship in Edmondson Village. Melvina missed seeing her best friend at church but remained at United in Victory, which was helping her to regain her lease on life. She and Earlene's voices continued to bring them praise and popularity at the church, which was always packed to capacity. Looking back at what happened there, my beautiful little girl's singing voice may have also brought her unwanted attention, Melvina thought.

On March 24, 1989, Melvina received some unbelievable news about Earlene. Melvina always remembered the exact date because it was the same day as the Exxon Valdez oil spill. The oil slick was all over the news, and she and Earlene talked about it. They were both sad to see so many oil-blackened dead mammals floating in the water. Melvina spoke to Bishop Just about what she was told about her 11-year-old daughter. He felt it was in everyone's best interest to send Earlene away, and as her spiritual leader, Melvina thought it was only right to take his advice. The decision was made to send Earlene to live with her relatives in Durham, North Carolina. Among other things, Earlene would receive tremendous singing opportunities in North Carolina, and her relatives were in a much better position financially to raise Earlene. Her aunt, Doris Graham owned a convenience store, and her husband Lou Graham was a musician who said he knew a lot of influential people in the music world including famed Motown founder Berry Gordon who had discovered the likes of The Jackson 5, Diana Ross, and The Supremes, and Marvin Gaye.

With the help of Bishop Just, Melvina purchased a one-way ticket for Earlene, and on May 11, 1990, tearfully put her on a Greyhound bus to Durham, North Carolina to live with Aunt Doris and Uncle Lou.

This is only a temporary situation, Melvina repeatedly told herself. Once everything dies down, I'm gonna send for Earlene.

The anguishing decision to send Earlene to North Caroline was the most difficult decision the 24-year-old Melvina had ever made. Angry, bitter, sad, and regretful over what happened to Earlene, Melvina left United in Victory. Sunday, May 13, 1989, marked the last time she attended the church. She fell out of fellowship and no longer sang in the choir. I don't want any part of church, she thought. And I don't want to sing. This is the lowest I have felt in my entire life. If I were to sing anything, it would be the Blues. Now I understand what Billie Holiday's song Good Morning Heartache was all about. Because right now, I feel nothing but heartache. However, Caroline stayed on Melvina about returning to church.

"M, I know you are dealing with 'church hurt' after what happened at United in Victory," said Caroline. "I tell you the Devil is some kinda busy! But M, don't give up on church altogether, and whatever you do, don't give up on Gawd! The Bible says forsake not to assemble! Not to mention you have stopped sangin' again! You got to continue to use the gift the good Lawd gave ya!"

On Sunday, January 7, 1990 – nearly seven months after leaving United in Victory, following a scandalous cover-up, Melvina began attending New Life Fellowship with Caroline and Carl. The couple would pick Melvina up and take her to church with them. She joined New Life on Sunday, January 28, 1990. Some Sunday afternoons, the couple would have Melvina over for supper. On many occasions, Melvina would gaze at Caroline and Carl at the dinner table and wish she were married too. Now in her mid-20s, Melvina yearned for a boyfriend, or better yet, a husband. One day, she shared this with Caroline.

"I'm 24-years-old now Caroline," she told her best friend. "You and Carl look so happy. I'd like to get married too. Especially before I turn 30. Do you think I'll ever find a husband?"

"Of course I do, M," replied Caroline. "But you can't just jump out there and accept any ol' thing! Just pray and wait on the good Lawd! 'He'll send you a good huuuuusband, just like He sent me one.'"

What Melvina yearned for, unexpectedly showed up the afternoon of Sunday, February 8, 1990. She was at Caroline and Carl's having supper when someone knocked at the door.

Caroline and Carl were puzzled. The couple was not expecting any company. Caroline walked over to a window and pulled back the drapes to see who was outside. She turned and looked at Carl with a concerned look.

"Lawd have mercy," said Caroline.

"What's wrong?" asked Carl.

"It's my bruuuuuther Michael."

Carl didn't look thrilled. He shifted his body and shook his head.

Melvina sat at their dinner table thinking about the story Caroline shared about her mother Annie Mae Adams years ago. It was the Sunday morning Melvina went to United in Victory with Caroline for the first time. In comforting Melvina, Caroline divulged what happened to her mother.

Caroline said one night back in 1981, her mother frantically awakened her and her older brother Michael from their sleep. "We ain't know what was going on with our mama," said Caroline. "But she was crying and upset…eyes bloodshot red and mascara just a runnin'. She hurried me and my bruuuuuther into the back seat of her car and drove like a bat outta hell from Mississippi to Baltimore."

Caroline went on to tell Melvina she, her brother, and mother temporarily stayed in the parsonage of United in Victory Tabernacle, and soon joined the church. That's when she met Miss Simpson.

"During a revival one Sunday, I became filled with the Holy Ghost and shouted all over that church," said Caroline. "What a glorious experience. I wasn't but 15 at the time. I have been saved ever since."

Caroline said she later became a youth usher, and that her mother served on the Missionary Circle and volunteered in the Soup Kitchen. Her mother got a job as a cashier at McCrory's department store.

"My mama moved out of the parsonage," said Caroline. "We moved into a large home on Liberty Heights Avenue, where my mama rented the third floor. Things were starting to look up. But my brother Michael always stayed in trouble. He was 17 at the time and also got kicked out of school. He drifted back and forth between Baltimore and Mississippi. He was so hard-headed. Mama couldn't do a thing with that boy."

"How did your mama die?" Melvina asked.

"Mama hanged herself," said Caroline.

"That's terrible!" said Melvina who was both shocked and horrified.

"Tell me about it. And my bruuuuuther Michael was the one who found her."

"Oh my goodness!"

"Thinking back, there were times my mama seemed so sad and depressed. But nobody saw that coming."

"I'm so sorry Caroline. That had to be very traumatic for your brother."

"It was. But Michael did his best not to show it. You know how some men are…they never cry on the outside…they see cryin' as a weakness. But they are cryin' on the inside. That's my bruuuuuther."

"And nobody knows what could have led your mama to take her own life?"

"Naw, nobody knows. But Michael did say he called Mama and told her he wanted to talk to her about something regarding his birth certificate. When he got to the apartment, that's when he found her hanging from the ceiling."

"How old was your mama?"

"She wasn't but 33."

Caroline took a deep pause and began to cry. 'Had it not been for the good Lawd, there's no way I would have made it,' she said of the experience. 'I had been through so many terrible things in my life.'

Caroline said after her mother's suicide, Miss Simpson took her in. She rarely talked about her brother Michael nor their family in Mississippi. Melvina had never met Michael, and this particular Sunday marked the first time she heard his name mentioned in a long time.

Caroline walked over to the door and turned the deadbolt. After a long pause, she opened the door, and in walked Michael.

So that's Michael, Melvina thought. I would have never guessed. He and Caroline don't look nothing alike.

"What in the Sam Hill brings you here?" asked Caroline as she flashed an uneasy look at Carl. "When did you get out?"

"About three months ago," Michael responded. "I was in the neighborhood, so I reckoned I'd stop by to holler at you and Carl."

"Is that so?" Caroline asked.

"That's right," said Michael. "And I also wanted to let you know that I got a job. And my own crib."

"That's good," said Caroline. "I'm glad to hear you're doing better for yourself. I hope you're staying out of trouble."

"I ain't plannin' on getting' in no more trouble. Got my Driver's License now, and I'm workin' as a delivery driver."

"You got a job?" asked Caroline.

"That's right," said Michael.

"Thank the Lawd for that," said Caroline.

"And I really like my job too. Just me, my deliveries, and the road. And the pay ain't bad either. Hey Caroline."

"Yes, Michael?"

"I guess Grandpa teaching us how to drive so early came in handy, huh?" asked Michael. "Remember how he would put us on the yellow tractor when we were little kids? I can still see him dressed in his dingy overalls plopping us on his lap and letting us steer that big, ole tractor. You remember that, Caroline?"

"How could I forget?' responded Caroline glancing at Carl apprehensively. "You want something to eat Michael?"

"Don't mind if I do," said Michael glancing at Melvina. "Who wouldn't sit at the table with such a purdy little lady. Caroline, ain't you gonna introduce us?"

"M, this is my bruuuuther Michael Adams, Sr.," said Caroline.

"Pleased to meet you, Michael."

"Pleased to meet you M."

"Hold it right there!" said Caroline giving her brother a squinty eye. "I call her 'M'. 'That's the nickname I gave my best friend, and only I call her that. You can call her by her first name, Melvina."

"Pleased to meet you Melvina," said Michael. "Hey, Carl." Carl acknowledged Michael's greeting with a silent nod of the head.

"Boy am I hungry!" said Michael, sitting next to Melvina. He immediately began eating. The minute Michael sat next to her - the fragrance of 'Polo' cologne making its way up Melvina's nostrils. She loved the smell of 'Polo' on a man.

"Michael!" snapped Caroline. "You can't just sit at the table and start eating like a hungry hawg before saying Grace. And take off your hat in my house!"

Michael looked annoyed, but took off his hat, bowed his head, and said his Grace silently.

After he held his head up, Caroline sniffed her nose in Michael's direction.

"You might have all that fancy cologne on," said Caroline. "But I still smell the stench of cigarette smoke on you."

"I'm gonna kick the habit one day," Michael replied.

"You better, or those Cancer sticks are gonna kick you!," warned Caroline.

"You'd think I'd never woulda picked up a cigarette in my life after Grandpa," said Michael. "But I did. And I tell you what…it's a hard habit to break."

"All habits are," said Caroline.

As he and Caroline bantered back and forth about his cigarette habit, Melvina gazed at Michael.

Caroline never told me her brother was so fine, Melvina thought. She checked Michael out from head to toe the moment he walked through the door. He was about 5'9'', had a medium build, a light complexion, striking emerald-green eyes, and curly sandy brown hair. Michael reminded her of Smoky Robinson, and she always had the biggest crush on the singer.

Melvina could still recall what Michael had on that day. A beeper was clipped to the waist of his black Adidas sweatsuit. He sported a black Kangol hat and a gold dookie rope chain. His dress reminded her of the attire worn by Run DMC, a popular rap group.

Supper that day was awkward. Typically, eating at Caroline and Carl's dinner table included lively conversation. They usually talked about church, the happenings in Baltimore, and other things. On this particular day, the conversation was limited. Melvina would have expected Michael and Caroline to catch up on lost time. They did converse, but Michael mostly talked about how much he enjoyed his new job. Caroline and Carl looked uncomfortable at the dinner table. The couple periodically glanced at each other when Michael spoke. Caroline seemed fidgety, which was highly unusual.

But Melvina was smitten. She kept looking over at Michael. During one of her glances, their eyes met. Melvina blushed. It was not her intent for Michael to catch her staring over at him. Michael smiled at Melvina. She shyly looked down towards her lap and saw Michael tap her on the thigh. Just the mere touch of Michael's hand on her thigh was arousing. He was slipping her a torn piece of paper with his contact information. Melvina didn't quite know what to make of all the secrecy, but she followed Michael's lead and eased the piece of paper into her dress pocket beneath the veil of the table. Yet, Caroline was not fooled and caught whiff of the hand-off. And like a referee spotting a foul play, Caroline gave Melvina a stern warning.

'I saw my bruuuuuther Michael sliiiiide you his number on the low yesterday,' said Caroline the following morning. 'Listen to me M, and you listen good. Tear that number up! Michael's my bruuuuuther and I love him. But M, you're my best friend, and I love you too. I don't want to see you get hurt. Don't play with that fire, or you gonna get burnt!'

Melvina remained silent as she listened to Caroline go on and on about Michael. At that moment, Melvina was holding the paper Michael scribbled his name and beeper (pager) number on in black ink.

Tear his card up? Melvina thought as she eyeballed the paper. I'll do no such thing. I'm gonna beep Michael and see what happens. Maybe, he'll call me back. Besides, it's about time I went out on a date. Melvina began to think about a night out on the town with the green-eyed dreamboat and could hardly wait to page him.

'Hello! Hello! M…are you there?!' shouted Caroline interrupting her thoughts.

'I'm here,' said Melvina.

'Do you hear what I'm saying?'

'Yes.'

'Well, I'm not convinced. Michael's no good for you, M'. Like I told ya before, just wait on the Lawd. He'll send you the right man. Take it from me. It ain't my bruuuuuther Michael. Do you hear me?'

"Loud and clear."

'You better take heed of what I'm tellin' ya. Don't be deceived! Michael might be good-looking and charming but beware. He can be as mean as a desert rattlesnake and just as vicious! Stay away from him!'

You have a man Caroline, Melvina thought to herself. I don't! What's the harm in at least talking to Michael? He seems nice enough and he is fine as can be!

Melvina disregarded Caroline's warnings, and as soon as the two hung up, she beeped Michael. With bated breath, she waited for Michael to call her back, and about 15 anxious minutes later, the phone rang.

They talked and made plans to go out after the two got off from work later that day, and on February 9, 1990, she and Michael went out on their first date. They went out again. And again. And again. Other than her close friend Caroline, Melvina had never spent so much time with a person outside of her family.

Melvina took great measures to hide from Caroline that she and her brother were dating. Melvina kept their phone conversations short by coming up with excuses to get off the phone, and sometimes avoiding Caroline's calls altogether. Consequently, there was no denying she and Michael were seeing one another after Caroline unexpectedly stopped by her house one afternoon and saw Michael there watching television with his feet kicked up on her new cocktail table and blowing o-shaped smoke rings while puffing on cigarettes.

Caroline's visit was brief. Embarrassed that Caroline's visit confirmed she failed to heed her best friend's warning, Melvina did not answer her repeated phone calls. She knew it was Caroline calling because of Caller ID, a new technology that allowed a person to see the phone number of a caller. Melvina was waiting on a customer one afternoon when she heard the tinkering of the small bell that hung from a string on the bakery door. The sound of the bell's clapper clanging against its rustic metal could be heard whenever someone entered or exited the bakery. On this occasion, the person walking in was Caroline who greeted Miss Moonie before asking Melvina if they could talk.

Melvina finished waiting on her customer and asked Miss Moonie if she could take a short break.

"Why of course you can Melvina," replied Miss Moonie. "I'll wait on customers. But don't be too long. It's nearing noon on a Saturday, and you know how busy things get around here."

"Thank you, Miss Moonie. I won't be long."

"Nice seeing you, Caroline."

"Nice seeing you too Miss Moonie."

Melvina and Caroline stepped off to the side so they could talk privately.

"I've been trying to call you for several days M, and I know you have been avoiding my phone calls," said Caroline. "That's why I came to the bakery...I knew I would find you here. Now M, we've been friends for almost ten years. And I ain't about to tear up our friendship over Michael. What good is gonna come out of that? You gonna do what you wanna do anyway. And with so many good men out here, I can't believe you wanna date my bruuuuuther. But I'm tellin' you, that boy has a dark side. And it looks like you finna find out the hard way. But don't ever say I ain't tell you.'

"Are you finished, Caroline? I have to get back to work."

"Yes, I'm done wastin' my precious breath. "While I'm here, I may as well buy something so this trip won't be a total waste of my time, gasoline, and energy."

Melvina walked behind the bakery's glass displays and Caroline made her way in front of them to peruse the baked goods.

"Give me two of them raisin buns," said Caroline pointing inside the case. One for me, and one for Carl. And give me a slice of that Pineapple Upside Down cake too. No! Not that piece! The one next to it...that piece is bigger. I'll eat that later, while I'm thinking about you and my bruuuuuther cause Michael is gonna turn your world upside down! Mark my word!"

Caroline is just mad because I'm dating her brother, Melvina fumed. Maybe she's jealous of me because now I'm dating someone who just so happens to be her brother.

"And while you're at it, give me a piece of Pound Cake," said Caroline. "I'll eat that while I think about how much I have tried to pound into that hard head of yours that my bruuuuuther is no good. But you won't listen."

"Is that it?!" seethed Melvina.

"That's it."

Melvina dropped Carolina's tissue-wrapped selections in a white paper bag and rang them up on the cash register.

"Keep the change," said Caroline. "You're gonna need it by the time my bruuuuuuther gets finished with you.

Melvina looked at Caroline march out the bakery; the bell tinkering as she went out the door.

The weeks moved along, and Melvina was having the time of her life. Michael was exposing her to a variety of fun, new experiences. He took her to Phillips Seafood and other restaurants at the Baltimore Inner Harbor, and afterward went paddle boating on its waters. They ate steamed crabs seasoned with 'Old Bay' from 'Bay Island' and 'Martinis from Crab Row' on Monroe Street and he showed her how to open crabs and use a crab mallet. He took her fishing along Patapsco Avenue and taught her how to fish. The more they went out, the more she wanted to spend time with him.

Sometimes, she and Michael would just sit and talk. She trusted Michael and confided in him about some of the hardships she had gone through in her life. Melvina felt they had a lot in common. She told him what life was like after having a child at age 12. He told her he had also gone through difficult circumstances as a child. Melvina told him about losing her parents at a young age and the insurance money she received after her mother's death. Michael told her about losing his mother at a young age. Melvina told him she dropped out of high school. Michael said he also dropped out of school.

"After my mama moved to Baltimore back in '81, she enrolled me and Caroline in school, but I wouldn't go," said Michael. "I kept hooking school and always stayed in trouble. Before Mama got her own place, we were all staying at a church parsonage, but I didn't like it there at all. I needed a way to make some fast money, so I started hustling. I stayed in motels for a while. Eventually, I saved up enough cash to enroll in driving school, get my Maryland Driver's License and buy me a Hooptie –"

"I can't even imagine you driving a Hooptie," laughed Melvina. "They are generally old, raggedy cars."

"My Hooptie was an old 1972 red, white and blue Ford Pinto," chuckled Michael. "But it got me where I had to go, and it was good on gas. Hell, when I bought it back in 1982, it took just five bucks to fill the gas tank. I began buying dope here in Baltimore and traveling back to Mississippi to sell it. I was making good money too, but I got busted for Possession a few times and sent to juvenile detention centers. But after I turned 18, I was being charged as an adult and was being sent to adult jails. By '88, I went in front of a judge who looked at my rap sheet and said that if I violated my probation again, I would be looking at a mandatory minimum of 10 years with no possibility of parole."

"Wow! One day in jail would be too long for me. Ten years is an awfully long time to be locked up."

"Damn right it is, and I ain't tryin' to do 10 years for nobody in the slammer! So, I thought it was best to stop hustling and get a regular job. My grandpa taught me how to drive when I was a little boy back in Mississippi. I always liked driving, so I started looking for driving jobs. Problem was, nobody wanted to hire me with my criminal background. So, I did what I had to do."

"And what was that?" Melvina asked.

"I lied," Michael replied. "That's how I got my job as a delivery truck driver. And I aim to do what I got to do to keep my job. It's a shame you gotta lie to survive, but that's the way of the world.'

She and Michael were spending more and more time together and they talked on the phone for hours.

Michael and I stay on the phone all night long. We even fall asleep talking on the phone. I have never felt this way about anybody before. I want to be with Michael all the time. I think I am falling in love. Michael is nothing like Caroline said.

Sex also became a part of their dating early into their relationship. This was a major change for Melvina. She had not been intimate with anyone in years. After being impregnated at a young age, she was apprehensive about sexual intercourse. Nevertheless, Michael changed her perspective about sex. After telling him her childhood pregnancy arose out of a very traumatic experience, he told her things would be different between the two of them.

"I'm gonna take my time with you Melvina," he said. "I'm gonna be real gentle. Being with me will be a totally new experience."

Michael was right, Melvina thought, reflecting on her and Michael's first time sleeping together. Being with him was a new experience. He kissed me all over…including in my private area…which is the first time anyone has given me oral sex. It tickled at first, but then it felt good. I've never had foreplay like that in my life. And then he took his time sliding that big penis in me. It hurt at first, but then it felt soooooo good. I've heard women talk about climaxing, but Michael is the first man to make me climax. And he makes me climax over and over again. At first, I was afraid to have sex again, and now I can't seem to get enough.

Once Melvina and Michael began having sex, which sometimes was two or three times a day, she went to her OB/GYN doctor who prescribed her birth control pills. While Michael initially started out gentle, he soon began to have rough sex with Melvina. This included introducing her to anal sex, which she found painful – but which he found highly pleasurable.

This hurts, but I'll do anything to please Michael. He really enjoys putting it in back there, and I'll do anything to please my man. Anything.

Soon, thoughts crept into her mind about having Michael's baby.

I know Michael can make some pretty babies, she thought. I want to give Michael a cute, little green-eyed baby. We'll be one little happy family.

Conversely, Michael did not want any children – a sentiment that reminded Melvina of Caroline's husband, Carl.

"Melvina, after the hell I went through as a child, I never want to have any children," Michael told her. "Never."

However, she was determined to give him a child and secretly stopped taking her birth control pills. Contraception made her periods irregular, but in March of 1990, they stopped altogether. The results of a pregnancy test given by her OB/GYN doctor confirmed it. Melvina was pregnant.

The followed day, Melvina cooked a romantic, candle-lit dinner to break the news to Michael. She shopped at Mondawmin after work and bought groceries and other items she needed to prepare the special meal. Mr. Billy drove Melvina home and helped her carry the bags into the house.

"You're my favor-right hack, Mr. Billy," she told him.

"And you're my favorite rider," said Mr. Billy, flashing a gold-toothed grin. "See you next time Melvina."

Melvina prepared a special meal of liver and onions smothered in gravy. To go along with the meat, she cooked buttered mashed potatoes and fresh green beans seasoned with smoked meat. She mixed a fresh batch of Sweet Tea for them to drink.

As she opened the oven door to check on the homemade chocolate cake baking in the oven, she heard Michael coming through the door with the key she gave him.

"Where are you Melvina?" he yelled from the living room. "You wanted me to get over here right quick. And mmmmmm. Is that liver and onions I smell?"

"That is liver and onions you smell. Your favor-right meat. Have a seat right at the dining room table Michael. I'll be right there."

Glancing at the cake in the oven which wasn't quite done, Melvina whispered, "Michael is going to be so happy when he finds out I got a cake in the oven…our own little baby."

"You got it all fancy in here," said Michael. "Candles lit on the table and everything. What's the special occasion?"

"You'll find out soon enough Michael. I'm about to bring the food in."

After setting their plates of food and tall glasses of Iced Tea on the table, Melvina said Grace, and they began to eat.

"Boy this food is good Melvina," said a jovial Michael as he chomped down on the food. "You and my grandmama make the best liver and onions. But a fancy meal like this on a Tuesday evening? You must got some big news to tell me. What is it? You got a promotion on the job? You hit the Lotto? You decided to get your Driver's License?"

"No Michael, it isn't any of those things."

"Well then, what is it?"

"Michael," she said with great excitement. "I'm pregnant."

"Pregnant?! How in the hell did you wind up pregnant?" he howled. "You told me you were on The Pill! What the hell did you do?! Stop taking them?!"

"What's wrong baby? I thought you would be happy."

"Happy? Happy about what? I told your dumb ass I ain't want no children Melvina! What the fuck is wrong with you?"

"I'm sorry Michael," Melvina cried. "But I –"

"Sorry my ass!" said Michael as he got up from the table. "I told you I ain't want no children Melvina! Now I'm gonna need for you to get to one of those clinics and get an abortion! I'll pay for it!"

"Baby, don't leave," she pleaded. "You haven't even finished eating."

"I don't want nothing else to eat! After that fucked-up news you just told me, I lost my appetite! And I ain't makin' enough money on my driving job to take care of a baby! Get rid of it Melvina! You hear me! Get rid of it!"

Melvina tearfully watched Michael storm out of the house. She had never seen Michael act like this. Melvina was stunned. His reaction was not what she expected, and marked the first time she witnessed Michael's raging temper. It was not only shocking to Melvina but scary. She sat down at the dining room table and continued to cry. Several minutes later, she smelled something burning.

"The cake!" she exclaimed, rushing to the kitchen. "I forgot all about it!"

Melvina opened the oven door and smoke came billowing out. Looking at the burned cake and then down at her stomach, she couldn't help but wonder if this was a bad premonition of what was to come.

Several days went by with Melvina desperately trying to reach Michael. He wouldn't respond to her pages and numerous calls to his cell phone went unanswered. *Michael's still upset with me about the baby. I know it. I wish he would answer the phone.* Melvina yearned to talk to Caroline about her dilemma but decided against it. *All Caroline is going to say, is 'I told you so. That's the last thing in the world I want to hear right now.*

After what Melvina shared with Michael about her first pregnancy, she could not believe he wanted her to get rid of this baby. During that conversation, she told him her family opposed abortion, and while she was incredibly young, terminating the pregnancy was not an option.

I didn't get rid of my first baby, and I'm not about to get rid of this one.

When Michael finally began taking her phone calls again, he repeatedly asked when she was going to the abortion clinic.

"I'm not getting rid of this baby, Michael," she said. "I plan to have this baby, and you're going to be a father. Just give it a chance."

"I don't want to be a father, and I don't want to give it a chance!" he yelled in the phone before hanging up on Melvina.

Weeks went by before Michael came by the house. They argued as Michael furiously objected to them having a child. However, they did make love before he left. However, it was particularly violent. He threw Melvina across the bed, got on top of her, and began to have rough sex with her. She laid beneath him wondering if he was attempting to cause her to miscarry. From that day on, sex with Michael was always that way. As she moved along in her pregnancy, Melvina decided to refrain from sex until after she gave birth, for fear he might cause her to lose the baby.

On July 10, 1990, Melvina gave birth to Michael Adams, Jr. He was born four months premature. Melvina nicknamed their newborn son, 'Lil' Mike', and began calling Michael, 'Big Mike.'

After the birth of their son, Melvina doted over Lil' Mike. Contrastingly, Big Mike was distant when it came to the baby. He rarely held him and always seems agitated whenever Lil' Mike cried. Big Mike was also coming to her home less frequently, and their fun outings all but stopped.

I miss the old Big Mike. I hope he snaps out of his funk.

Eventually, Big Mike seemed to warm up to Lil' Mike. Every now and then Big Mike changed the baby's diapers, and sometimes he even cradled him in his arms. He also resumed taking Melvina out to restaurants and other places, while Mrs. Brown babysat Lil' Mike. He told Melvina he wanted to take her to a club to go dancing.

"I've never been to a Club," said Melvina. "I wouldn't even know what to wear."

"I'll help you pick out some nice clothes to wear," said Big Mike. "We're going to Odell's nightclub, and you can't get in there lookin' any old kind of way."

Big Mike took Melvina shopping, picking out the clothes she should wear to the nightclub. She made an appointment with Henrietta to get her hair done Wednesday evening for their outing the following night.

"So, you're going to a club?" Miss Henrietta asked during the salon appointment.

"That's right," said Melvina. "This is my first time going to one."

"Whaaaaaat? Your first time?"

"Have you ever been to a club Miss Henrietta?"

"Doggone right and I still go to the club! Odells, Pascals, 32nd Street Plaza…you name it! I may be hittin' 50, but Miss Henrietta still gets her dance on! Check out these moves!" she said, dancing in the middle of the salon floor as Melvina and the other customers all laughed.

"I see you can still dance," said Melvina. "But can you do something different with my hair this time?"

"Alright," said Henrietta. "I'll hook you up with a French Roll and dress it up with some gold spray, silver spray and top it off with some glitter. You gonna be the Bomb girl!"

"Gold spray, silver spray, and glitter?" said Melvina.

"That's right child!" said Henrietta stopping to nibble on pickled pig's feet. "Time to get with the times. As of today, no more press and curl. That went out in the late 70s. This is 1990. We got relaxers now. I'm perming these beads and giving you a nice French Roll."

The entire salon erupted in laughter.

"I'll try it," said Melvina apprehensively. "But if I don't like it, you're taking it out and styling my hair over again."

"The hell I ain't!" declared Henrietta, putting her hands on her hips. "The Devil is a liar! I ain't putting a finger in that head of yours until we agree you gonna pay me!"

"Alright, Henrietta. I'll try it."

"That's more like it. Cause ain't nobody makin' you do nothin'!"

"Now Henrietta, I got to be at work in the morning."

"Join the club!" said another customer. "We all got to go to work in the morning."

"Seriously Miss Henrietta, I can't be sitting in here all night."

"Uh-huh," said Miss Henrietta nonchalantly as she wrapped a cape around Melvina to prevent anything from spilling on her clothes. "Now be quiet so I can enjoy the onion pickle I'm about to eat in peace before I bring these naps of yours up-to-date".

Miss Henrietta howled with laughter along with the other customers. However, Melvina did not find her comments amusing.

I should say something about that stinky pickled pig's feet and onion pickle breath of yours, Melvina silently fumed. I bet you won't find that funny!

Melvina left Miss Henrietta's Beauty Salon the wee hours of the following morning. She didn't like having to wait so long to have her hair done, but she really liked her new hairstyle. Several customers commented about how nice her new hairstyle looked. Miss Moonie said she liked it too, but that she needed to refrain from wearing the glitter.

"The glitter might fall in the cakes and pastries Melvina, and we don't want customers eating those."

"Yes ma'am."

Later that night, she and Big Mike went to Odells on North Avenue. They waited in a long line which stretched down the street under the watchful eye of a tall, muscular, imposing man everyone was calling "Karate." Once they were inside, a woman sitting behind the glass pane of a ticket booth eyeballed her and Mike down before waving them on in. Melvina breathed a sigh of relief.

"Why did I feel like I was just surveyed," said Melvina.

"Because you was," replied Mike. "If she don't like the way you look or the way you are dressed, you ain't getting in on Odells on a Thursday night."

Melvina and Big Mike danced beneath a large disco ball above the dance floor. She listened in amazement at the booming sound of House Music pumping through Odell's enormous speakers.

I've never seen such humongous speakers in my life, nor heard speakers this loud, marveled Melvina. The closest I've ever been to a club was going to the movies and seeing Saturday Night Fever when I was a little girl. Everyone here is having such a good time, and so am I.

By the time Melvina and Mike left Odell's, and he dropped her off home, it was close to 4 a.m. Miss Moonie expected her to arrive at work by 6 a.m., and this morning would be no different.

"I may as well stay up," Melvina concluded. "If I lay down, I may oversleep and be late for work. I'm going to shower, dress, and head to work. I'll call Miss Brown to apologize for leaving Lil' Mike overnight and let her know I'll pick him up after work."

Melvina made it to work on time, but she was tired. Between her late-night partying at 'Odells' and being in the salon until the early morning hours the previous night, she could barely keep her eyes open.

"Are you alright Melvina?" asked Miss Moonie.

"Yes ma'am," she replied. "I'm fine."

"Just checking. You seem sluggish."

"I'm fine Miss Moonie. Just a little tired."

"Okay young lady, but you got to pick up the pace. It's Friday morning and we got a shop full of customers in here."

"Yes ma'am."

I swear if I make it through work today, I won't stay out so late again. I got written up again, and the last thing I want to do is disappoint Miss Moonie.

Despite those sentiments, when Big Mike offered to take her clubbing again, Melvina obliged.

"I can't wait to go back to Odells," she told him. "I had so much fun the last time we went there. What a good-looking group of people all dressed up in fancy clothes and having a ball! Other than Soul Train and another dance show I used to watch called the Moonman Connection, I've never people dance so well in my life! They could really dance!"

"You didn't have any fun before you met me. You didn't do nothin'."

"I did plenty of things."

"Like what? Have a baby when you were just a kid, go to church all the time, sing, and work? That ain't no fun. What you need to do is use that voice of yours to sing R&B. Then you could stop kneadin' bakery dough and make some real dough."

"You need to stop being so critical of me Big Mike. Listen, I sing Gospel. That's what I sing. I'm not interested in singing any other kind of music."

"Suit yourself. But ain't no money or fame in singing Gospel."

"Apparently, you've never heard of gospel singers Mahalia Jackson, The Staple Singers, James Cleveland, or Shirley Caesar?"

"Nope."

Melvina continued to hang out with Big Mike at Odells on Thursday nights. By 1992, they were frequenting other spots stretching from Baltimore to D.C., including 32nd Street Plaza, The Five Mile House, Tiffany's, The

Classic, and Wolf Trap. One night, he drove to New York to take her to a club called The Paradise Garage. Consequently, they did not arrive back in Baltimore until late the following afternoon, causing her to miss work.

Her newfound nightlife was resulting in a high sitter bill with Mrs. Brown who was also scolding her for failing to pick Lil' Mike up on time. Moreover, Melvina was finding herself in hot water with Miss Moonie for her lackluster job performance.

"Melvina!" said Miss Moonie. "You are messing up customer's orders, not to mention you look like you are sleepwalking. I have no choice but to write you up for being late again today. This is the first time since I hired you 10 years ago, that I have ever had to write you up. I'm not sure what's going on in your personal life, but my advice is to get it straight quick!"

"I'm sorry Miss Moonie. But sometimes I'm really tired from being up late at night with the baby feeding him bottles and changing his diapers."

"That's called motherhood and it isn't an excuse for arriving to work late, burning up cakes and pastries because you're leaving them in the oven too long, and messing up orders. Not to mention you were dozing off while waiting on a customer the other day. I worked, put myself through school, and started my own business all while singlehandedly raising five children. Not to mention I baked and sold cakes and pies from my home until I was able to save up enough money to start my own business. I had to do that because no bank would give me…a single Black woman with a dream… but no credit…money to start a business. So while I understand what you are trying to tell me about juggling work-life with raising children, that's life for most single, working mothers…and single, working fathers because we have those too. Not to mention you were always punctual while you were raising Earlene. By the way, how is Earlene doing in North Carolina?"

"She's doing just fine Miss Moonie."

"That's good to hear. Hopefully, a big record label will pick her up. Now Melvina, Miss Moonie hates to be hard on you, but I'm paying you to do a job, and I need you to do it. Not to mention throwing away burned pastries and cakes, costs me money. You have always been exceptional, and that needs to continue. Is that understood?"

"Yes, Miss Moonie, and I'm very sorry."

"One more thing Melvina?"

"Yes, Miss Moonie."

"This change in your work pattern…this wouldn't happen to have anything to do with that boyfriend of yours, would it?"

"No ma'am Miss Moonie."

"I see him when he comes in the bakery for you…hardly opens his mouth to speak. Seems this unusual behavior of yours started after he showed up. I'm not trying to get into your business Melvina, but I'm 49-years-old and I've been around for a little while. You're like a daughter to me. I know you two have a baby together, but he seems offish to me. Be careful."

Melvina loved her job at the bakery and the last thing she wanted to do was lose it. Miss Moonie has been so good to me. So has Mrs. Brown. I can't keep messing up. Not to mention, I've been going so much I hardly spend time with Lil' Mike. I'm trying to burn both ends of the candle and it's catching up with me in a major way.

She decided to tell Big Mike she no longer would go clubbing on nights she had to work the following morning.

"Well I have to be to work by 9 in the morning and staying out late ain't bothering me," he said after learning of her decision.

"That's you, Big Mike. I'm not able to stay up all night and function well the next day. Not to mention the nights I am up with the baby. All of that is telling on me at work and I don't want to lose my job."

"Well Melvina, you were the one who decided you wanted to have that baby. Not me. You made that bed, and now you have to lie in it."

Melvina stuck firm to her decision. She stopped going to clubs when she had to work the following day. Soon, she stopped going to clubs altogether. Big Mike pressured her to continue to go out with him, but she stood her ground. She enjoyed the time she was spending with Lil' Mike and being in good standing once again with both Miss Moonie and Mrs. Brown.

Big Mike eventually stopped asking her about going out. On the contrary, he continued to pressure her to drink alcohol – something he had unsuccessfully tried to do since they first began dating. His drink of choice was forty ounces (Forty) of Colt 45 malt liquor.

"A little beer ain't gonna hurt you Melvina," he said holding the tall bottle in her direction. Take a swig."

"Big Mike, I have told you time and time again that after seeing what alcohol did to my daddy, I ain't touching the stuff. Drinking all that beer ain't good for you. Neither is that weed you are smoking right now or those cigarettes you love to smoke."

"You don't know what you are missing," he said taking a long drag off a marijuana joint and blowing it in her face.

"Yes, I do too," she said. "A good chance of getting cancer, becoming a Pot Head, and messing my liver up. Thanks but no thanks."

Big Mike used Cocaine occasionally and tried to coax Melvina into trying that too.

"Absolutely not," she said. "I heard you can get hooked the first time you try that stuff. I'm not trying to get hooked on nothing. I got a son to take care of, a daughter in North Carolina I plan to bring back home, and a good job with benefits. Not to mention I plan to get my Driver's License and earn my G.E.D."

"You drive?" laughed Big Mike. "You're 26-years-old now. If you ain't got your license all this time, you ain't gonna get it."

"Better late than never," she retorted. "I'm still young and I still got dreams. I plan to use the money I have saved in the bank for the children's college education and to start my own business one day. Miss Moonie has taught me everything she knows. Maybe, I'll open my own bakery…or maybe even my own restaurant. I'm not sure what I'm gonna do just yet, but I do know I don't have the time or the money to be messing with no drugs."

By 1993, Melvina decided it was time to return to church, calling Caroline to see if she and Carl would pick up her and Lil' Mike.

"Praise Him!" shouted Caroline. "Of course we'll swing by to get you and my little nephew. Me and Carl ain't never not wanted to take you to church! But ever since you started hanging out with my no-good bruuuuuther and dancing that little body of yours to the Devil's music all over those sinful clubs, you stopped going! Carl and I will be there bright and early Sunday morning to pick up you and my wonderful nephew."

Melvina wasn't quite sure how Caroline found out she was going to nightclubs, nor did she ask. She assumed Big Mike told her. She was just grateful to end her hiatus from church and jumpstart the worship experience she missed so much. She was also going to great lengths to prove herself again to Miss Moonie – arriving to work early, staying late, creating new pastry designs, and being extra courteous, friendly, and helpful to customers. Miss Moonie was so pleased with her performance she gave Melvina a raise and promoted her to Bakery Manager.

At home, Melvina was devoting as much time as she could to three-year-old Lil' Mike. On her days off from work, she took him with her to Mondawmin Mall where they ate pizza slices and she bought him clothes, toys, and sneakers. She pushed him along in the shopping cart at the supermarket while shopping for groceries. Once she was done shopping at the market, she pushed Lil' Mike and her cart full of groceries out front, her eyes scanning the procession of cars double-parked out front. They all belonged to the 'hacks' – men and a few women who made money driving shoppers home from the mall.

"There's Mr. Billy's Buick right there," said Melvina pointing to the car. "Mr. Billy is going to drive us home Lil' Mike. He happens to be my favor-rite hack. He's always friendly, has good conversation, and helps your mama with her bags. Mr. Billy is mighty good looking too…just like you my little man," she said tickling Lil' Mike's stomach causing him to giggle.

When they shopped at Lexington Market, Lil' Mike's eyes lit up at all the interesting sights. She recalled him curiously inquiring about the many things he saw there including shoeshine men, people eating oysters, seafood, and the fresh meats meticulously arranged in display cases.

And Lil' Mike sure loves sticky apples. I always make it a point to get him a big red sticky apple when I go to Lexington Market to shop. And I don't leave that place until I get Caroline a corned beef on rye and Big Mike a bag of hot peanuts. But Big Mike throwing the shells on my clean floors always plucks my nerves. Despite his inconsiderate ways, I love that green-eyed monster and I know he loves me. I just wish he were more father-like to Lil' Mike. He treats him so coldly at times.

Melvina took Lil' Mike to The Aquarium, The Baltimore Zoo, and The Maryland Science Center. She packed picnic baskets with ham sandwiches, juices, potato chips, pretzels, and other goodies and they sat on a blanket at Druid Hill Park and ate. She took him to play at Hanlon Park where they threw a ball. The two licked sweet marshmallow-whipped topping off snowballs from the snowball stand on Monroe Street on hot summer days. She got egg custard flavor and strawberry flavor for Lil' Mike and they smiled at each other with marshmallow mustaches.

On school-day mornings, she fixed Lil' Mike a hearty breakfast which included fluffy pancakes and orange juice. Afterward, they headed out the door and she walked him to school every day during his Pre-K and kindergarten school years before heading to work.

Caroline still vehemently opposed Melvina's relationship with Big Mike. Nevertheless, the best friends got their friendship back on track, making sure they carved out time to eat lunch at Double T Diner every other Wednesday afternoon and shopping together whenever their schedules allowed. Caroline had settled quite nicely into married life, and Melvina longed for the day she and Big Mike would tie the knot.

I can't wait until me and my green-eyed dreamboat walk down the aisle. One day, I'll be Mrs. Melvina Adams. Right now, I'm just happy that things are finally looking up for me. I have so much to be grateful for…a good man, a wonderful son, a true best friend, a house that's paid for, savings in the bank, and a promotion on the job.

Since reconnecting with the church, she joined New Life Fellowship's church choir. I love singing for the Lord…especially old, Gospel hymns. I thank God for the opportunity to be singing in church again. He is blessing me in a mighty way. Soon, I will enroll in Driving School and get into a G.E.D. program. I know things are going well for Earlene in North Carolina, but once I get through Driving School and earning my G.E.D., I plan to bring Earlene back to Baltimore. I miss my daughter and want her back home. Besides, I want her to finally meet her new little brother.

Despite Melvina's happiness about the way things were going in her life and optimism about her future, Melvina's dreams would be deferred.

※

By now, Melvina was no longer talking to her reflection in the downstairs bathroom, since making her way back to the couch. Time continued to tick by on this October 8, 1998, day while she laid on the filthy couch immersed in deep thoughts about her past.

Melvina's mind wandered back to the first time she ever got high. It was October 14, 1995 – nearly three years ago. She and Big Mike were watching a movie at her home that Saturday evening when a scene came on in which a mother tearfully waved goodbye as she watched her crying daughter pull off from a bus station. The scene evoked painful memories of the day she sent Earlene away aboard a bus that departed from the Greyhound station on Howard Street. The decision always saddened Melvina, and the movie scene only exacerbated those feelings.

Melvina needed to talk about it, and she always found Michael to be a good listener. After telling him she sent Earlene to live with her aunt and uncle in North Carolina, Michael asked, "Why did you decide to send her there?"

"I'd rather not say why," she replied, thinking about how she put her hand on The Bible under the watchful eyes of church leadership and swore never to divulge the secret. "But I can tell you this. My daughter is an exceptional singer, and my uncle knows a lot of people in the music business including Berry Gordy. Sending her to North Carolina was so hard to do, but I know it will give her all kinds of wonderful opportunities that I could never give her, but I miss her so much."

"Have you spoken to her?"

"No."

"Why?"

"Because I feel so bad about sending her away. But once I get my Driver's License and earn my G.E.D., I plan to go to North Carolina and get my daughter."

"Well, at least you ain't got to kick out no money to take care of her. They're doin' all of that for you. Might be best to leave her right where she is."

"My aunt and uncle are giving her a better life than I can right now, but trust and believe, I'm going to get my daughter back."

"That's the thing about having kids. Them little crumb-snatchers suck up all your money and too much of your time. I told your ass I ain't want none, but you got pregnant anyway."

"Don't start that again Big Mike."

"Hell, I got whippings you wouldn't believe when I was a child. That's another reason why I ain't want no kids."

"Were those whippings what caused you to have those black marks on your arms and legs?' she inquired.

'Some things ain't meant to be discussed, he muttered. "Now stop asking me about them."

The two had been seeing each other for several months before Melvina first saw the marks. Even on sweltering hot days, Big Mike always kept his arms and legs covered. Melvina saw the marks for the first time when she walked into the bathroom one day while he was taking a shower.

"I'm gonna surprise Big Mike and give him some lovin' while he's in the shower," she said taking off her clothes. Naked, she quietly pushed open the slightly ajar bathroom door and tiptoed in. She pulled back the shower curtains to climb in the shower with Big Mike and saw the marks. She was shocked to see them and based on his scathing reaction, it was clear Big Mike did not want her to see them.

"Git the fuck out!" he shouted. "What the hell is wrong with you comin' in here while I'm washing my ass! I know this is your house, but can't a man have some damn privacy?"

She eventually questioned Big Mike about the marks, but he didn't want to talk about them. She also asked Caroline about the marks, but she didn't want to discuss them either. Melvina found that odd because she and Caroline talked about everything.

The movie Melvina and Big Mike were watching ended. Despite the movie having a happy ending with the mother and daughter reuniting, the bus station scene continued to play in Melvina's mind.

"That movie reminded me so much of when I sent my daughter away," she told Big Mike crying uncontrollably."

"Take a hit off this," said Big Mike, handing her a lit marijuana joint. "A little weed always makes me feel better."

"You know I don't smoke," she said.

"I know you don't Melvina. But this will relax you."

"No, I better not," she replied shaking her head.

"Go on baby…a puff or two won't hurt. It'll calm you down."

"I shouldn't," said Melvina, a silent debate raging in her mind.

"Come on Melvina. Do it for me."

"Alright, Big Mike…but just this one time," she said, giving in to his request. "You know I'll do anything for you."

Big Mike handed her the joint. Unsure exactly how to smoke it, she put her lips around it and took big puffs.

"Oh that's terrible!" she said violently coughing. "My throat and lungs feel like they're burning! I'm about to gag!"

'That's not the way you smoke it,' said Big Mike. 'This is how you smoke it.'

Big Mike showed Melvina how to take small drags off the joint. Following his instructions, she puffed on the pot (marijuana). The coughs continued but were not as intense. A few minutes later, Melvina began to feel relaxed.

"Wow Big Mike," she said. "I feel like I haven't got a care in the world."

"Told you."

Big Mike reached for the Forty of Colt 45 and twisted off the bottle cap. He chugged some down and handed Melvina the bottle. Thoughts of her late father gushed through her mind like a high tide rolling to shore. After a long hesitation, Melvina put the bottle up to her lips.

"What the hell," she said. "You only live once."

This was Melvina's first time drinking beer, and she found the taste repulsive. Yet, she continued to drink the beer until she felt nauseated and dizzy.

"It looks like the room is spinning," she said. "And I better get to the bathroom. I feel sick."

Melvina rushed to the bathroom and vomited in the toilet. Despite the unpleasant effects of the beer and weed, she also found them pleasurable. Ultimately, the night turned into a thrilling rollercoaster ride of sex, drugs, and alcohol, burying sad thoughts about Earlene into the deep crevices of her mind.

The following morning, Melvina laid in the bed feeling sick and reflecting on the events of the prior night.

I have a terrible headache! My head is banging! My head hurts so bad, it feels like someone just hit it with a brick! The rest of me feels like I got run over by a freight train! Aw man, I feel horrible! I guess this is what a hangover feels like. Good thing I'm off today. I'm going to just lay here and think about the sex me and Big Mike had last night! It was the best ever! I don't know if it was the weed or what, but I lost count of the number of times I had an orgasm! I'll get up in about an hour or so to take some aspirin and fix Lil' Mike breakfast. Right now, I don't feel like moving.

Melvina heard a familiar car horn blowing outside.

"Oh my goodness! That's Caroline and Carl, and they are here to pick up me and Lil' Mike and take us to church! And I can't miss church today! Today is the Usher's Anniversary, and I am singing lead on a song."

Melvina stumbled out of the bed, falling over the covers in her haste to quickly head to the bathroom medicine cabinet to take two aspirin. Melvina pulled clothes out closets and drawers, getting herself dressed along with Lil' Mike as fast as she could amidst the ongoing blaring of Caroline and Carl's car horn.

"What took you so long to come out?!" asked Caroline. "Not only do you look terrible but now you have made us late to church! I'm an ursher and Carl is a deacon. We got duties which means outside of bein' in caskets, we should never be late for church! Not to mention today is the Ursher's Anniversary, and I've been workin' on my march for the last two weeks!"

After church that particular Sunday, both Caroline and Carl chastised Melvina during the drive home for singing the wrong words to a song and dozing off in the church's Choir Loft.

"Even Me begins with the words 'Lord I hear of showers of blessings…Thou art scattering full and free" Caroline yelled, turning to give Melvina a squinty-eyed look. "The words are not 'Lord after showering I need a blessing, thou art scattering full as can be!' That's my favorite hymn and you messed it all up! You normally sing that song like a songbird! But today you sang it like a dying crow! Up there coughing and gaggin' tryin' to sing stopping in the middle of the song asking for a glass of water! Lawd have mercy M! I ain't never been so embarrassed in my life!"

"Me neither," added Carl. "Not to mention you fell asleep in the Choir Loft which faces the congregation. The whole church was looking at you Melvina."

"M, I don't know what was going on up there, but that was terrible! Just terrible!"

"I'm sorry Caroline and Carl," said Melvina softly. "I didn't mean to embarrass you two."

"It ain't us you need to worry about embarrassin'!," said Caroline. "It's the good Lawd you need to worry about! He ain't bless you with that angelic voice you got to embarrass Him like that! You had better get yourself together M!"

"That's right Melvina," chimed in Carl. "God gave you that voice to use to His glory. With the anointing you have on your voice, Satan will do all he can to silence it. Don't let that happen."

"It will if she keeps messin' with that bruuuuuther of mines," said Caroline turning to roll her eyes at Melvina. "You need to leave Michael alone M. He will destroy you."

Melvina tearfully slumped down in the back seat and glanced over at Lil' Mike who looked back at her with his big innocent brown eyes.

※

Over the course of the following days, weeks, and months, Melvina continued to smoke weed and drink forties with Big Mike. Initially, it began with her engaging in such activities on the weekends. Gradually, Melvina's use of these vices became more frequent, and by early 1996, now included weekdays.

Once again, she began to experience problems on the job between her and Miss Moonie who was writing her up again for punctuality and professionalism issues. Despite her problems at the bakery, Melvina continued to smoke marijuana and drink beer with Big Mike, now accustomed to using both vices. Thus, the mother of two no longer coughed or felt nauseous like she did during her earlier experiences with them.

Melvina and Big Mike kept in constant contact, seeing, or talking to one another nearly every day. Surprisingly, communication between the two lovers went abruptly silent one spring week in 1996.

"I haven't heard from Big Mike in two days," she frantically told Caroline. "I would check to see if he's at his place, but I'm not sure exactly where he lives."

"Nobody knows exactly where Michael lives including me," replied Caroline. "Nor do I wanna know! The last thing I want to do is step foot in the devil's lair. Did you try callin' him?"

"I did, and his cell phone just rings. I have paged him numerous times and he hasn't called me back. I'm very concerned because this just isn't like him."

"It ain't too far of a stretch for my bruuuuuther to just up and disappear,' said Caroline. "That's the same thing he did when our mama was still livin'. Michael would just get up and go without sayin' a word. And mama would worry herself sick. Just don't go worryin' yourself the same way. Maybe he took a trip back home to Mississippi. Or maybe he got in trouble again. Who knows?"

"Give it a few more days. With Michael, ain't no tellin' what that boy is doing. I told you not to fool with him. I hate to tell you I told you so, but I told you so. Had you listened to me, you wouldn't be goin' through this. I told you to wait for the Lawd to send you a good Christian man, but you didn't want to do that. You wanted to be all fast and do it your way."

"Fast?!" said Melvina. "I was 24-years-old when I met your brother. Before you know it, I'll be 30. How long was I supposed to wait?"

"As long as it takes. Gawd don't move on our time, He moves according to His time. And for most people, that ain't never fast enough. But God don't work like a microwave. Put something in a microwave…and ding! It's done. Naw, that ain't how the good Lawd works. Gawd does things when he is good and ready to do them. And for good reasons. We don't know the reasons, but God knows. We just must be patient and wait for God to move at the appointed time. And most times, it ain't quick. Speaking of quick, don't be so fast in wanting that heathen bruuuuuther of mines to come back from whatever rock he's crawled under. If you ask me M, his bein' gone might be a blessing in disguise for you and my sweet nephew Lil' Mike."

A week went by before Melvina finally heard from Big Mike in the early morning hours of April 17, 1996. Calling collect, he told her he was locked up for drug possession.

"Can you get out some of that money you got saved up in the bank and bail me out of jail? I will also need a lawyer because I violated my probation."

"Of course I will Big Mike," said Melvina. "I miss you so much, honey."

Once Melvina arrived at work, she asked Miss Moonie if she could leave early that day "to take care of some personal business." Miss Moonie agreed to allow her to clock out early "just as long as she completed her work for the day." Melvina expeditiously worked to ensure her duties for the day were done and left the bakery around noon. She met with a bails bondsman who told her exactly how much was needed to bail Big Mike out of jail. She went to the bank, withdrew the money, and returned to the bails bondsman's office and handed him $2,000 cash – the required 10% of the $20,000 bail a court commissioner set for Big Mike.

The following day – April 18, 1996, Big Mike was freed on bond. He called Melvina and told her he was going to be meeting with a lawyer someone referred him to later that afternoon.

"I still need your help with that," said Big Mike. "I'll let you know how much the lawyer is charging once I'm through meeting with him."

"You know I've got the money in the bank," she told Big Mike. "Just let me know how much it is, and I'll take it out tomorrow."

On February 19, 1995, Melvina caught a cab from the bakery to the bank so she could make it back on time from her lunch break. She told the cabbie to wait for her until she came out of the bank.

"Alright Toots, the cabbie told her. "Keep in mind, this cab might be stopped, but the meter keeps right on running."

"I know…that's why I like using hacks," she grumbled under her breath.

"Oh, and one more thing," said the cabbie.

"What?!"

"No funny stuff. I've lost count of the number of times people have jumped out of my cab once I take them where they want to go. And the ones who tell me they'll be right back, casually walk in the front door of a place and run out the back…all while I'm sitting outside waiting. I've been burned enough times. But I see that little work badge you got on and the name of the bakery you were standing in front of when you flagged me down. I know where you work Toots."

"Well if you know my name from looking at my badge. You know that it isn't Toots. It's Melvina. I'll be out as soon as I'm done."

"Alright Tina or whatever you said your name is," said the cabbie looking at the meter. "Time is ticking, and this meter will be too."

Melvina scoffed as she climbed out of the double-parked cab and rushed into the bank.

"Thank God the lines aren't long," she said, walking up to the teller. She noticed her neighbor Mr. Hawkins was also in the bank and waved while wondering how his daughter and wife were doing and thinking about the rumor spread by their neighbor Violetta Jenkins.

That nosey Miss Jenkins told everyone Mr. Hawkins' wife left him and took their baby along with her, thought Melvina. That busybody can spread news faster than the World Wide Web.

After withdrawing $1,000.00 in hundred dollars bills, Melvina jumped back inside the waiting cab and headed back to work.

"Made it back just in the nick of time," she said pulling out her cell phone to call Big Mike while walking inside the bakery.

"I got the money for the lawyer," she told him.

"Thanks, Melvina. I'll stop past the bakery to get it so I can take it to the lawyer today," said Big Mike.

Less than an hour later, Big Mike walked into the bakery. Melvina took the envelope out of her purse and handed it to Big Mike under the glaring, suspicious eyes of Miss Moonie.

❀

A few nights later, Saturday, April 20, 1996, Big Mike sat talking to Melvina about being picked up by the police after copping some marijuana and being taken to Baltimore's Western District police station in a paddy wagon before being taken to Central Booking.

"The damn Po-Po locked my Black ass up for some bullshit!" Big Mike told her, taking deep drags off a cigarette. "People out here shootin', robbin' killin' and everything else, and they hustle me handcuffed in the back of a paddy wagon with those cold, hard, steel seats for a little weed! What the fuck?!"

"I'm sorry about that Big Mike. That must have been terrible. I've heard about those paddy wagons. Never been in one and don't ever want to be in one. But the important thing is that you're out now."

"That's right!' It's all good, and I still got my job. You can't keep a good Black man down!"

"You still got your job after not showing up for over a whole week?"

"Yep."

"How did you do that? I get in trouble if I miss as much as a day from work."

"I told my boss a bogus-ass story, and he brought it. I lied to get my driving job, and I lied to keep it. If I told the boss I got locked up, he probably would have fired me on the spot. I did what I had to do."

"But getting locked up…won't that mess you up, being on probation and all?"

"The lawyer said he could pull a few strings. He was using some fancy legal words, but the bottom line is that the lawyer was telling me he probably could work things out in such a way that I probably wouldn't even have to go to court. He's a Black lawyer with a spiffy office and walks around with fancy, expensive suits and shoes like he's Johnny Cockran or somebody."

"Sounds fancy-schmancy."

"Yep, he is. But he also warned me that if I got in trouble again, I best be prepared to be gone away for a long time. He ain't got to worry about that. I ain't gittin' in no more trouble. And I 'preciate you helpin' me get a lawyer Melvina by giving me that money."

"You know I'll do anything for you, Big Mike,' said Melvina as she threw her arms around him. "I'm just glad you're out of jail so you can come home to be with me and Lil' Mike."

"I got my own home, Melvina."

"I know that. It was just a figure of speech."

"Well, the bottom line is that after a little unexpected vacation at Western and Central," said Big Mike referencing the two police precincts, "I'm back! And it calls for a celebration!" Pulling out two bottles of Colt 45 out of a brown paper bag he told Melvina, "I got an ice-cold Forty for you and one for me.'"

"Thank you, baby."

"Where's Lil' Mike?"

"In his room playing the PlayStation I got him for Christmas. He loves that thing."

"Cool. I also got us some weed," said Big Mike pulling out a bag of marijuana and some Top paper. "I got something else special too."

"I think you're trying to turn me into a pothead," said Melvina. "What else you got?"

"Some Crack-A-Lack!" said Big Mike jiggling a bag of Crack he pulled out his jacket pocket.

"Crack?!"

"That's right. Crack. Listen Melvina, I was sprung from jail, and now I am free as a bird! That calls for a celebration and I want to get fucked-up! I might smoke weed, drink beer, and snort a little Coke every now and then, but I ain't never had no Crack. I figured we try it together."

"I don't think I want to try any Crack."

'You tried weed, and now you like it right?"

"Yeah Mike, but—"

"And you tried beer, and now you like it right?"

"Yeah, but –"

'Well then Melvina, try this Crack out with me. I wanna see if it's what it's all cracked up to be. No pun intended."

"But Big Mike…Crack? Weed and beer is one thing…but Crack is on a whole different level."

Melvina thought about the things she heard about Crack Cocaine. She first heard about the drug back in the 1980s when she was still in high school. Back then, folks began talking about a powerful new drug called Crack that had hit the streets of Baltimore. According to the news, Crack was highly addictive, cheap to buy, and sparked an unprecedented spike in killings around the city.

"I've heard a lot of things about that stuff and none of it is good," said Melvina.

"You can't believe everything you hear Melvina. One hit won't hurt. Do it for me."

"I don't want to do it, Big Mike."

"You would do it if you loved me."

"You know I love you, Big Mike. It's just that –"

"Well prove it then," said Big Mike looking at Melvina with his emerald-colored eyes. "I want us to experience this high together. Don't leave me hangin' out there by myself to try it alone. And after we get high together, you know what's going to happen."

"What's that Big Mike?"

"I'm gonna fuck the shit out of you!"

Melvina smiled, as thoughts raced through her mind about being with Big Mike sexually. The last time they were intimate was prior to his going to jail, and she longed to be with him.

And I just can't say no when he looks at me like that with those sexy green eyes, she thought. I'm like putty in his hands.

"Alright, if it means that much to you, I'll do it," said Melvina running her hands through his curly hair. But just this one time. That's it."

"That's all I'm askin'."

"I'd better check on Lil' Mike first. The last thing I want him to see is me and you down here snortin' drugs."

'We ain't gonna snort it Melvina. We're gonna smoke it.'

Prior to Big Mike finally contacting her, Melvina hadn't heard from him in over a week. During his absence, Melvina slumped into a dark hole of sadness. She missed Big Mike. She missed Earlene. She missed her parents. She thought about her failure to finish high school, and other matters which troubled her heart.

Melvina had also been reprimanded at work twice in recent months for showing up smelling of weed and beer. The reprimands marked the first time Melvina had ever gotten in trouble at work. She was upset about that too.

Walking up the steps to check on Lil' Mike, Melvina thought, I'm messing up at work. I still haven't gotten my Driver's License, nor my G.E.D. Not to mention I still miss Earlene and regret sending her away. I feel like such a failure…both as a person and a mother. Maybe Crack is just what I need to clear my mind. Besides, if he and I trying it together is how Big Mike wants to celebrate, then that's how we're going to celebrate.

Melvina stood at the door of Lil' Mike's bedroom watching him play his gaming console.

It took some saving up from my paychecks to buy that Playstation and those five games, she thought glancing at the console before turning her attention to the boxes which read, 'Cool Boarders', 'Oddworld: Abe's Odyssey, 'Crash Bandicoot', 'Gran Turismo', and 'Madden NFL 98'. But Lil' Mike enjoys playing on that system so much, which makes it worth every penny I spent. Reminds me of how much I enjoyed playing my Atari gaming system Mama bought me when I was in high school."

"Hey there little man," she said. "Are you doing okay?"

"I'm fine Mama," said Lil' Mike holding the controller, never turning away from the game's screen on the television.

"Mama."

"Yes, Lil' Mike."

"What are you about to do?"

"Go back downstairs with your father. Why do you ask?"

"I was wondering if you wanted to race against me on Grand Turismo."

"Not right now Lil' Mike. I don't have time right this second, but I will play the game with you, and that's a promise. I have to get back downstairs with your father."

"Hey, Melvina!" Big Mike yelled from downstairs. "Come on back down here!"

"Coming Big Mike!" said Melvina racing downstairs. Once she reached the living room, Big Mike patted the sofa, signaling Melvina to sit close to him. Melvina sat down, scooting close to him, and looking at the pebbly rocks inside the pipe. "I'll go first, and then you," said Big Mike, holding a lit cigarette lighter on one end of the pipe while inhaling from a stem on the other end. Melvina watched Big Mike inhale and exhale a few times before handing her the pipe.

"Careful," he said. "The pipe is hot."

Hitting that crack pipe was unlike anything Melvina ever felt before in her life.

"I can't even describe how I'm feeling right now," she told Big Mike. "The closest I can get to describing it is euphoric."

"Told you," said Big Mike. "But enjoy it while you can. I'm told the high don't last long."

Melvina found herself wanting to experience that euphoric feeling again. And again. And again. Consequently, since first trying Crack that April 20th day two years ago, Melvina found herself constantly chasing that high. For Ravens fans, April 20, 1996, was an important date in the team's history. It represented the day the team selected UCLA offensive lineman Jonathan Ogden with their 1st-ever NFL draft choice and University of Miami linebacker Ray Lewis as their second pick. For Melvina A. Thomas, this date represented the day she joined the ranks of Baltimore's crack addicts.

Melvina could hear the steady flow of vehicles outside her home on Gwynns Falls Parkway, a heavily traveled street in Baltimore. Vehicles travel along both directions of the busy road day and night, heading towards their perspective destinations. The sounds of cars, trucks, buses, and motorcycles were commonplace in her neighborhood. But for some odd reason on this August 8, 1998 day, these automotive sounds were helping to keep her mind immersed in her past.

"The drivers behind the wheels of those cars and trucks know exactly where they are going," lamented Melvina. "They're going Downtown. They're going to work. They're coming from work. They're going someplace, and they know where they are going. But me…I don't know where in the Hell I am going. I took a couple of wrong turns in my life…and right now, I can't seem to find my way back."

For Melvina, this day was turning into one of great reflection…and regret.

"Melvina, the condition of your house is just like the condition of your life. A fuckin' mess!" she muttered looking at the empty beer bottles strewn across the living room floor. Her eyes began circling the room, gazing at the once-beautiful, flowered wallpaper. Years ago, her mother plastered the wallpaper on the walls. It was now curling away from the walls, exposing blotches of old, dried, crusted paste.

"I want to be well again…I want to be a good mother again…I want to sing again…I want to go back to church again…I want my best friend Caroline back again…I want things to go back to the way they were before I …" she cried, stopping short of finishing her last sentence, instead glancing down at the couch on which she was spending so much of her days. "There was a time in my life where things were so nice…just like this couch. But now, much like this couch, my life is in ruins…filthy, stained, and unfit...ready to be thrown away. But I don't want to throw my life away. I need help. And I'm gonna get it. Yep, I'm gonna get it…as soon as I'm ready. I'll start looking into some addiction programs next week. Yeah, that's exactly what I'm gonna do."

She thought of losing her job at Ty's Bakery. In the days, weeks, and months leading up to her firing, her issues on the job continued to mount. She was not showing up for work, and failing to inform Miss Moonie she would not be coming in for her shift. She began stealing cupcakes and other baked goods to eat for satisfying her voracious appetite for sweets and staying alert at work after she began smoking marijuana.

She thought about the money from her mother's insurance policy. By December 1996, every penny of it was gone.

"Your dumbass dipped and dipped into that money until there was nothing left," she said, talking to herself. "I can't believe you went through that money like that! But I guess it wasn't hard between helping Big Mike out with his legal shit and giving him money every time he asked for it. I spent a little on Lil' Mike, but blew most of it buying Crack."

After she began smoking Crack, she was no longer stealing baked goods from Miss Moonie, but money. As her Crack addiction worsened, the money she made at the bakery, was no longer enough to support her insatiable habit. As soon as her Crack high wore off, Melvina wanted more. No longer able to withdraw money from her bank account, she looked at the cash register at Ty's Bakery as her new funding source.

At first, Melvina slipped out $5 and $10 bills here and there. But the more she got away with taking money out of the register, the more brazen she got. The frequency in which she was taking money increased along with the denominations of currency she was slipping out the register into her pockets. She was now taking $20 bills a few times a week. She was also stealing ingredients such as flour, sugar, and toilet paper to sell on the street.

Things came to an unforgettable crescendo one November day in 1997. Although it was an early Tuesday afternoon, Miss Moonie flipped the 'OPEN' sign on the door over to 'CLOSED' once the bakery had no customers before locking the door.

"Is everything okay Miss Moonie?" curiously asked Melvina. "I see you turned over the sign, and you generally don't do that until closing time."

"Hand it over," said Miss Moonie.

"Hand over what Miss Moonie?" asked Melvina.

"That money you just put in your pocket."

"Miss Moonie, I already had money in my pocket. Why would I steal from you?"

"I got my reasons as to why I believe you have been stealing from me…but only you and the Good Lord know the answer to that Melvina. But we can settle this right now. Take the money out your pocket."

"Yes Miss Moonie," said Melvina placing a crumpled $20 bill on a counter near the register.

Picking up the money, Miss Moonie said, "I marked this $20 with a red marker," "And I've caught you red-handed."

Melvina quietly looked down at the floor, not saying a word.

"You've been here for 15 years Melvina!" said Miss Moonie fighting back tears. "Fifteen years! How could you steal from me Melvina?! After all I've done to help you?! How?!"

"But Miss Moonie, I –"

"But nothing Melvina! I knew my register was coming up short too many times based on sales. Not to mention supplies I know I have been ordering are suddenly disappearing! I knew you were stealing from me, but I turned a blind eye to those things because you are like a daughter to me. I was praying you would stop, but you just kept right on taking…just like you did today."

No longer able to fight back the tears that welled up in her eyes, Miss Moonie said, "I took you under my wing like a daughter…taught you everything I know…and you steal from me! It hurts me to my heart to do this Melvina. But I have no choice, but to let you go."

Consumed with anger and embarrassment for Miss Moonie confronting her, coupled with great angst as to how she was going to get the money to buy Crack once she left work, Melvina shouted, "The hell with this job! I'll find another one! You can put my last check in the damn mail!!"

Melvina unlocked the bakery door and swung it open with great force, the bell hanging from it tinkering loudly in her wake, the cold winter air slapping her in the face.

Despite her body reminding her it needed Crack, Melvina continued to lay motionless on the couch thinking about her life this warm August 8, 1998 day.

"I've lost everything that was special to me…my parents…Earlene…my job at the bakery…Caroline…going to church…singing in church…the list goes on and on. All I have left is Big Mike and our children. But Big Mike is so mean now, I hardly recognize who he is. What happened to the man I fell in love with just a few short years ago?"

She shared thoughts of the Baltimore Orioles of ten years ago with herself.

"I remember back in 1988 when everybody was talking about the team being 0-21. My life's no different. No matter how hard I try, I'm always on the losing side. I guess that's why I like smoking Crack so much," she sighed. "It makes me forget about all of those things…at least for a short while."

Crack Cocaine made Melvina feel like she was on the winning side, even though she was losing everything. Despite the mounting losses in her life, she had to have it. And she would do anything to get it. "I took Caroline's money out of her purse. I even sold Lil' Mike's Sony PlayStation and video games for $50. I've gone through all the money in my savings account. I stole from Miss Moonie. I've sold or pawned everything in this house of value. Now, I'm even selling my ass. This shit is making me do things I never dreamed I would do."

Melvina began thinking about what Crack would drive her to do next when the pangs of addiction finally drove her up from the couch.

"I need a hit," she said. "But I don't have any money or nothing to sell...other than sex."

"Lil' Mike!" she yelled heading out the door.

"Yes Mama!" he replied from upstairs.

"Keep an eye out on Angel. She's sleeping in her bassinet."

"Are you coming right back, Mama?!"

"Yes, Lil' Mike."

Melvina headed out the door to turn a quick trick to buy Crack, the shrilling cries of a now-awakened Angel beating the air like a drummer ceaselessly hitting a broken cymbal.

CHAPTER THREE

MY FAVOR-RIGHT BOOK

Baltimore, Maryland
August 10, 1998

Two more days passed. It was now August 10, 1998, and the cheerfully bright sun was shining like an orange lollipop amidst skies the color of light blue rock candy. Nodding, Melvina was oblivious to the sweetness of the summer day's picturesque view. Earlier this Monday morning, she smoked Crack given to her by Big Mike.

Between a night of getting high and Angel's relentless crying, Melvina exhaustingly drifted off to sleep. Awakened by a loud voice, she sprang up from the couch up like a jack-in-the-box and marched over to the window. "That loudmouth Mr. Hawkins woke me up from my sleep," grumbled Melvina. "He's got the biggest mouth in Baltimore. Instead of being a mailman, he should be a politician. He's always talking." Melvina stood sneering at her longtime neighbor from the living room window, dressed in a purple Baltimore Ravens t-shirt and team cap. An overweight man, the shirt protruded from the girth of his big belly. She listened as Mr. Hawkins' mouth ran non-stop beneath the lid of his Ravens cap talking about the team. Throughout the years, Melvina saw him sitting in his backyard drinking Natty Boh beer and eating steamed, Old Bay seasoned crabs, smashing the legs of the orange crustaceans with a wooden mallet. He loved his beer, crabs, and the Baltimore Ravens.

"I was at the new stadium for the pre-season game on Saturday," he was bragging to a small group of neighbors. "Them Bawl'more Ravens beat the Chicago Bears. Keep an eye out on that boy out of Miami, Ray Lewis. He's something special. One day, he's gonna take them Ravens all the way to the Super Bowl."

"Who needs to watch television with a neighbor like Mr. Hawkins?," Melvina growled. "Out there bragging to everybody about being at the game. Who cares? He's such a loudmouth braggart. I wish he would shut up before he wakes up Angel."

Mr. Hawkins abruptly stopped talking; he along with the others turning and glaring sharply at Melvina.

"Thank goodness Mr. Hawkins finally stopped running that big mouth of his! But why is he, Miss Jenkins, and the rest of them out there all looking at me and shaking their heads? Miss Jenkins looked over at me first. She probably was the one who told them to look over at me. I'd better lay back down before I really give them something to look at," she smirked, walking away from the window.

Before plopping back on the sofa, she peered inside Angel's bassinet.

"Look at my little Angel sleeping like an angel," Melvina softly whispered. "She looks just like her daddy. Especially when those little green eyes of hers are open. She's such a fussy baby…fussy just like her father. But I love them both. It's nice to see her sleeping so soundly. My God, she looks so peaceful."

❀

Upstairs, Lil' Mike sat Indian-style in his bed, awakened by the sound of Mr. Hawkins' loud voice. Rubbing his eyes, he climbed out of the bed, still groggy from Angel's crying and fetching her bottles throughout the night. He scampered to the window and peered outside.

"Why does Mr. Hawkins always talk so loud?" he wondered, staring out at his neighbor.

Tweet! Tweet! Tweet! chirped the birds sitting perched on the tree outside Lil' Mike's window.

"I guess you all are fussy because Mr. Hawkins woke you up too," laughed Lil' Mike. "Good morning little birdies."

Lil' Mike often talked to the birds outside his bedroom window; pretending he could understand them, and they could understand him.

Tweet! Tweet! Tweet! Tweet! Tweet! Tweet!

"Yeah, I didn't get much sleep either. But it wasn't totally Mr. Hawkins' fault. I was up all night getting my kid sister her baby bottles. She probably kept all of you up too. I'm still sleepy, but I'm happy! Today is gonna be a really special day!" Skipping over to the calendar held up by a nail on his wall, Lil' Mike looked at the day's date.

"Monday, August 10th, 1998!" he stated blissfully. "The day I'm going to recite the poem I've learned for Mama!"

For weeks, Lil' Mike worked hard to memorize, Ursula V. Battle's I Rose ABOVE it All.

"I worked really, really hard! And now I know every word by heart!"

"You birds can be my audience," said Lil' Mike, before heading over to the dresser to grab his book. "I'm going to rehearse the last part one more time before I go downstairs and recite the whole poem to Mama."

Flipping to his bookmarker, Lil' Mike tightly closed his eyes, careful not to peek at a single word.

"Like ocean water gushing in during morning tide; Upon a wave of hope I will continue to ride, Lil' Mike chuckled, grabbing his bedspread, and flapping it up and down. "You seek to crush my spirit with your ploys and acts; Your words, your actions, your relentless attacks!" he yelled motioning as if he were striking someone. "You swing words like an ax to chop me down; You the lumberjack, me…the tree hitting the ground," he cried, falling backwards on his bed. "You tell me I have nothing to offer at all, saying what you can to make me feel small," he lamented, closely bringing his thumb and forefinger together, leaving a smidgeon of space between the two. "With the words from your lips, you whip me with your lashes; And with the lighter of your tongue, you burn me to ashes," cried Lil' Mike, his eyes darting to a cigarette butt his father snuffed out on the floor. "Despite your venomous spew, I hold my head up high; Determined not to believe nar' one of your lies," he declared pointing at the air as if his father was standing there. "I have goals and dreams, inner treasures so rich! But you seek to bury them all deep down in a ditch," said the youngster, digging with an imaginary shovel. "Aspirations you hope I never discover; You throw me in a pit like Joseph's brothers!" he bellowed, pretending he was heaving something. "Out of the cistern of your words, I will climb; It may seem unlikely, but give it some time," said Lil' Mike, glancing at his calendar. "You pummel me with your words to bring me down in defeat," he stated stooping, "But the Lord gives me strength to get back on my feet!" he declared, standing. "For my faith is in Him and not in you! God is the One who will bring me through!" he thundered, imitating the preacher at church. "Like the song of the birds high up in the trees; I too will sing a melody as free as can be," he chimed.

Tweet! Tweet! Tweet! Tweet! Tweet! Tweet! The birds loudly chirped. "I'm glad you like it," chuckled Lil' Mike. "Now let me finish the rest."

"You foolishly believe I am ink, and you are the pen; The author of my story 'til the very end," said Lil' Mike, jotting his name on the cover of his composition notebook. "Writing in the annals of your twisted mind; I will never escape from the lies of your binds," he exclaimed, putting his hands behind his back as though they were shackled. "That I'd never make it because of what you took; But there's another ending to the story of my book!" he said, looking at his name on the cover. "Despite all you did to cause me to stumble and fall," he said, stumbling to the floor, "I'm here to tell you, I rose! I rose! I rose…above it all!" he shouted, catapulting to his feet, and raising his arms victoriously. Chirp! Chirp! Chirp! Chirp! Chirp! Chirp! cried the birds wildly, as if they were an audience giving Lil' Mike rousing applause.

"Thank you for your standing ovation," giggled Lil' Mike taking a bow from the stage of his bedroom. "I'm glad you all like it. Mama's gonna like it too! She's gonna be so surprised!"

Lil' Mike put on his slippers and prepared to head downstairs, glancing at himself as he passed by his dresser mirror. He momentarily gazed at the caramel-skinned eight-year boy staring back at him.

"I look like Mama used to look," he softly said. "Before she started smoking that Crack stuff. Now she's all skinny and sick-looking."

Looking at his curly black hair, Lil' Mike said, "My hair is so long. I haven't had my hair cut in weeks. Mama needs to take me to Mr. John's barbershop. She used to take me there for a haircut all the time. Now I'm lucky if she takes me once a month."

Lil' Mike's barber was John Battle. "Mr. John" owned a barbershop on N. Mount Street in Sandtown-Winchester called Battle's Barber Shop. Lil' Mike began to think about the sights, smells, and sounds of the neighborhood shop. The barbershop always smelled of shaving cream, hair, and hair tonic. Taped to a wall, was a steadily growing collage of photos.

"Mr. John, who are all those people?" Lil' Mike once asked.

"My wife, children, parents, and other family members," replied Mr. Battle.

Every time he went there, Lil' Mike would check to see if any new pictures had been added to the wall.

Mr. Battle had been cutting Lil' Mike's hair ever since he could remember. Battle's Barber Shop was always full of people, and sometimes, Lil' Mike and his mother had to wait a long time for his turn. But Lil' Mike didn't mind. The wait was always lively and entertaining. There were always people coming in there selling movies, toys, household goods, and other things.

"Sometimes Mama buys me toys from the people selling them at Mr. John's. But if I don't hide them, she'll take them back and I never see them again."

Battle's Barber Shop was always abuzz with the sound of Mr. Battle's clippers and plenty of trash talking.

The men always kept Lil' Mike laughing. They talked about their wives, girlfriends, cars, money, jobs, and other things. They talked about whatever was playing on the television in Mr. Battle's barbershop. Unlike the ladies at Miss Henrietta's salon, the men did not watch daytime soap operas and game shows. They typically watched variety shows, sports, and the news. But like the ladies at the hair salon, the men cussed words too. Lil' Mike recalled a painful rebuke given to one customer after asking Mr. Battle to switch from a Maryland Terrapins basketball game to a daytime soap opera.

"You must have lost your damn mind!" roared a customer. "This is March Madness and the Terps are playing! Ain't nobody switching shit to watch no soupy ass soap operas! Go home and watch the damn soaps with your wife! And that right, John?"

"That's riiiiight!" said Mr. John stressing the word 'right' as he customarily did. Mr. John, the man whose hair he was cutting, and the rest of the shop's customers all laughed and teased the now sour-faced man who inquired about switching to the soaps.

Pimlico Racetrack, located in the Park Heights area of the city, was a place Lil' Mike often heard the men talk about.

"After I get my shape-up, I'm going to the track," said 'Mr. Joe', an old, grey-bearded man, marking up a horseracing program with a pencil. "I see some longshots I'm gonna bet on."

"Mr. Joe, I lost my ass the last time I was at Pimlico," commented Smitty, another awaiting customer. "I ain't going nowhere near that place."

"The racetrack ain't taking your money Smitty, said Mr. Joe. 'Trying to be a lady's man is what's taking all your money."

"Pops, you stick to handicapping instead of telling me how I'm spending my money. I ain't a never been a one-woman man."

"Young buck, I used to think the same thing…that I wasn't a one-woman man," said Mr. Joe. 'But I became one after my wife caught me at a motel with another woman and threatened to blow off my balls. After that, the only asses I mess around with are the ones at the racetrack!"

All the men in the shop howled with laughter.

No topic was off-limits at Battle's Barber Shop.

"They talk about all kinds of grown-up things there," chuckled Lil' Mike, thinking about the advice some of the men told him to keep in mind once he was old enough to have a girlfriend.

"Yuck, girls!" Lil' Mike said to them. "I don't want a mushy girlfriend!"

"You might be saying that now," said a man wearing an MTA uniform. "But you won't be saying that when you get older. Will he John?"

"That's riiiiight!" said Mr. John, holding steady, the head of a crying youngster now sitting on a booster chair in his barber chair.

"This is his first haircut, Mr. John," said the child's mother. "I'm sorry he won't be still."

"There's are reasons I'm a Master Barber," said Mr. Battle. "And one of them is because there isn't a head of hair that's too hard for John Battle to cut. No matter how old or young. Even if they won't hold still."

Lil' Mike recalled his amazement at how Mr. Battle cut the little boy's hair with precision perfectness despite the youngster's crying and constant movement.

Sometimes, Mr. Battle would let Lil' Mike sweep cut hair from the floor. Whenever he did, the barber paid Lil' Mike $2.

"Save your money and work hard," Mr. John told him. "Maybe one day, you can open your own business, just like I did. If a young Black man from Blakely, Georgia can open a barbershop in Baltimore City in the late 1960s, you can achieve your dreams too."

"Yes sir, and thank you, Mr. John," said Lil' Mike, stuffing the money in his pockets.

The time finally arrived. Lil' Mike and his mother's wait was over.

"Hop up in the chair little man," said Mr. Battle. "It's your turn."

Lil' Mike jumped into the barber chair like a rocket being propelled into space. Sometimes, Mr. John would spin him around in the chair.

"Wheeeeee! That's so much fun Mr. John!" said Lil' Mike. After a few spins, Mr. Battle would pump the lever on the side of the barber chair to make it taller, and drape Lil' Mike in a cape.

Lil' Mike recalled the times when he would cry in Mr. John's chair just like the other little boy did. But once Lil' Mike grew accustomed to getting his hair cut, he stopped crying and sat still. Initially, he was afraid of the buzzing sound of the clippers but now was used to it.

Once Mr. Battle finished cutting Lil' Mike's hair, he slathered on the green hair tonic. "That stuff smells good Mr. John," said Lil Mike.

"Good ole Jeris Hair Tonic," replied Mr. Battle, now swirling around the barber chair, so Lil' Mike could see himself in large mirrors mounted on the shop wall. Lil' Mike smiled, admiring his fresh, stylish, high-top fade.

"Now you're ready for the girls," said Mr. Battle.

"Yuck, girls."

"You won't be saying that ten years from now," laughed Mr. John, drawing commentary from other men in the shop.

Lil' Mike had not been to Mr. John's for a cut in quite some time, and his hair showed it.

"You can't even see my high-top fade anymore because the sides of my hair have grown back," he told his reflection.

Lil' Mike continued to stare at the sad little boy in the mirror. His unhappiness was short-lived, as he remembered how special the day was going to be once he recited the poem to his mother. A snaggle-toothed smile formed on his face. The boy staring back at him from the mirror now looked happy.

Lil' Mike's missing front teeth reminded him of something he forgot to do when he woke up. He sprinted over to his bed and lifted the pillows. There was nothing under either one.

"The Tooth Fairy still hasn't left me any money," he grumbled. "My tooth is still here. I can't believe she forgot about me again." Lil' Mike shrugged his shoulders. "Maybe, the Tooth Fairy will remember me tomorrow. Then, I can buy some candy from the penny candy store."

Clutching I Rose ABOVE it all, Lil' Mike skipped towards the door to head downstairs.

"Oh, I almost forgot the truck daddy bought me," he said turning around to retrieve the red replica from a small bin of toys. "I'm going to play with that after I say the poem for Mama."

Tweet! Tweet! Tweet!

Turning towards the window during his exit from the room, Lil' Mike said, "Bye little birdies, see you tomorrow."

Running his truck down the wood banister, Lil' Mike roared, "Vroom! Vroom! Vroom!" pretending it was a steep hill. He could see Angel was asleep, and lowered his voice, thinking, The last thing I want to do is wake Angel up. Then, I won't be able to say my poem for Mama.

Tip-toeing over to his sleeping mother, he gently pressed on her shoulder. "What is it, baby?" Melvina groggily asked. After setting the truck down on the cocktail table, Lil' Mike stood in front of his mother holding the book. A lazy smile formed on Melvina's face. "Oh yeah, I had that book when I was in elementary school," she told him. "That was my favor-right book."

"Favorite mama. Favorite." Lil' Mike watched his mother's chin dip down. Mama's dozing off. He again pressed her on the shoulder. "I know it's your favorite book mama. Don't you remember when you told me it was your favorite book? he asked, flipping to his bookmarker.

"Yeah…I remember son," she said.

"That's why I learned this poem just for you Mama!" Lil' Mike exclaimed pointing to the words on the pages. "You'll see Mama! I know it by heart!"

"That's nice Lil' Mike, I…" replied a dozing Melvina, her voice trailing off.

Flipping to the inside cover of the book and placing it directly in front of her face, Lil' Mike said, "Mama, wake up. I have something to show you." Melvina began to snore. He tapped her on the shoulder and repeated, "Mama, wake up. I have something to show you." Melvina sluggishly opened her eyes, looking at the cursive handwriting her son was pointing to in the book. A smile formed on her face; her eyes now fixated on the pages. "I was about nine when I wrote my name there…Melvina…A…Thomas.". she said, using her right index finger to write her name invisibly in the air. "But mama, that's impossible," countered Lil' Mike. "Santa Clause wouldn't have given me your book as a Christmas present." "Santa's magical Lil' Mike," she explained. "He can do anything. Even…"

"Mama, wake up," stressed Lil' Mike, now sitting on the fringes of frustration over his mother's constant dozing. "Listen mama!" he implored, shaking her shoulder. "I learned the whole poem! Just listen!"

"With the arrows of your words, you've shot me again; Piercing a piece of my heart so hard to mend," Lil' Mike exclaimed, gesturing his hands and arms as if he were releasing an arrow from its bow.

Lil' Mike's arms listlessly fell to his side. Melvina was asleep, prompting Lil' Mike to begin shaking her. Melvina opened her eyelids halfway. "Stay awake mama," he pleaded, looking at his mother's crescent-shaped eyes. "I want to finish reciting my poem for you. But since you keep falling asleep, I'll just recite the last part of it for right now," he said. "Writing in the annals of your twisted mind; I will never escape from escape from the lies of your binds," he exclaimed, putting his hands behind his back as though they were shackled." She dazedly replied, "Not right now Lil' Mike. Mama's tired. Recite it to your father. He's here." "Daddy's not going to listen," he asserted. "But you Mama…you always listen." Feeling himself getting choked up, Lil' Mike took a long pause and continued, "At least you used to listen. Until you started sleeping all the time." Melvina was drifting off to sleep again, and frustration was creeping in for Lil' Mike. *For weeks, I have worked hard to learn this poem for Mama, And all she keeps doing is falling asleep before I can even finish!* Lil' Mike began shaking her more forcefully, telling her, "Mama! Wake up so I can finish reciting my poem for you!" His mother fully opened her eyelids, revealing bulging, bloodshot eyes. She looked like an angry werewolf under a full, crimson moon. Scared, Lil' Mike slightly backed up, feeling like helpless prey about to be attacked. "Damnit!" Melvina howled, pushing Lil' Mike hard to the floor. "Why do you keep waking me up?! What the hell do you think I am?! A damn milkshake! Stop shaking me!" "But mama —" "But mama shit! I don't know what's gotten into you shaking me like that, but if you ever do that again, I'll beat the hell out of you!"

Angel's cries pierced the air.

"Shit! Now look at what you made me do! Wake the baby up! The last thing I want to hear right now is all that damn crying!" she screamed, rubbing her head as if she had a migraine. "Go get your sister's bottle outta the microwave! I warmed it up earlier." Lil' Mike's stomach growled as it had embarrassingly done in class so many times. "But Mama…I'm hungry too!" he pleaded, getting up from the floor. Melvina barked, "Look! I fixed you some Oodles of Noodles earlier! They're also in the microwave." "But Mama, I'm tired of eating Oodles of Noodles all the time." His mother shouted, "Well right now, that's all the food we got in the damn house! Some folks ain't even got that! There are a lot of starving children over in Africa and other places that would love to eat the food we have! And you got the nerve to be picky! Be grateful for what you do have!" she spat, closing her eyes. Dumbfounded and hurt, Lil' Mike was feeling like a wounded animal. *I can't believe Mama pushed me to the floor,* he silently yelped, his eyes filling with tears. *All I wanted to do was surprise her by reciting her favorite poem.* A few seconds later, his mother opened her eyes. "Why are you standing there looking at me?!" she bellowed. "Didn't I tell you to get your sister's bottle?! Now git before I slap the shit out of you!" Lil Mike, stammered, "Yyyyyes mmmma'am," before turning to start towards the kitchen, tears gushing from his eyes like a river of water bursting through a broken dam.

Watching Lil' Mike walking away with great dejection, Melvina immediately felt a sense of guilt, self-conviction, and remorse.

"Lil Mike," she softly called out to him, standing up from the couch. Lil' Mike stopped. "Come here, son." Turning slowly, Lil' Mike walked apprehensively over to his mother who raised her hand towards him. Lil' Mike cowered, throwing up both arms to defend himself. "I'm not going to hit you Lil' Mike," she assured him. "I just wanted to apologize. I'm so sorry baby. I don't know what came over me, but I didn't mean to talk to you like that or push you down. You know Mama loves you…and my crying little Angel," she said, turning to look at the wailing baby. "I know you love us, Mama," replied Lil' Mike. "We love you too." Melvina sniffled, "Mama just gets a little upset sometimes. But I would never hurt my babies. With open arms, Melvina smiled and said, "Now, Mama is gonna listen to you say your poem, Lil' Mike. But first, you have to give me a big hug. That'll let me know you forgive me." A smile returning to his face, Lil' Mike replied, "Okay Mama," welcoming the warm, motherly embrace only she could give. "I love you son." "I love you too Mama." Melvina couldn't help but wonder the last time she hugged her son or told him how much she loved him. I need to do this more often, she silently admitted. Wah! Wah! Wah! wailed Angel, her cries seemingly intensifying. "Get your sister's bottle, and then I will listen to you recite your poem." Complying, Lil' Mike replied to his mother, "Yes ma'am," setting both his book and truck down on the cocktail table.

Looking at Lil' Mike's hair, Melvina promised, "Mama's gonna take you to Mr. John's tomorrow for a haircut." Feeling the crown of his head, Lil' Mike said, I look like a werewolf Mama. Can't you take me today? Recalling the shop's hours, Melvina explained, "Mr. John is closed on Mondays. I'll take you tomorrow and that's a promise." Lil' Mike replied, "Okay, mama," starting towards the kitchen. Waiting for Lil' Mike to return from the kitchen, Melvina giggled, thinking about what a visit to Battle's Barbershop would bring the next day. Lil' Mike represented the second generation of her family who went to Mr. Battle for a haircut. Mr. John also cut her father's hair. When Melvina was a little girl, her father sometimes took her with him to the barbershop. Melvina recalled the story Mr. Battle once told the customers in the shop, sharing how he graduated from high school at age 16 and left his native Blakely, Georgia to attend Apex Beauty School in Baltimore. "After I graduated from Apex, I worked as an apprentice at Rivers Barbershop on Riggs Avenue," he said, shaping a man's 'Barbisol' shaving cream-covered face and mustache with a straight razor. "I opened my shop in the early 1970s." Melvina's father replied, "You know, I got a lot of respect for you, John. For a Black man to come to Baltimore and open his own shop up at that time is quite an accomplishment. Me and the guys down at The Point talk about you all the time. Not to mention you own property around here and a carry-out. That's remarkable John." Never stopping to look up, Mr. Battle, who was also a minister replied, "That ain't me, Melvin. That's God."

Having sat in the shop on many occasions, Melvina heard not only "Mr. John," but other men, talk about how they came into their livelihoods. Like Mr. John, some owned businesses or were also ministers, elders, or pastors. Others like her father were blue-collar workers and employed at Sparrows Point. Many of them worked in education and were schoolteachers, principals, and assistant principals. Others were gym teachers and coaches. Some were retired military men who fought in Vietnam. One, in particular, a man they all called 'Sarge', sometimes wore his old Army jacket and dog tags, and always shared stories of fighting in 'Nam.' The shop was always full of characters. Some of them had nicknames that were given to them based on their physicality or occupation. There was 'Short Man', 'Stickman', 'Ice Cream Man', 'Boss Man,' 'Trash Man', and 'Antique Man.'

However, not all of Mr. Battle's customers talked about their jobs. They didn't have to. Their uniforms told the story. They were postal workers, policemen, firemen, mechanics, and MTA bus drivers. Battle's Barber Shop was never short on people or talk. Situated at Mount and Mosher streets, this corner of the world was just as enlightening and entertaining now as it was when her late father took her there. The men were never short of topics. They talked about their wives, their girlfriends, politics, the happenings across the street at Phil's Bar and so much more. Melvina could never forget October 3, 1995. She had taken then five-year-old Lil' Mike to the barbershop for a haircut. She, along with everyone else, sat with bated breath, their eyes fixated on the television. The verdict in the O.J. Simpson trial was about to be delivered when one of the men in the shop started talking. "Shut up!," a customer yelled. "We don't want to hear you! We want to hear the verdict!" Another blurted, "The lady in charge of the jury is coming out now and she's about to read the verdict!" Mr. John shut off his clippers, something Melvina rarely saw him do during his workday, silencing the buzzing sound to clearly hear the verdict. Then came the long-awaited moment.

"We, the jury, in the above-entitled action, find the Defendant, Orenthal James Simpson, not guilty," announced the jury forewoman. After the verdict was read, Mr. John immediately turned his clippers back on. Meanwhile, his barbershop erupted into complete pandemonium, many of its customers morphing into 'The Hood's very own self-proclaimed legal analysts and experts.

"Told you The Juice would get off!" said one man, high-fiving another.

"Nigger, you know O.J. killed them folks!," commented a customer shaking his head in disgust.

A patron in the barber chair chimed, "O.J.'s Dream Team was the best! "If the glove didn't fit, they had to acquit!"

Another blurted, "White folks gonna be mad as hell that boy got off!"

Not only was Mr. John's barbershop entertaining, but his $5 cuts, were among the cheapest around.

Will I even have the money to pay Mr. John when I take Lil' Mike to the shop tomorrow? she wondered. Hopefully, I will. But he always works with me if I don't have enough money or no money at all. He does that for a lot of people... especially when it comes to their kids getting haircuts. Conversely, Melvina did not want to be at the mercy of people's benevolence. She wanted to get back to being able to pay people what she owed. As hard as it was to admit, she realized Crack was not only causing her to steal, but it had stolen her ability to be self-sufficient.

Things can't go on like this Melvina. Something's got to give. Every time you get your hands on some money, you smoke it up.

Internally, Melvina wailed, thoughts of Lil' Mike's disappointment about the 'Tooth Fairy', not showing up, now circling about her mind. She set aside change to place under her son's pillow when his first tooth came out. Nevertheless, she spent it. Most recently, when his other front tooth came out, she again set aside change. Yet, she spent that money too.

Watching Lil Mike starting towards the hallway leading to the kitchen, Melvina softly whispered, "Mama's gonna get herself together Lil' Mike. I promise."

※

Skipping towards the kitchen, Lil' Mike was thinking about the emotional rollercoaster ride he just stepped off.

When Mama cusses and fusses at me, I feel so sad because it makes me feel like she doesn't love me. And her pushing me down like she did today, makes me even sadder. Mama used to tell me she loved me all the time...and give me warm hugs...just like she did today. That hug made me so happy! I miss Mama's hugs. I know she loves me...and Angel...but that Crack stuff makes Mama so mean! Lil' Mike smiled, daydreaming about his mother's reaction once she heard him recite the poem. Mama's so tired and angry nowadays. But when I say the poem for her, she will be happy again!

The closer Lil' Mike got to the kitchen, the louder her crying seemed to be getting. Her bawling sounded more like screaming than crying. Angel's always crying! I wish she would shut up!

Lil' Mike reached the kitchen doorway. Instead of walking in, he suddenly stopped. Terrified, he was trying to scream, but no noise would come out. He could not believe what he was seeing. Unsure what to do, he darted up to his room, jumped in the bed, and buried himself deep beneath the dark sanctity of covers.

A few minutes later, Big Mike stood in the living room entranceway; his striking green eyes fixed squarely on Melvina. She was asleep sitting upright; the upper torso of her body positioned squarely between her legs, and her hair and arms dangling downwards towards the floor like a limp rag doll.

"That shit always got her messed up," Big Mike scoffed. "Fuckin' Crackhead."

Silencing his beeper and cell phone so that the two would vibrate instead of ringing, he quietly laid Melvina's crack pipe down on the cocktail table next to Lil' Mike's truck and book. His intention was to quietly leave for work, but seeing Melvina sleeping in such a compromising position made her easy prey, and aroused him. "Might as well get me some of that ass before I leave," Big Mike murmured, thoughts of ramming his penis into Melvina's anus quickly taking hold of his mind. Menacingly walking over to the couch, he began plotting how he would launch his surprise attack on her unsuspecting body. I'll get behind the couch, climb over it, get up under her, pull down her pants, and screw her as hard as I can. My dick is getting hard already at the thought of hearing her scream. Guess I'll kiss on her a little first. That'll be my goodbye kiss before I go to work. Hopefully, I can put up with the smell of the funky Bitch.

Melvina's senses were awakened by the sensual feeling of soft lips pressing against her neck. Smiling, she let out a giddy giggle.

"Damn, that feels good baby," Melvina cooed, inhaling the odor of Big Mike's caramel body, garnished with the delicious aroma of Polo cologne. "You ain't kissed my neck like that in a long time." Big Mike responded by running his moist tongue around her ears and his hands down her shirt towards her big breasts. "Mmmmmm Big Mike," Melvina purred, closing her eyes, and licking her lips whilst his fingertips tightly squeezed her nipples. Melvina's body was yearning for Big Mike but wanted Crack even more. Jumping up from the couch, abruptly interrupting their sensuous moment, Melvina cried, "Where's my Crack pipe?! Where's my Crack pipe?!," eyes frantically searching for the paraphernalia, hands tossing pillows on the floor in her wake. "Damnit Melvina, you can't remember shit!" Big Mike barked. "You'd forget where ya damn head was if it wasn't attached to your body!" Pointing to the Crack pipe on the cocktail table, he seethed, "Your Crack pipe is sitting right there in front of you! You left it in the kitchen near the stove." Puzzled, she replied, "I did? I don't remember taking my Crack pipe in the kitchen. I could have sworn I left it sitting right here on the table."

Melvina joyfully picked up the Crack pipe and kissed it, thoughts of where she put the Crack pipe dissipating like smoke. She began dancing, happy to see her pipe on the table. "Do a little dance, make a little love, Get down tonight, get down tonight," sang Big Mike, piping a tune from K.C. & The Sunshine's band's 'Get Down Tonight'. Grinning, Big Mike said, "Melvina, I see that Ready Rock you smoked earlier got you real nice." Consequently, his words reminded Melvina she wanted more of the drug, prompting her to stop dancing. "That was some good ass Crack-a-lack," she replied. But I need some more Big Mike...I need a hit real bad."

"I'll hit my man up for some more before I go to work," Big Mike promised. "He told me that's the best stuff on the streets right now."

Relieved, Melvina replied, "Okay honey. But make sure you drop it off to me before you go to work."

"Okay. Gotta go," said Big Mike looking at his watch before kissing her a final time on the neck. Big Mike's gonna take real good care of you. I'm callin' my man up right now."

Big Mike casually strolled out the door, pulling out his 'Motorola Startac' flip phone along the way. A few short years ago, the only people who could afford cell phones were rich people, recalled Melvina. And those were big clunky cases, bag phones, or installed in fancy cars. Big Mike sure looks smooth using his new cell phone. Kinda reminds me of Detective Tubbs on that TV show Miami Vice.

⚛

Mere minutes went by, but to Melvina, they seemed like hours. She was pacing back and forth, cussing and fussing, wondering out loud what was taking Big Mike so long to return.

"Where is Big Mike with my blast?! I'm fienin' and I'm fienin' bad," she hissed, scratching her arms and legs. "I need a hit now. What the fuck is takin' him so long to get back?!" Melvina walked over to the cocktail table and picked up the Crack pipe. She shook it, hoping it held even the tiniest trace of Crack.

"Shit! It's empty!" she roared, slamming the pipe down on the table. "Big Mike needs to hurry back with my Ready Rock!"

She resumed her pacing, looking over at the television in hopes it might take her mind off how bad she wanted to get high. She changed course during her travels about the room to slightly turn up the TV's lowered volume.

"Questions remain about the death of Lady Diana who was killed in a car crash last year," said a newscaster's voice. "The late Princess of Wales…"

The newscaster's voice faded away from her ears, his report sweeping her mind back to July 9, 1981. That day, Melvina was among the millions who watched Lady Diana Spencer (Lady Di) wed Prince Charles of Wales (Prince Charles) on television. When the school year resumed after summer break, many of her female classmates at Garrison Jr. High School were still talking about the wedding. She along with them, all dreamed of one day having a fairytale wedding – just like Lady Di.

"Once upon a time, I thought Big Mike would be my Prince Charles, and I would be his Lady Di," Melvina whispered, looking at photos of the Royal Couple flash across the television. "Lady Di is pictured here with Princess Caroline of Monaco," said the newscaster's voice, evoking thoughts of Caroline.

"I miss Caroline so much," sighed Melvina. "It's been a month since our big argument on Lil' Mike's birthday. I want to call Caroline. But after what she said to me, I damn sure ain't calling her! She's gonna have to call me first. But looking back at what she told me about Big Mike, I have to admit…she was right. But I still love him. And I really thought I could change him…that I could make him a better person…that I could make him love me. I thought giving him children would help. Damnit Melvina! That only made things worse! No matter how hard I try, I can't change Big Mike…I can't make him love me. He won't marry me, and he acts like the children don't exist!" A photo from the car wreck that claimed Princess Di's life, was now on the TV screen.

"Life just ain't fair," Melvina moaned, flicking off the television. "Man, I need a hit right now. Hopefully, Big

Mike will bring his ass back here soon." Stepping up her pacing a notch, Melvina's thoughts shifted to Big Mike's uncharacteristic recent actions. "A few weeks ago, Big Mike takes Lil' Mike to the store. And outta the blue, he buys him a truck. He buys me Crack last night, brings me more this morning…and didn't make me fetch it a single time. Now he's on his way back with more. And, before he left, he comes in here kissing me all over my neck and feelin' my titties. And, he left before ramming that big ass dick of his in my ass to get his jollies off. What gives?" A plausible hypothesis came to mind, causing a Grinch-like smile to form on Melvina's face. "I got it!" Melvina surmised. "That Nigga's tryin' to butter me up! Being all nice to me because I took his ass Downtown for Child Support for Lil' Mike and Angel! Big Mike ain't foolin' nobody! Tryin' to outsmart me! But I outsmarted him this time! That's right! And he's gonna pay me my damn Child Support money!"

Gloating over figuring out Big Mike's ploy, Melvina rushed over to the window hoping to see him coming up the walkway. Instead, she saw her neighbors standing around listening to Miss Jenkins. "Damn!" said Melvina. "They have been standing outside half the morning! Don't they have anything better to do than to stand outside all day gossiping?! And where the hell is Big Mike?! These cravings are kickin' my ass!" She stood at the window gazing at Miss Jenkins' movements. "Look at that nosey busybody out there, mouth moving a mile a minute!" she exclaimed. When Melvina was a little girl, Miss Jenkin's husband Linwood Jenkins died after a tragic accident on the job. Melvina recalled the words of her late mother, Margaret. "Violetta probably talked poor Linwood to death," her mother jokingly said. "He probably went on home to be with the good Lawd just to get some peace from all of Violetta's talkin." But on a far more serious note regarding Linwood Jenkins, Melvina overheard her mother one day tell her father, "There's more to what happened to Linwood than meets the eye. Sounds fishy to me. Violetta ain't buyin' that cockamamy story about that accident on the job, and neither do I. Not everybody was happy to see him get that big promotion."

Miss Jenkins' nosey tendencies were traits common to her, but following Mr. Jenkins's death, such behavior became more prevalent. The widow meandered around the block poking in everyone's business and even purchased a Police Scanner to keep up with emergencies happening around the city. Sometimes, Melvina would see the talkative woman handing their neighbors copies of The Baltimore Times or placing copies of the free weekly newspaper behind their screen doors. "All Colored folks ain't out here robbin', killin', and usin' drugs," Melvina heard Miss Jenkins telling neighbors about the free weekly publication. "Lots of us are doing wonderful things. And you can read all about it in The Baltimore Times."

Back when Melvina was still a recipient of Miss Jenkins' hand deliveries of the paper, she told Melvina, "A Colored woman named Joy Bramble owns it. Isn't that something? A Colored woman starting her own newspaper."

Melvina always wondered why Miss Jenkins still referred to 'Black' people as 'Colored.' This is the 1990s, Melvina thought, listening to Miss Jenkins go on and on about the wonderful things The Baltimore Times was doing for the city. Colored seems so outdated and discriminatory. This is the perfect time to ask Miss Jenkins why she still uses a term I feel symbolizes Jim Crow. With these things in mind, Melvina asked Miss Jenkins why she used the word 'Colored' as opposed to 'Black' or 'African American'. Miss Jenkins explained, "I was born in 1935 and came up during a time when our race was referred to as 'Colored', and in some cases by the 'N Word', but I won't dare utter that terrible word! And to think some of our own people call one another by the "N-word" now! I can hardly believe it! Anyway, I got used to being called Colored, calling myself Colored, and calling others Colored. Not to mention eating at counters, sitting at movies, or going to a show where we could only sit in areas designated for 'Colored', and the better of these areas designated for 'Whites'. Thank the Lord for Dr. King, Medgar Evers, Malcolm X, and so many other civil rights leaders who helped change that! And let me not forget Rosa Parks…and people always tell me I look like her –"

"And you do Miss Jenkins," interjected Melvina.

"Thank you Sugar Pie, because Rosa Parks is a beautiful woman and so courageous!"

"She certainly is," said Melvina, while thinking, I bet Rosa Parks don't talk half as much as you do Miss Jenkins!

"As I was saying, God sent us as Black people…see I said Black people, so as you can see Melvina, I'm working on it," Miss Jenkins winked, "So many champions to bring about change when it came to racial segregation. But for Miss Jenkins, after so many years of hearing, reading, and using the word 'Colored', it became ingrained in my mind…like a bad habit. And bad habits can sometimes be extremely hard to break…but not impossible."

"Yes ma'am," said Melvina. "Have a nice day, Miss Jenkins."

"You do the same!" Miss Jenkins replied.

These days, Miss Jenkins no longer gave Melvina copies of The Baltimore Times or dropped them in her door. Miss Jenkins barely looks my way, and when that busybody does, seems to me, she's whispering bad things about me, Melvina surmised. But ask me if I care? I don't give a damn what Miss Jenkins thinks about me!"

Miss Jenkins was also a longtime member of Melvina's former church, United in Victory Tabernacle. Even at that church, Miss Jenkins was into everything, Melvina silently recalled. Always gossiping and spreading rumors about everybody…even the Bishop."

Melvina's eyes stayed fixated on the group – Miss Jenkins' jaws moving up and down chewing on Wrigley's Spearmint Gum while she talked, the people gathered, attentively listening. Cassius Henderson was also among the neighbors standing outside. Mr. Henderson worked at Sparrows Point with Melvina's father and was President of the community's neighborhood association. A civic-minded activist, whose involvement earned him the nickname, 'Mr. Community,' Mr. Henderson oversaw the neighborhood's AFRO American Newspaper's AFRO Clean Block contest efforts. In prior years, their block was a regular winner of the famous campaign, aimed at encouraging communities across the city to keep their neighborhoods looking good. Winning the contest was a big deal, and gave communities bragging rights. People living in Black communities across the city went all out to beautify their blocks and earn the right for the contest's large winning banner to hang in their neighborhoods.

Up and down Fulton Avenue in Sandtown, women got down on their hands and knees to scrub their marble steps with Clorox Bleach and put plants in planters fashioned out of rubber tires. Along Edmonson Avenue in Edmonson Village women rose early in the morning to sweep their gutters, walkways, and sidewalks with their corn brooms. These were among the sights that could be found in preparation for AFRO Clean Block and Melvina remembered them all well.

On her own porch front, Melvina's mother planted green and white Hosta plants, accenting the ground around them with colorful begonias and petunias. Her father was a stickler for cut grass, bushes, and hedges. While the lawn sat on an incline, he mowed the Kentucky Bluegrass in a lined pattern and went to work on the greenery using his hedge trimmer, neatly shaping them with the precision of Mr. John's cutting hair. Her father went to great lengths to ensure no weeds were growing in the yard, putting down weed killer and plucking them out of the ground by hand. Melvina swept up the clippings with her mother's own corn broom. Under a keen eye, her mother checked behind her to make sure not one clipping was left on the ground. Her parents always kept the front and backyards nice, but they really went the extra mile for AFRO Clean Block. "This house won't be the one to cause us to lose AFRO Clean block," said her mother. The once-immaculate home and its yards were a stark contrast from the way they looked when Melvina's parents were alive. In watching her neighbors, Melvina obliviously looked past the overgrown bushes and hedges, and the grass, now overrun with Dandelions and other weeds.

"Look at that nosey ass Miss Jenkins talking Mr. Henderson's ears off…mouth running a mile a minute," said Melvina, shaking her head. "Always chewing that damn Wrigley's Spearmint Gum. Always in everybody's business. Always running that trap of hers." Melvina could see Miss Jenkins' eyes flashing quick glances at her house and then up at her standing in the window. "I bet Miss Jenkins is out there talking about me right now! She needs to get a damn life! And where the hell is Big Mike?! Let me go page his ass again!" Preparing to walk away from the window, Melvina noticed city police cars and a paddy wagon slow up and park on the block. "I wonder who the Po-Po is coming to lock up today?" she wondered, departing the window to page Big Mike.

Peering over silver-rimmed, cat-eyed styled eyeglasses attached to a chain around her neck, Miss Jenkins' eyes followed the parking police vehicles, careful not to blink for fear she would miss something.

The grey-wigged 62-year-old had her own suspicions as to who the police had come to lock up. She momentarily stopping looking at the law enforcement vehicles to stare at Melvina's house. Shaking her head, Miss Jenkins who pronounced the word 'child' as 'chile', commented to her neighbors, "Em, em, em," Look at that chile's house! I know Melvin and Margaret are turning over in their graves! That house never looked like that when they were alive."

"That's right Violetta," voiced Mr. Henderson. "That house is nothing but an eyesore. We have not won the AFRO Clean Block contest in years. If you ask me, that house is the reason why."

"That's part of the reason, Cassius. People around here don't keep up their property like they used to. Folks used to keep their houses up. But some of these younguns don't take pride in these homes like their parents did. They don't appreciate the hard work and sacrifices their fathers and mothers made to get these houses. Like me, many of them also had to deal with racist White folks who didn't want us Colored folks moving in. And when too many of us moved in, they moved out."

"This new generation takes too many things for granted," opined Mr. Henderson. "Just look at that house! Melvina should be ashamed of herself. She got that house free and clear after her parents died, and she has not done a thing to keep it up." Pointing towards the house, he noted, "Look at that raggedy porch and the crumbling steps. Look up there at that roof. It looks like it's about to cave in. And look at that grass. Looks like a forest. Melvin used to keep that grass cut. Even when he drank that booze, he still cut that grass. I was always afraid he was gonna cut off his own toes."

"That's right Cassius," chuckled Miss Jenkins, thinking about an intoxicated Mr. Thomas wobbly navigating the lawnmower. "And Margaret used to get out there every spring and plant pretty flowers. Now look at it. Ain't nothin' growin' in that yard but ugly weeds."

"Damn shame," Mr. Henderson responded, frowning at the weeds. "Melvina is dragging down our property value right along with her!"

"I remember when Melvina was born right over yonder at Provident Hospital," said Miss Jenkins pointing in the direction of the facility. "It's terrible how she messed herself all up behind them drugs. If you ask me, her place ain't nuthin' but a Crack House."

"I believe so too," agreed Mr. Henderson. "I tell you, Violetta, Mayor Kurt Schmoke got his hands full trying to deal with the drugs and crime in this city. You know, I read in The Sun paper the other day he was talking about legalizing drugs. He said if you take the profit away from the drug trade, the violence will come down."

"Is that so?" asked Miss Jenkins.

"That's what I read," replied Mr. Henderson. "Sounds radical to me, but that's what I read."

"Legalize drugs in this city?!" incredulously asked Miss Jenkins. "When pigs fly! That will never happen!"

"Hey, look over there," said Mr. Henderson pointing to a parking white, compact car prompting the small contingency to turn and look. The group watched two women emerging from the car. In tandem, the police began to exit their squad cars, slamming the doors behind them.

"Uh-oh," said Miss. Jenkins peering over her glasses.

"Uh-oh is right," said Mr. Henderson, his eyes trailing the contingency, he and the rest of the neighbors now speculating why the police and two conservatively women were heading to Melvina Thomas' house.

❧

Lil' Mike lay trembling, his entire body still submerged beneath bedcovers. His mind was now a place of bedlam, thoughts racing at warp speed as to what action he should take to address the terrifying sight playing over and over again in his consciousness.

I need to tell Mama, he decided, slowly and cautiously peeling away bedcovers from atop his small frame. Knock! Knock! Knock! Knock! Knock! The hitting of loud knuckles on the front door in rapid succession quickly brought Lil' Mike out of the bed. "Someone's at the door!". Quivering, he whispered. "Maybe Daddy left. I'd better hurry downstairs and tell Mama what I saw in the kitchen."

Running down the steps, the knocks at the door now growing louder, Lil' Mike rushed over to the couch. "Mama!" he gasped, trying to catch his breath. "I have something to tell you! Where's Daddy?!"

"Big Mike left, but that's him at the door," she replied. "It's about damn time he got back! But why is he bangin' on the door like that when he's got a key?!"

"Mama, I —"

"Wait a second Lil' Mike! I'll listen to you recite your poem after I —"

Knock! Knock! Knock! Knock! Knock!

"But Mama, I saw —"

Knock! Knock! Knock! Knock! Knock!

"Damnit Big Mike!" she yelled, turning towards the door. "Why are you knocking on my door like the damn police!"

Knock! Knock! Knock! Knock! Knock!

"Listen, Mama, I really need to tell you something before Daddy comes in. I saw —"

Knock! Knock! Knock! Knock! Knock! Knock! Knock! Knock!

"Quiet Lil' Mike!" shouted Melvina, putting her forefinger over her mouth.

Knock! Knock! Knock! Knock! Knock! Knock! Knock! Knock! Knock! Knock! The forceful knocks were now causing the door to shake along with Lil' Mike. I'm scared, he thought.

"Big Mike must have lost his damn mind knocking on my door like that!" Melvina hissed, marching to the front door. "He's about to send me to jail, knocking on my door like the damn police!"

"Mama, please! You have to listen to me I —."

"Shit! Not right now Lil' Mike! Go check on your sister!"

"Angel isn't in her bassinet mama. She's —"

"I can't wait to cuss his ass out!" fumed Melvina, turning the knob. "Big Mike, what the fuck is wrong with you knocking on my door like…"

Melvina abruptly stopped short of finishing her profanity-laced tirade, startled at the sight of four uniformed Baltimore City Police officers and two plainly dressed women standing on the door's opposite side.

❀

Standing at the door dumbfoundingly looking at the stone-faced group, Melvina asked, "Can I help you?"

"Melvina Thomas?" inquired one of the officers.

"What's going on and how do you know my name?"

"I'm Sergeant Daniel Vargas," answered the officer talking to Melvina before pointing to the others. "And this is Officer Joseph Brown, Officer Anton Hill, Officer Eric Long, and Officer Tammy Dennis. We're from the Baltimore City Police Department."

"I'm Stephanie Matthews," said the Caucasian woman.

"And I'm Anne Braxton," replied her African American counterpart. "We're from Child Protective Services."

"What!" shrieked Melvina. "The police! Child Protective Services!"

"Ma'am, we got a call about drug activity at this address," said Sgt. Vargas. "We were also notified of alleged child abuse and child neglect of two children residing at the home."

"Miss Thomas, we need to check on the welfare of your children," blurted Ms. Matthews, stretching her neck along with the others to peer inside.

"Drug activity?! Child abuse?! Child neglect!? I don't know who called and told ya'll that, but they lied! Ain't none of that going on up in here!"

Sgt. Vargas' roving eyes came to a sudden stop.

Shit! Melvina cursed in her mind. That officer sees my damn crack pipe!

"Ma'am is that a crack pipe lying in there on the table?" inquired Sgt. Vargas.

"Where are your children?" Miss Braxton demanded to know. "We need to make sure they are okay."

Before Melvina could say another word, the small group brushed past her, making their way inside. The group quickly dispersed, Officer Brown putting on latex gloves while walking to the cocktail table, Officer Dennis rushing towards the kitchen, and Miss Braxton making her way over to Lil' Mike.

"Y'all can't just run up in my house like this!" Melvina cried, watching Officer Long cover Officer Dennis with his gun drawn, cocked, and aimed in the direction of the kitchen door.

"Hey, officer! Why you got your gun out! Hey, you over there! Why are you going into my kitchen! Y'all ain't got no right to come up in my house like this!"

"Clear!" shouted Officer Dennis from the kitchen.

"I got the Crack pipe!" declared Officer Brown dropping it into a cellophane bag.

"Man, this place is filthy," commented Officer Hill putting on latex gloves before pulling pillows off Melvina's couch and tossing them to the floor. "You got your kids living like this?"

"Who gave you the right to ransack my house like this?! And right in front of my little boy!" shouted Melvina glancing over at a crying Lil' Mike. "What are you looking for? I know my rights! Where's your search warrant?!"

The officers did not respond to Melvina's questioning; instead, they continued to search about the house.

"With all the crime and murders going on in Baltimore, why y'all over here harassing me?!" Melvina screamed in dismay. "I might take a little hit every now and then! A little somethin', somethin'! So what?! I ain't hurtin' nobody!" Melvina's attention was snatched by Ms. Braxton taking Lil' Mike by the hand and coaxing him towards the front door. "Hey lady! Let go of my son!" she demanded, looking at Lil' Mike struggling to get away from the social worker.

"If I were you, I'd lower that tone," cautioned Sgt. Vargas.

"My boyfriend Big Mike will be here any minute!" Melvina informed them. "He'll straighten this mess out!"

A thought came to Melvina's mind. She knew who was behind all of this. She knew exactly who called the police and Social Services.

"Damn you, Caroline! I know that backstabbin' heifer is the one who called you all! Fuckin' traitor! She's behind all of this! Well, I've got news for all of you up in here! You won't find nothin' 'cause I ain't got nothing! And as far as my children are concerned, I take damn good care of my kids!"

"We sure got a loud one here Sarge," Officer Brown commented.

"Sure do," replied Sgt. Vargas. "But if I were her, I would change that attitude."

Officer Brown dropped to the living room floor. Holding a flashlight, he was crawling along the floor like a soldier on a covert operation in the jungles of Vietnam. Stunned, Melvina yelled, "Why are you crawling on my floor?! I have already told ya'll that I ain't got nothin' in here! Again, where's your search warrant?!" Officer Brown snaked across the floor to the old fireplace, reached inside, and began feeling around. "Y'all ain't got no right to do this!" shouted Melvina. "What are you all looking for?! I know one thing! I'm callin' a lawyer! And I'm gonna sue the hell outta the police and the city for this illegal search of my home!"

"I think I feel something in here. Yep, there's something in here," said Officer Brown pulling a large, clear baggie containing a powdery white substance from the fireplace. "I found the drugs! Looks like Cocaine!"

"Just like they said, this is a Stash House!" declared Sgt. Vargas.

"This ain't no damn stash house!" said Melvina, looking at the cellophane bag in disbelief. "Damnit, I use drugs! As a matter of fact, I would have used those drugs had I known it was in there! What are ya'll trying to do?! Set me up?!"

"Ahhhhhhhhhhhhhhhhhhhhhhhhhhhhhhhh!"

A blood-curdling scream was coming from the kitchen, prompting Melvina's heart to jump and all the officers to draw their guns.

※

Lil Mike was trying to desperately free himself from Ms. Matthews' tight grasp, but the scream proved to be an adrenalin boost to fight even harder.

"Let me go!" he yelled kicking and screaming. "Let me go!"

From the moment Ms. Matthews walked over to him and told her his name, she assured him nothing bad was going to happen and not to be afraid. I can't help but be afraid. Did all these people all come to our house because of what I saw? Is Mama in trouble now? he wondered.

Gently steering Lil' Mike towards the front door, Ms. Matthews told him, "We need to go son." But as far back as he could remember, his mother always told him never to go with strangers. 'If a stranger ever tries to take you, scream, fight, kick, and yell Stranger Danger!' she instructed him. Lil' Mike was doing all of these things. But Officer Dennis running back into the living room carrying Angel brought his frantic movements to an abrupt stop.

※

Melvina let out a deafening scream at the sight of Officer Dennis carrying Angel, the infant's arms and legs dangling limply before wailing, "Oh my God! My baby!"

"I found the baby inside the microwave!" Officer Dennis yelled frantically. "With a bad, bad, burn on her arm!"

"What?!" screamed Melvina hysterically. "Angel was in the microwave?! With a burn on her arm?! Is she okay?! Who put her there?! Why is she so still?! Give me my baby!"

"It looks like she may have gone into shock," said Officer Dennis, directing her comments to the other officers. "We need to get an ambulance here now!"

"Angel!" screamed Melvina. "Angel!"

"We need a paramedic here right away," Officer Brown yelled into his walkie-talkie.

"My baby sister!" yelled Lil' Mike trying to pull away from Ms. Matthews. "Why isn't she moving?! Angel please wake up! Please wake up!"

Angel let out a loud wail. Contrastingly different from the many times she heard Angel bawling, Melvina was never so happy to hear the baby's piercing cries.

"Hand over my baby!" Melvina demanded.

"Here's the baby," said Officer Dennis, gently handing Angel over to the waiting arms of Ms. Braxton.

"What are you all doing?!" asked Melvina. "That's my baby! Give me my baby! Nobody's taking my baby anywhere unless I'm going too."

"That's a real nasty burn on the baby's arm," said Sgt. Vargas, shaking his head. "Looks like a Crack pipe burn to me. Did you burn this little baby with your Crack pipe Ms. Thomas?"

In stupefied fashion, Melvina glanced around at the officers and social workers –all returning scathing looks.

She knew she needed to explain how Angel's injury happened and began a desperate backtracking of her actions. Come on Melvina! she silently yelled, her mind a brain fog of shock, fear, nervousness, and confusion. Think! Think! Try as she might, Melvina couldn't intelligently gather her thoughts, struggling to recount her actions earlier actions.

"Did you burn your baby with a Crack pipe Ms. Thomas!" repeated Sgt. Vargas. "Did you?!"

"Of course not!" Melvina fired back.

"Well, how did she get this burn?" inquired Ms. Braxton. "And how did she get in the microwave?"

"I don't know!" said Melvina, frustrated with her inability to focus and their line of questioning. "But what I do know is that I put my son's Oodles of Noodles and daughter's baby bottle in the microwave…not my little Angel." Pointing at the bassinet, Melvina rationed, "I put Angel in her bassinet sitting right over there," but began rubbing her forehead, unsure of her actions. "At least…I thought I thought I did."

"That's a damn shame!" chided Sgt. Vargas. "How can a mother be so high she puts her own baby in the microwave without even realizing it?!"

"I would never hurt my baby! You have to believe me!" pleaded Melvina, tears streaming down her face. "I love my children! Gawd knows I do!"

"Look at your baby's arm Ms. Thomas!" shouted Ms. Braxton, pointing at the large burn, a cringing, disturbing sight of seared flesh. "Look at it!"

Melvina sobbed, throwing both hands over her own face.

"Maybe you hurt your baby out of frustration because she wouldn't stop crying," asserted Ms. Braxton gazing at the screaming infant. "We see that a lot. And not only did you burn your baby, but you put her in the microwave. What kind of mother are you, Ms. Thomas?!"

"I told you, I would never hurt my baby!" Melvina protested, feeling as if her pleas were falling on deaf ears. "I admit…I did hit the pipe. But I wasn't smoking and holding Angel. At least…I don't think I was."

The two social workers looked at each other shaking their heads before Ms. Braxton declared to Melvina, "Ms. Thomas you are not in a mental state to provide care for these children. And your drug use exposed them to unreasonable risk and harm."

Melvina felt her arms being grabbed and placed behind her back. Next came the clicking sound of cold steel handcuffs being clamped around her boney wrists. "Melvina Thomas you are under arrest for possession with intent to distribute, endangering a child with criminal negligence, and being under the influence of a controlled substance," declared Sgt. Vargas. "You have the right to remain silent. Anything you say, can and will be used against you in a court of law—"

"I swear those drugs ain't mines!" Melvina cried. "I don't even know how those drugs got there! And I would never hurt my kids!"

"Tell it to the judge!" bellowed Officer Vargas. "Time to go!"

"I can't believe this is happening!" shouted Melvina closing her eyes hoping to wake up from a bad dream; the individuals in her home and her cuffed hands, serving as a sobering reminder this was a formidable reality.

She looked over at Lil' Mike, who was still struggling to get away from Ms. Matthews. Melvina felt like a shackled slave watching her children being torn away. But like the resistant slave, her children would not be taken without a fight, and she began struggling to break free from her captors.

"You better calm down Ms. Thomas!" Officer Dennis warned Melvina, who was now fighting, kicking, and screaming. "Keep this up, and we'll charge you with resisting arrest."

"You all are gonna have to carry me out of here, 'cause I ain't walkin' out!"

Melvina declared, bending her legs in defiance. "Not only did you all storm into my house with no warrant on false, trumped-up charges, but now you are locking me up? For what? This is a false arrest!"

"You burned your own baby, you're a Crack addict, and you're running a stash house," said Officer Long. "And all the while, with a little boy in the house. And you're hollering false arrest. What a crock!"

"I'm innocent!" screamed Melvina. "You all hear me?! I'm innocent! And you know something else?! My boyfriend Big Mike is going to get all this straight! He has the best lawyer in town! And when I sue the police department for every penny ya'll got, I'm going to laugh in your faces! And not only that! Mayor Kurt L. Schmoke is gonna hear about this!"

"Instead of your idle threats, you better figure out how you are going to explain your actions to the judge," said Officer Long. "And it's a good thing we got here when we did. That little baby probably would have died between being burned and potentially suffocating in that microwave."

"I'm a mother myself," said Officer Dennis dragging Melvina through the front door along with Officer Long. "Tell me, how could you do that to a helpless baby?"

※

Watching the chaotic scene between his mother and the police, Lil' Mike fought more violently to free himself from the tight grasp of Ms. Matthews.

"Stop fighting me son," the social worker urged. "Everything is going to be fine. All we're trying to do is get you someplace safe and help your little sister."

"No, I don't want to go with you!" Lil' Mike sobbed. "And where are they taking my Mama!"

Then, with all his might, Lil' Mike yanked away from Ms. Matthews, breaking free from the clutches of her arms. With outstretched arms, Lil' Mike dashed towards his mother, shouting, "Mama!" Just as he was about to reach her, Ms. Matthews grabbed Lil' Mike by the waist, picked him up, and carried him atop her shoulder. "Put me down!" commanded Lil' Mike. "I want my Mama! Put me down!" Lil' Mike observed Ms. Braxton picking up the family photo of him, his mother, and Angel off the table. Until now, it sat on the small table untouched, remaining there since Melvina placed it there following she and Caroline's big blow-up. Lil' Mike watched Ms. Braxton momentarily gaze at the photo before dropping it in a bag along with some of he and Angel's belongings. "Why are you taking our photo?!" Lil Mike inquired. Ms. Matthews was now carrying him by the cocktail table, shifting his attention to the book and red truck. Lil' Mike wanted to grab them both from the table, but his hands were buried between he and Miss Matthews' shoulder. He wriggled an arm free, but could only grab one. Which should I grab? My truck or my book? Lil' Mike agonized, thinking about the things his mother told him about I Rose ABOVE it all along with how much he loved playing with his new truck. Lil' Mike decided on the book, stretching his arm as far as he could, just enough to scoop it up from the table. Barely able to clasp the literary work with his small fingers, Lil' Mike held it tightly, fearing he might drop the book, and it would be left behind.

Ms. Matthews now carrying him through the front door, Lil' Mike's heart sank deeper, his view of the living room shrinking with her every step. When are we coming back home? he fearfully wondered.

Outside Melvina's home Miss Jenkins, Mr. Henderson, Mr. Hawkins, and several other neighbors were keeping a vigilant watch. Earlier, Miss Jenkins went house-to-house, knocking on doors, and telling them, "Something's about to go down at the Thomas house." Others she called on the phone.

The group was standing by the curb watching. Some of them like Miss Jenkins and Mr. Henderson had been outside eyeing the chain of events since they first unfolded. Others joined them later, Miss Jenkins bringing them up to speed. Still morning, some of the residents – still dressed in their slippers, robes, and housecoats, opted to observe the goings-on from their porches.

"I think the White woman and the Colored woman that got out of the car parked over there are social workers," said Miss Jenkins pointing to the white vehicle. "They're in the house too."

Melvina's babysitter Mrs. Brown and her husband Ned were among the group at the curb. The Browns were also members of United in Victory Tabernacle and were roused out of their beds by Miss Jenkins' persistent knocks at their door.

"I wonder what's going on in there now?" Mrs. Brown wondered out loud.

Dressed in a wifebeater and trousers held up by suspenders, Mr. Brown replied, "Both her and that mean-looking, light-eyed boy get high all the time."

"That's right," said Miss Jenkins. "Once that chile started foolin' around with him, she went straight downhill. That's why I stopped taking papers over to her. How she gonna read a paper all highed-up, face fallin' all down into the newspaper? That's a waste of a paper!"

"And I heard that boyfriend of hers sells drugs too," said Mr. Brown. "I bet those officers are about to do a drug bust!"

"Yeah, but I wonder who called the police on them?" asked Mrs. Brown, the group all turning in unison and looking at Miss Jenkins.

"Don't look at me!" said Miss Jenkins. "I ain't call nobody! My name is Bennett and I ain't innit!"

"I'm not buying that Violetta!" exclaimed Mr. Hawkins. "You're the one with the Police Scanner! Not to mention you're into everything but a hearse! You got the biggest mouth in Bawl'more. I bet you called!"

"I know you ain't talkin' Bigmouth!" bellowed Miss Jenkins. "Who runs their mouth more than you Rufus?! Instead of talkin' about me callin' somebody, you need to take that Ravens shirt you got on back to the store! It's waaaaaaaay too small!"

"What! Don't be talkin' about my —"

"Shhhhh you two!" said Mrs. Brown. "Somebody's coming out of the house now."

"The police are bringing out Melvina!" said Miss Jenkins, pulling her eyeglasses up to the crown of her nose. "Look at that gal's hair stickin' up all over her head! Lawd have mercy."

"And listen to Melvina makin' all that racket!" said Mrs. Brown. "And look! They got her in handcuffs!"

"See!" said Mr. Brown, stepping off the curb and into the street to get a better view. "I told y'all it was a drug bust!"

"Yep," agreed Mr. Henderson. "And they're taking her over to the paddy wagon."

"And look at the police draggin' her!" exclaimed Miss Jenkins.

"Guess they ain't got no choice," said Mr. Henderson. "Looks to me like she won't walk on her own. Maybe she's highed-up and can't walk!"

"Melvina's saying something. Can anybody make out what she's saying?" asked Mrs. Brown.

"I can't quite make out exactly what she's saying," said Mr. Henderson, "But sounds like she's saying something about not taking her babies."

"And she just said something about not burning her baby!" said Miss Jenkins. "Oh my Lawd, she done burned up her baby!"

The group could hear the wail of approaching sirens, an ambulance, and a firetruck now turning on the block and double-parking in the middle of the street.

"There's the ambulance and fire department!" shouted Miss Jenkins, watching paramedics rush into Melvina's house. "They must be coming to get the burned-up baby!"

"This is so terrible! I can't watch!" cried Mrs. Brown, throwing her hands over her face and parting two fingers just enough to peer through.

"I wonder if that baby is dead or alive?!" Miss Jenkins wondered aloud. "I'm gonna walk over there and find out for myself!"

"Oh no you don't Violetta!" said Mrs. Brown, gently taking Miss Jenkins by the arm. "I'm not about to let you go over there and meddle! You'll just be in the way! We'll find out soon enough."

"Let go of my arm!" said Miss Jenkins, yanking away. "You might be my best friend Essie Mae, but you ain't my Mama!"

Look!" exclaimed Mr. Hawkins. "One of the ambulance people is bringing out the baby now!"

"At least she's crying," said Mrs. Brown, "Thank the Lord for that! At least we now know she's alive!"

"Sounds like one of the paramedics is saying something about taking it to Johns Hopkins Children's Hospital," said Mr. Brown, who along with the group, was watching Ms. Braxton climb into the back of the ambulance for the ride to the hospital.

"The White woman is coming out with the little boy!" shouted Miss Jenkins, diverting the group's attention over to Ms. Matthews and Lil' Mike. "And look at him just a kickin' and a screamin'! Lawd have mercy! There's more action goin' on out here than on the stories!"

"Looks more like a crime drama to me," said Mr. Henderson. "And right here on our block! I ain't never seen nothing like this!"

Miss Jenkins slid her eyeglasses back down to the tip of her nose, peering over them at several of the men and women, before looking over at Mr. Henderson.

"See Cassius, I was right," said Miss Jenkins, chomping on her chewing gum. "I told you they were comin' to take them chil'ren. Lawd have mercy."

"You ought to have known!" asserted Mr. Hawkins. "You're the one who called!"

"I told you I didn't call nobody!" Miss Jenkins fired back. "Now Rufus, I ain't about to stand out here listening to you lying on me…accusing me of doing something I didn't do!"

"I bet you called!" said Mr. Hawkins.

"And you would lose that bet too, just like you lose all your bets, according to someone who shall remain nameless!" cackled Miss Jenkins.

"Ain't nobody told you that lie but that stuck-up wife of mines Lila Mae!' shouted Mr. Hawkins. "Since you two talk, tell her to give me back my money!"

"I don't know nuthin' about no money!" said Miss Jenkins. "But I do know one thing! You need to take that medium Ravens shirt back to the store and exchange it for a 4X!"

"What!" said Mr. Hawkins. "Now Violetta you need to —"

"You two need to be praying instead of arguing!" said Mrs. Brown. "This is such a sad moment...for Melvina...for me...for this block. And you two got the nerve to be standing out here arguing! The Thomas family is etched in the history of this neighborhood! We all knew Melvina's parents Melvina and Margaret...and I babysat not only Melvina but Earlene and Lil' Mike. Shaking her head, Mrs. Brown said, "Melvina's been through so much...having a child so young...losing her parents...and now this. I know she got strung out on drugs and all, but she doesn't deserve this. It looks like she's losing her children and her freedom right before our very eyes. And all on account of that no-good, green-eyed devil!"

Essie Mae is right, Miss Jenkins thought, watching Melvina struggle with the police. Instead of arguing with that little-shirt fool standing over there Rufus Hawkins, I should be praying for Melvina and them chil'ren. That gal and them kids need all the prayer they can get. 'Cause right now, it don't look good for her or them. Lawd have mercy.

※

Lil' Mike was bewildered by what he was seeing outside. Why are all these people out here looking at us? he wondered. He lost sight of Angel but could see the police leading his mother over to the paddy wagon. He silently read the words Baltimore City Police, on the vehicle, whose shape reminded him of the odd-shaped trucks Dog Catchers drove when they picked up stray dogs and cats off the street.

"Where are you taking Mama?!" Lil' Mike screamed at the top of his lungs at the officers. "And where is my sister?" His stomach full of butterflies, and flinging his arms and legs wildly to free himself from Ms. Matthews, he heard a loud thud. "My book!" Lil' Mike cried. Stooping down to the sidewalk, Ms. Matthews picked up the book and proceeded to the white car.

"Mama!" Lil' Mike screamed, watching the police officers open the rear doors of the paddy wagon. "Mama!"

"Please calm down young man," said Ms. Matthews, setting him down on the backseat and clicking the seatbelt. "Everything is going to be okay."

"Where are you taking me?" Lil' Mike demanded to know.

"We are taking you to a safe place, and your little sister is going to the hospital for treatment," shared Ms. Matthews.

"But Mama, where are they taking her? " he cried, pressing his face to the car window, and seeing the police hoisting his mother into the back of the paddy wagon. Ms. Matthews started the car, the breath of Lil' Mike's cries leaving a foggy imprint on the glass. "I'll find you, Mama!" Lil' Mike tearfully declared, catching one final glimpse of his mother before Ms. Matthews pulled out the parking space. "And Angel too. I promise."

❀

Through her screams and cries, Melvina heard the loud sound of the paddy wagon's big double doors being slammed shut. Light of day had been replaced with darkness. The softness of her warm sofa had been replaced with the coldness of a steel bench. The company of her children, and from time-to-time Big Mike, had been replaced with loneliness and seclusion. Such was the bleak environment offered by the paddy wagon.

Melvina had seen paddy wagons, their shape always reminding her of an old-fashioned Good Humor ice cream truck. As a child, she always looked forward to the tinkling ring of the Good Humor ice cream truck. That meant the truck would soon be turning down the block, and she could buy a Toasted Almond.

That was my favor-right ice cream. But this is no ice cream truck, but a paddy wagon. This is my first time ever being in one, and I hate it! Melvina scooted her butt as best she could towards the doors to peer through their barred windows.

"Nooooooooooooo! My baby!" Melvina screamed, catching one precious final glimpse of Angel before the paramedics closed the ambulance doors and sped off with its sirens blaring. She could see Lil' Mike's crying face in the window of the white car before it pulled off. "Lil' Mike!" she screamed, clenching her handcuffed hands. "Lil' Mike!" Her children no longer in sight, Melvina stared through the filmy windows at her neighbors. "My baby is being rushed to the hospital and my son is being taken God knows where, and they're all standing around out there like they are watching television!" she cried in the mobile lock-up. "I can't wait until Big Mike helps me straighten this shit out and I'm back home! I'm going to give all of them a piece of my mind!" Melvina heard the vehicle's engine start. "Wooooooooooooo!" she said, trying to steady herself; the momentum of the vehicle pulling off causing her body to shift and slide, but unable to grab ahold of anything because she was handcuffed.

The meager view the vehicle's windows offered of her neighbors now gone, Melvina could now see a blur of trees and rowhouses whiz by, the paddy wagon, now picking up speed. Soon, the Gwynns Falls Parkway neighborhood that had been home to Melvina all 32 years of her life, was no longer in sight.

The vehicle now making its way towards I-83 South, Melvina's mind shifted from fear and confusion to anger and resentment. "Caroline is behind all of this!" she vented. "Caroline called CPS on me, and she called the police. Someone must have told her Big Mike was stashing drugs in the house. I had no idea he was stashing drugs in my house! But I do know this…Caroline threatened to call CPS on me, and she did. I hate Caroline with every bone in my body…and I'll never forgive that backstabbing Bitch for what she's done!"

Melvina's thoughts now shifting to Angel, she found herself questioning the validity of her own memory. I could have sworn I put Angel's bottle and Lil' Mike's noodles in the microwave. But that Crack that Big Mike bought me really had me fucked up! Is it possible I put Angel in the microwave instead of her bottle and Lil' Mike's food and burned her with my pipe without even realizing it? Thoughts of Big Mike quickly brought Melvina some semblance of comfort. He'll get to the bottom of all this bullshit! And he's also gonna deal with that snake Caroline! Wait until he hears about this! Melvina felt the paddy wagon slow and come to a stop. Two police officers corralled her out of the vehicle and into Central Booking for processing. The police arrest me based on lies and bring me down here after that bumpy-ass ride! she silently hollered. Then they take my mugshot, after which time, I'm ordered to pull down my pants, bend forward, spread my cheeks, and squat and cough so they can search my butthole for drugs and weapons! I heard people talk about Squat and Cough, but now I have experienced it! I have never felt so degraded and humiliated in my life! Then I'm fingerprinted like a common criminal and now I'm being shoved into a jail cell! And for what?! Nothing?!

The unnerving sound of the cell door rolling shut behind her, cut to Melvina's very soul. She fell to the cold, hard floor and let out an agonizing cry that rang throughout the jail.

Several hours passed and Melvina was still in shock and disbelief. Over the years, she heard so many stories about Central Booking but never thought she would be here. It's hot as shit in here and I'm in this little ass cell with two other females!   There's only one nasty ass toilet in here for us to share, and our beds are nothing more than cold, hard steel. I'm sick of hearing flies buzzing around this shitty ass toilet and I'm about to lose my mind hearing these cell doors open and shut! And I'm tired of hearing the cries and screams of these women in here!

For Melvina, the sights and sounds all culminated into a melancholy chorus of sickening despair. To this tune, Melvina's body writhed in pain, crying out for Crack, her heart crying out for her children. Man, what I wouldn't do for a hit right now! I'm fienin' so bad! And what I wouldn't give to hear Angel's cries instead of these inmates! she lamented in silent despair. And boy do I wish I had listened to Lil' Mike recite his poem! I can hardly wait until we are back home, and he can say his poem for me!

Thoughts of Caroline soon returned, causing Melvina's stomach to knot up in anguish and anger. Having experienced so much loss in her life, hurt was nothing new to Melvina. I know Caroline and I stopped speaking, but we have been through so much together. Yes, we've had our ups and downs… highs and lows…and have been through peaks and valleys together. We've also had our river and mountaintop experiences…both together. How could she do this to me? Like David and Jonathan in The Bible, Melvina believed she and Caroline were knitted at the soul. This is the ultimate betrayal! thought Melvina. Caroline is more like Judas than Jonathan. Melvina sunk her face into her lap and began to sob. She could hear footsteps approaching her jail cell. Hopefully, that's one of the guards coming to get me so I can call Big Mike, she thought.

To Melvina's great disappointment, the correctional officer stopped in front of the cell and pushed a tray of food through an opening in the cell door. That looks like runny dog food! I'm hungry, but I'm not eating that shit! she declared looking at the unappealing meatloaf and mashed potatoes. Melvina spent the next several minutes trying to comfortably situate herself on the bed of steel. The task proved nearly impossible, and an hour or so passed before she cried herself to sleep.

The sound of a correctional officer yelling her name woke Melvina up from her uncomfortable slumber. "Melvina Thomas!" the officer again bellowed.

"Right here!" yelled Melvina rushing over to the cell door.

"You can make your call now Thomas," she informed Melvina.

Elated, Melvina replied, "Finally! Thank you! Now, I can call my boyfriend. He will get this all straightened out and get me outta here. I'm innocent you know."

"Sure you are," replied the officer with doubtful sarcasm. "That's what they all say."

Reading the officer's pin imprinted with the last name 'Lattimore', she and the correctional officer made their way down a maze of hallways before reaching another area of the jail. Pointing to a phone, the officer said, "There's the phone. Go on and make your call." With bated breath, Melvina dialed Big Mike's cell phone number, holding the handset tightly to her ear under the watchful eyes of the guard. The phone began to ring, Melvina silently pleading, Please, please Big Mike…answer the phone.

"Hello," answered Big Mike.

"Collect call from Melvina," do you accept?" asked the operator.

"Yes," Big Mike mumbled.

"Big Mike!" said Melvina, breathing a heavy sigh of relief. "Thank God you answered the phone! You won't believe this, but I —"

"You got a lot of fuckin' nerve callin' me collect Melvina after what you did to the baby!" Big Mike spewed, Caroline's voice fussing in the background. "How dare you call me!"

"But Big Mike, I'm innocent! The police came and locked me up and took the kids. Once I see a court commissioner, and bail is set, I will need you to bail me outta here! I don't know your lawyer's name, but whatever his name is, please get in touch with him! I'm gonna need one to straighten this mess out!"

"I ain't givin' you shit Melvina! You damn near kill the baby and now you got the nerve to want me to contact my lawyer! Hell no!" Shocked, Melvina dumbfoundingly looked at the guard, who lowered her eyes and looked the other way.

"But Big Mike, I didn't —"

"Yes, you did!" Big Mike roared through the phone. "Damnit Melvina! You listen, and you listen good! I may not be as close to them kids as I need to be, but they are mines! You had no right to hurt them the way you did!"

"Give me that durn phone!" Caroline shouted.

"M, my bruuuuuther is here with me and Carl right now!" cried Caroline. "He is so broken up and distraught! He told us all about what you did to my poor little ol' niece and nephew! He—"

"Caroline, you called the police and CPS!" Melvina shouted. "You—"

"Keep it down Thomas and you got two minutes!" warned the guard, looking at a clock on the wall.

"How could you do this to me Caroline?!" sobbed Melvina in a hushed tone. "You were—"

"The one who tried to help you and my poor little niece and nephew," shouted Caroline from the other end of the phone. "Lawd knows, that's all I ever tried to do! And how did you repay me? I'll tell you how! By stealing from me, by using the Devil's vocabulary to cuss me out, and by tryin' to attack me with one of your sinful, beer jugs!"

"And remember the time you told me you were about to throw Angel out the window 'cause she wouldn't stop cryin!" Big Mike shouted from the background.

"That's just terrible M, just terrible!" cried Caroline, her voice cracking. "I know those drugs turned you into a hot-headed heathen! But I never thought you would try to kill the children! You burned my poor little ol' niece like you were branding a pig! And then you tried to cook her! My nerves are so bad right now! M, I pray the Lawd has mercy on your wicked, wretched soul!"

"Your telephone time is just about up," the guard notified Melvina, glancing at the clock again.

"Sounds like she got to get ready to get off the phone," Melvina heard Caroline telling Big Mike.

"Wait! Give me the phone back!" demanded Big Mike. "I ain't through talkin' to her yet! I got somethin' else to say!" Numb, Melvina listened to the muffled sound of the phone changing hands. "How dare you snatch the phone outta my hand like that Michael?!" snapped Caroline. "Where are your manners you barbaric beast! I know what M did was evil, but you nearly snatched my wrist off! And don't be using those terrible curse words in my house when you talk to 'M' this time! In my house, we serve the Lord!" Big Mike replied, "Be quiet Caroline so I can hear myself talk!" to which Carl told him, "Hey man, hold it! I know you're upset, but you can't snatch the phone out of my wife's hand or talk to her like that! Disrespect Caroline again, and I'll put you out myself!" Screaming in the phone, Michael said, "You burned Angel, nearly starved Lil' Mike to death, and had drugs in the house! You never told me you were stashin' drugs in the house! Whose drugs were you stashing in the house Melvina?! Huh?! Whose drugs were they!?"

"I don't know who they belonged to or how they got there!" Melvina cried in anguish. "I swear Big Mike! You have to believe me! I didn't hurt Angel either! And I cooked food for Lil' Mike!"

"The police said you put Angel in the microwave! You were so high off that shit you didn't know what in the hell you were doin'!" Big Mike screamed, Caroline and Carl both yelling at him in the background to stop cursing. "And you know something else Melvina! I hate you for what you have done! Don't ever call me again! You hear me! I hope you rot in jail! Crackhead!"

"But Big Mike!" wept Melvina, I –" her words curtly cut short by the sound of a loud click followed by a dial tone.

"Time to go back to lock-up!" said the guard, leading a broken, shattered, and scared Melvina back to the jail cell.

CHAPTER FOUR

REFLECTIONS

Baltimore, MD – 20 years later
May 1, 2018
Morning

It was May 1, 2018, and the day was brimming with the sights and sounds of spring. The sun was shining bright against a backdrop of blue skies speckled with white clouds that resembled puffs of cotton candy. The buds of flowers were blooming, bees were busily buzzing about, lawnmower engines were roaring, butterflies were swirling around, and the smell of fresh mulch being laid by nearby landscapers filled the air.

Exhilaratingly taking in all these things walking to the church house door, the Rev. Al B. Wright, Just, Jr., Pastor of United in Victory Tabernacle took a deep breath and exhaled. "Lord, I am always in awe of the changing of the seasons," he whispered. "Always a thing of beauty, always wondrous, and like You, the Creator of all of these things, always Marvelous."

Inserting the key in the church house door, he heard a familiar voice crying out "Pastor! Pastor!" It was the mailman, Rufus Hawkins.

"Here's the church's mail," said Mr. Hawkins, rushing up to him and handing him a small stack of letters, bills, and other correspondence.

"Thank you, Mr. Hawkins," Pastor Just gratuitously responded while thinking about how much the mailman reminded him of 'Mr. Brown' from Tyler Perry's Meet The Browns. Pastor Just and his wife Jacqueline also saw the dark-complected, white goatee-wearing character with ashy knees in one of Tyler Perry's plays at The Lyric Opera House, and both commented on how much Mr. Hawkins looked and acted like the comical character.

"You're welcome Pastor," gasped the winded mailman. "Whew! That was quite a jog right there!"

"Why Mr. Hawkins, you only ran a few feet," exclaimed Pastor Just looking at Mr. Hawkins bent over with his hands on his knees trying to catch his breath and debating whether he should ask the mailman if he needed some lotion.

"Look at how bad I am sweatin'!" declared Mr. Hawkins wiping his face with a face cloth. "Sweat just a pourin'! Let's face it…I ain't as young as I used to be. I get tired much quicker now."

"None of us are as young as we used to be Mr. Hawkins. We get older by the second, and sometimes our bodies remind us of that," chuckled Pastor Just. "Nevertheless, we should be grateful. Things could be worse."

"Hey Pastor, speaking of grateful, did you hear the Bawl'more Ravens picked up Lamar Jackson in the NFL draft a few days ago?"

"So I hear," commented Pastor Just. "Everyone's talking about it."

"I believe he's just what the Ravens needed," said Mr. Hawkins. "Ozzie Newsome has always had a knack for picking the hidden gems. Ray Lewis, Ed Reed, Jonathan Ogden, the list goes on and on."

"That's right, Mr. Hawkins. They don't call Ozzie the Wizard of Oz for nothing."

"Oz is stepping down as General Manager of the Ravens after this season," commented Mr. Hawkins. "I hate to see him go. But they say he's still gonna be involved with the team in some capacity. But me, once I leave my job, I'm gone! And that's in less than a month."

"You're retiring Mr. Hawkins?"

"That's right. Knees have gotten so bad, I need knee replacements. And luggin' this heavy mailbag ain't helping matters," said Mr. Hawkins glancing at the mailbag slung over his shoulder. "And to make matters worse, now the Post Office got me delivering packages people are ordering online that are being shipped from all over the world! Hong Kong, Australia, China, New York, California…you name it! Too doggone heavy! And speaking of doggone, I can't tell you how many pit bulls, bulldogs, Chihuahuas, Yorkies, and other dogs have tried to chew my legs like they were beef jerky! The heck with this! I just celebrated a birthday and I'm almost 70 now! I can't run like I used to! And as bad as these Bawl'more streets have gotten, I need more than a can of Mace for protection!"

Laughing, Pastor Just quickly seized the moment to extend a church invitation.

"Well Mr. Hawkins, since you are retiring, maybe now you can join us for Sunday service."

"Oh noooooo, I can't do that!" replied Mr. Hawkins. "Once I retire, I plan on going to the Ravens games every Sunday they play at Home. I also plan to do lots of fishing. Besides, it's best I keep my distance from one of your church members. If you know what I mean."

"Yeah, I know what you mean and exactly who you're talking about," said Pastor Just. "But you never know what might bring you two back together."

"If I wasn't standing in front of a preacher, I would have cussed to hear you say such a thing!" balked Mr. Hawkins. "Me and Dr. Lila Mae ain't never getting back together!"

Pastor Just replied, "One thing I have come to learn in this life is to never ever say never."

"Well I'm saying it!" said Mr. Hawkins. "I ain't never, never, never, never, never, ever reckon'cilin' with that high-falutin' woman! Walkin' around with her nose in the air!"

Chuckling at Mr. Hawkins' statement and his pronunciation of the words reconciling and highfalutin, Pastor Just reflected on his long-time church member, Dr. Lila Mae Hawkins. Mr. Hawkins is right about his ex-wife even though I would never tell him that, Pastor Just thought silently. Dr. Lila Mae Hawkins is indeed a proud peacock.

"And Pastor Just, when you see that stuck up Dr. Lila Mae, tell her to give me back the money she owes me!"

said Mr. Hawkins.

Money? wondered Pastor Just. I have no idea what money Mr. Hawkins is talking about.

"And Pastor…"

"Yes, Mr. Hawkins?"

"Give Dr. Lila Mae this message too! Tell her Rufus Hawkins said, 'she can kiss my mail!'"

"I'll do no such thing," laughed Pastor Just.

"Work has been going on over here at this church house for quite a while," said Mr. Hawkins, squinting his eyes under sunbeams observing the church house. "Looks nice."

"Thank you, Mr. Hawkins."

Deep in thought, Mr. Hawkins started, "A lot has gone on in t…" the rest of his words trailing off in unintelligible gibberish.

"What was that Mr. Hawkins?" inquired Pastor Just, puzzlingly. "I'm sorry, but do you mind repeating what you just said?"

"Oh, it was nuthin' Pastor," said Mr. Hawkins looking at his mailbag. "I'll best be moving on now. Lots of mail to deliver."

"Have a Blessed Day Mr. Hawkins," said Pastor Just watching the postman make his way down the street. "Go Ravens!"

"Go Ravens!" exclaimed Mr. Hawkins, turning and giving the thumbs-up sign.

"That invite to join us for service is an open invitation," stressed Pastor Just.

"Alright Pastor!" yelled Mr. Hawkins, climbing into his mail truck. "But, don't hold your breath!"

Pastor Just watched Mr. Hawkins drive off, still wondering what the mailman uttered under his breath. That was mighty strange, he thought, turning the key, and walking into the church house. "I wanted to take another look at the place which will soon be home to United in Victory's new transitional housing program!" the preacher shouted gleefully, his thoughts about Mr. Hawkins now behind him.

Thinking about all it took to reach this point, he began walking about the church house, the bottoms of his shiny, black Florsheim shoes clonking against the freshly waxed wood floor with every step.

Working with Hal Arnold of H.A.C.E. Consultants to get the proper building permits, Bob Harris of Gambino Construction Company for the needed structural improvements, and Joshua Cornelius Matthews of JCM Controls Systems, Inc. for the HVAC (Heating Ventilation and Air Conditioning). Just a few of the many people that had to be contracted to complete all the needed work to bring the building up to code, and I had to handle them all. There was also the matter of purchasing beds, dressers, and other furniture…not to mention getting information out to various agencies to identify potential clients. And let me not forget the process of hiring the right personnel including the program's Clinical Social Worker…and we have the perfect one. It's been a long and arduous process, but soon we will be opening. The building has been approved for residential housing, and we can begin taking applicants. So much was involved in this entire process, and it took years to get to this point. But thank God, we made it." Looking upwards with a smile, Pastor Just exclaimed, "God, you did it again! Now, the only thing left for me to do is to find a House Mother. And I'm believing You are going to send us that person too."

The son of the church's founder, Bishop Wright Just, Sr., Pastor Just had been a member of United in Victory all his life. He was Christened there, baptized there, and ordained thereafter receiving the Call to Preach. Now, 55-

years-old, he has painfully watched the community surrounding the church slowly crumble under the weight of poverty, drug trafficking, gangs, violence, and addiction.

"When I was a kid, we played outside and our parents never had to worry about us being hit by a stray bullet," he pondered out loud, walking over to a window. "My, my, my have things changed."

❀

Observing the view outside, Pastor Just went into deep thought about the evolution and popularity of drugs.

Back in the 1970s, Angel Dust, Acid, and Marijuana was the thing. In the 1980s and 1990s, it was sniffing glue, Cocaine, Crack, and Heroin. In the 2000s, many of these drugs are still around, but now we are dealing with Opioids such as Fentanyl, and the pain relievers Oxycodone (OxyContin), Hydrocodone (Vicodin), Codeine, and Morphine. In researching Opioids, I learned they are legally prescribed and highly addictive. I also know this from personal experience…I nearly got entangled with OxyContin myself. But God.

Years ago, Pastor Just tore a ligament in his right knee and underwent surgery to repair the tear.

I was prescribed OxyContin as needed for pain after the surgery, and man, was I in a lot of pain. The inside of my knee felt like it was being pulled like taffy and being kicked repeatedly, and the surgical incisions on the outside of my knee felt as if someone was jabbing a knife in it. Even though I wore a knee brace to help my knee straightened, even the slightest bend or movement caused unbearable pain. I still cringe thinking about it. But I had that little bottle of OxyContin to take whenever I needed it. Up until then, the only pills I ever took for pain were Tylenol, Bayer, and Advil. While they all relieved pain, these over-the-counter aspirin paled in comparison to OxyContin. Not only did OxyContin relieve my excruciating post-surgical pain, but the pills also relaxed me. I would pop one of those pills, lay across my bed or couch, and peacefully drift off to sleep in no time… pain gone and lights out.

But about two weeks into taking the prescription, I felt a slight, tug…and I'll never forget that tug of OxyContin discreetly enticing me to take one. But there was really no need to take one. By then, the pain in my knee had subsided. I couldn't help but wonder, 'Am I becoming addicted to these pills?' But my fear of dependency scared me, and I decided I would not take another single one of those pills. I can still remember just as clear as day, taking the OxyContin bottle out of the bathroom medicine cabinet, walking over to the toilet, unscrewing the top of the bottle, and turning it downwards towards the toilet. And just as I was about to flush the rest of those pills down the toilet…as crazy as this now sounds, they all seemed to whisper to me, 'Al, you might need to keep a few of us around…just in case the pain comes back.' Of course, that wasn't OxyContin talking to me, but my own mind…and as I see it, a last-ditch effort by Satan himself to lure me into dependency."

Continuing his silent retrospect, Pastor Just recalled his reluctance in flushing the pills. My thoughts were causing the hesitation. Thoughts like…'What if that excruciating pain comes back? What will I do? How will I rest?' But the good Lord gave me the wherewithal to resist what my own mind was telling me, and flush them all. The sounds and images of the toilet bowl flushing, and pills swirling around and around in its water until they were no longer in sight rushing to mind, the minister professing, I looked at the empty bottle in my hand and thought, 'No more OxyContin.' But one look at the label, and I knew I was wrong. The bottle was empty, but the label informing me I still had 2 more refills left was still there. I will never forget how I got my toolbox from the shed, took out my hammer, and laid the prescription bottle down on the kitchen counter. Drawing his arm back as if he held a hammer, Pastor Just proclaimed, "And then I smashed it!," bringing the imaginary tool down swiftly. Looking back, I have to admit to myself that seemed quite excessive…but I was taking no chances…you cannot play with the Devil. I picked up the pieces of the cracked bottle and threw them in the trash can. Bringing his hands together as if he were wiping them clean, Pastor Just said, "That was the day I swept OxyContin out of my life, marking the end of my personal experience with the pills. Thank the Lord for that! But the experience made me realize there was only one thing that separated me from those who have fallen into addiction — a decision. Yes, the Lord gave me the strength to deny myself. But He also gives us the free will to choose. And the truth of the matter is that when it comes to satisfying what our fleshly bodies want, it's so easy for us to make the wrong decisions. And the Devil does a good job of helping that along."

Shaking his head, while continuing to look inward, Pastor Just pondered, Had I kept on taking those pills, where would my ministry be? Would I still be preaching the Gospel? Would I still be leading others to Christ? Would I have become pastor of my father's church? After carefully examining these questions, he concluded, I have no way of knowing the answers to those questions. Thank God I never had to find out. Had it not been for the Lord on my side, where would I be? Only God knows."

Continuing to peer through the church house windows' glass panes, Pastor Just commented, "My brush with OxyContin opened my eyes to just how easily one can fall into the ditch of addiction. And once a person falls in, it's hard as hell to climb out…and the evidence of those who are stuck in its miry ditch are everywhere."

Pastor Just and his wife Jacqueline were foster parents and had cared for many children – some of them birthed from the addicted. In some cases, one or both parents were strung out on drugs. In other cases, one or both parents died of overdoses.

I have delivered numerous eulogies for men and women who have succumbed to overdosing on all kinds of drugs, lamented Pastor Just. Much to my hurtful surprise, a few of them have been members of my congregation or relatives and friends of our members. But I was particularly shocked by the number of those OD'ing on Opioids. That, along with my own personal experience is what prompted me to start doing all that research.

In conducting his research, Pastor Just combed through news articles, medical journals, and other resources to learn more about Opioids. He discovered Fentanyl, a synthetic opioid pain reliever, had been especially deadly. Fentanyl was similar to Morphine but 50 to 100 times more potent. Like Morphine, it was a medicine that was typically used to treat patients with severe pain, especially after surgery. While it was a prescription drug, it could also be made illegally by street pharmacists.

He read some of the street names for Fentanyl were 'Apache', 'China Girl', 'China White', 'Dance Fever', 'Friend', 'Goodfellas', 'Jackpot', 'Tango & Cash' and 'Murder 8'. Oddly enough, if word hit the street that someone had overdosed on the drug, people wanted it. The same held true for other drugs. Seems, some people believe the deadlier a drug is, the stronger it is, and the better it is. I could never understand this ideology. Why would someone want to use a drug so potent it killed somebody? That's baffling to me, but a chance many are willing to take.

Pastor Just's train of thought led to his best friend and confidante, Deacon Roy E. Jackson. The two grew up together in United in Victory. Pastor Just referred to Deacon Jackson as 'Roy', and Deacon Jackson called him 'Al'. Throughout the years, the two longtime friends discussed Baltimore's drug problems.

"Drugs are really taking a lot of folks away from here Al," said Deacon Jackson during one such conversation. "Especially those Opioids."

"You're right Roy. I preached two eulogies last week for people who overdosed on those pills."

"Well Al," said Deacon Jackson, "To tell you the truth, Black folks have been dying of overdoses for years. But now that so many White folks are overdosing on the same drugs, it's a crisis…an epidemic."

"That's right Roy. The Opioid Epidemic."

"Well Al, as long as folks' minds are all tangled up in drugs, they can't see their way to salvation," said Deacon Jackson. "No matter what color they are. If there was ever a time for United in Victory to offer transitional housing, it's now."

"Amen to that!" replied Pastor Just. "And if it's the Lord's will, it's going to happen no matter what. Nothing or no one will stop it from coming to pass."

※

Leading up to United in Victory's quest to offer a transitional housing program for those struggling with addiction, Pastor Just started an Addiction Outreach Ministry in September 2011 at the behest of Deacon Jackson. Through this ministry, A.A. and N.A. meetings were hosted in the basement of the church. Deacon Jackson oversaw the ministry, which offered counseling, prayer, and moral encouragement to those seeking help. Many people sought help through the church's Addiction Ministry.

"We are helping a lot of people, but so many are still dying," Pastor Just once shared with Deacon Jackson. "Overdoses and gun violence are the culprits behind so much loss of life. And then there's also the issue of the grieving families left behind, which is another tragedy. They are victims too. I can't tell you how many people I've referred to Roberta's House for grief support."

"I know," agreed Deacon Jackson. "Mothers, fathers, sisters, brothers…and so many children left with one or no parents. I know many grandparents as well as uncles and aunts who have had to step in and raise their young relatives. But this all contributes to the breakdown of the traditional parental structure of a father, a mother, and a child or children. And then there are some kids who have absolutely no family support and turn to the streets not only seeking people to connect with but a way to survive. As you know, I had my own experiences with the lure of the streets…and that's even with being raised in the church and having a God-fearing, evangelist as a mother."

"The Devil doesn't care who your parents are, or how you were raised," opined Pastor Just. "The Bible says the Devil roams the world seeking whom he may devour, and that applies to all of us."

"That's the truth," agreed Deacon Jackson. "But I admit Al…one of the things that bother me the most is when innocent little children die as a result of gun violence. Little boys and girls and even babies mowed down before they've even had a chance to live."

"That's right Roy… and every Eulogy I preach is always hard. But the most difficult eulogies are the ones I've had to deliver for children. And I've done three for youngsters who have lost their lives in the crossfire of gun battles. The Bible says, 'A little child shall lead them.' But Roy, how can a child lead when their lives end so violently at the hands of those who have no right to cut it short?"

"A question I've thought about many times," said Deacon Jackson. "And one I just can't answer."

With great sadness, Pastor Just said, "I'll tell you this Roy. When I step into the pulpit to give a eulogy for a child, I have to be strong to give an encouraging Word to the grieving. But my stoicism is nothing but a front because privately I am crying many tears over the senseless loss of so many young, innocent, promising lives."

Pastor Just's and Deacon Jackson's conversations about the state of the city also included talks about the Freddie Grey riots of 2015. Located on North Avenue, United in Victory was in short proximity of Sandtown-Winchester, one of the many areas in the city where rioting had taken place. Sandtown-Winchester was also the neighborhood where Grey lived, and on April 12, 2015, was arrested. Grey died of injuries he sustained while in police custody on April 19, 2015, sparking outrage in Baltimore and across the nation.

"It was really something how Freddie Grey suffered spinal cord injury while the police were transporting him in that police van," said Pastor Just. "If you ask me, that should never have happened."

"I've rode in a police van before…as a prisoner," said Deacon Jackson. "Back then, we called them Paddy Wagons. Probably the most uncomfortable ride I have ever experienced…sliding on those steel seats and feeling every bump in the street. Solitary confinement on wheels if you ask me. And if the arresting officers didn't secure Freddie Grey during that ride…which I heard they did not, I can see how injuries like that could have happened. Not much you can do to keep your body stationary if your hands are in handcuffs."

"So much destruction happened in the city during the protests," recalled Pastor Just. "Businesses were looted, including Mondawmin Mall, a place near and dear to my heart. My parents took me there to shop when I was a little boy, and I took photos with the mall's famous black Santa Clauses."

"My mother took me there too," added Deacon Jackson. "I can still remember when Sears & Roebuck was in the mall. A lot of history and fond memories lie within Mondawmin Mall. But in the wake of all the rioting, a mall where Black folks have been shopping for generations, had to be closed for over a week."

"That's right. Many buildings were set ablaze and some totally destroyed," recalled Pastor Just. "Even churches weren't spared. Three of our stained-glass windows were broken during the civil unrest. Thank God that's all the damage United in Victory sustained."

Deacon Jackson replied, "Amen to that. Things got so bad Mayor Stephanie Rawlings Blake had to impose a curfew, Governor Larry Hogan declared a State of Emergency in the city and had to deploy the National Guard."

"But through it all, we kept the church doors open," recalled Pastor Just. "I wanted United in Victory to continue to be a safe haven for all to come."

"You certainly did, and that was important because the city needed prayer, hope, and healing, and what better place to come than the church?" replied Deacon Jackson. "Hey Al, you remember our walks along North and Pennsylvania Avenues during the protests?"

"How could I forget us being down at Penn-North?" said Deacon Jackson. "By that time, people were calling the area 'Ground Zero'…and people…thousands of them all representing various colors, religions, nationalities, and groups from all over the world, all came together in a show of solidarity."

"And many of them carrying Black Lives Matter signs in support of the movement," interjected Pastor Just, referring to Black Lives Matter (BLM), a Black-centered political will and movement building project that spearheads demonstrations worldwide protesting police brutality and systematic racism that overwhelmingly affects the Black community."

"And all of the Media coverage," said Deacon Jackson. "There were news cameras everywhere…CNN, MSNBC…you name it. There was also a heavy city police presence. And so many famous people including Rev. Al Sharpton came to the city to denounce Grey's death."

"That's right," Pastor Just agreed. "And not only did we walk North and Pennsylvania Avenues and surrounding blocks, but we were also encouraging people not to protest violently, along with the likes of Congressman Elijah Cummings and Pastor Jamal Bryant. It reminded me of how my father told me he took to the streets to stop people from rioting when Dr. King was assassinated back in 1968. And there I was doing the same thing nearly 50 years later."

"History truly repeats itself," said Deacon Jackson. "And I will never forget when we walked over to the neighborhood CVS at the corner of North and Pennsylvania…members of the National Guard standing watch in front of the building. I can still smell the char and smoke of the building…all boarded up…totally destroyed after being set ablaze during the rioting."

"And so many people…," mentioned Pastor Just, "Many of the seniors who attend this very church, were no longer able to go there…or to the CVS on Franklintown Road, which was also vandalized…to get their prescriptions or other needed items."

"And when the neighborhood store is all you got and you don't have transportation to get around, that can be devastating," commented Deacon Jackson. "So many businesses were destroyed…some of them Black-owned. When we tear down what somebody's blood, sweat, and tears worked hard to put up, we not only hurt them but ourselves."

"You got that right," said Pastor Just. "Thank the Lord both CVS stores have since reopened along with many of the other stores that had to close as a result of the vandalism and looting."

"Yes, that's a blessing," replied Deacon Jackson. "But some stores never reopened."

How Baltimore City got to this point troubled the two men. A young, Black man died while in police custody. Angry, young Black men had run amuck with destruction on their minds demolishing businesses and cars, and some even attacking people. The wall of mistrust between the city's police department and Black citizens widened even more.

"Freddie Grey's death right here in Baltimore," said Pastor Just. "Michael Brown's death in Ferguson, Missouri. Sandra Bland's death in Waller County, Texas. The list goes on and on of Black people who have died at the hands of police. Baltimore and other cities across this nation are bleeding…our youth and young adults crying out for help and screaming for justice. They were tired of being beat and profiled for being Black."

"You are speaking the truth. And if things weren't bad enough, there was the death of Sean Suiter last year," Deacon Jackson replied, referring to the shooting death of Baltimore City Police Detective Sean Suiter on November 15, 2017. "I know some people who live in that area, and it was put on lockdown to search for the killer.

They told me they had a time coming and leaving from their homes. And distrust of the police grew even more because no arrests were made. I understand that the police are saying it was a suicide, but many people aren't buying that. Many believe it smells of a cover-up."

Slipping into deep thought, Pastor Just commented. "Cover-up…such a racy word…one full of mystery, concealment, and deception."

"But The Bible tells us 'For there is nothing hidden that will not be disclosed, and nothing concealed that will not be known or brought out into the open,'" said Deacon Jackson referencing Luke 8:17. "In other words, what's done in the dark, comes out in the light."

Pastor Just sat silently, prompting Deacon Jackson to call out his name.

"Al," said Deacon Jackson. "Earth to Al."

"Oh yes, I'm listening," said Pastor Just snapping out of the deep pondering. "Sorry about that Roy. My mind momentarily went someplace else."

In talking about the state of things in their beloved hometown of Baltimore, Maryland, as well as around the world, Pastor Just and Deacon Jackson discussed ways in which they could help, particularly through the church.

"United in Victory can't save the world, but we can certainly do more," said Pastor Just.

"I wholeheartedly agree," replied Deacon Jackson. "We just need to zero in on a specific need and focus our outreach efforts in that area. No point in trying to spread ourselves thin trying to do a bunch of things and not being able to do them well."

"That's a valid point," said Pastor Just. "Right now, United in Victory already has a drug and alcohol addiction outreach ministry. I say that 'Addiction' should be our focal area."

"Agreed," replied Deacon Jackson. "We should step up our efforts to help those struggling with addiction. And I believe a transitional housing program is the way to go. I know we can't help but so many at one time through such a program, but it will definitely make a difference in people's lives. And that's what ministry is all about…letting our lights shine through what we do to help others."

What began as a conversation between the pastor and deacon would progress to plans to move forward with the bold initiative. United in Victory would offer a three-month transitional housing program. It would provide safe housing, and a supportive environment to help prevent those in recovery from relapsing. The program would be housed in United in Victory's church house and would serve as an extension of the church's Addiction Ministry.

"I've got just the name," said Deacon Jackson. "It will be a name that represents peace, hope, and tranquility. We should call it 'Serenity House.'"

CHAPTER FIVE

SERENITY HOUSE

May 1, 2018,
Later that morning

A few more minutes going by, Pastor Just was still thinking about his lifelong friend Deacon Jackson and the church house being named 'Serenity House'.

Pastor Just thought the name was perfect for our transitional housing program. I liked it so much I decided to go with it. The hope is that those in addiction will come here to live in a peaceful, supportive environment and ultimately transform their lives. And if anybody knows about transformation it's Roy. He reminds me so much of the Apostle Paul. There had been a time in Paul's life that he peddled a message of death and destruction, Paul persecuted believers of Christianity. But The Bible tells us the very same man that persecuted Christians, was the very same man that came to steer sinners and unbelievers towards Christianity. Paul not only became a follower of Jesus Christ but also taught the Gospel of Jesus Christ. What a miraculous transformation! And like Paul, Roy had a miraculous transformation! To change from someone who once peddled Heroin to someone who speaks against drug use. To change from someone who sold heroin to addicts, to someone who is steering addicts towards treatment. To change from someone who was behind bars to someone who ministers to those behind bars as a member of United in Victory's Prison Ministry. Don't tell me what God can't do!

Through the Prison Ministry, members of United in Victory regularly visited incarcerated men and women and conducted church services behind prison walls. Roy told me that during the days he was a drug dealer, he was locked up for possession many times. Now, Roy's on the other side of prison bars, encouraging inmates…giving them hope…and letting them know there's a better way. To metamorphosis from a dealer to a deacon is amazing. And like Paul, so was the experience in Roy's life that led to his conversion.

❈

Walking away from the window, reflections of all it took to reach this point resurfaced in Pastor Just's mind.

Bringing the building up to code, hiring staff, identifying clients, buying furniture, and handling other matters that needed to be addressed to open Serenity House was just half the battle," thought Pastor Just. The other half of the battle involved some of my very own church members.

Pastor Just weathered staunch criticism from several members about his decision to start the Addiction Ministry. Plans to start a residential treatment program drew even greater opposition. So many of my congregation were already upset about unfamiliar people struggling with drug and alcohol addiction coming into the church and I was sharply criticized for the Addiction Ministry. But when we began moving towards opening the transitional residential program, I was subjected to even greater condemnation.

His reflections called to his remembrance, a conversation he had with Dr. Lila Mae Hawkins – the wife of the church's mailman Rufus Hawkins. She pulled the pastor to the side one night after seeing some N.A. meeting participants leaving the church.

"There are programs out there for those drug people," said Dr. Hawkins. "Those derelicts have absolutely no business in this church!"

"Judge not," Pastor Just told Dr. Hawkins. "And they are not derelicts...but people. And one of those people could have just as easily been me or you."

"Certainly not I," Dr. Hawkins retorted, marching off in a tiff, dismissing the notion she would ever need the services of an addiction program.

As a condition of staying at Serenity House, clients are required to attend sessions every Wednesday night, called "Serenity Meetings". The meetings will be conducted in the large front room of Serenity House where Pastor Just is now standing. The space formerly housed the church's Youth Bible Class, which had since been relocated to the basement of the church. Although the space in the basement was much larger, the relocation did not sit well with Deacon Larry Williams who taught the class. Walking with a quick stride with Bible in hand over to Pastor Just one Sunday after service, Deacon Williams thundered, "Now Pastor, for years we have conducted the youth's Wednesday night Bible classes in that room! And out of the blue, you are going to just up and move us! At my last church, the pastor would have never done a thing like that! He would have brought it before the congregation first!"

"Well Deacon Williams, the Bible tells us in Matthew 5:16, 'Let your light so shine before men, that they may see your good works, and glorify your Father which is in heaven," replied Pastor Just. "Sometimes, those good works require going outside the church walls. And sometimes, those good works mean bringing folks inside the church walls. In this case, it means bringing them inside the church house...an extension of the church, which is the best place for us to meet their needs. Ultimately, we are charged with telling a dying world there is a better way. In life, sometimes we must lose something in order to gain something. Change is always difficult, but true faith is trusting God even when we don't understand. Wouldn't you agree, Deacon Williams?"

At a loss for words, Deacon Williams stood with his mouth agape, looking at The Bible he held then at Pastor Just. "Well Pastor, I,I,I,I, suppose you're right," the deacon stuttered, glancing at his watch. "I best be heading home. The missus cooked a good supper today." Watching Deacon Williams scurry away, Pastor Just could not resist the opportunity to raise a point. "Deacon Williams," he called out.

"Yes Pastor?" he grumbled.

"Well, Deacon Williams, seems to me that your last church was a mighty fine place. Makes me wonder why you would ever leave such a wonderful church to come here."

"Pastor, why I left my last church is of no concern of yours!" snapped Deacon Williams. "Instead of meddling in my business, what you should be concerned about is the business of the church and how you are treating its members to accommodate those drug addicts and alcoholics! You're treating them better than us, and they're not even members! That's the problem with you young preachers! Think you know everything! That's why I was against you becoming Pastor of this church in the first place! I sure wish your father Bishop Just were still the Pastor!"

"I'll be praying for you, too, Deacon Williams," Pastor Just responded congenially, watching Deacon Williams marching off and shoving his way past church members standing in his path – both young and old.

Despite the backlash and pushback from Dr. Hawkins, Deacon Williams, and other members of his congregation, Pastor Just was undaunted. I thought I would be burned at the stake, he thought. But if God is leading me to do something, I'm going to do it. Dr. King once said, 'The measure of a man is not where he stands in moments of comfort and convenience, but where he stands at time of challenge and controversy.' I have found that to be true."

Ring! Ring! Ring! The shrill of his cell phone halted Pastor Just's thoughts. The call was coming from Deacon Jackson's cell phone. He briefly hesitated before answering,

"Hello?"

"Pastor, it's Sister Jackson. Can you please come over right away?" she asked, her voice reflecting a degree of urgency. "Roy would like to see you."

"Of course Sister Jackson. I'll be right there."

Worried, Pastor Just thought, That call from Sister Jackson from Roy's phone is concerning to me. I'm going to swing by the house and pick up Jacqueline and take her over there with me. I hope Roy is okay.

Flickering off the lights, Pastor Just glanced around Serenity House one last time before stepping out the door.

Now mid-afternoon, the voices of Pastor Just and his wife Jacqueline along with Deacon Jackson and his wife Audrey Jackson chimed through the air. Several hours passed since the Just's arrival at the Jackson's Northwest Baltimore home, and the four were all still laughing and talking, sharing story after story.

Pastor Just was in the trusted company of his spouse and closest friends and felt comfortable talking about anything. He and Jacqueline talked about how they met. Deacon Jackson and Sister Jackson talked about how they met. He and Deacon Jackson talked about growing up in United in Victory.

"Me and Roy here shared a great deal in common growing up in United in Victory," said Pastor Just. "We were both the same age –"

"Born one day apart," interjected Deacon Jackson. "I was born April 18, 1963, and you were born April 19, 1963, which makes me the oldest."

"That is correct," chuckled Pastor Just. "We have so many things in common my friend. That also includes being 'Preacher's Kids,' also known as PKs. We were also both raised by one parent."

"And we were always both getting into trouble," interjected Deacon Roy with a labored laugh. "And just because we were raised by one parent didn't mean we got less beatings than kids being raised by two."

"Spare the rod, spoil the child," was definitely the mantra of both my father and your mother," laughed Pastor Just referencing a saying derived from Proverbs 13:24.

"And Proverbs 23:13 which says, 'Withhold not correction from the child: for if thou beatest him with the rod, he shall not die.' quoted Deacon Jackson. "But I have to admit, there were times when my mother beat me with that switch of hers so bad, I thought I would die," he said, prompting them all to burst out laughing.

❦

Pastor Just lost his mother Amanda Just when he was a child and was raised by his father Bishop Wright Just, Sr. A great deal of speculation swirled around exactly what happened to Mrs. Just, who seemingly disappeared without a trace sometime Friday, June 20, 1973. Not having any 'concrete' information as to what happened to their "First Lady," left many members coming up with their own baseless conclusions.

Over the years, Pastor Just got wind of some of the rumors that floated around the church about the mystery surrounding his mother. Some believed she ran off and left his father. Others believed she lost her mind, and that the family secretly committed her to a mental institution. One of the congregants who believed the latter was church usher Gertrude "Gertie" Green who always kept the engine of the church's rumor mill running on all cylinders. Her gossiping ways earned her the nickname 'Gossippin' Gertrude.' When he was a little boy, Pastor Just overheard a conversation between Usher Green and longtime member Violetta Jenkins in the church hallway.

"If you ask me, I believe the Bishop shipped the First Lady out to Crownsville somewhere," said Usher Green referencing the now-closed mental institution located in Jessup Maryland, once referred to as the Hospital for the Negro Insane of Maryland. "Don't nobody just disappear into thin air like that. I ain't buying it.' Motioning her forefinger in a circular motion towards her forehead, Usher Green added, "I heard through the grapevine that Amanda was good and crazy. Cuckoo for Cocoa Puffs! But you didn't hear that from me, cause I ain't one to gossip!"

Miss Jenkins, who was referred to as 'Sister Jenkins' within church circles, noticed the younger Just and began tapping Usher Green on the shoulder while motioning her head in his direction. Neither woman realized the youngster had been standing there all along. Confused and saddened, the youngster told his father what he overheard.

"Usher Green said those things, son?" his father asked, his light-complexioned skin turning beet red.

"Yes, Daddy."

"They were nothing but silly rumors, Al," his father assured him. "What Usher Green said were simply a pack of mean lies. Don't pay that cackling, old woman any mind."

Looking back, my father must have given Usher Green a firm scolding, thought Pastor Just whenever he reflected on what he heard her telling Sister Jenkins. For years, I could feel the heat of Usher Green's sharp gaze whenever she looked my way or whenever I looked her way. She always made sure she walked far away from me and whispered to whomever she may have been talking to whenever I was around. I always believed she was upset with me because she figured I went back and told my father what I overheard.

While Usher Green had her own unfounded beliefs about what happened to his mother, others conjectured her disappearance was the result of something far more sinister.

Deacon Jackson was raised by his mother Evangelist Christine Jackson. While she passed away years ago, many at United in Victory still talked about her powerful prayers. "Al, your mother Evangelist Jackson was a praying woman. I was just a child, but I can still remember her praying…sweat pouring from her face…her body trembling, and her ability to speak in tongues," recalled Pastor Just referencing the spiritual gift The Bible talks about in Acts 2:4. "She would set the church on fire whenever she prayed."

"Indeed my mother was a Holy Ghost filled Saint," replied Deacon Jackson. "She was a firm believer prayer could change any situation. I can still remember people falling out on the pews and onto the floor whenever my mother prayed. So many people told her they were healed of physical infirmities and experienced remarkable turnarounds involving challenging situations in their lives. All I can say is thank God for a praying mother."

No one was certain about the identity of Deacon Jackson's father including Deacon Jackson. His mother never divulged who his father was, and she named him after her father. Conversely, Usher Green claimed she knew the answer. She said, "inside sources," told her Deacon Jackson's father was a Puerto Rican mailman named Ricky Martinez who delivered mail to Evangelist Jackson's home. Sister Jackson shared the story with Deacon Jackson, Pastor Just, and Mrs. Just about the time she heard Usher Jenkins and Sister Jenkins discussing the matter.

"I was using the stall at the far end of the women's bathroom in the basement of the church," Sister Jackson told them. "Neither of them realized I was even in the bathroom. Not only could I hear the two, but I could see them through the opening between the stall door and its metal hinges."

"Oh my," said Mrs. Just.

"Oh my, is right," replied Sister Jackson with a hearty laugh. "I overheard Usher Green telling Sister Jenkins, 'Roy was the mailman's Special Delivery. She went on to say, 'Of course, Evangelist Jackson didn't want nobody to know that, because she had him out of wedlock…when Evangelist Jackson was still a hellion! Before she got saved, sanctified, pressed down, and filled with the Holy Ghost!' Then, Usher Green got to hoopin' and a hollerin' in the bathroom…jumping all over the place doing her slapstick imitation of Evangelist Jackson praying. The two started cacklin' and bam! That's when I flung the stall door open!"

"What did they do?" asked Mrs. Just laughing.

"They both looked like they had seen a ghost! said Sister Jackson, chuckling. "And Sister Jenkins was so surprised to see me standing there, that her mouth dropped open and her dentures fell clear outta her mouth. That was one of the funniest things I've seen in my entire life…and I've seen some things."

"Priceless," said Deacon Jackson.

"Good ole Sister Jenkins," said Pastor Just.

"Not according to Mother Pearl Carter," giggled Mrs. Just. "She would beg to differ when it comes to Sister Violetta Jenkins." Mrs. Just's comment began a discussion amongst them regarding the ongoing controversy between Sister Jenkins and Mother Carter. Evangelist Jackson, Mother Carter, and Sister Jenkins were among the church's first original members. However, when Evangelist Jackson joined the church, Mother Carter – who was Sister Carter at the time – and Sister Jenkins were already members. Sister Carter said she joined before Sister Jenkins, while Sister Jenkins claimed she joined before Sister Carter.

Without a church charter or other form of supporting documentation, the church relied on verbal accounts. However, it would be Bishop Just's memory that would settle the matter once and for all.

Years ago, before becoming senile, Bishop Just said Sister Carter joined the church prior to Sister Jenkins. Citing Sister Carter being United in Victory's oldest member, he named Sister Carter as the rightful "Mother of the Church." However, bestowing the highly-esteemed title upon Sister Carter did not sit well with Sister Jenkins.

Despite Sister Jenkins' objections, Bishop Just stood by his decision. Not only was he certain Sister Carter joined before Sister Jenkins, he noted that she was also a widow. With these things in mind, Bishop Just gave specific instructions pertaining to Mother Carter. As United in Victory's Church Mother, she would be receiving perks and benefits. Among other things, Mother Carter would be supported financially by the church; the church's Food Committee would deliver home-cooked meals to her home; the church's Cleaning Committee would ensure her home was cleaned each week, and the men had to cut her grass and trim her hedges.

"After Mother Carter began using a wheelchair to get around for health reasons, she requested my father to send someone over to her home to set out her trash," recalled Pastor Just. "And man oh man was Sister Jenkins mad about that!"

Bishop Just was drawing on The Bible to justify his decision in providing financial and other support to United in Victory's first Mother of the Church. Specifically, 1 Timothy 5: 9-10, which calls for the church to look after a widow if she was at least 60 years of age, and was:

'Well reported of for good works; if she has brought up children, if she has lodged strangers, if she has washed the saints' feet, if she has relieved the afflicted, if she has diligently followed every good work.'

Nevertheless, Sister Jenkins was also a widow and felt Mother Carter did not meet the criteria outlined in Scripture and shared this sentiment with Deacon Jackson. "'Hogwash!' Sister Jenkins told me," said Deacon Jackson recalling the conversation with his wife and the Justs – imitating Sister Jenkins by chewing on imaginary gum and pretending to peer over eyeglasses. "'Pearl Carter don't meet the criteria of 1 Timothy 5! While she may be over 60 and had one husband — as far as we know — she sure ain't take in no strangers, wash nobody's feet, or help the afflicted! And she sure ain't follow every good work! I know that because not only is she a bald-faced liar, but she also cusses like a sailor!'" Snickering along with the others, Deacon Jackson continued, "So I said, to her, 'Sister Jenkins, Mother Carter is so meek and nice. I don't believe she has a cussing bone in her body,' to which she said, 'You're right...Mother Carter doesn't have a cussin' bone in her body...she has whole a lot of them...not just one!'"

"Man, that's funny!" said Pastor Just, trying to catch his breath from laughing so hard. "They have been feuding about who came to United in Victory first for years."

"That's right," said Deacon Jackson, coughing. "And she also told me, 'That phony Mother Carter knows I came to United in Victory before she did! As far as I'm concerned, she's gotten the royal treatment all these years because she and the Bishop's wife Amanda were best friends!'"

"And don't forget about Bishop having Mother Carter's name inscribed on a special seat on the front row of the church!" giggled Mrs. Just. "That further fueled the fire. That's Mother Pearl Carter's seat...and Mother Pearl Carter's seat only. Anyone else is forbidden to sit there. And after Mother Carter started using her wheelchair, Bishop had an area next her seat reserved for her wheelchair...beneath the stained-glass windows personalized with her name of course."

"That's right," said Pastor Just. "And my father saw to it that the instructions concerning Mother Carter would still be carried out even when he was no longer the church's pastor…something else Sister Jenkins is not a fan of. Even after all these years, the resentment Sister Jenkins has towards Mother Carter has not waned one bit event they both are now in their 80s."

CHAPTER SIX

THRILLER SUNDAY AT UNITED IN VICTORY

May 1, 2018,
Later that evening

Outside the Jackson home, the sapphire skies of morning and afternoon were now darkened to a deep hue of royal blue. Inside the Jackson home, the couple was still swapping stories with their company of the last several hours, Pastor and Mrs. Just. The lively conversations included stories of Pastor Just and Deacon Jackson flying kites and playing 'Skully' on the church's grounds when they were little boys. Mrs. Just talked about playing 'Hopscotch' when she was a little girl and Mrs. Jackson recalled the high spring in her step when she 'Jump Roped'.

"Those were the days," said Deacon Jackson. "Hey Al, do you remember the time we were playing Hide and Go Seek with the other children one Saturday afternoon and discovered where the Communion wine was kept?"

"How could I forget?" chuckled Pastor Just.

"Back in those days, real wine was served for the sacrament," said Deacon Jackson with a labored laugh. "Not only did we get drunk from drinking the wine, but we ate all the Communion wafers. Communion Sunday was the next day, and there was nothing to serve. When our parents found out what we had done, I got the beating of my life."

"And so did I," added Pastor Just. "Who told on us anyway?"

"That greedy, tattle tale Pat Parker," said Deacon Jackson. "We used to call her 'Fatty Patty'. She was the one who ate most of the crackers. Of course she left that part out."

"That's right," said Pastor Just. "And it just so happens that she's a relative of Sister Green…also known as 'Gossippin' Gertrude.'"

"Telling everything must be in the blood," said Deacon Jackson.

"Must be," laughed Pastor Just, their talks now prompting him to reflect on his entry into Ministry.

❀

Pastor Just's father, the Rev. Dr. Al B. Wright Just, Sr., founded United in Victory Tabernacle in 1956. Consecrated as a Bishop in 1970, Bishop Just was known throughout Baltimore as 'The Singing Preacher', possessing dynamic singing ability and delivering parts of his sermon through song. Bishop Just was also a Civil Rights activist and active member of the NAACP, openly criticizing racial discrimination from the pulpit.

"My father still talks about meeting Dr. King back in 1955 after hearing him preach, said Pastor Just.

"What did your father say the sermon was about?" asked Sister Jackson.

"He said it was called 'The Impassable Gulf', said Pastor Just. "Using the parable of Dives and Lazarus –"

"Found in Luke 16:13-31," interjected Deacon Jackson.

"That's right," said Pastor Just. "God has truly blessed you with an incredible memory when it comes to precisely referencing Scriptures.

"I sure wish I could call them off like my Roy," said Sister Jackson. "But I am working on it."

"Yes, you are honey," laughed Deacon Jackson. "You may not be able to precisely recall Scriptures, but my baby sure can sing."

"Amen to that!" said Pastor Just. "In his sermon, Dr. King referenced Dives – a rich man, and Lazarus – a poor man, a story told by Jesus. In using the parable, Dr. King highlighted the disparities of racism and told those in attendance they should work to close that gap."

"We've come a long way in bridging that gap," said Deacon Jackson. "But nearly 60 years later, that work continues…because racism still exists."

"Sadly, it does," agreed Pastor Just. "But many people…both Black and White have made great sacrifices to change that great wrong because we are all God's children and in His great artistry, he did not make us all the same color, but different hues."

"Beautifully said," replied Sister Jackson. "Pastor Just, how did your father get to speak with Dr. King?"

Laughing, Pastor Just exclaimed, "My father told me that getting to Dr. King was like the widow woman in The Bible trying to reach Jesus because so many people were crowded around him. But like the widow woman, he was determined, and managed to make his way through the crowd to get to Dr. King."

A highly educated man, Bishop earned a Ph.D. in Theology from Loyola College (now University) in Baltimore, a Master's degree from Bowie State University, and his Bachelor's degree from Morehouse College.

"My father told me that when he got to Dr. King, he informed him that he was also a graduate of Morehouse and an Alpha," continued Pastor Just. "He said they immediately connected…kinsmen through their schooling, fraternity, and Civil Rights work. Meeting Dr. King was one of the proudest moments of my father's life. We still have the piece of paper Dr. King wrote his personal phone number on and handed to my father. The two became friends, eventually leading to Dr. King preaching at United in Victory…another crowning moment of my father's life."

As a college student at Morehouse, Bishop Just also met the church's famed musical genius Malachi Madison.

"During my dad's days at Morehouse, he sang on the school's choir," said Pastor Just. "That's how he met Dr. Madison. The two were students at Morehouse, and Dr. Madison played the organ for Morehouse's choir. My father said Dr. Madison's talents on the Hammond B3 made him quite the celebrity on that campus."

"Well I'm no fan of his," mumbled Sister Jackson.

"What was that?" asked Pastor Just.

"Oh don't mind me," said Sister Jackson. "That slipped out…but I should not have said that. I apologize. But that Dr. Madison can be a little extra sometimes."

"Over the years, I have found that to be true," admitted Pastor Just. "But he and my father are very close…even after all these years. And he credits Dr. Madison with the tremendous success of our Music Ministry."

During his collegiate days at Morehouse College, Bishop Just also met his wife, Amanda. She was a 17-year-old student at Spelman College and a member of Alpha Kappa Alpha (AKA). The two met during a fraternity party, and the 18-year-old fell head over heels for the pretty 17-year-old with jet black bouffant hair who liked wearing pink and green sweaters and poodle skirts embroidered with 'AKA'.

The two married in 1954, and on April 19, 1963, had Al B. Wright Just., Jr.

Bishop Just had been grooming his namesake for the pastorship for many years. But the younger Just assumed the position unexpectedly sooner than he or anyone else thought once Dementia began creeping into his father's mind.

Pastor Just, his wife, and Deacon Jackson all began recounting the collective nervousness they felt seeing the Bishop stepping into the pulpit on Sunday mornings to deliver a sermon. "I didn't know what to expect," Pastor Just recollected. "I didn't know what my father might say or do. He has never been one to mince his words, hold his tongue, or sugar-coat anything. But once he began suffering from Dementia, there were no filters. If a thought came to his mind, he was going to say it. I sat in the pulpit behind him on many Sundays with bated breath hoping and praying nothing offensive would come out of his mouth."

Sometimes, Bishop Just preached and sang the resounding and moving, fire and brimstone sermons he was known for delivering. Other times, his sermons were nothing more than nonsensical ramblings.

"I'll never forget the Sunday he was preaching, and no one could understand what he was saying," said Pastor Just. "I guess he didn't like the fact that he wasn't getting any response, and so he started singing 'Get on Up," laughed Pastor Just referring to the song by James Brown.

"Including the part about…'like a sex machine', recalled Mrs. Just.

"And dancing, and yelling out 'Yeah', 'Ha' and 'Yeah' in the vernacular of James Brown," said Pastor Just. "I couldn't believe it."

They recalled June 9, 2009 – the Sunday everyone realized it was best the Bishop no longer preach.

"Pardon my French," said Deacon Jackson looking up at the group. "You all know I don't use curse words. But that Sunday, I knew where things were heading when the Bishop opened his Bible, glanced down at the pages, and looked out at the congregation, and yelled, 'How am I supposed to read this small writing? Where the hell are my damn reading glasses?' I can still see myself and several other deacons scrambling to find those eyeglasses."

Pastor Just commented, "I had never heard my father use a curse word in his life," said Pastor Just. "Although I saw signs my dad might have been suffering from Dementia, I brushed them off because I didn't want to believe it. Watching the deterioration of a loved one's mind is a hurtful thing." Shaking his head, he added, "I sat there behind my father along with the congregation listening to him ramble on and on about how Jessie Jackson, Mahalia Jackson, President Andrew Jackson, Samuel L. Jackson, Reggie Jackson, our very own Evangelist Christine Jackson and of course her son…you Roy Jackson…" – glancing at Deacon Jackson – "And Michael Jackson were all first cousins. It was 2009, and Michael Jackson died in June of that year. I remember jumping up from my seat in the pulpit and rushing over to my father to escort him to his study in the back. It hurt me to my heart, but I was afraid of what my father might say next. As we all know, I didn't get to him soon enough."

Before he could reach his father, the elderman began blurting out things referencing his wife's disappearance. The last time anyone saw Mrs. Just was June 8,

1973. Her disappearance, which prompted some in the church to refer to the day as 'Black Friday', was shrouded in mystery and had kept the church's rumor mill turning for years. Consequently, Bishop Just's outburst took place on June 9, 2009, one day after the 36th anniversary of his wife's disappearance, and what he said rocked the church.

"You all believe that Michael Jackson died of an overdose!" he screamed at the congregation. "He didn't die of a damn overdose! It was all a cover-up! Just like Amanda's death! That was a cover-up too! That's right! A cover-up! Somebody killed her ass!" he announced, while also belting out a variety of lyrics from some of Michael Jackson's most famous songs including 'Smooth Criminal,' and 'Billie Jean' and screaming 'Hee-Hee!' while attempting to do the pop singer's infamous 'Moon Walk' dance, nearly tripping over his preacher's robe. Gazing out at the congregation, the Bishop zeroed in on one of the church's married couples – Mr. and Mrs. Johnny Jacobs and their son Junior Jacobs – a musical prodigy. He began singing, "I'm not the one! The kid is not my son!" lyrics from Billie Jean whilst looking up at Dr. Madison who was watching in shock from the organ loft.

"I didn't even know my father knew all of those Michael Jackson songs," said Pastor Just. "When and where he learned them, I'll never know. All I know is that we were trying to get my father to the back…and that was quite challenging," Pastor Just recalled, images coming to mind of him and several deacons including Roy Jackson, struggling to get his father out of the sanctuary. "We finally managed to wrestle my father to the back, but not before he unloaded accusations and obscenities at Mother Carter."

With a scathing look, Bishop Just glared at Mother Carter and bellowed, "You are sitting over there like you are Mother Theresa! Acting like you're a Saint! But you ain't! Blackmailing me just like Billie Jean tried to do Michael Jackson!" Unleashing a laugh like Vincent Price from Michael Jackson's 'Thriller', while they were ushering him out of the church, Bishop Just also told Mother Carter, "As far as I'm concerned, you are nothing but a lying, conniving, blackmailing Bitch! And I had the nerve to name you Mother Carter! You're a mother alright! More like a mother –". Before his father could utter another profane word, Rev. Just., Jr. covered his father's mouth with his hand. That memorable 2009 worship service which many in the church came to call 'Thriller Sunday', marked the last time Bishop Just preached in United in Victory's pulpit.

On Sunday, September 20, 2009, Rev. Just, Jr. was installed as Pastor of United in Victory Tabernacle at the age of 45, succeeding his then 74-year-old father.

The minutes of the day continuing to tick by, Pastor Just was now recalling the 'Tom Thumb Weddings' at United in Victory; highly celebrated pageants in which children acted out the marriage ceremony. Tom Thumb weddings were a big deal at the church, and parents went all out to make sure their children were the finest dressed.

"Jacqueline was my Tom Thumb bride," Pastor Just recalled, smiling at Mrs. Just.

"And you were my Tom Thumb groom," she said, returning the smile.

"I can still see us walking down the aisle of the church," recalled Pastor Just. "We couldn't have been any more than seven or eight years old." Turning and looking at the Jacksons he admitted, "Jacqueline did not know it at the time, but I had the biggest crush on her. I knew one day I would marry her, and I did. The Bible tells us in Proverbs that he who finds a wife finds a good thing, and he sure blessed me with a good thing."

"Amen to that," agreed Deacon Jackson, turning his head to look at Sister Jackson. "I got my good thing too."

"And the good Lawd knows I am thankful to be blessed with a husband like you," replied Sister Jackson. "But those ladies at the church sure didn't like the fact that you married me...and some still don't like the fact you married me."

Deacon Jackson's black hair, bronze skin, hazel eyes, thick brows, and long eyelashes – striking features contributing to his handsomeness, made him the affection of many females. When he and Pastor Just were children, many little girls had crushes on him, and in their teenage years, that trend continued. Now, middle-aged men, Deacon Jackson was still the object of many women's affections and desires – even though he was married.

"When we were little, the female ushers and other ladies at United in Victory always kissed you, Roy," teased Pastor Just, images of women hovering around Deacon Jackson when they were little boys flashing in his mind. "They left lipstick marks all over your face and pinched you on your cheeks. You got more peppermints, chewing gum, and nickels than any other child at the church."

"I didn't mind the peppermints, gum, and nickels," laughed Deacon Jackson. "But it was all those slobbery kisses that I didn't like...especially Sister Lilly Atkins' kisses. She would kiss me with those big, wet, nasty lips of hers," recalled Deacon Jackson. "And she always bent down to talk right in my face before she planted one of those slobbery kisses on my cheek. I hated it. I could only hold my breath for so long. God rest her soul, but Sister Adkins' breath was so bad, I can still smell it."

After a belly-whooping laugh, Sister Jackson lovingly looked down at Deacon Jackson and giggled, "And some of those ladies still want to pinch your cheeks. And not just the ones on your face."

"Come on over here so I can pinch cheeks," mused Deacon Jackson with a sly grin.

"That's a whoooooole lot of pinching," said Sister Jackson with a hearty laugh.

"And a whoooooole lot of fun," chuckled Deacon Jackson.

"Stop it, Roy," blushed Sister Jackson. "You're making me all giddy...just like some of the ladies at the church when you talk to them...talk about some bold women. Some of them flirt with you right in front of my face...as if I can't tell what they are doing."

"I know exactly what you're talking about," Mrs. Just chimed in. "Al has his fair share of unscrupulous admirers, too. A marriage band means nothing to them. I've walked up on some of them talking about how tall, well-built, and fine Al is.

"Did they say that?" Pastor Just asked cynically.

"You know they did," answered Mrs. Just. "Talking about your smooth dark skin, wavy black hair, white teeth, and stylish dress. I've caught many women salivating over you. They just didn't realize I was looking right at them. Some of them are worse than hungry alley cats stalking mice."

"Ain't that the truth!" exclaimed Sister Jackson.

"You two are over-exaggerating," laughed Pastor Just.

"That's right," chuckled Deacon Jackson.

"Oh no we're not," said Jacqueline. "How about Sadie Crenshaw?"

"Who's Sadie Crenshaw? asked Sister Jackson.

"Sister Crenshaw used to attend United in Victory," said Mrs. Just. "One Sunday after service, she walked up to Al and told him that the Lord had spoken to her and said that he was her chosen husband. There was just one problem. Al was already married to me."

Pastor Just interjected, "And then you told her 'The Lord didn't tell you no such thing!' Well, that was just before you asked Sister Crenshaw if the Lord told her she was about to get knocked out!"

"You just had to tell that part!" jeered Mrs. Just, laughing along with the others.

"And you just had to tell that story," snickered Pastor Just. "And speaking of the ladies, how about Bible Study? Roy, no one can draw them out to Bible Study like you. On nights when someone other than yourself teaches, about six or seven women attend Bible Study. But when you teach, that number jumps up to 20 or more."

Deacon Jackson's skill at quickly referencing Scripture and his knowledge of The Bible made him an excellent Bible Study teacher.

"I love teaching Bible Class," said Deacon Jackson. "However, there was a time in my life I never would have thought I would be teaching The Bible…because I was too busy doing things that went against it."

Deacon Jackson's mind began drifting back to the 1980s. He and Pastor Just shared many commonalities, but by the time they were in their early 20s, their lives took vastly different turns.

"It was the mid-1980s. Al had graduated from Baltimore Polytechnic Institute and was heading off to college. Likewise, I also graduated from Poly, but had plans to learn HVAC (Heating Ventilation and Air Conditioning)," recalled Deacon Jackson. "But I didn't go to a trade school…instead I went to 'the school of hard knocks', heeding the lucrative call of the drug trade. I was making thousands of dollars a week selling drugs on the streets of this city. I was known in the streets as 'Pretty Boy Roy.' In my mind, I would stay in the drug game long enough to buy a new, shiny black Camaro IROC-Z that I had been eyeing on a car dealership lot on Belair Road. The price tag…$10,000.00. Back during that time, the new 'Air Jordan 1' tennis shoes had debuted, and I had to have those. At $100 a pair, I couldn't afford them…and neither could my mother. A hundred dollars was a lot of money for a pair of tennis –"

"And it still is," said Sister Jackson.

"I suppose so," replied Deacon Jackson. "But at the time, I just wanted them. I also wanted some big gold, braided chain ropes. We called them 'Dookie ropes,' and rappers of the day like Big Daddy Kane, L.L. Cool J, Public Enemy, and Ice-T wore them in their music videos. I thought they were so cool, and I wanted to wear them too…along with the big, gold and diamond-encrusted medallions that hung from their rope chains. Pretty soon, I was making enough money to buy all those things. I still remember riding through Druid Hill Park on Sunday afternoons feeling like a celebrity…showing off my new car and wearing all my glitzy jewelry…laid back and leaning to the left behind the steering wheel blasting my booming, custom-installed speakers. Druid Hill Park was the place to show off your vehicle, hang out, and meet singles. And all the young ladies wanted to sit in the passenger seat next to 'Pretty Boy Roy.'"

"I bet they did!" interjected Sister Jackson.

"They did sugar plum," said Deacon Jackson. "But I'm all yours now, and the only lady sitting in the car next to me is you!"

"Flattery will get you everywhere darling," giggled Sister Jackson. "Go on baby…finish telling your story."

"Well, along with the money I was making, came the opportunity to help my mother financially. What young man doesn't want to help their mother who is single-handedly raising him, and struggling in the process? When I was growing up, she dressed me in hand-me-downs or bought secondhand clothes for me to wear from thrift stores, but always made sure I looked my best. When my elementary school had Book Fairs, Bazaars, and Santa's Christmas Shop she would give me what little change she had so that I could buy things…carefully counting out each penny and nickel. Chuckling, Deacon Jackson said, "I'll never forget the time she dressed me up in a black suit and velvet tie and sent me to school carrying a brown sandwich bag. Inside that bag were pennies wrapped in paper coin wrappers to pay for my third-grade school photos. 'Ma', I told my mother, 'I don't want to take all of these rolls of pennies to school to pay for my pictures.' 'Roy, how many pennies equal a dollar?' she asked. 'A hundred', I replied. 'That's right son', she told me. 'Now take all seven hundred of those pennies to school and pay for those pictures.'"

Laughing along with the others about the story, Deacon Jackson added, "I was embarrassed paying for my school photos with all those pennies, but looking back, I realize my mother had probably been saving pennies for weeks to pay for them. Money was always tight in our house, and my mother stretched and saved every dime…and of course penny…she made by any means possible. That included using S&H Green Stamps," said Deacon Jackson, referring to a rewards program offered by Sperry & Hutchinson, in which customers received stamps at the checkout counters of retailers and redeemed them for products in the company's catalog.

"Oh, I remember them," recalled Mrs. Just. "My mother did the same thing. When we shopped at supermarkets and other stores, she always made sure she got those Green Stamps. I can still see those stamps…green in color and the initials 'S' and 'H' written cursively in the middle. That's back when people did a lot of their shopping out of Spiegel and other catalogs."

"That's right," said Deacon Jackson. "Now people are shopping online. How things have changed over the years! But my mother got things for the house like our toaster thanks to S&H Green Stamps. She was big on those. She was resourceful and wasted no money. Laughing, he said, "My mother pinched pennies so tight, she could squeeze a tear out of Abraham Lincoln's face from the penny! But on a more serious note, even with everything she did to keep the lights on, it still was not enough to keep the lights from being turned off. Whenever our gas and electricity were turned off, Ma used the fireplace. And thank God for that fireplace, because when our utilities were turned off during the winter months, it was brutally cold. She bundled me up along with herself and used that old hearth fireplace to heat the house and cook. In my mind right now, I can still see her holding her old, worn black iron skillet over the flames cooking beans and hotdogs."

"Something about an old skillet that brings out the best in foods," said Sister Jackson.

"That's the truth," replied Deacon Jackson. "And baby, you are one heck of a cook! And so was my mother, God rest her soul.

Deacon Jackson continued to recount the struggles of growing up in a poor household.

"When I was a teenager, I had to wear 'Fish Heads', said Deacon Jackson, using a term that was used at the time to describe tennis shoes that weren't considered fashionable. My mother could not afford to buy me the more expensive 'Jack Purcells' like many of my classmates were wearing. In terms of food, my mother stretched those blocks of 'Government Cheese'. We ate Grilled Cheese Sandwiches, eggs and cheese, bologna and cheese, and her own delicious version of Mac and Cheese. She would put scraps of leftover food in that Mac and Cheese. Sometimes, I didn't know what those bits and pieces were, but it was good. She didn't believe in throwing leftover food away. She always scrimped and scraped, but despite all the hardships, my Ma always kept a roof over our heads, food on the table, and clothes on our backs. So while I'm not saying that selling drugs on the streets was right…at the time I also saw it as means to help my mother by giving her money. That was something I always wanted to do, and I was making enough money to do it. That's why we cannot judge the actions of others…we don't know the impetus behind them doing whatever it is they are doing. I was making a lot of money through my lifestyle and stashing it away in tennis shoe boxes arranged neatly in my bedroom closet. I lied and told my mother I had gotten a job working as a cook at McDonald's. Every day, I would leave out the house as if I were going to work. But my hustle wasn't flipping burgers…my hustle was selling dope."

Coughing and shaking his head, Deacon Jackson began recalling one unforgettable day in 1985.

"Ma was sizzling bacon in a skillet over the fireplace flames," he remembered. "I proudly handed her ten, one-hundred-dollar bills…a thousand dollars. I figured she would be happy getting that kind of money…especially with our gas and electricity being off at the time. She sat down the skillet, looked at the money, then at me, and then back at the money and threw it in the fireplace! 'I don't want no parts of your dirty money!' she screamed. I should have known better than to give my mother so much money at one time. Call it motherly intuition, but she knew there was no way I could have been giving her that kind of money on a Mickey D's paycheck."

"Mickey D's?" asked Mrs. Just.

"That was a slang term we used back then for McDonald's," explained Deacon Jackson.

"That's right honey," teased Pastor Just. "You bougie people wouldn't know that."

Laughing and playfully hitting Pastor Just on the shoulder, Mrs. Just replied, "I'm not bougie…far from it. Now, go on and finish your story Deacon Jackson."

"While my mother may not have had much education, she was very astute and smart. She also had Godly intuition and favor, so there was no pulling the wool over Evangelist Christine Jackson's eyes. 'That fancy jewelry and clothes you are wearin' don't mean nothin' Roy if your soul ain't right!' she yelled in that soul-stirring voice of hers. 'You're just sin all dressed up! You think I don't know what you are out in those streets doing?! You ain't working at no McDonald's! You are out in the streets working for the Devil! I know that for a fact because some people from church told me they saw you on the corner selling drugs!"

"We church folk don't miss much," commented Sister Jackson. "Gawd has us dispatched all over the place."

"Now that's the Gospel truth," laughed Pastor Just. "About three years ago, I thought I was getting away with eating a small piece of steak at the Golden Corral. I-"

"Oh yes!" interrupted Sister Jackson. "I love going there to eat! Oh, Lawd Pastor! You got my mouth watering for some of those hot rolls, cakes, cookies, and other sweets! My, my, my, my, my! I enjoy dining there! Sorry Pastor, I didn't mean to interrupt…go on and finish telling your story," she said, opening a box of donuts sitting on a table.

Resuming the story of his experience at the restaurant, Pastor Just continued, "I could not resist the temptation of just one tiny, itty bitty piece of steak. No sooner than I put the fork in my mouth, I heard someone yell 'Pastor!' I turned around, and there stood Usher Green alias 'Usher Gossippin' Gertrude.'"

"So what was wrong with eating a piece of steak?" inquired Sister Jackson smacking on donuts. "Lawd knows, I eat my belly full every time I go there…and that includes several pieces of steak!"

"The problem was, the church was on a 21 Day Daniel Fast," laughed Pastor Just. "That meant no meat. And there I was chomping on a piece of steak. Needless to say, Gossippin' Gertrude spread that news faster than I could put the fork down."

"God is always watching," said Mrs. Just. "I told you not to eat that steak, but you wouldn't listen to me."

"You are right honey," said Pastor Just. "But even Men of the Cloth get tempted."

"We all do," said Deacon Jackson. "Especially when it comes to money. That's what lured me into selling drugs in the first place…money. And to tell you the truth, I was furious at my mother for throwing that thousand dollars in the fireplace! 'Ma, how could you do that?!' I asked. 'What difference does it make how I got the money! The gas and electric man came here and shut off the power! That money was more than enough to get it turned back on!' 'Roy, I'd rather go without power in this house than accept your ill-gotten money! Money is the root of all evil!' Grabbing my jacket to leave because I was backtalking my mother and I knew that was wrong to do, I said to her, 'You say money is the root of all evil, and I say money is what pays the bills!' However, my mother began pleading with me not to leave. 'Roy, don't go back out in those streets! Something bad is gonna happen!' But I was leaving, and that was that. I began walking towards the front door, listening to Ma praying to God and asking Him to keep His 'Hedge of Protection' around me. You see, my mother would have visions about things, and through them, she said God would reveal things to her. She would say those visions sometimes came through dreams, and at other times, she could see things in her mind when she was fully awake. I left the house, despite her pleas and cries for me to stay. I would later learn my mother received a revelation that something terrible would happen to me on that day, and it did."

Tightly closing his eyes, Deacon Jackson's mind took a trip back to August 16, 1985.

"It was a warm summer Friday night I was standing on my usual corner in front of a convenience store peddling drugs along with some of friends…my homeboys as I called them," he recounted to his wife and the Justs. "We were laughing and talking when suddenly, a car pulled up and came to a screeching stop. Two guys wearing bandanas jumped out and began spraying the corner with bullets. I took off running while hearing groans and what sounded like people falling to the pavement. I didn't look…I was too scared to turn around. Amidst the hail of bullets, I could hear the footsteps of somebody chasing me. I tell you, I was running like Olympic Track and Field star Carl Lewis! I ran Track in both junior high and high school, and that experience came in handy! But this time, I wasn't running for ribbons, trophies, or medals…I was l running for my life! Although I was in a familiar area, I was so scared, I couldn't even remember where I was! I completely lost my sense of direction along with my bearings as to where I was exactly and what street I was on! All I could think was to keep running! And that's what I did. Rounding a corner, my heart feeling like it was beating out of my chest…I came upon the mouth of an alley. I was hoping I alluded my assailants…but I was too afraid to turn around and look. Noticing a dumpster down the dark alley, I ran towards it, jumping inside. Easing the lid of the dumpster down so it would not slam shut for fear the noise would give me away, I huddled inside the terrible bowels of that dumpster as still as I could, holding my breath. I had never been so terrified in my life. Fear took control of my body, and I was no longer able to my control my bodily functions. Hot urine was trickling down my legs, perspiration was rolling from my armpits and forehead, and no matter how hard I tried, I couldn't stop trembling. I was so afraid that my assailant would hear my shaking. I'm sure it was little to no sound, but at this moment, it was magnified one thousand times. I was thinking, 'I don't want to die like this! Not in this dank, smelly dumpster! And for the first time in my 21 years of living, I thought about my own mortality. I thought I was invincible, and thoughts of dying never crossed my mind until now. I screamed out in grim silence, wondering what death would be like. I thought about Bishop Just's sermons about the hot flames of Hell, and not wanting to go there. And here I was inside of a dumpster…my only shield of covering! My life hanging in the balance. I began thinking about all the advice, cautions, and warnings my mother had given me throughout the years. I thought about Bishop's teachings about the rewards of obedience and the consequences of disobedience. I thought about the legacy I would leave behind…another young, Black man killed on the streets of the city. I figure I probably had been in the dumpster for just a few minutes, but a lifetime of things along with the prospect of dying…were all running through my mind. My thoughts were interrupted by squealing sounds."

"Ewwww…don't tell me it was what I'm thinking," grimaced Mrs. Just.

"Yep, rats," Deacon Jackson replied, "And they were scampering over my legs. Talk about squirming, it was sickening my stomach, but what could I do? I was trying to remain still, but feeling the long, skinny tail of a rat slither over my face, I shifted my body hoping it would move away from me. We had a lot of rats in the city back then…and it felt and sounded like every one of them was in the dumpster with me…listening to all that squealing and feeling them running over and around me. I was desperately trying not to move…despite their clamoring and squealing near my face. But when I felt their teeth-gnashing on my skin, I could no longer hold still. Screaming, I began punching to drive them away. But thanks to the rat pack, I gave myself away! Talk about ratting and squealing on somebody! Now hearing two people discussing me being in the dumpster and approaching footsteps, my heart began pounding faster and faster and louder and louder. Awaiting my fate, I didn't know what else to do but to begin calling on Jesus. All my life, I had been hearing people talk about calling on Jesus in times of trouble. It was something I heard many times both at home and in church, and it stuck."

"There's power in the name of Jesus!" shouted Sister Jackson.

"That's right," said Deacon Jackson, "John 1:5, tells us 'And the light shineth in darkness; and the darkness comprehendeth it not'. In this dark place…a rat-infested dumpster, I could see the light because even in my filthy sinfulness, I knew I could call on the Father in the name of Jesus to deliver me from my perilous plight. So that's what I did…promising God that if he spared my life, I would give up my life of drug-dealing and serve Him. My eyes tightly shut, I was praying silently, but at some point, I began praying out loud…and my pursuers could hear me. I assume there were two of them…but I really don't know because I never saw them. Laughing, they taunted, "No one can help you now!" They represented the darkness John 1:5 talks about because they could not comprehend…could not understand…how someone they were about to kill could be praying in such a situation. Hearing the rat-a-tat of bullets now hitting the dumpster, I began scrambling about…along with the rats, whom I assume didn't want to get shot either…digging my way through the dumpster's mess of contents until I felt the bottom. My side was burning, so I knew I had been shot. Listening to their feet clamoring atop the dumpster, I heard the dumpster's creaky lid being lifted. Figuring my end had come, I thought about my mother and how she would cope without me…her one and only child. I closed my eyes, awaiting my fate! But then came the sound of a car speeding down the alley along with the wailing of approaching police sirens! Normally, I would have hated those sounds, but in my predicament, I could not have been happier! 'Shit! The Po-Po!' one of them shouted, 'C'mon let's go!' I heard the lid slam shut…and my assailants scrambling off the dumpster. Then I could hear the pitter-pattering of their feet running away…and the police cruiser screeching off behind them in hot pursuit. Petrified with fear, I remained in the dumpster…bleeding and situated amidst its trash, critters, and unfathomable stench… all the while, those rats biting my toes…hands…you name it…and me fighting them back. It was a rat race, and they were winning! However, I was too afraid to climb out…afraid those who chased me, were somewhere outside the dumpster lying in wait. After much contemplation about my tribulation, I finally climbed out…figuring and hoping…by now they weren't coming back. I'm not sure how long I hid in there. But I do know it was many hours, because when I finally opened the lid of the dumpster…I could see dawn's morning light…a perfect symbol for the turning point of my life…because this was the day that I finally saw the light! For like the blind man The Bible talks about in John 9:26, I used to be blind, but now I could see."

More minutes lapsed by, and Deacon Jackson's listeners were discussing the wondrous story he was telling them. His wife and the Justs were familiar with the story, but on this evening, Deacon Jackson felt he was telling the story with even greater conviction, thereby garnering all the more astonishment.

"I climbed out of the stank dumpster wounded…but alive…which was miraculous in and of itself," said Deacon Jackson coughing – prompting his wife to get him a glass of water. "Limping home, bleeding, and fully determined I was leaving my life of dope dealing behind me, little did I know another astonishing event awaited. It had been a hellish night…and I looked the part. I had on just one shoe…losing the other one sometime during my unfortunate adventure. Stained with blood, my new Puma jogging suit clung to my body…held there by pee and perspiration, which had come together to form a funky adhesive. I still could smell the terrible odors of the dumpster! I was no longer in it, but its stench was still with me! I was reeking so bad, I felt myself about to throw up and that's exactly what I did! So now my horrid odor also included the smell of vomit! Running in that terrible state, I realized I did not feel the weight of my ropes and medallions around my neck. Every last one of them was gone…apparently, they snapped or fell off sometime during my calamitous night. But I didn't care about that…they were materialistic things…and when you nearly lose your life…you realize those things mean nothing. I was just glad to be home. I walked through the door hoping my mother was asleep in her bed upstairs. The last thing I wanted her to see was me looking like this! But to my disappointment, I found her sitting in her favorite chair…a rocking chair with worn grey cushions, reading the large Bible resting on her lap. She looked up from its pages…and I'll never forget what she said, serenely gazing at me with joy and relief. 'Thank you, Jesus!' she shouted. 'Thank you, God for answering my prayer! I praise your Holy and Righteousness name my Father in Heaven for delivering my son out of that dumpster!' I stood there dumbfounded, wondering… how could my mother have known that? How did she know I had been in a dumpster? I thought about that…but didn't ask at the time. All I wanted was for her to hold me. With tears streaming down her face, she held out her arms and we cried together…my mother giving me the maternal hug that only a mother could."

Deacon Jackson's moving recollection…particularly the latter part, brought both his wife and Mrs. Just to tears.

❀

Deacon Jackson sat silent, feeling a bit uneasy about finishing his story, given the emotional response it was drawing from his wife who was now reaching for a pack of cookies, and Mrs. Just who was now in distant thought.

"Go on and finish your story, honey," said Sister Jackson, wiping tears from her eyes."

"Yes, Deacon Jackson," sniffled Mrs. Just, dabbing her eyes with a Kleenex. "Please tell the rest of your story."

"Are you both sure?" he asked. "The last thing I wanted to do was make anyone cry."

"Yes, honey…please go on with your story," muffled Sister Jackson, her mouth full of cookies. "I'm just a big, ole baby when it comes to that story."

"It's a remarkable story Deacon Jackson," commented Mrs. Just. "I would very much like to hear the rest. Tell me…did you ever go to the hospital?"

"Yes, my mother took me to the hospital after she put some kind of homemade salve on my wound and on my bites and cleaned me up." Chuckling, Deacon Jackson said, "My mother told me she wasn't taking me out in public looking like that. Once we got to the hospital, I was treated for a graze wound on my side and rat bites and released. Sadly, one of my friends who was standing on the corner with me died, and another was left paralyzed from the waist down. I would later learn that we were shot at because some other dealers wanted our lucrative drug turf. As far as I was concerned, they could have it! Don't get me wrong…making money was good. But what good is it to me if I lose my life in the process? I was thankful and blessed to be alive, but I couldn't stop thinking about what my mother said about me being in a dumpster. It was weighing so heavily on my mind, that one day, I finally decided to ask her about it. 'Well son,' she told me, 'Early one morning, I was laying in my bed. But I wasn't asleep…I was awake. God showed me a vision…and in that vision, I saw you hiding in an old, filthy dumpster that was dark as midnight inside. Your eyes were closed, and you were so still, I couldn't tell if you were dead or alive. And Roy baby…that's why I was begging you to stay home that day. I ain't have but one child and that was you. All I could do was pray to God to bring my son back home.' My jaw-dropping open, I told my mother, 'Ma, the day I was shot, I hid in a dumpster. I literally swam through trash to position myself all the way at the bottom of the dumpster where I was as still as a statue. The fact that you saw that in a vision before it happened…is unbelievable.' 'Son, when you have unwavering faith and are intimately connected with God, He can show you things you can't see with human vision,' she told him. 'God is real, and He can do miraculous things.'"

Outside the Jackson home, an ominous but beautiful skyglow of oranges and greys emanated from the evening skies. Inside the Jackson home, Deacon Jackson was now talking about his professional and spiritual growth, earning his HVAC certification in 1988 at age 24, and returning to United in Victory in 1990 at age 26.

"I promised God I would never sell drugs again, and I intended to keep that promise," said Deacon Jackson. After graduating from HVAC school, I worked for a heating and refrigeration company for about five years before leaving to start my own HVAC business in 1993 at the age of 29. As an employee, and eventually an entrepreneur, I could help my mother financially. But this time around, I was legally earning my money. While I strayed away from the church, I eventually found my way back to United in Victory. 'You're like The Bible's Prodigal Son', my mother once me before she passed away in 2000. 'You were out in the world, but now, you've come back home.' Looking at the Justs, Deacon Jackson pointed out, "Al, by the time I rededicated my life to Christ and re-joined the church, you and Jacqueline were married. And of course, you had gotten that fine education."

"That's right," said Pastor Just. "I had earned my undergraduate and graduate degrees from Howard University's School of Divinity and had begun working on my doctorate at Loyola College, now Loyola University. Earning my doctorate from Loyola like my father was something I was really looking forward to doing."

"What kept you from doing it?" inquired Sister Jackson.

Glancing at Mrs. Just who was gazing sharply at him, Pastor Just cleared his throat and replied. "I had just begun serving as an Associate Pastor under my father. "I put my doctoral studies on hold, but earning my doctorate is something I still intend to do."

"And you should," said Sister Jackson. "It ain't never too late to earn an education."

"That's right," said Deacon Jackson. "And we've got to pursue our dreams and goals while we still have a reasonable portion of health. I can't tell you all how happy I am that I made the necessary decisions to change the trajectory of my life when I was in a position to do so. And I am so thankful my mother not only lived to see me earn my certification in HVAC and eventually start my own business but that she also witnessed Bishop Just ordaining me as a Deacon. She was so proud. After my Ordination, she told me, 'I'm so proud of you son. You have a special purpose in your life! That's why the Adversary was so hard on your trail! The enemy wanted to snatch you away, but God had other plans.'"

Sitting at Deacon Jackson's bedside, Pastor Just began reflecting upon the faithfulness and loyalty of his longtime friend. Through so many challenging times, the two had stood by each other's side.

"Roy, you have been with me during the good times and the bad," said Pastor Just. "God gave me a true friend when he blessed me with you…my brother from another mother!"

"I concur," said Deacon Jackson. "And right back at you!"

"I have friends…but there's something special about having a Best Friend," said Mrs. Just. "I really don't have a close friend."

"You've got me, honey," said Pastor Just.

"I know sweetheart," said Mrs. Just. "But I am referring to a good, good girlfriend. A 'ride or die.' Someone who had your back no matter what. I thought I had one, but the one I had turned out to be a fake."

"I honestly believe true friends are sent by God," commented Sister Jackson putting a handful of cookies in her mouth. "But I have to agree," she said pausing to chew on the cookies, "There are some real backstabbers out there."

"I thank God for Roy," said Pastor Just. "I believe that when you are in Ministry, you have to have a Best Friend…someone you can trust. Serving in the Ministry has been a great joy. It has been my life's work…and I would not trade it for anything else in the world. But anyone who goes into it thinking the work is easy will find that not to be true. I've always had my fair share of detractors at the church. Many of them were comfortable with us operating the food pantry, serving the hungry, preparing meals for families on Thanksgiving, taking toys to children living in shelters during the Christmas holiday, and the church's other great works. But many did not approve of my views on the church taking a more aggressive approach to helping the community to save souls outside of it. That was hurtful. I might have become disparaged about the way they felt, but I was not discouraged. Roy, you always had an encouraging word for me, and using God's Word, you inspired me never to give up!"

"That's what friends are for," said Deacon Jackson. "And you did the same for me."

Pastor Just began reflecting on the lack of support he received after launching United in Victory's Prison Ministry in January 2010.

 "I remember when I opened up the opportunity for the members to serve on the Prison Ministry," recalled Pastor Just. "I explained the process, which included a background check and training, and told them that Prison Ministry services would take place bi-monthly, every third Sunday at 4 p.m. Although I was hopeful many members would agree to serve on the new ministry, Roy, and only a handful of others volunteered. Instead of a lot of participation, all I got was a lot of excuses. Speaking in both male and female voices, Pastor Just mimicked, 'Pastor, I work on Sundays', some members told me, although I knew they were retired or had no jobs. 'Pastor, I'm not comfortable going to jail with all those prisoners!' 'Pastor, I'm not comfortable with being frisked and patted down! Pastor, I would join, but I just don't have the time!'"

Pastor Just continued to talk about The Prison Ministry, detailing how it got underway with a small group, traveling to the Maryland Correctional Institute for Women (MCIW) in Jessup and other facilities to have church service with the inmates.

"Most of the time, Roy and I rode together to the various jails," recounted Pastor Just. "We talked about so many things. Well one Sunday, our worship services at the prison fell on Roy's birthday. As we were riding to the prison, I said, to him, 'Man, you just turned 47 years old, and you still don't have a wife yet…despite having all of those dreamy-eyed admirers. What are you waiting for?'"

"I replied, 'I'm waiting on the good Lord to send me the right lady,' said Deacon Jackson lovingly looking at Mrs. Jackson.

"That's right," chuckled Sister Jackson. "I didn't think you would ever get married. Boy, was I wrong! Little did I know, that would be the day you would meet the future, Mrs. Roy Jackson."

CHAPTER SEVEN

FRIENDS 'TIL THE END

May 1, 2018,
Later that night

The skies of night were now indigo. By now, the Jacksons and the Justs had spent a considerable part of the day sharing reflections, along with eating, singing, and praying. This was all especially endearing for Deacon Jackson. He wanted to stretch this time as far as he could.

This has been such a beautiful day, he thought. Sitting here sharing fond memories with my wife and friends. Life has been quite a journey for me…it has come full circle. But the Lord is telling me the time has come.

Cancer. The disease that had silently invaded and wreaked havoc inside Deacon Jackson's body was about to claim his life. He knew the moment he put off as long as he could – had arrived. It was time for him to have the difficult – but necessary conversation with his best friend, Pastor Just. Believing he would not make it through the day, Deacon Jackson had his wife to call Pastor Just and tell him to come to the house. No use putting off what I got to say any longer. I need to talk to Al right now. Turning to Sister Jackson, Deacon Jackson said, "Honey, me and Al need to talk privately."

"Sure sugar," she said trying to avoid looking him in the eyes. "Do you need me to get you anything?"

"No honey, I'm fine."

"Are you sure Roy?" Mrs. Jackson asked with a look of concern.

"Positive honey," replied Deacon Jackson.

"Alright, Roy…I'll be cleaning the dishes in the kitchen. Just give me a holler if you need me."

"I'll give you a hand with those dishes," said Mrs. Just.

Sister Jackson and Mrs. Just made their way out of the bedroom, turning and looking at Deacon Jackson before exiting.

"Close the door, Al," Deacon Jackson told his longtime friend.

CHAPTER EIGHT

THE HOURGLASS

May 1, 2018,
Minutes later

Flipping another page in what had become the final chapter of his life, Deacon Jackson and his trusted friend Pastor Just quietly wept for several minutes, neither saying a word. Deacon Jackson broke the silence, asking Pastor Just to prop his pillow slightly, his words now hoarse and raspy.

"Thank you for adjusting my pillow," said Deacon Jackson. "That helped me to sit up a little better. You know me, Al…I'm not one who likes to ask for help with anything. I would have done it myself, but these boney hands and legs of mines have little to no strength left…and I'm just too weak."

"You're welcome Roy," sniffled Pastor Just. "Are you comfortable? Your neck looks a little awkward."

"Just a tad," said Deacon Jackson, prompting Pastor Just to pick up the control for the hospital bed. Studying his dear friend raising the bed, the hum of its components being heard in a room where Death was about to enter, Deacon Jackson thought about what he was about to tell him.

"That's perfect right there," said Deacon Jackson, signaling the adjustment of the bed was good. "Thank you, Al."

"Your welcome Roy," said Pastor Just. "That's what friends are for."

"Al, my friend, life is like sand in an hourglass," said Deacon Jackson. "Before we come into the world…situated in the womb of our mothers…granules of sand fill the top half. As soon as we are born, the hourglass is flipped over, and the sand begins to tumble slowly through the neck of the hourglass. Days, weeks, months, and years pass by. Next thing we know, more sand fills the bottom half than the top. Now, none of us knows exactly when that last granule of sand will fall through the neck of the hourglass and hit the bottom. But this much I do know. I don't have much sand left in the top of mines."

Pastor Just took him by the hand and squeezed it; Deacon Jackson gripping his hand back with the little strength he could muster up.

"This is so symbolic of our friendship," whispered Pastor Just, tears streaming down his face. "An unshakable tight bond that will never be broken."

"Not even by death," replied Deacon Jackson. "And while we will no longer be together in the physical realm, don't cry for me. I am going to be fine. I know where I'm going…and that's to be with The King. And I'm not talking about Elvis either."

"Al, you always did have a sense of humor," laughed Pastor Just.

"Like they say, laughter is good medicine," said Deacon Jackson.

"It is," said Pastor Just. "And you have doled out a lot of it. Thank God for you, Roy. You have brought so much joy and happiness in so many people's lives."

"That's a blessing, Al. I can't say that was always the case. Thank God for His mercy! I could have died years ago in a dumpster. Had I died back then, I believe I was headed straight to a burning Hell. But the good Lord gave me a chance to get myself together…to save me from myself through the blood of his Son, Jesus Christ! My work here is done, and I have absolutely no fear of dying. 2 Corinthians 5:8 tells us, 'We are confident, I say, and willing rather to be absent from the body, and to be present with the Lord.'"

"Amen," said Pastor Just. "You are still quoting Scriptures."

"Until the day I die," replied Deacon Jackson. "And for me, that day is today."

"Roy, how do you know that?"

"Because my mother appeared to me in a dream early this morning. And in that dream, I was a little boy, and she and I were sitting near the fireplace on a cold winter night. She turned to me in the dream and said, 'Roy are you warm?' I said, 'Yes Ma, I'm warm.' And then she said, 'That's good Roy. And Mama is sorry we have to huddle like this near the hearth because the gas and electric man shut off the power because I didn't have the money to pay the bill. But son, the day will come when we both will live in a place where we ain't ever got to worry about being too hot or too cold…well depending on where you are going…because the bill has been paid! Paid in full by the shed blood of Jesus for the remission of sins through which we receive salvation! Roy, that place is our Eternal Home, and son, this will be the day you will join me here.'"

Deacon Jackson was diagnosed with Cancer in 2017 at age 54, but the warning signs dated back to 2014 when he began feeling the urge to urinate more frequently than usual. He found himself rushing to the bathroom, but once he got to the urinal, only a small amount of urine would trickle out. He found that strange but dismissed it as a part of being diabetic and chose to ignore it. However, he could not ignore the traces of blood now showing up in his urine weeks later. The red-tinged toilet bowl was scaring him, but he brushed it off. Whatever this is will clear up, he thought. It's the heat of summer, and I have too many air conditioning jobs to complete. I can't fall behind on my work. I don't have time to take off to see a doctor, and I definitely don't want to worry Audrey. But his wife had taken notice of his frequent trips to the bathroom and questioned him about it. "Roy, you're running back and forth to the bathroom every time I turn around. Is everything okay" she asked. "Yes honey, everything is fine. My Diabetes is just a little out of control," he told her. But as the days and weeks and passed by, his condition worsened. I'm peeing out more blood now than urine, he thought. And sometimes, it's painful to urinate. On top of that, I am experiencing excruciating back pain. That's not normal…I've never had back problems before in my life. But I've got to push myself to get my work done. It's winter and I've got a lot of heating jobs to do. Deacon Jackson couldn't dismiss that whatever was happening inside his body was also affecting he and his wife's typically busy sex life. What's going on with me? he wondered. I can't even get it up anymore. I seem to be experiencing some sort of erectile dysfunction. But why? As the old saying goes, 'Happy Wife, happy life.' But it's hard to keep her happy if I can't perform in bed. I'll get myself checked out sometime in the spring.

But Deacon Jackson's trip to the doctor came sooner than he planned one day, after using the bathroom throughout the night and forgetting to flush it. "Roy!" Sister Jackson screamed from the bathroom. "This toilet bowl is full of blood!" Deacon Jackson could not explain away the occurrence, unable to come up with a logical explanation. Sister Jackson immediately called Pastor Just who drove them to Sinai Hospital. Deacon Jackson was admitted, and a battery of ultrasounds, exams, biopsies, and other evaluations and tests were conducted. In the coming days, with his wife and best friend in the hospital room, Deacon Jackson received the grim news – he had Stage IV Prostate Cancer, and his prognosis was poor. The cancer had spread beyond his prostate to other organs, and even Chemotherapy treatment would not help. "The Cancer is too far gone," said the doctor, also telling him, "If you had sought medical attention sooner, it would have made a tremendous difference. We could have caught the cancer before it spread to other areas from your prostate and had more options for treatment." Swallowing a gulp of spit, numb from what he was hearing, Deacon Jackson asked, "How long have I got Doc?" With a somber face, his doctor replied, "Three months…give or take a few days," the devastating news serving as a catalyst for a loud, tearful outburst from his wife and groans from Pastor Just. Deacon Jackson received his diagnosis and the subsequent three months to live estimate in 2017. But to the great surprise of the doctors, he surpassed the life expectancy they gave him, for more than a year had passed.

"I prayed like Hezekiah did in The Bible," he said to Pastor Just, now sitting in a chair near his bedside. "I prayed to be healed of Cancer, but God said 'No.' So I prayed for additional days on this earth, reminding the good Lord that while I was not perfect, I had been a faithful steward. We don't understand why God sometimes gives us what we ask for, and sometimes He does not. And that's a tough pill to swallow when we are going through whatever it is we are going through…because we so desperately want whatever it is we are asking for. But what I do know is this…God knows best. And while He did not heal my Cancer, I prayed to Him for the opportunity to spend whatever time I had left at home. I prayed to God that I would spend my final hours with my wife and best friend at my side…and that I would be alert enough to talk with you all. I prayed to God for the opportunity to live long enough to see Serenity House…a place that will be a blessing to many… come to fruition. God allowed all of those things to come to pass, seeing fit to allow me to live much longer than the doctors ever expected. And Al, I not only have joy in my soul, but I am at peace.

The Cancer had spread through Deacon Jackson's body like an uncontrollable wildfire raging through a forest and just as fast; in its wake causing massive weight loss, claiming his ability to work, stealing his self-dependency, and unleashing irreparable damage to his organs. He had grown weary of the suffering, reaching a point in recent weeks where he was ready to die. God, I am ready to be called Home, he prayed. And now he was dying. His surroundings growing dimmer and dimmer, Deacon Jackson knew he had to discuss another matter with Pastor Just while he was still alive to do so, for death was inching even closer.

Looking at Deacon Jackson propped up in his hospital bed, was painfully tearing at the soul of Pastor Just. He sat there at his friend's bedside, wanting to tear his own hair out and run out of the room while knowing he had to remain steadfast in the seat.

"Hey buddy," said Deacon Jackson.

"Yes, friend," responded Pastor Just.

"Al, I tell you…we labored long and hard for Serenity House," shared Deacon Jackson.

"We certainly did," said Pastor Just. "I was by there earlier today, and things are moving along very well. I recently hired a highly qualified woman by the name of Claire C. Voyant to be our Licensed Clinical Social Worker. She heard about the position and applied for the job. I tell you, Roy, she's really something special. Now, all we need is a House Mother."

"Funny you would say that," said Deacon Jackson. "The House Mother job at Serenity House…that's exactly what I wanted to talk to you about. There's someone I would like for you to consider for the position."

"Who did you have in mind, Roy?" asked Pastor Just.

"My wife, Audrey."

Pastor Just was trying to mask his surprise but could tell from the look on Deacon Jackson's face he was not doing a good job.

"Audrey?" asked Pastor Just.

"Yes…Audrey," responded Deacon Jackson.

"Hmmm," said Pastor Just. "I never thought about her."

The two momentarily were silent, Pastor Just thinking to himself, Sister Jackson? I know she's Roy's wife, that she is a Godly woman, a faithful member of the church, and one of the most talented people I have ever met, but serving as House Mother? I don't know about that. Sister Jackson is always messing up Scriptures and eating all the time. I don't know if I know anyone who eats as many sweets as much as she does! I'm not saying she's not up to the job…she certainly has the experience. I know I shouldn't judge, but how can Sister Jackson work if she's eating all the time? But how can I tell Roy, no?"

"Al, if it's a problem, I –"

"Roy, who said it was a problem?" said Pastor Just. "I was just thinking…that's all. It just might work. But the question is, how will Audrey feel about it?

"She's not going to be crazy about the idea," admitted Deacon Jackson. "That's the reason why I wanted to talk to you about it privately. And I'm not asking you to consider Audrey because she's my wife. I'm asking you to consider Audrey because I know she's equipped for the job."

"Consider it done," said Al. "Consider it done."

"Now she's gonna be stubborn about it," said Deacon Jackson. "She's pretty hard on herself. Honestly, she's too hard on herself. But I know she can do it. She'll be fine as long as she doesn't try quoting Scripture."

"She does have a way of misquoting scripture," laughed Pastor Just.

"That's an understatement," chuckled Deacon Jackson. "Quoting from The Bible is definitely not one of her strong suits. His laughter stopping abruptly, Deacon Jackson added, "Al, some of the folks at the church won't be happy about Audrey serving as House Mother of Serenity House. They are going to raise Cain."

"Now, Roy, you let me worry about that," said Deacon Jackson. "I have had my fair share of experiences dealing with unhappy members. Besides, they were crazy about the clinical social worker either."

"No? Why is that?"

"She's blind."

"Really?"

"Yep."

"But Roy my friend…believe me when I tell you…she can see better than most people."

CHAPTER NINE

THE MIDNIGHT HOUR

May 1, 2018

More time lapsed by, and Deacon Jackson was now observing the sights around him, first looking at the hospital equipment he was hooked up to near his bed, followed by the armoire, fondly looking at the framed photos situated on top of it of he and his wife and him and his mother. I've had some good times, he thought, gazing at the photo's smiling faces. God has blessed me with a good life.

Deacon Jackson began thinking about something a former girlfriend once told him. Years ago, Jill Tinsley told me she was pregnant with my child. Then she stopped coming to school, and I never heard from her again. I wonder if there was any truth to what she told me? Was she really pregnant? And if she was, that child's photo should be sitting up there on the dresser too.

Afraid of what his mother might do if she found out he was sexually active at 16, and worse yet, that he may have possibly impregnated someone, Deacon Jackson never divulged to anyone – not even his wife nor Pastor Just, what the 16-year-old Western High School sophomore told him. The possibility that he might have a child lingered in his mind over the years, but he never investigated the matter. Now on his death bed, Deacon Jackson wanted to divulge his long-kept secret and spent the next couple of minutes confessing it to Pastor Just.

"I'm not asking you to do anything, other than to keep it to yourself," said Deacon Jackson. "I just wanted to get it off my chest. As far as I know, Jill could have made the whole thing up…she really liked me. And with Poly and Western High School being so close together, we would meet up after and get realllllll close and personal in our own secret area out there in the grass if you know what I mean."

"I remember you telling me you and your girlfriend were messing around," recalled Pastor Just. "But you never told me you may have gotten her pregnant."

Deacon Jackson sighed, "I was young, but it was really irresponsible of me to sleep with her without using protection. I never mentioned that part about her possibly being pregnant to no one…not even you…until now. I just moved on with my life, and I guess Jill moved on with hers…and I never took up the responsibility of finding out if it was true or not. I preferred to leave things just as they were…and her moving away made things simpler, yet at the same time more complicated."

"I understand," said Pastor Just. "A lot of us do crazy things when we're young…and sometimes the same applies to when we're old. But I must admit my friend, this is quite a shocker."

"I know it is. But I had to tell someone," said Deacon Jackson, turning to look out the bedroom windows, the moon now strung against pitch-black skies. "What time is it Al?"

"A little before midnight," responded Pastor Just.

"Tell them to come on back in."

"Okay Roy," replied Pastor Just with an uneasy look before leaving the room and returning a short time later with their wives.

❀

By now, Sister Jackson was sitting on the bed tightly grasping Deacon Jackson's hand, while Pastor Just stood on the opposite side holding his other hand. Mrs. Just held Pastor Just's other hand, doing what she could to comfort him. Looking at the small contingency gathered around him, the moment became one of silent introspection for Deacon Jackson.

The last time I faced Death, I was inside a filthy, rat-infested dumpster…and all alone. But God saw fit to allow me to get my life together and to die peacefully and with dignity…my wife and friends right here by my side. And my previous go-round with Death, I was afraid to die…but this time, I have absolutely no fear of dying.

The breath in his lungs now leaving him, Deacon Jackson looked upwards and cried, "Ma!," now seeing his late mother Evangelist Christine Jackson above the bed with outstretched arms.

"I see my mother!" he told the others in astonishment. "I see my mother!"

"You see your mother?" Sister Jackson asked incredulously.

"Yes!" gasped Deacon Jackson pointing upwards. "Can't you all see her?"

Telling from the looks on their faces, Deacon Jackson concluded only he could see his mother, but just as quickly as she was there, she was gone. Squeezing the hands of his wife and best friend with the little strength he had left, Deacon Jackson whispered, "I am about to join my mother on the other side of eternity…and must now leave this side of eternity. Farewell for now…I love you all so much."

"We love you too," they cried amidst other sentiments of adoration.

Their crying faces now fading away from his eyesight and their voices phasing out from his ears, Deacon Jackson began to see a bright, marvelous light, unlike anything he had ever seen before.

❧

Pastor Just felt Deacon Jackson's tight grip loosen, the late hours of the night now slipping into the next day.

Lifting the arm of the 55-year-old, the preacher began feeling his wrist for a pulse, but there was none.

"Roy is gone," he wept, looking at his watch. "12:05 in the morning…five minutes after the midnight hour. It is now Wednesday, May 2, 2018…the day my friend went home to be the Lord…the day I lost a friend with whom I will always be knitted to at the heart."

Amidst his grief Pastor Just and his wife turned their attention to comforting Sister Jackson.

Sister Jackson was laying on her husband's chest; this cavity of his body no longer heaving up and down, but instead as still as time seemingly had become. Overcome with sorrow, she knew the terminal illness her husband had been battling the last few years would claim his life, but nothing prepared her for the grief she would be feeling when it happened.

"My Roy!" she sobbed. "What am I going to do without you? I feel so empty right now…like my heart has been ripped out! My helpmate…my soulmate…my everything is gone! Lawd, please help me!"

"It's going to be alright, Sister Jackson," assured Pastor Just. "It's going to be alright because –"

"No Pastor!" she cried. "It's not going to be alright! My baby is gone!"

"I know Sister Jackson…I know," said Pastor Just, he and his wife giving the grieving woman consoling pats and rubs on her shoulders and arms. "I don't quite have the words to express how I am feeling right now, and I can only imagine how you are feeling right now. But Sister Jackson, Roy has fought the good fight that The Bible talks about in 2 Timothy 4:7. He has finished his course and kept the faith, and a crown of righteousness has been laid up for him. And as hard as it is to say goodbye, our beloved Roy has been called from labor to reward."

Still holding Deacon Jackson's hand, his fingers and palms now beginning to grow cold, Sister Jackson began singing the old Hymn written by Sullivan Pugh, 'May the Work I've Done Speak For Me.'

After singing a few verses, Sister Jackson whispered, "Rest on my baby…rest on," closing Deacon Jackson's eyelids, while praying to the Lord for strength to call her husband's longtime friend Carlton C. Douglass, owner of Carlton C. Douglass Funeral home to pick up his body.

CHAPTER TEN

WIDOWED AND WORRIED

Wednesday, October 10, 2018
6 Months Later
5:00 a.m.

It was still dark outside, as the sun had not yet risen this October 2018 morning. Inside Serenity House, the shades strung from the windows in Sister Jackson's room were pulled down and every light was turned off; synonymous with her wanting to cloak herself in darkness – a subliminal attempt to prolong what light of day might bring.

Be-beep! Be-beep! Be-beep!

The shrill of the alarm clock awakened Sister Jackson. Rolling over and slapping her fingers on the snooze button for the seventh time this morning, she murmured, "In a little while, I will have to get up. I know it was Roy's dying wish that I would serve as House Mother for this program, but Lawd knows I am dreading it."

Laying in her King-sized bed, Sister Jackson lamented about her lack of sleep. I tossed and turned all night long thinking about today. When something's on your mind…and your stomach is all knotted up… it's hard to get any sleep. I know I shouldn't have any fear…but I do…because I just don't know what to expect. The truth of the matter is that I'm grateful for this job but can't help but wish I hadn't taken it.

In these foreboding moments, Sister Jackson began reflecting on her acceptance of the House Mother position.

When Pastor Just offered me this job six months ago, I accepted…but I had my reservations back then...and I still do. I know I shouldn't…because this is such a wonderful opportunity. As House Mother, I get to stay here at Serenity House with our new clients. It's so nice…I got this big, ol' comfortable bed, she thought, tapping her fingers on the cushioned mattress. There's new furniture and shiny floors throughout Serenity House…Pastor made sure the entire place was redone beautifully. The job pays good, and I can stay here as long as I am employed with the program. I also get to cook meals for our new clients…and Lawd knows…I love to cook. I also get to help people struggling with addiction which was something Roy was passionate about. All those things are good, and I know I should be thankful. But it's not about the pay or free room and board. Between the money I received from Roy's life insurance policy and his monthly Social Security death benefits, I am fine, financially. Then there's the money in the bank from the business, she thought referencing the hefty sum Deacon Jackson received after selling his company Jackson HVAC after becoming too ill to work. And that's on top of the money he saved over the years. Before he died, he also made sure his funeral expenses were all paid for, sitting down with Mr. Douglass to pre-arrange everything so I would not have to do it. He also purchased a burial plot next to his mother…even getting me one alongside his. He picked his own casket and even wrote his obituary. Roy took care of everything. He made sure I would be well taken care of, even leaving me this house which is paid for.

However, living in the house without her husband had been challenging for Sister Jackson. Roy's imprint is all over that house, she thought, her eyes wide open staring into the darkness. His worn, brown leather Laz-Z-Boy chair he loved sitting in when he watched television in the living room now sits empty. His favorite Raven's coffee mug now hangs in the kitchen, his lips no longer sipping coffee from its rim. His work truck still sits in the driveway, not having been moved since the last time he drove it…and that was over a year or so ago after he got too sick to drive. His greeting is still on the answering machine at home. His greeting is still on his cell phone too… which I kept on just to call and hear his voice. I sometimes call that number thinking that somehow…someway Roy will pick up the phone and answer…although I know he will not. His suits, shirts, ties, shoes, and coats remain hanging in our closets. I can't bring myself to donate them…not just yet. From time to time, I still like to pick up an article of clothing, put it close to my nose, and deeply inhale the smell of his favorite cologne Cool Water, and his natural, sweet body odor. What a sweet aroma! And laying here in this bed, I can't help but think about the bed at home Roy and I have shared for five years. The bed I slept in before we got married was nowhere near as comfortable as that bed. He bought the best Sealy Posturepedic mattresses money could buy to make sure I slept comfortably. I had the bed moved to the basement after we had to put the hospital bed in the bedroom, but I just can't bring myself to get rid of that bed. Roy and I slept in that bed, talked in that bed, and made love in that bed. Truth be told, no one had ever made love to me like Roy.

Be-beep! Be-beep! Be-beep!

The alarm clock sounding off again, Sister Jackson again quieted it with the slap of her hand, resuming thoughts of she and Deacon Jackson's lovemaking. Roy was patient enough to wait until after we were married to have sexual intercourse…and when we did…it was beautiful. I appreciated that because unlike my previous sexual experiences, Roy was patient…just like he was with everything…he took his time. He never rushed…and foreplay was just as important to him as was intercourse. He kissed me from head to toe and everywhere in between. No one had ever done that before. And he sure loved sucking on this big bosom of mines. 'My special milk jugs' he would say. He massaged every inch of my body not only with those large, firm hands of his but his warm tongue. He always wanted to taste every bit of this big, ol' body of mines, and I let him. My size may bother me, but it never bothered him. He always joked, 'More lusciousness for me to have all to myself,' He always wanted to make sure I was good and wet before he put that nice-sized penis of his into my vagina. Oooooh! I could hardly wait for him to put his 'Johnson' as he called it, inside of me. And sometimes he would tease me when I got to this point by rubbing the tip of his 'Johnson' at the tip of my vagina as if he were about to put it in me…and then pull it back. He always thought that was funny, but it wasn't to me. I wanted that Johnson inside of me and I didn't want to be teased while I was waiting for it. Once he put that rock-hard Johnson into my awaiting vagina, I would scream with ecstasy, enjoying every minute of what would become another enjoyable lovemaking journey. What I wouldn't do to have him here to take another one of our sexual rides! Referring to her obesity, she added, 'And I sure gave him a lot to ride!'

While Deacon Jackson had been accepting of her weight, Sister Jackson was not. She struggled with insecurity brought on by trust issues, guilt, and a plethora of other reasons. But one of the major reasons behind her insecurity was how she felt about her weight. I know I'm a large woman, she laid in the bed thinking. That's one of the reasons why it took me so long to allow Roy to see me nude. He was a fit man. And there I was — all blubber and fat. I thought he would be repulsed to see me in my birthday suit. I would darken the room...much like this one is now...to make sure he didn't see me naked...making sure I also put on a robe and covered myself with sheets when I got out of the bed after we made love — anything to prevent Roy from seeing my body. He noticed that and after sharing my anxiety with him he kissed me on my forehead and told me. 'I love you...all of you. I remember just sitting there in his arms crying like a baby...I was so moved. It took some time but after a while I finally let Roy see my large birthday suit. Then, I got used to getting in and out of the bed naked and his seeing me in all my glory.

However, while Sister Jackson eventually shed the sheets and other things she used to keep herself covered-up, the 52-year-old could not shed the weight, eating high-fat food dishes, guzzling down sodas, and always snacking on what had become comfort foods for her – a variety of sugary snacks such as cakes, cookies, pies, and donuts. Although Deacon Jackson encouraged her to eat healthier, she always kept a multitude of snacks all over the house.

I tell you, she said, still stretched out in the bed, despite my flaws, shortcomings, and mistakes, God sent me a wonderful husband. Roy accepted me – weight and all, loving me...just for me. I remember wanting to pinch myself so many times. I found it so hard to believe that I was blessed not only with a good-looking, talented, hardworking man who owned his own business, but a God-fearing one. I didn't deserve someone like Roy...and if someone told me I would have married a man like that, I wouldn't have believed them. And now, the best thing that ever happened to me is gone. And now...I am a widow. So many times, I've heard women talking about trying to cope and adjust to life after losing their husbands. And now I'm one of them.

Over the course of the last few minutes, Sister Jackson's ponderings had once again shifted back to today's 10 a.m. Serenity Meeting. This morning would mark the first of these gatherings, and thoughts about what the experience would be like were swirling around in her head like soft-serve ice cream being placed on a cone.

Although I had my personal concerns about accepting this position, it seemed like a logical one, thought Sister Jackson. I felt lonely and depressed in the house all alone without Roy...and this job took me out of the house. Being House Mother also keeps me busy... which helps take my mind off of thinking about Roy's loss day and night.

As House Mother, Sister Jackson's day-to-day responsibilities included cooking the residents' meals, posting, and enforcing the House Rules, maintaining order, and delegating chores.

I've got years of work experience and I know I shouldn't be so worried. I worked for years as a cook and have an extensive background...which includes helping Roy with his business. And in helping Roy with Jackson HVAC, I filed papers, wrote up work orders, answered the phones, and scheduled his appointments. But now, I am a middle-aged woman who hasn't worked a full-time job in years.

I can also clean a place from top to bottom just like my mother, and I also have the residents to help around the house…well with exception of two who refuse to clean. But am I adequate for this job? Can I really do it? Can I handle this? Am I really qualified? And then there's the matter of how much has changed over the years in the workplace. I'm used to files and file cabinets and the old-fashioned way of keeping paperwork…pen…paper…and a bottle of good ol' Bic Wite-Out and Wite-Out pens to cover my mistakes when I wrote down the wrong things. I love Wite-Out products…they can blot out anything. But now, paperwork is all computerized, fancy, and high-tech. Even transportation is high-tech now with people using Goober and Lists, she thought referring to the ridesharing services 'Uber' and 'Lyft'. Who would have thought you could have a program on your phone that would allow someone to come and pick you up? I'm still using a flip phone. This is all like the cartoons I watched growing up. We are now in the age of The Jetsons…but I'm still stuck in Bedrock with The Flintstones. So much has changed over the years. Will I fit in? Lawd, I am worrying myself sick! I know I shouldn't be so worried…also having provided counseling and encouragement to many women and some men who have been in addiction...talking to people one-on-one, and in small and large group settings. I have worked with all kinds of people…easy going-people, difficult people, nice people, and mean people…many of them sitting down with me having good attitudes…like the new resident Willie Jones, Jr., even although he's a lazy lout…and others having bad attitudes…like the new resident…Miracle Smith…my Lawd that's a nasty child! I have worked in pressure-filled environments full of restraints and constraints. I know I've got the experience…but it's the meetings that worry me…especially the setting. As soon as Pastor Just told me these meetings were part of the job responsibilities, I didn't like it.

The weekly meetings are a part of the Serenity House program and are being held every Wednesday morning at 10 a.m. in the 'Deacon Roy E. Jackson Room'. An area located on the first floor near the entrance of Serenity House, the large room is named in loving memory of Deacon Jackson. The meetings are mandatory for staff and all residents and will be run by Sister Jackson and the program's Clinical Social Worker Claire C. Voyant. Comprised of prayer, dialogue, and discussion, the hope is that through these meetings, the residents will open up about their struggles with addiction and face them head-on. Although they all have been alcohol or drug-free for at least the past three months, all the residents have a history of relapsing. The goals of the Serenity Meetings are to identify the trigger points for their relapses and help the residents move past them.

This is the first time I have worked in a setting like Serenity House, lamented Sister Jackson. Living under one roof with residents who have all struggled with addiction is something I am not comfortable with. We all have a past of some sort. But when it's ugly, who wants to show it to anybody? I know the meetings are for our clients…and not me. But they all have difficult, painful pasts, and these meetings will force them to face their pasts. I can't help but believe that talks in these meetings will cause me to think about mines…and that's something I'd rather not do. Sometimes it's best to let sleeping dogs lie.

Sister Jackson's apprehension about these gatherings, far exceeded her concerns about performing her day-to-day responsibilities – worrying she would have little to no wiggle room for escape. Usually, I can slip away from conversations I find uncomfortable. I go to the bathroom and just stay for a long time…even when I don't have to go. I step outside to make a phone call…and pretend I am talking to someone on the other line. I excuse myself from parties and other social gatherings…saying I have previous engagements or urgent matters that need my prompt attention and leave early. But with these meetings, I cannot slip out. Being in them for their entirety is part of my job and my usual excuses just won't do.

The meeting time drawing ever closer, Sister Jackson continued worrying; the prospect of climbing out of bed and   facing   the   inevitable   looming   like   a   swinging   pendulum.

CHAPTER ELEVEN

THE CLIENTS

Wednesday, October 10, 2018
Ten Minutes Later

The clock at her bedside now reading 5:10 a.m., Sister Jackson was again silencing the snooze alarm. Plopping her head down on the pillows, her thoughts now shifted to Serenity House's first group of residents – Dancer Hawkins, Willie Jones, Jr., James Franklin, Hank Riley, Jr. Miracle Smith, and Sharon Torres.

The transitional home opened just over a week ago, and all the residents had settled in by now. Sister Jackson told the residents they could call her "Mama Jackson," the title making her feel motherly. All the clients except for Miracle referred to her as 'Mama Jackson.' Except for Dancer and Willie, the residents had been referred to Serenity House by their caseworker, Anthony Jenkins.

Dancer Hawkins was the daughter of fellow church member, Dr. Lila Mae Hawkins. However, Sister Jackson had not seen 34-year-old Dancer in years. Dancer grew up to be such a beautiful young woman, thought Sis. Jackson. Anytime she believes someone is feeling sad or down, she wants to give them a hug.

Sister Jackson reflected on a conversation the two had after Dancer's arrival to Serenity House.

"How did you get the name Dancer?" asked Sister Jackson.

"People ask me that all the time Mama Jackson," Dancer giggled. "My mom told me she named me Dancer because she took one look at me after I was born and said…'Look at this beautiful thing!' Dancer stated, imitating the crisp, highly-proper enunciation of words like her mother. She's going to grow up and become a dancer!"

Dancer's so sweet and has such a childlike innocence, thought Sister Jackson. She's the exact opposite of her mother Dr. Hawkins! What a conceited, prideful woman! Strolling around like she's a queen and the rest of us are her royal subjects!

One morning, Sister Jackson observed Dancer's eyes trailing a ladybug that found its way inside the house. Gingerly scampering over to the ladybug and picking it up, Dancer opened the front door, gently placing it outside in the grass.

What a thoughtful, caring young lady, Sister Jackson was thinking. I can't help but wonder how in the world she went from being a ballerina dancer to dancing nude on The Block.

⚘

Sister Jackson began thinking about Dancer's whimsical tendencies and her servitude ways.

I remember the very first day Dancer arrived. She was immediately drawn to the wooden coat rack near the front door with all the unclaimed hats, coats, jackets, and scarves left behind from church services. That girl tried on everything on that rack! Just-a-dancing as she masqueraded around like a little girl playing dress-up! And she's always singing that old Willie Armstrong song 'What A Wonderful World' while doing her chores. And that child sure don't mind cleaning! She'd clean the tar off the bottom of a shoe if someone asked her to! She has such as servant's heart and is always going out of her way to please others. It sure didn't take that self-proclaimed 'Casa Nova' Willie Jones, Jr. to try and take advantage of Dancer's kindness. I know he's the pastor's nephew, but I got to keep an eye on him! I can spot a womanizer a mile away.

Sister Jackson reflected on the day the group was all eating lunch. Dancer got up from the table, singing while waltzing to a corner of the kitchen and picking up the broom. Dancer began sweeping the floor although that was one of Miracle's chores.

"Dancer, I notice you like to clean, and I'm a neat freak," said Willie. "Tell me this Dancer. Do you do manicures and pedicures? Do you iron clothes? I need a woman to do those things for me while I'm staying here."

"Yes! I do!" Dancer eagerly responded. "I'll be happy to do those things for you!"

Intervening, Sister Jackson said, "Dancer will do no such thing! And Willie...you'll be responsible for your own upkeep while you're here!"

"But Mama Jackson, I've never had to iron my own clothes...or cut my own nails and toenails," explained Willie. "I'm used to women doing all of those things for me,"

"Well, that won't be happening here," replied Sister Jackson. "You'll have to do those things for yourself! And if you don't know how to do them, it's about time you learned!"

And upon learning his chores would include taking out the trash and cleaning the bathrooms, Willie replied, "Ooooooh no! I don't do trash or bathrooms."

"Oh, you don't?' asked Sister Jackson.

"Absolutely not!" declared Willie.

"Well, if you are going to continue staying here, that's going to change," Sister Jackson snapped, handing him the scrub brush and cleaner for the bathrooms.

Every time I turn around, that Willie is trying to weasel his way out of chores by convincing Dancer to do them for him. But Dancer certainly has found an ally in Sharon. Between me and Sharon, we make sure that slick, ol' Willie doesn't have Dancer doing his chores or tending to his personal upkeep. Somebody spoiled that boy by doing everything for him. And now he doesn't know how to do a thing for himself!

❧

Willie Jones, Jr. stood about 6'4'' tall, had smooth, peach-colored skin, striking hazel eyes, wavy hair capped off with a widow's peak and a radiant smile. The 42-year-old reminded Sister Jackson of Terrance Howard, the star of one of her favorite shows 'Empire.'

That Willie is a good-looking man just like my Roy, thought Sister Jackson. But unlike Roy, Willie likes to flaunt his good looks and use them to get what he wants…along with that smooth, sweet-talking tongue of his! I know all about those kind! And Willie sure likes to get all dressed up! Walking around here in expensive shirts, slacks, suits, and even Gucci loafers. I'm quite familiar with those shoes and their high price tag. My Roy was quite a dapper dresser too, and I remember the time he treated himself to a pair of Gucci loafers…much like the ones Willie wears around here. That was the first time in my life I ever saw someone shell out over $1,000 for a pair of shoes. I couldn't believe it! Roy told me he was paying for the name and craftsmanship, and I told him he was crazy! recalled Sister Jackson, mustering up a chuckle amidst her apprehension about the day's forthcoming meeting. From the time Willie stepped into Serenity House, I could tell he considered himself a 'Lady's Man.' And every time I turn around that cell phone of his is constantly ringing…hopeless women clinging on the other end to every lie he says until I tell him to get off that phone! And just as soon as he puts the phone away, it's ringing again! Clearly, he deals with a whooooooole lot of women! But the funny thing about Willie is that he can be just as silly and immature as he is suave and debonaire. Instead of a standard cell phone ring, Willie has one personalized in the form of a female voice. 'Pick up Big Daddy!' the ringers shrieks until he answers it. What an annoying ring! And he always goes out of his way to let everyone know it's one of his women friends calling because he puts the person on speakerphone so we all can hear. One of the problems with that is when the person on the other end says too much.

Sister Jackson was referencing what happened over breakfast a few days ago. She and the others were enjoying a light-hearted conversation over breakfast when Willie's phone interrupted with its distinct ring.

"Chellooooo," Willie answered, imitating 'J.J. Evans' of the 1970s television show 'Good Times'.

"Hi Big Willie," sensually replied the woman's voice on the other line. "When am I going to see you? I miss you, baby. I miss the reason why I call you Big Willie. When are you going to come over here and give me some of that big d—"

"Doggone dollar I owe you?!" said Willie quickly taking the phone off speaker before moving the phone away from his mouth. Sheepishly looking at the group, Willie cackled, 'Ahe...ahe' attempting to sound like 'James Evans' of Good Times – a laugh the father sometimes did on the sitcom when he found himself in embarrassing situations. Such occasions included looking at the glaring eyes of his wife 'Florida Evans'. And at the breakfast table on this particular day, nearly everyone was staring back at Willie with the same glaring look.

"Don't nobody want to hear your nasty ass conversations with your freaks Willie!" Sharon shouted across the table.

"Watch your mouth, Sharon!" sternly warned Sister Jackson. "Remember the House Rules. No profanity."

"I'm sorry Mama Jackson," apologized Sharon. "But don't nobody want to hear all of that!"

"Mind your business!" Willie said to Sharon in a hushed tone, now covering the earpiece of his phone.

"I'm trying to!" Sharon fired back. "We're all trying to! But you won't let us eat our breakfast in peace!"

"Put the phone away at the breakfast table!" Sis. Jackson instructed Willie. "And change that ridiculous ring!"

Willie raised the phone back to his mouth and ear attempting to explain the voices fussing at him in the background. "I'm still on vacation and right now, I am sitting near the indoor pool. There are a lot of people around me, and they are a loud bunch. They are so loud, I can hardly hear you, so I will have to call you back when I return. When? Did you say when? As soon as I'm back from vacation."

"Vacation? That's a laugh!" shouted Sharon. "He'll be gone for six months!"

"Shut up Sharon!" grumbled Willie covering up the mouthpiece.

"You shut up!" yelled Sharon.

"Listen, I'll have to call you back. And yes, of course, I still have those Gucci loafers…and the new iPhone you brought me. I'm talking on it right and I have on those shoes," said Willie glancing beneath the table at the loafers on his feet.

"Freeloader!" bellowed Sharon.

"Gotta go, baby," Willie told the caller. "Big Willie loves you too." After ending the call, Willie looked at Sharon and said, "Stop hating on a brother! That was Janet Jones. Or should I say, Mrs. Jones? And we got a thang going on." After singing a few verses from the 1970s song 'Me and Mrs. Jones' by Billy Paul, he and Hank began laughing and high-fiving one another.

Hank and Willie are quite the opposites, but the two have become unlikely friends, thought Sister Jackson. Willie's late mother was Pastor Just's sister…and died tragically…but Pastor never went into detail about what happened to her. And Hank also suffered a family tragedy. Perhaps that's the commonality that led them to bond, she speculated, lying in her bed thinking about the residents and the meeting that awaited them all.

Hank Riley was 29-years-old and the only Caucasian among the residents. Hank told me he was a former star athlete who once had a promising sports future, thought Sister Jackson. Looking at Hank, it's hard to believe he ever was an athlete! That little White boy don't look like he weighs 120 pounds soaking wet! He's as skinny as a rail! And he was born with a silver spoon in his mouth…his family being rich and all. But looking at him, you sure can't tell! Most days I see Hank…he is wearing raggedy t-shirts with faded, worn dungarees full of holes and beat-up sneakers. That long, stringy blonde hair of his looks like it ain't seen clippers in months or washed for that matter. I sure hope he ain't got the lice! And my Lawd…that boy's teeth are starting to turn black with rot…I assume from those drugs he was using. His nose is slightly crooked. Did someone punch him in the nose and break it? And he looks kinda scary with those raised pinkish, black lines running across his wrists…the old scars of a suicide attempt. Not to mention those green veins protruding from his forehead, those big ol' blue eyes, and those large, dark circles beneath them! He looks like he has experienced many sleepless nights. I can tell…because I have had my fair share of those…including last night. Hank has been through a lot, and it shows. But I've found Hank to be friendly, personable, respectable, and very well-mannered. He also likes to laugh and joke with Willie all the time…and seems to be quite the prankster, she thought, reflecting on what Hank did to Willie just the other day.

"Has anyone seen my other Gucci loafer?" asked Willie, walking into the kitchen with one shoe on while she and some of the other residents ate breakfast. "I've looked everywhere, and I can't find it."

"Have you tried looking up your ass?" mused Sharon, quickly turning to Sister Jackson and apologizing.

"Very funny!" replied Willie with a fake laugh. "What am I supposed to do with one shoe?"

"Are you looking for this?" asked Hank, walking into the kitchen wearing Willie's loafer on one foot, and his own sneaker on the other. Modeling a sports jacket, jeans, a t-shirt with Willie Nelson's picture on the front, and a blade of straw stuck in his mouth, Hank inquired with a fake southern drawl, "How do I look? I couldn't' decide if I wanted to be GQ or a hillbilly, so I dressed up as both!"

"Gucci doesn't become you man!" Willie laughed. "Now take my loafer off that funky foot of yours! I was looking all over the place for that shoe!"

"I know," Hank laughed. "I saw you."

"Those two laughed so hard about that...and it was pretty funny, thought Sister Jackson. They sure love goofing around and laughing at one another's silly antics. They remind me of 'Felix' and 'Alex' on that old television show, The Odd Couple...another show I watched growing up during the 1970s...two totally opposite men becoming friends...that's Willie and Hank.

Hank was from Clarksburg, West Virginia, a city located about 250 miles from Baltimore.

I've never been to Clarksburg, thought Sister Jackson, still thinking about Hank. But I've sure heard a lot about that place...and read a lot about it too. How those pharmacies, doctors, and who knows what else got all those people hooked on those pills was just terrible!

 Sister Jackson was referencing news reports that many of Clarksburg's doctors had treated their patients with a steady dose of pills; ultimately hooking many of them on Opioids. Roy talked about that quite a bit, she recalled. He felt what happened there was a travesty. I remember reading somewhere that deaths from Opioid overdoses in West Virginia led the nation in 2017...just last year. Hank is the first person I've ever met from Clarksburg. I guess his family still lives there. Hank never talks about them...and when I asked about his relatives, he told me they have not spoken in years. I wonder why?

CHAPTER
TWELVE

FIVE DONUTS & A SNOOZE ALARM

Wednesday, October 10, 2018
15 Minutes Later

It was now 5:25 a.m., and five minutes ago Sister Jackson again quieted the snooze alarm, the meeting a little over four hours away. Her mind still swirling around the residents, she was now thinking about native New Yorker, Sharon Torres.

"I'm from The Bronx, but my mother moved here to Baltimore when I was a teenager," the 40-year-old detailed to Sister Jackson in her strong New York accent. "So, I grew up in Cherry Hill. I used to fight all the time when I was a kid in New York and when we moved to Cherry Hill, I fought even more. I had to show those girls who was boss, and that I wasn't no punk! I'm from The Bronx!"

That Sharon ain't but 5'3'' with a medium build, but she sure is a tough cookie! thought Sister Jackson, turning over in the bed. She don't hold her tongue, and my goodness can she cuss! That child uses profanity like it's a language! I get on her all the time about that…but I understand…I once had a terrible mouth too. Old habits are hard to break, but they can be broken. Sharon's always on the defense…just like Miracle. Sharon's quite a hellcat, but she's nowhere near as ornery as Miracle. They both are very guarded…and in Sharon's case, she seems to always be ready for a fight. She may be 40, but I wouldn't put it past her to still fight somebody! She's a scrappy little thang! But I've been around enough people to know that beneath that tough exterior of hers, she has a soft side. But I guess she's been hurt a lot…I understand that too. And much like Willie and Hank, Sharon and Dancer have become friends here at Serenity House. Sharon is like a protector for Dancer…making sure that Willie doesn't try to take advantage of her. It's safe to say Sharon makes sure nobody messes with Dancer. I see them walking around the house…Dancer talking…and Sharon listening to her go on and on about whatever…never cutting her off or interrupting her. That tells me that Sharon is not only a good listener, but also has a degree of patience…although it's hard to see because she's so short-tempered. The other thing about Sharon is that she is also receptive to the hugs that Dancer wants to give everyone…although some like Miracle…turn them away.

Again, thinking about Sharon's physical features, Sister Jackson thought, Sharon's a pretty girl with that long black hair of hers she keeps pulled back in a ponytail trailing down her back. She reminds me of that singer…what's her name? C'mon Audrey you ain't that old…that's right…I got it K-Lo!, she thought referring to actress, singer, and dancer Jennifer Lopez also known as 'J.Lo.' That's who Sharon reminds me of…K-Lo…just a hardened version. Sharon bears the scars of her past fights…with those old scratch marks on her face. She's a small woman with a big mouth. I assume that mouth of hers probably got her into a lot of fights. The Bible tells us that our tongues will burn us up! Sister Jackson rattled off in her mind, inaccurately referencing James 3:6 which says, The tongue also is a fire, a world of evil among the parts of the body. And I guess Sharon's addiction didn't help either…that's hard on a woman…and a man too. She don't wear no make-up. I get it…I don't wear any either. And after all these years, why even start? I guess she figure like I figure…take it or leave it. And that child has needle marks running up and down her arms…telling me she shot up Heroin for years.

"Juicy introduced me to Heron," said Sharon referencing Heroin.

"Juicy?" Sister Jackson asked. "Who's that?"

"I can't tell you who Juicy is," said Sharon. "But you do know her."

"I would not have forgotten a name like Juicy," Sister Jackson told Sharon. "But that name doesn't ring a bell. All that's coming to mind for me regarding the name Juicy is a big, ol' juicy steak…and a juicy pork chop!" she said, clasping her hands together in sheer delight. "And hot, juicy chicken drizzled in hot sauce…and a juicy, jelly-filled donut…and juicy lamb chops! My Lawd! I'm making myself hungry!"

"I'm not talking about food, Mama Jackson," Sharon replied. "Juicy is definitely a person. I just can't tell you who the person is right now."

Sharon not divulging the identity of Juicy left Sister Jackson wondering, Who is Juicy?

Sister Jackson's thoughts were now directed towards 20-year-old Miracle Smith. Miracle may be the youngest of all the residents, but she is the angriest and most combative. She is disrespectful and walks around here with a scowl on her face all the time. What a mean young woman! Clearly, she doesn't want to be here so why did she come? She pulls the chair out from under the table when we eat with such force, she rocks the table. Then, she sits down all mad with her arms crossed and slumps down in the chair. She's always rude and never has anything nice or pleasant to say to anyone. I don't know much about her background, but I do know this…she has a terrible disposition! And she has such strange tendencies. Right now, it's Indian Summer…and still fairly warm outside. So much so, we don't even have to turn on the thermostat. But she always wears large, oversized, dark coats that are more suitable for winter. She's a petite little thang, but the coats she wears are large enough to fit me! Beneath the coat she always has on a hoodie…its hood pulled down over her face as far as it will go. And the sweatpants she tends to always wear are far too big. They too, look like they are large enough to fit me. She goes out of her way to put on heavy layers of oversized clothing which look frumpy on Miracle…with her being so small and all. With her being tiny, I can't help but wonder why she seems to go out of her way to cover herself up? If I were her, I would be showing my body off! But despite all she does to keep herself covered up, Miracle cannot hide the fact that she is an attractive young woman. I try not to stare, but I've seen enough of her face to see that smooth, light-brown skin of hers, thick eyebrows and lashes, those coal-black colored eyes, long brown hair, and that perfectly straight nose. Miracle reminds me of that model…Sarah Banks, Sister Jackson thought referring to model and television personality Tara Banks. "The only difference is that Miracle's eyes are dark-colored, and Sarah's eyes are light. And to say Miracle has a chip on her shoulder would be putting it mildly…she has a boulder on her shoulder. I guess all the residents do…to a certain degree…but Miracle's is the biggest of them all…and that keeps her and the others fussing all the time. The others haven't gotten off to a good start with Miracle, concluded Sister Jackson, now reflecting on a prior evening.

"Miracle, please allow me to give you a hug," Dancer offered with outstretched arms. "You seem to be very upset about something."

"She's always upset about something," mumbled Sharon.

"Don't touch me Twinkle Toes!' Miracle warned Dancer. "Now get the hell away from me!"

Dancer heeded Miracle's command, turning away from her, and sitting at the kitchen table wearing an expression of a sad child who had been chastised.

"I've had about enough of you!" Sharon shouted, banging her fists on the kitchen table. "I'm about to bang you in your damn face!"

"I wish the hell you would!" Miracle snarled.

"Listen here little girl…because you're a little girl to me!" screamed Sharon. "All Dancer is trying to do is give you a hug! That's all! What the hell is your damn problem!"

"Watch your mouth Sharon," cautioned Sister Jackson. "Now I need for both of you to be quiet and eat your breakfast!"

Standing up from the table, Miracle screamed, "I don't want anything to eat! And as far as my problem…I'll tell you what my problem is…all of you!" she said, pointing at them all with one swoop of her hand before storming out of the kitchen to the yells of Sharon and several others.

"Crazy ass Bitch!' hollered Sharon. "Oops, sorry Mama Jackson."

After warning Sharon yet again about her mouth, Sister Jackson, and Sister Voyant who was also eating with the group, managed to calm them all down. Willie broke the ice of the moment by stating, "Well Sister Voyant, I know you didn't see it, but Miracle pointed at you too," prompting them all to laugh. The remainder of breakfast was filled with light-hearted conversation with Sharon cheering up Dancer with a hug.

"Thank you for the hug Sharon," said Dancer. "I feel much better now."

"Hugs are good pain medicine," Sister Voyant told them. "And they don't cost one dime."

However, Miracle's behavior that day along with her action on so many others, left Sister Jackson wondering, Why is Miracle so toxic?

❧

At 60, James Franklin was the oldest of the group. But Sister Jackson felt James looked much older than his age.

James ain't but eight years older than me…but he looks old enough to be my father. I can't believe he's just 60! The little hair he has left on that bald head of his is as white as snow…and so are his mustache and goatee. If I didn't know any better, I would have sworn James was at least 70! I know men that age who look younger than James! My Lawd he looks old! They say Black don't crack…but James sure did! But on the other hand, he's in good physical shape. He said he exercises, and his body is still fit from his days as a member of the Downtown Athletic Club…DAC he called it. I ain't never been there, but I heard that gym was exclusive and that famous athletes, successful business owners, Corporate America people, and folks like judges and lawyers go there to workout. I believe Pastor Just mentioned going there too. I wonder if James was ever any of those. I can't say because he never talks about what he used to do. He mostly stays to himself, but I've found James to be helpful, knowledgeable, and highly intellectual. I can tell by the way he speaks that James is an educated man. And with that strong, baritone voice of his, I figured he must sing, and I was right.

"James are you a singer?" she asked him one day while he was sitting in the den quietly reading his Bible.

"Why I am," replied James. "I haven't done any singing in a while, but I used to sing with my church's choir."

"Your voice is so resounding," said Sister Jackson. "Like that actor from long time ago –"

"Paul Roberson," said James.

"That's right!" said Sister Jackson.

"I've been hearing that just about my entire life," chuckled James.

On the contrary, while Sister Jackson liked James, there was something about him that rubbed her the wrong way.

I love to encourage the residents by quoting Bible scriptures, thought Sister Jackson. I'm no Bible scholar like Roy was and I might be off a word or two. After all, I am saying them off the top of my head. But as soon as I flub a Scripture even a tiny bit…here comes James! Rushing over to me with his Bible in hand to correct me and recite whichever verse I've said word for word! And he's doing it in front of the others! That irks me to no end! I don't like his public display of correction! I play it off laughing…he-heeing and ke-keeing…acting like what he said is exactly what I meant to say, but I don't like it one bit! He's a man of few words, but James did tell me he used to be active in the church…and I can tell.

James knows that Bible like the back of his hand…much like my Roy. I know James is spiritual and all, but he has a dark side too. I can tell from that run-in he had with Willie. Push James too hard or say the wrong thing, that twin within him is coming out.

Sister Jackson was thinking back on an incident that happened a few nights ago. She and the others – except for Miracle who opted to stay in her room, were all watching a movie in the den. James sat reading his Bible, and occasionally looking up at the television.

"I don't need no addiction help," Willie told them after a commercial aired about a recovery program. I haven't drunk one drop of alcohol in over three months. That taste has completely gone out of my mouth!"

"Will you shut up!" shouted Sharon. "We don't want to hear you! We want to hear the movie!"

"She's right," said James, closing his Bible. "But I am curious about one thing you just mentioned. Since you do not need addiction help, why are you here?"

"Yeah!" shouted Sharon. "Why are you here Willie!?"

"I called my Unk up," explained Willie.

"Unk?" asked James. "Who or what is an Unk?"

"My uncle man…Pastor Just," replied Willie. "I told Unk I needed a place to stay because one of my lady friends put me out. She thought I was cheatin' on her."

"Well, where you?'" asked James.

"Can't put all my eggs in one basket," gloated Willie like he was jive-talking with a buddy about women. Standing up from his chair, Willie told James, "You know how the game is played Player!" and began doing the 'Cabbage Patch Dance', Hank cracking up laughing at Willie. James laughed too, standing to join Willie in doing the dance, leading them all to believe he agreed with Willie's assertion. But James abruptly stopped dancing, firing a ballistic look at Willie and shouting, "No! I don't know how the game is played, Player!"

Willie's face dropped, and he began embarrassingly looking around at the group who were all laughing. Sharon ran over to Willie, stooping down to pick something up from the floor. "Here's your face!" she told him, acting as if she were putting his face back on. "I picked it up for you because it was cracked and on the floor!" Howling with laughter, Sharon rushed back to her seat, her antics causing the others in the room to cackle even louder. "Willie, you got egg all on your face!" laughed Hank pointing at Willie. Willie, however, was not amused, yelling, "James, you need to stop perpetrating! Stop acting like you're all faithful and everything!" James charged towards Willie like a fierce bull rushing towards a matador, and before they all knew it, was grabbing Willie by his shirt collar. "Oh shit!" Sharon said gleefully, ready to see them fight. "It's about to go down up in here! Get him, James!" Between heavy breaths, James shouted in Willie's face, "Listen here, man! I was faithful to my wife! Do you hear me?! I was faithful to my wife!" Sister Jackson and Hank rushed over to intervene, but Willie managed to free himself from James' grasp, coughing from the choke. Grabbing James by the arm, Hank began walking him back to his seat. James yanked his arm out of Hank's clutch and hollered, "Get off me man! I'm cool! But if that Bozo ever disrespects me like that again, I'll rip him apart!" Dusting off his suit jacket with his hand, Willie coughed, "James, man, I don't know what your problem is! But Lucky for you, I'm a lover and not a fighter!' Jumping back up out of his chair, James taunted, "There's nothing between us but space and opportunity Willie! Nothing but space and opportunity! Now you had better sit your rapid ass down!" Scurrying back to his seat like a scared squirrel, Willie said, "Sitting down!" And Mama Jackson did you hear him cuss at me?! James broke a rule!" Sharon began clucking like a chicken, telling him, "Look at you running away like a chicken! Cluck! Cluck! Cluck! You are a punk, Willie! Cluck! Cluck! Cluck!" Hank joined Sharon by flapping his arms like a chicken and walking around in circles shouting, "Sharon's right, Willie. You are a punk! Cluck! Cluck! Cluck!" Looking at them both, Willie said, "I ain't no punk! And James be glad Mama Jackson jumped between us when she did!" James yelled, "You're the one that better be glad! Idiot!" Chastising them, Sister Jackson said, "That's enough! You all are acting like children! Since you want to act like children, I have to treat you like children! Everyone to your rooms! Our Movie Night is now over!"

Disgruntled about the early end of the gathering, the group fussed, while James gathered his things, keeping his eyes fixated on Willie. Dancer noticed, scooting over to James with open arms to give him a hug. "James, you still look mad. Looks like somebody needs a hug!" she said melodiously. Pushing Dancer's arms away, James replied, "I don't want a damn hug!," drawing a dejected look on Dancer's face. Sharon walked over to Dancer, giving her a hug, immediately cheering her up. Before they all left the den, Sister Jackson pulled James to the side and told him, "James you know the rules. Grab someone like that again, and you'll run the risk of being put out of Serenity House." With a disappointed look, James replied, "That should have never happened and I'm really sorry Mama Jackson. I deeply apologize. I am grateful to be here at Serenity House and thank God for the opportunity. The last thing I want to do is mess up. But I'm not going to stand for that fool Willie or anyone for that matter, accusing me of not being faithful to my wife! I was a faithful husband! Proverbs 18:22 tells us that that 'He who finds a wife, finds a good thing.' I loved my wife…but I lost her…and I would do anything…anything to have her back!" he exclaimed fighting back tears.

I was told James lost his wife and daughter tragically, thought Sister Jackson shifting again in the bed. I don't know the circumstances, but clearly Willie struck a painful nerve.

Amidst the stormy relationship of the residents, and Sister Jackson's own sea of doubt was an anchor of encouragement — Claire C. Voyant. Sister Jackson had deep admiration for Sister Voyant and was completely enamored with her abilities, wisdom, and insight. The two had also struck up a friendship of their own, referring to one another by first name and talking all the time. Awaiting the unwelcoming toll of the snooze alarm, Sister Jackson began thinking about her blind counterpart.

In all my 52 years, I have never met anyone like Claire, she thought. I love being in her space. The way she acts, and dresses remind me so much of…my goodness what are their names? C'mon Audrey…you can remember! You ain't that old! Oh! I got it! Iyana Trasvant and Sister Mary! she said, inaccurately referencing television personality and life coach 'Iyana Vanzant' and the late, legendary Baltimore griot 'Mary Carter Smith'.

An eclectic woman, Sister Voyant dressed in unusual, fascinating garb, wearing colorful dashikis, baggy pants, clogs, and a wide assortment of gaudy jewelry which included turquoise rings and bracelets, necklaces, and earrings. She always wore head wraps, and large, dark glasses, making sure she kept her eyes covered.

I just love the way Claire dresses, thought Sister Jackson. It's so unique! She also has such a commanding, regal, yet mysterious way about her. She told me she's not a minister but everything about her spirit is Ministry. And she can speak in Tongues," said Sister Jackson referring to a spiritual gift that allows a person to speak a language unknown to them, referenced in Acts 2:1-12.

Sister Voyant possessed a rich Performing Arts and Human Services background. Her impressive resume including training at Julliard in New York, earning a Master's Degree in Public Health from Johns Hopkins University, and a second Master's Degree in Social Work from the University of Maryland. She spoke oratorial-like, announcing her words in a fashion reflective of deeper inner-spirituality and impeccable education. Her diction was precise and poignant, and she had a distinct way of pronouncing words that began with the letter 'r.' often rolling the letter off her tongue like someone of foreign descent.

The way Claire talks…I've never heard anyone talk like that, thought Sister Jackson. It's so intriguing. And the way she moves around without needing any assistance is amazing! She has a walking stick but doesn't use it much. She told me she was going to school to earn one of those fancy doctorate degrees but stopped going after something happened and she lost her eyesight. I wonder what in the world happened?

A few more minutes ran by, and the pitter-pattering of rain was softly knocking on Sister Jackson's bedroom window. Looking at the bright, red numbers on the digital clock, now displaying 5:28 a.m., she repositioned herself; now laying flat on her back. Still – not moving in an attempt to stay swallowed up in the sanctity of her bed.

I can't hit the snooze button no more, she agonized staring up at the ceiling, now lightened by the early morning sunrise. Pretty soon, I got to get up…although I don't want to. Sister Jackson found herself again questioning her ability to handle the meetings, the rain outside providing the perfect accompaniment to her internal Blues.

How am I going to handle these meetings? she asked herself. What if these meetings are too much for me? What if I disappoint Pastor Just? He and Roy placed a huge amount of confidence in me. They believe in me more than I believe in myself. I really didn't want to take this job, but how could I turn down Pastor knowing this was what Roy wanted?

Be-Beep! Be-Beep! Be-Beep!

"Oh, shut up!" blurted Sister Jackson slamming her hand down on the alarm as if the beeps were taunting her. My Lawd! She thought. I didn't mean to hit the clock so hard. I hope I didn't break it! I just don't want to get out of this bed…but I got to…it's 5:30 now…and I'm usually up at 4. As much as I hate climbing out of this bed, I got to wash myself, brush my teeth and get dressed. Then I've got to cook breakfast and get ready for this meeting. I can't just lie here feeling sorry for myself. I've got to get up. Sister Jackson sat upright and swung her legs on the side of the bed. After turning on the light on the nightstand, she looked at the donut box sitting on top of it, taking out one after another. "My Lawd, I've eaten five donuts!" she whispered to herself, rolling her body out of the bed, and lowering her knees to the floor to pray. I start my day every day with prayer, she thought. I've got to thank God every day for his tender mercies and for allowing me to wake up to see a new day. Sister Jackson went into prayer, asking God out loud, "Lord, cover me with your Hedge of Protection…cover my family, and Lord please give me the strength." Staying on her knees much longer than she normally would, Sister Jackson hoisted herself up from the floor, using the bed to do so, and headed to the bathroom stating, "God, it's time for me to face whatever lies ahead today. Only You know what the day will hold."

CHAPTER THIRTEEN

A ROUGH START

Wednesday, October 10, 2018
Later that morning
The First Meeting

It was now 9:40 a.m. and the group's 1st Serenity Meeting would be starting in the 'Deacon Roy Jackson Room' in 20 minutes. A line of chairs was arranged in a half-circle, with Sister Jackson and Sister Voyant seated directly in the center. The two would have been seated directly next to one another, were it not for a table sitting between them. Sister Jackson placed the table there earlier, and on its top, sat many snacks.

I got my potato chips, pretzels, cookies, cupcakes, and donuts right here next to me at arm's length, she thought gazing at the table. If I want to snack on something, all I gots to do is reach over and grab it.

"Good morning, Willie and Hank," said Sister Jackson, the two being the first residents to arrive. "Have a seat in any of those chairs," she said pointing to the empty seats.

The two greeted both Sister Jackson and Sister Voyant before sitting down next to one another, Hank listening intently to Willie brag about his many girlfriends. Meanwhile, Sharon and Dancer arrived together. Before deciding on two chairs to sit in next to one another, Dancer gave the others a hug. After sitting, they began listening to Willie talk to Hank.

"That's right, Hank. My women buy me clothes, shoes, jewelry, cell phones…you name it," said Willie using his fingers to count off his list of things. This diamond stud you see in my ear…one of my ladies brought that too. And stud is very fitting…ha-ha…because that's what I am…a stud. The ladies take very good care of me. You see

Hank, the ladies gots to pay to play with Will-lay."

"Oh please," interjected Sharon with a sarcastic laugh. "You're nothing but a narcissistic womanizer."

"There you go again, hatin' on a brother," said Willie, turning to look at Sharon. "Well guess what Sharon? You would be taking care of me too if you had some of this!"

"Some of what?!" Sharon inquired.

"Some of this!" replied Willie gyrating his hips as if he were having sex.

"Negro please!" said Sharon. "You must have bumped your head!"

"Not mines," said Willie with a sly smile. "But I've sure bumped a lot of women's heads…against headboards that is!" he laughed, high-fiving Hank.

"That was a good one!" yelped Hank, joining Willie in laughter.

"You are one nasty man!" said Sharon. "Sex is always on your mind!"

"What else is there to think about?" asked Willie.

"That's enough!" said Sister Jackson. "Hush up and stop all that X-Rated talk Willie!"

James walked in toting his Bible, taking a seat. As the group awaited the meeting's start, they talked amongst themselves, James, Dancer, and Sharon seated to the left of Sister Voyant and Sister Jackson, and Willie and Hank seated to their right. But one empty chair remained, signaling someone was missing.

"It's 9:45," said Sister Jackson looking at her wristwatch. "Where is Miracle? The meeting will be starting in fifteen minutes."

"Hopefully, she won't show up," commented Sharon. I am sure the meeting will be a lot more peaceful without her here!"

Ain't that the truth! Sister Jackson thought in her mind, but said, "Well, these meetings are mandatory, and she needs to be here. If she doesn't get here in the next five minutes, I'll have to send one of you to get her."

"Count me out!" said Sharon, leaning all the way back in her chair."

"Count me in!" said Dancer. "I'll get Miracle for you!"

"Why thank you Dancer!" smiled Sister Jackson. "Let's give it a few more minutes and –"

Blowing in like the wind now raging outside, Miracle stomped into the meeting.

"Hurricane Miracle has arrived," muttered Sharon.

"Miracle, baby, take off your coat and make yourself comfortable," suggested Sister Jackson.

"No!" barked Miracle, drawing stares and whispers from the other residents. "I don't want to take my coat off! And I can't get comfortable because I don't want to be here!"

"We leave attitudes at the door, Miracle," stated Sister Jackson. "Don't bring it in here. Now have a seat right over there!" she directed, pointing to the lone chair. Huffing and puffing, Miracle headed to the chair, grabbing, and sliding it at least six feet away from the group before sitting down.

James, Dancer, and Sharon were now seated to Sister Voyant's and Sister Jackson's left, and Hank, Willie, and Miracle were now seated to their right in that order – a seating order they all kept to for this meeting and all the meetings to come. Clearly, Miracle does not want to be in this meeting, thought Sister Jackson looking at Miracle. Truth be told, neither do I. How in the world am I going to help these people? I should never have agreed to do this! But there ain't no point in second-guessing myself now, she conversed silently glancing at her watch. "It's 10 of 10, and soon we will be starting this meeting.

Sister Voyant reached over and gave Sister Jackson's hand a reassuring squeeze. "It's going to be alright my Beloved," Sister Voyant softly whispered, sensing her nervousness. "You're going to do just fine."

"Thank you, Claire," said Sister Jackson, reaching for the assorted donut box and removing one. Biting into the sweet pastry, she began savoring its flavor, the delicious taste of sweet raspberry jelly filling her mouth and arousing her palate. Mmmmm…this is good…raspberry-jelly…delicious! Sister Jackson thought – momentarily staring at the donut before sinking her teeth into it again to relish another bite.

Willie sat looking at Sister Jackson noticing how much she was enjoying her donut.

"Hank," whispered Willie, tapping him on the shoulder. "Did you see Mama Jackson eating that donut? She was looking at it all dreamy-eyed like she was about to have sex with it!"

Speaking in an equally low tone, "Hank shook his head whispering, "Sharon's right, Willie. All you think about is sex."

"That may be true Hank," replied Willie. "But damn…Mama Jackson is already big as a house. And every time I turn around, she's gobbling down sweets. If I didn't know any better, I'd swear she was Aunt Jemima."

"Aunt Jemima?" inquired Hank. Who is Aunt Jemima?"

"Oh, I forgot, Hank. You're a rich White boy…born with a silver spoon in your mouth so you wouldn't know. Aunt Jemima is the fat, Black woman on the pancake box. Here, let me Goggle her picture," said Willie taking out his cell phone. "Then, you can see who I'm talking about."

"Gee Willie, you're right," said Hank looking at the image of Aunt Jemina on Willie's phone. "They do resemble. But Mama Jackson is a dead ringer for Mammy."

"Mammy?! What's up with you Hank man?" You racist or something?! Just because Mama Jackson is fat and Black, don't make her nobody's Mammy!"

"No Willie, of course I'm not racist! I'm talking about Mammy of Gone with The Wind."

"Man, I ain't never watched no 'Gone With the Wind'."

"Put a search in Google for Mammy of Gone with The Wind," directed Hank. "Then you can see the woman I'm talking about."

After typing the name in on his Goggle search bar, photos of actress 'Hattie McDaniels' popped up.

"That's her right there," said Hank pointing at one of them.

"Wow, you were right Hank!" said Willie staring at the photo. "She looks just like you know who!" he said nodding his head in Sister Jackson's direction.

"I told you."

"Instead of calling her Mama Jackson, maybe I should call her Mammy Jackson."

"I wouldn't do that if I were you," warned Hank with a laugh.

"It says here that Hattie McDaniels was the first black entertainer to win an Oscar for her role as Mammy."

"Righto," said Hank. "I know the movie well. My grandma Emma used to watch Gone With The Wind all the time. She loved Gone With The Wind. It was her favorite movie."

"Oh yeah?" asked Willie. "What's so special about it?"

Not receiving any response to his question, Willie again asked about the movie. Hank again failed to respond.

Noticing Hank now looked distant and immersed in deep thought, Willie tapped him on the shoulder, again asking what made 'Gone With The Wind' so special.

"Fuck!" Hank hissed under his breath.

"What's wrong Hank?" asked Willie.

"Thinking about my grandma and that movie just messed me up man," said Hank. "She used to call me her Hanky."

"Her Hanky?" asked Willie.

"Leave me alone Willie!" demanded Hank. "I don't want to talk about it."

Willie was puzzled, thinking, I can't believe how Hank's mood changed. Just a minute ago, he was happy-go-lucky like the Lucky Charms Cereal leprechaun. Now he's gone all Fruity Pebbles on me!' I remember him telling me he was bipolar, but geez!

Observing Hank starting to bite what was left of his fingernails, Willie told him, "Hank you might want to stop biting your nails. There ain't much left to chew on. You've already gnawed them down to the nubs."

"My grandma is a very sensitive subject for me, Willie," said Hank, continuing to bite his nails. I chew on my nails every time I think about her, so let's not talk about it anymore."

"Sure man," said Willie.

Clearing her throat, Mama Jackson announced, "It's now 10 a.m. and time to start our Serenity Meeting. Now put that phone away Willie!" she commanded, prompting Willie to quickly stick the cell phone back in his pocket.

"Welcome to our first Serenity Meeting my Beloveds," said Sister Voyant with open arms.

The meeting now underway, Willie continued wondering why Hank's family was such a sticky subject for his newfound friend.

James gazed at the words of The Serenity Prayer. Seconds ago, Sister Jackson handed out photocopies of the prayer to the group. Now Sister Voyant was explaining its purpose.

"We will open every Serenity Meeting by joining hands and saying the Serenity Prayer," said Sister Voyant. "We want each of you to commit this prayer to memory."

I do not want to seem ungrateful about being here, thought James. Lord knows I am thankful to be here at Serenity House! But I still cannot believe I am actually here…physically, mentally, and financially. Thank God I am well spiritually…that's the only thing that has kept me together. But I still find it hard to believe I am here. Me! A former defense attorney!

Sister Jackson and Sister Jackson continued talking about the prayer and other matters regarding the Serenity Meeting. But James was paying little attention to what they were saying, his mind wandering off in the past.

I never thought I would be in such a place! A lawyer with a successful law practice located in a skyscraper overlooking Baltimore City! A husband with a beautiful wife…my Pauline and our beloved daughter Tiffany…all living in a sprawling, million-dollar estate in Columbia, MD. Turning his neck to look at his surroundings, James silently groaned, The master bedroom of our house was larger than the entire first floor of this place! I had walk-in closets larger than this room! Pauline and I parked our luxury Mercedes Benzes in a four-car garage. The many amenities on our property included tennis and basketball courts, a workout room, sauna, and an Olympic-sized swimming pool for days when I opted not to drive to the Downtown Athletic Club. I had a membership with the Center Club and hobnobbed with the elite! I had everything and lost it all on account of a woman! Now look at me! This is incredulous! A man once regarded as one of the city's top attorneys whose company once included the likes of judges, counsel colleagues, politicians, and other influential and wealthy members of society sitting here with these weirdos! he lamented scratching his bald head and glancing at the others. Me of all people staying in a transitional home with a morbidly obese women who can't stop eating sweets or quote a scripture correctly to save her life! he silently shouted leaning forward to look at Sister Jackson and her table of snacks. And sitting in here with us is a highly intellectual blind lady who speaks with great magniloquence, but dresses like some kind of hippie! Now directing his attention to Willie and Hank, he introvertedly barked, And the cast of characters also includes that immature, idiotic playboy who has already pissed me off...and his sidekick...that crazy-looking White boy who acts like he is bipolar...paranoid schizophrenic, or both! And look at those two! he fussed internally, looking at Sharon and Dancer. That Sharon is a hot-headed Puerto Rican from New York who curses all the time, and that flighty girl Dancer wants to hug everybody! Then let me not forget that Miracle! he said frowning in her direction. She needs much prayer, walking around here dressed like an Eskimo with a persona that's as cold as the temperatures in Alaska! Unbelievable! All those years of law school! All that studying to pass the Bar Exam! All the sweat and tears I put into opening my very own law firm! Me, James L. Franklin, Esquire! Here with them all because I refused to –"

"James!" said Sister Jackson, ending James' silent lamentation.

"Yes, Mama Jackson?" he replied.

"You're so busy looking around, it doesn't seem like you're paying a bit of attention to a word we are saying," said Sister Jackson.

"Oh, but I am Mama Jackson," said James. "I am just meditating on what you both are telling us."

"Sure you are," said Sister Jackson sarcastically. "Did you read over the Serenity Prayer along with the others?"

"Certainly, I did," said James looking down at the photocopy of the prayer he held in his hand and speed-reading it.

"Now that you've all read over The Serenity Prayer," said Sister Jackson stressing the word 'all', while peering over at James, "Let's all join hands and recite the prayer together."

Sister Jackson noticed that everyone was holding the hand of the person next to them except for Miracle. She remained seated – turned away from the group with her arms crossed and a frown on her face. While Willie extended his arm in an attempt to join hands with Miracle, he held nothing more than air, for she refused to interlock their hands.

"Miracle, aren't you going to join us?" asked Sister Jackson.

"No!" shouted Miracle, drawing stares and whispers from the residents.

"I didn't want to hold your hand anyway!" exclaimed Willie.

"No you didn't just yell at me again!" said Sister Jackson. "Miracle, you had better –"

"Let her be," Sister Voyant leaned over and whispered to Sister Jackson. "Sometimes, what comes easy for us is difficult for others to do. We must be patient. Give her some time." Directing her attention back to the group, Sister Voyant said, "Let us begin."

Everyone except Miracle began 'The Serenity Prayer' stating:

The Serenity Prayer

God, grant me the Serenity
To accept the things I cannot change...
Courage to change the things I can,
And Wisdom to know the difference.
Living one day at a time,
Enjoying one moment at a time,
Accepting hardship as the pathway to peace.
Taking, as He did, this sinful world as it is,
Not as I would have it.
Trusting that He will make all things right
if I surrender to His will.
That I may be reasonably happy in this life,
And supremely happy with Him forever in the next.
Amen.

❀

By now, the residents had recited 'The Serenity Prayer' and were introducing themselves in the group setting at the behest of Sister Jackson. Sharon and James had already talked about themselves, with Hank, Willie, Dancer, and Miracle yet to come. Hank told them his name and that he was from Clarksburg, Virginia, afterward thinking, Keep your head in the meeting man. Stop thinking about what happened back in Clarksburg.

"I'll go next!" said Willie, standing and dusting off the shoulders of his suit jacket as if he were the coolest man alive. "The name's Willie Jones, Jr., but all you ladies can call me Will. Because I will sweep you off your feet!" he declared mimicking sweeping the floor.

"In your dreams!" jeered Sharon, looking Willie up and down and rolling her eyes.

"Sharon, you drink too much Hater-Aid!" said Willie.

Turning to look at Miracle, Sister Jackson urged her to go next. Miracle responded by mumbling her name inaudibly.

"What was that?,'" asked Sister Jackson, putting her hand up to her ear. "I couldn't make out what you said."

"You hard of hearing or something?!" Miracle yelled. "And why do I have to tell you all my name again anyway! You already know my name! Miracle! Miracle Smith!"

Man, that's one mean chic, Hank thought.

"Miracle, you are gonna have to watch that tone young lady!" chastised Sister Jackson. "Now, I know that being here might be an adjustment for you! But we have rules around here, and one of them is that we will respect one another at all times!"

"Whatever!," hissed Miracle sucking her teeth.

Meanwhile, Dancer was waltzing around wiping off furniture with an old rag.

"Dancer, you are quite the performer and cleaner," said Sister Jackson. "But right now, we are in the middle of a meeting…and we don't have much time. Have a seat and tell us a little bit about yourself."

"Yes ma'am, Mama Jackson!" said Dancer stutter-stepping back to her seat. "Sorry…but sometimes it's hard for me to sit still." Sitting down briefly, and then popping back up, Dancer said, "My name is Dancer…Dancer Hawkins. And I'm here at Serenity House because I'm a recovering addict." Hank could feel Willie nudge his side before whispering, "Hey Hank…instead of Dancer Hawkins, her name should be Dancer Huggins as much as she likes to hug!" prompting them both to laugh. "What's so funny over there?" asked Sister Jackson glaring at them both. "Oh nothing Mama Jackson," replied Willie trying to contain his laughter. "You two need to let us in on the joke so we can laugh too," said Sister Jackson. "It's nothing Mama Jackson," said Hank. "Willie is just over here acting silly again," he explained, prompting Willie to poke him on his side.

"Now, Dancer baby," said Sister Jackson, "We haven't gotten to why we are here, but I rebuke the label you have placed on yourself in the name of Jesus! The Bible says life and death are in the power of the lungs!" Rushing over to Sister Jackson with his Bible in hand, James said, "That's not what the scripture says, Mama Jackson. "I believe you meant…'Life and death are in the power of the tongue'...Proverbs 18 and 21." With a flabbergasted look, Sister Jackson asked, "Ain't that what I said?," to which James replied, "No ma'am." Sister Jackson then declared, "Well that's exactly what I meant." James walked back to his seat looking puzzled while Sister Jackson directed her attention back to Dancer, saying, "Now Dancer baby, you've got to speak healing over yourself. Now repeat after me…My name is Dancer Hawkins, and I have been delivered." Dancer stared at the group like a nervous performer suffering from stage fright looking out into an audience. "Go on my Beloved, you can do it," encouraged Sister Voyant. "Okay…I'll try," said Dancer. Closing her eyes and taking a deep breath, she exhaled, "My name is Dancer Hawkins and I have been delivered." Opening her eyes and looking at Sister Voyant and Sister Jackson, Dancer nervously twiddled her fingers awaiting their reaction.

Sister Jackson said elatedly "You did it, Dancer!"

"Splendid job, my Beloved!" added Sister Voyant.

"Yah!" said Dancer clapping her hands and smiling. Then she curtsied as if she had just finished a dance routine. After sitting down, Dancer tapped Sharon on the shoulder, crying out, "I did it!" Sharon replied, "Yeah, you did it…good for you Dancer."

Sister Voyant was now talking to the group, but once again, Hank felt Willie's elbow nudging his arm. "Hey Hank," Willie whispered, "Looks like they are supplying us with snacks for these meetings." Looking at the potato chips and other items sitting on the table situated between Sister Jackson and Sister Voyant, Hank whispered back, "Willie, I don't think those snacks are for us," to which Willie replied, "Well then, who are they for?" Hank surmised, "I believe they are all Mama Jackson's snacks." Snickering, Willie told Hank, "Listen man…I know Mama Jackson is greedy. But there's no way all those snacks are only for Mama Jackson. I mean look at that smorgasbord of snacks! There's chips, donuts, and cupcakes. I'm willing to bet they're for everyone. Watch…I'm going to walk over to the table and get a donut." Hank cautioned, "Dude, I wouldn't do that if I were you." Willie dismissed the warning, telling him, "Hank man, you worry too much. Watch this." Hank watched Willie casually stroll over to the table, prompting Sister Jackson who was speaking to the group, to stop talking. Hank and the others watched Willie open a donut box and remove a chocolate donut. After momentarily staring at him in disbelief, Sister Jackson slapped his hand so hard the donut fell out of Willie's hand, landing on the table. "Put it back!" she demanded. "Whatever you say, Mama Jackson," said Willie, his face reflecting both embarrassment and surprise. Quickly picking up and dropping the donut back inside the box, Willie said, "Sorry Mama Jackson. I thought these snacks were for everybody."

Pointing at Willie, Sharon laughed, "Now that was funny! "Well Wil-lay, it sure doesn't look like you're going to be helping yourself to Mama Jackson's goodies!" Hank and most of the others laughed, while Sister Jackson pointed Willie back to his seat like a kindergartner being reprimanded by their teacher. "Here's another rule!" declared Sister Jackson. "And my memory must have failed me…because I don't know how in the world, I forgot this one. It's my own personal, unwritten rule! And that is never, and I do mean never ever, touch anything on this table!" she told them looking down at the snacks. This is my table! Is that understood?" Nearly all the residents acknowledged what Sister Jackson told them by simply nodding their heads or saying something. Miracle, however, looked Sister Jackson Mama up and down, shook her head, and snickered. "Make no mistake about it," continued Sister Jackson, looking at the group before pointing at the items on the table. "These are my snacks! Now let's move on!"

Willie who had since sat down was now telling Hank, "I hate to see what Mama Jackson would have done had I actually ate the donut." Hank snickered, "I told you not to go over there, man." In a booming voice, Sister Jackson told Hank and Willie, "Hush up!" I hear you two talking over there! This is our meeting period, and we ain't got much time! Go on Claire." Hank could hear Sister Voyant resume her discussion with the group. However, he was not paying attention to anything she was saying, because his mind had left Baltimore and traveled back to Clarksburg. Grandma Emma loved baking, and all that talk about donuts and sweets has stirred up a batch of bad memories, thought Hank. First, it was talking about her favorite movie Gone With The Wind, and now this! Every time I try to file away what happened somewhere in the far back of my mind, here comes something or someone re-opening that folder! I know this is the first one, but I hope these meetings are not always a source of painful reminders…that scares me.

Sister Voyant was now talking to the group about how blessed they all were to be at Serenity House; her words prompting Dancer to drift off into daydreams about how happy she was being one of them. I've made so many friends here, thought Dancer. I like all of them…even Miracle…although she's angry all the time and refuses my hugs. But out of everybody, I like Sharon the most. I remember growing up wishing I had a big sister to play with…and to guard me from the bullies at school. Sharon is like the big sister I never had. I always hoped that my mom and dad would get back together and have more children…but they never did.

The only child of the church's recently retired mailman Rufus Hawkins and United in Victory church member

Dr. Lila Mae Hawkins, her mother packed up and left her father years ago, taking Dancer too. Dancer was a baby at the time, and after years of separation, her parents divorced. As a little girl she was curious as to why her parents were not together and asked both. Reflecting on such conversations sitting in this meeting, she recalled how different each of their stories was.

"Dad, why did you and Mom split up?" she asked one day sitting in the living room of their Gwynns Falls Parkway home.

"Well Dancer, after your Mama…that high-siddity Dr. Lila Mae Hawkins got all that education, she became too good for your Papa," explained her father. "She packed up her things, took you, and left me. They talk about White Flight, but there's a thing called Black Flight too…'cause she moved out of our home and ran out there to the county. As I see it, she felt our home in the city wasn't good enough for her anymore and neither was I. So, she moved out to Randallstown where her kind lived."

"Her kind?" Dancer asked.

"Yes, her kind," said her father, sticking his nose high up in the air. "In my book, they are snooty, educated Black folks who leave the city and move out to the county or far out to the suburbs because they feel they have arrived."

"Arrived?" she inquired.

"Meaning they have reached the mountaintop of success and look down on other folks," her father explained. "I hate talkin' about your mother, but I'm just tellin' the truth! Between that fancy title she had in the school system and earning that doc'rate degree," he told her referencing doctorate, "Lila Mae's head got so big it could no longer fit in this house. That's why she left."

Posing the same question to her mother one day sitting at the kitchen table of their Randallstown home, she asked, "Mom, why did you and Dad split up?"

Shaking her head, her mother responded, "Dancer, it was all your father's fault. You see, all he wanted was mediocrity! All I wanted was for him to do better for himself! To be the best! And that is where we bumped heads. Rufus never aspired to be anything beyond a mailman. And for your mother, that just was not good enough! Besides…that house was not big enough for me, him, you, and football!"

"Football?" questioned Dancer.

"Yes, football," her mother replied. 'That's all Rufus ever wanted to do…lay on his tush watching football! Football was his wife – not me. He gave more attention to the Colts when they were here than he ever gave me! Darling, who wants a marriage like that? Rufus left me with no alternative but to leave! Funny thing," snickered her mother, "He loved those Colts more than anything. But they left him, and so did I!"

I love both my parents, thought Dancer looking at Sister Voyant talking, but not listening to a word she was saying. They blame one another for the break-up of their marriage and can't seem to forgive one another. My Dad talks to his friends about some money my Mom owes him. I have no clue what that's all about. I just hope one day my Dad and Mom can come together and mend their differences…but they aren't even on speaking terms. I pray that changes one day. As I see it, they both are alone and could really use each other's companionship. They need one another. I love my parents soooooo much! Every time I think about what I put them through…it makes me sad! They did everything they could for me and look at how I treated them! C'mon Dancer stop thinking about that! she urged herself, quickly ending such thoughts and tuning her mind back to the meeting.

"Serenity Meetings are held here each week and are a time of healing and rrrrrrestoration," said Sister Voyant, rolling the 'r' in the word 'restoration.' "We won't pressure anyone. However, we are hopeful each of you will share your stories of addiction...to be transparent."

Marveling at Sister Voyant's manner of speaking, Dancer thought, I love listening to Sister Voyant speak! It's so regal! Regal... mused Dancer, "That's one of Mom's favorite words.

Biting into a cupcake Sister Jackson said, "Amen! That's right! We won't pressure anyone."

Mama Jackson sure likes sweets, thought Dancer, watching Sister Jackson gobble down the confection.

"Now, let me forewarn you my beloveds," cautioned Sister Voyant. "These meetings won't be easy. As a matter of fact, they're going to get downright ugly! Because this is where you meet you. Where you take off the mask!"

Pondering what Sister Voyant told them, Dancer thought, I wore masks as a child when I dressed up for Halloween. I could be whatever character I wanted. A beautiful princess...a mean witch...a goofy clown...a superhero. But the mask that Sister Voyant is talking about...I'm not sure what she's talking about. I had better ask. Raising her hand, Dancer said, "Sister Voyant, I have a question."

"Yes, my Beloved," responded Sister Voyant.

"What do you mean by 'take off the mask'?" Dancer asked.

"Well, my Beloved," replied Sister Voyant, "I'm not referring to a physical mask, but an emotional one. I'm referring to that pretend mask we sometimes hide behind to cover up the things inside of us that we don't want to face...or don't want others to see. And when those masks come off, those are trying moments indeed."

"Why?" pressed Dancer.

"Because during those moments, we may be revealing the very thing or things that have us bound up," explained Sister Voyant. "We are exposing things like our vulnerabilities...weaknesses...and past mistakes....and that my Beloved...is not an easy thing to do. But pouring out can be cleansing. It can even help us to unload the burdensome things we are carrying around that are keeping us shackled."

"My Lawd!" shouted Sister Jackson, throwing up both arms in praise-like fashion, while holding cookies in both hands.

"But freedom is available to you Dancer," continued Sister Voyant. "Freedom is available to all of you my Beloveds," she said opening her arms in welcoming fashion. "I can't see any of you...but I know you all are yearning to be free from the plantation of addiction! And if you face its evil Master head-on, calling on God to strengthen you where you are weak, He will give you the strength to break the chains and bits that have you shackled, help you escape to freedom, never turning or being taken back!"

Sharon sat in her seat reflecting on the things she just heard, silently saying to herself, Wow, that Sister Voyant is such a deep Sister! I am so impressed with her...and I am not easily impressed. She is full of wisdom and every word she says is so poetic and means something. Turning her attention to Sister Jackson who was nibbling on a cookie, Sharon inwardly said, Damn! Mama Jackson is always eating! Every time I turn around, she's stuffing something in her mouth! She reminds me of Ms. Pac-Man chomping on those pellets! surmised Sharon, referencing the classic arcade game. If Mama Jackson keeps it up, that food is going to get catch-up with her just like those ghosts trapping Ms. Pac-Man! Ber-bup-bup! her mind imitating the annihilating noise of the Miss Pac-Man character being overrun by one or more chasing ghosts before popping off the screen.

"Hallelujah!" rejoiced Sister Jackson. "Claire, what you just said was so moving! I tell you that was something powerful! You really gave everybody, including me something to chew on!"

She sure did, thought Sharon. But you're sitting over there chewing on cookies with your greedy self!

"Now I want you all to keep in mind that what's talked about in these meetings, stays in these meetings," said Sister Jackson. "And no matter how difficult these meetings might get, we must and will respect one another."

"We are going to laugh together… cry together…sing together…shout together… and celebrate together," added Sister Voyant prompting Willie to mimic childishly, but silently each of the actions she was describing – opening his mouth chortling; making a sad face and wiping his eyes; singing into his hand as if it were a mic; smiling gleefully from ear to ear; motioning his arms like he was running, and throwing up his arms in celebratory fashion. Hank sat next to him smiling, trying to contain his laughter.

To be so fine, that Willie is one immature, silly-ass man, thought Sharon watching his antics.

"Willie! Stop your foolishness!" bellowed Sister Jackson. "I see you over there!"

"My Beloveds, at times, it might seem like an emotional roller coaster ride," said Sister Voyant. "But we will work through our issues together! As we move towards total healing, rrrrrrestoration, and rrrrrreconciliation to God, family, friends, and self! Now at the completion of your three-month stay here at Serenity House, we will have our Graduation Ceremony. During that ceremony, we will have our 'Purging The Wound' session. That is when you can apologize to the person or persons you have hurt the most. And my Beloveds…it will probably be one of the hardest things you have done in your entire life."

"Apologize? Ha! That's a laugh!," seethed Miracle sucking her teeth and slouching down further in her chair, her arms folded.

Sharon did not like Miracle. She was disrespectful, mean, and always angry.

There she goes again! thought Sharon, eyeing Miracle. I'm old enough to be that little girl's Mama! I'm also old enough to know that what she needs is a good, old-fashioned ass whipping! Always walking around here like everybody in the world owes her something! Miracle hasn't had a positive thing to say about anything or anyone since we got here! Maybe she's been hurt or has trust issues or something. I know about that myself. I trusted Juicy, and look at where it got me! A 17-year love affair with Heron! Now Juicy is all cleaned up and looks at me as if I am a complete stranger! Every time I think about how I listened to Juicy and where it got me, makes me want to chew nails!

Miracle's mind was boiling over with frustration and resentment. I hate everything about Serenity House! she yelled in her mind. I hate all these people! she thought looking at the others. I hate my room! I hate being here in this meeting! All I want is for my three months in this prison to be over! No longer able to contain her emotions, Miracle jumped up from her chair and blurted, "Why did we have to come to Serenity House?! We just completed a residential a residential treatment drug program! We are all three months clean!"

Agreeing with what Miracle said in her outburst, Hank added, "She's right! Why are we here?!"

Sister Voyant calmly replied, "You all are here because you aren't ready my Beloveds."

"Not ready for what Sister Cleo?!" Hank asked jokingly while high-fiving Willie.

"Sister Cleo!" hooted Willie. "That's the phony television psychic that was on television years ago! Aw man, that was a good one Hank!"

Sister Cleo? wondered Miracle. "Who is that? It doesn't matter. All that matters is the day I get out of here! It won't come soon enough for me! I've been around a lot of men…and those two, she thought looking at Willie and Hank, have to be among the biggest goofballs I've ever met! Someone get me outta here!

"Hank," said Sister Voyant. "Let me give you my name again since you seem to have me confused with someone else. The name's Claire C. Voyant. That's Claire, spelled C-L-A-I-R-E. My middle initial is 'C'… and I see everything. And my last name is Voyant, spelled V-O-Y-A-N-T."

Nudging Willie, Hank proceeded to walk over to Sister Voyant. He stood in front of her chair shaking his head and smiling while waving his hands in front of her dark glasses.

"How can you help us?!" he inquired sarcastically. "You're blind! You can't even see!"

"The blind leading the blind," Willie chimed, slapping his own knee, amused by his comment.

"That's not funny Willie!" said Sharon.

"Go back to your seat Hank!" commanded Sister Jackson.

"Yes ma'am," said Hank obligingly. "Sorry."

Sister Voyant stood up from her chair and commenced to walking behind the chair of everyone, gently placing her hand on their shoulders as she moved along. Watching Sister Voyant make her way in her direction, Miracle thought, That Voyant lady is touching everyone! She even touched that fat Jackson lady even though she's not a resident! Well, one thing for sure…I don't want her to lay a single finger on me! That goes for any and everybody! I've been touched enough! Sister Voyant reached Willie and touched his shoulder. Willie closed his eyes and limply slid down in his seat to depict being 'Slain in the Spirit' before sharing a quiet laugh with Hank. Seeing Sister Voyant now heading towards her, Miracle hissed, "Don't come over here! I don't want anyone touching me!" Honoring what she said, Sister Voyant bypassed Miracle uttering a prayer and making her way to the front of the group.

"Ah,," purred Sister Voyant. "Hank, you and Willie joke and laugh about me being blind. But led by the Holy Spirit, I see everything. It is no mistake you are here. The purpose of Serenity House is to arm you…each of you…with the spiritual tools you will need to defeat the spirit of addiction. The spirit of addiction may be lying dormant…silent right now…but it's still lurking…," she said bringing up one arm. "And the first opportunity it gets…that thing is going to strike!" she thundered, bringing down her arm like a hammer striking a nail. "Tell me, what defense will you have Hank? You need God to help you beat this thing. And we're going to teach you how to fight this spiritual battle and gain the victory in the name of Jesus!"

"Amen to that!" agreed Sister Jackson. "Addiction has stolen so much. Weeks, months, years, and for some of us, decades of time. Now, we may not be able to reclaim the time that is behind us, but we can do something to claim the time we have in front of us. ...now you all listen…we ain't got much time, so let's use this time wisely."

Jumping up from his seat, Hank said, "Look! I just want to get on with my life! I don't know about them!" he added, looking around at all the residents. "But I do know that I am not going to relapse. I am done with using. It has caused me enough problems!

"Have a seat, man!" said Willie pulling Hank back down into his seat.

"What's up with you dude?!" Hank fired back. "You should be mad about being here too!"

"Why should I be mad and mess up my rent-free arrangement?" smirked Willie, nestling back in the chair and crossing his legs. "I got it made in the shade being here. Why should I complain?"

"Who cares about Serenity House being rent-free you Moocher?!" snarled Sharon. "You want everything to be about you, Willie! But this isn't just about you! It's about every one of us beating our addictions once and for all! Now shut the hell up!"

"Watch it Sharon!" cautioned Sister Jackson.

"There you go again Sharon," chuckled Willie shaking his head. "Can't we all just get along?" he added in the vernacular of Rodney King, a Black man beaten by officers with the Los Angeles Police Department (LAPD) in 1991.

"Man, why don't you grow up with your immature ass!" balked Sharon, prompting Willie to begin arguing with her and Sister Jackson intervening. Their kafuffle was cut short by the front door flying open and Pastor Just and Social Worker, Anthony Jenkins bursting into the room.

"Is everything alright?!" asked Pastor Just looking at the group.

"We could hear shouting coming from here all the way outside," added Mr. Jenkins.

"What's going on in here?" inquired Pastor Just.

"Minor disagreements, that's all," explained Sister Jackson. "Nothing that we can't handle."

Pastor Just and Mr. Jenkins momentarily glanced at one another before walking towards them and greeting everyone. Miracle's eyes were fixated on Mr. Jenkins, inwardly boiling like a pot turned up high at his very sight.

I hate Mr. Jenkins' guts for sending me to Serenity House! Miracle silently screamed. I hate every bone in his body! I hate everyone here! Beginning with Sister Jackson and ending with James, Miracle began her loathing perspective, while glancing at each person she was describing in her thoughts. I don't want to be here with a fat lady who eats more cookies than Cookie Monster, and more donuts than Homer Simpson! A strange blind lady who dresses like a Gypsy or some sort of Fortune Teller! A wannabe Playboy who thinks he's the answer but he's not! A psycho-looking White guy who looks like he might go off on the deep end any minute! A big-mouthed New York lady who always has something smart to say! A dingbat who wants to hug all the time! And a deep-voiced man who's old enough to be my grandfather! I need to get out of here! Miracle surmised continuing to peer out of the corners of her eyes at Mr. Jenkins.

CHAPTER FOURTEEN

TRIED AND TESTED

Wednesday, October 10, 2018
A few minutes later

Sister Jackson was shifting her body in the metal folding chair. The only thing more uncomfortable than this meeting is this itty- bitty chair, she thought whilst twisting and turning. I've been trying to situate myself in this chair since we started this meeting, and I ain't got comfortable yet! Directing her attention to Mr. Jenkins who was dressed in a blue suit, shirt and tie, and crisp shiny, black patent leather shoes, Sister Jackson thought, What a clean-cut young man! Noticing the worn duffle bag he was carrying, she surmised, To be so nicely dressed, that sure is a raggedy bag he is carrying. But he looks very fit…like he works out in the gym. Maybe that's his gym bag. Hearing Miracle loudly sucking her teeth, Sister Jackson looked over at her thinking, That Miracle Smith needs her hineparts spanked. Her parents must not have taught her any manners!

Meanwhile, Dancer rushed over to Pastor Just and began hugging him, exclaiming. "Thank you so much Pastor Just for letting me come to Serenity House! It's so wonderful here!"

"Yeah right!" muttered Miracle.

"You're welcome, Dancer," said Pastor Just, looking flustered and uncomfortable with her clinging onto him. "But I can't take the credit. God made it happen."

Smiling, Dancer loosened Pastor Just, held her arms upwards, and tightly closed them, explaining, "God is everywhere! I can hug Him too."

"What a sweet way of expressing your gratefulness to the Lord," replied Pastor Just. "And Dancer, you are right. God is omnipresent."

"Hey there Unk," waved Wille. "I appreciate being here too. This is a real nice, rent-free, set-up."

Pastor Just set his keys down on the table, casually walked over to Willie, and firmly began squeezing his shoulder, causing him to grimace and slide down in his chair.

"That's Uncle Just, Willie…not Unk," said Pastor Just. "Now Nephew, I hope you are behaving yourself, and taking full advantage of Serenity House. There's more to being here than just free room and board."

"Oh, he's taking full advantage of it alright!" blurted Sharon laughing sarcastically.

"I've had about enough of you woman!" said Willie. "Mind your business!"

Abruptly stopping her laugh, Sharon replied with a stern look, "It's hard to mind my business with you telling all your business about your mooching off women and bragging about it!"

Snickering at their exchange, Pastor Just patted Mr. Jenkins on the shoulder. Pastor Just snickered at Willie and Sharon's exchange before patting Mr. Jenkins on the shoulder and walking closer towards Sister Jackson and Sister Voyant, the younger man following closely behind him. "Sister Jackson and Sister Voyant, do you remember the group's caseworker, Anthony Jenkins?"

Mr. Jenkins looked vaguely familiar to Sister Jackson, but before she could open her mouth to speak, Willie stood and began loudly clearing his throat.

"Corrrrrrection!" said Willie, rolling the 'r's' off his tongue.

"Willie, I do believe you are mocking me!" exclaimed Sister Voyant, turning in his direction.

"Mr. Jenkins is their caseworker!" said Willie pointing at the other residents. "Not mines! Big Willie don't need no caseworker!"

"Corrrrrrection!" said Sharon, also rolling the 'r's' off her tongue.

Turning in her direction, Sister Voyant remarked in sing-song fashion, "Sharon, I do believe you are mocking me too!"

Walking over to Willie, Sharon ridiculed, "That would be Little Willie!" gesturing her thumb and forefingers to imply he had a small penis. "Because in your case Little Willie, you are a worker of women! But not up in here! You hear me?! Not…up…in…here!"

"Little Willie, huh?" he asked. "Well Sharon,

"Well, you got it all wrong Shorty!" said Willie referencing Sharon's height, standing, and looking down into her face. "Because everything…and I do mean everything about me is tall! So why don't you climb up on this tree and find out for yourself!"

"Stop all that filthy talk!" chided Sister Jackson. "Both of you have a seat!"

"That's right!" tag-teamed Pastor Just. "Willie and Sharon, this is not the place for sexual innuendos!"

Sharon sharply turned to walk away from Willie, flinging her long hair in his face, a portion of her ponytail smacking him in the mouth. Overdramatizing, Willie began rapidly smacking his lips and pulling strands of hair from his mouth as if he had eaten something distasteful. Sharon began marching off, Willie stretching his long arm atop her head like he was plucking fruit from a tree. Bringing his hand up to his mouth, he began chewing and making a sound with his tongue and teeth to indicate he was cleaning remnants of food from between his teeth.

Watching Sharon walk back to her seat, Sister Jackson thought, Every time I turn around, Sharon and Willie are coming for one another! I have to scold those two like they are children! But I must admit…Willie may have met his match in Sharon. He is so accustomed to having his way with women...and she ain't having it! Sharon is surely time enough for him!

"Sorry for interrupting the meeting," said Mr. Jenkins. "Miracle, you left your duffle bag in my car when I brought you here. But you can really use another bag because the zipper on this bag is broken and some of the contents spilled out onto the floor of my car. But I picked up everything and put them back inside."

Snatching the bag out of Mr. Jenkins' hand she snapped, "Don't worry about the zipper on my bag! I've been looking everywhere for this! You should have brought it to me days ago Mr. Jenkins! Everything had better be in here!"

Sister Jackson along with the others watched Miracle drop down to her knees, and turn the bag upside down, dumping its contents onto the floor. frantically sifting through the items.

"Where's my jewelry box?!" she screamed at Mr. Jenkins, frantically sifting through the items. "You stole my jewelry box!"

"I put everything I saw back in your bag Miracle."

"Well, it's not here Mr. Jenkins!"

"I will check my car again Miracle," sighed Mr. Jenkins. "If I find it, I will bring it back."

"You had better find it and bring it back!" Miracle demanded. "You have no idea how much that jewelry box means to me!"

"Miracle, I have no clue why you would think I would steal something from you," said Mr. Jenkins.

"Because everybody steals from me, Mr. Jenkins!"

"Everybody is a strong word," he replied. "But I am here to help you Miracle...not hurt you...that's why you are here. But I can see you really treasure your jewelry box and if I find it, I will bring it back to you. I promise."

"Uggggghhhhhhhhhhhh!" growled Miracle. "Why am I here Mr. Jenkins?!"

"Miracle, when Anthony brought the stack of applications to my office, yours was the first Sister Voyant pulled from the pile," interjected Pastor Just.

"Well, she shouldn't have done me any favors!" hollered Miracle. "I don't want to be here!"

"My Beloved, this is the place that God wants you to be at this time," said Sister Voyant. "You can fight God all you want...but you can't beat Him."

"Amen to that," said Pastor Just. "Miracle, this may be hard for you to understand right now...but you should be grateful. You are among the inaugural residents of Serenity House...and our maximum intake was only six. And you were one of the chosen six."

"Chosen by God — all of you," added Sister Voyant.

"Miracle, you have no idea how fortunate you are to have gotten into Serenity House," Mr. Jenkins told her. "There's a long waiting list of people in need of transitional housing who want to come here. I'm sure any one of those folks would love to trade places with you right now."

"I'll happily trade places with them!" Miracle shouted. "Besides, if you hadn't brought me here, I would still have my jewelry box!"

"I had better get going," said Mr. Jenkins glancing at his watch. "I have an appointment with a client at my office. Everyone enjoy the rest of your day. Again, my apologies for interrupting your meeting."

"Hey, Mr. Jenkins!" Miracle yelled watching him turning to walk away. "Make sure you bring back my jewelry box!"

"Have a good day Miracle," replied Mr. Jenkins. "And please behave yourself."

"I'll see you out Anthony," said Pastor Just, the two proceeding together to the front door, and he pulling the door shut behind them.

"Thief!" Miracle snarled Miracle, sneering at the door. "Mr. Jenkins has my jewelry box! I fuckin' know it!"

"Oooh! Oooh! Oooh!" yelled Willie throwing up his arms as if he were a pupil about to squeal on a fellow student. "Miracle broke a rule, Sister Jackson!"

"It looks like someone needs a hug!" chimed Dancer, heading towards Miracle.

"Don't touch me Twinkle Toes!" said Miracle. "Stay the hell away from me!"

"I'll take the hug you were going to give her," suggested Willie.

"No, you won't!" Sharon told Willie, adding, "You'll probably try to get your jollies off with your sex-crazed self! Come on over here Dancer, I'll give you a hug." The two hugged, Sharon stretching her neck to peer over Dancer and asking, "Miracle! What the hell is your problem?! All the girl is trying to do is give your trifling ass a hug!"

"Sharon and Miracle stop all that cussing!" fussed Sister Jackson.

"I'm about to wash your mouths out with soap like the old folks used to do years ago! My grandmother and mother both did it to me, and it sure made me watch what I said growing up!"

Getting up from her chair and stomping over to Sister Jackson, Miracle yelled in her face, "Try it Fat-so! I ain't your daughter! And you sure as hell ain't my Mama!" screaming with such force Sister Jackson felt sprinklings of spit wetting her face.

Standing up from her chair and drawing back her hand, Sister Jackson seethed, "Why you little –" stopping short of calling Miracle a name while being egged on by Hank, Willie, and Sharon, who were shouting, "Slap her! Slap her! Slap her!"

"I can't look!" quivered Dancer covering her eyes.

"No, my Beloved!" shouted Sister Voyant.

"Don't let that rascal take you there, Mama Jackson," urged James. "Remember self-control…one of the fruits of the Spirit."

Listening to the advice being hurled at her from both sides, Sister Jackson thought, Sister Voyant and James are right! I can't allow this disrespectful young woman to cause me to act out of anger! I nearly called her a Bitch! Me! Of all people! I hate the fact that she called me Fat-so! I hate it! But even at that…I can't stoop down to her level…especially with all these people looking at me. I'm supposed to lead by example.

"You got that hand up…now slap her, Mama Jackson!" yelled Sharon. Giving in to the temptation of hitting Miracle, Sister Jackson slapped her.

✿

The group sat looking at Sister Jackson and Miracle in utter disbelief; most of them not believing what they were seeing and hearing. Sister Jackson had slapped Miracle not with her hand, but a song, reaching and looking upwards while belting out:

Precious Lord, Take my hand

Lead me on, let me stand

I am tired, I'm weak, I am worn

Through the storm, through the night

Lead me on to the light

Take my ha-and, precious Lord

Lead me home

Written by the Rev. Thomas Dorsey, the preacher penned 'Precious Lord, Take My Hand' in the 1930s after his wife and son died during childbirth. Turning to the piano in his grief, Rev. Dorsey wrote the famous Hymn, which Sister Jackson always found to be a source of inspiration and hope amidst turbulent times. It was also through this song she met Deacon Jackson. After hearing her performance of the song at a concert in 2010, he approached her, and the two eventually married. Perhaps the most well-known version of the song was sung by Mahalia Jackson. Sister Jackson was not the late gospel singer, but the group all sat looking at her starstruck.

❧

Walking back to her seat, Miracle broke the silence of the awe-filled moment, taunting, "That's what I thought! I wish you would have hit me! They would have been picking your fat butt up off the floor! That's if they could pick you up!" she snickered. Despite Miracle's curtness, it did little to change the temperament Sister Jackson's singing brought to the room.

"You could have taken my hand!" said Willie. "But Mama Jackson, you sure got a set of pies on you!"

"I would have slapped that spoiled brat!" added Sharon. "But Willie's right! You sure can sing Mama Jackson!"

"Mama Jackson!" exclaimed James, "I didn't know you could sing like that! Your name might be Mama Jackson, but my God...you sure sound like Mahalia Jackson. I haven't heard anyone sing like that in years! Hallelujah! You took me back to church on that one!"

"Mr. James is right! Wow wee! Mama Jackson, you sing like Jennifer Hudson!" said Dancer likening her to the former American Idol contestant, singer, and actress. "Bravo! Encore! Encore!" cried Dancer standing and clapping.

"Hearing you sing made me feel better," said Hank. "And I was feeling pretty lousy."

"My, my, my, that was breathtaking my Beloved," said Sister Voyant. "So calming...so reassuring...so uplifting. Indeed, that was music to my soul!"

"Why thank you, everyone...I am flattered and humbled," replied Sister Jackson, while thinking, Lawd am I grateful for passing that test with Miracle! I nearly failed it! But by not losing my composure, I believe God allowed me to encourage the residents. Lord thank you! I nearly slipped, but You gave me the strength to bite my tongue and hold on!

❧

Sister Jackson's short rendition of 'Precious Lord, Take My Hand' kept the residents talking for the last several minutes – James sharing how much he loved to sing in his church and Dancer chatting on and on about her ballet performances.

Sister Jackson was listening, and then she wasn't – her mind still entangled in not only escaping the snare of Miracle's words but also questioning if she would be up to the task of coping with such moments if they were to come up again. I figured these meetings would be difficult, she thought. That mean child, Miracle, didn't prove me wrong…and nearly took me to an ugly place! I can tell she's going to be an ongoing thorn in my side! How can I get through three more months of these meetings? I'm gonna talk to Pastor Just about finding another House Mother. I just don't think I can do this.

Sister Voyant began calling her name, ceasing Sister Jackson's doubtful thoughts.

"Yes, Claire?" she answered.

"Audrey, my Beloved, can you give everyone here a pen and a sheet of paper?"

"Sure I can Claire," she answered, while silently thinking, Oh Lawd! I gots to get up out of this seat after finally finding a halfway decent seating position. But I guess it's just as well…my butt hurts from sitting on that hard chair.

Sister Jackson retrieved paper and pens, Dancer assisting her with distributing the items to the group. The two distributed the items, Miracle exhaling loudly while snatching them out of Sister Jackson's hands.

I was going to conduct this exercise later, but I think it's important to do it now. Many of you have heard the old saying about sticks and stones breaking bones and words not hurting. Now I don't know who came up with that saying, but whoever it was didn't have a clue what they were talking about. Words can hurt…they are a powerful thing. And when we shoot mean, degrading words out of the bows of our mouths, they are like arrows…piercing the hearts of those we aim them towards. Words can hurt people's feelings. Words can start wars. Words can cause people to lose their lives. Words can cause people to give up. Words can start long-lasting feuds. Words can make a person who is already feeling bad, feel worse. Words can kill a person's confidence. Words can cause a person to give up. Words can tear down a person's self-esteem. Words –"

"And words can trick us into sinning…like the serpent did to Eve in the Garden of Eden," interjected James.

"That's right," said Sister Voyant. "Words can lead us to do things we know we shouldn't do. Overall, I believe everyone gets the big picture…when used in a degrading, cunning, way…words…a small five-letter word…can cause great harm. But on the contrary, my Beloveds, while words can speak death into someone, they can also speak life! Words can encourage. Words can stop wars. Words can save lives. Words can stop feuds. Words can make a person feel better. Words can instill confidence. Words can cause people not to give up. Words can build a person's self-esteem. So, my Beloveds…remember, there is great power in words. Be careful how you use them. Now, for our Exercise. I want everyone here to write down the word 'sword' in all-caps. After momentarily pausing to give them time to write down the word, Sister Voyant continued, "Now move the 's' from the end and place it on the front. Now, what does that word spell?"

"Sword!" exclaimed Dancer.

"That's right Dancer, my Beloved," said Sister Voyant. "James, come up here with your Bible and stand here next to me." Getting up from his chair, James replied, "Yes, Sister Voyant," and walked up next to her. "James, hold up your Bible," she told him, James proceeding to hold it up high. "The Bible that James is holding up is our sword!" she declared. "When people try to kill your spirit by tearing you down with their words, use your sword! Why? Some of you may ask…well I'll tell you. God has given us all the weaponry we need to fight back, and it's in His Word!"

"Amen!" said James. "How poignant!"

"Hallelujah! Thank the Lord for His Word!" said Sister Jackson. "The way you put that Sister Voyant…was mighty special."

"Thank you," said Sister Voyant, "And James you can go back to your seat now."

James headed back to his seat, while Sister Jackson glanced at her wristwatch, realizing she needed to check the time. "Oooh, it's a little after 11 o'clock," she said. "This concludes our first meeting. We've run a few minutes over our one-hour meeting time. I will see you all in the kitchen at noon for lunch."

The group began dispersing, Miracle leaving out first in a huff, followed by the others – Willie and Hank snickering behind her. Sister Voyant remained, walking over and sitting next to Sister Jackson, taking ahold of her hand.

"Audrey, my Beloved, are you alright?" asked Sister Voyant.

"I'm okay," said Sister Jackson reaching for the snack table and unwrapping a Little Debbie chocolate cupcake. "I knew these meetings would not be easy, but I –."   Sister Jackson was interrupted by Pastor Just, who returned, stating, "I came back to get my keys. I mistakenly left them sitting over here on the table," he told them, the keys jingling when he picked them up.

"Excuse me, Claire," Sister Jackson whispered to Sister Voyant. "But, I really need to talk to Pastor Just," she said, wanting to seize the opportunity to talk with him privately.

"I understand my Beloved," said Sister Voyant, giving Sister Jackson's hand a reassuring squeeze. "I know some mean things were said to you in today's meeting by Miracle Smith…and I know those things hurt. But do not let her words dissuade you, my Beloved. Rather, let them persuade you to stand firmly on God's Word."

"Thank you, Claire," replied Sister Jackson, softly squeezing Sister Voyant's hand. "I really appreciate what you just said."

"You are welcome, my Beloved. I just say what I believe God is telling me to say," she told Sister Jackson before leaving the room. Sister Jackson centered her attention on Pastor Just who was preparing to leave, saying, "Just one minute, Pastor. I'd like to have a word with you before you go."

Watching Sister Jackson walking in his direction, Pastor Just replied, "Why of course Sister Jackson. Taking notice of the rest of a cupcake she was popping in her mouth, he thought to himself, Sister Jackson is a glutton. Roy used to tell me how he would stay on her about eating a lot of sweets. That was highly concerning to him. Apparently, she didn't listen. But I am going to keep praying for her. I know she's been through a lot.

"That young man that walked in with you…Mr. Jenkins," said Sister Jackson. "He's quite impressive."

"Yes, and I am very proud of Anthony," said Pastor Just. "During the time Jacqueline and I were doing foster care, Anthony stayed with us. But after deciding to devote my time to full-time ministry, time just would not allow me to continue being a foster parent. But I sure loved it."

"After we stopped doing foster care, Jacqueline and I lost contact with many of the children, including Anthony," said Pastor Just. "By the time Anthony and I reconnected, he was a grown man. I'm so blessed to see he did so well for himself. Anthony's a licensed clinical social worker, earned his bachelor's and master's degrees in Social Work, and is now working on his Doctorate."

"That's wonderful Pastor," said Sister Jackson. "It doesn't take rocket science to see that you are very proud of him. And working on a Doctorate too! That's a big degree and one I've heard you talk about earning yourself. You are such an intelligent man Pastor…what stopped you from getting it?"

After earning his undergraduate and graduate degrees from Howard University, Pastor Just enrolled in Loyola College to earn a Ph.D. in Theology. Sister

Jackson's question caught him by surprise, causing him not only to reflect on his educational credentials but his past marital problems. *Jacqueline is the reason I had to step out,* he thought. *I had to put a lot of things on hold running behind her, trying to make sure she was not laid up in a shooting gallery dead somewhere. What a trying time that was! Jacqueline's addiction nearly cost us our marriage! However, I cannot divulge any of this to Sister Jackson…Jacqueline is very guarded about her prior drug use.*

"Yoo-Hoo!" said Sister Jackson, waving her hand in front of his face. "Earth to Pastor!"

"Oh sorry Sister Jackson," said Pastor Just. "My mind went someplace else. You were saying?"

"Never mind that Pastor," said Sister Jackson. "These residents…what a challenging bunch…none of them seem to really want to be here with the exception of your nephew Willie."

"Willie's not fooling me," chuckled Pastor Just. "I know he's here to mooch off the program. Always looking for a free ride…that's Willie. But I believe this program can really help him. He's my oldest sister Mae's son."

"Mae?" inquired Sister Jackson. "The one that —"

"Yes, her."

Glancing down at her watch, Sister Jackson said, "Pastor, there is something I need to discuss with you, but I need to run in the kitchen to start preparing lunch. Do you mind waiting just a few minutes? I promise I won't keep you long."

"Alright," replied Pastor Just, now taking out his cell phone and glancing at the time. "It's 11:15, and I have to get back to my Study to finish working on my sermon for Sunday. I can't stay much longer."

"Okay," Sister Jackson told him. "I'll be back in five minutes."

After watching Sister Jackson rush off to the kitchen, Pastor Just sat down and began scrolling through the pictures on his cell phone; their conversation prompting him to search for the photo of his late sister Mae Jones.

Pastor Just sat gazing at his sister's picture thinking, *My big sister Mae…I miss you so much. There's not a day that goes by that I don't think about what happened. You didn't deserve to die the way you did…and to be honest…I still find myself struggling with my thoughts about Willie. Helping him to get his life on track is what I know you would have wanted…and I know it's the right thing to do. But honestly, I still find it hard to look him in the eye after what he did.*

Mae Jones was married to Willie Jones, Sr., and had one child – his nephew, Willie Jones, Jr. You would have had two children…maybe even more…had it not been for what happened back in '89. Even after all these years, I still have a hard time accepting it. Up until her death, his sister Mae lived in Raleigh North Caroline with Willie, Sr. who had also passed away. For years, you suffered terrible physical abuse at the hands of Willie, Sr. I wish I had known what was going on, but you kept that abuse hidden from the family. We had no clue…with you being all the way in North Carolina…and you never complained. We didn't find out about the severity of the beatings until after you died at nine months pregnant.

After the death of his parents when he was 13-years-old, Willie went to live with his mother's sister Rose Harvey and her husband, Dan Harvey, whom Pastor Just referred to as 'Aunt Rose' and 'Uncle Harvey.' The couple resided in Baton Rouge, Louisiana, his aunt owning a daycare center, and his uncle working as a mechanic.

Aunt Rose and Uncle Dan never had any children, but they raised Willie as their own, recalled Pastor Just, reflecting on his aunt's successful court petition to adopt Willie. After Mae and Willie, Sr. died, Aunt Rose felt it was best to get him out of Raleigh…to give him a fresh, new start after his traumatic experience. Uncle Dan was a quiet man…Lord rest his soul…but he sure talked a lot about Willie being spoiled…And Uncle Dan was right. Pastor Just began reflecting on some of the things his uncle told him when he visited their home in Baton Rouge. He recalled one such conversation taking place in his uncle's garage while working on the engine of an old Ford Galaxie.

"Your Aunt Rose ain't doing nuthin' but spoilin' that boy," said Uncle Dan, his head buried under the car's hood. "Rose won't even let Willie Jr. wash a dish. I tried teaching him how to work on cars. But Rose said that was too much for Willie, Jr. Pass me that wrench over there, Al," he directed, pointing to the tool, and Pastor Just retrieving and handing it to him. "Your Aunt Rose presses that boy's clothes, brushes his hair, cooks for him. You name it…she does it. You see these hands? he asked, raising them. "My nails and hands are full of grease and grime from working on cars…doing what I love to do while making an honest living. Hell, Willie is 17 now… and don't know a doggone thing about what it means to work because Rose won't let him do a thing for himself. He doesn't even know how to fix a bowl of corn flakes. Al, get in the car. I want to see if it turns over," he said referring to the car starting.

"Sure Uncle Dan," said Pastor Just climbing in the Ford.

"Now turn it," instructed Uncle Dan, gesturing his hand in a twisting motion signaling him to start the ignition.

Pastor Just turned the key, and the engine roared immediately. "She wouldn't start at first," said Uncle Dan referring to the Ford Galaxie. "But she's cranking now! Just listen to that engine! You see Al, everybody who lives in these parts brings their cars to me because I'm the best mechanic around here. I know what I'm doing. I've worked on cars since I was a boy…my father taught me. That's why I was trying to teach Willie, Jr. It's best to teach kids things while they're young. But all your aunt wants to do is baby him. I told her I smelled Corn Liquor on his breath too. That ain't good either. Rose don't want to believe me...but I know what I smelled. I've made enough of it myself. I tell you, Al, I don't know what that lazy lout is going to do when Rose and I go Home to be with the Lord. He's going to be in trouble, 'cause he ain't gonna be able to survive out in this world on his own."

By the time Willie was twenty-five, both his aunt and uncle had passed away. He inherited a little over $27,000 from a life insurance policy his aunt kept up, along with their house and other possessions. Willie went through all that money and lost the house because of careless living, recalled Pastor Just.

Drinking…gambling…and women…a surefire way to blow through money. And after he lost everything, he used the only things he had left…good looks and charm…to manipulate and take advantage of women. All of them believing everything he said…all of them falling for his deception…all of them taking care of him. I remember him calling and bragging to me about such things. I told him to settle down with one good woman. 'Me, settle down with one woman?! I can't do that Unk! All of them are good to me!' I also warned him materialistic things were temporary and that usury was not of God. I encouraged him to go to school…take up a trade…do something. But he preferred living off a woman. Now he's 42, and it looks like his womanizing ways have run its course. The lady woman he stayed with put him out in the street. With no place to go, he called me, recollected Pastor Just. I circumvented the normal applicant process and got him in. He came here from Baton Rouge with only the clothes on his back…staying with me and Jacqueline until Serenity House opened.

"I've dried out," Willie told Pastor Just. "No more drinking for me. I've given up gambling and living off women too.

While Pastor Just had not seen any indications that Willie was still consuming alcohol and gambling, he suspected his nephew came to the city still carrying one of his old habits – using women.

I see Willie dressing up in those expensive clothes and shoes, thought Pastor Just, images of his nephew's high-end suits and accessories coming to mind. I saw him in a pair of Gators one day and in Gucci loafers the next! He even has a new iPhone. Still up to his old tricks when it comes to using women. I've told him numerous times there's a reason behind the saying, 'Love hath no fury like a woman scorned.' But he doesn't believe me… and one day it's really going to catch up with him. Based on his activity at our home, he's running the same game here in Baltimore that he ran back in Baton Rouge! And those phone calls Sister Jackson told me he's always getting confirms it. Looking at the time on his cell phone he wondered, That reminds me…where is Sister Jackson? It's 11:35! Now turning his eyes towards the kitchen, he thought, I've been sitting here waiting for her close to 20 minutes. I'm pretty sure she wants to bellyache and complain about her new job! However, she will need to speak with me at another time. No sooner Pastor Just stood up to leave, Sister Jackson pushed through the kitchen door, taking off her oven mitts while rushing towards him. Oh Lord, thought Pastor Just, sitting back down. I sat here daydreaming all that time and didn't get up to leave soon enough, he concluded, watching Sister Jackson situate herself in the chair next to him.

After apologizing to Pastor Just for her lengthy stay in the kitchen – attributing it to trying to locate some of her cooking ingredients – and he believing it was due to Sister Jackson cooking and eating – based on the grease around her mouth, she spent the last several minutes recalling the difficulties of the day's meeting.

"Pastor, I just don't believe I'm cut out for this job," she told him grabbing a handful of potato chips. "These people are really hurting, and I'm not sure if I can help them. I've got my own issues I'm dealing with, and this job is a lot on me. I don't think I can handle it on top of everything else."

For the next five or so minutes – between annoying crunches, Pastor Just listened to Sister Jackson run down a plethora of reasons as to why she was not fit for the job. They included the death of her husband, and how her ankles swelled from time to time.

"I know you miss Roy, and I do too," said Pastor Just. "But we must remember he's in a better place now. And as far as your ankles, perhaps it's too much salt."

"Oh no!" exclaimed Sister Jackson with a mouth full of chips. "That's definitely not it! I ain't got high blood pressure or nothing! My ankles are probably swelling from too much standing."

Looking at her swollen ankles, Pastor Just replied, "Hmmm...okay Sister Jackson," while privately thinking, She ain't fooling nobody but herself.

"And Pastor," continued Sister Jackson, "As I see it, Claire is far more qualified than me. She has way more education. She has a Bachelor's degree...two Master's degrees...and was working on a Ph.D. As for me, all I got is a G.E.D. and I ain't too long ago got that."

"And Sister Jackson, you worked hard to earn that G.E.D.," said Pastor Just.

"Lawd knows I did Pastor! And during a very difficult time in life at that."

"Indeed it was, but you persevered."

"Pastor not only is Claire far more educated, but she has far more work experience. You don't need me because she could run this program all by herself. She is a Social Worker, Counselor, and who knows what else. I just don't think I have what it takes to do this job. I don't believe I bring enough to the table."

Pastor Just replied, "Sister Jackson by man's standards, Sister Voyant does have more educational degrees and work experience. However, God has a different standard. A standard that He uses to elevate us like no man can. God can qualify a person who never went to college."

"Amen Pastor...He can do anything."

"That's right Sister Jackson. Just look at what God did in Roy's life. And there are examples all throughout the Bible of ordinary people the Lord used to do extraordinary things. Moses had a stuttering problem. And not only that...but he killed an Egyptian. But God used Moses to lead the Israelites out of bondage, and through him, communicated 'The Ten Commandments.'"

"That's true Pastor."

"David was a young, meek teenager who kept watch over sheep. But God used him to slay a giant by the name of Goliath. David also became King of Israel."

"True Pastor."

"Rehab was considered a harlot, which is a prostitute by today's standards. However, God used Rehab to assist two spies sent by Joshua to Jericho. Through her assistance, she not only helped them but saved herself and her family.

"That's remarkable."

"That's right. And in our modern world, just take Michael Jordan. Had he walked away from basketball after not making his high school varsity basketball team, he never would have won six NBA championships."

"That's true Pastor...he wouldn't have given himself a chance."

"That's right Sister Jackson! And just look at Oprah Winfrey. I've read that she was molested as a child –"

"Oh Lawd, that's such a terrible word! I hate hearing it!"

"I know Sister Jackson...I know. But think about it. Had Oprah allowed molestation to mold her future, she probably would not have become a Black billionaire and one of the biggest celebrities of all times."

"That's right Pastor! And I love me some Oprah! I remember when she was right here in Baltimore on 'People Are Talking' with Richard Scher with his curly-headed self!"

"I remember that show too," laughed Pastor Just. "And Sister Jackson, there's also Barack Obama. Had he dwelled on the fact that no Black had ever served as President of the United States of America, perhaps he never would have not become the first to do so."

"I never thought about that Pastor, but you're right! And that Michelle Obama always looks so good!"

"That's right…and you know something Sister Jackson…she reminds me so much of my mother Amanda. I don't want to get off talking about that because my mother disappeared when I was just a lad…and that haunts me. But I just remember her being tall, slim, attractive, and stylish!"

"I have heard so much about her," said Sister Jackson. "But by the time I came to United in Victory, she had already…well…had been missing for years. I hope one day you will get some closure."

"And so do I…not only for my sake…but my father's sake. I do believe the truth will one day surface," his voice trailing off. "Oh!" he stated, the volume of his voice picking back up, "Here's another example I want to share with you – Tyler Perry. I've read that his first-ever production 'I Know I've Been Changed', flopped. Now had he walked away from writing –"

"Maybe there would have never been a Madea!" shouted Sister Jackson. "And I love me some Madea! And here's another one Pastor. That tall, good-looking Judge Greg Mathis. When I had a lot of time on my hands, I would do a lot of reading. And I read a story about how he overcame a troubled past as a youth growing up in Chicago to become a famous television judge. Judge Greg Mathis is my number one show! I'm a huge fan! Not only because of his show but because of his story. It's so inspiring to me!"

"He's another great example, Sister Jackson. Now, I have to get going, but I wanted to take the time to share these things with you. Always keep in mind that God has a wondrous, strategic way of placing people in our lives at the appointed time to get us to the place where He wants us to go. Perhaps your being here is part of God's divine assignment for you. You see, God has a miraculously strange way of doing things that supersedes man's thoughts and ways of how something ought to be done. Who knows? God in His infinite wisdom could be preparing you for something much bigger than you or I could ever imagine."

"That sounds very exciting," said Sister Jackson with a smile. I guess sometimes the Devil sets our minds on all that went wrong, is going wrong, and could go wrong in our lives. It's easy to forget what God fixed, is fixing, and can fix."

"Amen," said Pastor Just. "I couldn't have said it any better. And Sister Jackson… I know what you've been through. You have what it takes to do this job. Do not give up prematurely! In doing so, whatever it is that God has planned for you may not come to pass if you quit! Think about all the people we talked about."

"Pastor, today's meeting was tough…very tough. But I gave you my word that I would do this, and I am a woman of my word. I have to admit…I was ready to walk away from this job. But thanks to your pep talk, I'm not gonna quit. I'm staying on as House Mother."

"Amen Daughter of Zion!" responded Pastor Just. "Roy believed you could do it, and so do I."

"Thank you, Pastor. I miss my Roy so much. He always had more confidence in me than I had in myself. He accepted me and loved me despite…well, you know the story."

"Yes, Sister Jackson. I know the story. And I also know the story of how Christ died on the cross for our sins…for we all have messed up. And The Bible tells us in Second Corinthians 5:17 'Therefore if any man be in Christ, he is a new creature: old things are passed away; behold, all things are become new.'"

"Amen Pastor," said Sister Jackson. "And despite my faults, God has taken good care of me…and He saw fit to bless me with a man like Roy. Grinning, she added, "Listening to you quote that Scripture just now reminded me of how Roy would churn them off his lips word for word. That man could quote Scriptures like the back of his hand. He got on me something terrible when I messed one up."

"Roy was a Bible Scholar in his own right," said Pastor Just.

"Indeed, Roy was a Bible Scholar. He would always tell me, 'Audrey, The Bible wasn't written for you to tear up Scriptures,'" she said deepening her voice to sound like Deacon Jackson. "'So if you're gonna reference them, say them right.'"

"That was Roy," Pastor Just chuckled. "He was a stickler for God's Word."

"Now, I might miss a word or two here and there," said Sister Jackson. "But I know my Scriptures. Ain't that right pastor?"

"Some of us are really gifted in the area of quoting Scripture, and others…well…are more gifted in other areas," replied Pastor Just, treading carefully – not wanting to lie, while gingerly stating the truth. "Lord knows you are a fine singer! Right up there with Shirley Caesar!"

"Why thank you Pastor!" exclaimed Sister Jackson.

"Well, that settles it, Sister Jackson. Now if there's anything I can do to make things a little easier around here, please don't hesitate to let me know."

"There is one thing Pastor. Could you please look into getting me another chair to sit in? There is no way I will be able to sit in one of these itty-bitty folding chairs during these meetings," said Sister Jackson looking down at the one she was sitting in. "They are just too uncomfortable…even with this extra padding I have in the back," she chuckled, glancing around at her hindside.

"Why of course I will get you another chair," promised Pastor Just. "Consider it done."

"That's wonderful," said Sister Jackson glancing down at her watch. "Ooh! It's almost noon…I have to hurry back in the kitchen…I've got food cooking on the burners."

"Yes, I need to be moving along too," said Pastor Just, standing and beginning to make his way to the front door. Abruptly stopping, he chuckled, turning to tell Sister Jackson, "Oh, and one more thing just came to mind."

"What is it Pastor?" asked Sister Jackson.

"Well, Roy once told me that Serenity House would be a place where miracles would happen," he said. "And one miracle has already happened."

"It has?" she responded with a perplexed look.

"That's right," said Pastor Just. "Miracle Smith! Although I don't think she's the type of miracle Roy had in mind," Pastor Just mused, he and Sister Jackson sharing a hearty laugh. "But we're going to keep the faith!"

"That's right, Pastor," Sister Jackson replied. "Because faith without works is in the head!"

Cringing inside, Pastor Just replied, "Sister Jackson, I believe you meant, faith without works is dead."

"Ain't that what I said?" she asked.

"No, Sister Jackson…it wasn't."

"Well, that's exactly what I meant. And Pastor…"

"Yes, Sister Jackson?" replied Pastor Just, while thinking, Please don't tell me she's going to try to quote another Scripture!

"Whatever it is that God has in store…well…I guess we'll just have to wait and see. Huh, Pastor?"

"That's right Sister Jackson," replied Pastor Just, looking upwards. "Because only God knows what's in His Divine Plan."

CHAPTER FIFTEEN

PRIDE AND LIGHT-SKINNED PRIVILEGED

Friday, October 12, 2018
Morning

On this brisk fall day, Dr. Lila Mae S. Hawkins stood in the living room of her modest Randallstown, Maryland home staring at her cell phone.

"My dear Dancer has called and invited me to Serenity House's Commencement Ceremony. Magnificent! I am going to place this date on my calendar right now," she stated to herself, retrieving her calendar book, and writing down the February 8, 2019, graduation event. "Dancer is sticking with this program, and I am so incredibly proud! When we spoke, she insisted I pick up eight purple, personalized teddy bears…purple wrapping paper… bows…and tags. She insisted I drop those things over to her well before the Christmas holiday. Let me jot down a reminder to do that too."

Dr. Hawkins placed her cell phone back on its charger, sat her calendar on a table, and proceeded to the sofa. She sat down, kicked off her mink Marabou pink slippers, and steeped the teabag in her mug before setting it down on an end table. Picking up the remote control to the television, she stated, "A Golden Girls' marathon is coming on today. I just love that show!" Flipping through the channels, she heard 'The Golden Girls' theme song 'Thank You For Being A Friend' playing and laid down the remote next to her. "Oh goody…an episode is coming on now. I plan to sit here relaxing while I watch episode after episode," she said, picking up her fine pearl-colored, bone China teacup and saucer. Raising it up to her mouth, she took a deep breath, inhaling and savoring the Chamomile aroma of hot tea vapors. "Ahhhhhh," she said exhaling before taking short sips from the cup. "That's good, but I'd better let this tea cool down some," she said. "It's piping hot."

Dr. Hawkins was always a huge fan of 'The Golden Girls' – watching the television sitcom since its inception back in the mid-1980s. At that time, she was about 33 and worked as an administrator in the Baltimore City Public School System. She enjoyed watching widows 'Blanche' and 'Rose', live under one roof with 'Dorothy', who was divorced, and her wisecracking mother 'Sophia'. The lives of the four women gave Dr. Hawkins insight into both the joys and challenges of being a mature woman – namely a single older woman.

Those four have always kept me in stitches, thought Dr. Hawkins. Thirty years later, and I am still laughing at this show. The only difference is now I am actually one of them. I am a 66-year-old divorcee. I am a Golden Girl. Sipping from her tea, she continued her train of thought, marveling at how the years flew by so quickly. I went through Childhood…followed by Young Adulthood…then I was a Middle-Aged Adult, and just like that…I am now a Senior. The stages of aging are like the seasons Summer, Spring, Fall, and Winter. Just a minute ago, I was in Summer, and just like that, the Winter season of my life has arrived. Grabbing onto the long white hair flowing down her shoulders, Dr. Hawkins looked at the bunch in a beholding manner, thinking, In the Summer stage of my life, my hair was coal black. People would ask, 'Do you dye your hair? It's so black.' Now, that I'm in the Winter stage of life, it's white as snow and people ask, 'Why don't you dye your hair? It's so white." But why dye it? Letting my hair take on its natural color makes me look refined and distinguished…like the woman I am.

After watching several episodes of 'The Golden Girls', Dr. Hawkins sat silently juxtaposing her life with those of its characters. Sitting here watching this show back-to-back, has me realizing I have more in common with Blanche, Rose, Dorothy, and Sophia than just being a mature, divorced woman, she thought. Like them, I find myself cautious…even apprehensive about certain things…like dating for example. I have not dated a man since Rufus. But The Golden Girls live together and have one another…to talk to…to confide in…to keep each other company. Contrarily, I live alone and really do not have those things. I used to watch this show all the time years ago…until I just could not find the time to watch it. But as a retiree, I now have some spare time… and now…looking at this show through a different lens, I not only see the beauty of friendship…but its importance. Yes, I do have many, many friends I suppose…but not any real close ones. I am talking about the type of friend you can trust your life with…the ones that by today's standards would be called a Best Friend Forever…or BFF. I do not have one of those.

She sat thinking about her Delta Sigma Theta Sorority sisters – many of whom she had known since her college days before starting her 40-year career in the Baltimore City Public School System. Me and my Sorors attend conferences, volunteer in the community, and host beautiful events, she thought. I get together with a few of them once a month to play 'Bridge' and 'Pinochle'. Some of them like Rose – she reflected, referring to former Frederick Douglass High School Principal Rose Backus-Hamm – graduated from Coppin with me and also worked for years in the school system.

Dr. Hawkins began her tenure in the school system as a teacher – serving in a multiplicity of other positions including Assistant Principal and Principal before retiring in 2013 at age 61 as an Assistant School Superintendent.

"I have many highly successful friends," she said, conversing with herself, whilst halfway listening to the show. "But in my own success, I never really wanted to get too close to people...or allow them to get too close to me. I seemed to have managed just fine not having close friends or a Best Friend. But oddly enough, I am quite bothered today by not having either one. The last and only best friend I ever had was my old Western High School classmate Kate Bowers-Tinsley. However, Kate and I lost contact with one another years ago after she and her husband moved away with their daughter. My goodness...I wonder how Jill is doing? Maybe one day, I'll learn how to put up a Facebook page and look her up."

Dr. Hawkins' high school days not only marked when she met her long, lost best friend, Kate Bowers-Tinsley, but it was when met her now ex-husband, Rufus Earl Hawkins.

❀

The voices coming from The Golden Girls show began fading from Dr. Hawkins' ears – her mind floating back to the year 1968. She was among a handful of Blacks who attended the then predominately White Western High School. The all-girls school had recently relocated from North Howard and Centre Streets to Falls Road where it still sits. Mr. Hawkins attended the all-black Frederick Douglass High School located on Gwynns Falls Parkway. She thought about what she told Dancer years ago when the inquisitive youngster asked, 'Mom, when and how did you and dad meet?'

Dr. Hawkins began by telling the then ten-year-old, "Well Dancer, your father and I met during the unforgettable 1960s. What a psychedelic time! Not just in terms of the wide color spectrum of clothing...but because so many things happened during that time that shaped our history. There was The Civil Rights Movement, The Vietnam War, hair and fashion trends, and groundbreaking music and TV shows. I can see it all just like it was yesterday...young men barely out of high school leaving the neighborhood to fight in Vietnam...some never coming back. There were the Freedom Riders and the Sit-Ins, Afros and Bell-Bottoms, and the early careers of singers like Stevie Wonder, The Beatles, The Supremes, Aretha Franklin, and James Brown. There were Lava Lamps and Hippies, Go-Go Boots, and Miniskirts...I wore those myself...and two of my favorite TV shows, 'I Spy' and 'I Dream of Jeannie'...the list goes on and on...so long ago...yet still so memorable. There was the assassination of President John F. Kennedy in 1963...I was 13 and attending Lemmel Junior High School at the time. Then in 1968 while I was attending Western came the assassination of Dr. King. The rioting and looting that followed led to my meeting your father," she explained to Dancer recalling the violence that erupted in Baltimore following the Thursday, April 4, 1968, assassination of Dr. Martin Luther King, Jr. in Memphis, Tennessee. "Mother and father warned me not to venture to certain areas of the city because it wasn't safe, recalled Dr. Hawkins referencing her parents Jessie and Madeline Cross. "But I didn't mind Mother and Father and was walking along Gay and Monument Streets on April 6, 1968, when looting broke out. People were running through the streets yelling and breaking the windows of retail stores with bricks and bottles. In my mind, I can still hear the smashing of glass and the ripping of protective iron gratings from storefronts. I had never seen anything like it, and I was petrified."

"Gee Mom," replied Dancer. "I bet that was really scary!"

"It was Dancer," Dr. Hawkins replied. "The next thing I knew, I could hear footsteps behind me...lots of them.

It sounded like a stampede. I turned around and saw a mob of young men wielding stones, bottles, and baseball bats heading in my direction. I didn't know what to do. I just stood there frozen like a deer in headlights."

"Wow!" said Dancer. "And then Dad came along like a Superhero and rescued you?!"

"Something like that," chuckled Dr. Hawkins. "That terrible mob knocked me down, and the next thing I knew, I was sprawled out on the sidewalk. I laid there crying…confused and dazed. I heard a friendly voice say, 'Hello Miss. Are you okay? C'mon. Let me help you up.' I looked up at the stranger while grabbing ahold of his outstretched hand. It was the hand of your father. He helped me up to my feet, offering to get me somewhere safe. I decided to chance it…knowing it was not wise to venture off somewhere with a stranger…but not knowing what else to do." Dreamy-eyed, she told Dancer, "Besides, I thought your father was cute standing there looking like Bill Cosby as 'Scotty' on I Spy…but with a touch of militance; nice build…a metal-teethed, black-fisted pick comb nestled in his hair, wearing a t-shirt which read 'Black Power!', jeans, and a short-waisted black leather jacket."

Observing her mother, Dancer told her, "Mom, you look so happy talking about the day you and Dad met. Your face lit up!"

"Nonsense!" replied Dr. Hawkins. "I was just adding a little bravado to the story! Anyway, your father took ahold of my hand, and he whisked me off. We hurried along the street… people rushing by us carrying furniture, televisions, clothing, and other goods they swiped during the looting. Fire was coming from buildings that had been set ablaze and billowing smoke filled the air. We retreated to the safety of 'Brown's Moving', a Black-owned furniture moving company. Your father knew the owners and they let us in. They were praying the looters wouldn't attack their store, and they didn't, thank God! It was inside the store that your father said, 'By the way, my name is Rufus. What's yours?' I told him, 'Lila Mae.' He replied, 'That's a mighty purdy name,' We stayed huddled inside the store until it was safe to venture outside…the company owners being kind enough to drive us home. Before parting ways, Rufus and I exchanged phone numbers. Needless to say, when I walked into the house that evening, my mother gave me a scolding. Back then, we did not have cell phones and she was worried sick about me. Father was out working at the time…he was an Arabber you know. And even with everything that was going on out in the streets with the looting and rioting, he was out there on that donkey-drawn cart of his, selling produce not only to make money…but to make sure his customers got the fruits and vegetables they needed. I told Mother what happened…and when Father arrived home…he gave me a terrible beating for my disobedience…telling me I could have been trampled to death. However, on a brighter note, your father called the following day…not only to check on me…but to ask me out on a date…and I accepted."

"That's so romantic Mom!" exclaimed Dancer.

"Your father and I both were 17 at the time. Back then, most parents did not let their children go out on a school night. So, Rufus picked me up the following Saturday afternoon…Father taking a break from work to meet him…parking his cart in front of our house. After Rufus arrived in his father's Chevy convertible, Father told him, 'Now son, you'd better treat my Lila Mae right, and you'd better have her home by 9 p.m.' laughed Dr. Hawkins. "On our first date, we went to a little Luncheonette…a Black-owned one…because in those days, most of the White-owned ones didn't want Blacks eating there. Your father called those, 'Lyncheonettes', noting a Black man might get lynched for eating at one of them. But such perilous danger didn't stop him from participating in sit-ins at such places."

"Dad is so brave!" said Dancer.

"He is," replied Dr. Hawkins. "But quite hard-headed too. That is why we aren't together now. That man just won't listen! I am working myself into a tizzy! Let me continue with the story. So, your father dropped two straws in a glass, and we shared a tall chocolate milkshake garnished with whipped crème and a cherry. Of course, he let me have the cherry. After we finished our shake, we did a little shaking of our own after he walked over to a Jukebox, pushed in a nickel and we began doing Chubby Checker's 'The Twist' while the song 'Let's Do The Twist' blared from the jukebox. Your father told me I was a great dancer and was really light on my feet. I explained to him I was a trained dancer. We had such a great time. That would be the first of many dates. We began dating or as we called it back then, we started 'going steady.'"

"What a wonderful story Mom," said Dancer. "But why were you and Dad down in that area where you met in the first place.

"I was about to get to that," said Dr. Hawkins. "I went against my parents' orders, leaving school and not going directly home. Instead, I ventured down to Gay and Monument Streets to buy a purse…using the money I saved up from my allowance. Your father, on the other hand, had gone to the area to loot, explaining he and the other young men he was with were expressing their anger and outrage over Dr. King's death. During one of our dates, he told me, 'After turning around and seeing you had been knocked down, I couldn't help but run back and help you up. You were the prettiest gal I had ever seen…I actually thought I was looking at Lena Horne.' I told Rufus, 'I get that a lot. My grandmother is a dead-ringer for Lena Horne.'

In reflecting on her conversation with Dancer, Dr. Hawkins' thoughts traveled to Bel Air, MD, the birthplace of her father Jessie Cross. Her maiden name was Lila Mae Sudie Cross, and she was the only child of her parents Jessie and Madeline Cross. Her father graduated from Central Consolidated High School in Bel Air, while her mother was born in Baltimore City and earned her high school diploma from Frederick Douglass High School. Her father's parents Jefferson and Lila Mae "Lily" Margaret Cross owned a farm on Vale Road on the outskirts of Bel Air, MD near the Hendon Hill Cemetery. Reflecting on these things, a picture album containing old snapshots of how her late paternal grandparents looked and their lives in Bel Air, formed in her mind.

My grandfather Jefferson Cross, stood about 5'9'' and had thick, coarse hair that he always kept neatly parted on the side. He was a bricklayer and was nicknamed, 'Midnight' because of his dark complexion. Grandfather was quite the character. He would always say, 'The blacker the berry, the sweeter the juice' when it came to his skin color. He also told me he built half of Bel Air…even helping to build the town's first courthouse. And he sure looked like it with those bulging biceps of his! One of his favorite pastimes was going to the Beer Garden on Bond Street in Bel Air. Grandfather enjoyed going there and always talked about its owner Hannah Moore…the town's first Black millionaire. 'White folks ain't the only ones who can become millionaires' he always said. Everyone hung out at The Beer Garden and on its parking lot…well except Grandmother Lily. She never went there. And then there was Ronnie's Barbershop on the corner of Alice Ann and Bond Streets! I still remember my Grandfather taking me there when I was a little girl. Ronnie's was a house fashioned into a Barber Shop and Beauty Parlor. Men got their hair cut on one side of the house and the women got their hair fried, died, and laid to the side on the other side of the house! Grandfather went there every week to get his haircut…Mr. Ronnie always precisely etching the part in Grandfather's hair. Most of the Black women in the area went there to get their hair done…but Grandmother Lily would not have been caught dead at Ronnie's Barbershop! Now Grandmother and my namesake…Lila Mae 'Lily' Margaret Cross was of mixed heritage…part Black and part White. Grandmother's name was Lila…but people called her Lily because she was lily White. She always kept her hair dyed blonde when she lived in Bel Air. I remember Grandmother Lily telling me how she passed for White…White by day and Black by night she called it. Grandfather grew up on Alice Ann Street and visited his side of the family often, but Grandmother rarely visited the relatives on her side for fear of being found out. I can still recall the stories Grandmother told me of how she shopped for groceries at Caucasian markets, and how she worked for years as a saleslady in a White-only women's retail clothing store until her employer found out she was a 'Negro'. Grandmother told me many of the White women pitched a terrible fit when they found out that a 'Nigger' had helped them try on clothes…and that it was rumored some of them got rid of the items they bought…considering them 'dirty' because she touched them. After it was discovered that Grandmother was of Black lineage, she and Grandfather fled the town in the early 1960s and moved to Baltimore after some Klansmen burned a cross in the front yard and set their farmhouse ablaze. She told me it was best that they left town anyway…not only for the family's safety…but because of some of the things that happened there. I remember Grandmother telling me there were more secrets buried back there than the bones in Hendon Hill Cemetery. I had no clue what she was talking about. Grandmother said she was never going back there, and she never did. Oddly enough after Grandmother left Bel Air, she kept her natural black hair color, never dying it blonde again. She said that is when everyone started telling her she looked like Lena Horne.

Dr. Hawkins' late grandparents had 15 children – a creation of offspring with varying skin colors, features, and grades of hair – traits passed down to their children and the generations that followed. Lila Mae's father Jessie inherited his father's dark skin and his mother's straight hair. I remember people telling Father he looked like a darker-skinned Cab Calloway, Dr. Hawkins recalled, referencing the famed 'Cotton Club' singer and Big Band leader. But of all the grandchildren, I favored Grandmother Lily the most. I remember my cousins telling me I thought I was better than they were because of my light skin. 'Grandma's Favorite!' they would yell as they pinched me! They were all very jealous. There was a great deal of friction between some of us growing up. Grandmother Lily often referred to me as her 'light-skinned', 'red-boned', 'pretty', or 'favorite' grandchild. Looking back…certainly, that would have angered my cousins! Grandmother also made sure she always gave me larger scoops of food, the better of her Christmas gifts, extra cookies, candies, and other treats. Such displays of favoritism strained the relationship between me and my cousins…some of whom I have not seen or spoken to in years. So much of the family was divided over skin color. I even remember overhearing Grandmother's sister Aunt Peggy telling someone she was a member of the 'Blue Vein Society', a group of Blacks who considered other members of the race as being 'lower-class' if their veins could not be seen beneath their skin. I wonder if Aunt Peggy still lives in Bel Air? My, my, my…Bel Air…a quaint town chock full of intriguing stories. I have not been there in years. Now that I am retired, I have a little more time on my hands. Maybe one day I will take a drive out to Bel Air and pay the town a visit. It would be interesting to see what Alice Ann, Archer, George, and Lee Streets are like now and if the people I so vividly remember…still live in Bel Air.

Dr. Hawkins glanced at the television. Another episode of 'The Golden Girls' was about to go off, but her thoughts were still on Bel Air. She thought about something else her grandmother told her years ago while sitting at a sewing machine mending her husband's trousers.

"Now Lila Mae darling, when you are old enough to start seeing young men, don't date anyone darker than a brown paper bag," Grandmother Lily said, her bony, blue-veined hands carefully gliding the pants under the needle of the sewing machine. "I know that's harsh honey, but I'm telling you the truth."

"But why Grandmother?" she asked. "After all, you married Grandfather, and he's jet black."

"He is," chuckled her grandmother. "Funny thing…as white as I am…I have always been attracted to dark men and fell madly in love with your grandfather. But dear, if you date and marry a light-skinned man…or are fortunate enough to nab a White one…although that's highly unlikely…and highly risky…and that's a whole 'nother story…you won't have to fret about having any dark children. Life is much harder for the darker-skinned of our race. You don't want to bring offspring in this world having to contend with such maladies…that is…if you can help it."

"I don't quite understand Grandmother."

"Think of it this way Lila Mae…when your grandfather and I go different places, we are treated differently because of our skin color. I am seated first, waited on first, greeted first, and served first with a smile. And that's within the Black race."

Lila Mae replied, "But I always thought that White people were the only ones that treated us differently because of skin color."

"That is not always the case," said Grandmother Lily. "I will tell you about something very daring your grandfather and I once did after we moved to Baltimore. We came here in the late 1960s, so this was around the mid-1970s. I convinced him to let me cover him in white make-up. We put on fancy clothes and went out for dinner…masquerading as a White couple. Of course, I could not do a thing to straighten that nappy hair of his…not even perm would lay it down enough… so he wore a hat. Before we left, I reminded Jefferson no matter what you do, remember not to take off your hat! When we arrived at the restaurant, we were immediately seated…despite the fact, there were Black people waiting who arrived before we did. We received impeccable service…the waiter giving us special attention. Our caper went off without a hitch until your father took off his hat to say Grace. The waiter stood at the table looking at this white-looking man with permed Black hair and a part showing a dark scalp! Jefferson paid the tab, we boxed up our food, and got out of that restaurant quicker than we left Bel Air! We still laugh about that!"

"But none of that seems fair Grandmother."

"It's not," said Grandmother Lillie. "But fair or unfair, believe me when I tell you…racism does exist…and within our own race 'Light-Skinned Privilege' is not fiction but fact. Colorism is a part of our everyday lives. Rest assured many in your own race will hate you for your complexion. I've been called every name from A to Z meaning everything from 'A House Nigger' to 'Mud' to 'Zebra Woman.'

Despite the things her grandmother told her, the future Lila Mae Hawkins would not be able to resist her handsome suitor, Rufus Hawkins. Rufus was a shade or two darker than a brown paper bag, thought Dr. Hawkins, her mind now circling back to the story she told Dancer about her and Rufus' courtship.

"Me and your father went out every chance we got," she shared with Dancer. "He used his father's car to drive us around when we went out on dates. We went to 'Carlin's Drive-In' to see movies like 'Godzilla' and 'Sinbad the Sailor' movies and fed each other popcorn and drank soda pop under the stars in his father's convertible. And he was always such a gentleman...opening the car door for me...pulling the chair out from under tables whenever we ate...and covering me with his jacket whenever I got chilly. He was such a gentleman. They say chivalry is not dead...but in your father's case...it is! I don't know what happened to him!"

"What do you mean by that Mom?" Dancer asked.

"Never mind that!" replied Dr. Hawkins. "I'm about to go off on a tangent again talking about that man! Anyway, my dear, your father and I dated throughout high school. We both graduated in 1969...he from Douglass...and I from Western. I guess I thought I was pretty hot stuff...Western High School has rigorous standards for getting in...and there were not that many of us Blacks there. Most of us who attended did extremely well...even better some of our White counterparts. I graduated in the top 10 percentile of my class. Your mother's one smart cookie Dancer!"

"And you still are!" said Dancer.

"That's right!' Dr. Hawkins grinned.

"And so is Daddy!" exclaimed Dancer.

"I don't know about that," replied Dr. Hawkins, the grin now gone from her face. "By the time your father and I graduated from high school, we were madly in love. Talk of marriage began to spring up in our conversations, and before long, your father proposed to me. We decided to find jobs and save up some money before setting a wedding date. Your father jumped on a hiring opportunity at the U.S. Post Office, and I was hired as a cashier at F.W. Woolworth's 5&10 at Reisterstown Road Plaza or 'The Plaza' as some call it. We eventually set our wedding date for Saturday, June 20, 1970."

Once again, Dr. Hawkins' thoughts deviated from her conversation with Dancer – her mind flashing back to objections Mr. Hawkins raised regarding their wedding.

Rufus argued against everything! she thought. He did not want to get married at United in Victory even though his parents and mines all attended the church. Once I insisted that we get married there, he went along with it, but stood firm on his position that we not use United in Victory's church house...the current site of Serenity House...for the wedding reception although we could use it free of charge. But the church house was not needed, as the church had a large enough banquet area downstairs. But I still could not understand his contrariness. Rufus also did not want Dr. Madison to play the organ at our wedding...although Dr. Madison's talents are impeccable. As a result, another musician played for our wedding. That particular musician did a good job...but paled in comparison to how Dr. Madison would have played The Wedding March! Rufus did not want this! Rufus did not want that! He complained about everything regarding our wedding! He always told me I was spoiled, but he was the one who acted like Bridezilla! His fits raised many an eyebrow! His bizarre behavior back then should have told me something! But I married that lout anyway! How foolish of me! But I was blinded by love.

§

By now, Dr. Hawkins had retrieved she and her ex-husband's wedding album, the hardcover book, and its clear plastic pages still preserving the photos taken of the two during their June 20, 1970, wedding ceremony. Flipping through the pages, she recalled how she pointed each of the pictures out to Dancer years ago, describing what was taking place when the photos were snapped.

"I always wanted to be a June bride, and there I am marrying your father on a beautiful June day," Dr. Hawkins told the inquisitive youngster. "Bishop Just officiated, and that's him giving us our wedding vows."

"He looked a lot younger back then," said Dancer.

"We all did," laughed Dr. Hawkins. "And that's your father and I posing near the church altar after the ceremony with the wedding party and your grandparents."

"Your dress was beautiful, Mom," replied Dancer. "Look at that long train!"

"Thank you, honey," said Dr. Hawkins. "My dress was tailor-made. And when you grow up and get married, it will be waiting for you along with the pearls and locket I am wearing in these photos, and other family heirlooms."

"Do you think I will marry the prince of my dreams like you did?" Dancer asked.

"Well Darling, my prince turned out to be a toad, but hopefully your prince will be a prince."

"Why Mom, Dad's not a toad!" exclaimed Dancer.

"To you, he's not," said Dr. Hawkins, "But I don't want to get into that. Pointing to another photograph, Dr. Hawkins told Dancer, "That's me and your father taking our First Dance at the wedding reception. We danced to The Dixie Cups' The Chapel of Love."

"I've never heard of that group or song," said Dancer.

"Of course not," said Dr. Hawkins. "You're too young." Pointing to another photo, Dr. Hawkins told her daughter, "That's me and Rufus in your grandfather's convertible about to drive off from the church. Back then, the words 'Just Married' were written in big bold letters on the windows of cars, and cans attached to string were hung from bumpers. I can still hear the sounds of those cans rattling against the street when we pulled off from the church."

"Mom, you and Dad really look happy," commented Dancer, gazing at the photo.

"We do," acknowledged Dr. Hawkins. "But as unfortunate as it might be, not all marriages have happy endings. In the case of me and your father, you can thank him for that! Had it not been for his stubbornness, perhaps we might still be together."

§

About an hour or so had passed, and Dr. Hawkins had since put away she and Rufus' wedding album. 'The Golden Girls' marathon was still playing, and she resumed sitting in front of the television. Back-to-back episodes featuring Dorothy's adulterous ex-husband 'Stan' had just gone off, prompting Dr. Hawkins to think out loud about married life with Rufus.

"Rufus did not run around on me, but he was…and still is…just as annoying to me as Stan is to Dorothy on this show," said Dr. Hawkins. "Rufus just could never get past the fact that I had more education than he did! Some men are threatened by strong-willed, success-driven women! I wish I had known that before I married him! To think that all I tried to do was push Rufus! To be the best! To shoot for more! To not settle for mediocrity! But he resented that! What a waste of so many good years of my life! Talking about I owe him money! He should be paying me for mental anguish! The nerve! And why am I sitting here talking to myself?! I'm just as bad as Rufus!"

Dr. Hawkins thought about how she and Rufus saved up enough money to move into their home on Gwynns Falls Parkway. The newlyweds' home was in close proximity to Coppin State College (now Coppin State University), the school the young bride set her sights on attending. She enrolled, and between Rufus' postal income and money her parents saved up for her 'college fund', Dr. Hawkins was able to leave her job at F.W. Woolworth's to focus on full-time studies at Coppin.

Continuing her stroll down Memory Lane, Dr. Hawkins began to recall college life at Coppin.

Coppin has since undergone a major expansion, she thought, thinking about her occasional drives past the school. Now the campus stretches along North Avenue, Warwick Avenue, and along Gwynns Falls Parkway and has several buildings and dormitories. But during my 'Coppin Days', the college had no dorms, she reflected, now walking to the den to grab her college yearbook from a bookcase shelf. The school consisted of just a few buildings. Returning to the living room and sitting on the couch, she glanced at a photo of Connor Hall, named after the school's first president Dr. Miles W. Connor. "Many of us students, along with the faculty and administrators walked from Connor Hall to Mondawmin Mall between classes or during breaks to buy lunch or shop," she said, now thinking out loud. "A little group of us always walked together…Vashtied Battle-Brown, Valerie 'Val' Fraling, Rose Hamm…who reigned as 'Miss Coppin' back then, Dr. Priscilla Smothers, and Koretha Cumberbatch. We shopped at Sears, Reed's Drug Store, G.C. Murphy 5&10, Lerner's, and other places in Mondawmin Mall. From time to time, we would buy lunch at a small, memorable eatery at Mondawmin called The Elevator Café. What fun we had! All those places are gone now, but I shall never forget them! I have such fond memories!" Flipping through more pages of the yearbook, Dr. Hawkins came across a photo of Dr. Calvin W. Burnett, who served as the President of Coppin from 1970 until 2003. "Look at this photo of Dr. Burnett! He was a young, brand new President when I started attending and remained there for 33 years. He was an excellent leader who enjoyed walking the campus, interacting with the students, and telling jokes. And here are photos of some of the faculty and administrators…Dr. Flossie M. Dedmond, Dr. Leroy Fitzgerald, and Dr. Luke Shaw. Oh my goodness, here is a photo of Dr. Leon Holsey, who taught Social Science. I will never forget him! He always dressed in colorful dashikis with matching hats…just like he is in this photo. He always encouraged us to embrace and celebrate our heritage. And my, my, my, here are photos of some of my other professors…Dr. Guilbert A. Daley, Dr. Peter Valletutti, Dr. Jerusa Wilson, Dr. Elias Taylor, Dr. Gilbert Ogonji, and Dr. Judith Willner. They, like so many of the school's administrators and faculty, demanded the best from their students, and every grade was hard-earned. That school was no cakewalk. No…no…no. From academics and articulation to dress and diction, to penmanship and professionalism, to zest and zeal, the school inculcated excellence into its entire student body. Flipping to another page, Dr. Hawkins said, "And just look at his photo of me, Rose and Val standing along Sorority Row on the campus dressed in our crimson and cream Delta Sigma Theta colors! I forgot all about this photo being in the yearbook! Oh my! We all looked forward to being a part of such a community-centered sisterhood! I remember the silly things we had to do to pledge!" she chuckled. "But we did what we were told to become members, and are still proud, active Sorors!"

❀

Another hour went by, and Dr. Hawkins had since placed her Coppin Yearbook back on the shelf. Another episode of 'The Golden Girls' was playing and included tensioned, but hilarious exchanges between 'Dorothy' and 'Stan.' Their banter prompted Dr. Hawkins' mind to revert to thoughts about her and her own ex-husband.

"Rufus and I were so happy at first," she thought out loud. "We even gave each other 'Pet Names.' I called him my 'Chocolate Superman', derived from his saving me from the hooligans who knocked me down on the sidewalk during the riots. And he called me 'Kitten' because he said I purred when I talked," she recalled, letting out a soft purr. "How romantic! And Rufus was so caring back then. He did not like me walking to school from our house, so he saved up enough money to buy an old Plymouth Valiant. Not only that, but he adjusted his workday so he could take me to school and pick me up. He also taught me how to drive in that car, and I passed the Driving Test and got my Driver's License. I was so proud and so was he! He began letting me drive the Valiant, while he caught the bus or rides to work until he saved up enough to buy a second car." Slapping herself on the wrist, Dr. Hawkins chastised herself saying, "Oh Lila Mae! Why are you sitting here talking to yourself about Rufus! Stop it!"

In May of 1973, Dr. Hawkins graduated from Coppin, earning a Bachelor's Degree in Early Childhood Education. Shortly thereafter, she was hired as a teacher in the Baltimore City Public School System. "We moved on up like 'George' and 'Weezie'," she laughed, referring to characters 'George and Louise Jefferson' from the TV sitcom 'The Jeffersons.' "Between the salary Rufus made at the Post Office and my own, I began shopping at more exclusive places like 'Pauline Brooks'. The boutique was located upstairs in Mondawmin Mall and was named after its pioneering Black owner, Pauline Brooks. That was the place to shop for chic, New York fashions! I would also patronize other upscale stores like Franklin Simon, Stewart's Department Store, Hutzler's Hamburgers, and Benton's Tweed Shop. Some of these stores were located at 'The Plaza,' and when I worked there, I could only 'window shop' at these stores. But after Rufus and I started making more money, I became a paying customer. Sometimes I would stroll into Woolworth's at 'The Plaza', just to buy something to show off the fact that I was no longer a cashier, but a customer. I took great satisfaction in doing that. The cashiers who still worked there always rolled their eyes at me."

Dr. Hawkins began recalling some of the places she dined during her shopping excursions or when she and Mr. Hawkins went out to eat. "I dined at Hot Shoppes Restaurant and at King's Court in Westview Mall. Most people probably don't remember this, but Westview Mall originally opened as an outdoor mall before being turned into an indoor shopping center. Sometimes, Rufus and I would eat together at King's Court, which cooked steaks to order on a sizzling grill. The cafeteria-style dining experience allowed us to personally select our own pre-prepared salad along with dessert…an array of puddings, Jell-O, cakes, and pies dolloped with whipped cream. We would place our selections on a tray, which we would slide down a metal bar leading to the cash register. Oh, and then there were our favorite steakhouses…Sizzler's, Ponderosa, and Rustler. Oh, how Rufus and I loved the smell and taste of their steaks cooking on a flaming grill! Things were going so well for Rufus and me…until our marriage began to unravel."

❀

Time continued to tick by. What began as a morning of drinking tea and binge-watching 'The Golden Girls' had become a day of reflection for Dr. Hawkins – spurred on by the lives of the show's characters.

"As a young woman, I never thought their storylines would one day become my own," sighed Dr. Hawkins gazing at the television screen. "I would have never thought Rufus and I would one day divorce. But we did."

Dr. Hawkins soon found herself coming up with things she felt contributed to the disintegration of her marriage. Things were going so well for me and Rufus, she thought. Albeit there was no denying the fact that Dance was something I enjoyed immensely…and I set it aside once we got married.

As a little girl, Dr. Hawkins learned the art form at The Zelma Cole Brown School of the Dance, a renowned Black-owned dance studio in the Grove Park area of Northwest Baltimore. Mrs. Brown or 'Mrs. Z', operated the studio from 1965-1977, as a Black female business owner in an era where there were few Black dance studios in the area. Mrs. Brown was among Frederick Douglass High School and Morgan State College (University) and New York University's many distinguished graduates. Mrs. Brown taught generations of young girls various forms of dance including Ballet (point), modern dance, interpretive dance, jazz, calypso dance, Latin dance (salsa), tap, and African Dance. Every year, I was so excited to put on my tutu and ballet tights to perform in Ms. Z's annual Dance recitals, thought Dr. Hawkins, recollections of her in the attire dancing through her mind. At a time when the Black culture was being shunned in a racially segregated society, Mrs. Z exposed me and other students to the rich tradition of Caribbean and African Dance and African American rhythms. Her instruction went beyond Dance, as she also taught us grace, poise, and instilled in us that we could strive to reach our goals, achieve, and become leaders. She encouraged us to take pride in our culture and ourselves. She also introduced us to 'Pilates' and emphasized the importance of strengthening and increasing muscle tone which would improve our confidence. 'Don't slouch and walk with your head up properly', Mrs. Z always told us. I never forgot her instruction, and still, sit and walk in such a manner till this very day. Noting my natural dancing ability, Mrs. Z encouraged me to pursue Dance. I wanted to take her advice and aimed for a Dance career…setting my sights on dancing in shows On Broadway. I also aspired to join the Alvin Ailey Dance Company. I saw the group perform live, and never forgot their moving piece, 'Revelations.' But alas! I was a young bride with a strong desire to earn additional college degrees, while Rufus was ready to have children. Somehow, Dance got lost in the shuffle. It took some convincing to persuade Rufus to wait for us to start a family. I convinced him…but it was not easy at toll. I told him I wanted to work on earning a Master's Degree. Truthfully, that was part of the reason. The other explanation was something I never shared with Rufus…and that was the fact that I did not want to mess up my girlish figure.

Years of dancing, watching her diet and exercising sculpted her body into a nice, curvy shape. During her undergraduate days at Coppin, she often heard the young mothers who attended the school talk about the difficulty of shedding baby fat after pregnancy. I was not ready to put blubber on my flat stomach, nor ruin my figure, Dr. Hawkins recalled. No, not at toll! Of course, this was something I could not tell Rufus. After telling him I wanted to put off motherhood to further my education, he was terribly upset! But in my own best interest…a Hawkins baby would have to wait. Rufus honored my decision…but he was not happy about it.

While her husband drove and walked Baltimore's neighborhoods delivering mail, she worked as a schoolteacher while aggressively furthering her education. In 1975, she earned a Master's Degree in Early Childhood Education from Coppin.

Again, Rufus pressed me to have our first child, thought Dr. Hawkins. And again, I asked him to wait…this time citing the fact that I wanted to earn my Doctorate. That was a half-truth, she conceded, touching her slightly-protruding stomach. Back then my stomach was flat as iron and just as solid…due mainly in part to those Pilates that Mrs. Z taught us to do…and which I still rigorously practiced. I wasn't quite ready to give up my hourglass figure. I was still the envy of most women. Letting out a deep sigh, Dr. Hawkins continued with her thoughts, recalling, Rufus stubbornly went along with my wishes. Consequently, he was even more upset about my desire to put off having a child to focus on earning my Doctorate than he was when I pursued my Master's. He put up such a fuss! We argued on several occasions about my going back to school to earn that Doctorate. That was the first time Rufus called me 'selfish'…but certainly not the last. The nerve of that imbecile calling me of all people selfish!

In 1979, she earned a doctorate from Morgan College (now Morgan State University) in Urban Educational Leadership. The then 28-year-old had reached her educational pinnacle. The girl who grew up poor in West Baltimore not only owned the distinction of being the first in her family to earn a college degree, but now she had earned a doctorate. The former Lila Mae Cross was now Dr. Lila Mae Hawkins.

Dr. Hawkins' parents Jessie and Jimmie Lee Cross had not gone beyond an eighth-grade education, forgoing school to work. The two along with young Lila Mae – their only child, lived on Appleton Street in Baltimore City. Mr. Cross, who was known as 'Fruit Man Jessie', was an 'A-rabber', peddling fruits and vegetables from a horse-drawn cart in neighborhoods throughout West Baltimore. Her mother Jimmie Lee worked as a housekeeper, cleaning the homes of affluent Jewish women living in Pikesville, Maryland. "I tell you," said Dr. Hawkins recalling her late parents, "Father and mother did not have much…but they sure made much of what they had. I am not sure what they were making in terms of salaries, but it could not have been very much. Despite what had to be meager incomes selling produce and cleaning, Father and Mother managed to become homeowners, owned a jalopy, and exposed me to various cultural experiences, which included paying for me to attend Mrs. Z's highly-acclaimed dance school. Attending Mrs. Z's studio further fueled my interest in etiquette and modeling, so my parents paid for me to attend Flair Studio operated by Willia Bland, which provided me with even greater knowledge about style, poise, and grace. How proud I was to have been taught by the legendary Willia Bland! I didn't think about it at the time, but I have come to realize that my parents had to have made tremendous sacrifices to afford me such opportunities. Not to mention we also ate good meals, which often included chicken, lamb, steak, and a variety of roasts with an accompaniment of fresh vegetables and fruits from Father's cart. Collectively, my parents tried to give me the spoils of life. I did not even know we were poor until I reached adolescence."

More minutes lapsed by, and morning had given way to afternoon. Episodes of 'The Golden Girls' were still airing, and Dr. Hawkins was still sitting on her sofa reflecting on her early years.

When I was a little girl, Mother would sit me between her legs on one of the lower front steps of our house and do my hair, recalled Dr. Hawkins. She would adorn my long black hair with colorful bows and ribbons. Mother hot-combed her own hair using the stove, but she never had to do that with me…because my hair was already straight. I can still recall the smell of hair grease sizzling in her head as she ran that hot comb through her hair. And Mother always kept me dressed in beautiful dresses, pristine white knee-hi's, and shiny, black patent leather shoes. As far as I was concerned, Lila Mae Cross was the best-dressed girl in elementary…Coppin Demonstration School #132 on North Mount Street. I felt the same way when I matriculated to Lemmel Junior High School on Dukeland Street. Dr. Anne Emery was the school's Assistant Principal at the time, and she often commented on my manner of dress and walk. That made me feel extra special! She was such a strict educator, who demanded nothing short of excellence from the school's students. When we saw her coming down Lemmel's hallways, everyone straightened their posture. Slouching was not an option when it came to Dr. Emery. Nor was backtalk or failing grades. She was such a stickler for high standards. I must admit that even now…as a woman in my late 60s, I still revert back to my days as a junior high school student when I run into Dr. Emery. That's how imposing her very presence was…and still is. She demanded respect and she got it.

When she was a little girl, Dr. Hawkins thought her parents were very well-off, and that her mother kept her so well-dressed because they could afford to do so. Nevertheless, she discovered otherwise after listening to her mother Jimmie Lee talking on the house phone to her Jewish employer. Dr. Hawkins began reflecting on what she overheard as a 14-year-old standing behind the stairwell banister of their home.

"Thank you for the dress, Mrs. Steinberg! I just took it out of the box!" said her mother, joyfully holding up a bright yellow chiffon dress adorned with yellow roses and lace. "It's exquisite! she declared, gripping the house phone between her chin and shoulder to hold the dress. "Lila Mae will love it! I can hardly wait to show it to her! I plan to let Lila Mae wear it to church on Easter along with those beautiful black patent leather shoes you gave me." After pausing to listen to Mrs. Steinberg talk on the other end of the phone, her mother said, "Mrs. Steinberg, you are such a kind, giving woman. I just want you to know how much I appreciate your generosity. All the dresses, shoes, purses, barrettes, and other things you have given that Isabella and Sarah no longer wore or outgrew, have helped me to keep Lila Mae so beautifully dressed all these years. Lord knows, my husband and I would have never been able to purchase such expensive things. Thank you, Mrs. Steinberg…I'll see you bright and early tomorrow morning."

Young Lila Mae stood grasping the banister in utter shock and disbelief. Her mother barely had a chance to hang up the phone before the youngster threw a temper tantrum.

"Mother!" she yelled, "You mean to tell me that all this time I have been wearing some other children's hand-me-downs?!"

"How dare you take that tone with me young lady?!' shouted her mother. "Standing up there on the steps being nosy and signafyin' while I'm talking on the phone! What I tell you about all that signafyin?!'

"Mother, the word is pronounced signifying and not signafyin'! But that's beside the point! I can't believe you've been dressing me in used clothing! And to think you have been putting things that were in another girls' hair in my head! Mother! How could you?! All this time, I thought all those things were new!"

"Child, I will slap you to Kingdom Come! How dare you correct my diction! I may not have gone all the way through school, but I know how to talk! I talk in a professional manner…watching my diction when I talk to Mrs. Steinberg, like this…'Why hello Mrs. Steinberg, isn't it a beautiful day," she said, enunciating every syllable. 'But when I'm home in my own house, I ain't got to talk that way!" she boomed. "Now listen here you ungrateful little girl, and you listen good! The reason you thought all the things Mrs. Steinberg has given to me were new, is because everything is in such good condition! You should be happy that Mrs. Steinberg is nice enough to give me such nice things for you to wear! If it weren't for her, there's no way you could dress so nicely! Your father and I can't afford to buy such expensive things…like the dress I have in my hand" – her mother started looking at the dress, "With the money we make! We work hard, but we are still poor Black folks!"

"What!?" exclaimed young Lila Mae. "You and Father work all the time and you two are still poor?" she shouted, placing special on the word poor. "Well, I don't like being poor! And when I grow up, I will never accept clothes or other silly donations from someone for my little girl to look nice! Who wants to wear hand-me-downs?! Besides, Grandmother Lily tells me I'm her lightest grandchild…and the prettiest! That makes me better than everyone else! I should never be dressed in hand-me-downs!'

"What!?" exclaimed young Lila Mae. "You and Father work all the time and you two are still poor?" she shouted, placing special on the word poor. "Well, I don't like being poor! And when I grow up, I will never accept clothes or other silly donations from someone for my little girl to look nice! Who wants to wear hand-me-downs?! I am light and I am pretty! That makes me better than everyone else!"

"What!?" roared her mother, tossing the dress to the couch. "Who told you that!"

"Grandmother Lily," replied young Lila Mae. "She also tells me I'm her favorite grandchild because I look just like her, and that being light with pretty hair makes me privileged. Therefore, Mother, you should never ever dress me in hand-me-downs!"

Before young Lila Mae could blink, her mother rushed over to the stairwell and slapped her so hard across the face, the youngster thought she would pass out. Pulling the crying youngster by the arm down the steps to the living room landing, her mother told her, "If you think that was bad, wait until your father hears about your disrespectful behavior young lady!" she cried in a cracking voice, fighting to hold back tears. "The nerve…thinking you are better than everyone else because of your light skin and straight hair! I shall speak to your grandmother…filling your head with that garbage! Mother-in-law or not, I'm gonna give that devilish woman a piece of my mind! As for you young lady, that big mouth and nasty, vain attitude of yours is going to get you in a lot of trouble one day! Mark my words! Vanity and ungratefulness will only bring you disappointment, heartache, and pain! Now go to your room!"

Young Lila Mae's face still stinging from her mother's slap, she tearfully stormed to her bedroom, slamming the door shut. Bawling in her pillow, she cried herself to sleep, hoping her father would be too tired to beat her when he arrived home. However, he roused young Lila Mae from her sleep with the lashes of his belt and gave her a terrible beating. About two weeks after the skin-weltering whipping, her father sat her down for a talk.

"Lila Mae, your mother and I get out here and work long hours so that you ain't got to struggle like we struggle," he said. "Both of us had to drop out of school to work. Your momma scrubs toilets, iron clothes, cooks, and everything else for those rich Jewish folks to make a living. I hustle up and down these streets with my cart in all kinds of weather day and night selling fruits and vegetables to make money to take care of you, your mother, and this home. I'm up at 3 a.m. getting ready for work, and sometimes I don't get home until 9 or 10 o'clock at night. I work so much, I can still hear the clip-pity-clop of my mule's feet pulling my cart along the streets of this city in my sleep. "Look my hands," directed her father, holding up his big, dry, ashy, cracked, hands. "See these big callouses and dark marks? Well pulling my donkey's reins for hours on end makes my hands turn raw and bleed. You wouldn't know about that because you don't hear me talking about it. I get out here and do what I got to do to take care of my family. The same holds true for your mother. She gets down on her hands and knees to scrub floors and irons clothes six days out of a seven-day week for her employer. Sometimes, she has to take Epsom salt baths on account of her back hurting from all of that bending. But you wouldn't know about that either 'cause she never complains about it. Your mother and I don't want you to have to make a living cleaning up after nobody or peddling produce on the streets. All we want Lila Mae, is better for you. Now just because we want better for you don't mean you are better than anyone else because of your skin color and hair…'cause you ain't. That kind of thinkin' makes you just like White folks. Now I ain't talking about all White people…because there are a lot of good White people. Some of my best customers over in Pig Town off Monroe Street are White people. I'm talkin' about White folks who hate Black folks on account of our skin color. Don't be like them, Lila Mae. White privilege…light-skinned privileged…it's all the same. But as I see it, in some ways, light-skinned privileged is worse…'cause it's discrimination within your own race. And we as Black people already got enough issues to deal with in our lives. Do you understand what I am trying to tell you, Lila Mae?"

"Yes Father," young Lila Mae replied.

"Good," her father replied. "And Lila Mae, don't pay no mind to what my Mama has said about you being more privileged because you got her hair and light-skinned genes. She may pass for White…but make no mistake about it…she's still Black…and so are you. Now, Lila Mae, you are beautiful…and beauty is good. But you got to have brains too. Me and your Mama work hard…not only to take care of our home and family…but to save up money to enable you to go to college when you grow up. Whatever we make…10 percent of it goes to God first…then we pay bills and other expenses…and set aside money for your college fund. We want our Lila Mae to be the first person on either side of our family to go to college."

And young Lila Mae did. Before the death of her parents, they attended Commencement Exercises for her Bachelor's, Master's, and Doctorate degrees. It was an especially shining moment in her life – and theirs, for her to walk across the stage in her graduation regalia adorned with velvet doctoral bars.

"Imagine that!" her father told her a few weeks after the ceremony. "My daughter Lila Mae, the great-great-granddaughter of sharecroppers earning a doctorate! "I'm so proud of you Lila Mae! I brag about you all the time to my customers. But a word of caution…no matter how successful you become, don't ever get the 'big head.'"

"Why would you ever think that Father?" she asked.

"Let's just say it's always a possibility," said her father. "Education can sometimes make people prideful. Don't ever let that happen to you. Pride cometh before a fall. That's The Word of God."

Dr. Hawkins' parents and grandparents had died years ago, but memories of them – and their divide, were very much alive.

I still remember the day Mother marched into Grandfather Jefferson and Grandmother Lily's house toting me by the hand to speak to her about telling me I was privileged because of my skin color and hair, thought Dr. Hawkins. Mother did not use a single curse word, but she sure gave Grandmother Lily a severe tongue-lashing! 'How dare you fill Lila Mae's head with such prideful untruths about her skin color and hair you conceited old coot!' Mother told Grandmother Lily. 'Get out of my house Jimmie Lee! Before I throw you out!' screamed Grandmother Lily. 'Try it!' shouted Mother. You might look White right now, but you are going to be black and blue by the time I finish with you!'" Chuckling over her mother's words, Dr. Hawkins said, "Grandfather had to pick Grandmother Lily up by the waist and carry her out of the room kicking and screaming to keep those two from fighting! My Lord what a mess that was! Father came to the house to calm down Mother and take her home. Poor Father…after their big blowup, he was always caught in the middle of Mother and Grandmother Lily's disagreement…having to choose sides between his wife and mother. He did everything he could to get those two to make amends. "'Mama, why can't you and Jimmie Lee just bury the hatchet?' Father told Grandmother Lily. 'After all, Jimmie Lee is my wife.'" I remember Grandmother Lily replying "I'll be happy to bury the hatchet alright! Right in Jimmie Lee's back! You may have forgotten, but I am your mother and I told you not to marry that woman in the first place!' Bug-eyed, Father asked, 'Why? Because Jimmie Lee was darker than a brown paper bag?! Well, in case you didn't notice, despite being your son, I'm darker than a brown paper bag too! Does that make me any less than a person?' For a while, things were tense between Father and Grandmother Lily after that conversation. But they eventually worked out their differences. On the contrary, Mother and Grandmother Lily never did settle their dispute. They had a real-life family feud, which in my opinion further divided the family. They never spoke again and went to their graves still mad with one another."

The Golden Girls episodes continuing to roll along, Dr. Hawkins nibbled on a buttered croissant she retrieved from the kitchen. Sipping another cup of hot tea, memories of her professional and married life, returned to her thoughts.

After working as a teacher for a few years, I became an Assistant Principal, and by 1982, I was an elementary school Principal. That same year, Rufus took me to Schwartz Cadillac in Pikesville, (now Frankel & Chesapeake Cadillac) and brought me a spanking new Cadillac Coupe de Ville. The following day, Rufus bought me a full-length mink from Mano Swartz furriers and had my initials 'LMH' monogrammed in the coat's lining. She recalled a conversation the two had in which he explained why he chose Mano Swartz.

"When I was a little boy, my mother would walk past Mano Swartz," said Mr. Hawkins. "Back then, the store was located on Howard Street. When we walked by, she would talk about wanting to try on one of the store's fur coats, even though she couldn't afford to buy one. At the time, Baltimore was segra'gated," he explained, referencing the word 'segregated.' Most stores wouldn't allow a Black inside their store, let alone try something on. But one day…and I don't know why… Momma decided to walk inside Mano Swartz. Holding my hand, we walked on in. I recalled being scared. But to my shock, not only did the store owner welcome us, but he allowed Momma to try on a coat. I will never forget the look Momma had on her face when she looked at herself in the mirror with that coat on! She was beamin' with joy! Once we left the store, Momma said, 'Son, I might be po', but I sure felt like a rich woman with that mink coat on.' Well Lila Mae, I never forgot how happy Mano Schwartz made my mother. She really cherished that experience. I promised myself back then that if I could ever afford to get a coat from the store, I would. So, I put aside money to buy Momma a coat from there…the one I gave her a few Christmases ago, and now Lila Mae honey…I am buying you one!"

Unlike his mother's Lucille Hawkins' mink, Mr. Hawkins did not purchase his wife's fur coat with money he earned from his postal job. Nor did he purchase Dr. Hawkins' new Cadillac with his income. Dr. Hawkins would later learn her husband had purchased the pricey items from his 'Street Numbers' winnings. A popular, but rather secretive, illegal numbers game, 'Street Numbers' was a decades-old tradition in Baltimore. Dr. Hawkins recalled the conversation she and her husband had one morning after Mr. Hawkins told her he woke up with a 'hunch' about a number.

"I'm going to place a large bet through Smitty," said Mr. Hawkins referring to his friend Malcolm 'Smitty' Green.

"Rufus, I'm not interested in hearing about your hunch or bet," she replied. "Not only are you playing an illegal game, but you are frivolously throwing away our hard-earned money. I do not know how that game works, and I don't want to know. But what I do know is that you are wasting money away on that silly game."

"Say what you want Lila Mae," said Mr. Hawkins. "But my palm is itchin', and that means that a lot of money is coming. On top of that, when I was out on my route yesterday, a bird doo-dooed on my head. I was mad, but after I thought about it, I remembered that a bird poopin' on your head means good luck…and I feel lucky!"

"There's nothing good about a bird disposing of their waste on your head, and there's no such thing as luck," she scoffed. "I've heard enough. I'm going to work."

"Too-da-loo!" he chuckled. "You won't be saying that if I win!"

Dr. Hawkins left for work fuming over the fact that her husband would be spending money on an improbable bet.

A few days later, Mr. Hawkins summoned his wife into the kitchen.

"What is it?" she asked.

"Take a look!" he replied, pointing to stacks of cash on the table.

Her eyes popping out of her head, she asked, "Rufus! Don't tell me –"

"That's right Lila Mae honey! I won and Baby, I won big! I hit the Street Number!"

"What?!" she gawked.

"Well Lila Mae, what you consider to be a silly game earned me a whole hell of a lotta money!" he laughed. "I hit the number, and I hit it big! Count it, baby!'

After counting the money, Dr. Hawkins told her husband, "I can't believe it! There's $75,000 on that table!"

"Believe it," he grinned. "Cause it's true."

At first, Dr. Hawkins had reservations about her husband taking her shopping with what she considered to be 'ill-gotten gains.'

Silly me, she thought of her decision. But thoughts of a lavish shopping spree excited me, so I gave in. Not only did Rufus buy me a Cadillac and a fur, but he also gave me $5,000 cash to spend at my discretion…which I happily excepted. I had never seen that much money before in my life! Rufus brought himself a new, state-of-the-art big-screen color projection television from Luskin's electronics store to watch football, some clothes, and a used Ford Thunderbird. He deposited the rest of his winnings into our joint account at the Mondawmin Mall branch of Maryland National Bank. Letting out a deep sigh, Dr. Hawkins lamented, On so many occasions, I have regretted the decision I made to move my money out of that bank.

❀

The excitement surrounding her husband's winnings along with the expensive purchases the money afforded, soon faded. Despite his large financial gain, Dr. Hawkins was losing patience with Mr. Hawkins on several fronts. Another episode of 'The Golden Girls' now mid-way through along with half of the afternoon, Dr. Hawkins thought back on her festering discontent.

As time went on, I began to feel that Rufus needed to raise his personal bar…by several notches. Every day, I was exposed to professional, educated, successful men…school administrators, college professors, politicians, pastors, and business owners. In comparison, I felt Rufus was underachieving. Yes, he had a good-paying job at the post office working as a mail carrier. But I felt he could attain so much more. I had grown tired of taking him to Balls and other social affairs and being embarrassed by his terrible grammar and lack of etiquette. My colleagues, Sorors, and socialite friends…along with their husbands, were both articulate and classy. Rufus on the other hand was uncivilized and uncouth. When we attended social gatherings, I cringed whenever he spoke. He had picked up a considerable amount of weight, and there he stood with his belly hanging over his unbuttoned, too-small tuxedo pants yelling loudly across the ballroom of places like The Forum Caterers or Martin's West for the Wait Staff to bring him a can of that God-forsaken beer, 'Natty Boh!' Once they brought him his beer, he would pop open the can and start talking loudly about his 'Bawl'more Colts' as he called them, between belches. How embarrassing!

In comparing her husband to the husbands of other women, Dr. Hawkins also compared him to other male graduates of his Alma Mater, Frederick Douglass High School. Douglass had so many notable graduates…Thurgood Marshall, the first Black to sit on the U.S. Supreme Court…Parren J. Mitchell, the first Black congressman…Kweisi Mfume…who succeeded Parren J. Mitchell. Why couldn't Rufus be more like them? I just couldn't understand it. I suggested he take a portion of the money he had sitting in the bank from his street winnings and start a business. He did not want to do that. I suggested he further his education by attending college. I really pushed that! But he pushed back! He did not like the idea. 'Lila Mae', he would tell me, 'I love you. I also make a good, steady income, and pay all the bills around here. That allows you to spend the income you make on just about anything you want. I'm a good husband who treats you like the Queen you are Honey. But I'm content with what I'm doing. I love working at the Post Office. I'm proud to be a U.S. Postman! I don't want to start a business or go to school. Just be happy with what I'm doin', 'cause I am."

Nevertheless, Dr. Hawkins continued to press her husband about college and aiming for a higher-paying, higher-profile career. I thought Rufus could be more than a mailman, reflected Dr. Hawkins. That's all he wanted…but I wanted more. On top of that, I felt Rufus was becoming a fat slob. His flat stomach had started to expand like a gluttonous blowfish! I would come home from weekend shopping excursions, brunch, afternoon tea, and church to find Rufus sitting on the couch crunching on fried chicken and eating large containers of spicy rice and fries from Chicken George in Walbrook Junction! The more I saw him sitting on the sofa eating and watching football…dropping crumbs everywhere and popping open cans of Natty Boh, the angrier I became! He went from looking like a young Bill Cosby to Fat Albert, she thought referencing the cartoon 'Fat Albert and the Cosby Kids' created by Bill Cosby. Grumbling silently, I would leave out the house or walk back in, thinking, Just look at Rufus on that couch! Him and his smelly feet and filthy socks! Instead of sitting in front of the television, he could be sitting in a classroom or lecture hall at a fine school like Coppin or Morgan where he could take a Public Speaking course to improve his horrendous vernacular! He does a hatchet job on the simplest of words! But no! On weekends, Rufus would rather sit home on his flatulated ass, eating and passing gas all day, watching football, and jotting down street numbers on pieces of paper! I get that he works during the week, but why not use his off days more wisely?! What a foolish man!

During the early years of their marriage, the Hawkins rarely argued, and when they did, they talked through their differences and quickly made up. But the more frustrated Dr. Hawkins grew about Mr. Hawkins' unwillingness to further his education or become an entrepreneur, the more her thoughts silently festered like infection in a sore. And like puss in a sore, Dr. Hawkins' internal feelings came to the surface, as she began to verbalize what she thought to her husband. This birthed the start of ongoing arguments between the couple. She reflected on one of their many verbal disagreements.

"Rufus, when are you going to take the initiative to start improving yourself?!" she asked one day heading out the door for church. "Instead of laying on your ass watching television in your spare time, why not go to college?! Don't you want to be more than a mailman?!"

"I'm just fine bein' a mailman Dr. Lila Mae!' he snarled with an air of sarcasm, popping pub pretzels in his mouth. "I love what I do and I ain't about to change my job or oca'pation to please you!"

"The word is occupation!" she barked.

"Ocu'pation…smoc'upation…whatever you want to call it!" sneered Mr. Hawkins. "You know what I'm sayin'! That's your problem! You're always criticizin' me!"

"I do not! All I am trying to do is help you…to motivate you to do more! I hardly consider that criticizing you!"

"Listen here Dr. Lila Mae, I'm a man!" he bellowed in frustration. "A Black man living in America who got to work extra hard to get ahead! A Black man who was once told by a White postal customer, 'I don't like a Nigger touchin' my mail, let alone deliverin' it! I wanted to knock him out, but I love my job and I wasn't about to lose it on account of him so I told him he could 'kiss my mail!'

"Why Rufus!" said Dr. Hawkins with great surprise. "You never told me that!"

"There are just some things a person would rather not talk about," Mr. Hawkins replied. "I'm sure that had I told you that back then, you just would have used that to remind me that I needed another job!"

"Is that so?" she asked.

"You damn skimpy!" he shouted, jumping up from the couch, the bowl of pretzels sitting on his lap falling to the floor. "Lila Mae, I've been put down enough out there in the world! Do you ever think about how it makes me feel when I come home, and my wife puts me down! It hurts like hell! Always comparin' me to other men! You married me…Rufus Earl Hawkins…not them! Since we got hitched, I have bent over backward to treat you like a queen and you still ain't satisfied! You're a queen alright…a Queen B! Now I ain't gonna call you out of your name on account of it being Sunday and my mother taught me better…even though you cussed at me! Now go on out that door to church before you make me change my mind!"

"I'm not leaving out this door until you apologize!"

"Apologize for what Dr. Lila Mae?! questioned Mr. Hawkins. "If anybody should be apologizin', it should be you!"

"I beg to differ!" she said, marching over to him.

"You can beg all you want!," said Mr. Hawkins. "Can't a man have some peace?! After working all week, all I was doin' was sittin' in here on the couch eating snacks, drinking a beer, and watchin' the pre-game football news, and here you come!" Motioning his hand for her to move Mr. Hawkins added, 'Move outta the way! You're standing right in front of the television, and I can't see!"

"How dare you tell me to move out of the way!" she screamed. "You and your dirty socks and funky feet!"

"These are the same funky feet that walk mail routes day in and day out!" he blasted. "The same funky feet that pay all the bills around here and helped to support you getting that fancy education of yours! These feet smelled just fine back then! Now leave me the hell alone Lila Mae!" said Mr. Hawkins, prompting her to storm out of the house, slamming its door behind her.

For Dr. Hawkins, there was also the matter of her husband not attending church. That proved to be another area of growing resentment for her when it came to Mr. Hawkins.

"No matter how hard I tried, I could not get that man to go to church on Sunday mornings, she recalled, thinking out loud. "When I left the house for Worship Service at United Victory dressed to the nine in my fine attire…one of my large, plumed church hats from Hochschild Kohn, a dress suit from Stewart's, and my heels from Hess Shoe Store, I would invite Rufus to get dressed and come along with me. But no! He would opt to stay home, remaining dressed in his own Sunday attire for the day's football games…a dingy white 'wifebeater' soiled with food and ketchup stains, pajama pants, and dirty socks. At arm's length were his chips, dip, and buffalo wings. And of course, there was his six-pack of Natty Boh beer in the refrigerator! Him and those cans of beer with that one-eyed man 'Mr. Boh' on them! Talking to that silly Mr. Boh as if he were talking to a person! For the life of me, I never understand why Rufus would do that?" Momentarily thinking about what she was doing, she stated to herself, "Come, come now Lila Mae! Here you are doing the same exact thing!"

Dr. Hawkins ceased talking to herself, now reflecting on her desire for her and her former husband to move out of their home in the city to the county.

Our salaries afforded us the income to move to what I considered to be a better neighborhood, she recalled. I made it clear to Rufus my desire to sell our home in the city and move to the county…specifically Randallstown, Maryland. Many of my colleagues had moved to the area, and I really liked the area with its ranchers, split-levels, Cape Cods, and other varying styles of homes. But no! Rufus would not hear of that either!' she recollected, her mind recalling yet another one of their arguments.

"I don't want to move to Randallstown with those 'Crackers' and uppity Black folks!' he expressed. 'I'm keeping my black ass right where I'm at! I ain't mean to cuss at you Lila Mae, but I'm tired of you needlin' me about movin' out of this house. I like it here, and this is where I intend to stay!"

"That's your problem now Rufus!" she bellowed. "You want to stay right where you are! You have absolutely no gumption or umph to do better in life! No desire to be more than a mailman! No desire to live in a better neighborhood! No desire to want more out of life! No desire to be successful!

"Well Dr. Lila Mae," said Mr. Hawkins, his pronunciation of her name stinging with sarcasm, "As far as I'm concerned, I am successful! I've achieved the American Dream! I got a house, a car, all my bills are paid up, I don't owe nobody nothin'… 'cause unlike you, I don't believe in credit cards, and I got a nice chunk of money in the bank!"

"And what good is that money in the bank if you don't invest it or make it work for you?" she asked. "You could use that money to finance a business or go to school."

"And be like those snooty people you know?" he asked. "That's what you want…not me! And as far as my money, I like my cash being in the bank for safekeeping! It's in Maryland National gaining interest, and I ain't got to worry about spendin' it all or nobody stealin' it!"

"Rufus, you are making much ado about nothing!" she said. "All I want is for you to do better…to achieve more."

"Nothin' to you Lila Mae, but somethin' to me because all you have been doin' these past few years is complainin' and puttin' me down!" Mr. Hawkins yelled. "You are married to a mailman…something you seemed to have forgotten! But let me remind you of a few things since you seem to have forgotten! My bein' a mailman was fine and dandy when you were in college! Back when you had that little job working at the Five and Dime! Oh, you loved my good government job back then! It even allowed you to leave the post office and go to school full-time!"

"Shut up Rufus!"

"No, I'm not shuttin' up!" he declared. "I'm not finished! The health and dental insurance that came with my government job paid for your doctor's and dental appointments until you were able to get your own insurance with the school system –"

"That's right!" she yelled. "Blue Cross and Blue Shield."

"I don't care what the name of it is…you were on mines at first! That's why your teeth look so good now! And not only that, but my little postal job helped us to get this house! It also helped put you through school and provided the income for me to buy us a car so you wouldn't have to walk or catch the bus to school! Hell, I even changed my work schedule to drop you off at the campus and pick you up! But I guess you forgot all that! And do you know why? Well, I'll tell you why! Because Dr. Lila Mae Hawkins, after you got all that education, especially that fancy doc'rate, you got the big head!'"

"The word is doctorate!" Dr. Hawkins fired back, while momentarily being taken aback by her husband telling her she had gotten 'the big head.' Mr. Hawkins' words sparked memories of her father's warning about not getting 'the big head', and here was her husband telling her she had 'the big head.'

"Your head done swolled up so much, it won't even fit in this house anymore because you think you are too good to live here now! But I've got news for you, Lila Mae…I like it here, and I ain't goin' nowhere until I am good and ready. Not even for you!"

"I do not have 'the big head' Rufus! All I want is for you to attain more!"

"There you have it right there!" he told Dr. Hawkins. "This is all about what you want…not what I want! Well, I've got news for you, Lila Mae…I love my job, and I ain't got no intention of changin' that! Yeah, I've had a few bad experiences…as most people do on their jobs from time to time. But I love what I do, and rain or shine…and in snow and ice… I'm out there bustin' my ass doin' my job! The peoples along my routes show me more love and appreciation than you do! They give me cold ice water and sodas when it's hot in the summer, and pippin' hot coffee and tea when it's cold in the winter. They even offer me lunch, and some even give me tips. You used to pack me a lunch box for work! When's the last time you did that Lila Mae? My postal customers appreciate my hard work, and you should too! But you don't because you are too busy takin' me for granted! And on top of that, you're spoiled and selfish!"

Appalled, she shouted, "Rufus, just because I want you to do better for yourself, and for us to move to a better neighborhood in Randallstown does not make me spoiled and selfish! How dare you tell me that?!"

"You asked for it, Lila Mae! I'll tell you what…since you like Randallstown so much, and this neighborhood ain't good enough for you no more, go on and move out there!"

"I just might do that!" she threatened. "And then I won't have to hear or smell your rancid gas! The smell would put a skunk to shame!"

"And if you moved way out there, I won't have to hear that loud snorin' of yours, Dr. Snores! You snore louder than Fred Flintstone! You're just mad because I won't do what you want me to do! I'm my own man! I don't need a bossy woman tellin' me what to do with my life! Go on and move out to Randallstown since that's where you want to go! As for Rufus Earl Hawkins, I'm keeping my black ass right chere in Bawl'more City where I was born, bred, and belong!'

"Rufus, maybe if you ever decided to get up off your ever-growing rump roast to further your education, you would get that screwed up vernacular of yours together! The word is pronounced 'here' not 'chere' …and the name of the city is pronounced Bal-ti-more…and not Bawl'more! And while we're at it, here's another word you screw up all the time that gets under my skin! Our kitchen has a sink and not a zink!"

"Well Dr. Lila Mae, where I come from, we say chere, Bawl'more, and zink!' he screamed plopping back down on the sofa and picking up the remote control. "That's how some folks pronounce it where you come from too. Oh…silly me…I forgot…you got that doc'rate now! You forgot where you came from!"

'It's doctorate!" she hollered.

"Say it any way you wanna say it!' he bellowed. "You and your high-yellow ass!"

"Well, you sure loved my high-yellow ass when we met!" she countered.

"And I still do!" he said. "But I damn sure don't like the woman your high-yellow ass has become!"

"I haven't changed! I have always been this way!" she said.

"Well, you damn sure fooled me!" he said, flipping through the television stations. "But one thing for sure, once you got all that education, your nose went straight up in the air! I've got another name that fits you better now…Dr. Sudie Snooty!"

"How dare you call me by that name!" she ranted. "You know I hate my middle name Sudie!"

"I know you do!" he laughed. "But no matter how much you hate it, that's your birth name! And that'll never change…well unless you change it along with the way you are trying to change everything…including me."

Dr. Hawkins' birthname was Lila Mae Sudie Cross. While her parents named her 'Lila Mae' after her paternal grandmother, they gave her the middle name 'Sudie' after her maternal grandmother Sudie Perkins – the wife of Lionel Perkins who was the parent of her mother Jimmie Lee Cross.

I have always used the first initial of my middle name Sudie because I thought it was too old-fashioned, Dr. Hawkins recalled, continuing to think back on her and her ex's arguments. I told Rufus how much I hated my middle name…something I came to regret. That man always did have a way of pushing just the right buttons to ruffle my feathers. And one of the things he used to do to annoy me was referring to me by that distasteful nickname he concocted…Dr. Sudie Snooty!

Their arguments growing more contentious, the husband and wife would swap insult after insult – Dr. Hawkins tired of Mr. Hawkins calling her selfish or referring to her as 'Dr. Sudie Snooty', 'Dr. Snores' and 'high-yellow'. Meanwhile, Mr. Hawkins up to his eyeballs in frustration hearing her complain about his refusal to further his education or start a business and watching football on the weekends. Their volcanic disagreements erupted one Saturday afternoon after Mr. Hawkins shouted, "Dr. Sudie Snooty, you need to come down off that high-yellow horse of yours because you're acting like a real ass!" In response to her husband's comments, she replied, "How dare you continue to speak to me in that manner?! I'm sick and tired of it, Blackie!"

That's how Grandmother Lily referred to dark-skinned people, Dr. Hawkins recalled. I remember calling my Cousin Genevieve by that name because she wouldn't let me play with her doll. I remember her bursting into tears, and she would not stop crying. Not to mention Father gave me a painful spanking after learning I called Cousin Genevieve by that name. Calling Rufus 'Blackie' years later, marked the first time I had called anyone that name since I was a little girl. Rufus made me so mad…but I instantly regretted calling him such a derogatory and demeaning name. But I could not take it back…it had already slipped out my mouth…I had already said it. I apologized…but the damage was already done, she thought, recalling what came next.

Livid and hurt, Mr. Hawkins yelled, "Save your apologies Lila Mae!," while grabbing his coat out of the closet. "You just confirmed what I realized but didn't want to believe…and that is…that I'm not smart enough…talented enough…or light enough for you!"

"Rufus…Honey, I'm sorry!" she cried. "That's not it at all! I never meant to call you that name!"

"You're not sorry!" shouted Mr. Hawkins. "You just confirmed what has been in your heart all along! What I can't understand, is why you married me in the first place? Why didn't you marry a light-skinned man, or better yet a White man?! Why did you marry a man you didn't love?"

"But Rufus, I do love you!"

"How is that love?! You walk around this house complainin' all the time…puttin' me down…naggin' me every weekend! A man can't even come home and get peace in his house! And now you got the nerve to come out of your mouth with the name 'Blackie?!'" he yelled, putting on his brown, Fedora-style hat. "I got to get out this house before I say or do somethin' I regret!"

Following Mr. Hawkins to the front door with tears streaming down her face, Dr. Hawkins pleaded, "Rufus please don't leave! I'm very sorry! I didn't mean to call you that name! And the only man I've ever been in love with you! You must believe me!"

"Well I don't!" he bellowed, "And don't wait up for me!" he added, opening the front door, and slamming it shut behind him in her face.

Things really blew up between Rufus and me that day, recalled Dr. Hawkins. I thought all my pushing and prodding would motivate Rufus…but all it seemed to do was anger him more…and pull us further apart. However, all I wanted was for Rufus to be the best that he could be.

❧

Another hour or so went by. Dr. Hawkins was now stretched out on the sofa – 'The Golden Girls' marathon still on, and her mind still tuned to thoughts about her now-nullified married life.

My, my, my, she thought. Rufus and I did get past my calling him that awful name. Thank God! But I always felt that we lost something after I called him that. And there was no denying the fact that our disagreements...that one being the coup de grâce in some ways, had taken a toll on our once wonderfully busy sex life. When he and I met, I was a virgin. He respectfully honored my wishes to wait until after we were married to have sexual intercourse. I lost my virginity to him on our wedding night…I'll never forget that! Having never 'done it' before, I was nervous. But he was gentle and took his time with me. After our first encounter, I wanted to make love to him all the time. We made love all the time and everywhere…in our bed…on the floor…even in the backseat of the car. Whenever our libidos raged hot, we did it! And I'll never forget that adventurous night we made love outside on the ground at Druid Hill Park as I looked up into the nighttime stars. On another daring occasion, we made love at Holiday Inn's well-known circulating restaurant Circle One. Rufus worked there for a short while as a busboy before he got the job at the post office, and knew about a hidden area inside the restaurant. I will never forget how we made love as the restaurant circled while providing a breathtaking view from its location at the corner of Lombard and Howard Streets. Thinking back, it amazes me that we took such a chance, risking the fact that we could have been caught! But I guess that's what made it so thrilling! Sadly, we got to a point in our marriage where we argued more than we made love. We intertwined our bodies so rarely, that I stopped taking my Birth Control pills on a regular basis. And it was during one of our increasingly rare sexual encounters I became pregnant with Dancer.

❧

Dancer was born on February 3, 1984, at Provident Hospital. The Hawkins – both 32 years of age – were proud new parents. Unfortunately, even after birthing their daughter, 'Colorism' shaded the prism of Dr. Hawkins' heart.

Dancer inherited most of my features, thought Dr. Hawkins. However, she has Rufus' darker skin color. I thought she would inherit me and Grandmother Lily's lighter complexion. But that was not to be, she sighed, her mind traveling back to the day she first laid eyes on her newborn daughter.

Dr. Hawkins was sharing a room in the maternity ward with a dark-skinned woman who had also given birth. The two women were recuperating in their hospital beds, avidly waiting for a nurse to bring in their newborns so they could see and hold their child for the first time. The nurse – Patricia Martin, RN, whom she knew from United in Victory, walked in with a light-complexioned baby. At the time, Mr. Hawkins had stepped out of the room to use the bathroom. After Nurse Martin walked in with the newborn, Dr. Hawkins automatically sat up and reached out to take the child in her arms. However, Nurse Martin passed by her bed and handed that baby to the other mother. A short time later, the nurse returned with a much darker baby and handed her to Lila Mae.

"Are you certain this is my baby?" asked Dr. Hawkins, glancing at the baby's dark ears. "There must be some mistake."

"She's definitely yours Sister Hawkins," said Nurse Martin. "Congratulations on your new, healthy, bouncing baby girl! She's a real cutie!"

"Are you positive this is my little girl?" questioned Dr. Hawkins, glancing over at the baby in the other mother's arms. "Perhaps there has been some type of mix-up."

"Yes, I am positive," said Nurse Martin, with a puzzled look. "I can assure you, there was no mix-up. That beautiful baby girl you are holding is yours."

Looking down at her baby, Dr. Hawkins replied, "Well, in that case, I'll just have to dress her up and make her look as pretty as possible."

Looking at her strangely, Nurse Martin asked, "Can I get you anything else?"

"No, that will be all Nurse Martin," replied Dr. Hawkins. "I will summon for you if I need anything."

"Very well," said Nurse Martin, her mouth agape, at Dr. Hawkins' subservient comment. "I'll be just outside at the Nurse's Station."

Why was Nurse Martin looking at me side-eyed? wondered Dr. Hawkins, watching the RN leave the room. Enough of that! I have far more important things to think about. I am a new mother! Cradling the newborn, Dr. Hawkins said to the baby, "Just look at these long, slender legs of yours…just like mines," – gliding her hand along her legs – "You're going to be a dancer. Therefore, I shall name you Dancer! And your middle name will be Angela…because you are Mommy's little angel…Dancer Angela Hawkins! I love your name! Hopefully, your Daddy will too."

Soon thereafter, Mr. Hawkins returned, rushing over to the hospital bed when he saw Dr. Hawkins holding their new baby. "My little Sugar Cup!" he said joyfully after she handed him their little girl. "Coochie-coochie-coo!" giggled Mr. Hawkins, gentle tickling the baby's tiny stomach. "Look at Daddy's little girl! I'm so happy I could kiss this floor! Just look at her Lila Mae! Our first baby!"

The arrival of Dancer Angela Hawkins would prove not only to be the Hawkins' first child, but their last.

The couple was overjoyed at becoming parents. The two cuddled together, holding their new baby, and went on strolls in Druid Hill Park, pushing Dancer in the stroller. They took turns feeding Dancer and changing her diapers. They had a family portrait taken at Olan Mills Studio of themselves and Dancer. However, tender, blissful moments with their new family member proved to be short-lived. The couple's fiery disagreements resumed, with Dr. Hawkins using their growing family as a basis for them needing to move and to chide her husband for not making the grade professionally.

I came to realize that my wanting more for Rufus was simply 'visions of grandeur', she thought, still reflecting on their marriage. He was complacent with mediocrity, and that was something I could not change. I, on the other hand, continued to climb high! In 1983…a year before Dancer was born, I reached the pinnacle of my career, having become an Assistant Superintendent in the city's public school system. Meanwhile, that bull-headed Rufus had not advanced at all! He was still a mailman! Not even a postal supervisor! An Assistant Superintendent for Baltimore City Public Schools married to a mailman! I thought that was very droll! But on the other hand, Rufus was a firm believer that a man should pay all the bills...and he did. He took care of the mortgage...utilities...automotive repairs...etcetera...etcetera. But I began to feel I could make it on my own. My handsome salary very easily afforded me the means to move to Randallstown...with or without him! On numerous occasions, Rufus articulated to me in his shabby words that he did not have an ounce of interest in moving out of that house! On top of that, I really felt his job and watching football was clearly far more important to him than me! I had had enough! So I secretly decided I would leave him...and take Dancer with me.

Dr. Hawkins' secretive thoughts about leaving her husband began to take tangible shape. Unbeknownst to him, she contacted a real estate agent Nina Harper, letting her know she preferred a home in the Randallstown area. One fall day in 1984, the realtor called and told her there was a home for sale in Kings Point Estates in Randallstown.

"Are you available this evening around five-ish?" asked Ms. Harper.

"I will make myself available!" replied Dr. Hawkins, afterward jotting down the address of the property.

Reflecting on the experience, Dr. Hawkins thought, The moment we pulled up to this house, I knew it was perfect! And once she showed me the inside along with the backyard, that sealed the deal! Before long, I had a contract on the house and was signing closing papers. And Rufus did not have a clue as to what was going on! He was too busy working, eating, playing Street Numbers, and watching football! Meanwhile, I devised a plan to move out of our home on Gwynns Falls right under his nose.

Dr. Hawkins retained the services of Ferguson Moving Company, owned and operator by Edward Ferguson, who was also a minister. After deciding on a moving date, she gave Rev. Ferguson specific instructions regarding the move, which included pulling the moving truck in the rear of her home.

"I don't want to chance my nosey neighbors – namely that busybody Miss Jenkins who lives across the street, to see my things being moved out the house," she told Rev. Ferguson. "I want it done as discreetly as possible, which is why I am not taking any large furnishings...just boxes. Tell your men to keep the noise down. No loud talking! It is also crucially important that all my belongings are out of the house by 4 p.m. My husband generally arrives home from work around 6 p.m. and I want to be long gone by then."

"I know it's not any of my business," he asked, "But –"

"You're right! It's not any of your business!" she snapped, "But go on."

"Well Miss Hawkins, you –"

Correcting him, she stated, "That's Dr. Hawkins! You were saying?!"

"Well Dr. Hawkins, you might want to think twice before leaving your husband," he continued. "Perhaps you two can work it out. Separation sometimes tends to lead to divorce, and The Bible tells us that God hates divorce."

"I hired you to move my things...not to tell me what to do about my marriage!" she scolded. "If I wanted that, I would have consulted a marriage counselor!"

"Yes ma'am," replied the reverend, biting his lip. "I just felt the need to tell you that. But maybe it wasn't me...maybe that was God tryin' to tell you somethin'."

Dr. Hawkins did not bat an eye over what the minister told her. Instead, she rolled them while proceeding full steam ahead with details concerning the move.

Looking back, I suppose I could have just told Rufus what I was going to do, she thought. Nevertheless, I found it somewhat thrilling to go about it in such a covert way. In some ways, I guess it was my way of getting back at Rufus for not listening to me. But at the time, I did not see it that way. I felt I had no other alternative but to leave Rufus. There was also a part of me that believed that my moving out would force him to do more with his life…and from there, we could work things out. But I was wrong.

𝔊

Tuesday, October 16, 1984, the day of the move soon arrived. Dr. Hawkins reflected on the events of the day.

Everything went off without a hitch, she thought. I had to chastise the movers a time or two about talking too loud for my liking. But overall, I was highly pleased with the move. The movers expeditiously carried out the boxes I packed containing clocks, jewelry boxes, and other bric-a-brac and whatnots, along with clothing, and other items I packed, including my most prized possessions…my academic diplomas…my expensive artwork…and my Delta elephant statues. With these hands, she thought– holding out her slender, frail-like hands in front of her – I gleefully emptied my closets and dresser-drawers and removed items from walls and shelves thinking about the look on Rufus' face when he arrived home to find me gone along with my things. 'This will teach him to listen to me!' I thought. I did, however, leave a few old housecoats in the top dresser drawer in our bedroom, as I had already purchased new ones along with many new household things. 'No point in taking these old things' I thought. I even left Rufus all the furniture. I had already picked out and paid for fabulous new Art Deco furniture for the new house. In terms of the expensive items he bought me when he won all that money, my monogrammed mink was in refrigerated storage at Mano Schwartz, and as far as my Cadillac, I decided I no longer wanted that car. I no longer wanted that vehicle, as I had set my sights on a newer, more expensive car…a new Mercedes Benz convertible. So I left the keys to the Cadillac…and the house on the kitchen table along with a handwritten note to Rufus. After the movers took out the last box, I walked through the house to ensure I was not leaving anything behind I wanted to take. Walking through Dancer's room, I recalled how barren that room looked after the movers took apart her crib and took it outside along with boxes containing her baby toys and other belongings. After I was satisfied that I was not leaving anything I needed behind, I recall letting out a deep sigh and softly shutting the door behind me. But the door of my heart was still ajar! I knew I still loved Rufus and the sense of satisfaction I felt in successfully pulling off my elaborate plan was quickly being replaced with guilt and doubt. I began to have second thoughts about leaving him. 'Get it together Lila Mae!' I told myself. 'You've come too far! There's no turning back now!' I also told myself that there was still the handwritten note on the kitchen table explaining why my moving out was necessary. I also considered that note to be my last plea to convince Rufus to agree to change his stubborn ways, and if he did, perhaps our marriage could be salvaged. The note also included my new residential phone number, which I indicated he could call once he decided to follow my good advice. I figured once I moved out, he would realize I meant business and beg me to come back home! I waited for my new house phone to ring…and when it did…I ran to it believing Rufus had a change of heart. But alas! Rufus' conversation that evening was not one of regret, reasoning, and reconciliation! On the contrary, it was dastardly, distasteful, and downright disrespectful! I certainly did not expect that!

The Golden Girls marathon now creeping into the early hours of the evening, Dr. Hawkins recalled the phone call – and the conversation that followed.

"I read your damn note on the table, Lila Mae!" Mr. Hawkins shouted. "How could you do this to me after everything I've done for you?! Not only did you move out of here without my knowin' but you took the baby too! Where's Dancer?!"

"She's with me!" shouted Dr. Hawkins.

"I'll take your ass to court for full parental custody!" he threatened. "You spoiled, selfish, self-centered, connivin', back-stabbin' Bitch!"

"How dare you call me a Bitch you ignoramus!" she shouted in the phone. "I wish I had never married you!"

"And I damn sure wish I had never married you!" Mr. Hawkins screamed, his voice breaking. "I should have left your ass on the ground right where you belonged!"

For several minutes, the two threw painful jabs at one another during their verbal telephone phone fight, hitting below the belt with painful insult after painful insult. The bout did not end until Dr. Hawkins slammed her new Victorian-style French rotary telephone down on the receiver so hard it broke.

From that day forward, Rufus and I only communicated when it came to Dancer, she recalled. I did speak to a lawyer just in case Rufus was serious about pursuing sole custody of Dancer. But I knew he would not do that. He was not about to give up football and going to bed after getting off work to tend to a toddler. But I thought it was best to speak to a lawyer just in case. We began to move on with our lives…me in my house in Baltimore County…and he in the house we once shared in Baltimore City. With each passing day, my hope that we could reconcile began to dim…we had become estranged. Over the years, I heard both men and women talk about being estranged from their spouses. But even with that coupled with all my educational degrees, I was not quite sure what the word meant, so I had to look it up in the dictionary. I recall reading, 'Estranged…a husband or wife is not living with the person they are married to.' I never thought Rufus and I would find ourselves in such a place, but there we were…married, but living in two different residences. I thought about what my mover Rev. Ferguson said to me about separation leading to divorce. I scoffed at what he said but realized Rufus and I was on its road. I did not like the word or meaning of estranged, and I detested the word 'divorced' even more. But as much as I did not like the prospect of Rufus and I divorcing, there was no denying we had made significant headway down its path. I had hoped we could work things out…but Rufus would have to make the first move.

CHAPTER SIXTEEN

EATING CROW

Dr. Hawkins' trek down Memory Lane this October day resumed with thoughts of her early days in the house – which she settled in comfortably by December of 1984.

Everything was just lovely, she recalled. Every room in this house was decked out, including Dancer's, which was pink, and accented with ballerina wallpaper. I had a new sleek, black two-seater Mercedes Benz parked in my two-car garage. But as much as I wanted that car, sadly, it marked the first time in my life I owned a car with a note. Rufus always paid cash for our cars…along with paying for car insurance and maintenance. He even took our cars to the car wash. But after I left him, unfortunately, all those responsibilities fell squarely on me…along with my mortgage and other household bills. I never paid a single, solitary mortgage payment until I moved into this house. Rufus took care of that, and before I married him, my parents paid the mortgage for the house they owned. I did not anticipate the expenses I would incur having to pay for things all by myself. But I did not fret about it too much. I made more than enough money…although I could not help thinking about how much I missed spending all my money as I pleased. I could not do that any longer…I had bills to pay. Nevertheless, I was doing very well financially with my salary. I also had money in the bank from the sale of my parents' Lanvale Street home after they died. While Rufus and I had a joint checking account at Maryland National Bank, I also had an account at that bank solely in my´name that Rufus knew nothing about…and in that account, I had accumulated a little over $75,000. And since I had so much money in my secret account, I did not see the need to continue to have my name listed on our joint bank account…especially since for the most part…that money was his. So, I called Rufus and demanded that he remove my name off our joint account. He happily obliged, and I carried out the necessary procedures to do so. It did not matter to me. I had my own money.

Conversely, Dr. Hawkins grew tired of driving from her new residence in Randallstown as opposed to Maryland National's Mondawmin Mall branch. That drive was eight miles and took about 20 minutes, she remembered. *It was more sensible for me to bank with an institution closer to my home.*

There was one – 'Old Court Savings & Loan', located at the corner of Liberty and Old Court Roads. *Not only was Old Court Savings & Loan less than two minutes away from my home, but I heard the bank offered the best interest rates around,* she recalled. *I remember paying a visit to the bank one December day to find out if what I had heard about the excellent interest rates were true. A banker at the branch told me what I heard was indeed true. 'Wow!' I thought. An 11-percent interest rate on my $75,000 will net me an excellent return each month! After my visit to Old Court Savings & Loan, I immediately made plans for the following day. I would withdraw every dime of my money from Maryland National and deposit it into Old Court Savings & Loan.*

Beginning with her morning activity, Dr. Hawkins retracted the day's events in her mind.

It was Friday, December 14, 1984...I'll never forget that date! During that time, I watched 'Dynasty', and loved 'Dominique Deveraux,' she recalled, referring to the wealthy and ruthless character played by actress Diahann Carroll on Dynasty, a primetime soap opera that aired during the 1980s. *I figured that when I walked into Maryland National Bank, I would fashionably strut in there like Dominique Deveraux and look the part. After all, I was taking out a small fortune! After putting on my make-up, I selected a fine red outfit to wear. Red exudes power and it was also fitting for the Christmas season. I slipped on my crisp, freshly dry-cleaned 'Talbots' red pants suit, under which I wore a winter white wool 'Calvin Klein' turtleneck. I draped a pearl necklace around my neck and clipped on matching earrings. I pulled on my knee-highs and stepped into my fiery red 'Salvatore Ferragamo' pumps. I recall pulling out numerous hatboxes from my walk-in closet until I opened the one containing the specific hat that I was searching for...my exquisite, red-plumed church hat. I put the hat on and stood in front of the full-length mirror in my bedroom so that I could position it just right. After many adjustments, I settled on slightly pulling the hat down and tilting it a smidgeon for a little bravado. I recall telling my reflection, 'Dr. Lila Mae Hawkins, you look marvelous darling!' Finally, I grabbed my black patent leather 'Anne Klein' purse and slipped on my mink coat. Looking like a million dollars, I sashayed down the street to my two-seater Mercedes and drove to Maryland National to take out every penny. Once I was inside the bank, I exercised the great penmanship taught to me at Coppin, and cursively wrote my name on the sign-in sheet. While waiting to talk to a banker, I recall impatiently glancing down at my Movado watch thinking, 'What is taking them so long!'*

The bank was busy was bustling with activity that cold December day. Customers were standing in lines curved around stanchions waiting to see tellers, and Dr. Hawkins was sitting amongst several customers waiting to talk to a banker. All the bankers were with customers. Despite sitting for just a few minutes, Dr. Hawkins was antsy and did not bridle her impatience. She huffed and puffed, continuously glanced at her wristwatch, and gazed sharply at the bankers and the customers sitting at their desks. "My God, what's taking them so long?!" she mumbled under her breath. "I need to get my money out of here as

expeditiously as possible! If they knew who I was, they would not have me sitting here burning up in this mink coat waiting all this time! And just look at them over there laughing and talking!" she vented, glaring at the bankers. All they are doing is sitting in their cubicles chit-chatting with customers!"

About a half-hour later, Dr. Hawkins saw a banker stand along with a man and woman. "Finally!" she said, realizing her name was next to be called. After the man and woman turned around, Dr. Hawkins immediately recognized the two. They were her neighbors – 'Mr. and Mrs. Tucker'. The couple introduced themselves to Dr. Hawkins after she moved to Randallstown and lived on the same block. While they lived just a few doors down from her, Dr. Hawkins did not know them very well. All she could remember was their last name, and that she sometimes would see Mr. Tucker puffing on cigarettes – assuming that the hoarseness of his voice was due to years of smoking. During their comings and goings, Dr. Hawkins would give them an occasional nod when they greeted her and waved. She would sometimes hear Mr. Tucker coughing, and would think to herself, *What a nasty smoker's cough! And his voice sounds so gravelly! My guess is that he has ruined his vocal cords with all that smoking! What a terrible habit!*

Dr. Hawkins watched the dapper banker walk the couple as far as the sign-in book while telling them, "They made a wise choice." They noticed her and spoke, prompting Dr. Hawkins to give them her usual nod. After thanking the banker and shaking his hand, the couple and the banker exchanged goodbyes, and looked at the sign-in book.

"Dr. Lila Mae –"

"Hawkins!" interrupted Dr. Hawkins, standing. "That would be me!"

"Thanks for coming in today. My name is Michael Howard. Come on back."

"My goodness you people are slow," commented Dr. Hawkins strolling behind him.

"My apologies," said Mr. Howard. "It's been very busy today…especially with the holidays right around the corner."

Once they reached his desk, Mr. Howard pulled out a chair for Dr. Hawkins and said, "Please, have a seat. How can I help you today?"

Mr. Howard sat intently listening to Dr. Hawkins inform him of her desire to not only withdraw all her money but also close her account.

"Are you sure you want to take out all your funds and close down your account at this time?" he asked.

"I am quite sure," she smugly replied.

"You've been banking with us for such a long time," said Mr. Howard. "You're a good, loyal customer…one we would hate to lose."

"I bet you are! With all the money I have in the bank along with what my hus…" said Dr. Hawkins, stopping short of saying the word 'husband' in its entirety. "Listen…what did you say your name was?"

"Howard," said the banker. "Michael Howard."

"Well Mr. Howard, I am very clear on what I want to do, and that is to take every dime of my hard-earned money out of this branch and close my account."

"Do you mind my asking why you want to withdraw all your money out of Maryland National?" he asked.

Appalled by what she considered to be nosiness on the part of Mr. Howard, she replied, "Not that it's any of your business, but since you were brash enough to ask, I must tell you that I plan to put my money out at Old Court Savings and Loan. Not only is the branch a few blocks away from where I now live, but they offer a much higher interest rate than Maryland National Bank."

Clearing his throat and loosening his blue and white pinstriped tie, Mr. Howard replied, "Take it from me…I wouldn't do that if I were you. I'm not being facetious, but it would be in your best interest, to leave your money here in Maryland National Bank," he urged, stressing the word 'interest'. "Our interest rates may not be as attractive, but it's fair to say your money is much safer with us. Besides, it's not good to put all your eggs in one basket. That basket might tip over," he told her deliberately enunciating the 'p' in the word tip.

Dr. Hawkins caught on that Mr. Howard was making it his business to emphasize certain words. She did not know why, nor did she care.

Incensed, she hissed, "You don't tell me what to do with my money!' drawing stares from those sitting in close proximity. "I didn't ask for your advice! I asked for my money! Now, Mr. Howard, if you decline to do what I have asked, I'll get someone else over here to help me! Better yet, I'll ask for the branch manager!"

"That won't be necessary," said Mr. Howard. "Please accept my sincere apology for offending you, Miss Hawkins."

"Well Mr. Howard, once again, I must chastise you. My name is Dr. Lila Mae Hawkins…not Miss Hawkins! I will have you to know that I worked hard to earn my doctorate and will be addressed by the title afforded by my degree!"

"Yes, Dr. Hawkins," he replied. "Now if you would excuse me, I will move forward with processing your request."

"That's more like it!" she replied. "And I'll take my monies in the form of a Certified Cashier's Check!"

"Very well, Dr. Hawkins," said Mr. Howard, remaining polite and accommodating despite her arrogance. "Just sit tight. I'll be back in a few minutes."

While waiting for Mr. Howard to return, Dr. Hawkins reflected on something her mother once told her.

"Mother, when I grow up, I'm going to put a million dollars in the bank!" said young Lila Mae.

"Lila Mae, chile, don't ever put all your money in the bank," warned her mother. "There are too many crooked people. Do like me and your Daddy do…hide it somewhere."

The Cross' didn't trust banks and would place money in secret places throughout their Lanvale Street house. The two once told their daughter their apprehension about banks dated back to living through 'The Great Depression'. Considered the worst economic downturn in U.S. history, the trying time period spanned from 1929 to 1939. Wall Street crashed, causing investors to be wiped out, and half of the country's banks to fail.

I disagreed with Father and Mother's home banking system, and still do, she thought sitting in the bank. I hate to admit it, but they just don't know any better. Money in the bank earns interest. It can't earn interest tucked under a mattress, in a drawer, or sitting inside a coffee can or cookie jar. Banks are safe-houses for money. A person would stand a better chance of having their money stolen inside a house than in a bank.

Mr. Howard returned, interrupting the daydream she was having about her parents. Handing her an envelope, he stated, "Here's your certified check, Dr. Hawkins." Opening it up, she looked at the Certified Check, reading it aloud, "Pay to the order of Lila Mae Hawkins…Seventy-five thousand dollars and two cents."

"That is correct," said Mr. Howard, after which time the two took the necessary steps to close her account. Dr. Hawkins stuck the envelope inside her purse and stood up to leave.

"Thank you for your patronage over the years," said Mr. Howard. "We hate to lose your business. On behalf of Maryland National Bank, we wish you all the best," he said extending his hand to give her a handshake. Still seething over what she considered to be Mr. Howard's cockiness in trying to retain her business, she did not respond and left his hand hanging in mid-air. She turned, threw up her nose, and sauntered out of Maryland National Bank clutching the purse holding her life savings. Feeling exhilarated, she climbed into her two-seater and raced her Mercedes up Liberty Heights Avenue until it transitioned into Liberty Road.

I drove so fast that I made what normally was a 20-minute ride in about 10 minutes, she recalled. I wanted to open an account at Old Court Savings and Loan and deposit that cashier's check as quickly as possible! I could hardly wait for all that money to start drawing such handsome interest! Gloating during my drive, I thought about how smart my decision had been. Little did I know that one decision would bring me to ruins...proving to be the most unwise and by far, the costliest mistake I made in my entire life.

❀

Dr. Hawkins continued with her reflections – 'The Golden Girls' marathon continuing to play on.

"I will never forget when I turned to the morning news that May day in 1985," she recalled out loud. "And it truly was Mayday! For me, it was a day of great distress! I remember sitting down with a cup of fresh, brewed coffee and a buttered croissant. I took a long sip of coffee and heard a newscaster say something I will never forget!"

In what would become a day of infamy in Dr. Hawkins' book, the voice of a newscaster blared from her television set, "The Baltimore Sun is reporting that Old Court Savings and Loan has hired a new chief executive to clear up unspecified difficulties caused by rapid growth! Stay tuned more on this breaking story!"

Shocked, Dr. Hawkins spat coffee all over her clothes.

"Old Court Savings and Loan?!" she cried. "Why that's my bank!"

Flipping to hear the news on another channel she gasped, Let me turn to another station! What I just heard had to either be a mistake or a false report!"

Dr. Hawkins turned to all four of the local news stations – channels 11, 13, 2, and 45 respectively, only to discover they all were reporting the same story. She rushed to the front door of her home to grab the city's daily news publication, The Baltimore Sun. The paper was delivered to her home every morning, but she had not yet brought it in the house. Grabbing the paper, she rushed back inside.

I couldn't get the rubber band from around the paper fast enough! she recalled, reflecting on her actions that day. Unrolling that paper and seeing the bold, glaring headlines surrounding troubling practices at Old Court Savings and Loan shall forever be etched in my mind! By that time, I had nearly $80,000 in that bank! I called the bank repeatedly and kept getting a busy signal. I remember thinking that I needed to get to that bank as fast as I could no matter how I looked! I had not yet done my make-up or hair, which was still in sponge rollers, and was dressed in a housecoat. I grabbed a pair of slippers, put on a light jacket, grabbed my keys, and ran to my car. I didn't care how I looked. All I was concerned about was getting to that bank as fast as I could to withdraw every penny of my money! However, as I drove along Old Court Road towards the bank, I could already see the people...hundreds of them standing in a line that wrapped around the bank and extended along the street! Horrified, I drove along slowly...staring in disbelief at all those men and women...who like myself were in a frenzy. I parked my car, walked several blocks, and stood in line with them...all of us there for the same reason...to take our money out of that bank. I didn't get any of my money out of the bank that day…most of us didn't. I, along with so many others, would come to learn that we were among the victims of the biggest, white-collar crime in Maryland's history: The Old Court Savings & Loan Scandal.

Dr. Hawkins and other shocked depositors would discover that Jeffrey A. Levitz, executive of Old Court Savings & Loan, stole millions from the bank. We went broke, while he enjoyed the spoils of our money! I read he owned some 20 vehicles, homes not only here in Maryland, but in Florida, and even sported a custom-made golf cart with a 'Rolls Royce' front! All courtesy of our money, which financed his luxurious lifestyle! Just as clear as day I can still see myself along with other desperate depositors standing in line trying to withdraw our monies! Blacks, Whites, Jews, Asians…people of all nationalities. We stood under clear skies. We stood under cloudy skies. We stood in the sunshine. We stood in the rain. What a poor soul I was! On so many occasions, I cried myself to sleep wishing I had simply left my money in Maryland National Bank!

Dr. Hawkins reflected on the day she and her neighbor Mrs. Tucker, pulled onto their block at the same time. After parking, Mrs. Tucker got out of her car carrying a bag of groceries and rushed over to Dr. Hawkins' car, waiting for her to exit.

What the hell does this heifer want? Lila Mae silently grumbled. It's Saturday afternoon, and I've spent a good part of the day standing in line again at that God-forsaken bank! I don't want to talk to anybody! Maybe if I take my sweet time getting out of the car, she'll take her ass on in the house!

For several minutes, Dr. Hawkins sat in the car looking busy. Nevertheless, Mrs. Tucker stood and waited for her to exit. When that didn't work, Dr. Hawkins took out her 'Motorola Bag Phone' and pretended she was answering a call. Undeterred, Mrs. Tucker patiently continued to wait. My God! She is still standing outside my car! Dr. Hawkins screamed in her mind. I have fooled around in this car for at least 15 minutes, and Mrs. Tucker is still standing there holding her bag of groceries, smiling and waving! Damnit, I'm ready to go inside my house! I don't know why Mrs. Tucker feels it's necessary to bother me, but I may as well get this over with!

Dr. Hawkins pretended she was finishing her pretend call, closed her bag phone, and climbed out of the car.

"Why hello Mrs. Tucker," said Dr. Hawkins, mustering a weak smile.

"Why hello Dr. Hawkins!" said Mrs. Tucker. "And just call me Christine! We're neighbors you know! I was hoping to catch you coming or going into the house, and it looks like today is that day!"

"Whoopie!" replied Dr. Hawkins dryly. "Mrs. Tucker…I meant Christine…please excuse my forwardness, but it's been quite a day and I'm fairly tired. Is there something you would like to tell me?"

"Oh yes, there is!" said the bubbly woman, hardly able to contain herself. "That day my husband and I saw you at Maryland National –"

"Yes," interrupted Dr. Hawkins, "What about it?"

"Well, before leaving the bank, my husband Mark and I noticed Mr. Howard…the same banker who served us, taking you back to his desk."

"He did," said Dr. Hawkins. "Go on."

"Well," continued Mrs. Tucker, "Mark and I had gone to the bank that day to pull all our money out of

Maryland National to put out here at Old Court Savings and Loan. However, Mr. Howard strongly advised against it. At first, we thought he was telling us some mumbo-jumbo just so we wouldn't take out our money. But then we thought, 'what if this guy knows something?'"

Sickened by what she just heard, Dr. Hawkins thought, I really feel like throwing up!

"Dr. Hawkins, God sure has a way of warning us about things without us even knowing it!," continued Mrs. Tucker. 'I can't tell you how grateful Mark and I are for listening to Mr. Howard. With everything going on out here at Old Court Savings and Loan, I am sure you are very relieved that you bank with Maryland National Bank. Shaking her head, Mrs. Tucker added, "What a mess! Well, it has been nice talking to you, Dr. Hawkins. Enjoy the rest of your day."

Dr. Hawkins watched Mrs. Tucker trot off, thinking, I really feel sick now.

Prior to the Old Court Savings & Loan debacle, Dr. Hawkins had already earmarked her savings, planning to use a portion of the money to have an addition added to her house, and saving the rest of it for Dancer's education and her own retirement. But the crisis involving the bank was having a rippling effect on her life.

Harry Hughes, who was Maryland's governor at the time imposed a $1,000-a-month limit on withdrawals at Old Court Savings & Loan. Up until that time, Dr. Hawkins had not been able to withdraw any money from the bank. Withdrawing $1,000 a month is better than nothing, but that's hardly enough to pay my contractor the $10,000 I owe him for completing the new addition to my home! she thought. I had planned to write him a check against my checking account, but thanks to Mr. Levitz's thievery, I cannot do that now! That bank has put me in an awful predicament! And what about my retirement?! What about Dancer's education?!

The time she allocated to straightening out her affairs at the bank coupled with mounting stress surrounding the situation, led Dr. Hawkins to take a short leave of absence from work. Adding to her growing dilemma, footage of her standing in line at the bank aired on a local television newscast. People called and told me they saw me on the news waiting to get inside the bank, she recalled. I looked horrid with my hair in rollers and no make-up! Me...an assistant city school superintendent on television looking like Helga the Housemaid! They showed that news clip every single day! Oh, the embarrassment! My life was in shambles! I would stay up all night thinking about my quandary! I really thought I would have a nervous breakdown! My doctor prescribed me Quaaludes to calm my nerves and to help me sleep. I was downing 'Bloody Mary' after 'Bloody Mary' at Nick's Place, she remembered, referencing a bar and restaurant once located in the area. I would tell the waitress to make sure she told the bartender to make my Bloody Mary's strong. And then I would sit there in my favorite booth...drowning my sorrows in those alcoholic concoctions thinking about all the warnings people gave me ...what Mother said about putting all my money in the bank and people stealing...what the banker Mr. Howard told me about not putting my money in Old Court Savings and Loan. But that was all for naught because I didn't listen, and I paid a terrible price! I nearly became a lush! But after a great deal of prayer, and countless mornings waking up with head-banging hangovers, I reached a sobering conclusion. I would have to do the unthinkable. I would have to call Rufus.

Dr. Hawkins reflected on how day after painstaking day, she painfully pondered making that call to her husband. Still separated at the time, he was the last person she wanted to call.

Being on my own, I came to realize I had bitten off more than I could chew financially…even with all the money I was making. There was unexpected expense after unexpected expense on top of the mortgage, Dancer's private school tuition, my private psychiatrist, and other costs! I was in dire straits financially, and Rufus was the only person I knew who had the money on hand that I needed to catch up on my bills and pay the people I owed. The contractor was threatening to sue me for nonpayment, and I was even beginning to receive letters from my mortgage company threatening foreclosure. The company that financed my Mercedes was calling me relentlessly threatening repossession. I resorted to parking my car around the corner from my house under the cloak of darkness for fear I would wake up and find it gone from my driveway. On top of that, my car needed maintenance, but I could not afford to pay for oil changes and other needed services. Not only had I maxed out every one of my credit cards, but I had fallen behind on my credit card payments. Those creditors rang my phone non-stop – day and night, threatening to take me to court. What a mess I was in! There was no other spousal income or savings to fall back on. There was just one income – mines. But my bills and mounting expenses were outpacing my income, and thanks to Old Court Savings & Loan, I could not access the amount of money I needed to satisfy all my obligations. I could not even pay my Delta Sorority dues! Oh, the embarrassment of it all! As much as I didn't want to admit it, I realized just how much of a blessing it had been to have a husband who took care of all the bills. Not only did it allow me to spend my money any way I pleased, but I was able to set aside a portion of my salary, which I deposited in my savings account. I laid in my bed so many nights asking myself the question, 'Did I take Rufus for granted?' Sadly, I had to admit to myself, the answer was, 'Yes.' And now it appeared that Rufus was just about the only person I could turn to for help in my dire situation. I tried to come up with every possible alternative, but there were none. The last thing I wanted to do was ask Rufus for anything. But as I saw it, if I didn't go to him, I would lose everything.

Despite their estrangement, Mr. Hawkins made sure he remained an active part of their daughter's life – picking Dancer up, dropping her off, and sending Dr. Hawkins financial support in the form of money orders to support their daughter.

We hardly said a word to one another, Dr. Hawkins recalled. Rufus asked me how much I needed for Dancer's clothes, childcare, and other expenses. After I gave him a figure, he would send me money orders in the mail each week. He never put money in my hand. I recall him telling me he needed to make sure he had a record of what he was giving me in case I lied about him taking care of his daughter. We argued about that until I hung the phone up in his ear. And when Rufus picked Dancer up, or dropped her off, our words were limited to simple hellos and goodbyes.

After her name was removed from their joint bank account, Dr. Hawkins was no longer privy to how much Mr. Hawkins had in the bank. However, she firmly believed that if she went to him for a loan, he had the money.

Rufus did not believe in buying things with credit, she recalled in her reflections. When we were together, he didn't have one credit card. He always felt that if he couldn't pay for something with cash, it wasn't needed. He didn't like owing anybody. He is a simple man who rarely indulges in buying himself lavish things. For years, he drove the Thunderbird he bought with his 'Street Number' winnings. And even when he purchased that car, it was used. At the time, I thought he was being too frugal…a cheapskate…a tightwad. But on the contrary…there is no denying the fact that when it came to me, he always bought me new…never used. 'Only the best for my Kitten,' he would say, winking his eye. Rufus was a firm believer in saving money…not frivolously spending it…which is the reason why I was certain he had more than enough money in the bank to help me out. The truth of the matter was that I would have rather chewed rusty nails than have gone to him for help. I was abhorred by the thought. But I was so engulfed in debt that I knew I would have to swallow my pride and give Rufus a call…and I did.

That day came Saturday, August 17, 1985. Dr. Hawkins rehearsed what she would say once Mr. Hawkins answered. Picking up her residential phone, she began dialing, only to hang it up before the call went through. Dr. Hawkins did this several times, until she concluded, "Oh Lila Mae! You are overthinking this! Just call the man and get this over with!"

Dr. Hawkins again picked up the phone and called Mr. Hawkins.

"Hello," he said.

"Yes, hello Rufus, this is Lila Mae."

"Who?!"

"Lila Mae."

After a brief pause, Mr. Hawkins replied, "Lila Mae?! What do you want?!"

"Rufus, there's an urgent matter we need to discuss."

"An urgent matter we need to discuss?! Is something going on with Dancer?!"

"No, not a toll…Dancer is fine."

"Well, what is it then?!"

"I'd rather not discuss it over the phone. I'd rather talk to you in person. When can I stop by?"

"I'm pretty busy," said Rufus – Dr. Hawkins hearing through the phone what sounded like him flipping through a calendar or some kind of book. "It will be at least another week before I can fit you in."

"Not for another week?!" asked Dr. Hawkins, surprised at hearing he had a busy schedule.

"That's right," he replied.

"A week from today…let's see, that Saturday, August 24, 1985," said Dr. Hawkins looking at her Weekly Planner.

"Yep, you can stop by then…let's say 'round 3 p.m.," said Mr. Hawkins.

"Alright, I will be there," said Dr. Hawkins, jotting the date and time down in her Planner. I will see you then and thank –"

Before she could finish thanking Mr. Hawkins for agreeing to talk with her, he hung the phone up in her ear. Dr. Hawkins hung up her phone. She recalled thinking, Given my financial predicament, August 24th won't arrive soon enough…but at the same time, I am dreading its arrival.

✻

A week went by, and August 24, 1985, arrived. I recall my stomach turning, Dr. Hawkins thought, reflecting on the day. I laid in bed that morning thinking about how much I dreaded going over to the house and asking Rufus for money. But I dragged myself out of the bed and dressed myself along with Dancer who was about a year-and-a-half at the time. I dropped her off at the sitter's thinking it was best to limit any distractions such as Dancer crying or needing to change her diaper when Rufus and I talked. I parked my car, looked at nosy Miss Jenkins standing in her doorway, walked up the walkway, took a deep breath, and knocked on the door. I could hardly believe what I saw when Rufus opened the door.

Dr. Hawkins' visit to the house they formerly shared, marked the first time she had been inside since she left. It also marked the first time in about two years she had seen Mr. Hawkins in dress clothes. He wore a blue Oxford button-down shirt, pressed slacks with sharp creases, a black leather belt, and dressy shoes with tassels. His hair was freshly cut, and he was clean-shaven, having paid a visit to his barber John Battle earlier that morning.

When Rufus opened the door, I couldn't help but notice how handsome he looked, she recalled. And he not only looked good but smelled good. As soon as Rufus swung open the door, the inviting scent of 'Irish Spring' soap and 'Drakkar Noir' cologne filled the air. I love the smell of both…which was something I shared with Rufus when we were still together. From the looks of his girth, I noticed he had even lost weight! He invited me in, asking why I did not bring Dancer, and I explained I thought it was best to take her to the sitter so that the two of us could talk uninterrupted. After walking in, I was surprised to see the place did not look like a pigsty! Instead, It was clean and tidy! I was also shocked to see weights and an exercise bike sitting in a corner in the living room. 'My God,' I thought. Rufus is exercising?! Taking all these things in…I was quite bewildered. But I snapped out of my bewilderment, quickly reminding myself why I was there, and not to get off track.

Dr. Hawkins reflected on how they sat down, and how she kept 'beating around the bush' until Mr. Hawkins finally said, "Lila Mae, would you mind just sayin' whatever it is you're tryin' to say!" After several anguishing seconds, she got up enough gumption to blurt out "Rufus, I need a loan!"

"A loan?! Let me get this straight…you Dr. Lila Mae Sudie Hawkins are coming to me…a lowly mailman for a loan?" Mr. Hawkins asked, emphasizing her name.

"That's correct," she replied, squirming in her seat.

"So…er…Dr. Lila Mae…" how much money are you talkin' about?"

"$25,000," she replied in an incoherent mumble.

"What?!" said Mr. Hawkins. "I can't understand a thing you just said! Can you repeat that again?!"

"I said…twenty…five…thousand…dollars!" replied Dr. Hawkins sitting in angst awaiting his response.

"Woo-wee! That sure is a lot of money, Dr. Lila Mae. When you moved out there to that house on 'Sugar Hill' you had a lot of money. What happened to it?"

Dr. Hawkins did not want to get into the sordid details of what became of her money. Gritting her teeth, she provided scant information to him about what led up to her financial dilemma.

After listening to her quick overview, Mr. Hawkins replied, "I know what happened. I was just testin' to see if you was gonna lie," he snickered, "'Cause I saw you on television with them other peoples trying to get your money outta that bank! Hell, a lot of people saw you! Especially after the news camera zoomed in on you and gave your fancy title! And to think that Dr. Lila Mae now has to come to me… an ig'nant, stinky-footed Bawl'more mailman who talks to his beer cans and farts all the time to get a loan! Em…em…em," he laughed, shaking his head.

Offended, Dr. Hawkins replied, "Rufus! I did not come here to be humiliated! I simply —'

"Pull back your fangs Sudie…pull back your fangs!" he said. "Ole Rufus is gonna help ya out. You outta know that I'll never let our daughter be in a bad situation or lack anything because her mother made bad decisions and lost all her money! Now here's what I'm gonna do. I'm gonna loan you the money. But you are gonna pay me back every red cent! I should charge you interest, but I ain't gonna do that!"

Annoyed at his snide remarks, but greatly relieved he would loan her the money, Dr. Hawkins was moved to give Mr. Hawkins a hug to express her gratitude. But after having second thoughts, she decided against it.

"Sit tight Sudie," he chuckled, "While I go get my checkbook."

Mr. Hawkins got up from the sofa, excused himself to retrieve his checkbook, and during the brief moments he was gone, Dr. Hawkins glanced around the living room.

Letting out a deep sigh, she glanced around the living room and thought to herself, Despite the skirmishes that Rufus and I had in this house, this is still a place of endearment. Sitting here, I can't help but think about the wonderful times we had in this house. I find myself struggling not to admit there's a part of me that misses being here.

Mr. Hawkins walked back into the living room, interrupting her thoughts. Dr. Hawkins listened and watched while her estranged husband began writing out the check.

"Pay to the order of Dr. Lila Mae Hawkins," he gloated, "Twenty-five thousand dollars. Let's see…on the memo line what shall I say?" he asked himself out loud. "Loan!" he snickered, writing down the word. After tearing the perforated check from the checkbook, Mr. Hawkins stretched out his hand to take the check, and she stretched out hers to take it.

"Not so fast Sudie!" said Mr. Hawkins pulling back his hand. "Your hands might be itchin' for money, but right now, my back is itchin'! You scratch my back, and I'll scratch yours!" he said, sitting down on the couch and turning his back in her direction.

Abhorred, Dr. Hawkins thought, The nerve of Rufus asking me to scratch his back! I really want to tell him where to stick that check! After one of our arguments, I swore to him that I would never scratch his hairy back again! But if I do not scratch his back, he might change his mind about loaning me the money. I had better do it. I will just have to chalk this up to being a life lesson about never saying never.

Mr. Hawkins unfastened the buttons on his shirt so that he could lift it up along with his undershirt. Dr. Hawkins grimaced and began scratching his back.

"Ahhhh, that feels good Sudie," said Mr. Hawkins, letting out a loud exhale, followed by a burp. "This reminds me of how you used to scratch my back after we got married. But go a little easy. Feels like you're trying to claw my back instead of scratching it. Hit the top shoulder blade… that feels nice. Now get that middle part. Oh yeah, that's it right there!"

I could just die! she thought, continuing to scratch his back.

SERENITY HOUSE

After several more minutes, Mr. Hawkins said chuckling, "I'll put you out of your misery. You can stop scratching my back now Sudie."

If he calls me Sudie one more time, I swear I'm going to clonk him over the head! she silently shouted. Keep calm Lila Mae…keep calm. Wusa! Wusa! she repeated, closing her eyes.

"Here you go Lila Mae," said Mr. Hawkins, handing her the check. "Now I expect full payment. I'm not gonna impose a deadline or nothin' like that on you, but when do you think you will be able to repay it?"

"I believe it's safe to say that I can start paying you monthly installments in another three to four months and I —"

"Naw Sudie," interrupted Mr. Hawkins. "I don't want no piecemeal payments…too much time and trouble tryin' to keep up with all of that! I'm giving you the whole $25,000 chunk at one time, and I want the whole $25,000 chunk repaid at one time."

"Alright Rufus," said Dr. Hawkins, folding up the check and placing it in her purse. "I believe it's safe to say that I will be able to repay you all the money back in about three years…maybe before then if I'm able to recoup my money from Old Court Savings & Loan."

"That's fine," Mr. Hawkins agreed. "Just don't try to swindle me," he laughed.

"I don't find your sense of humor funny at all!" said Dr. Hawkins, standing up to leave. "But I am greatly appreciative of you helping me out. Thank you, Rufus."

"You're welcome," he replied.

"Well, I guess I'll be on my way," stated Dr. Hawkins, making her way to the front door.

"Let me get the door for you," said Mr. Hawkins, rushing to the front door to open it. "You may have forgotten, but I'm still a gentleman."

"Why thank you, Rufus," said Dr. Hawkins, walking through the door and onto the front porch.

"You're welcome," he said. "Get home safely."

"I will," she responded, making her way down the porch steps.

"Oh, and one more thing 'Kitten'," cooed Mr. Hawkins.

Dr. Hawkins stopped dead in her tracks, thinking, Oh my! Rufus just called me by my pet name! Seems to me, he is finally making the first move! He wants to reconcile! Why else would he be calling me 'Kitten' in such a sexy manner? I guess Rufus simply could not go on living without me. I assume he is about to call me back inside the house, fall to his knees and beg his Kitten to come back home. As much as I hated scratching that hairy back of his…I must admit…it not only brought back memories of the good ole times we had together…but it was nice to touch him after such a long time. I am feeling like a giddy teenager right now…enough to answer him back by saying, 'Yes, my Chocolate Superman?' But I had better not…I don't want to seem desperate.

"Yes, Rufus?" she replied alluringly, turning around to face him.

"Kitten if I were you, I wouldn't cash that check at Old Court Savings and Loan!" he teased.

Watching Mr. Hawkins bursting with laughter, she hissed, "Indeed! Rufus, I did not find that funny at all!"

"It was funny as heck to me!" he laughed. "Aww, lighten up Lila Mae! It was just a joke!"

"Well, I found it to be in extremely poor taste!" she replied. "I will leave it at that!"

Marching to her car Dr. Hawkins fumed, The nerve of that man leading me on and then telling such a terrible joke! But I will not act indignant by stooping down to his level! Rolling her eyes at Miss Jenkins who stood on her porch, she thought, I will only make a spectacle of myself in front of that nosy Miss Jenkins! Doesn't that woman have anything better to do than stand on her porch staring at me?!"

"Why you rollin' your eyes at me Lila Mae?" yelled Miss Jenkins. "I ain't do nothin' to you!"

"Just ignore that busybody!" Dr. Hawkins mumbled, trekking down the street to her car. "After all, you are leaving with what you came to get…and that's the $25,000 check you have inside this purse!" she said, tightly squeezing the clutch-style purse beneath her arm. "And I plan to repay Rufus every penny of this money back if it's the last thing I do, because if I don't…he will never let me live it down!" she surmised, pulling off in her car so fast, the wheels screeched.

The day continues to move along, Dr. Hawkins had prepared herself lunch consisting of French Onion Soup Au Gratin and a Chef Salad drizzled in her favorite Poppyseed dressing. Another episode of 'The Golden Girls' was on. As she sipped her soup and crunched on her salad, Dr. Hawkins immersed herself in another one of Blanche, Rose, Dorothy, and Sophia's capers. But before long, she was simply staring at the television, her mind roaming off to the affairs of her own life. Thank God for the $25,000 loan from Rufus! she thought. Despite his childish mockery of my financial difficulties, I am glad he loaned me that money. Those funds kept me from losing my home, not having to file for bankruptcy… which I thought I would have to do, and allowed me to catch up on my credit card debt! I was also able to pay the contractor, which got him off my back! I believe it's fair to say I don't know what I would have done without it! Looking back over what happened at Old Court Savings and Loan, it would take years before I was able to recoup some of it. And some of the poor souls who banked with them died before they could get anything. That situation was the source of so much heartache and pain! And how could I ever forget that dreadful evening at Nick's Place!

Dr. Hawkins' mind called up the past, going back to October 7, 1985. She was sitting in her favorite booth at Nick's Place when she overheard two men the waiter seated behind her discussing a familiar name.

I was downing a Bloody Mary and thinking about that damn swindler Jeffrey Levitiz, she recalled, images of the evening assembling in her mind. Sitting there, I could hear the two men laughing and talking. Naturally, when I heard the name Levitz, I began to eavesdrop.

"Jeffrey Levitz sure messed a whole lot of people up," said one of the men.

"Tell me about it," said the other. "He ruined a lot of lives."

Sitting there listening to their conversation, Dr. Hawkins' eavesdropping was momentarily interrupted by a cautionary voice in her mind – it was that of her mother. Lila Mae, what I tell you about all that signafyin'? Keep it up, and one day you are gonna hear something you don't want to hear.

But just as fast as her mother's voice popped in her mind, it popped out just as quickly. I just could not help myself, she remembered. I wanted to hear more of what those men were saying about Levitz. Dr. Hawkins continued to listen to the monotonous voice of one man, and the gravelly voice of the other. I know that raspy voice anywhere! she thought, taking another sip of her drink. It belongs to that smokestack neighbor of mines Mr. Tucker! The other man sounds familiar too, but I can't quite put my finger on who he is…if I continue to listen, I am certain I can figure it out.

"Quite honestly, I had been scooped that Old Court Savings and Loan was in serious trouble," said the man with the monotonous voice. "Some of the employees who worked at the bank knew Levitz was spending money like water. That raised some eyebrows. But a few of them were also suspicious of how Old Court did business….one of them being a young lady I used to date. She worked there as a banker and told me things were eventually going to hit the fan. She also let me in on the fact that when things hit the fan, some bad shit was going to go down at that bank."

"And it damn sure did," replied Mr. Tucker.

"Now as you very well know, I tried to warn people about Old Court Savings and Loan," said the man, his comments instantaneously telling Dr. Hawkins exactly who he was and where she knew him from. My God! That's that guy from Maryland National! she silently yelled to herself. "That's Michael Howard…the banker who tried to convince me to leave my money in that bank! My gut is telling me to pay my tab and leave. No, no, no. Why should I leave? I was here first. Besides, I'm going to finish my drink and leave once I'm good and ready. Moreover, I'm curious to hear what else they are going to say.

"We had many customers coming to Maryland National who either wanted to take a portion of their money out, or all of it," continued Mr. Howard. "Knowing what I had been told along with the fact that money is so hard to come by, I wanted to alert people before they put their money in that bank. Now of course I could not come right out and tell our customers what I heard about Old Court Savings and Loan. So, I tried to do it discreetly. Some listened. Some did not. If I can be candid, those who didn't listen lost their shirts…their drawers…and their asses."

"That's some fucked-up shit," said Mr. Tucker. "And my wife and I could have just as easily been one of them."

"I know," replied Mr. Tucker. "But you two listened…many didn't. All you can do is try. You can't make people listen…especially the ones who think they know everything."

"You got that right," responded Mr. Tucker with a cough-filled laugh. "And one of them happens to be my wife."

"I know what you mean," chuckled Mr. Howard. "But you know the old saying, "Happy wife, happy life.""

'I'll drink to that!' agreed Mr. Tucker raising a glass of Rum and Coke followed by the two men clanging their glasses together. "Well Michael, I just wanted to treat you to dinner and drinks for what you did for me and Christine. Christine and I were prepared to take our money out of Maryland National and put it out at Old Court S and L. You really saved our necks. Had it not been for you, we would have lost our retirement."

"Hey man, I don't deserve the credit," replied Mr. Howard. "The credit goes to God. Don't thank me…thank Him."

Dr. Hawkins continued sitting in the booth, now squirming, and taking big swallows of her Bloody Mary while listening to the men.

"Thank you, Lord!" said Mr. Tucker, coughing repeatedly. "Man," he said to Mr. Howard, "I really need to give up these cigarettes. I can hardly get out a few words before I start coughing trying to catch my breath. Oh, and by the way…I've been meaning to ask you something.'

"What is it?" asked Mr. Howard, sipping Vodka and orange juice.

"That day Christine and I were at the bank, we saw you taking one of our neighbors back to your desk."

"Hmmm," said Mr. Howard. "So many people come through the bank. Describe her to me…maybe that will refresh my memory."

"She's a tall, light-skinned Black woman with long hair who thinks she's White," said Mr. Tucker. "The day my wife and I saw her in the bank, she was wearing a mink coat."

"Oh…that Bitch!" exclaimed Mr. Howard, prompting Dr. Hawkins to gawk in the booth on the other side. "I will never forget her! I can still remember her name because she made sure I didn't forget it…Lila Mae Hawkins…Doctor Lila Mae Hawkins," he said, emphasizing the word 'Doctor'. She nearly bit my head off for mistakenly not addressing her by her doctoral title."

Mr. Tucker replied, "What a stuck-up Braud! Me and Christine speak to her, and all the snooty heifer does is nod her head…won't even open her forward mouth to speak. What a piece of work!"

"Well, I tried to warn her too in an indirect way," said Mr. Tucker. "Not only did she not listen, but she threatened to ask for the branch manager because I was advising against taking all of her money out of Maryland National. Come to think of it, she said she was planning to put it all out at Old Court Savings and Loan. She withdrew her money from our bank and closed the account. I don't know if she put her money in that Savings and Loan or not…hopefully she didn't."

"She did," Mr. Tucker disclosed. "My wife saw her on television trying to get her money out of the bank. She's some bigwig in the school system too."

"Sorry to hear that happened to her," said Mr. Howard. "Despite her arrogance, it's very unfortunate."

"Well, I don't have an ounce of pity for anybody whose head is so swollen with pride, it can barely fit in a room," coughed Mr. Tucker. "If you ask me, she got what she deserved."

Dr. Hawkins sat in her booth stunned for several seconds before deciding she heard enough and needed to leave. After swallowing down the remainder of her drink, she left the money to pay her bill, grabbed her purse, and slid out of the booth. All I want to do is get out of here without them seeing me, she thought. However, there's no way to exit this place without walking past their booth. With her face turned away, Dr. Hawkins quickly walked past the booth where the two men sat. She was about four feet past them when Mr. Tucker cried out, "Well, I'll be doggone! I believe that's my neighbor Dr. Hawkins! I would recognize that walk anywhere!" His comments prompted Dr. Hawkins to abruptly stop her quick stride to turn around and look at the two – their necks outstretched, peering over their booth. "What a coincidence!" said Mr. Tucker, unaware she had been sitting directly behind them. "Me and my friend Mr. Howard here were just talking about you!"

Flustered, embarrassed, and upset, Dr. Hawkins rushed out of Nick's Place crying while thinking, I could just pull my hair out! The only thing I want to do right now is take a Quaalude and go to sleep!"

Bringing her mind back to 2018, Dr. Hawkins concluded, Levitt and his cronies…which also included his wife, caused my life to plummet into a horrendous financial crisis. Drunk one night and feeling totally hopeless…I had even contemplated suicide by overdosing on Quaaludes. Thank God I did not do that! I realized I had too much to live for…including my daughter…and that the tide of my financial situation could change at any time. I felt like I was thrown off a boat that capsized. But how would I know the tide had calmed and that I could climb back aboard the boat if I drowned myself?

Mr. Levitt pleaded guilty to stealing $14.6 million from Old Court Savings & Loan and was sentenced to 30 years in prison; serving 7 ½ years before being paroled in 1993.

I did get to see justice served…but as I saw it…Levitt got off too easy…considering he destroyed so many dreams and lives, she thought. But at least I was able to recoup some of my money. I was also able to eventually regain control of my financial life. I had to learn how to better balance my budget and drastically cut back on lavish clothes and other items to pay my mortgage and others bills. I had to account for every penny I made. I also had to let my Mercedes go and buy a car outright with the money Rufus loaned me. I did not like driving around in that red, white, and blue 1972 Ford Pinto one bit…talk about humbling! But it was what I had to do to get around…and that car was great on gas. Thank God for allowing Rufus to loan me that money! It helped me to regain a sense of normalcy in my life. By 1991, between setting aside money from my paychecks, and recovering a portion of the money I lost in the scandal, I finally was able to save up enough funds to repay Rufus his $25,000…and had every intention of doing so. That is…until I called the house one day to let him know I would be dropping off the check…and a woman answered the phone.

Remembering how flabbergasted she was to hear the voice of a female answering Mr. Hawkins' phone that June 27, 1991 day, she thought, It was a Thursday evening, and I knew by that time Rufus should be home from work. I never expected some woman to answer his phone! I guess I was about 39 at the time…and I can still vividly recall a pit immediately forming in my stomach the moment I heard her voice! I did not say a word…I simply hung up and called Miss Jenkins to find out what was going on. Miss Jenkins hasn't earned the nickname 'Sister Two-Faced' at church for nothing! We all call her that because of her notorious tendency to run her mouth and stir up drama by straddling the fence between people in the congregation who are at odds with one another. I absolutely loathed calling that nosy woman! But if anybody knew what was going on at Rufus' house and if he were seeing another woman…it would be Miss Jenkins, Dr. Hawkins surmised, her mind drifting back to the call she made to her former neighbor and their conversation.

In preparing to make the call to Miss Jenkins that 1991 day, Dr. Hawkins stood in her Randallstown home holding her phone, ready to dial – but hesitated. I wanted to hear the truth, but at the same time I did not want to hear the truth, she recalled. When I left Rufus, I never gave any thought to the fact that he might possibly take up with another woman. I always assumed he would stop being so stubborn and we would get back together. But I was wrong, she concluded, recalling the things Miss Jenkins told her once she made the call. The phone barely rang once before Miss Jenkins answered, "Hello?"

"Hello, Miss Jenkins, this is Dr. Lila Mae Hawkins," said Dr. Hawkins.

"Chile, I know who this is," replied Miss Jenkins. "Not only did I catch your voice as soon as I heard it, but your name came up on my Caller ID. Chile, I started to call you, but figured I better mind my business."

"You did?" asked Dr. Hawkins.

"That's right," said Miss Jenkins.

"To tell me what?" inquired Dr. Hawkins.

"Well since you asked…and you did call me," said Miss Jenkins, "I might as well tell you…Rufus is seeing some young hussy named Anna."

"Anna?!" Lila Mae, asked, feeling both angst and anger over what her neighbor just divulged.

"That's right," said Miss Jenkins.

"I can't believe it!" Dr. Hawkins shouted in the phone.

"You had better believe it!" replied Miss Jenkins. "At first, she would spend the night, but now the young heifer done moved right on in."

"They live together?!" Dr. Hawkins asked.

"Yep," said Miss Jenkins. "Shacking up! And Rufus needs to be 'shamed of himself too. He is old enough to be that gal's father!'"

"Is that so?!"

"Sad to say, but I'm afraid so," said her former neighbor. "I see her out my windows all the time. And just the other day I just so happened to be looking out the window, and I saw Rufus park a new car. I guess he got rid of the Thunderbird. I was gonna call you about that too, but I figured I'd better keep it to myself and mind my business."

"What!?" asked Dr. Hawkins. "Rufus has a new car?! What kind of car?"

'Chile, a black convertible sports car. A nice one too. Looks like one of them Mar-sadees Benz's…kind of reminds me of the one you used to have."

"I believe you meant Mercedes Benz," said Dr. Hawkins.

"However you wanna pronounce it, I'm standing at the door looking at the car right now," replied Miss Jenkins. "That car is a two-seater…just like the one you used to have. I guess he brought that one he got parked outside for him and that woman to ride in."

Dr. Hawkins was speechless, images of her husband riding around with another female coming to mind. She tried to paint a picture in her mind of how the person might look. A few seconds went by without either she or Miss Jenkins saying a word.

"Hello?!" said Miss Jenkins. "Hello Lila Mae, are you still there?!"

"Yes, Miss Jenkins," answered Dr. Hawkins. "I am still here."

"Maybe Rufus is going through some kind of mid-life crisis," said Miss Jenkins. "All men go through that."

"But Rufus is only 39," replied Dr. Hawkins.

"That might be right," said Miss Jenkins. "But some men go through it sooner than others. Just like some women go through menopause sooner than others. I wasn't but 40 when I stopped getting my periods. I know women a lot older than me who still get their periods. They are still on the rag and –"

"Really Miss Jenkins! I hate to be rude, but I really don't want to hear about when you stopped getting your period!" said Dr. Hawkins.

"You ain't got to be so nasty about it!" said Miss Jenkins. "I was only –"

Before Miss Jenkins finished, Dr. Hawkins heard a loud noise through the telephone, prompting her to ask, "Miss Jenkins are you still there? Is everything alright!"

"Oh Lawd!" shouted Miss Jenkins. "I just saw something that made me drop the phone!"

"You did?" asked Dr. Hawkins. "Well, what did you see?"

"My Lawd," replied Miss Jenkins. "I better not say."

'What is it, Miss Jenkins?! Tell me…what do you see?"

"Are you sure you want me to tell you, Lila Mae?"

"Yes, Miss Jenkins! Whatever it is, please tell me!"

"Well, since you insist, I'll tell you. That heifer is standing at the screen door right now wearing one of your old housecoats!"

"What?!" roared Dr. Hawkins. "You mean to tell me that not only has Rufus moved some slut into our house, but she's wearing the clothes I left behind?!"

"I'm afraid so," said Miss Jenkins, smacking on her spearmint chewing gum. 'Lawd have mercy. Em…em…em."

Nearly 30 years between when she called Miss Jenkins to ask about her estranged husband and today, Dr. Hawkins could still remember how upset she was at the time, thinking to herself, I was so infuriated, I slammed the phone down in Miss Jenkins' ear! I told myself, 'I'll be damn if Rufus and some cheap whore named Anna are going to spend my hard-earned money…$25,000 to be exact…frolicking around!' And then I tore the check in half and ripped it into shreds.

Justifying her unwillingness to repay the loan to her estranged husband on his purported infidelity, Dr. Hawkins just could not fathom Mr. Hawkins seeing another woman. I felt that since we were not together per se, he would remain faithful to me. I assumed he would always be there. After all, while we were separated, we were still Mr. and Mrs. Hawkins…living in separate households…but as I saw it…still married. And the thought of some bimbo wearing the housecoats I left behind made me even madder! I figured I would leave those things in my drawers just in case I spent a night or two there leading up to us getting back together…that is…after he made the first move. But little did I know at the time that he was making moves on some young woman…who…according to Miss Jenkins was half his age! That explains why Rufus was all spiffed up the day he loaned me the money! It also explains why the house was so clean…she cleaned it up! It also explains Rufus' weight loss and the exercise equipment I saw! That was his attempt to get in shape to keep up with that young woman! And to think the two of them had the unmitigated gall to be scooting around town in a two-seater Mercedes convertible! The nerve! I'm certain she was using Rufus for his money! What a fool! Nothing more than a Sugar Daddy! It took me nearly six years to save up enough money to repay Rufus! I'll be damned if I was going to give Rufus $25,000 of my hard-earned money to spend on some harlot!

As punishment for Mr. Hawkins' seeing another woman, Dr. Hawkins used her daughter as a pawn to get back at her husband, refusing to drop her off at their Gwynns Falls Parkway home as she sometimes would do in the past, and minimizing the time they would normally spend together. If Rufus wants to see our daughter, he will have to drive to my house and pick her up! Dr. Hawkins declared. I am not burning my gas to drop Dancer off and Rufus is galivanting around with some woman! I will also make sure I schedule Dancer's dance and etiquette classes during Rufus' days off! I'll teach that two-timing gigolo to mess around on me!

Mr. Hawkins eventually caught on to her ploy, threatening to sue her for the money she owed him. Although Rufus said he would take me to court, he never did...albeit I still have not paid him his money, thought Dr. Hawkins. I had justifiable reasons not to! On top of him seeing some floozy named Anna, that woman had the nerve to call me and demand I repay Rufus his money! The unmitigated gall of that winch to call me... his wife of 21 years at the time...and curse me out about that money! Not to mention she called me the same week of Rufus and I's wedding anniversary! And while I always carry myself in an upright, dignified way as a church-going woman, I had no choice but to get indignant, she admitted. I just could not hold my tongue that day!

Reflecting on Thursday, September 26, 1991, Dr. Hawkins thought, I was sitting in the lunchroom at work chatting with my colleagues and eating lunch when my cell phone rang. I looked at the number and saw it was the telephone number from our house on Gwynns Falls Parkway. Wondering why Rufus was calling me while I was at work, but thinking it might be an important matter, I answered. But it was not Rufus at toll! Instead, it was that bimbo of his Anna...calling me from the house phone! 'This is Anna! Is this Lila Mae?!' she screamed in my ear. I said, 'Yes, it is. Please hold on.' I politely excused myself from the lunchroom to resume the call.

For privacy, Dr. Hawkins walked outside to her car to resume the call with Anna, whose full name is Anna Barnes.

"Yes, hello, what do you want?!" asked Dr. Hawkins.

"I want you to pay my common-law husband Rufus back his money!" said Ms. Barnes.

"You've got some nerve calling me on my cell phone!" snapped Dr. Hawkins. "And who gave you my phone number!"

"Don't worry about who gave me your phone number!" Ms. Barnes shouted in the phone. "When do you plan to give my man back his money!"

"Your common-law husband?! Your man?!" Dr. Hawkins sarcastically asked. "Ha! That's a joke! Are you aware that Rufus and I are still married? You're nothing but a side chic! I'm still his wife!"

"I don't give a damn about that!" said Ms. Barnes. "The bottom line is that you two aren't together and he's in love with me now!"

"I hardly believe that!" yelled Dr. Hawkins, looking around to make sure no one was within earshot of her car. "Perhaps he's having some cheap fling with you because he's going through a mid-life crisis of some sort, but he's not in love with you!"

"Whether you believe it or not, it's true!" shouted Ms. Barnes. "Even if you wanted to come back to him, he wouldn't take back your snooty ass...Sister Sudie Snooty! Ain't that your name?!"

"How dare you call me that?!" hollered Dr. Hawkins. "If I could, I would come through this phone and slap the shit out of you!"

"And I would whip your ass too!" lashed Ms. Barnes. "You're just mad because Rufus has moved on! He's with me now!"

"Listen here you cheap whore!" Dr. Hawkins yelled. "Rufus and I are still legally married!"

"Like I said before, I don't give a damn about him being married to you! That don't bother me at all! All that means is that I took him from you! Ain't no shame in my game! I like em' married!"

"It doesn't take a rocket scientist to see that, you homewrecker!" said Dr. Hawkins. "But that doesn't change the fact that Rufus and I are still married! Therefore, if I decide not to take him back, you're just getting my leftovers!"

"Leftovers?!" said Ms. Barnes. "Bitch, you can kiss my ass!"

"Who are you calling a Bitch?!" asked Dr. Hawkins.

"You!" replied Ms. Barnes.

"How dare you call me that insidious name you Jezebel slut!" bellowed Dr. Hawkins. "You listen, and you listen good! I am and always will be the first wife! You got that! The first wife!"

"And look at you 'First Wife'! laughed Anna sarcastically. "A miserable 40-year-old lonely bag that nobody wants!"

"40-year-old bag?!" screamed Dr. Hawkins. "I beg your pardon! I'm only 39!"

"Round it off and you're 40!" screamed Anna.

"Where are you?!" yelled Dr. Hawkins. "I might live in Randallstown now, but I grew

up on Appleton Street! I'll meet you right now and whip your ass!"

"You know where I am!" yelled Anna. "In your house, wearing your negligee, laying in your bed, waiting for your man to come home so I can do all the things for him that you would never do!"

"Argh!" Dr. Hawkins screamed, hanging up the phone. She could now hear the faint tap of someone's knuckles lightly rapping against her car window. Dr. Hawkins looked up and there stood Dr. Walter Amprey, Superintendent of the Baltimore City Public School System.

"Dr. Amprey!," she said, rolling down her window. "I didn't know you were standing there!"

"Are you okay Dr. Hawkins?!" he asked with a perplexed look on his face. "I could hear you cussing…er' I meant fussing after I walked out the building…just checking on you."

Flustered, Dr. Hawkins explained, "I just had an incredibly challenging call. I'm terribly sorry you caught me acting in such an ugly manner Dr. Amprey."

"No problem," he replied, "It happens to the best of us."

The two bid each other goodbye. Embarrassed and irate, Dr. Hawkins set her sights on personally confronting Mr. Hawkins. *I was minding my business at work, and here comes the devil! I cannot believe Rufus gave that woman my cell phone number!* Dr. Hawkins thought, marching back into the building to return to work. *And not only that, but Rufus put her up to calling me about the money I owe him because he does not have the balls to confront me about it himself! That foul-mouthed winch also cussed me out and called me Dr. Sudie Snooty! Who else could have told her that name but Rufus? And on top of everything else, my boss heard me cursing and acting a fool! Oh, the humiliation! Well since Rufus gave that hussy my personal number, and she called me while I was on my job, I'll be sure to pay him a visit on his!*" she decided. "I know Rufus' mail route, and I will make it my business to speak to him face-to-face about this on tomorrow!"

The Golden Girls Marathon still playing, Dr. Hawkins momentarily pondered what she would prepare for dinner that evening, while briefly recalling her confrontation with Mr. Hawkins on Friday, September 27, 1991. *I left work early, tracked down Rufus' mail truck, and gave him a piece of my mind! We had quite a kerfuffle before*

he took off in his mail truck like a bat out of hell! That was the first time I ever saw a mail truck turn the corner on two wheels! she chuckled. I'm laughing now, but it was hardly funny to me at the time. After our blistering argument, that day, Rufus and I drifted further and further apart, she sighed. I immersed myself in work, sorority activities, social events, and Dancer, making sure she received the finest education along with the necessary training to become a professional dancer. I also sent her to both Flair Studio of Dance and Modeling and Travis Winkey Studios. Under the tutelage of Willia Bland, Andrea Bland, and Travis Winkey, my Dancer modeled in fashion shows all over the city. As far as dancing was concerned, I wanted to see to it that my daughter would become the best of the best! The crème de la crème! I never achieved my dream of becoming a professional dancer. But that didn't mean Dancer could not become one. So, I pushed her! I felt that if she was going to become a professional dancer, she didn't have time to play Hide and Seek and other silly games with the neighborhood kids. Nor did she have time to play Nurse with her dolls. I remember her telling me she wanted to be a nurse when she grew up. I dismissed those aspirations with something she gathered from a conversation with her father. But I would not hear of her becoming a nurse…I wanted her to become a dancer, Dr. Hawkins admitted, feeling a sense of self-incrimination while remembering the day Mr. Hawkins dropped Dancer off after taking her shopping at Toys "R" Us on Baltimore National Pike.

"Mommy! Mommy!" Dancer exclaimed, skipping through the front door carrying a large plastic bag imprinted with the toy chain's bright, multi-colored logo. "Look at my new dolls!" she cried, pulling 'Raggedy Ann' and 'Andy' dolls out of the bag along with two 'Cabbage Patch' Kids dolls.

"How nice," replied Dr. Hawkins rather dryly.

"I've always wanted Raggedy Ann and Andy dolls! And boy oh boy did I want a Cabbage Patch Kid! And Daddy got me two! And look at what else Daddy got me!" Dancer giggled, showing her mother a children's doctor's bag, and opening it to reveal a pretend stethoscope, candy vitamins, and other items inside. "I'm going to play 'Doctor' and 'Nurse' and 'Raggedy Ann' and 'Andy' and my 'Cabbage Patch' dolls are going to be the newest patients in my hospital!" Dancer announced, referring to her bedroom, which was her imaginary hospital ward.

We'll just see about that, Dr. Hawkins thought, watching her daughter dart upstairs to play with her new toys. Those things will only divert her attention away from dancing.

A few days later, while Dancer was in dance class, Dr. Hawkins disposed of Dancer's new dolls, doctor's bag, and other items. Now, I feel bad about what I did, admitted Dr. Hawkins. But back then, I thought I was doing the proper thing as it related to Dancer's future. But sitting here and really thinking back on it, begs two questions. Did I dispose of Dancer's toys because I felt they would somehow divert her attention away from Dance? Or could it have been because it was another way of punishing Rufus? I guess it was a little bit of both. But in doing what I did, I have no choice but to silently admit that Dancer was the one being punished…although that was never my intention.

Dr. Hawkins continued to sit in silent reflection.

As time went on, Rufus and I were doing all kinds of things to ruffle each other's feathers, which included me going out of my way to be nasty towards him…and him going out of his way to be nasty to me. Anytime he found the opportunity to call me 'Dr. Sudie Snooty' and ask me about the loan, he did. And anytime I found the opportunity to call him 'A Dumb Sugar Daddy', I did that. Eventually, we stopped speaking altogether. I reached a point where I felt our marriage was irreparable. Not only had he taken up with another woman, but he had allowed her to move into our house! The two eventually broke up…serves him right…but we had been separated for 16 years. I thought, 'Why waste more precious years of my life waiting for him to come to his senses?' By that time I was pushing 50 and had given up on trying to save our marriage. As I saw it, our only option was divorce…and in 2000…some 18 years ago…we divorced.

᳜

After hours of sitting in her home reflecting on her engagement, marriage, separation, and divorce, Dr. Hawkins exhaled loudly and softly whispered, "During Rufus and I's many disagreements, I lost count of the numbers of phones I broke and had to replace after speaking to that man. However, after the ink dried on our divorce, I eventually came to realize that phones were quite easy to replace. But on the contrary…a good, hard-working husband…even one who belches, passes gas, has smelly feet, watches football every weekend…with a beer can in one hand and a Buffalo wing in the other…are not so easily replaced. I suppose Rufus has his flaws. But I'm 66 now…and it took me this long to realize that I have a few flaws too. I am sure that Rufus having to get up at the crack of dawn to go to work after hearing my snoring all night was no cakewalk either. I suppose we both had our flaws and shortcomings. Perhaps we should have tried harder to work through them. But when one's mind is made up about something…it's hard to unmake it. But not impossible if a person is willing to be open-minded and try. You also have to be willing to compromise."

᳜

It was now going on 6 p.m. and Dr. Hawkins was sitting alone in her kitchen eating the dinner she prepared for herself – salmon, asparagus, and a tossed salad with poppyseed dressing splashed with a touch of vinaigrette and olive oil.

"Ah, that was delicious," she mumbled, chewing on the remaining morsels of her dinner before chasing it down with a tall glass of homemade lemonade. "When life gives you lemons," she said, looking at the lemons sitting at the bottom of the glass, "Make lemonade. Beyoncé made a song about that…and I have to agree."

Dr. Hawkins picked up her dish and glass and washed them at the sink. "All these years, I've had one less dish to wash…one less meal to cook…one less of everything…which reminds me of Marilyn McCoo singing that old 1970's song," she said, referencing The 5th Dimension's 'One Less Bell to Answer.' "Rufus and I married the same year that song came out. But never in a million years did I see myself having so much in common with the lyrics representing the woman of that song. I suppose it speaks for many women. But on the song, her man left her…but in my case…I left him."

'One Less Bell to Answer' playing in her mind, Dr. Hawkins decided, I think I'll play that song…just for old times' sake. I have the CD. I loved that song back then…and still do. It's quite sad…but absolutely beautiful.

After retrieving the CD, she placed it in her player and sat down on the sofa. Listening to the melody, she thought, I'm not knocking the new music, but there's a certain truth about those old songs that hold true despite the test of time. Tearing up, she inwardly admitted, Unfortunately, my marriage did not. But I can't help but admit like the woman says in the song… I still love him.

Time now ticked to a little after 6 p.m. and once again Dr. Hawkins sat perched in front of the television. No longer listening to her musical CD, her ears were now paying rapt attention to 'The Golden Girls' theme song, 'Thank You For Being A Friend'.

My God, she thought. I've heard that song so many times over the years. I guess I was listening and not listening. I was hearing the song, but not really paying attention to what the song was saying. But sitting here and finally listening to the words…I mean really listening to the words…I realize that song is all about friendship.

Glancing around her home she thought, I was always very particular about letting people in my personal space. The last best friend I had was Kate Bowers, my old classmate at Western. But we lost contact after she married and moved away. I guess I came to believe that I really did not need a best friend…or even a close circle of friends. But right now, I sure could use one for a little pick me up…because I am feeling low today…starting with that call from Dancer. I'm both happy and sad about that and wish I could pick up the phone and call someone. A good girlfriend who would immediately detect something was wrong by merely the sound of my voice…one who would make it her business to come over…one who I could share private thoughts with and not worry about her blabbing my business in the streets…one I could call in the wee hours of the morning and cry in her ear about a problem or other misfortune in life…and she would listen and provide encouragement that everything will work out. A best friend who would go to the ends of the earth with you…a ride or die as the young folks say now. A friend you can chit-chat with over tea or brunch and just talk and with whom you can be real. That is what this show is about…that is what that song is about…friendship…something that Blanche, Rose, Dorothy, and Sophia all share. But I don't have that. Yes, I do have friends…but not any close ones. I never felt I needed one. But now I realize I do.

It was now 6:30 p.m. and a different television show was coming on. 'The Golden Girls' marathon had ended, prompting Dr. Hawkins to pick up her remote control and flick off the television.

"I cannot believe I spent the entire day watching television," she thought out loud, slipping her feet back into her mink Marabou pink slippers. "As much as I have always enjoyed watching The Golden Girls, I must admit…today it was rather painful because it got me thinking about two things I am lacking in my own life…friendship and companionship."

Standing up from the sofa, she fixed herself another cup of tea before heading to the den. She gazed at the mahogany wood shelving holding a myriad of books along with her 'Delta Sigma Theta' elephant statues. Her eyes making their way up the wall, she stared at her framed collegiate degrees hanging from the wall along with a plethora of honorary certificates and awards. Among these things were photographs of her pictured with former colleagues, sorority sisters, business owners, politicians, and other prominent members of the community. These were among some of her most prized possessions, but the dust had settled on much of it.

My goodness, these things are dusty, she thought running her fingers across one of the frames. They could use a good dusting off. They're turning into nothing more than dust collectors.

Dr. Hawkins took a long sip from her tea, continuing to take in the highly decorated room. Like the pin of a valiant solider, each item represented a special achievement, milestone, or moment. But these things coupled with the sea of emotions she floated and floundered in throughout the day caused her to land in an unsuspecting place of painful realization.

"My goodness Lila Mae…you are a miserable lonely old bag that nobody wants…just like Anna said almost 30 years ago," she whispered to herself. "And all of these grand things are of little company to you right now. What a fool you have been! So many remarkable accomplishments you have attained. And what do you have to show for it? You're a lonely divorcee whose only child is living in a transitional home for recovering addicts."

Tearing up, Dr. Hawkins picked up a portrait that she, Mr. Hawkins, and Dancer had taken together at Olan Mills when Dancer was two months old. No longer able to contain her tears, she grabbed a Kleenex and dabbed her eyes.

I cannot even remember the last time I cried, Dr. Hawkins thought. I have always been one of stoicism. But looking back over my life…and some of the decisions I made…I cannot help but look at this family portrait and get emotional. I am feeling a gut-wrenching sense of regret right now.

With tear-soaked eyes, she talked to the images captured from the lens of the photo studio's camera some 34 years ago as if they could talk back.

"Oh, Rufus and Dancer," she said. "I am so sorry! If only I had compromised…even just a tad. Maybe… just maybe if I had simply considered what you two wanted for your lives…and not what I wanted for your lives…maybe…just maybe…things may have turned out differently…for all of us."

A few more minutes lapsed by, and Dr. Hawkins was still gazing at the photo – her eyes fixated on Dancer. "Oh Dancer," she said. "It seemed it was just yesterday that you were a baby, and now you are a grown woman of 34 years. I am so optimistic after hearing your voice this morning. You were so happy and excited about your upcoming Serenity House graduation! You were upbeat and sounding like your old self! You said you gained your weight back and were healthy again! That was music to my ears because you lost so much weight when you were on those drugs, I hardly recognized you were my child! You've also made a best friend named Sharon. It was so nice to hear you have a good friend to journey with as you continue down your road to recovery. I could use a friend like that myself to be perfectly honest. Oh, Lila Mae don't go back down that road again! All you will do is depress yourself even more with the 'should have' and 'would haves' and 'could haves.' You've done that enough for one day."

Dr. Hawkins proceeded to place her thoughts back on the things her daughter shared over the phone about the graduation. "I shall buy special outfits for me and Dancer to wear for the occasion!' she declared. "I will shop for them at 'Wear It's At' in Reisterstown, Maryland. I just love that Boutique and Joyce Newsome who works there! Joyce is always so helpful in assisting me with picking out clothing and accessories! And that voice of hers! My

God! It's so melodious! It sings when she talks! The majestic manner in which she speaks reminds me of my former high school classmate…Claire…who works at Serenity House. I told Claire about that position…and was delighted to hear she got the job! And Dancer simply loves Claire! And Dancer, after the graduation, I shall shower Dancer you with accolades and present you with a beautiful bouquet of fresh-cut purple lilacs," said Dr. Hawkins, talking to her daughter's infancy image. "I know how much you love purple! I wanted to tell you how proud I was over the phone today…but prefer to tell you that in person…right after the commencement."

Moments ago, Dr. Hawkins gently placed the portrait back down on an end table. She now stood in the quietness of the den surrounded by her academia, occupational, and social artifacts – her thoughts now reflecting upon the new that replaced the old. She began with a recent drive past the former site of Old Court Savings & Loan.

It took a long time for me to drive past that building, she thought, wiping her eyes with the saturated Kleenex. It would evoke such painful memories…but eventually I began to drive past there. Now…some 33 years later, it's a healthcare facility," she thought referencing ExpressCare Urgent Care Center operated by Northwest Hospital. You can't even tell a bank was ever there. The building bears no structural resemblances that it ever was a financial institution. All that remains of what once sat there are bad memories… for me and a whole lot of other people that got swindled by Levitz and his shameful shenanigans. I sometimes sit at the red light at the corner of Old Court and Liberty Roads thinking about the hell I went through thanks to that bank! It's nice to see that a location that caused so much financial misery and sickness, is now a place of medical treatment and care. I thought I would never trust another financial institution again until I was introduced to Ramsey Harris and Karen Burley of PNC Bank. I am extremely pleased with PNC Bank, and they are taking exceptionally good care of my money. Nick's Place is also gone, she thought, continuing to reflect on the changing landscape of the Randallstown area. Now it's called Identity Ultra Lounge. So many places that were in this area when I first moved out here are now a thing of the past. Some changed hands, while some went out of business…unable to compete with Walmart and other retailers that opened stores out here. But the area is still thriving and busy and has many Black-owned businesses such as Harbor Bank, Vaughn Green Funeral Home, and Wylie Funeral Home. There's so much out here to do and everything is convenient. Phoenix Salon and Suites where my beautician Tarusa Pennick does my hair is just a stone's throw away from where I live. I absolutely enjoy going to the Liberty Senior Center and the Randallstown Community Center for Ursula V. Battle's plays, exercises, and other activities. I am also a member of the Liberty Lites Book Club. My church member Patrician Martin, who recently retired from nursing encouraged me to join that club and I am glad I did. I told Patricia I would like to write a book one day…and she encouraged me to do so…maybe I will. Since retiring last year, I have the time. Hmmm…what will I write about? Perhaps I shall write a Memoir? No, she thought shaking her head, a Memoir probably would not be a good idea. I would have to tell my business, and there's no way I'm going to do that! Maybe one day I'll settle on something and discuss it with Patricia. Oh! That reminds me," said Dr. Hawkins, snapping her fingers. I need to call Patricia. When Dancer and I spoke earlier, she talked about the things she wanted to do to work towards achieving the goals and dreams she had for her life. That included enrolling in a GED program and immediately afterward going to Coppin to study nursing. Having worked as a nurse for many years, Patricia…who brought Dancer to my hospital room and handed her to me after she was born…would be an excellent person for Dancer to talk with about a career in nursing. I will call Patricia now and arrange a date and time for her and Dancer to chat about it over lunch.

᪥

After speaking to Ms. Martin who agreed to talk with Dancer, Dr. Hawkins added the lunch date to the calendar on her phone. "Saturday, January 12, 2019," Dr. Hawkins said aloud while typing the event on her calendar. "Exactly one week after Dancer finishes the program. By that time, Dancer will have finished the program and will be back home with me. We'll drive out to Owings Mills to Granny's Restaurant where we will be meeting Patricia. "Funny thing," said Dr. Hawkins now heading upstairs to turn in for the night, "there was a time when I did everything I could to extinguish the bright light that burned inside of Dancer to grow up and become a nurse. Now, with all the hell she's been through with her addiction, I want to do anything I can to keep that fire lit. It was good to hear Dancer hadn't given up on becoming a nurse. It's something how life works. Sometimes you find yourself going back to the very thing you tried your best to avoid."

Dr. Hawkins turned off the downstairs lights and began proceeding upstairs to her bedroom - but veered to the bathroom.

"I am just happy that my Dancer is getting another chance at life," said Dr. Hawkins, opening the medicine cabinet and unscrewing the top from her pill bottle. After popping two Quaaludes in her mouth, she turned on the faucet, cupped one of her hands to catch some of the water, brought the water up to her mouth, and used the liquid to swallow the pills.

"This is the longest Dancer has gone without using and Serenity House is exactly where she needs to be right now," said Dr. Hawkins. "I know I had to eat crow to get her here in that program…but I have come to realize that sometimes you have to eat crow before you can eat steak. Nevertheless, she got in…thank God for Serenity House."

CHAPTER SEVENTEEN

THE ROOT (RUT)

October 17, 2018
The Second Meeting

It was a brisk fall day. Leaves of varying hues of orange, brown, green, and burnt yellow clung to tree branches, while others drifted listlessly to the ground. Inside Serenity House, the residents were well into their weekly meeting. Sister Jackson was addressing the group. Just behind her stood Sister Voyant gripping a vestige of plant remaining from a cultivation season long past - a long weed stretching some four feet long, clumped with dirt at its root.

Before I lost my eyesight, I dug up this weed…the longest I ever unearthed, Sister Voyant silently recalled. I decided to save it but did not know why. In meditating on what I would discuss with the group for today's meeting, God brought this weed to my remembrance, revealing to me exactly why He had me to save it. This weed is the perfect visual to illustrate what I will be sharing with them this morning.

Willie felt Hank tapping him on his shoulder.

"Hey man," whispered Hank. "What's Sister Voyant holding in her hand?"

"Looks like some kinda tree or flower root or something," said Willie. "I don't know."

"Well, what do you think she's going to do with it?" asked Hank.

"She's probably going to grind it up into some kind of potion," Willie mused. I hope it's loooooove potion" he said, grinning at Sharon, prompting her to roll her eyes at him.

"I wonder what's in that pouch around her waist?" asked Hank.

"Don't know," said Willie. "But check out Mama Jackson's new, supersized Laz-Z-Boy chair. It's a good thing she has another chair to sit in. It looked like the chair she sat in during our meeting last week was about to buckle under all that weight."

"Man, you are crazy," chuckled Hank. "But I thought the same thing too."

"Hush all that talking and laughing over there Willie and Hank!" scolded Sister Jackson, biting into a cupcake. "Sister Voyant is about to speak!"

Sister Jackson waddled her way back to her chair while Sister Voyant held the weed and its root up high. There was complete silence in the room, the others wondering what she was about to do.

Sister Voyant began, "Listen closely my Beloveds because I'm about to take it real deep. Now, I like food from the earth, so in the summer I grow my own vegetables and herbs. Well, one summer, a patch of weeds began growing in my garden, and they were choking out my vegetables and herbs. Well, I wasn't having that, so I would pull weeds every chance I got…and they would grow back worse than before. I tell you my Beloveds…you can learn a lot from a garden. So, one day, instead of pulling the weeds, I decided to get my shovel and dig them out the ground…one by one. Once I started digging, I discovered that all those weeds were growing from this loooooooooooooooooooooong rut that ran deep beneath the ground. Most pronounce the word root, but my grandmother was from the deep South. She used to call it a rut, and that pronunciation stayed with me. Anyway, I kept digging and pulling and digging and pulling, and I thought I would never get to the end of this rut. But I was determined, so I kept digging and pulling and digging and pulling until I got this ugly rut out of the ground. Once I got this rut out of the ground, those nasty weeds no longer had its source…a lifeline to grow from. Therefore, they could no longer grow and choke out my beautiful vegetables and herbs. What am I saying? Why am I talking about weeds and ruts? Because it's cultivation time my Beloveds! You're here!" declared Sister Voyant, pointing at the plant. "You've pulled the weeds of addiction. You're drug-free…and some of you have been drug-free before, but the first chance you got, you ran right back to that drug! You relapsed! Why? Because ladies and gentlemen, you pulled the weed…but you did not pull the rut…and the rut was still there. A rut, which grew from a tiny, ole seed…" she said reaching inside the fanny pack around her waist and feeling around inside. "Ah, here it is," said Sister Voyant, removing the pack of seeds from the fanny pack and tearing it open. "It could be the seed of hurt," she said, pulling a seed out of the pack and holding it up. "Or it could be the seed of unforgiveness," she announced, holding up another. "It might be the seed of anger," said Sister Voyant displaying yet another seed. "And now, you're walking around all mean, nasty, and mad with the world. "Perhaps, it's the seed of rejection or disappointment," she said, displaying two more seeds. "The seed of whatever your issue is. The seed rrrrrrepresents that event…that moment in your life that triggered your addiction…where you turned to drugs, or alcohol, or sex —"

"Did she say sex?" asked Willie jumping up from his chair.

"Sit down man," growled James.

"Were you turned to drugs, or alcohol, or sex to deal with the pain and allowed the spirit of addiction to come in and have its way," continued Sister Voyant. "Sometimes, we don't even know how that seed got there. But it sprang forth a rut that tricked you into believing the lie that you had to have that crack...that heroin...that alcohol...that pill...that sex...for everything to be okay because it kept you from facing your reality...your inner-fears —"

"Tell it like it is!" commented Sister Jackson chewing cookies.

"Now my Beloveds," said Sister Voyant, "It's time to remove that bitter rut. Because until you do...that rut is still there," she said grabbing the root end of the weed and holding it up. "And the first thing that upsets you once you're out of here...or sends you back to your old neighborhood where your old friends 'Addiction' and 'Dependency' are waiting to welcome you back...will take you right back to your drug of choice. So, you've got to dig deep down inside to dig out that rut that put you in a rut! The rut that gave life to all those weeds that are choking and killing you. But you don't have to go about it alone! You don't have to toil by yourself! No...no...no! God...The Master Gardener is right there with you! If you allow Him...if you give God a chance...He can help you dig up that rut once and for all so that you can become the beautiful persons, He created you to be."

CHAPTER EIGHTEEN

THE HYMNAL

October 17, 2018

Sister Voyant's demonstration to the group was finished. Sister Jackson sat in her comfortable, new chair mesmerized, along with the others.

"Hallelujah!" shouted Sister Jackson, raising both arms. "That was so inspirational!"

"Powerful!" said James holding up his Bible.

"I'm just a vessel," replied Sister Voyant, taking her seat.

"Wow wee!" chimed Dancer. "That was neat how you used a garden and weeds to talk about addiction! I've never heard it explained that way before. Hanging her head, she said sadly, "But Sister Voyant, no matter how hard I try not to…I keep going back to Heroin…I just keep going back."

"Dancer baby, you have to get to the root," replied Sister Voyant. "Don't give up…and whatever you do…don't give in! We're going to get there."

"Well," piped Willie standing up and primping, "I must be a drug, because all my women keep coming back!"

"Shut up and sit down you played out Player!" yelled Sharon.

"Call me what you want!" replied Willie jovially. "I've been called worse. But all women love me!"

"Shut the front door, Willie!" said Sister Jackson. "This is serious business and we ain't got much time!"

Willie acted as if he were plucking lint off his suit jacket and sat down while Sister Jackson told Dancer, "Honey, you don't have to keep going back to using. No siree! Gawd has given you everything you need to resist that temptation. It's all about casting down laminations and imitations so that we can obey Christ!"

James immediately jumped up from his chair. Here comes that Know It All! Sister Jackson silently yelled.

"Mama Jackson," said James. "I believe you meant 'Casting down imaginations, and every high thing that exalteth itself against the knowledge of God, and bringing into captivity every thought to the obedience of Christ'. That's 2 Corinthians 10:5."

"Ain't that what I said?" Sister Jackson asked incredulously.

"No ma'am," responded James.

"Well, that's exactly what I meant," Sister Jackson declared while trying her best to mask her growing frustration with James' constant corrections. In thought she vented; I don't like when James does that. I don't like it one bit! I am the House Mother. Not only that, but I am a Christian woman! And when James nitpicks my little mistakes like that, it makes me look as if I don't know The Word of Gawd! I've been wanting to know more about his own church experience…and this is a good time to ask! Let's see how 'Mr. Know It All' answers that!

"So, uh, James," said Sister Jackson with a pinch of sarcasm. "I see you are well-versed in The Bible. So, tell us James…were you uh…active in the church?"

"Yes, I was very active in my church," responded James. "I sang in the choir and taught Bible Class. My Bishop was even about to make me a deacon. I was a faithful member until…"

"Until what James?" inquired Sister Jackson.

"Until I lost my faith," said James sadly, looking down at the floor.

"James…my Beloved," said Sister Voyant. "I can feel the tears of sadness welling up in my spirit! We're going to have to use a spiritual scalpel to surgically extract that sadness and implant it with the joy and happiness that comes from God."

James sniffled, and began to weep, prompting Dancer to get him a Kleenex.

"Where does your sadness flow from James?" asked Sister Voyant. "Pour out James…share my Beloved."

Without saying a word, James left the room, leaving the others to wonder if he would return. A short time later, he returned, carrying a worn leather briefcase. Standing before the group, he reached inside the case and pulled out an old burgundy Hymnal book.

That bag and songbook look like they've been through a war, Sister Jackson opined, her thoughts interrupted by the piercing, moaning cry James let out after opening his Hymnal.

CHAPTER NINETEEN

JAMES' STORY – I REST MY CASE

October 17, 2018
The Second Meeting

James stood before the group thinking about his actions a few moments ago. I didn't mean for that cry to rip from my throat like that, he thought. It just came out. Continuing to weep, he could taste his sorrow, the salty flavor of tears dribbling into his mouth.

I have never shared the story hidden inside my Hymnal, James silently admitted. But in opening it up…today will be the day I will open up and tell my story. Bowing his head and closing his eyes, James whispered, "God give me strength as I prepare to give my testimony. The truth, the whole truth, and nothing but the truth…so help me God."

With tears running down his face, James began to tell the story within the Hymnal - its pages holding a piece of history that told the painful song of his past.

"Twenty years ago, I was on top of the world," James told them. "I was a successful lawyer—"

"A lawyer!" said Willie with great surprise.

"Yeah right!" hissed Miracle with a sarcastic laugh, her chair once again sitting apart from the group.

"You were a lawyer?" Sharon asked doubtfully. "Yeah right! And I'm Diana Ross!"

"Well, whether you believe it or not, I was a lawyer," said James, annoyed by their disbelief and interruptions. "The truth of the matter is that I was a lawyer –"

"Well in that case…Counsel…give me twenty dollars man!" said Willie, standing and holding out his hand.

What a jerk! thought James.

"Quiet Willie!" said Sister Jackson. "Now sit down!"

"He said he was a lawyer," Willie grumbled childishly, sitting back down in his chair.

Pleased at Sister Jackson's admonishment of Willie, James continued, "I was an attorney, and owned a highly successful law firm...the law offices of James L. Franklin, Esquire...located in a skyscraper in downtown Baltimore."

"Hmmm," I've heard of that firm," said Sister Jackson. "Can't quite place where, but I've heard that name before. Go on James."

"What a place that was!" said James, reflecting on the practice's stylish décor. "Rich mahogany wood furniture...plush leather chairs...a huge conference room...exquisite crystal pieces, expensive artwork...all complemented with a breathtaking view of Baltimore City." Walking over to a window, James said, "Sometimes, I would just stare from my window out at the city through the humongous glass panes of my office...like a prideful king looking out at my kingdom. But instead of a royal cape, I was dressed in expensive tailored, monogrammed suits accented with just the right bowties and suspenders. But as 'The Good Book' says in Jeremiah 49:16 regarding pride, 'Though you build your nest as high as the eagle's, from there I will bring you down,' declares the LORD. And I was brought down," said James, walking away from the window.

In preparing to remove an envelope wedged between two pages of the Hymnal, James' stomach tied up in knots, beads of sweat dampened his forehead, and trickles of sweat poured beneath his underarms. My heart is beating like a sledgehammer against steel and my stomach feels like every butterfly in nature has flown inside of it, he thought. His hands shaking, James proceeded to flip through the Hymnal's pages until he reached the envelope. Despite every effort to keep his hands steady, they trembled uncontrollably. Pulling the envelope from the Hymnal, James opened the flap and pulled out a photograph. Pictured were he, his wife Pauline Franklin, and their daughter Tiffany.

"This is my beautiful wife Pauline and our pride and joy...Tiffany," said James holding the photo up high for the group to see.

"Wow, what a great photo!" exclaimed Dancer. "Look at those smiles! You all look really, really, really happy!"

"Thank you, Dancer," said James. "And you are right. We were happy. We had everything. The three of us lived in a sprawling mansion in Columbia, Maryland. Pauline and I drove luxury cars...owned a boat docked on the waters of Annapolis, MD...and wore the best high-end clothing money could buy. I sported fine haberdashery and she carried Gucci, Louis Vuitton, Chanel, and other designer purses and accessories. We bought what we wanted. I was making a lot of money and –"

"Making money like 'The Franklin Mint' – Willie laughed, making light of James' last name.

"Yes, I guess you can say that," chuckled James. "I was earning a fortune, and we lived a very lavish lifestyle. "We were very blessed. We were also very active members of the church we attended. I taught Sunday School and sang on the Mass Choir. Pauline –"

"You sang on the Mass Choir?" asked Sister Jackson.

"I certainly did," replied James.

"I should have known with that strong baritone voice of yours," commented Sister Jackson.

"That's right…one of the choir's lead singers," said James. "Pauline was on the Missionary and Usher Boards. Tiffany, who was 18, was a Youth Usher, and had been ushering since she was about eight or nine."

"What a beautiful family," said Sister Jackson, reaching for a donut. "You know, I have…"

"You have what, Mama Jackson?" asked James, simultaneously wondering why she was always eating sweets.

"Don't mind me, James," said Sister Jackson. "My mind went someplace else. Go on and finish Sugar."

Speaking of sugar, James thought to himself, You certainly eat a lot of it. I sure hope you aren't diabetic. Resuming his story, James said, "Well, one evening, I settled comfortably in my recliner in the living room after a long day's work. Shortly thereafter, Pauline and Tiffany rushed through the door. They both were excited about something. Pauline dropped the shopping bags she was carrying down to the floor and rushed over and kissed me on the cheek. Tiffany ran over to me holding this envelope in her hand, said James glancing at the envelope he removed from the Hymnal. "Pauline told me they were going out to dinner and wanted me to come along. She also wanted me to drive. But I told them to go on without me…that I would have dinner with them another time. It had been a long, arduous day in court, and all I wanted to do was rest. Tiffany tried her best to convince me to go, asking a few more times. But I was not budging…I was totally exhausted. I told her, 'Sweetheart, Daddy's tired…I'm in no shape to go anywhere. I need to get some shuteye.' I could tell Tiffany was disappointed, but she told me, 'Okay, Dad. But I wish you were coming along with us.' I replied, 'I'm sorry Honey, but I'm wiped out.' Well, Pauline was furious! 'James, I can't believe you are too tired to have dinner with us!" she shouted. "When it comes to your law firm and your clients, you have all the energy in the world! But when it comes to your wife and daughter, you're always tired! Let one of your clients call! I bet you'll get your butt out that seat then!' I yelled back, 'Pauline, that practice and its clients are what pays the bills! Their money finances those minks you like to wear, those designer bags you love to tote, and your shopping excursions at The Village of Cross Keys, Saks Fifth Avenue, Nordstrom, and other places! Thanks to my income…derived from the money from my clients, you don't even have to work!' I remember Pauline's voice starting to crack when she yelled back, 'I see that law practice of yours has given you a short memory! You forgot about the fact that I supported your dream of becoming a lawyer…while at the same time deferring mines! Well since you have amnesia, let me remind you…I wanted to become an airline stewardess after college! But no, I –"

"Gee, interrupted Dancer. "I don't know your wife, but I sure know how that feels…not doing something you dreamed of doing to help or please someone else. My apologies Mr. James, I didn't mean to interrupt."

"Well, Pauline went on to remind me of all the sacrifices she made in her own life to appease me, while also supporting my law aspirations. Things like finishing her undergraduate degree at Towson a year later than she planned because I wanted to have a child, while I completed my studies at Johns Hopkins on schedule. How she juggled motherhood and work to help put me through the University of Maryland's JD Program…and how seeing an airline stewardess on an airplane always reminded her of how she missed her destination in life…all to satisfy me. I heard Pauline out, but explained to her that all I was trying to do was make sure she never had to work…never had to answer to a boss…never had to hold down a 9 to 5…that all I wanted was for her to live a life of privilege as the wife of James L. Franklin, Esquire."

On that June 17, 1998, day, the argument between the Franklins would escalate.

"James, all you have been talking about is what you wanted!" screamed Mrs. Franklin. "I have lost count of the number of times you said 'I', referring to yourself. It's always about you, you, you! But what about me? What about us?" she said looking at Tiffany. "The reason you and I are having a disagreement is because of what you want! And right now, instead of spending a little time with us, all you want to do is rest!"

"Damnit, Pauline!" shouted James. "You are making a much bigger case of this than what it is! Why are you standing there prosecuting me when all I am trying to do is get some sleep! I argued enough today in court! Why can't I come home and get some peace! Shit! Can't you see I'm tired!"

"How dare you curse at me?!" Mrs. Franklin fired back. "Sitting there arguing with me as if I am an attorney you are arguing against in court! Well since your life seems to revolve around the courtroom, I'll put it this way…the fact remains, that you James, L. Franklin, Esquire…are prideful and selfish!"

"Me, prideful and selfish?!" James shouted, jumping out of his chair. "How ungrateful you are! After all, I've done for you…our family…the community through my philanthropy…and the church…giving of my time, tithes, and talents…how dare you call me selfish?!"

"Because you are!" shouted Mrs. Franklin. "And you're too blind to see it!"

"Mom and Dad, please don't argue," said Tiffany.

"I'm done arguing with your father!" said Mrs. Franklin storming towards the door. "C'mon Tiffany, let's go."

"Coming Mom,," said Tiffany, grabbing a bright yellow Post-It Note and jotting something down, before affixing it to a letter inside the envelope.

"I'll be outside waiting…so hurry up!" shouted Mrs. Franklin walking outside, the keys on her keyring jiggling in her hand. "Or we'll be late for our reservations."

"Okay, Mom," said Tiffany. Directing her attention back to her father, Tiffany handed me the envelope and instructed, "Dad, please promise me you won't open this envelope until we get back."

"Sure honey," said James. "I promise not to open it."

A former Girl Scout, Tiffany held up three fingers and asked, "Scout's Honor?"

"Scout's Honor," replied James.

Tiffany smiled and the father and daughter shared a warm hug.

"Bye Daddy," she said, leaving out the door to the sound of Mrs. Franklin blowing the car horn. "And no peeking!"

"Okay Honey," said James. "I promise not to peek."

Upon her leaving, James paced the floor wondering, Should I call Pauline on her cell phone and apologize for what I said? Should I just find out where they are going and meet them there? No, I think I will just wait. Pauline needs to simmer down anyway. And after all, she's the one who's wrong…not me, he concluded, before settling back in his recliner, never looking at…or opening the letter his daughter handed him.

James continued to tell his account of what happened to the Serenity House group. "Even with all the years that have passed, I can still hear those sounds…the horn…the car door closing…the car starting up…and the car backing out of the driveway, recalled James. "A short time after getting quite comfortable in my recliner, my cell phone rang. I thought it might be a client, so I jumped up from my chair to grab the phone. Looking back, I realized that I did exactly what Pauline said I would do if I thought a client was calling…get my butt up from the chair…and that's exactly what I did. However, it wasn't a client at all, but my Bishop. He was calling to request that I sing his favorite song at church that coming Sunday. I replied, 'Why Bishop, I would be honored,' said James, sticking out his chest and demonstrating a proud stride." I made my way to the den and pulled the Hymnal in my hand off the shelf, flipping its pages to the song he asked me to sing…'Great is Thy Faithfulness.' I was looking at the words of the song when…when…oh my God! When…" said James with a petrified look, his voice trailing off.

"Go on my Beloved," urged Sister Voyant. "Finish your story. I know it's extremely difficult my Beloved…I can feel your pain. But you can do it."

Feeling a sense of reassurance from Sister Voyant, James took a deep swallow and continued, "When I heard the sound of brakes screeching and a loud crash," said James, the ruckus of a wreck playing in his mind. "The unforgettable sound of screeching brakes and metal meeting metal. Seconds later, someone began clanging the heavy brass knocker on my front door and ringing the doorbell repeatedly. I opened the door and there was my neighbor Jim…frantic and out of breath…to tell me that Pauline and Tiffany had been in a car accident at the corner…and that it was bad…real bad. I was still holding the envelope Tiffany handed to me. I stuck the envelope inside this Hymnal, put it down on an end table, and rushed out the door behind Jim!" said James, running out of Serenity House's door, reliving the moments he ran behind his neighbor. "I was right on Jim's heels," he said. "Fearing what I was about to face…but knowing I would have to face it. It all felt so surreal…but it was real. I continued running behind Jim before stopping dead in my tracks," said James, halting his steps at the doorsteps – standing in the crisp fall air, looking around at his North Avenue surroundings as if he were standing in his Columbia, Maryland neighborhood. His heart pounding faster, his breathing now more labored, James momentarily stood there, visualizing the accident scene that unfolded two decades earlier. "We had reached the corner where the crash occurred. I can still see what remained of the cars…mangled, twisted metal that resembled two trains colliding at a high rate of speed," described James. "And then came the wailing sounds of emergency vehicles and their hues of blue and red flashing lights. Pauline! Tiffany! I yelled trying to get over to them. But Jim and several neighbors held me back…telling me it was best that I did not…some of them having already looked inside the car. Clenching his fists, James said, "But the driver of the other car…the drunk driver…he was still very much alive… I recognized that scumbag as soon as I saw him and I —"

"You knew him?!" interrupted Sister Jackson, nibbling on a cookie.

"Yes," answered James. "He was one of my clients…Jack Reynolds. I represented him in a drunk-driving case about a year or so before the accident. He was young, spoiled, reckless, loved to party, and enjoyed driving fast cars. His parents were rich…filthy, stinking, rich!"

"Just like mines," said Hank.

"Look at you Hank!" said Sharon. "There's no way your parents are rich!"

"Don't judge a book by its cover," said Hank.

"That's right," agreed Sister Jackson. "Go on James."

"Although he was just 24, Jack was no stranger to drunk driving, having already been arrested several times for DWIs," said James. "But his parents always paid his way out of trouble. Each time he was charged with a DWI, Jack's parents got him the best lawyers that money could buy…myself being among them. But Jack would turn around and do the same thing again. After getting off so many times without any real punishment, I guess Jack thought he could keep drinking and driving and getting away with it. And here he was again…driving under the influence of alcohol! But this time, he was involved in a head-on collision involving my wife and daughter!"

"My goodness, Mr. James!" exclaimed Dancer. "That's terrible!"

"That's really awful James, and I'm so sorry," said Sister Jackson. "You said you recognized him. Did he recognize you?"

"Despite his drunkenness, he did recognize me," responded James. "I heard him tell the police, 'There's my lawyer over there! I told you cops my parents would take care of this!'" said James sluggishly, mimicking Jack Reynolds' intoxicated voice. "Then Jack looked over at me with a big, dumb smile on his face and yelled, 'Hey Mr. Franklin! Over here!' yelled James, gesturing his hands as if he were signaling for someone to walk over to him.

"Wow," sighed Hank. "That had to be a real punch in the gut."

"It was," said James. "That drunk actually thought his parents sent me there on his behalf! And there was my wife and daughter in a vehicle he hit mortally injured! And that bastard was so drunk…he couldn't even stand on his own…stumbling and falling to the street during a sobriety test…the officers helping him to his feet. Weakened with devastation…I fell too…my legs completely giving out beneath me…my neighbors and officers helping me up to my feet. The officers on the scene even had to assist Jack during his walk over to the backseat of a patrol car. And that drunkard was driven away from that scene without as much as a broken bone...not even a fracture! Me on the other hand, driven away with a broken heart…my life forever fractured! Part of me praying that my wife and daughter would pull through. The other part of me thinking about what happened those final moments before they left the house that night. The only thing that could save me from myself was if Pauline and Tiffany pulled through. What if they somehow, had survived that terrible accident I could have the opportunity to apologize…to smooth things over…to make things right!" James cried in anguish. "Pauline and Tiffany were rushed to Maryland Shock Trauma Center…but I believe they were already gone! I sat down at that hospital waiting to hear something…numb…fearful…and my stomach knotted up in anxiety for an update on their condition. I knew what was coming by the somber look on the doctor's face when he walked over to me and delivered the terrible news…they had both passed away!" announced James drawing collective gasps from the group."

"Oh no!" shrieked Sister Jackson, shaking her head.

"Awww man," said Hank, "I know how you feel…I've been there before…"

"I can't even imagine going through something like that," said Dancer softly. "That's really sad Mr. James."

"Jim and some of the other neighbors were right there with me," continued James, "And they tried their best to console me…but I lost it! I cried, screamed, and threw whatever I could get my hands on! My God, that was the worst night of my life! I would come to find out that Jack Reynolds had gone barhopping with some friends and afterward bought more alcohol…an empty bottle of whiskey along with beer cans cars strewn all over the floor of his car! He had no business being behind the wheel of an automobile! His blood alcohol content was off the charts, and his actions took away my wife and daughter! Well, guess what?! I was drunk too! Drunk with guilt for representing him in the first place! However, I went from being a defender to a victim! I got Jack probation, which kept him from going to jail! You see, I saved him from prison, but he sent me to prison! Jailed by the words 'if only' If only I had not represented him…If only I had gone with Pauline and Tiffany…If only…'"

"What happened wasn't your fault James," said Sister Jackson. "It was their time."

James threw up his arms in frustration and slammed the door shut.

"Everyone tried to tell me that Mama Jackson!" he yelled, starting to pace the floor. "But they didn't know what went on between me, my daughter, and my wife that night! Pauline and Tiffany asked me to do a simple thing...to go with them...and I didn't. Nothing no one said could ease the pain...the guilt...the overwhelming grief I felt. I kept playing that evening over and over again in my mind...like a broken record. I couldn't sleep...couldn't eat...and every time I got a moment's rest...guilt would visit my bedside causing my heart to race and sweat to pour...tormenting me with images, thoughts, and sounds. Images of the last time I watched them walk out the door...thoughts of how I talked to Pauline that day...and the deafening sounds from the crash."

"My Lawd," said Sister Jackson, rocking in her seat.

"And do you know something else Mama Jackson?" asked James.

"What's that James?" Sister Jackson replied, feeling remorseful for asking the question that sparked him to tell his story.

"As a defense lawyer, I had defended so many clients who stood accused of something. My job as a defense attorney was to defend them in a court of law. Sometimes, I believed they were innocent. Sometimes I did not. What I did know was that I was paid handsomely to defend them. That was my job! Do you all understand? That was my job! But then I found myself on the other side. I was the victim and not the defender. And I hated Jack Reynolds with every bone in my body!" yelled James. "Do you all hear me! I hated him! Sometimes I sat in my bed plotting how I would get my revenge by somehow killing him. I felt I had to do something. Jack Reynolds had to pay! Imagine that...me of all people...a lawyer...plotting how I could kill someone...someone who killed a part of me! But thank God I realized that was not the way to go. Taking his life, would not bring back the ones that were taken away from me. All it would do is lead to my being jailed...and more heartache and pain for another family."

"That was a wise choice, my Beloved," said Sister Voyant.

"That's right," said Sister Jackon. "The Bible tells us, revenge is mines, I will not delay, saith the Lawd!"

"Mama Jackson, Romans 12:9 says, 'Vengeance is mine...I will repay, saith the Lord', quoted James stressing the word 'mine.'

"Ain't that what I said?" asked Sister Jackson.

"No ma'am Mama Jackson," said Sharon. "That's not what you said...not at all."

"No, Mama Jackson," said Hank. "That's definitely not what you said. Sorry."

"Well, that's exactly what I meant," declared Sister Jackson. "Now go on James...we ain't got much time."

Mama Jackson shouldn't say Scriptures if she cannot adequately quote them. That burns me up! thought James before picking up on his story where he left off. "Well, the only person I hated more than Jack Reynolds was myself! I didn't think I could never forgive either one of us! You can't imagine what that was like...sitting on the front pew of a church...looking at my wife in one casket and my child in another!"

Willie let out a deep sigh and said, "James, I've been at a funeral like that...and it involved relatives of mines too..."

"I'm sorry to hear that Willie," said James. "Very sorry...because it's an indescribable seat to sit in...and none that I would ever want anyone to experience. After the funeral, I slumped into an abyss of deep depression...subsequently succumbing to the weight of guilt I carried around."

"Ooooh Lawd!" said Sister Jackson. "Guilt will eat you alive!"

"From the inside out," added Sister Voyant. "If you let it...go on my James...finish sharing your story."

"Well, to relieve some of that guilt, I began looking elsewhere…anywhere…to shift the blame. The devil convincing me that God was to blame! And the more I blamed God, the angrier I became at Him. Sometimes, while I was driving, I would bang my hands on the steering wheel and yell, 'God, why didn't you stop that accident from happening! Why?'"

"Oh, my Beloved," interjected Sister Voyant. "I know exactly how you feel…and that's a deep, dark, lonely place."

"You know how that feels, Sister Voyant?" James asked. "To blame God for something bad that happened in your life?"

"Yes, I do," Sister Voyant replied softly. "But that's another story James…continue on with yours my Beloved."

"The way I saw it…my 40-year-old wife was gone along with our18-year-old daughter," said James. "In a matter of minutes…22 years of marriage…being a devoted husband who loved his wife with all his heart…and 18 years of experiencing the joys of fatherhood…were gone in an instant. All that was left were memories. I remember standing in my mansion yelling at God. 'Where are you, God?'" I screamed at the top of my lungs. 'Nowhere to be found! The way I served You! After all I've done for You! What about all the tithes I paid! What about my service to the church! What about my philanthropic efforts in the community! I honored Your Word! I gave! I helped! I served! How could you allow this to happen after all I've done for You!' I felt so alone! I was also convinced that had God abandoned me. I stopped praying and going to church. I stopped singing. What was there to sing about? The Bible tells us in John 15:1 that Jesus is the true vine. I cut my own self off that vine…and by cutting that connection, in essence, I was dead…nothing but dry bones, which Ezekiel 37 talks about in The Bible. I no longer wanted anything to do with God…that included hearing the preached Word or reading it."

"Oh, my Beloved," said Sister Jackson. "You are on my street…that's where I was many years ago."

"Sister Voyant, I can't even imagine you being in such a place," said James. "But me…I was among the walking dead…dead in spirit, but physically alive. And my fleshly body needed something…it needed somebody…and I found it! Oh, did I find it! A new comforter…a new companion…a new friend…a new lover!"

"Oh yeah!" said Willie gleefully.

"Yes, that is what I was looking for…and I found it," said James.

"Now, this woman was really something. I met her a few weeks after the funeral. I needed some relief, so she and I got together."

"My man!" commented Willie.

"She was just what I needed to take my mind off what happened…and I will never forget our first encounter. Just thinking about it gives me chill bumps!" exclaimed James quivering his body and rubbing his arms. "She kissed me," he whispered, puckering, and sounding out a kiss. "She touched me," he cooed, gliding his hands all over his body. "She hugged me," he declared sexily, wrapping his arms around himself. "She fondled me," he stated, grabbing his crotch.

"Yes!" shouted Willie, jumping up from his chair. "Now that's what I'm talking about!"

"Sit down Willie!" said the group.

"Listen, I can't help if James was getting me worked up!" rationalized Willie, taking his seat.

"She blew my mind!" said James. "And after she and I shared one another that first time, I fell in love all over again! And I wanted to be with her again…and again…and again…and again…it was never-ending. The more I got of her…the more I wanted. I could never get enough!"

"That lady sounds like my kind of girl!" blurted Willie. "I would sure like to meet her! What's this sexy mama's name?"

Looking at James squarely in the eyes, James announced, "Her name is 'Cocaine'.

Shaking his head 'no,' Willie responded, "Naw man, that's okay. I'll pass on her!"

"I sure wish I had," said James. "But I didn't! I fell for her and I fell for her hard!

I loved her and would do anything for her! But she didn't come cheap! Cocaine was a $1,000-a-day drug habit!"

"Whew!" said Willie. "That's a lot of money!"

"That's right," replied James. "And it didn't take long for me to empty my bank accounts. I ran through $300,000 in savings…and spent the $1 million in insurance money paid out to me after Pauline and Tiffany's death!"

"A million dollars!" said Willie jumping up from the seat, prompting the group to all say, "Sit down Willie!"

"That's right…a million dollars," said James. "Mindboggling when you think about it! But when you are addicted, you don't stop to think about how much that particular vice is costing you…all you think about is having whatever that thing might be…and for me…that was Cocaine. I blew through all that money and found myself completely broke. I began selling everything I owned for money…the artwork in the house…the artwork at the office…clothes…shoes…jewelry…appliances, furniture…cars, you name it!"

"Lawd have mercy!" said Sister Jackson unwrapping a pack of white powdered donuts. "I used to know somebody like that, and it was a terrible situation."

"I was able to cover my addiction for a while, but the time ultimately arrived whereas I could no longer conceal it," said James. "My life spiraled out of control! I was no longer the lawyer I once was in court…standing in front of judges sniffling…my nose constantly running. I was frazzled and forgetful…no longer effective…rambling on and on in the courtroom about things that made no sense. Things really hit the fan one day when I bought some Cocaine. What I didn't realize was that I was buying it from an undercover cop! Well, I knew some powerful people and had powerful friends…which included politicians and judges…who managed to get me out of that bind. But when I was busted four more times, there were no more favors to call on. Before long, I was disbarred and was no longer able to pay my bills! I lost everything…including my prized mansion. I tell you…once that viper Cocaine sunk her fangs into me, she sucked away everything I worked for and owned. And she didn't give a damn about me! Fast forward to 2014. Broke and homeless I was living in complete obscurity amongst the homeless in Tent City near I-83…underneath the Jones Falls Expressway…a harsh underbelly of Baltimore City…a world away from where I once lived in Columbia. Far away from everyone I knew…and I wanted it that way! I didn't want to be around nobody because the devil filled my head with all sorts of things...that Pauline's family and our friends were all secretly thinking…secretly whispering…that I was responsible for the accident…because I refused to join them for dinner."

"Wow," said Hank, biting his nails and letting out a heavy sigh.

"In the universe of homelessness and hopelessness where I found myself dwelling, I discovered a totally different way of living. Talk about humbling! I never realized people lived like this! Cold when it was cold outside…and I knew one or two people who froze to death. Hot when it was hot outside…I knew people who died of heat exposure. I found myself having to wholly depend on people's generosity not just to survive…but to get high. I stood at intersections panhandling and washing windshields to earn money to buy Cocaine. I could no longer afford to buy $1,000 worth of Cocaine, but I was spending upwards of $300 each day. Can you believe it? From an attorney with a lucrative practice to a panhandler and squeegee man. Hard to believe, but that's what happened to me. I tell people all the time…when you see a homeless person…or a squeegee kid…or a squeegee adult…don't judge. You don't know their story."

"That's very true," said Hank.

"Sometimes, you got to do something a little straaange, to get a little chaaange," said Willie with a grin.

"Shut up Willie!" said the group.

"Addiction changes you," said James. "I have never been a violent man. Maybe a little testy…but not violent. But I had changed into a totally different person without even realizing it."

"When did you realize it?" asked Sharon.

"One day I was in my tent about to get high when another homeless man by the name of Harvey came into my tent bumming a cigarette," recalled James. "I was very annoyed because he just walked right into my tent."

"Was he supposed to knock…or ring the doorbell first?" quipped Willie with a laugh, joined by Hank.

"That's not funny Willie," said Sharon.

"I didn't find that joke amusing at all," said James, flashing a distaining look at Willie before going on with his story. "Anyway, I told Harvey I was not a smoker, so he left. Afterward, I looked for my vial of Cocaine and could not find it. The only person who had been in my tent other than me was Harvey…so my mind automatically went to him. I was furious! I ran Harvey down and accused him of stealing my Cocaine. He said, 'Man, I didn't take your drugs! It was impossible to take them! I only stepped a few feet inside your place!' I told Harvey, 'You liar! I don't know how you did it, but you stole my Coke!" said James, using one of the slang terms for Cocaine. 'You know you got a bad Meth habit Harvey, and you'll steal anything you can get your hands on to get it!' Harvey continued to deny…and I continued to accuse…and before I knew it, I punched Harvey in the face as hard as 'Iron Mike' Tyson hit Michael Spinks back in the day," said James demonstrating an uppercut. "Harvey went down just as fast as Spinks did, and after getting up, he cursed me out, running back to his tent, bleeding from the nose.

"You punched him in the face?" asked Sharon.

"Yes, I did," admitted James. "It's not something I'm proud of either."

"We've all done things we're not proud of James," said Sister Jackson. "I think we all can think of something we did that we wish we could take back. Go on James…finish your story."

"I got back out on the streets and made enough money to buy some more. A few days later…I'll never forget the date…October 5, 2015, I was sitting outside my tent with Jake and Otis – two of my homeless buddies," said James with a smile. "We struck up quite a friendship during my time in Tent City. Jake said he was a realtor before he hit rock bottom after he became addicted to gambling. Imagine that…a realtor who sold homes and winds up homeless."

"Hard to imagine a lot of things," said Hank.

"And Otis served in the Army before he became homeless. He would tell us his war stories about his heroism in Vietnam, or 'Nam' as he called it. He said he suffered from PTSD or Post Traumatic Stress Syndrome. Didn't seem right that a man who served his country was living on the streets…but there he was."

"Very sad indeed," said Sister Voyant.

"What great guys," smiled James, reminiscing about the two men. "They nicknamed me 'James Earl Jones' because they said my voice sounded like the actor's voice and I had his demeanor."

"They were right," said Sister Voyant. "Your voice is so …so rrrrrich…so rrrrrresounding….so rrrrrregal! Just like that of James Earl Jones. You two share more than just your first names. Go on my Beloved."

"Well on this specific October day, it was fall, but unseasonably cold," said James. "A few weeks prior to that, I received a coat from a nearby church. With winter on the way, I needed a coat and was thankful for the church's generosity. After I was given the coat, I took it back inside my tent, folded it neatly, and dropped it inside a large cardboard box that housed my few possessions. There it remained until I got chilly sitting outside with Jake and Otis. I remembered the coat and went inside my tent to get it. I removed it from the box…the same coat you see hanging over there," said James pointing to his hooded Bomber coat hanging on the coat rack. "The one that looks a lot like the coat you are wearing Miracle."

Miracle looked down at her coat and then at James – but did not say a word.

"After taking my coat out of the box, I peered inside. Nestled beneath some toiletries and a few other items were my Bible and Hymnal," said James, moving as if he were taking the books out of a box. "I had no desire to read my Bible or sing songs from a Hymnal…so they laid buried away inside the box…just like I had buried myself away from anyone or anything that had some connection to my old life. Quite frankly, I didn't even notice my Bible and Hymnal inside the box anymore…I looked right past them…despite going inside that box many times. But on that October 5th day, the Bible and Hymnal caught my attention. I picked up the Hymnal and opened it…seeing the envelope Tiffany gave to me the night of the accident tucked inside," said James, removing the envelope from the Hymnal. "For years, the pages of my Hymnal had served as a placeholder for this envelope. At some point, I placed the photo of the three of us inside the envelope…but never read the letter inside," James lamented, again picking up his family photo. "Sometimes, I would just stare at this photo of me, Pauline, and Tiffany and cry until I couldn't cry anymore. It represented such a wonderful, joyous time in our lives, and I missed them more than any word could ever convey."

James could hear someone sniffling and was surprised to see it was Miracle, who was crying.

"Sometimes," whispered Miracle, twiddling her fingers, "A photo is all you got…"

Miracle's rare show of emotion and words prompted everyone to stare at her, including James.

Sister Jackson said, "Miracle baby, do you –."

"Listen, I just made a comment about a photo!" Miracle blurted, wiping tears from her face. "I didn't say I wanted to talk! So don't ask me any questions! You got that?!"

"Don't take that tone with me young lady!" said Sister Jackson. "I thought you wanted to say something else."

"Well, I don't!" she yelled, crossing her arms, and sliding down in the chair. "The only thing I want is for this meeting to end!"

"Go on James," said Sister Jackson, cutting her eyes at Miracle.

"As I mentioned earlier, at some point I placed the photo inside the envelope with the letter and sealed it up," said James. "After a while, it pained me too much to look at the photo and I could never bring myself to read the letter. So there the two sat inside my Hymnal for years."

James walked over to the coat rack and lifted it off the hook.

"It's hard to explain, but once I put on this coat," said James, slipping on the coat, "came a feeling of empowerment…not entitlement…but empowerment. There is a difference between the two I will elaborate on later. The amazing thing is that after I put on this coat, I felt somehow…someway…I could handle whatever the letter. A coat I received through the benevolence of a church of which I was not a member, nor ever attended. I believe it was God's way of reminding me that while I no longer knew Him, He was still covering me," said James glancing at Miracle. "The letter was still folded in the manner in which Tiffany creased it," stated James, flipping back the flap of the envelope, and removing the letter inside. "The envelope and letter both bearing the historic seal of my Alma Mater…the great Johns Hopkins University," noted James, raising the envelope, and pointing to the emblem. "I opened the letter," he said, unfolding the 8 ½ x 11 sheet of parchment paper. "I will read you all a short portion," he informed them, the popular commencement tune Sir Edward Elgar's Pomp and Circumstance playing along in his mind.

"'Dear Ms. Franklin, Congratulations, it is with immense pleasure that I inform you of your acceptance into the Law program at Johns Hopkins University, with a full, four-year academic scholarship,'" read James, his mouth forming into a smile. Pointing to the Yellow Post-It-Note that clung to the letter, he said, "This sticky note was still attached. While the ink has faded, you can still see the message Tiffany jotted down before she left. It reads, 'Walking in the footsteps of my Daddy. If you are reading this…I know you opened this envelope before Mom and I got back.' Beneath the three smiley faces she drew at the bottom, my beautiful princess wrote, 'Daddy, I hope you are proud. Love Always, Tiffany.'" said James, the smile on his face no longer visible.

"How precious," said Sister Voyant.

"I know," said James. "Pauline and Tiffany were both such gems. I took for granted how precious they were…until they were gone. That's a nice segue into explaining the difference between empowerment and entitlement. The Bible tells us in Acts 10:34 that God is no respecter of persons. After I lost my wife and daughter, I finally saw my view on life for what it was – I walked around with a false sense of entitlement. Entitlement because of my success. Entitlement because I was a big-time philanthropist who wrote big checks to organizations. Entitlement because of my support of the church through my tithes, time, and talents. However, I failed to realize that while all these things were good, they did not exempt me from trials, tribulation, and tragedy."

"You are so right my Beloved," said Sister Voyant.

"James, your story is so deep," said Sharon.

"For once I agree with you Sharon," said Willie. "James man, your story is deep."

"My Lawd it certainly is," said Sister Jackson, munching on a cookie. "Go on James. We ain't got much time."

"After reading the letter and its sticky note, it instantly brought back memories of Pauline and Tiffany's excitement the night of the accident. I felt like a ton of bricks had toppled on me. That night was supposed to have been a special evening…to celebrate Tiffany's achievement. That is why they both were so adamant I go. Tiffany was going to surprise me with her full-ride acceptance letter to Hopkins."

"Gee, that's really sad Mr. James," said Dancer, rushing over and giving James a hug and returning to his seat.

"Thank you, Dancer," said James. "Well after reading that letter and sticky note, I cried out the words of Apostle Paul wrote in Romans 7:24…'What a wretched man I am! Who will rescue me from this body that is subject to death!' Looking at each face of the captivated group James told them, "You would think my answer to

Paul's question would have been 'God.' But it wasn't. My answer was 'Cocaine.' She and only she would be able to come to my rescue and again help me to escape my captors 'Torment' and 'Guilt.'"

"Jesus!," shouted Sister Jackson with white-powdered lips, throwing her arms in the air. "I know what you are talking about! Lawd have mercy! I almost dropped my box of donuts on that one!'

"Uh…Mama Jackson," you might want to wipe your lips," said James, while thinking to himself, How disgusting.

"My lips?" asked Sister Jackson.

"Yes," replied James. "Your lips. They are covered in white powder…from the donuts you are eating."

"Oh Lawd," said Sister Jackson, using her hand as a napkin to wipe her lips clean. "I'm sorry. That had to look nasty."

"It did," said Willie with a grimace.

"Ain't nobody ask you all that Willie!" snapped Sister Jackson. "Now go on James…finish your story. We ain't got much time."

"I got ready to leave my tent to make some money to buy some Coke," recalled James. "But before leaving, I inserted the envelope with Tiffany's letter back into the Hymnal. But in doing so, I looked down at its pages. Glaring back at me were the words to the song my Bishop requested me to sing. The name of the song…'Great is Thy Faithfulness.' I stood there just looking at those words….and then I did something I had not done in years," said James, falling to his knees. "I laid prostrate on the ground and began to pray! In anguish I cried out, 'God, I need you!" he shouted, stretching his arms upward. "Please God, I cannot take any more! I repent for turning my back in You…for being angry at You…for denying You! Please help me! I cannot go on like this! I fully surrender myself to You! And Lord, I promise that if you deliver me from my living hell, I will give up Cocaine! God…I am no longer seeking her for deliverance…but you."

"Glory be to God!" said Sister Jackson.

"I tell you at that miraculous moment, I could hear the weighty shackles of 'Torment' and 'Guilt' snap…and the loud, ugly sounds that came with them…silenced! No distractions…just me and God. In the marvelous quiet of those precious moments, I could hear God's voice…like a soothing breeze on a hot summer day gently whisper to me:

"'James, can you receive good and not bad? Do you serve me when things are going good, but turn away from me when things are going bad? There is a time to live...and there is a time to die. It was already destined for Pauline and Tiffany to come Home to be with me...there was nothing you could have done to change that. In good times and in bad times…you must trust Me. You thought I left you...but James…it was you who left Me. You know my Word...I will be with you always...even until the end of time. James, where is your faith?'

"In that miraculous moment, I began to remember who I was…and whose I was," James boomed. "Something on the inside of me began welling up …and my faith began to rebuild again! My Bishop called me 20 years earlier to request that I sing 'Great is Thy Faithfulness' for him at church…but God already knew the day would come when I would need the words of that song to minister to me!"

"Praise God!" said Sister Voyant.

"What should have been another low point in my life, became the turning point in my life," said James. "I made my mind up that I would go to a Mission, where I hoped to stay and get help with my addiction. Well, the great tempter – the devil himself immediately showed up…because, at that very moment, something laying on the floor of the tent caught my attention. In actuality, it was the ground, but for me…it was my floor. I walked over and picked it up," recounted James, walking a few steps, stooping down, and picking up an item he alone, saw in his mind. "You'll never guess what it was in a million years."

"What was it?" asked Hank.

James stood and stared silently at his right thumb and forefinger as if they were clasping something.

"What was it, Mr. James," asked Dancer. "Money…oops that reminds me…I know somebody named Money. I don't want to think about him right now. Let's see…what else. Was it a ring? A watch? A rare coin?"

"A vial of Cocaine…the same vial of Coke I accused Harvey of stealing," said James glaring at his fingers as if he were holding it. "Right there in plain sight, but I did not see it until that moment. Apparently, it must have fallen out of my pocket. He was telling the truth and I punched that man in the face for nothing."

"Like Tyson did Spinks" Willie chimed.

"Shut up Willie," they all said in concert.

"I managed to break the chains of 'Torment' and 'Guilt' and there stood another giant by the name of 'Temptation'," said James staring at his imaginary vial. "And right after I made a promise to God that I would give up Cocaine. I had a split decision to make. "In one hand, was Cocaine," he said, holding up the invisible vial. "In the other hand, I held my Hymnal," he added, holding up the book as if it were evidence in a courtroom. "Metaphorically, I was my own Scale of Justice, having to decide for myself…which I would choose…the choice was solely mines. This may sound a bit hyperbole, but the words of the song seemingly jumped off the pages. It was like they were preaching to me…reminding me of God's faithfulness. The vial, on the other hand, reminding me of its futileness. My mind scrolling back to all the tribulation it has caused in my life…the hurt…the loss…the embarrassment…the pain. Taking all these things into consideration…now with a clear, sound mind… my choice was easy. I chose life over death…blessings over curses… just like God tells us to do in Deuteronomy 30:19," declared James holding his Bible up high.

"Praise God!" said Sister Voyant.

"I began singing the song," said James belting out the first few verses:

Great is Thy faithfulness
O God my Father
There is no shadow of turning with Thee
Thou changest not
Thy compassions they fail not
As Thou hast been
Thou forever will be

"And then," said James, "My God, something came over me! Because I threw that vial of cocaine down on the floor as hard as I could…and crushed it beneath my shoe!" he shouted, twisting his foot back and forth in a crushing motion.

"You did that?" Dancer asked in astonishment. "You actually threw your drugs down on the floor…oopsies…I meant ground and smashed it?!"

"That's right Dancer," said James. "You see Dancer, once I surrendered everything to God and made up my mind that I was through with Cocaine, I had the power to tell Cocaine, 'No!' and I did!"

"Wow Mr. James," said Dancer wide-eyed. "That's pretty unbelievable! The fact that you actually stepped on your drugs like that."

"Put it under my foot and destroyed it," said James. "You can do it too Dancer. All things are possible. To him who believes…Mark 9:23. But you have to believe Dancer…you have to believe."

"It's hard to believe that I could ever find it in me to stomp on my drugs like that Mr. James," replied Dancer.

"Dancer, addiction is a powerful stronghold," said James. "Take it from me…I know. But the key is fully surrendering that addiction over to God and deciding that come hell or high water, you won't turn back! Believing by faith, God can help you do what you can't do for yourself! The Bible tells us in Matthew 17:20 that if we have faith the size of a mustard seed, we can move mountains! And I know with God's help, I moved the mountain in my life that glorious day! And in those miraculous moments, I felt myself reattaching to the vine of Jesus. It was just like The Bible tells us in Ezekiel 37:4-6, which is 'I heard the word of the Lord and he made breath enter me and I came back to life! I know He is the Lord!' Because I tell you Dancer…along with everyone sitting here today…these dry bones of mines…which for so long lay buried in a place the prophet talks about in Ezekiel 37, came alive again! I no longer resided in 'The Valley of Dry Bones!' I was alive again!' James exclaimed, many in the group responding with "Hallelujahs" and "Amens".

"And after God stood me back on my feet like the vast army described in Ezekiel 39:10, I stepped outside my tent feeling like a conqueror!" bellowed James, "Storms were now moving through the area and torrential rain was pouring down! But I didn't care! I was full of hope and a new sense of purpose! Drenching wet but feeling the warmth of God's presence in the cool, damp air, I commenced to singing the remainder of Great is Thy Faithfulness.

With the group staring at him in a trance-like state – mesmerized by the story he was sharing, James summoned up his singing voice – awakening a baritone bonanza of power that had slumbered since reverberating through 'Tent City'. Taking a deep breath, he exhaled the words of the old hymn written by Thomas Chisholm and composed by William M. Runyan singing:

Great is Thy faithfulness
Great is Thy faithfulness
Morning by morning new mercies I see
And all I have needed Thy hand hath provided
Great is Thy faithfulness
Lord unto me
Pardon for sin
And a peace that endureth
Thine own dear presence to cheer
And to guide
Strength for today

and bright hope for tomorrow

Blessings all mine, with ten thousand beside

Great is Thy faithfulness

Great is Thy faithfulness

Lord every morning new mercies I see

And all I have needed Thy hands hath

provided

Great is Thy faithfulness

Great is Thy faithfulness

Great is Thy faithfulness

Lord unto me

So faithful to me

Throughout James' rendition, some in the group outwardly showed displays of praise. Some were clapping, yelling out words of encouragement, or singing along with him. The rest cried – overcome with emotion, or simply sat quietly. After his performance and to the applause that filled the room, James told the group, "It was as if God Himself was in my lungs that day!"

"Sounds like He's still in your lungs!" exclaimed Dancer. "Wow, Mr. James, you sing like Reverend James Cleveland! My Mom would listen to him all the time when I was growing up."

"Thank you, Dancer," replied James. "Rev. Cleveland was quite the singer. He's known as the 'King of Gospel.'"

"Man, you can really sing," said Willie. "You have a voice like Isaac Hayes and Barry White."

"You would say R&B singers who sang sexy songs!" said Sharon.

"So what?" asked Willie. "They were some singing dudes too."

"They were," said James. "And thank you, Willie. I'm a fan of their music too. Me and Pauline would listen to their songs all the time."

"Beautiful rendition James," said Sister Voyant. "Beautiful rendition."

"Thank you, Sister Voyant," replied James. "The devil silenced my singing voice for a looooooong time, seeking to keep it quiet forever. But glory be to God! I came through the fiery furnace of my life singing with more power and anointing than ever!"

James walked over to a window – the sound of applause still filling the room. Leaning on the windowsill and staring through its panes, he said, "That October 5th day, my voice drew people out of their tents, and there was great rejoicing. And something else quite remarkable happened. At the exact moment I finished my song, the driving rain stopped, and the winds calmed. Rays of sunshine began to peek through the grey storm clouds…and then came a rainbow. To me, this was God's way of illustrating with His majestic paintbrush, this wondrous day would mark a new beginning. That day, wearing my new coat and carrying the cardboard box housing everything I owned, I walked away from Tent City and never looked back. To be perfectly honest, I did not keep up with calendar days or time back then. To me, each day was just another passing day…simply morning, noon, and night. But on that day…that glorious day, I walked out of my tent and never looked back, walking to The Helping Up

Mission," said James referencing the faith-based recovery shelter for men in Baltimore City. "It was there that I was told it was October 8, 2015. I was overcome with joy and began to cry, immediately recognizing that the number eight is a symbolic representation of new beginnings. There, I was comforted, consoled, and clothed not just physically, but emotionally and spiritually. They took me in…free of charge…and their charitable act of love and kindness changed my life. During my three-year stay at the Helping Up Mission, or HUM as we called it, I completed their Spiritual Recovery Program, finishing in 2016. Afterward, HUM's generosity allowed me to stay there for two more years. It was during my stay at the Mission that I met our social worker, Mr. Jenkins. I felt I was washed up in terms of my talents and abilities, but Anthony reminded me I still had much to offer. He also told me that I needed to start thinking about life outside of the Mission and that I needed to have a plan of functionality afterward. He told me about Serenity House, feeling it was just what I needed. He explained to me that he believed that as a good, Christian-based residential program, Serenity House would not only keep me grounded in the things I learned at the mission, but would also offer safe transitional shelter."

"I am familiar with their great work," commented Sister Voyant. "They have helped so many people. HUM was a beautiful gateway for you to walk through en route to God leading you here."

"Amen to that!" declared James. Walking away from the window, he made his way back over to the group. Standing in front of them, he said: "When I first started using Cocaine in 1998, I was 40-years-old. When I went to HUM in 2015, I was 57. I came to Serenity House this year…2018, and now I am 60. For 17 years of my life, I was locked up in the jailhouse of addiction!" James shouted, clenching his fists as though they were wrapped around jail bars. "But I have taken the stand here today as a 'Living Witness' that God, the most powerful 'Judge' of all, through His son 'Jesus Christ', the most wonderful 'Counselor' of all, set me free! That is my 'Testimony!'"

Walking closer to the captivated group, he spoke to them as if they were jurors in a jury box.

"Men and women of this court," he said to them. "I stand before you today to say you can believe the non-believers and naysayers if you want! But I know for myself God is real! I know what I saw, and I know what I heard! I know without a shadow of a doubt that God spoke to me that day in 'Tent City', He gave me supernatural strength that day in 'Tent City', and I know it's only because of His enduring grace and mercy I am here at Serenity House. I rest my case."

CHAPTER TWENTY

MASKED PAIN

Wednesday, October 24, 2018

A week passing since James shared his story, the group was several minutes into their third Serenity Meeting. Willie shifted back and forth in his seat – his mind still occupied with James' story. Sister Jackson was speaking to them, eating pretzels as she talked. Nevertheless, Willie wasn't listening to a word she was saying.

I thought about what James said all week, Willie thought, again shifting his body. I know he and I got off to a bad start, but we have a lot in common. His story really hit home for me, and I just can't seem to get the things he said out of my head. Had it not been for these meetings being mandatory, I would have skipped coming today. Hearing James' story last week dusted off bad memories I would rather keep hidden in the attic of my mind.

Willie again shifted, propping his head up with his arm.

Hank leaned over and whispered, "Hey dude, are you okay?"

"Yeah Hank, I'm okay," said Willie. "Why do you ask?"

"Because you aren't looking or behaving like your normal, jovial self," explained Hank. "You look down and you've been unusually quiet. No wise-cracks or talking about Mama Jackson eating, which she's doing right now," he said, glancing at Sister Jackson nibbling on pretzels. That's not like you at all, Willie."

"I'm cool man."

"Are you sure Willie? You don't seem to –"

"Damnit Hank!" blurted Willie, jumping up from his chair. "I said I was fine!"

"Willie! What's wrong with you hollering out like that?!" asked Sister Jackson. "What the devil has gotten into you?!"

Taken aback, Hank said, "Yeah, Willie. What was that all about?! All I did was ask if you were okay!"

"I apologize for my outburst," replied Willie, his eyes welling up with tears. "Hank, I didn't mean to yell at you like that. It's just that…"

"What is it, Willie?" asked Sister Jackson. "What is it that you are trying to say?"

Wille didn't respond, instead thinking, I'm sure they all believe I'm the smoothest, most debonaire man they've ever met. The last thing I want them to see me do is cry. And here I am standing right in front of them crying.

"Let me get you some Kleenex!" said Dancer, jumping up from her chair, grabbing the Kleenex box, and handing several to Willie. She hugged him and skipped back to her seat.

"Thank you, Dancer," sighed Willie, wiping his eyes with the Kleenex.

"You're welcome Willie," said Dancer.

"Ooooooh my Beloved," said Sister Voyant, extending her arms in Willie's direction. "The hurt…the sadness…the unforgiveness…I can feel your pain from where I sit."

"Since the last meeting, I've been thinking about what James told us," cried Willie, blurting out the emotions he held inside all week.

"You have?" James asked in astonishment.

"Yes, I have," replied Willie. "And damn James…I know just how you feel."

"You do?," said James, his mouth dropping open with surprise.

"Yes James, I can relate…" said Willie, his voice trailing off.

"Share my beloved," urged Sister Voyant. "Share Willie. The time has come for you to take off the mask."

Take off the mask? Willie asked himself. I remember when Sister Voyant told us that in the first meeting. But am I ready to take off mines?

At 42 years of age – 29 years after the night that forever changed his life – Sister Voyant's words pricked his mind, prompting him to ask himself, Am I masking the pain of what happened years ago?

While Sister Voyant's words helped unveil this revelation to Willie, he was oblivious to the various styles of masks he wore. He was like the revelers of New Orleans' 'Mardi Gras' – donning a wide variety of colorful, eye-catching, glitzy masks. But for Willie, these were not physical masks, but psychological ones –changing them at will to suit the occasion.

There was 'The Mask of Vanity' – a narcissistic love affair with his own handsome self. 'The Mask of Folly' – living wreckful and carelessly with little or no consideration for consequences. 'The Mask of Deception' – manipulating people, most notably women by lying to them. Then there the most decorative of them all – his 'Jester's Mask'. Behind this extravagant mask, Willie could be jovial, happy, and funny. Nevertheless, beneath this mask, like all the others, lived a sad, fragile man. Walking before the group, their eyes trailing along, this man of many masks prepared to unmask.

Sharon sat watching in astonishment, asking herself a barrage of questions. Why is Willie is standing there with tears streaming down his face?! Willie crying?! I can't believe it! What's going on with him? Why is he so upset?

Sharon's attention was diverted by the rattling, shaking sounds of a paper bag. She turned and looked at Sister Jackson – seeing her hand digging inside a large, Utz potato chip bag.

Look at greedy Mama Jackson over there eating! Sharon thought. And right when Willie was about to open up about something! Watching Sister Jackson pop a handful of chips into her mouth, proceeded by loud crunching, she silently screamed, No Mama Jackson isn't over there chomping on those chips like that! That don't make no sense! What a glutton!

Sister Voyant's dark glasses faced Sister Jackson's directions, along with the gaze of the group.

"Oh Lawd, I'm sorry!" said Sister Jackson with a sheepish look, noticing their stares. "I didn't realize you all could hear me over here chewing," she explained, closing the potato chip bag.

That chewing was loud enough to wake the dead! Sharon thought before placing her attention back on Willie. He couldn't even tell us whatever it was he wanted to say…thanks to Mama Jackson interrupting him with her loud crunching! Hopefully, Willie will still tell us whatever it was…with his fine ass self! Did I just call Willie fine? I did call him fine! No Sharon don't go there! she thought, admonishing herself.

"Willie, you walked up there to say something," said Sister Jackson. "Go on Sugar."

"Yes Willie," said Sister Voyant. "Share what's on your heart, my Beloved."

Willie stood silently, tears continuing to run down his face.

"I don't like seeing you sad Willie," said Dancer, walking up to hand holding a box of Kleenex. "Please don't cry," she said, wiping the tears from his face.

"Thank you, Dancer," said Willie. "This is very kind of you."

"You're welcome Willie," said Dancer, throwing her arms around Willie and hugging him. "I hope you feel better."

"I do," said Willie, giving Dancer a warm squeeze.

Watching them, Sharon thought, I can't believe I'm sitting here wishing I were the one up there with Willie…and that he was hugging me. Could it be…that I'm falling for Willie?!

CHAPTER TWENTY-ONE

WILLIE'S STORY – SONNY'S JUKE JOINT

A few minutes lapsed by. Dancer had taken her seat, and Willie was gathering himself to start his story.

"Take your time Willie," said Sister Voyant. "Pouring out pain isn't always an easy thing to do my Beloved. But it can be good for the soul."

Swallowing a gulp of spit amidst fear and nervousness, Willie closed his eyes tightly, his mind traveling back to his birthplace – Raleigh, North Carolina.

"I was born in North Cackalacky," started Willie.

"North Cackalacky?" asked Hank. "Where is that?"

"I should have known you didn't know," said Willie shaking his head. "North Cackalacky is a nickname for North Carolina…got some of the best corn liquor you'll find anywhere. And my father, Willie Jones, Sr. loved his corn whiskey! 200-proof 'Moonshine'! That stuff was so strong, you could probably start a car with it. Now he and my mother May Jones were married and –"

"Pastor Just's sister?" asked Sister Jackson.

"That's right," replied Willie. "Although he was married, Daddy loved running women. And he had his fair share of them. He was a good-looking man," he said, posing for the group. "Look at Willie, Jr.!" he exclaimed. "Can't you tell?"

Exhaling loudly, Sharon replied, "Give me a break!"

"Sharon, you are always hatin' on a brother!" said Willie. "Don't hate…celebrate!"

"Pah-lease!" replied Sharon referring to the word 'please' and rolling her eyes.

"Anyway," continued Willie after grimacing at Sharon, "Daddy was a lumberjack. He stood six-foot-six and weighed about two hundred and forty-five pounds. A massive man, he was bulging with muscles."

"Wow," said Dancer. "That's how my grandfather was built. But he was a bricklayer. Go on Willie...sorry for interrupting."

"When I was a child, Daddy reminded me of Paul Bunyan, the legendary lumberjack I read about in my storybooks," recalled Willie. "They both had big muscular chests and arms and chopped down trees. But in Daddy's case, he had a head full of coal-black curly hair and smooth, light, red-colored skin. Some of his buddies called him 'Red Bone'. Daddy may have been easy on the eyes, but so was Mama. She was beautiful! A real looker! She had the prettiest, most radiant eyes. She probably could have been an actress out in Hollywood starring in movies. I got my good looks from here too. See my hazel eyes?" asked Willie, pointing to his eyes. I got my eye color from her and –"

"Don't nobody want to sit here listening to you talk about you and your Mama's stupid eye color!" blurted Miracle. "Why are people so into eye color!?"

"Girl, don't you know to keep your mouth shut when grown folks are talkin!'" yelled Willie.

"Miracle, I don't know what prompted your outburst, but you will respect Willie and let him finish his story! Uninterrupted!" said Sister Jackson.

"I hate these meetings!" screamed Miracle, folding her arms, and slumping down in the chair.

"Anyway, before I was so rrrrrrrrudely interrupted," continued Willie, rolling the 'r' in the word 'rudely' in Voyant-like fashion. "Mama was a gorgeous woman with gorgeous eyes which I inherited," he sniped opening his eyes wide, and pointing to them while gazing at Miracle. "But having a wife who looked like a model wasn't enough for Daddy. He loved fooling around with a whole lot of women. He –"

"At least you got it honestly," said Sharon, laughing sarcastically.

"Very funny!" said Willie. "A-he-he," he sounded, returning her sarcastic laugh with his own. "Be quiet woman and let me finish my story!"

"Thank you, Mama Jackson!" said Willie. "As I was saying...he was what you ladies would call a tall glass of water, and Daddy was willing to quench every thirst. Women loved him...just like they love me. Daddy had this habit of starting his sentences with 'I say, I say'...just like the cartoon character 'Foghorn Leghorn'. I'm not sure why Daddy did that...but as far back as I can remember, that's how he prefaced a great deal of his talk. Anyway, Daddy kept his Moonshine high-up in a kitchen cupboard. Every time I turned around, Daddy was stretching his arm towards that shelf for some Moonshine and chugging down a swig. I thought 'It just looks like water. Why does Daddy love to drink that stuff so much? Eventually, my curiosity got the best of me, and I decided to try some. At the time, I was 13 and wasn't quite tall enough to reach the cupboard shelf. So, I grabbed a kitchen chair, scooted it over to the kitchen counter, stood on top of it, stepped onto the counter, and took the Moonshine off the shelf. Looking around like a mischievous child, Willie told the group, "I knew Daddy was at work, and Mama was sleeping on the couch, but I still looked around to make sure no one was coming. I knew if Daddy caught me sneaking in his Moonshine, he would skin me alive...especially if he had been drinking. He could be charming when he was sober...but when he drank...he was as mean as a rattlesnake...so I was afraid of him. I tried my best to mind him and stay out of his way...the last thing I wanted to do was anger him. Despite my fear, I unscrewed the top off the bottle and took my first taste of Moonshine," said Willie, demonstrating by grasping an imaginary bottle, putting it up to his mouth, and swallowing. "'Ugh! Yuck!' Willie grimaced. "It tasted terrible! I thought it tasted like that nasty Castor Oil that Mama would spoon into my mouth whenever I caught a cold."

"Oooh Lawd!" cried Sister Jackson. "My mother used to do that same thing to me. It tasted terrible, but it worked!"

"Well despite the horrid taste, I forced down a few more sips," gasped Willie. "Afterwards, I screwed the top back on, climbed atop the chair, and tried my best to make sure I put that bottle back in its exact spot. I may not have liked the way that Moonshine tasted…but I sure liked the way it made me feel! The next day, I climbed back up to that cabinet, repeating what I did the day before. The next day, I did the same thing…and then the day after that…and then the day after that…and then the day after that. Until…"

"Until what Willie?" asked Dancer. "What happened?"

"Until June 24, 1989," replied Willie. "On that Saturday afternoon, I decided to pour some Moonshine into a little shot glass. "Daddy and his buddies would sometimes drink out of shot glasses at the house, so I figured, 'What the hay?! I'll try that too! That'll make me grown-up like Daddy! Carefully holding the bottle, I stepped off the kitchen counter, back onto the chair, and lowered my feet onto the floor, preparing to pour some Moonshine into a shot glass, recalled Willie, demonstrating these actions to the group. "I turned around, and to my shock, there stood Daddy! I nearly jumped out of my skin! I never heard him come into the kitchen. All I could think to do was hide the bottle," said Willie, placing an arm behind his back, reliving the moment. "I can still see Daddy standing there…with those massive arms of his…wearing a blue and white flannel shirt, suspenders, and faded Levi jeans," recalled Willie. "I was terrified because my father was a real-life 'Dr. Jekyll' and 'Mr. Hyde'. He was the kindest man you'd ever wanna meet when he didn't drink — 'Dr. Jekyll'. But when he got that oil in him, he was the meanest man you'd ever met — 'Mr. Hyde.' And on that day, I could look at Daddy and tell he was 'Mr. Hyde'. I knew that mean, crazed, sneering look…eyes shifting and blood-shot red…and I knew that smell…the strong stench of alcohol seeping through his pores. He probably went drinking with his buddies after work that day. I stood there trembling in my pinstriped pajamas," said Willie, his mind at age 13, now reuniting with his 43-year-old self.

After a long pause, Willie continued, "I can still hear Daddy clear as day saying to me in that deep, gruff voice of his…'I say, I say Junior!" said Willie imitating his father's deep Southern vernacular, 'Don't you hear me talkin' to you! I say, I say, what you got there, son?!' 'Nothing Daddy', Willie whispered in a child-like voice. "Daddy walked behind me, grabbed the bottle of Moonshine out of my hand, and said, 'I say, I say Junior, you ain't being honest boy!' I was so afraid, that I was about to piss my pants. I can still hear Daddy say to me in that in that gruff voice of his…'I say, I say Junior!" said Willie imitating his father's deep Southern vernacular, 'What you got there, son?' 'Not…not…nothing Daddy', Willie stammered, whispering in a child-like voice. "And then Daddy walked behind me, grabbed the bottle of Moonshine out of my hand, and said, 'I say, I say Junior, you ain't being honest boy!'. I was so afraid, that I was about to piss my pants. Then Daddy stood in front of me, took the top off the bottle, and took some swigs of Moonshine. 'I say, I say, Junior,' he told me, 'I know you've been sneaking in my Moonshine 'cause I marked the bottle when I first noticed it looked a little low. I guess you were so busy stealing away at my Moonshine that you didn't notice these little pencil marks, huh boy?' Daddy asked, pointing at the tiny markings. 'And I say, I say, Junior, it looks like I caught you red-handed!', he shouted, slamming the bottle down on the kitchen counter so hard I thought it would break. Daddy raised one of those big hands of his," said Willie cowering and completely covering both eyes with his hands. "I waited for him to wallop the daylights out of me. He beat me pretty good when I got into trouble… but that was nothing compared to how bad he beat Mama. Sometimes, he would whup her with his belt," said Willie, lashing the air with his hands. "Sometimes, he slapped her around," he told the group, slapping the air several times with his hands. Sometimes he punched her," said Willie, balling his fists up and hitting the air. I loved my father, but I hated when he beat on my mother! And he beat her a lot…especially when he drank. He was always giving her black eyes. As a little boy, I wished I would hurry up and get older…so I would be big enough and strong enough to protect my Mama from my father," recalled Willie – stopping his story abruptly after he noticed Sister Jackson weeping.

"That's so sad Willie," said Sister Jackson, wiping her eyes with a Kleenex handed to her by Dancer. "I'm having a moment right now…go on Honey."

Resuming his story, Willie recalled, "I was just a lanky, skinny kid barely into puberty and certainly no match for Daddy's brute strength. 'I'm sorry Daddy!' I cried, waiting for him to dole out bruising punishment for sneaking into his Moonshine. Finally, I felt his big hand! But to my shock and surprise, it wasn't a hit, punch, lash, or even a slap!"

"It wasn't?" asked Dancer.

"No, it was not," replied Willie. "Instead, it was a pat! I couldn't believe it!" said Willie, lowering his hands from his face. "Daddy was patting me on my shoulder! With a big grin on his face, Daddy said. 'I say, I say, Junior, no need to apologize son. I say, I say, Junior, alcohol will make a man out of you boy! It'll grow hairs on your chest! It'll help you keep your women in line…'cause every now and then you gotta slap 'em around!'" said Willie slapping his hands together. "'And Junior, alcohol gives you the courage to do it. And women like for a man to sing to them too. I say, I say, you hear what I'm saying, boy?' 'Yes Sir', I said, relieved that he didn't beat the living daylights out of me. Now Daddy could carry a tune, and he loved to sing 'Cause I Love You', by Lenny Williams. He would sing that song to Mama all the time…especially when she was mad at him…and he was trying to make up with her. Most of the time, her anger stemmed from her suspicions about women. Mama would turn her back to Daddy, dismissing his idle excuses and explanations about whatever she found, heard, or saw. He would wrap his arms around her waist, and slow dance with Mama, and softly sing that song in her ears. It always worked, 'cause the next thing I knew, Daddy was picking Mama up, and carrying her in the bedroom. They would close the door and proceed to have sex. I could always tell because I could always hear them. Their headboard would hit against the wall harder than a Major League slugger knocking a fastball out of the park! I could hear Mama screaming in ecstasy, totally oblivious to the fact that I was listening."

"A lot for a youngster to take in," commented Sister Jackson.

"That's right," agreed Hank. "I don't think most kids like to hear their parents…uh doing it."

"That may be true," replied Willie. "But after a while, I just got used to it."

❀

After a few seconds of silent reflection on such moments, Willie resumed telling the group about being caught with his father's 'Moonshine.'

"Daddy talked another fifteen minutes or so, picked the jug of 'Moonshine' up from the counter, and gulped down more," recalled Willie, tilting his head back to drink from an invisible jug he held in his hand. "Afterwards, Daddy put the bottle back inside the cupboard and said, 'I say, I say, Junior, I was about your age when my daddy schooled me. Now get your jacket and shoes, son. I'm fittin' to take you to 'Sonny's Juke Joint' for your first visit.' Mama had gone shopping for groceries and wasn't home at the time. I had on pajamas…but I didn't dare to question Daddy…I just did what he said. So, I put on my jacket and shoes like he told me, and then we left. Daddy proceeded to drive his old Ford down a winding country dirt road until he reached a place that looked like an old shack. He parked the car and we walked over to the door. Daddy rapped on the door with his knuckles in short, rapid succession, which must have been a secret knock. An eye peered through a crude hole that looked like it had been fashioned by a jackleg. 'I say, I say, it's Willie! Open the door and let us in!' yelled Daddy. The door swung open, and in we walked. The place was little more than a hole in the wall, but it was packed. Everyone was having a good time drinking, dancing, and kissing," said Willie, his mind visualizing the haze of cigar and cigarette smoke hanging in the air. "An old jukebox was blaring Duke Ellington's 'Satin Doll'".

"Oh, Satin Doll," said Sister Voyant. "I just love that tune!"

"And I tell you those guys and gals were just a dancin'!" said Willie shuffling his feet and swinging his arms. "Daddy weaved through all those folks on that makeshift dance floor… and I stuck close behind him… mesmerized by this secret world of merriment. 'I say, I say, Junior, we're gonna have a seat right over yonder', said Daddy pointing to a small table with two empty chairs. After grabbing one of the chairs like so," said Willie grabbing a folding chair and turning it backward, Daddy sat down, telling me, 'I say, I say, don't just stand there lookin' like a fraidy cat!' he said. 'Have a seat Junior.' Minding what he said, I immediately sat down in the other chair, continuing to take in all that was going on around us."

"Hard to imagine a 13-year-old sitting in a place like that," said James.

"It may sound hard to believe, but that's what happened," said Willie. "Looking around, I noticed a barmaid taking orders from customers at another table. However, the moment she laid eyes on Daddy, she stopped waiting on them and rushed over to our table. They started fussin' and a cussin' but she paid them no mind. All that mattered to her was getting' over to Daddy," recalled Willie, an image of the floozy-looking barmaid coming to mind. "'What can I get for you Big Will?' she asked Daddy', Willie imitating the seductiveness in her voice. "Grinning from ear to ear, Daddy looked at her and said, 'I say, I say, bring me some of that Moonshine gal! And bring me a shot for my boy here too!'

"'Anything for you Darling,' said the barmaid winking at Daddy. Turning to me, she asked, 'And what's your name little man?' I replied, 'Junior'. 'Pleased to meet you, Junior,' she said extending her hand to shake mines. 'My name is Flo.' Looking down shyly, I replied, 'Nice meeting you ma'am'. Smiling she said, 'Aww, I see you're shy! Well, Junior, you ain't got to be shy around me…I don't bite!' With a hearty laugh, Daddy looked at her out the corners of his eyes and said, "Yes, you do!' Giggling, she told him, 'Shut your mouth, Willie! That ain't for everybody to know! Now you two handsome boys stay put. I'll be back in a sec with those drinks.'

"'Hey Flo! Get your ass back over here and finish taking our drink orders!' someone hollered from the initial table she was waitressing when we sat down. 'Kiss my ass J.T.!' she screamed back, slapping at her butt heading over to the makeshift bar counter that looked like two long pieces of wood adjoined by hinges and nails.

"A short time later, Flo returned with two shot glasses of Moonshine – one for my father and one for me. 'Bottoms up Junior!' said Daddy, gulping down his alcohol. I followed suit and drank mines. The night wearing on, we drank shot after shot of Moonshine. That stuff was so strong, it felt like fire going down my throat! I don't even know how I stomached so much alcohol that night. I guess I may have built up a little tolerance from sneaking in Daddy's Moonshine at home.

"Daddy talked for hours about women, sex, and his lumberjack adventures. I knew it was getting late because folks were starting to leave. I was ready to leave too, because my head was spinning, and I felt like I was about to throw up. But Daddy just kept right on drinking and talking. Then, right in mid-sentence, he stopped talking and looking at me...his eyes shifting elsewhere. Something or someone got his attention. I turned to see what it was or who it was, and behind the crude bar counter stood Flo signaling with her finger for Daddy 'to come here.' Daddy winked at her and stood up, telling me, 'I say, I say, Junior, I'll be right back. You stay put. Daddy's got some business to take care of.' I replied, 'Okay, Daddy'...feeling uneasy about his leaving me and uncomfortable that a woman other than my mother was summoning him in such a flirtatious, sexy manner. I watched Daddy hastily make his way over to Flo, pushing chairs and people out of the way. After he reached her, they both disappeared someplace in the back. I'm sure Flo dropped her drawers for Daddy, and they got it on real good someplace in that backwoods, barnyard watering hole. I guess it was about 20 minutes or so later when they emerged from the back...both straightening their clothes. Daddy walked over to me and said, 'I say, I say, Junior, let's go.' He made eye contact with Flo and signaled for her to come to our table. She walked over, prompting several customers to start fussing and cussing at her again. Daddy pulled out his wallet and handed some money to Flo, telling her, 'I say, I say, this cash settles my bar tab. I already gave you your tip' grinning and placing emphasis on the word 'tip.' Snickering, Flo said to my father, 'Why, yes you did Willie Jones, and it was a big tip too!' glancing down at his crotch, before walking away. Daddy helped me to my feet, and we made our way out the door. I could hardly stand up, let alone walk. I was good and drunk from drinking all that Moonshine. During the drive home, I fell asleep in a drunken stupor. When Daddy woke me up, he was pulling in our front yard. 'I say, I say, Junior! Wake up, boy! We're home!'

"Uh-oh," said Sharon. "I'm sure Mama was waiting!"

"I'm getting to that part," said Willie. "Now stop interrupting me, woman!"

"Go on man," said Sharon.

"Daddy parked, and we staggered towards the front door," continued Willie. "The rooster began to crow...'Cock a doodle do! Cock a doodle do!' Like clockwork, that rooster always crowed at the same time every morning. 'Shit!' said Daddy looking at his watch. 'It's 5 a.m.!' Meanwhile, I was staggering behind him humming Satin Doll. 'I say, I say, hush up Junior!' he said, snatching his cap off his head and using it to whack me across the top of my head. 'I don't want to wake Mae'. If she catches us coming in this time of morning, she's gonna pitch a fit! Daddy fumbled through his keys until he found the one for the front door...quietly sliding it in the lock before slowly opening the door. We staggered on in...and there was Mama...wide-awake and waiting...pacing the floor with big pink sponge hair rollers in her head, white slippers on her feet, and wearing a pink terry cloth robe, which sat way out here," sighed Willie demonstrating how far his mother's belly stuck out. "Mama was pregnant at the time. And I'll never forget the look she gave Daddy. It was the meanest, angriest look I ever saw her give anybody.

Boy was she mad! You could have fried an egg on her head! Typically, Mama didn't give Daddy much lip. A housewife, she was a quiet, docile woman who pretty much did his bidding. She took a great deal of verbal and physical abuse at the hands of my father...oftentimes saying very little. But this time, things would be different."

Willie paused for several seconds – closing his eyes and taking a deep breath – before recounting the events of Sunday, June 25, 1989.

"Mama shouted, 'Where the hell have you been Willie?!' Where did you take Junior?' Daddy bellowed, 'I say, I say, who the hell are you hollerin' at woman?! I know good and damn well you ain't talkin' to me like that!' 'The hell I ain't!' Mama screamed. 'You stayed out all night and kept Junior out with you! Now, I'm gonna ask you again...Where did you take Junior?!' Daddy stood there on wobbly legs looking at Mama dumbfounded. After a few seconds of trying to figure out what to say, Daddy pulled out the lucky charm that always worked...scooting behind Mama, lovingly wrapping his arms around her, and singing, 'Cause I Love You' in her ears. But the luck of the charm didn't work this time. Mama yanked herself away from him and shouted, 'Don't touch me, Willie! And I don't want to hear your sorry ass sangin' either! Now once and for all, where did you take Junior?!' 'I say, I say, Mae, you need to calm your ass down!' yelled Daddy. 'You're seven months pregnant! You shouldn't be getting yourself all worked up and excited like this! And I don't feel like standing here answerin' a whole bunch of questions either! Now looky here Mae! It ain't none of your damn business where I took the boy!' 'The hell it ain't my business, Willie!' Mama whooped. 'I'm his mother! It is my damn business!'"

"Sounds like your father was pretty drunk and your mother was very angry," commented James.

"That's an understatement," said Willie. "Daddy was so many sheets in the wind I don't even know how we made it home...and Mama was inflamed with rage. She kept right on him about our whereabouts until he shouted, 'Leave me the hell alone Mae! I'm tired and I don't feel like hearing no more of your mouth! I'm goin' back in the room to lay my black ass down!' Daddy stutter-stepped towards their bedroom...like so," said Willie, grabbing ahold of chairs and tables to hold himself up in demonstrating his father's stagger. 'Everything was on one floor in that house...and Daddy was trying his best to get back to that bedroom. But Mama wasn't having it. She ran behind Daddy, grabbed ahold of one of his arms, and screamed, 'Oh hell no Willie! You ain't laying your ass down! I ain't get no sleep, and neither will you!' 'Woman, you better take your hands off me!' Daddy thundered, ripping Mama's hand off his arm. 'And I know damn well you ain't cussing at me! 'You damn right I'm cussin' at you!' cried Mama. 'What the hell is wrong with you keeping Junior out all night! He's just 13! He ain't got no business stayin' out all night! And the smell of that stinkin' Moonshine is jumpin' off you Willie!' My mother rushed over and sniffed me a few times. She stepped back looking at me standing there all topsy-turvy. Wide-eyed, she screamed, 'Junior! You're drunk!' I remember mumbling something incoherently to Mama, and I started dancing around. 'What the hell is this?!' she asked, turning to look at Daddy. With tears streaming down her face, Mama shouted at Daddy, 'You bastard! Junior smells just like a distillery! He can hardly stand up!' 'I say, I say, Mae, the boy is fine!' he told Mama. Slurring, I told my mother, 'Yes...yep... I...I...I...am fffffine Mama. I ccccccan...can...wwwwwwalk mmmmmama...Mama...wwwwwatch.' I walked a few steps before stumbling and falling. Daddy staggered over and helped me up from the floor. 'Willie! Have you lost your motherfuckin' mind!'

Mama yelled at Daddy. 'How could you take Junior out drinking!' she asked. 'He's just a boy!' 'I say, I say, shut the hell up Mae!' replied Daddy, his anger increasing, his patience decreasing. But the same can be said about Mama, who said, 'Shut the hell up my ass!' Grabbing ahold of Daddy's face and turning it directly at me she screamed, 'Look at Junior! He's drunk!' 'Take your fuckin' hands off me!' said Daddy, yanking her hand from his face. You're gonna look at Junior in the face and then you're gonna look me in the face and tell me where you took him!'"

"Sounds like your mother wasn't backing down," said Sharon.

"She wasn't," replied Willie. "To tell you the truth, that was the first time in my life I ever saw Mama that mad. It was also the first time I ever heard her say the words that came out of her mouth that day. It also marked the first time I saw her stand up to Daddy like that. Mama was going toe to toe with him, and she wasn't about to throw in the towel, telling Daddy, 'How dare you keep my son out all night and bring him home the next morning drunk?! 'Where did you take him, Willie?! Where did you take him, Willie! I said, where–did–you–take–him–Willie! Answer me damnit!' My mother stood there seething over her questioning while refusing to tell her where we had been. Drunkenly dancing around, I said, 'Sonny's Juke Joint', singing the words. 'Daddy popped me upside the head real hard and hollered, "I say, I say, shut up Junior!' But it was too late. I had already let the cat out of the bag. 'What!'" roared Mama pop-eyed. 'You took my Junior to the whorehouse!' 'I say, I say, Junior's my son too!' shouted Daddy. 'You need to stop babyin' the boy! He's a teenager now! So what we had a few drinks?! The boy had already been sippin' on my Moonshine in the cabinet anyways! Now Mae, I ain't got nothin' more to say! It's Sunday mornin', I'm tired as a motherfucker, and I'm ready to go to bed! And make sure you have my lunch ready when I git up! You got that?!' Daddy turned, once again heading towards the bedroom. But Mama ran in front of Daddy, blocking his path. 'Naw Nigga!' she shouted. 'You still think you fittin' to get some sleep after keeping me up all night worrying about you and Junior! Hell naw! Like I said, I ain't get no sleep, and neither will you!' 'I say, I say, Mae, I've had enough of your mouth! Now move!' Daddy shouted, shoving Mama out of his way. Mama grabbed ahold of Daddy's shirt to keep from falling, ripping some of the buttons. That's when she noticed something red on his collar. 'I see one of those two-bit whores you screwed over there at Sonny's left her lipstick on your shirt!' Mama screamed. 'And I can smell her cheap perfume on you too! All the booze in the world couldn't cover the smell of that Five and Dime toilet water!' 'I ain't been with no woman Mae!' Daddy told Mama. 'Oh yeah?!' she said. 'Well in addition to that lipstick, how did you get those passion and bite marks on your neck?! Huh, Willie! Explain that! How the fuck did you get those!' Spit flying from his mouth, Daddy hollered, 'I say, I say, Mae, I ain't screwed nobody but you!' Your damn stomach ain't sittin' out like that for nothin'! Now you had better shut the hell up and leave me alone or else –' 'Or else what!?' Mama asked. 'You no-good, lyin', two-timin', Son of a Bitch!' 'Or else I'm going to take my belt to your ass!' roared Daddy, taking off his big, black, leather belt. 'Try it you drunk!" Mama screamed. "You've ruined your life and mines on account of that alcohol...or Devil Juice as I call it! But I'll be damned if I'm going to let you mess Junior's life up too! I'll meet you at the gates of hell before I allow that to happen! Without saying a word, Daddy drew his back arm and cocked his fist to hit Mama. But just as he was about to strike her, Mama reached into her robe and pulled out her arm...a firearm that is...a .347 Magnum. Shocked, Daddy slowly backed up a few steps...his eyes staring into the barrel of that gun. 'What you got to say now nigga?!' Mama asked. "'I say, I say, oh, so you're a badass Foxy Brown bitch now!' said Daddy.

"Oh, I remember seeing that movie!" exclaimed Sharon. "Foxy Brown was a baaaaaaad chic! Pam Grier played that role back in the 1970s."

"That's right," said Willie. "My father used to watch that movie all the time. "Well anyway, my mother told my father, 'You can call me whatever you want Willie!' 'But what I won't allow you to do is mess up Junior's life! He's gonna be better than a cheatin', no good, drunk like his Daddy!' After Mama said that, Daddy lost it! He went charging towards Mama screaming, 'I say, I say, Foxy Brown, meet Super Fly!'"

"I remember that movie," said James. "That was another 1970s movie…actor Ron O'Neal played 'Super Fly.'"

"You got it," said Willie. "And Daddy was flying towards Mama. Before she could react, Daddy grabbed Mama by the arm, which caused her to drop the gun, which spun clear across the floor. "'Who's bad now!' hollered Daddy, slapping Mama so hard across the face she fell to the floor. He straddled Mama to the floor so that she couldn't move. Mama tried to fight back, but she was no match for Daddy's size and strength. All she could do was lie on the floor kicking, screaming, and scratching while Daddy repeatedly hit her in the face.

"Oh my Lawd!" said Sister Jackson stuffing pretzel after pretzel into her mouth. "That's terrible!"

"'I can still hear my mother pleading, 'Stop Willie! Stop! Before you make me lose the baby!'" recalled Willie with a frightened look. Daddy kept brutally hitting Mama in the face, shouting 'I say, I say, Mae, you must have lost your damn mind thinkin' you gonna shoot me! I'm the baddest motherfucker around here!' Scared to death, I stuttered "'Sssssstop Dddddaddy! Ppppplease ssssssstop!' said Willie, his voice quivering. "'Shut up and stay out of grown folks' business Junior!' Daddy hollered at me. 'But you are gggggoing to hurt Mama!' I cried. 'And the bbbbbbaby! Ppppplease ssssssstop!' I pleaded. But Daddy wouldn't stop. He just kept right on hittin' Mama like she was a punchin' bag. I rushed over and jumped on his back," said Willie – demonstrating by taking a running leap. 'I say, I say, git the hell off me, Junior!' Daddy shouted, throwing me off his back like he was The Hulk. He threw me with such brute force, it sent me sprawling clear across the floor…and I landed right next to the gun. In that dark moment of drunkenness, all I could hear was Daddy pummeling Mama, and her bloodcurdling screams. I just wanted him to stop beating Mama! I was so afraid he was gonna kill her…because Daddy was punching Mama like he was hitting a man. I laid on the floor staring at the gun…finally deciding it was my only means of stopping him. Picking it up, I ran towards them…and with my hands shaking like a leaf, I aimed the gun directly at Daddy," said Wille, cupping his trembling hands together as if they were a pointed gun. "Standing behind him, I pleaded 'Sssssstop Dddddaddy! Ppppplease ssssssstop!'. It was as if Daddy were in another world…oblivious to the one he was in…because he just kept right on punching Mama…who was barely fighting back. I assumed by that time Daddy beat her so bad about the head, she was starting to slip into unconsciousness. 'Mama!' I screamed. From there everything happened in slow motion. I closed my eyes and squeezed the trigger. Pow! After the loud blast, everything went quiet and I momentarily blacked out," said Willie going down to the floor with closed eyes.

For several seconds, Willie sat crying on the floor, the group riveted by the devastating nature of his story. Opening his eyes, Willie told them, "When I came to, I dropped the gun…now sober with the somber reality of what I had just done! I ran over to my parents and saw the bullet had ripped a hole in Daddy's back! He was slumped over Mama and neither one of them was moving! 'Daddy! Mama! Get up!'" said Willie, frantically moving his hands to show how he shook his parents. "'Please get up!' Their eyes were open, but blood was trickling out of their mouths." With great sorrow, Willie rose to his knees and sobbed, 'I looked upwards to the Heavens and cried out, 'God, I need you! What have I done?!' That bullet…that one bullet…went through Daddy's body…and hit Mama! And in an instant…that bullet changed the course of all our lives…because Daddy, Mama, and the unborn baby…all died…the trajectory of a split-second decision shattering my life…and ending theirs."

❃

Looking at Willie laying on the floor in a fetal position, Sharon could hardly believe what she just heard. I never would have thought in a million years that Willie had gone through something like that! she thought. I thought my experience was bad! But James' and Willie's stories are even more traumatic than mines!

Sharon looked on a few moments longer thinking, Why am I feeling an uncontrollable urge to comfort Willie? Before she could answer her silent question, she rushed over to Willie, got down on the floor, wrapped her arms tightly around him, and slowly began to rock a man who up until this tender moment – had been her nemesis.

"All I was trying to do was help Mama," Willie wept. "I never meant to hurt them." Willie opened his tear-filled eyes and looked up at Sharon with great surprise. Then, to Sharon's greater surprise, Willie buried his head in her bosom and continued to weep.

Is Willie trying to be slick and get some free feels with his face, or is he so tore up from telling his story he doesn't realize he just put his entire face smack-dab in the middle of my cleavage? Sharon wondered. Should I pull away from him or continue to allow him to use my breasts as a crying pillow? I guess I can allow them to give him some comfort…at least for now.

The two remained that way until Dancer knelt beside them, tapping Willie on the shoulder.

"Willie…," said Dancer.

"Yes, Dancer?" said Willie, slowly unburying his face from Sharon's chest.

"You're going to be okay Willie," said Dancer gently patting his eyes with Kleenex. "Really you are. I know it hurts. But it was an accident. You didn't mean to shoot your parents."

"Dancer's right my Beloved," said Sister Voyant. "In my years of experience…I've been exposed to the ugliness of domestic violence. What happened wasn't your fault."

"Willie," said Dancer with a warm smile. "Now I know why you are always trying to make us laugh. It seems the saddest people always try their darndest to make people happy because deep down inside, they feel like they have no value…nothing to offer anybody that's worth a thing. So they do whatever they can, whenever they can, and every time they can, to make sure no one else ever feels that way."

"Hmmm, Dancer," said Willie. "I never looked at things that way. Maybe you're right. There's a part of me that loves clowning around. Laughter helps me to mask my pain."

"I know how you feel, Willie," said James. "But God!"

"My Beloveds," said Sister Voyant. "I too, have had my own share of difficult circumstances in the past relating to alcohol intoxication," said Sister Voyant, her comments drawing surprised gazes from the group.

"What!," said Sharon. "You were hitting the bottle Sister Voyant?

298

"No, not me," said Sister Voyant. "But somebody who was very close to me. And Willie my Beloved, thank you for sharing your story. That goes for you too James…thank you for sharing your story at the last meeting. I know that sharing your stories was not an easy thing to do."

"Your welcome Sister Voyant," said James. "And you're right…it wasn't easy…but telling it amongst our group helped me to get out some things I had been holding in."

"James is right," said Willie. "It's been years since I have told that story. But right now, I feel a weird sense of release…in a funny weird sort of way that's hard to explain."

"And that's the way it should be," said Sister Voyant. "The truth of the matter, my Beloveds, is that our stories are not meant for everyone's ears. Each time someone opens up and shares a story, we should be thankful. Why? You might ask. Well, I will tell you the answer. That person thought highly enough of you to allow you in their space and shared a piece of their lifetime. That, my Beloveds, is not a right, but a privilege."

"I guess everybody's got a story," whispered Miracle, prompting everyone in the room to look in her direction. "I don't know all of your stories, and you all sure as hell don't know mines. But one thing's for sure…everyone's fighting a battle no that one else knows nothing about."

❀

Sister Jackson began coughing, now prompting the group to all look in her direction. James and the group watched her cough with such force the bag of 'Utz' pretzels in her hand went sailing in the air. With an effort comparable to an outfielder trying to catch a fly ball, Sister Jackson quickly jumped up from her chair trying to grab the bag.

I've never seen Mama Jackson move that fast!' thought James watching the bag hit the floor, causing the remainder of the pretzels to spill out.

"Lawd have mercy!" Sister Jackson exclaimed, still trying to catch her breath between coughs.

"Let me get you some water Mama Jackson!" said Dancer racing to the kitchen.

"Are you alright Mama Jackson?" asked James, while thinking, My goodness Mama Jackson is a glutton! This is the second time I've seen her drop a bag of something! But this time, she sounded like she nearly choked!

"I'm alright James," said Sister Jackson, still coughing to clear her throat. "I can't believe I dropped my bag of pretzels!"

And I can't believe you are worried about those pretzels when you nearly choked to death eating them! thought James.

"I think one of my pretzels went down the wrong pipe!" said Sister Jackson, beating her chest.

One of them went down the wrong pipe alright! thought James. You were putting those pretzels in your mouth faster than you could chew them!

"Audrey, my Beloved, are you alright over there?" asked Sister Voyant, her face turned towards Sister Jackson.

"Yes, I'm okay," coughed Sister Jackson.

"Here's some water!" said Dancer, handing Sister Jackson a glass of water.

I'd better go on over and help, thought James getting up from his seat. The last thing I want to do is sit here and watch a fat woman choke off a pretzel! James walked over and began patting Sister Jackson on the back.

"Oh, I'm fine James," said Sister Jackson, "Really I am. I guess I got a little choked up. And thank you for the water, Dancer. It was just what I needed."

"You're welcome Mama Jackson," said Dancer. "And don't worry about these pretzels. I'll clean them up."

"Why thank you, Dancer," said Sister Jackson, finally getting her breath fully back. "You are such a servant!" Looking at her watch, Sister Jackson declared, "My Lawd, look at the time! We've run over our meeting period, and I've got to get lunch started!"

The residents got up from their seats and began to gather up their belongings.

"Same time…same place here next week my Beloveds," said Sister Voyant.

"Oh, and one more thing!" said Sister Jackson. "Please remember…if you haven't already done so…invite your guests to our upcoming Graduation Ceremony. Time flies and that date will be here before you know it."

CHAPTER TWENTY-TWO

INTO THE FLAMES

October 31, 2018
Clarksburg, West VA

Down the road a little over 200 miles away from Baltimore, was Hank's hometown – Clarksburg, West Virginia. On this Halloween morning, Ghosts strung from trees danced in the wind of the nippy air, Jack-o-lanterns of all shapes and sizes sat grinning on porches, and images of cackling witches aboard broomsticks or stirring cauldrons were plastered on windows. These were among the sights along Country Club Road, a stately neighborhood of multi-million-dollar mansions in this exclusive area of West Virginia.

Inside 89 Country Club Road, Hank's father – Hank Riley, Sr. stood in his living room staring at a letter that arrived amongst the stack of the day's mail. Earlier, Mr. Riley read the correspondence – a handwritten letter from Hank, Jr. inviting him and his wife Chelsea to Serenity House's February 8, 2019, Graduation Ceremony.

 Sighing, the 55-year-old real estate tycoon slid the letter back inside the envelope, thinking: This letter is postmarked from Baltimore, Maryland. So…Hank, is staying in a place called Serenity House. While Chelsea and I have not seen or spoken to Hank in five years, I have mixed feelings about this letter. It lets me know our son is alive and well. But on the other hand, hearing from Hank fills me with angst…especially this time of the year.

Stroking his greying beard, Mr. Riley glanced around his luxurious home. The elegant brick estate included seven bedrooms, heated floors, a wet bar, a workout room, and a four-car garage. On many winter nights, Chelsea and I snuggled and watched those orangish-red flames shoot up and crackle into the air, he thought gazing at the home's massive stone fireplace. But I cannot quite remember the last time we cuddled near the fireplace. We often entertained, hosting ritzy dinner parties attended by politicians, CEOs, and other influential people. But we stopped throwing such lavish soirees. And on Halloween, our home was a favorite gathering place for the neighbors and their children. But those days too, are a thing of the past.

Hank and Chelsea Riley were college sweethearts at Princeton University. Mr. Riley was a star Rugby player and an aspiring businessman. Mrs. Riley was a standout on the Women's Lacrosse team with aspirations to become an accountant. They graduated from Princeton in 1985 and married in 1987. Mr. Riley would become a successful real estate investor, while Mrs. Riley would go on to open an accounting firm. In 1989, the Rileys had their first and only child – Hank, and eventually moved into their home on Country Club Road.

In his reflections, Mr. Riley recalled, It didn't take long for Chelsea and I see that our rambunctious baby boy inherited our athleticism. Hank, or Hanky as Mother would call him…would go running after any and every kind of ball he could get his hands on…especially a Rugby football. That boy was barely out of pampers before I decided to have a small Rugby field installed just for him in the backyard. As he grew into a lad, I began teaching him the fundamentals of Rugby. Sometimes we spent hours in the yard playing Rugby…Hank was such a natural. He eventually became a standout 'hooker' on the area's youth Rugby teams. There was not a single, solitary player around who could match Hank's skills in that position. Nearly every collegiate Rugby team in the nation was trying to recruit Hank out of high school. They rang our phone non-stop and letters from universities and colleges across the country flooded the mailbox. Hank settled on my Alma Mater…Princeton University. My son was walking in my footsteps! I could not have been prouder! Images of his mother Emma Riley coming to mind, Mr. Riley thought, Everybody was proud of Hank. Especially Mother. A smile forming on his face, Mr. Riley recalled, Mother called herself 'Hanky's Number One Cheerleader.' She even stitched the title in big, colorful letters on several of her sweatshirts. She attended every Rugby game Hank played in. She was small in stature but had the biggest mouth in the stands! he chuckled. 'Go Hanky!' she yelled from the top of her lungs, prompting Hank to smile and wave at her from the field.

An avid baker Emma Riley once owned a popular bakery in Clarksburg, West Virginia called 'Emma's Homemade Delights.' After every game, Mother handed Hank a snack bag filled with her homemade cookies. He loved those cookies. Mother always did dote over Hanky. In Mother's eyes, her Hanky could do no wrong.

When she turned 70, Emma Riley sold her bakery business and retired. After retirement, she lived an active lifestyle – traveling, driving wherever she wanted to go, bowling on a league, shopping, and attending the neighborhood Catholic church where she volunteered in the Soup Kitchen. She also continued baking and other activities.

Mother was quite a woman, thought Mr. Riley. Independent, confident, warm, spunky, nurturing, and loving. A matriarch any family would love to have. But despite her independence, with Mother getting older and living alone after Father died, I wanted her to move in with us. We certainly had more than enough space. But being the woman that she was, she felt that was an imposition, and refused. She also did not want to leave that house. She had been there for so many years. 'I'm fine right where I am,' she once told me sitting in her favorite paisley chair. 'This home holds so many fond memories. Your father…God rest his soul…and I…raised you…along with your brothers and sister in this home. You all grew up here. I have lived here for well over 50 years. I can't imagine living anyplace else.'

Mr. Riley moved to the den, now sitting behind a cherry wood desk listening to 'Wolfgang Amadeus Mozart'. Reclining in a beaded leather executive chair, thoughts about his mother still occupied Mr. Riley's thoughts. Mother was such a spry woman. She was in excellent health, save for a few aches and pains that sometimes popped up with her arthritis. She enjoyed playing bridge with her friends and volunteered at a nursing home. Mother was as sweet as the desserts she loved to bake.

When she died in 2012 at the age of 77, Mr. Riley's mother lived in a modest home on Farland Avenue in Clarksburg – her husband Wilbur Riley preceding her in death a few years earlier.

All my life that house possessed nothing but fond, happy memories, recalled Mr. Riley. But all that changed.

Mr. Riley's mind re-winded back to June 23, 2007.

What a day! he thought. Picture perfect. Chelsea and I could not have asked for better weather in having Hank's sendoff…a grand bash celebrating his leaving for Princeton. For the lavish affair here at our estate, Chelsea and I pulled out all the stops…hiring a Party Planner to take care of logistics, catering, and other matters concerning the Rugby-themed party…sparing no expense! We wanted the day to be a memorable one…and it was…but for all the wrong reasons after Hank and some of his old Rugby teammates decides to horse around in the backyard. Hank and some of those kids had been playing together since they were little boys. Even with all the preparation that went into the party, no one was prepared for what happened. I watched in absolute horror as Hank's foot went into a beaver hole in the backyard. No one saw that beaver hole there…not even the groundskeeper. Hank's leg twisted like a Twizzler. He couldn't even walk…me and his friends had to help him up. To everyone's shock and disbelief, we would later learn that Hank had broken his ankle. The break was so severe, Hank needed surgery…the doctors informing us that his recovery would take months. After the surgery, Hank was prescribed OxyContin for pain. Those damn OxyContins! swore Mr. Riley, pounding his fist on the desk. I didn't know much about that medication at the time…but God knows I came to learn a great deal about them…after Hank became addicted to those pills. Initially, Chelsea and I simply thought they were helping Hank with his pain. But Chelsea and I became concerned after we noticed that days, weeks, and then months had gone by, and we were still picking up medication from the local pharmacy. We found that strange. No sooner than Hank finished one bottle…another refill was ready to be picked up from the pharmacy. Always a spunky, cheerful kid who loved to joke around, Chelsea and I noticed Hank was increasingly becoming more and more sullen…down…and withdrawn. He was extremely sad and upset about his ankle injury…and hated the fact that he was getting around on crutches. He was becoming more and more introverted and began keeping his bedroom door closed. Chelsea and I did all we could to encourage Hank and remind him he could play Rugby again after rehab. The last thing we wanted him to do was to give up on playing…and even worse…give up on college. But all Hank seemed to want to do was stay in his room. Chelsea and I began to wonder if he was addicted to those pills. I would come to learn that Hank was not alone. I began to hear my friends talking about how OxyContin did wonders when it came to relieving nagging back pains, sprains, chronic headaches, toothaches, and post-surgical discomfort. Chelsea and I checked into the pills and discovered OxyContin was highly addictive. We asked Hank if he might be addicted to the pills…something he got angry about and vehemently denied. Chelsea and I stopped picking his pills up from the pharmacy. But Hank still found a way to get over there to pick them up. Things just got worse. Hank became unkept, more reclusive, and more depressed…sulking and moping around about his injury. Eventually, he got off the crutches…but he did not get off those pills.

Reclining back in his chair, Mr. Riley recalled the day he confronted Hank's physician - Dr. Carl M. Daniels. At the time, Dr. Daniels was standing in the waiting area of his office seeing a patient out the door. Mr. Riley grabbed Dr. Daniels by the collar of his white lab coat – the physician's receptionist and patients all looking on in shock.

"Listen here Dr. Daniels" Mr. Riley shouted. "If you write one more prescription for my son Hank Riley, I'm going to break your fucking neck! Do you hear me!"

"Take your hands off of me!" demanded Dr. Daniels, attempting to un-wrangle Mr. Riley's hands off his collar. "Let go of me before I call the police!"

"Write another prescription for my son, and somebody is going to be calling an ambulance for you!" screamed Mr. Riley, letting go of the doctor's collar. "What the hell is wrong with you?! I am not sure what kind of practice you are running here Doc, but don't you realize those prescriptions you are nonchalantly writing for OxyContin are hooking people on those pills! I am warning you! Write another prescription for Hank, and I'll break your damn neck!" Mr. Riley threatened before storming out of Dr. Daniels' office.

Dr. Riley did heed my warning. He did not write another prescription for Hank. Hank was furious when he found out I demanded his doctor not to write him any more prescriptions for OxyContin. He argued with me and Chelsea over the matter. She and I hoped that with him no longer getting prescriptions for the pills he would turn away from them. But things got worse. Desperate, he did whatever he could do to get his hands on those pills. That included lying and stealing. Over time, he grew increasingly combative with me and Chelsea. By 2009, Chelsea and I would learn Hank was no longer taking OxyContin. He was on something far worse than either of us could ever imagine. Our son was now using Crystal Meth.

Mr. Riley's longtime friend Todd Mahoney delivered the startling news. According to Mr. Mahoney, he caught Hank and his son Matt Mahoney smoking Crystal Meth in Matt's room.

I really did not want to believe what Todd told me, Mr. Riley recollected. And when I told Chelsea…it broke her heart. She cried for days. We both hoped that Todd made some mistake in concluding Hank and Matt were smoking Crystal Meth. But when we asked Hank about using Crystal Methamphetamine, he furiously denied it…walking out the house and slamming the door in a rage. But Chelsea and I had no alternative other than to believe what Todd told me because everything about Hank continued to deteriorate…his looks…physique…attitude…you name it. Chelsea and I no longer recognized this person. Is this our son?' we asked one another. Hank's thievery ramped up…he was stealing everything he could get his hands on in this house…money, jewelry, coins, antiques, sports memorabilia, art. We pleaded with Hank to get help…offering to send him to the Betty Ford Clinic in California for treatment. But he refused, shouting at us that he did not have a problem. His tendency to 'fly off the handle' was also very unsettling. Chelsea and I stopped inviting our friends to the house…not wanting them to see Hank. We stopped going on vacations for fear we would return and find everything gone. Not to mention Hank began to bring suspicious, seedy-looking people into our home. Hank even outfitted his bedroom door with a lock to keep me and Chelsea from entering his room. I could not believe it! In our house where we pay all the bills…our son who was not paying one dime put a lock on his door! Between the stealing, Hank's company, and his erratic behavior, Chelsea and I felt like prisoners in our own home! Our arguments with Hank only intensified. Our lovely estate – thought Mr. Riley gazing around – had become nothing more than a battleground between us and our son.

Mr. Riley continued to reflect, his mind still recounting the events leading up to his son's great descent. I do not even know why I'm sitting here dredging all of this up, he thought. I try my best not to think about these things…because it still hurts. Perhaps I am doing so because of Hank's letter…maybe it's because today is Halloween…or perhaps it's a little bit of both.

Looking at the picture sitting on his desk of him, Chelsea, and Hank – in his Rugby uniform at eight, and smiling ear-to-ear, Mr. Riley lamented, Hard to believe things went awry with Hank the way they did. He had so much promise. Taking a deep breath and exhaling, he recalled, Then, there was the crux of why our arguments with Hank progressively got worse…money. Hank was receiving a weekly allowance. But Chelsea and I stopped giving him money…knowing he would spend it on drugs. That made him more irate and violent. I will never forget the day Chelsea told me Hank picked up a television and hurled it across the room because she refused to give him money. I rushed home to confront Hank and he raised his hand to hit me but instead punched a gaping hole in the wall before rushing out the house. In addition to such episodes of fury, Chelsea and I would sometimes hear Hank talking to someone who was not there. This led us to believe that Meth was causing him to hallucinate. Chelsea and I feared where all of this might lead. As hard as it was to admit, we were now afraid of our own son.

A few more moments went by, and Mr. Riley was now gazing at Hank's letter – which he placed on his desk. Before long, his thoughts returned to the place they left off.

Chelsea and I were at the end of our rope. Hank's behavior had gotten to be far too much for us to handle. I convinced Chelsea that we must give Hank an ultimatum. Either he would get help, or he would have to leave the house. She did not want to do that, but we had no choice. She tearfully…and hesitantly went along. We knocked on the door of his room and I demanded he let us in. Once we were inside…we looked around…in disbelief his room was in such disarray! It looked like a slob had been living in there…clothes everywhere…snack and candy paper wrappers all over the floor…empty cellophane bags. But we stepped over these things and sat down with Hank on his bed…and I gave him our ultimatum. Chelsea could not even look at Hank…she kept her head turned away. However, we got the answer out of Hank that we wanted…he said he would get help with his Meth addiction…but he didn't. Chelsea and I believe he genuinely wanted to get help. But he just couldn't seem to get that monkey off his back. It had taken total control of him.

By March 2011, the Rileys made what they felt was the most difficult decision of their lives.

After Chelsea and I came home and found Hank ransacking the house looking for money, I told him to leave the house. He refused, in profanity-laced tyranny, prompting me to call the police although Chelsea begged me not to call them. They commanded Hank to leave the house…and he did. He eventually returned, but I had every lock changed and made sure every window was closed and latched so that he could not get in. It was tough love, and Chelsea and I hated kicking Hank out of the house. We did decide that if there was some sign he would get help, our offer to send him to Betty Ford…or any clinic for that matter…still stood. But Hank displayed no signs he wanted help. I also warned family and friends not to fall for Hank's lies…not to give him money…or worse yet…take him in. All of them heeded our warnings…except for one…my mother Emma.

Picking Hank's letter up from the desk, Mr. Riley hastily walked back to the living room.

So, Hank is graduating from someplace in Baltimore called Serenity House, scoffed Mr. Riley. Well, I don't plan on attending! Nor will I share this letter with Chelsea! She's suffered enough! We both have! I told that boy he was dead to me…and he still is! Gazing at the letter with fiery eyes, Mr. Riley snarled, "Hank can go to Hell!," tossing it into the flames of the fireplace.

CHAPTER TWENTY-THREE

THE GHOSTS OF HALLOWEEN PAST

Wednesday, October 31, 2018
Baltimore, MD

Down the road in Baltimore, Maryland - a little over 200 miles away from Clarksburg, West Virginia – Hank and most of the others sat waiting for the group's fourth Serenity Meeting to start on this Halloween day.

Thinking to himself, Hank lamented, All I can do is sit here and think about how much I hate his day! I sure wish things could go back to the way things used to be on Halloween. Growing up in Clarksburg, I always looked forward to this day! And so did my parents! Mom would go all out for Halloween! She dressed me up in a wide variety of costumes…including 'Spider Man', 'Super Man', and 'Power Rangers' – all of which she made herself. And every year, she and Dad opened our home up to all the neighbors and their kids for a big Halloween Open House. Wearing costumes made by Mom, she and Dad greeted everyone at the door to the sound of spooky sounds and music blaring throughout the house. One year, Dad and Mom were The Munster's 'Herman' and 'Lily.' Another year they dressed as The Addams Family's 'Gomez' and 'Morticia'. Even Granddad and Grandma got into the act that year, showing up dressed as The Addams Family's 'Uncle Fester' and 'Grandmama.' Another year, Mom and Dad dressed as 'Frankenstein' and 'The Wife of Frankenstein.' Everyone always looked forward to our Halloween Open House. Not just to see what costumes Mom and Dad would wear, but also to see the decorations inside the house. Dad

strung orange and purple lights throughout and put fake spider webs in the ceiling. He and Mom placed life-sized figures of mummies, witches, and monsters throughout, along with cauldrons, broomsticks, and other decor. They even outfitted the front and back yards with replicas of coffins and headstones. Me and the other kids – who came dressed as aliens, superheroes, villains, sorcerers, witches, cartoon characters, and other costumes – bobbed for apples, played games, gobbled down toasted marshmallows, and made S'Mores. We filled our Halloween bags with all kinds of candy and other treats and listened to the older kids share ghost stories. While we did all of this, our parents sipped on warm apple cider and shared their own spooky stories huddled near the fireplace. They also talked about all that went into making or buying their children's costumes. We could always hear them laughing about that…what good times they were! Everyone always had a blast at our Halloween shindigs and couldn't wait until the next one. They were the talk of the town. But little did we know our family would become the talk of the town for another reason.

❀

"Where's Willie?" asked Sister Jackson, halting Hank's daydreams. "Everybody's here except for him. We need to get started, and we ain't got much time."

"Oh, I forgot to mention that Willie told me he would be a few minutes late," replied Hank. "He ran back to his room to get something. He should be down any minute."

"We'll get started, but I'm gonna speak to Willie about being late for our meeting," said Sister Jackson, digging into a large bag of assorted Halloween candy. "Tardiness at our Serenity Meetings are a no-no," she noted, opening a Hershey's chocolate miniature.

"Let us join hands and say the Serenity Prayer my Beloveds," said Sister Voyant, prompting Hank to stretch his hand towards Miracle in Willie's absence. Looking at Hank's hand, and then up at him, Miracle turned away. "Have it your way," said Hank, closing his eyes and reciting the prayer with the rest of the group. While the group prayed, Willie – wearing a frightful 'Ghostface' mask– crept into the room – tip-toeing so they could not hear him.

❀

After the group finished their prayer, Hank opened his eyes to the raucous sound of Willie standing behind them shouting, "Boo! Rahhhhhhhhh!" startling everyone in the group.

Bowled over with laughter, Willie told them, "I got you all good!" taking off the mask, made famous by the movie, 'Scream.' "Man, oh man, I got you all good!" he hooted, pointing at them. "You should have seen your faces!"

"Oh my," said Sister Voyant, placing her hand on her chest, "You startled me, Willie."

"What the hell is wrong with you Willie!" Sharon yelled. "You scared the shit out of me! Sorry Mama Jackson," she said, glancing at Sister Jackson. "I didn't mean to cuss. But that didn't make no damn sense! You really need to grow up Willie!"

"Whew," said Dancer, her eyes flickering left and right. "You scared me too."

"That wasn't funny Willie," said James. "That was a knucklehead move."

"Simpleton," snarled Miracle, rolling her eyes at Willie.

"Sit down Willie!" shouted Sister Jackson. "I can't believe you came in here and scared us like that! I nearly jumped out of my skin!"

"C'mon Mama Jackson," said Willie, still laughing. "Today's Halloween. Can't we have a little fun? Oh...and I see you have a bag of Halloween candy. Can we have some?"

"I guess I can share a piece," said Sister Jackson, passing the bag to Hank. "But just one piece...I'm watching."

Hank who sat fuming since Willie's antics, threw the bag of candy on the floor, grabbed the mask out of his hand, and hurled it across the room.

"Why did you do that man!" Hank screamed, wrapping both hands around Willie's neck. "Why did you do that Willie! Why!"

"No you didn't just throw my candy across the room!" said Sister Jackson. "Now let go of Willie!" she ordered, attempting to pull Hank away from Willie. James and Sharon rushed over to help, and the three pried Hank's hands from around Willie's neck.

"What the hell is wrong with you Hank?" gasped Willie. "You nearly choked me to death! It was just a Halloween prank!"

"Don't do that ever again Willie!" Hank screamed, his chest heaving up and down. "Do you hear me, Willie! Don't you ever-fucking-do-that-again!"

"I'm sorry Hank," said Willie. "I didn't mean to upset you. I was just joking around. I was only playing...it was a Halloween prank."

"Don't play with me like that!" Hank yelled. "What you did may have been amusing to you...but it scared the crap out of me! Not only that...but I hate Halloween! I fucking-hate-Halloween! And that prank of yours just made me feel worse! All it did was conjure up terrible memories!"

Watching James, Sharon, Dancer, and Sister Jackson coax Hank back to his seat,

Miracle thought, That fool Willie may have jolted me just a tiny bit...but not much. After the hell I have gone through, there's not much that scares me. I have lived in houses of horror...and survived! It's gonna take more than that to scare me like Willie scared the rest of those scaredy cats!

To Miracle's great surprise – and the others, Hank jumped up from his chair and flung it across the room – his skin beet red – and greenish-blue veins protruding from his forehead and arms. Going on a rampage, he turned over more chairs and Sister Jackson's table, causing all her snacks to fall to the floor. The White boy is acting like a maniac! thought Miracle.

"Maybe we should call the police!" suggested James.

"No!" shouted Sister Jackson. "There's no need to call the police! Help me get Hank back to his seat!" she said, causing James and Willie to rush over and assist her with forcibly getting Hank back over to his chair, and sitting him down.

Dancer scrambled about in a frenzy, trying to clean up and organize the things disrupted in Hank's wake.

"Dancer Baby...don't throw that candy away...put it right back in the bag." directed Sister Jackson, watching

Dancer pick the candy up from the floor. "And please set my table back up and put my snacks back on it. I'll organize them."

"Yes, ma'am Mama Jackson," said Dancer, who was also turning chairs upright.

"Hank!" exclaimed Sister Jackson, "What the Devil has gotten into you?! Going off like that?! I understand you are upset with Willie…but to tear the house up like this?!"

"You guys can let go of me!" said Hank. "And I'm sorry. I didn't mean to go off like that…I guess I lost it," he told them, sinking his face into his hands and sobbing.

"I'm sorry Hank," said Willie apologetically. "I'm really sorry."

"What should I do with this?" asked Dancer, holding the mask with the tips of her fingernails.

"Throw that evil-looking thang in the trash!" said Sister Jackson.

"My ma –" started Willie.

"That mask is going in the trash!" said Sister Jackson. "And don't backtalk me, Willie! It's not even up for debate!"

"Yes, Mama Jackson," Willie pouted.

Sister Voyant walked over to Hank, placing a hand on his shoulder.

"Shhhh…calm down Hank," she said. "Calm down my Beloved. Everything's going to be alright."

"I can't calm down!" screamed Hank, beating his fists against his head. "You don't understand!"

"No, Hank," Sister Voyant whispered, taking ahold of Hank's balled-up fists. "Please don't beat yourself up. It's time my Beloved…time to put the old ghosts and goblins who are haunting you…to rest."

Hank immediately stopped beating himself about the head – staring through tear-filled eyes at Sister Voyant.

"The ghosts of my past?" Hank asked with bewilderment. "How…how did you know that?"

"God allows me to see all kinds of things, Hank," said Sister Voyant. "I don't have to see you to see the pain of your past. It's written all over your heart."

CHAPTER TWENTY-FOUR

HANK'S STORY - GRANDMA, OXY & CRYSTAL

Comfortable that Hank calmed down, the others returned to their seats. Sister Voyant remained – still holding Hank's hands – loosened, no longer balled up into fists. Without realizing it, Hank gently let go of Sister Voyant's hands and walked in front of the group. Willie immediately ducked.

"Why are you ducking Fool?" Sharon asked, shaking her head.

"In case Hank decides to start throwing things again," said Willie. "Something might hit my handsome face. And I have to protect it at all costs."

"Shut up Willie!" said the group.

Gulping a ball of spit and taking a deep breath, Hank prepared to take a six-year journey back to October 31, 2012.

Nervously biting his nub of nails, Hank began, "I'm from Clarksburg, West Virginia where I was a star Rugby player and –"

"Rugby! interrupted Willie. Who the hell plays Rugby?!"

"Shut up Willie!" yelled the group.

"Ever since I can remember, I played Rugby," sniffled Hank. "According to my Dad, I was barely out of pampers and already kicking a Rugby ball. Dad loved the game and so did I. A former Rugby standout at Princeton, Dad even had our backyard outfitted with a Rugby field. I grew up playing the game. But I wasn't your average

Rugby player. I was good…I mean really, really good! I was the best player around in the hooker position."

"Hooker position?" inquired Dancer.

"Hooker position?!" asked Miracle, twisting her body around to look at Hank.

"Ha-ha," laughed Willie with a smirk. "A Hooker, huh?"

"Yeah, the hooker position," Hank replied. "I should have known you guys didn't have a clue. In Rugby, the hooker is the forward position on the team. The name comes from hooking the ball with the back of the foot. Like so," demonstrated Hank, using his foot to hook an imaginary ball. The move instantaneously brought back memories of his Rugby days.

"I can still hear the crowds cheering in the stands," said Hank. "And my Grandma Emma…well she was always the loudest in the stands. She never missed me play…and always handed me a nice, warm bag of cookies after every game. She made the best homemade cookies! And she –"

"Cookies?!" asked Sister Jackson. "Lawd have mercy, Hank! Homemade?!"

"That's right…homemade cookies Mama Jackson," said Hank. "My Grandma baked all kinds of things. Cakes, cookies, pies, you name it. She once owned a small bakery in Clarksburg. Everyone loved her desserts."

"My Lawd! A bakery!" commented Sister Jackson. "Well, isn't that something!"

"I got a lady friend who bakes too," said Willie. "I like her cakes and pies, but I really love her cookies!" joked Willie. "She is one sweet thing. Every time I talk to her, I sing 'Sweet Thing to her," said Willie humming the 1970s song by 'Rufus featuring Chaka Khan'.

"Oh, hush up Willie!" said Sister Jackson.

"Thank you, Mama Jackson!" said Sharon. "None of us want to sit here listening to you sing about your women Willie!"

"Please go on Hank," said Sister Jackson. "We don't have much time. I didn't mean to interrupt you. I got a little distracted when you started talking about them good ole cookies your grandmother used to bake. Emmmmmmmmmm! I bet they were some kinda good!"

"They were Mama Jackson," said Hank. "Chocolate chip, chocolate chip with walnut, cranberry, peanut butter –"

"Ooooooooh! Shut your mouth Hank!" said Sister Jackson. "I can't take hearing about those cookies! But here's the next best thing…store-bought ones," she said picking up a bag of Stauffer's Ginger Snaps. Take it from me! I know a thing or two about homemade desserts!"

I can tell, Hank thought silently, watching Sister Jackson tear open the bag and pop a cookie in her mouth.

"Lawd these are good!" Sister Jackson exclaimed. "Go on Baby!"

"Well, my granny was proud of me," said Hank. "She nicknamed me 'Hanky'.

"Hanky-panky!" said Willie, prompting the group to tell him, "Shut up Willie!"

"I was her Hanky!" said Hank, again bursting into tears. "I can still hear Grandma in the stands shouting, 'Go Hanky!' while waving our team pennant Go Hanky! Go Ha…" his voice trailing off.

"Go on my Beloved," urged Sister Voyant. "You can do it, Hank."

"I can't!" Hank cried. "I can't!"

Dancer rushed over to Hank and handed him a Kleenex. After wiping his eyes, she hugged him, prompting Hank to hug her back.

"I know it hurts my Beloved," said Sister Voyant. "Pouring out about something that hurts deeply is never easy. But you can do it, Hank."

"That's right Hank," Dancer chimed. "You can do it."

"I'll do my best," said Hank. "But it grieves me to talk about this."

❀

After a long pause, Hank continued: "There were also lots of Rugby recruiting scouts sitting in the stands…all wanting me to come play for their schools. I must admit…it was pretty neat to know they were all there watching me. Not to mention the stacks of mail at the house from schools all over the country. Academically, I also had good grades and scored high on my SATs, so for them…I was an ideal prospect. I decided on Princeton. The school was offering me a full-ride scholarship. My dad Hank Riley, Sr. and my mom Chelsea Riley are both alumni of Princeton and played sports at the school. My Dad is a real estate tycoon and Mom owns an accounting firm."

"So, your parents are really rich?" asked Willie.

"That's right," said Hank.

"I sure wish I was rich," said Willie. "I would be so happy!"

"Being rich is good," said Sister Voyant. "But riches do not always bring about happiness. Go on Hank."

"My parents were ecstatic I was going to Princeton!" continued Hank. "And I couldn't wait to go! So, there I was…privileged, popular, and headed for Princeton…until…"

"Until what Hank?" asked Sister Jackson snacking on Ginger Snaps.

"Until I broke my ankle playing during a party my parents were hosting for me at our mansion," Hank replied.

"Wow, a mansion?!" asked Willie. "My lady friend Mrs. Jones lives in a mansion!" he said singing the first few lines of the 1970s song by Billy Paul. "She's married…but we definitely have a thang going on!"

"Shut up Willie!" they all yelled.

"During the party, Russ…one of my old teammates yelled, 'hook the ball, Hank! For old time's sake!' I couldn't resist. But Dad heard what Russ said and told me not to do it. 'This is a party, Hank. No horseplaying', he warned. 'There are too many guests here. Somebody might get hurt.' Proceeding to run towards my friends, I said, 'Stop worrying Dad'. I figured this would be a keepsake memory from the party to take with me to Princeton. Many of the guests stopped to watch us…excitedly waiting for me to do what I did best…hook the ball. I felt my foot go down into a hole in our yard and twist awkwardly…all the guests gasping while watching me go down to the ground. I grabbed my ankle, writhing in pain…my Dad yelling 'Hank!' while Mom and Grandma screamed 'Hanky!' The party ended there. I hoped my injury was nothing more than a sprain…but I would later learn I had broken my ankle in three places."

"That's messed up," said Willie.

"Messed up is right," agreed Hank, looking at Willie. "Not only would I have to undergo surgery, but my doctor…Dr. Daniels said the recovery time would take weeks…maybe even months. I scoffed at his prognosis. I guess it's hard to tell now," said Hank looking down at his skinny frame, "but I was buff and in great shape. I figured being so young and athletic, I would undergo the surgery, do some aggressive rehab, and be back on the field in no time. Dr. Daniels scheduled my surgery. Instead of starting school in the fall as scheduled, I figured it was best to wait until spring. By then, I would be ready. The surgery would be behind me, and I would take the extra time to do what I needed to be in tip-top shape. I had the surgery…which seemed to go well. But I was on crutches…which I did not like…and I was in great discomfort after the surgery. Dr. Daniels jotted down a prescription. Handing it to me, he said, 'Hank, here's a prescription for Oxycontin. You can have it filled down the street at the neighborhood pharmacy. Take one every four to six hours as needed for pain.' I responded, 'Sure Doc.' My parents dropped off the prescription and waited for it. A few minutes later, my dad emerged from the pharmacist with my prescription, and we drove home. To be perfectly honest, I didn't know very much about OxyContin or 'Oxys' as I came to call those pills. As an athlete, I worked hard to keep my body in shape and went to great lengths to watch what I drank and ate…that included not ingesting pills or other medication. But achy and sore from the surgery, I opted to take the pills. And they did the trick! Oxy was my chill pill. I would take one of those babies and poof! The pain was gone, and before I knew it…I was out like a light! And Oxy was foxy! Those pills were so soothing and relaxing. Without even realizing it, Oxy had lulled me into believing I had to have them…not only for pain…but to sleep. Oxy also took my mind off the fact that instead of getting around like some handicap on my crutches, I should have been at Princeton playing lacrosse. Oxy was my escape because it took my mind of that. To make matters worse…not only was my ankle causing me a great deal of pain…it was taking longer than expected to heal. So, I repeated the same routine every day…several times a day. Go in my room, shut the door, pop an Oxy. Go in my room, shut the door, pop an Oxy. Go in my room, shut the door, pop an Oxy. Before long, that's all I wanted to do. Somewhere amidst all of this, Princeton took a back seat to Oxy. There was a lot less pressure hanging out in my room popping Oxys as opposed to going away to school in New Jersey, studying, getting up early to go to class and other rigors associated with going to college. In retrospect, I'm pretty sure had I just rehabbed like I was supposed to and kept a level head, I could have still attended Princeton in the spring and played Rugby. But all I wanted to do was pop those damn Oxys. And that was another thing…the thought of having to give up Oxy once I arrived at Princeton also crossed my mind. 'What if I'm tested for drugs and Oxy shows up?' I asked myself. Although I was not ready to give up Oxy…I still had every intention of going to Princeton, telling myself, 'I'll go next semester.' Soon, weeks turned into months, and finally…I lost my scholarship. Once that happened, I became moody and withdrawn. The more depressed I became, the more I popped those pills."

"Wow," said Dancer.

"And here's something else," said Hank. "Getting refills was easy. Once I finished one bottle, another refill was available at the pharmacy. If my refills ran out, Dr. Daniels would write more. My parents sensed something was wrong…questioning me about possibly being addicted to the pills. They were very upset about all of it…and crushed that I had not gone to school. They refused to pick up any more prescriptions from the pharmacy…but I always found a way to get them. That included having them delivered by the pharmacy to the house. After a while, I wasn't getting the deliveries. I discovered my parents were intercepting my prescription deliveries and disposing of my pills. I also believe they were going in my room looking for bottles to get rid of when I wasn't home. I was livid! I bought a padlock from a hardware store and put it on my door to keep them out. We got into a heated argument about that! I hardly ever argued with my parents…until I started wiling out on those pills. Well, my best friend Matt had a car…his father and mines were good friends. I began hopping rides with Matt, and we drove to the pharmacy to pick up our Oxys together. Matt had a rad sports car Mr. Mahoney bought him as a graduation gift. Well one day, we went to pick up our Oxys from the pharmacy. We joked around and perused a few comic books and 'Hustler' magazines during our wait. We couldn't help but notice the wait was taking much longer than usual. The pharmacist made his way back over to us. But he was carrying just one prescription bag…which he handed to Matt. Turning to me, the pharmacist said, 'I'm sorry Mr. Riley…but there's no prescription here for you.' I couldn't believe it! I yelled at the pharmacist, 'What do you mean there's no refill here for me! There must be some mistake!' Shaking his head in adamant disagreement, the pharmacist said, 'There's no mistake. Dr. Daniels did not call in or fax over a refill for your OxyContin. I checked all the shelves…three times…that's what took me so long.' 'Fuck!' I yelled, storming out the drug store door. Matt caught up with me and asked, 'Why do you think your doctor didn't write your prescription?' I replied, "I don't know! But I'm going to find out!' I had Matt to drive me directly to Dr. Daniel's office. 'Wait here,' I told him, rushing into the building where Dr. Daniels' suite was located. 'I'll be back once I get some answers."

Inside Dr. Daniel's suite, several patients sat waiting to be seen. Some read magazines, a few watched a TV mounted on the wall, and others chatted with one another. Conversely, they all stopped whatever they were doing once Hank swung the door open with great force.

"Where's Dr. Daniels?!" Hank yelled to the receptionist.

"Seeing patients," she said. "Do you have an appointment today, uh –"

"Riley!" screamed Hank, barging through a door leading to the back of the practice. "Hank Riley!"

"'No!" shouted the receptionist. "You can't come back here, Mr. Riley! Dr. Daniels is seeing patients."

Disregarding the receptionist, Hank went room to room searching for Dr. Daniels, until he found him.

"'I told Mr. Riley he couldn't come back here!" the receptionist explained to Dr. Daniels. "But he charged right past me! Should I call the police Dr. Daniels?!"

"That won't be necessary Roslyn. I can handle this matter myself." Momentarily excusing himself from his patient, Dr. Daniels stepped outside the examination room – shutting the door.

"Now what seems to be the problem, Hank?" asked Dr. Daniels in a hushed tone. "Certainly, you know better than to ram your way into my office in such an unorderly fashion."

"The problem Doc…is that when I went to pick up my prescriptions for Oxys today from the pharmacy, I was informed there was none. Tell me Doc…why was that?!" yelled Hank. "My ankle is still killing me?!"

"Lower your tone, Hank," said Dr. Daniels. "Now…the reason there was no OxyContin prescription for you at the pharmacy is because your father bogarted his way back here in the same manner that you have and threatened to break my neck. With that said, I won't be writing you any more prescriptions for OxyContin."

"What!?" said Hank. "My Dad is behind this?"

"I'm afraid so," said Dr. Daniels. "Now, if you would excuse me, I need to get back inside my exam room and finish seeing my patient. I am terribly sorry Hank. I know how much those pills have been helping to relieve your pain."

Hank turned and walked away.

"Take this," said Dr. Daniels, jotting down something. "This is my personal cell phone number. Call me…and

I'll see what I can do."

Hank stood before the group staring blankly in the air – thinking about his encounter with Dr. Daniels.

"I ran out of Dr. Daniels' office, and hopped back in Matt's convertible yellow and black Camaro," recalled Hank. "He called it 'Bumble Bee', after the 'Transformer movie'. That car was a thing of beauty…and blazing fast. The special-order exhaust pipes Matt had installed on that car were so loud you could hear him coming a mile away. And the sound system could blow your eardrums out. 'Where to Hank?' asked Matt. 'To my house', I told him. 'And get me there…quick!' 'Sure dude', said Matt. 'I looked over at Matt's prescription bag sitting on his lap, and said, 'Let me get a couple of your Oxys man.' Matt tossed his bag over to me, replying, 'No more than two Hank. I need my Oxys…I can't function without them.' I opened his pills…chucking two in my mouth and sneaking another four or five into my pocket. Matt turned up his 'Iron Maiden' heavy metal CD, revved up 'Bumble Bee' and took off towards my house on Country Club Road in Clarksburg."

Hank paused, images of Matt screeching into his family's driveway revving in his mind. "I couldn't wait to confront Dad," said Hank. "I hopped out the car before Matt even stopped and sprinted towards the house. I could hear Matt yell, 'Hey Hank!' I turned and stopped to see what he wanted. 'Go easy on your old man!' said Matt before pulling off. 'Mad or not…Mr. Riley is still your dad.' But Matt's advice went in one ear and out the other. All I could think about was the fact that my dad stopped my flow of Oxys! I needed them! 'How does he expect me to get through the day?!' I asked myself. I couldn't get inside the house fast enough. 'Where's Dad?!' I asked Mom who was sitting in the living room working on her laptop. 'Your father's in the den' she said. 'What's wrong, Hank?' Without saying a word, I marched into the den…Mom stepping away from her laptop to follow behind me. I didn't say a word. I went marching towards the den to confront Dad, who was sitting behind his desk talking to someone on the phone while listening to Beethoven…he loves Classical Music."

Little did Mr. Riley know…Hank was about to shatter the calm of the moment.

Rushing over to Mr. Riley, Hank hollered, "Why did you go to Dr. Daniels and tell him not to write me any more prescriptions! You know I need those pills for my pain! Why did you do that Dad!"

"Hanky!'" said Mrs. Riley, "How dare you talk to your father in such a disrespectful manner?!"

"'I'm going to have to call you back J.B,'" said Mr. Riley. "I've got a situation over here I need to handle. We'll wrap up that mall deal tomorrow."

Slamming the phone down on the receiver and jumping up from the chair, Mr. Riley shouted, "Hank Riley, Jr.! Have you lost your mind?! How dare you take that tone with me?!"

"Why did you threaten Dr. Daniels?" asked Hank. "Now he won't write me any more prescriptions! You had no right to do that!"

"'I had every right Hank!" bellowed Mr. Riley. "Look at you! Just look at you! Behaving badly…looking badly…smelling badly…the list goes on and on!"

"What am I supposed to do now that I can't get any pills? asked Hank. "Huh, Dad! Tell me that!"

"I'll tell you how!" screamed Mr. Riley. "By taking us up on our offer to send you to a clinic to get help! Betty Ford or any clinic for that matter! You need help, Hank! Your mother and I have watched you literally throw your life away behind those pills!"

"'Your father's right Hanky," said Mrs. Riley, her voice breaking. "We want you to do better…to go to school…we want our old Hanky back…one with dreams and aspirations."

"I should have known you would agree with Dad!" Hank yelled at his mother. You always take his side! Just go right ahead you two! Just go right on and gang up on me! Maybe it'll make both you of feel better!'"

"Honey, your father and I aren't ganging up on you," said Mrs. Riley. "We just don't want to see your life go down the drain on account of those pills!"

"That's a laugh!" said Hank. "You don't want to see my life go down the drain behind Oxys?! I guess that explains why you and Dad were flushing my pills down the drain to get rid of them…or grinding them in the garbage disposal!"

"It was for your own good Hanky," explained Mrs. Riley. "You are dependent on those pills…and that's just not healthy. Your father and I love you…and all we're trying to do is help you, Honey.'"

"Help me?!" said Hank with a sarcastic laugh. "What a crock! After all, what happened to me was all you and Dad's fault!"

"Our fault?" said the Rileys simultaneously while turning to look at one other.

"That's right! Your fault!" yelled Hank. "If you two hadn't thrown me that stupid party, I wouldn't have fallen in the first place!"

"'What?!" screeched Mr. Riley. "Why that's absurd!"

"You're blaming us…when all we were trying to do was have a nice party for you Hanky?" asked Mrs. Riley.

"Well just look at where that party got me Mom!" blasted Hank. "I fell and messed up my ankle! If I hadn't broken my ankle, I wouldn't have a reason to take Oxys! Now, would I? Instead, I would be at Princeton right now…in a classroom or playing Rugby…instead of arguing with you two!"

"That's a barrel of bullshit Hank and you know it!" fired Mr. Riley. "I see you conveniently left out the part about me warning you not to horse around in the first place! But did you listen! No!"

"'Well, Dad, if you guys hadn't given me a party, then that scenario wouldn't have presented itself!" argued Hank. "Now, would it?!"

"Keep telling yourself that lie Hank!" shouted Mr. Riley. "Keep believing it! But here's the truth! No one told you to horseplay that day Hanky! No one told you to keep taking those pills! No one told you not to rehab your ankle like you were supposed to! No one told you not to go to Princeton! Those were all your bad decisions! Now own them and stop blaming us! All your mother and I have ever done is shower you with love! We gave you everything! And this is how you repay us?"

"Hanky, you need to get some help," pleaded Mrs. Riley through tears. "Before it's too late."

"What I need are my Oxys, Mom! They help me with the pain caused by the injury that you two caused!

Thanks to you two…I'm damaged goods…no longer able to play Rugby!"

"You can still play!" said Mr. Riley. "But right now, you're not in shape to do anything! First, you need some serious intervention!"

"What I need…is to get out of here!" yelled Hank heading for the door.

"'Come back here Hank!" shouted Mr. Riley. "I'm not finished talking to you!"

"There's nothing else to talk about Dad!"

"'Hanky! Honey come back!" pleaded Mrs. Riley.

"Go to Hell!" Hank shouted at the top of his lungs.

Hank stood silently in front of the group, remembering how he turned around and looked at his parents before leaving the house.

"Mom's face was sunken into Dad's chest…and his arms were wrapped around Mom…trying to console her…I'll never forget that as long as I live," said Hank solemnly. "They both looked so hurt…disappointed…and broken. I looked at them briefly before slamming the door shut behind me. After that, I walked to Matt's house where I crashed for the night…and the next night…and the next night…and the next night. Between my laying around in Matt's room, eating up his parents' food, worrying Matt for Oxys, and not lifting a finger to clean up behind myself…it didn't take long for me to wear out my welcome. When I left my parents' house that day, I was dumb enough to think I was going to prove something to them. All it proved was that I couldn't survive without them. Well after being at Matt's for over a week, his parents sat me down and told me I needed to go home and straighten things out with my parents. With my tail between my legs, I scampered on home."

Pausing momentarily, Hank continued with his story. "I was able to patch things up with my parents…but it was just that…a patch because I still needed my Oxys. I didn't have a single pill! Remembering what Dr. Daniels told me, I rustled through my dirty clothes hamper…pulling the piece of paper with his number on it from the pocket of some jeans. I dialed Dr. Daniels' number…hoping he would answer. He did. I explained my plight…which included the fact I had no money. 'Alright Hank,' said Dr. Daniels, 'I have some OxyContin at my office. Meet me there at 8 p.m. sharp…and Hank…keep this between you and me.' 'Sure Dr. Daniels! 'I'll be there!' I met Dr. Daniels later that evening. I was a little uneasy because we were the only ones there. He flicked the lights on, and we walked to his office in the back. After telling me to have a seat, he sat a tall bottle of Oxys on his desk. 'Gee, Dr. Daniels, thank you!' I said, ready to grab the bottle of pills. 'Not so fast Hank' said Dr. Daniels quickly picking up the bottle. 'Before you grab that…I need you to grab this', he told me, unzipping his pants and taking out his pecker. I was startled by his proposition! I thought, 'Sex for Oxys?!' But I did it," said Hank, feeling embarrassed about his admission to the group.

"Seems to me…that doctor took advantage of you, Hank," said Miracle looking up at him. "There are those who prey upon the vulnerable."

Surprised at Miracle's reaction, Hank thought, Miracle hardly says a thing...and when she does...it's always something mean...but this time...she didn't sound so mean. She almost sounded...compassionate. Looking at Miracle, Hank said, "Despite my drastic change and what my parents tried to tell me, I didn't believe I was addicted to Oxys...but I was...and I was willing to do anything to get them to relieve my ankle pain and the 'high' they brought. So, you're right Miracle...I was vulnerable...and young. I was 18 when I started taking Oxys...and 20 when I stopped."

"You stopped?" asked Dancer.

"I did," replied Hank. "I turned away from Oxy for good...but only after I was introduced to Crystal."

"Crystal?" inquired Willie. "Was she pretty?"

"That's right, Willie," said Hank, looking down at the floor. "Crystal Meth."

❀

For several seconds, Hank stared silently at the wood floor of the Deacon Roy E. Jackson Room, thinking about his matriculation from OxyContin to Crystal Methamphetamine.

"I was at Matt's house one afternoon," Hank continued, "when he handed me a small glass pipe and said, 'Try this Ice, Hank...it will really fuck you up!' 'Ice?' I asked. 'Yeah, Ice', Matt replied. 'Glass' man.' 'Glass?' I asked. 'Yeah...'Glass'...Crystal Meth', he told me. I told Matt, 'I didn't know you used Meth.' 'I only use 'Ice' occasionally...it's not something I run around blabbing my mouth about', he explained. 'Here...try it.' I sat staring at that pipe trying to decide if I was going to try it or not...I heard some bad things about Crystal Meth. But I was out of Oxys...and was tired of doing Dr. Daniels' sexual bidding to them from him. But I figured, 'What the hell? What have I got to lose? Hey...it might even relieve my ankle pain.' So, I took the pipe out of Matt's hand and smoked that Meth. And Matt was right! It did fuck me up! It was a euphoric high...unlike anything I ever experienced before in my life! It was so potent," said Hank licking his lips. "So scrumptious...so tasty...so pleasing to my palate! One time...and this former Rugby hooker was hooked on Meth."

"I know what that's like Hank," said Dancer sadly. "I got hooked on drugs my first time too."

"I thought I was going from good to gooderer," said Hank.

"Gooderer?" asked Dancer with a puzzled look.

"Yep, gooderer" responded Hank, "That's a word I made up...meaning in my mind I thought I found something better than Oxy. But things didn't get better...they got worse. Much worse. It did take my mind off Oxy...but my desire to have Crystal was even greater. Once I experienced my initial high...I wanted that high again and again. And I didn't have to go through Dr. Daniels or some pharmacy to get it...the street pharmacists took care of that part. I smoked that shit all the time. The arguments with my parents intensified along with my desperation for money. Crystal would literally talk to me...I began to hear voices after I started using it. And it told me to do whatever it took to buy more. My lying and stealing really got bad when I got on Crystal. I stole any and everything...including my Dad's prized Princeton class ring...which I pawned at a pawn shop.

"His Princeton ring?!" asked James.

"His Princeton ring," replied Hank. "Terrible, isn't it? Thank God he got it back...but only after he paid a handsome sum to the pawn shop. And when I couldn't get my hands on something to steal…I reverted back to selling another asset…something that people like Dr. Daniels paid good money for…my body. And Crystal was my pimp."

Nervously biting his remnants of fingernails with his reflections on the past, Hank commented, "Life is funny, isn't it? From a star Rugby Hooker to a Hooker for Crystal! She demanded I make and give her all my money. By that time, I was about 22…and there were lots of anxious customers willing to pay good money for a young male to satisfy their voracious and sometimes perverse sexual appetites.

"Nasty men!" seethed Miracle.

"Not just men Miracle," explained Hank. "Women too…lots and lots of women…mostly older ones…looking for companionship and sex."

"I can definitely relate to that!" said Willie.

"Shut up Willie!" said the group.

"So yes…the majority of people I exchanged sexual favors with were women…but there were a few men too…"

"I definitely can't relate to that!" commented Willie.

"I learned never say what you won't do…because you just might find yourself doing it," said Hank. "I slept with anybody…anywhere… for money to buy that drug. I even began bringing all kinds of people into the house…taking them to my room… where we would smoke, fuck, or both. Sorry for my language Mama Jackson…just being honest…but please," said Hank, gazing into the faces of the group, "please don't judge me."

"Ain't nobody is here to judge you Baby!" said Sister Jackson. "The Bible says…Fudge not, or you will be judged…speaking of fudge…where did I put my fudge cookies? Oh, here they are," she said, opening the package and eating one.

"Mama Jackson, I believe you meant…'Judge not, that ye be not judged', said James pointing at the scripture in his Bible. "It's right here…Matthew 7, verse 1."

"Ain't that what I said?" asked Sister Jackson.

"No!" said James.

"Well, that's exactly what I meant," said Sister Jackson. "Now, go on Hank."

"Finally, my parents gave me an ultimatum," recalled Hank. 'Tough love'…they called it. Either I would get help with my addiction, or they would put me out of the house. They were prepared to pay whatever amount of money needed to get me into a good program. I said I would take them up on their offer…and I wanted to…but never did. My desire to get high on Crystal was much stronger than my desire to quit. By 2011, my parents had reached the end of their rope. They kicked me out of the house and changed all the locks. I had no money, no job, and no place to stay. I found out Dad told family and friends not to take me in…that I had changed and wasn't myself. But despite such warnings, my Grandma Emma took me in. To her, I was still her Hanky. But little did she know…Crystal had turned me into a monster."

Hank inhaled, exhaling a deep, long sigh, now approaching the most agonizing part of his story.

"It was Wednesday, October 31, 2012…Halloween," recounted Hank. "Although I wasn't in costume…I was a fiend…feigning bad for some Crystal. I would even say I was experiencing the worst cravings I ever experienced. I was coming down off my high, and I needed some quick money to buy more Crystal. A voice whispered to me 'Grandma Emma…she'll be back soon. Ask her for the money. She'll give it to you.' I replied, 'That's right…Grandma never tells me 'No.' I anxiously waited in the living room for Grandma to come through the door. Once she arrived home, she set her purse and groceries bags down on the table. Some Trick-or-Treaters rang the doorbell, and she dropped some baggies of homemade cookies and along with some candy in their Halloween bags. No sooner than she closed the door, I ran behind her. 'My goodness Hanky!' she said, putting one hand on her chest. 'You nearly scared me to death! Now help your grandmother put up these groceries. Afterward, I'm going to fix you a nice hearty meal because you are too skinny.' Mimicking the voice of a pirate she smiled and said, 'Argh! You need some meat on them bones mate!' said Hank, imitating the high seas vernacular. "But I didn't want to help put up any groceries. Nor did I want any food to eat. All I wanted was Crystal. After telling my grandmother I wasn't hungry, I asked her for ten dollars. 'No Hanky' she said. I couldn't believe it! I thought to myself, 'Did Grandma just tell me, 'No?' It was always 'sure Hanky'… 'okay Hanky'…'yes, Hanky'…but this time…the answer was 'No Hanky.' 'Now, your Grandma Emma will do anything to help you Hanky'," she told me. 'You know that. But I already know what you are going to do with the money. Your father and mother are worried sick about you and that drug habit. Honestly Hanky, I didn't want to believe it. But since you've come to stay with me…I've seen the signs for myself. Things disappearing out of this house. Money missing out of my purse. And my neighbors have told me you have strange people coming in and out of my house when I'm not home or late at night when I'm asleep. This all must stop Hanky…it all must stop'…" Hank's voice trailed off, his nose running and tears rolling down his face, prompting him to wipe them with the sleeve of his shirt.

"Ewwww man!" said Willie, grimacing. "No you didn't just wipe your snot with your clothes! That's nasty!"

Dancer handed Hank some Kleenex. After wiping his face, Hank continued with his story.

"Grandma also told me, 'Now I want to help you, Darling. Because Grandma loves you. But giving you money for you to use to buy drugs…isn't helping you…it's hurting you. So, I will feed you some good, nutritious, stick-to-your-ribs food…but not that habit of yours. Don't worry about the groceries Hank…I'll put them up', she said carrying her groceries into the kitchen. 'You just stay right there…while Grandma fixes you a nice, hot meal. I'm even going to whip up one of those protein shakes you used to drink. I know you like those. I'll be back in a jiffy!' And then something terrible came over me that Halloween afternoon! I began hallucinating badly. Of course, no one was there but Grandma Emma and me, but I began to hear a voice…a raspy…dark…evil…demonic voice. 'There's her purse!' it shouted, prompting me to look at Grandma's purse, sitting on a table. 'Hurry up before she comes back!' I rushed over to Grandma's purse and began rummaging through it. I heard her push the kitchen door open and say, "Oh Hanky, I forgot to ask you if you wanted…" stopping short of finishing what she was going to ask me after seeing me going through her purse. 'Hanky! Put my down my purse!" she yelled. But the voice inside my head was also yelling, telling me, 'Don't put that purse down until you get some money out of it, Hank! Go on! She can't stop you!' 'No!' She's standing right there!' I shouted. 'I can't do that! Bump that Hank! Take the money!' the voice screamed back. Startled, she asked, 'Hanky, who are you talking to? You are scaring me!' But the voice shouted even louder, 'Didn't you hear me? I said take the money! You need that Crystal more than she needs that money!' 'No!' I screamed,' said Hank, demonstrating how he covered his ears. "But covering my ears didn't work…because I could still hear that twisted, terrifying voice coming from the depths of my own deranged mind. 'Hank!' the voice shouted with shattering treble and bass, 'The only person standing between you and Crystal is her!

Stop worrying about that 'old battle ax' and take the fucking money, Hank! Now!' I continued digging through Grandma's purse looking for money, and she made her way over to me. 'Give me my purse!' she yelled, grabbing it out of my hands. 'Now, I'm going to call your father and tell him about this!'" she hollered, walking towards the phone. 'Get that damn purse back before she makes that call!' screamed the voice in my head. I ran behind Grandma and snatched the purse back out of her hand. Then, I ran over to the other side of the living room to get away from her!" – said Hank demonstrating by dashing to the other side of the room. "The last thing I wanted to do was hurt her! I found a handkerchief with some money inside…and took it out. I wish I had just taken her purse and ran out of the house. Running over to me she screamed, 'Give me back my money! It doesn't belong to you!' Then she tried to take the money out of my hand. I pushed her away and turned my back to count the money. And then I heard her hit the floor. The push caused her to lose her balance, and when I turned around…she was trying to get up…but couldn't. 'Grandma, I…I…I'm sorry! I didn't mean to push you down! Are you okay?" I asked. But the voice in my mind screamed, 'Get out of there Hank! 'You can come back and check on her later! You got the money! Now go get your honey!' I darted towards the door to the wails of my grandmother. 'Hanky!' she cried. 'I hit my head pretty hard! Please don't leave! Call for help!' I heard her…but at the same time, I didn't hear her because my warped mind wanted to go get that Crystal! I ran out the door and bought some Crystal and headed over to Matt's house…oblivious to what I had done! I had my Crystal! We were in his room smoking it when we heard loud knocks at his front door. The police came there looking for me…and locked me up. Turns out, Dad kept calling my grandmother and could not reach her. Concerned, he stopped by her house to make sure she was okay…and found her laying unconscious on the floor. She was rushed to the hospital…but lapsed into a coma and died."

Sobbing, Hank buried his face in his hands – some in the Serenity House group moved to tears by his story.

"Oh, my Lord Hank," said Sister Jackson, wiping tears from her eyes. "I am so sorry about your grandmother."

"Me too," said Willie. "I should have never pulled that Halloween stunt. I'm so sorry, Hank. Believe me…I know how you feel."

"Hank, I know the things you told us today were not easy to say," said Sister Voyant. "Your grandmother's death has been eating away at you like piranha eating away at flesh. But my Beloved…you've got to let go…and let God."

"I didn't mean to hurt my Grandma!" cried Hank. "I didn't mean to kill her!"

"You didn't kill her," said Sister Jackson nibbling away on a donut. "It was an accident."

"That's right Hank," agreed Sister Voyant. "Some people do things intentionally to hurt others…to harm them. You weren't trying to cause any injury to your grandmother."

"I served jail time for what I did," said Hank. "But understandably, my family…my friends…everybody… all shunned me…haven't spoken to me…never forgave me for what happened. My father disowned me…saying 'I was dead to him.' And I can't blame him…or any of them…because I couldn't forgive myself! I hated myself for what I did! I was convinced that the only way to kill the monster that lived inside of me…to make sure it never hurt anyone again…was to kill myself. Just days after my release from prison in 2014…I decided to end it all. And at just 25 years of age, I told myself, 'You have nothing to live for, Hank. You ended the life of your 77-year-old grandmother, ruined your chance to go to college and play sports…and on top of that…everyone hates you!' And with that, I bought a box of razor blades and went to the dankest, darkest alley I knew…and prepared to take my own life."

"Gee Hank," said Dancer. "An alley wouldn't have been a nice place to die."

"You're right Dancer," said Hank. "But that was my setting. I scooted down on its pavement with my back propped up against a building. I closed my eyes and watched the performance of my own life being performed on the stage of my mind. Its title! 'The Tragedy of Hank Riley, Jr.!" announced Hank as if he were introducing a Shakespearean play to an audience. Playing the role of 'The Main Character'…the star of the show…Hank Riley, Jr.! My dialogue beginning with the words… 'To Be...or Not To Be!'" he bellowed as if he were 'Prince Hamlet'. "And I!" said Hank, was choosing 'Not To Be!', while also imagining the action and dialogue of others once I took my life! Those supporting characters in my real-life tragedy…my parents…other family members…friends…coaches…players…all…who in their perspective roles…were familiar with the plot of my story…shaking their heads…delivering lines that stated, 'What a sad ending to a once-promising life!' I prepared to close the curtains on my life…convinced… again by a voice in my mind…that the world's stage…would be better off without me. My dying would be just recompense for what I did to Grandma. Suicide would be my 'Final Act.' I prayed to God for forgiveness for what I was about to do…and then swish!" said Hank sweeping his left hand over his right wrist and then his right hand over his left wrist. Bleeding, I closed my eyes expecting to wake up in a burning Hell. But instead, I awoke in a hospital bed."

Hank spent the new few seconds silently reflecting on his experience – the group anxiously waiting for him to elaborate on his miraculous turn-of-events.

"I was told someone found me unconscious and bleeding in the alley and called 911," said Hank. "That person saved my life. While I was being treated in the hospital, I met a man named Charles Diggs who moved to Clarksburg from Baltimore. He told me about a program in Baltimore called Project PLASE. Mr. Charles was a complete stranger…but he helped me. Not only did he encourage and pray with me during my hospital stay, but he was able to set things up for me at Project PLASE. After I was released from the hospital, he provided me with a Greyhound bus ticket to Baltimore. Not only did he pay for that ticket, but he arranged for Dr. Gregory Branch…a Board Member of Project PLASE to pick me up from the bus station. I was nervous…I had never been outside Clarksburg. But Dr. Branch greeted me with open arms…telling me to just call him 'Doc.' Well Doc drove me to

Project PLASE, where emergency housing awaited. They also got me help for my addiction, along with counseling, and other services. They also got me into more permanent housing, where I stayed for a couple of years. From there, I came here to Serenity House…which is further helping me to beware of the haunted house of addiction!"

"Praise God, my Beloved!" shouted Sister Voyant.

"I'm not going to lie…even with all I've gone through…it's still a struggle," admitted Hank. "But I am starting to feel I can finally beat this thing."

"That's right!" said James. "Speak it! Death and life are in the power of the tongue!"

Holding his wrists up high, Hank said, "So now you all know the story behind these scars on my wrists. I wasn't much of a religious person…but I've come to believe! I may not look like…or always act like a Believer…but I am! I had written my own ending…but little did I know…God had already rewritten it!"

"Well, I do declare!," said Sister Voyant, "Hank…you just sounded like a preacher!"

"Whoa?! Me a preacher?!" chuckled Hank incredulously. "I can't ever see being worthy of such a calling. Just look at me…and after the things I've done?! I can't ever see myself doing anything like that!"

"Oooooh Hank," said Sister Voyant. "We all are sinners called into God's marvelous light! And there's no denying the calling I just heard in your voice."

CHAPTER TWENTY-FIVE

MR. AND MRS. EX

Sunday, December 2, 2018
Afternoon

Atop the neat line of rowhouses along Gwynns Falls Parkway, black chimney smoke dissipated into the cold, gusty December air. Just below one of the houses, a large Baltimore Ravens flag donning the team's red-eyed bird logo flapped in the blustery wind. Inside the home sat Rufus E. Hawkins. Dressed in a soiled wife-beater, pajama pants, and grungy white socks, the retired postman laid reclined in his new, expresso-colored cinema-style recliner seat.

I sure am glad I got these chairs, he thought. They sure are comfortable. I liked this one so much, I went back to the store and bought two more.

All three chairs sat side-by-side and faced his 80-inch flat-screen television, covering nearly an entire wall. Sitting in the chair to the left, he sat the recliner upright and reached for his favorite beer and Baltimore's own hometown brew – 'National Bohemian', also called 'Natty Boh'.

"Here's to you Mr. Boh," said Mr. Hawkins, looking at the can's iconic, one-eyed, handlebar-mustachioed mascot as if it would talk back to him. "Can't wait until the summer gets here so I can eat me some jumbo Maryland male crabs seasoned with Old Bay and chase them down with you buddy".

Mr. Hawkins guzzled down the remaining beer, let out a loud burp, and sat the empty can back in the chair's cupholder. Pointing the remote control at the television, he turned it off, having watched the 'Baltimore Ravens' defeat the 'Atlanta Falcon's by a score of 26 to 16.

"Them Bawl'more Ravens look like they might win the AFC North this year," Mr. Hawkins thought out loud.

Mr. Hawkins typically would have been elated with a win like today coupled with the team's playoff hopes. Despite his team's win, Mr. Hawkins felt deflated.

Dancer called me back in October and invited me to her Graduation Ceremony at Serenity House, he thought. Back when I was a kid, Daddy and Momma attended United in Victory, and me and the other kids attended Youth Bible Class in that same building. I still got bad memories of what happened to me in there...I ain't even want to have our wedding at the church when I married Lila Mae. The closer Dancer's graduation gets...the antsier I'm gettin'. And I don't want to see my Princess sitting in that place with other recovering drug addicts! On top of that, Dancer said Lila Mae's coming too! I ain't happy about seeing that snooty woman either! Looking at the one-eyed

'Mr. Boh', he belched and said, "The thought of seein' her at that gradu-ration" – referring to graduation, 'makes my blood pressure shoot straight up! Dr. Lila Mae is gonna be sittin' up in there with her nose in the air acting as snooty and stuck-up as ever!" he declared, 'breaking wind'. "Gives me gas just thinkin' about it!" he shouted, reaching for the can of 'Glade' sitting next to his chair and spraying it. "But I'm gonna be there for my baby Dancer! This is the longest I can remember her not going back to drugs and I'm gonna be sitting right there watching her gradu-rate!"

Mr. Hawkins got up from the chair, slid on his purple and black Ravens slippers, and headed towards the kitchen. After grabbing a can of 'Natty Boh' from the fridge, he plopped back into his recliner. With the television off, and no one in the house but him, all was quiet. The silence was momentarily cracked by Mr. Hawkins tearing open the can and chugging down gulps of beer.

"Ahhhhhh," said Mr. Hawkins wiping dribbles of beer from the corners of his mouth. "This beer is ice cold! Just like I like it! The only thing colder than this can of beer is that doggone Lila Mae! I don't even know why I married that woman in the first place!"

Deep down inside, Mr. Hawkins knew why he married his ex-wife – but fought against feelings to admit it.

"I sometimes wish I left Lila Mae on the ground during those riots," he said, talking to his beer can. "I fell in love with that woman the first time I laid eyes on her. And I still got feelings for her...hell...I still love her! Can you believe that Mr. Boh? I still love that woman...even after she left me, ruined me and our daughter's lives, and still hasn't paid me back a dime of my money! Imitating Dr. Hawkins whilst the one-eyed man on the can stared unblinkingly back, Mr. Hawkins threw his nose up in the air and said: "'Rufus, you need to do this! Rufus, you need to do that! Rufus, I don't like the way you talk! Rufus, I don't like the way you walk! Rufus, you need to go to college! Rufus, you need to stop watching all that football on Sundays! Rufus, you need to go to church! Rufus your gut is getting too big! Nag, nag, nag! That's all Lila Mae would do! But she was nuthin' like that when we got married! No, not at all! She cooked for me, scratched my back, and was kind, loving, and considerate. You want to know what happened? Well, I'll tell you what happened Mr. Boh? Those damn degrees she got! That's what happened! After she earned those and got with them fancy sorority girls and other folks, I wasn't good enough for her anymore!"

After a few seconds of fuming silently, Mr. Hawkins resumed laying his case out to 'Mr. Boh'.

"I pay all the bills, help put that ungrateful woman through school, let her spend her paycheck on whatever she pleased…gave her money…bought her cars…furs… …you name it…and what did she do Mr. Boh?" asked Mr. Hawkins pointing at the front door. "She walked right out and left me! Dancer was just a little thing…but she took her too. Mr. Boh, there's an old sayin' about not buyin' a woman shoes cuz she might walk out on you. Thanks to me, Lila Mae owned a helluva lot of shoes. Maybe there's some truth to that old sayin', 'cause she damn sure left my Black ass! Shucks, why am I wastin' my time talkin' to you Mr. Boh?!" asked Mr. Hawkins frowning his face. "This is some 'Boh-shit!' All you can do is sit on that can lookin' at me with one eye. Hell, you can't talk!"

Placing the can back in the cupholder, Mr. Hawkins reclined his seat, nestling his body against its tufted leather and digging his feet into its supple footrest.

"This chair is mighty comfortable," he said closing his eyes. "It's like sittin' on a cloud. Worth every dime I paid for it."

Mr. Hawkins's thoughts soon returned to Dr. Hawkins.

That woman insisted I go to college. Now I ain't got nothin' against a college education. That's a good thing. I could have gone to college if I wanted. I got good grades at Douglass. But after I finished there, I had no desire to attend college. I wanted to go to a vocational school or work as a mailman.

Since childhood, Mr. Hawkins aspired to be a postman. After finishing high school, he learned of job openings at the U.S. Post Office and seized the opportunity. He was hired and worked as a mail sorter until becoming a postman in 1972.

I sure loved my job as a mailman. I carried mail for 46 years before retiring in June.

Mr. Hawkins' co-workers threw him a surprise retirement party at 'The Forum Caterers' on Primrose Avenue. The festive event included a delicious buffet, a photo slide show, and stories of his love for football, sense of humor, and work ethic. During his many years on the job, Mr. Hawkins never called out sick or arrived late.

My Retirement Party was quite an event. My co-workers really showed their appreciation for me, Mr. Hawkins thought, running his fingers through his hair. When Mr. Hawkins started working for the post office, he wore his hair in a large 'Afro' or 'Fro' as they called it back then. Also referred to as a 'bush,' his hair was jet black and thick. Now, it was grey and had thinned considerably. To help camouflage the balding area on top of his head, Mr. Hawkins parted his hair on the side and brushed it upwards. After his longtime barber John Battle passed away in May, he opted not to find another barber to cut his hair. Instead, he purchased razors and a pair of clippers and did his own grooming. I sure miss ol' John, Mr. Hawkins thought. Ain't a barber around who can cut hair like John Battle.

Mr. Battle was among the many longtime friends Mr. Hawkins lost just this year. Sighing the 66-year-old whispered, Every time I turn around, it seems as if one of my buddies is passing on.

Mr. Hawkins was roughly seven months into retirement – retiring due to his bad knees. He was now drawing Social Security, his house was paid off, and still had a considerable amount of money in the bank. He still banked in the same location at Mondawmin Mall. However, it was no longer Maryland National, but Bank of America.

I lost count of the number of times that bank changed hands, he thought. Nuthin' ever stays the same. Even my driving habits have changed. That cranberry-colored Buick I bought last year stays parked more than it moves. I still drive from time to time, but with my eyesight dimming, I don't drive at night. I leave early to get back before dark and get my parking space. And as crazy as people drive now, I stopped taking beltways and driving over bridges. Zoom! Zoom! People flying by me all crazy and giving me the eye 'cause I obey the 55-mile-per hour speed limit! Some of 'em tailgate so close, they damn near run me off the freeway! But I remember doing some of those same things when I was a young whippersnapper! I guess I'm just reaping what I sowed.

Mr. Hawkins continued to ponder life after retirement. So many times, I would walk the streets of this city delivering mail or drive along in my mail truck thinking, 'I can't wait to retire!' I wouldn't have to get out of my comfortable bed in all kinds of weather to report to work, I could sleep as long as I wanted to…could go anywhere I wanted to…when I wanted to. I could watch NFL games all day Sunday, and on Monday and Thursday nights and not have to worry about being tired the next day. But I gotta admit…while I'm enjoying retirement…and the freedom that comes along with it…sometimes…I get pretty bored. I would drive to Mondawmin Mall and sit on the benches near the fountain…but after a while, that got old. Then I started driving to Druid Hill Park and sitting on the park benches under the tree. But after a while…that got old too. Every now and then, I would take the ride out to Woodlawn Cemetery to visit the gravesites of relatives and friends who have passed on…and feed the birds. But that made me sad…so I stopped. Rev. Daniel Worthy who runs the Forest Park Senior Center on Liberty Heights Avenue encouraged me to join the center. Maybe I will. Maybe I will do some traveling. But what's the fun in traveling alone? When we were still married, Lila Mae and I talked about the things we would do once we retired. Back then, retirement was a long way off. We even talked about moving to Florida after retiring. But instead, she's living in one place, and I'm living in another. We are supposed to be spending our 'Golden Years' together…not apart. I never thought we would wind up like this. But after she left me, it was hard to repair the damage…not only to my ego…but to my heart."

Nearly 35 years later, the pain of coming from work and finding his wife gone, still lingered.

As soon as I set foot in this house, I knew Lila Mae left me, he thought, reflecting on the fall 1984 day. I remember just standing in the doorway with my mouth open. When I didn't see those elephants of hers, said Mr. Hawkins referencing Mrs. Hawkins' Delta Sigma Theta elephant figurines, "I knew she was gone. To me, they were just a bunch of elephants…but to Lila Mae…they meant the world."

One evening, Mr. Hawkins asked Dr. Hawkins what the elephants represented.

"Lila Mae," said Mr. Hawkins, "I ain't never seen somebody so crazy about elephants that can't walk or talk," he said watching her polish one of the figurines. "If a speck of dust settles on one, you are wiping it like I wipe our cars parked outside. What do they stand for? What do they mean?"

"My dear Rufus, these elephants represent strength and determination," Dr. Hawkins explained. 'The uplifted trunk represents high goals. The right foot forward represents forward movement. As you know, I pledged at Coppin. You would only be helping yourself if you were to go there too. You can join the Kappa Alpha Psi Fraternity. That brotherhood will do you a lot of good. They are high-achieving, professional Black men."

Mr. Hawkins' inquiry about the elephants and her answer led to an argument. To him, it seemed as if his wife would take any conversation and use it as a gateway for telling him what he should and should not be doing.

Every time I turned around, we were arguin' about something, recalled Mr. Hawkins. I guess she got tired of it and decided to move out. I knew the deal when I saw those elephants gone. I remember thinking, 'First them no good Colts snuck out of town on me, and now Lila Mae has done the same damn thing! I figured she was up to something actin' all 'spicious. And she took the baby too!'"

❦

Mr. Hawkins ran through every room in the house – each missing things that confirmed what he already suspected – his wife was gone.

I remember seeing the keys to the Cadillac I bought Lila Mae sitting on the kitchen table next to a note, he recalled. The note included a new home phone number and an ultimatum talking about I could call her once I decided to do more with my life. I 'I'll call her alright!' I hollered. 'To see about my daughter!' I was so mad I could have chewed steel! I was a postman, and I wanted to go postal, but I knew better than to do anything stupid!

Mr. Hawkins would call his wife, grabbing the wall phone and dialing the number. The two argued until she hung up. In a profanity-laced tirade, Mr. Hawkins ripped the phone's base off the wall and threw it at the refrigerator, denting its steel door.

I really took my frustrations out on that 'frigerator, he thought. It's still sitting in the kitchen with that big ole dent in it. Wasn't no point in replacing a 'frigerator that still worked. Hell, they don't make things like they used to anyway. Shaking his head, Mr. Hawkins thought, Man, it sure was rough coming home from work and finding Lila Mae gone. I ain't no what to do with myself, other than to get drunk. I drove to a cut-rate liquor store on Monroe Street to buy a bottle of booze, came home, and listened to Otis Redding's Sitting On The Dock of The Bay. I played that 45 on the record player over and over again while I cried like a baby. The words of that song represent a broken man. And I sure was one….'cause I damn sure was heartbroken. I nearly became an alcoholic over that woman 'cause I wanted to drink every day. But then I got to thinking about my old neighbor Melvin Thomas. Melvin was a good man…but alcohol took him to an early grave. I was afraid the same thing would happen to me. So, I stopped drinking hard liquor when I came home from work and start exercising.

Mr. Hawkins bought a variety of exercise equipment which included weights, and an exercise bike.

'I'll show Lila Mae!' I would shout, peddling that bike as fast as I could. Rufus ain't gonna sit back and die on account of her! I'm gonna get back in shape! That bike helped me to build up my stamina, and I wasn't so winded on my mail routes. I also started doing Tae Bo with Billy Blanks. The fast pace of the routine's punches and kicks helped me to lose weight and burn off a lot of steam…and I needed it… because I was still angry as hell with Lila Mae! I also cut back on fatty foods and cut back on cans of Natty Boh when I watched football. Before long, I could feel my trousers weren't fitting as snug around my waistline. Soon, my co-workers and postal customers were noticing my weight loss and telling me how good I looked. I was so proud of myself I bought a scale…and the needle kept goin' left. I'll never forget the morning when I slipped on my work pants, and they fell straight to the floor.

❦

The day waning on, Mr. Hawkins continued to reflect on his weight loss. His thoughts led back to Dr. Hawkins, and the meeting the two had back in August 1985. Once again, he started talking to his beer can.

"Mr. Boh, when Lila Mae called and told me she wanted to talk, I was so happy, I could have burst!" expressed Mr. Hawkins. "I figured 'Kitten' wanted to talk about coming back home to her 'Chocolate Superman.' And I cleaned this house up like Superman too! I wanted everything spic and span and smellin' good when she got here! I drove over to the Diplomat Shop and got me a whole bunch of fancy clothes and new shoes too. I showered with a bar of Irish Spring because I knew she liked the way that soap smelled. I even put on some of that Dracula cologne! she bought me one Christmas," recalled Mr. Hawkins, referencing Drakkar Noir. "I know Lila Mae liked the way that smelled too. I even dabbled a little behind my ears just in case she wanted to nibble on them. And then I put on my duds. By then, I had lost just over 50 pounds and I have no problem buttoning my shirt over my belly! No sooner I fastened the buttons on a shirt like that, as soon as I exhaled, my belly popped all the buttons!" he laughed. "I tell you…me and the place were looking mighty good for Lila Mae. I even thought we might git in on! But after Lila Mae got here, she got down to the real knitty-gritty! She needed money! Sudie Snooty needed some green to pay off those liens! How stupid it was for me to think that Lila Mae wanted to talk about anything other than what was best for Lila Mae. I loaned her the money but just couldn't resist the chance to rub it in her face, when I told her not to deposit that check at Old Court Savings and Loan. Boy did I ruffle her feathers! Kitten was mad as a hellcat!"

Looking at the can of beer before sitting up to gulp down what remained, Mr. Hawkins said, "And that woman has yet to pay me back my money! I'm not pressed for the money…but Mr. Boh…it's the principle. Speaking of principle, I should have charged that trif'lin woman interest! Lila Mae never told me why, but I'm willing to bet she never paid me back on account of Anna."

❀

Mr. Hawkins met Anna Barnes in 1991. The two met at 'Brice's Hilltop Inn', a popular lounge and bar. With their separation dragging on, his thoughts of reconciling with his wife began to diminish.

Mr. Boh, my buddies kept telling me to get out more…to date other women. I didn't want to do it because I was still married to Lila Mae. But she wasn't showing no signs of wanting to work things out…so I started hanging out with the boys a bit to check out the females. 'They're right!' I told myself. 'I'm single and ready to mingle!' Even though…I really wasn't quite single. But once I lost that weight and got a little swag going…I felt more women were checking ole Rufus out! So when Anna came over and introduced herself to me, I figured, 'Rufus, boy, you still got it!"

The two talked, drank, and danced to the sounds of music being mixed from the deejay booth by popular disc jockey 'Frank Ski'.

"Mr. Boh, I couldn't help but think how strange it felt dancing with a woman other than Lila Mae," he told the mustachioed icon. "We left together. She told me she didn't drive, so I offered to take her home. Mr. Boh, that woman got to rubbing my crouch. Then she unzipped my pants, pulled out my penis, and gave me 'head' while I was driving! I nearly ran off the road, zigzagging during the drive to my house. I parked the car and glanced across the street. And who was standing in the bedroom window looking but Miss Jenkins! But I didn't give a damn! I was horny as hell, and I was finally getting' me some!" I carried Anna up to my bedroom, threw her on the bed, slid down them drawers, sucked them big titties of hers, gapped them legs open, and gave it to her as hard as I could. I was finished in two minutes…I was a little embarrassed about that…but it had been so long since I had some booty. I felt good that night. But the next morning, I felt terrible because after I married Lila Mae, I hadn't slept with any other woman. But after a while, a man gets tired dealing with his sexual urges by watchin' porno flicks and 'jerking off.' Now I was a little older than Anna, but she gave me just what I needed…even oral sex…Lila Mae would never do that…telling me the only thing she put in her mouth was food. I offered to put some whipped cream on my thing, but she still wouldn't do it. But Anna ain't have no problem. Looking back over all that Mr. Boh, I should have known Anna was a crud ball from the start. She sucked on my Johnson and rode to my house so we could have sex. That says a lot about a woman who does that to a man she just met. I guess it said a lot about me too."

❈

The Sunday afternoon continuing to tick on, Mr. Hawkins typically would have been watching more football. Nevertheless, the television remained off, and he continued to rattle off thoughts to his empty beer can.

"Mr. Boh I was 39, and Anna was 24," recalled Mr. Hawkins. "I was feelin' pretty good…because I had a young thang. But I was 15 years older than Anna. I tried not to dwell on that too much…telling myself…age is just a number. And the sex was good…especially the oral sex! I loved that! called her my 'Sweet Thang' and she called me 'Sweet Daddy.' I liked Anna a lot…and we had some good times together…but I still loved Lila Mae. I even called her Lila Mae one night while we were making love! Anna was mad as shit about that! I tell you, Mr. Boh, I had to do a lot of making up to smooth that one over! But it was just another reminder I still hadn't gotten past Lila Mae…although I tried to convince myself otherwise. But I was knocking on the door of 40, and Anna made me feel like a young stud! I even got rid of my Thunderbird and got me a nice, sleek Mercedes Benz for us to ride around in…just like the one Lila Mae got after she left me. I guess I did that out of spite.

Now every now and then Mr. Boh, Anna stayed overnight. I didn't mind that so much. But the next thing I knew…she moved right on in! Shaking his head, Mr. Hawkins said, "She even started wearing the clothes Lila Mae left behind! Can you believe that?! She ain't have no business botherin' those clothes! I thought to myself, 'What the hell kind of mess have I gotten myself into?! I talked about it to ole Smitty, along with the fact that I thought that Anna was some kind of nimpo-maniac," he recalled, referring to the word nymphomaniac. Mr. Boh…one thing I learned from Smitty is to watch what you tell your friends…'cause not everybody who says they're you're friend…is a friend."

❈

Mr. Hawkins played his 'Street Numbers' through Malcolm "Smitty" Green. A flashy dresser who loved wearing Big Apple caps, Mr. Green considered himself a 'lady's man'. He often bought his clothes from 'The Diplomat Shop' at Old Town Mall, 'Cookies', 'The Red Shed, and other popular Black men's clothiers of the day. He and Mr. Hawkins were the same age and enjoyed each other's company.

One evening after work, the two men were doing some trash talking over beers at Brice's when Mr. Hawkins began talking about Anna.

"Smitty, I can barely my uniform off before Anna wants ol' Rufus to give it to her hard in the bed! I mean that girl wants it from the front, from the back, from the side! Up! Down! Upside down! Rightside up! You name it! I almost threw my back out one time foolin' with her! As soon as we finish having sex, she's ready to go at it again!"

"Sounds like she can't get enough" laughed Mr. Green.

"She can't!' said Mr. Hawkins. "And she loves to give that head too!"

"Whew!" said Mr. Green. "I've seen her over at the house when I've stopped by to get your numbers. Got a nice plump ass on her…and big boobs too!"

"And I'm wearin' them both out!" said Mr. Hawkins. "And Smitty…she gives some good 'head' too! A lot of women don't do that…including Lila Mae! But Anna damn sure ain't got no problem with it!"

"Sounds like quite a woman!" chuckled Mr. Green. "But man, you gotta be careful. One man ain't never enough for a freak like that."

Mr. Hawkins ran his hand through his balding head, reflecting on Mr. Green's comments.

"When Smitty made that comment about one man never being enough for Anna, that should have told me somethin' right there," Mr. Hawkins explained to his silent beer can. "But Smitty was my friend…and I trusted him. I trusted Anna too…but she also turned out to be a lowdown, dirty snake!"

Mr. Hawkins recollected the September day in 1991 Dr. Hawkins confronted him on the job about giving Anna her cell phone number.

"Mr. Boh, I ain't give Lila Mae's number to Anna! I couldn't get home fast enough to find out how Anna got Lila Mae's phone number and why she called her up! And do you know what Anna had the nerve to tell me? She said, 'it was her job to get her man back his money!' I asked, 'How did you know about the money I loaned Lila Mae?! I never talked to you about that!' Anna said she overheard me talking about the $25,000 loan and was trying to help me get my money back. She also admitted going through my cell phone until she found Lila's Mae's number. Imitating Anna's sultry voice he mimicked, 'I'm so shorry…Sweet Daddy. I was just trying to look out for you. That Bitch needs to pay back your money!' Well, I told her, 'That's between me and Lila Mae! You ain't got a damn thing to do with it! And don't be dis'respectin' my wife by calling her no Bitch! She might act like one, but that don't give you the right to call her one!' Faking crying, Mr. Hawkins said, "Anna started cryin' croc-a-dial tears," said Mr. Hawkins referring to the word 'crocodile' and wiping away phony tears. She wanted to know how I could take up for Lila Mae after she left me, borrowed money, and never paid it back! I told her this…'Fiddle with my phone again, that front door is gonna be hittin ya…where the good Lawd split ya!' 'I'm sorry Sweet Daddy' she boohooed. 'I was just trying to help. It won't happen again.' I told her, "It better not!" and left it at that."

Mr. Hawkins pulled the recliner lever, sitting the chair up. Grabbing his empty beer cans, he said, "I vented to Smitty a few times that Lila Mae borrowed 25 grand and never paid it back. But he and I never discussed it at the house…or over the phone. And I never told Anna that Lila Mae left me. In the back of my mind, I kept wondering how Anna knew these things."

By now, Mr. Hawkins had gone to the kitchen to grab another beer and was again enjoying the comforts of his favorite chair.

"Mr. Boh, even though I enjoyed the sex with Anna, my mind was still on Lila Mae. You see Mr. Boh…me and Lila Mae made love. But me and Anna…well we had sex. At the time, I guess I didn't understand the difference between the two. As I see it, that difference boils down to being with someone you love and love to make love to, as opposed to being with someone you like, and like to screw. And I guess because Anna felt she was paying me with booty…boody…or whichever you want to call it. She even did a little cooking and cleaning. That was all fine and good, but I told her, she had to get up off that ass and go to work. 'You're an able-bodied young woman,' I told her. 'You can't lay around here on my dime. You gotta get a job.'"

Mr. Hawkins began thinking about the summer day in 1992 when Miss Jenkins signaled for him to walk over to her porch. Tired from a long day's work, he thought: What the hell does that motor-mouth want? She's home all day and ain't got nuthin to do but meddle in everyone's business. I'm tired! I don't even feel like screwin' Anna tonight! The last thing I want to do right now is listen to Miss Jenkins run her trap! I'm gonna act like I don't see her!

But Miss Jenkins picked up a bullhorn she kept on her porch and started calling Rufus' name.

"Hey Rufus, come on over here!" she shouted in the bullhorn.

"Damnit!" Mr. Hawkins muttered under his breath, making his way over to her porch. "Where in the hell did she get that thing from?!"

"This is my new bullhorn," she told Mr. Hawkins. "I knew it would come in handy. I bought it just in case I need to rouse the neighbors during an emergency." Placing the bullhorn down on the porch, she began looking around, telling him: "I want to make sure none of these nosey people around here can hear what I'm about to tell you," she said, chewing on 'Wrigley's Spearmint-flavored gum.'

"Still chewing that Spearmint gum? Huh, Miss Jenkins," asked Mr. Hawkins.

"Been chewing it for years," replied Miss Jenkins. "Helped me stopped smokin'".

"I never knew you smoked," Mr. Hawkins commented.

"Sure did," said Miss Jenkins. 'And I'm glad I gave up them 'cancer sticks.' They killed a lot of people. Em…em…em...such a shame. You should be glad I gave 'em up. If I hadn't, I might not have been around to tell you what I'm about to tell you."

"And what's that Miss Jenkins?" he asked.

"That gal you got over in the house…"

 "What about her Miss Jenkins?"

"Lawd have mercy, maybe I better not say…"

"Go on and tell me…what about her?"

"Maybe I need to mind my business," said Miss Jenkins. "I don't want to see nobody get hurt."

"You called me over here Miss Jenkins…so it must be pretty important," said Mr. Hawkins, growing impatient.

"Lawd…how can I say this?" said Miss Jenkins. "It's terrible…just terrible. Emmmmmm…emmmmmm…emmmmmm."

"It's been a long day, Miss Jenkins," said Mr. Hawkins. 'Please tell me whatever it is you wanna tell me. I'm real tired…walked around half the city delivering mail."

"Well since you twisted my arm, I reckon I'll go on and tell you," said Miss Jenkins. "Lord…help me to say this…" she said looking upward and putting her hand on her chest. "I guess there ain't no way to say it other than to come right on out and say it…Rufus, that chile you got livin' over there with you got some man sneaking in the house while you're at work.'

"What!?" he shouted.

"That's right," said Miss Jenkins. "She thinks nobody is lookin'. But Miss Jenkins is always lookin.' Whoever he is, parks around the corner and sneaks through the back wearin' some phony get-up. Who wears a coat and hat during the summer when it's blazin' hot?"

"Ain't this some s-"

"Now don't curse now Rufus," said Miss Jenkins. "That ain't of God! Now, being a good neighbor and all, I thought it was best to tell you what was going on. That gal be turnin' your place into a whorehouse when you ain't home."

"Are you sure Miss Jenkins?" he asked.

Peering over her cat-eye-styled eyeglasses, Miss Jenkins shook her head and said: Positive. And I ain't got no good reason to lie. But I'll tell you this Rufus. I ain't never like that gal no way…'Adulterous Anna' I call her! She ain't got no business foolin' around with no married man and ain't no married man got no business foolin' around with her! Apparently, you didn't tell that Jezebel heifer you were still married!"

"Lila Mae and I –"

"Miss Jenkins don't want to hear it, Rufus! You and Lila Mae are both bein' stubborn. You two are married…not divorced. Therefore," said Miss Jenkins, putting her hands on her hips, "you are still a married man and –"

'But we – '

"Let me finish Rufus," said Miss Jenkins. "Not only are you old enough to be that chile's father, but you got the AIDS and everything else out here now. That's why I'm scared to date anybody. You can't just jump in the bed with some floozy! If you want to roll in the hay…work things out with your wife!"

"With all due respect, Miss Jenkins," said Mr. Hawkins. "But Lila Mae has been gone about seven years now. She's not coming back."

"Have you two tried talking out your differences?" asked Miss Jenkins.

"If she wants to talk, she knows where to find me," replied Mr. Hawkins.

'I'm gonna say this, and then I'm gonna mind my business,' said Miss Jenkins. 'I know you still love Lila Mae, and Lila Mae still loves you. If you approached saving your marriage half as hard as you break your neck to watch them football games, you might be able to save your marriage."

"Lila Mae left me, so she's gotta make the first move," said Mr. Hawkins.

"Somebody gotta be the bigger person," said Miss Jenkins. 'I'm 57-years-old now, and I've lived long enough to know that being bull-headed and stubborn leads to more losses than victories. Don't lose your wife over pride.'

"Pride?! Lila Mae put the p in pride!" You should be having this conversation with her…not me."

"Now Rufus, I know Lila Mae left you, and that wasn't right," said Miss Jenkins. Naw, that wasn't right. But you two need to get back together. Not only for you two's sake, but for your daughter's sake. Children hate to see when their parents ain't together."

Mr. Hawkins knew Miss Jenkins was right but simply thanked her for letting him know what was happening at his house when he was at work. He bid her goodbye and began making his way down her porch steps.

"Rufus!" she called out.

"Yes, Miss Jenkins! What is it now?!'

"Listen, I know you want to get over to that hussy in your house, but you better lower that tone sonny!" said Miss Jenkins. "There are two more things I need to say. One…I been meanin' to ask you about your weight loss. Lawd have mercy, you ain't sick are you?"

"No ma'am Miss Jenkins, I'm not sick. I've been watching my diet and exercising."

"Thank the Lawd for that," said Miss Jenkins. 'I've been to March Funeral Home – East and West locations, Joseph Brown Funeral Home, Wylie Funeral Home, and Carlton C. Douglass Funeral Home viewing bodies to see if there were any people that I knew. I would hate to see yours up there too."

"I'm in good shape, Miss Jenkins. What's the second thing you wanted to say?

"I would be happy to contact you the minute I see that man slithering up in your house again...if you get my drift," said Miss Jenkins winking her eye. "I got your phone number…but write down your pager number too," she told Mr. Hawkins, handing him pencil and paper. "Now when you see my home number on your pager followed by 9-1-1, you'll know just what time it is."

"I sure will, and I'll be here quicker than you can hang the phone up."

Mr. Hawkins again thanked Miss Jenkins and went home. Once he arrived, he didn't say anything to Anna pertaining to what Miss Jenkins told him. She cooked dinner for them earlier and placed his plate of food on the table.

"There you go Sweet Daddy," she said. "I put my foot in that food."

And I feel like putting my foot in your ass! Mr. Hawkins yelled in his mind.

About two weeks later, Mr. Hawkins was delivering mail when his beeper started going off. He read the digitalized message that was scrolling across. It was Miss Jenkins' number followed by 9-1-1.

"Time to go!" he said, jumping in his mail truck and speeding home.

❀

Recalling the speed of his mail truck, Mr. Hawkins chuckled: "'Damnit!' I said, 'Can't you move any faster?! A snail can move faster than you!' I'm laughing about it now Mr. Boh, but there wasn't a cotton-pickin' thing funny about it at the time!"

Once Mr. Hawkins reached his neighborhood, he parked his mail truck around the corner from his home, quietly entered through the basement door, and tiptoed upstairs. An orchestra of sexual sounds filled his ears – squeaking mattress springs, knocks of a headboard against the wall, and bedposts banging against wood floors, all accompanied by moans and groans.

Listen to them! he silently screamed creeping up the steps. Screwing in my damn house! In my damn bedroom! And in my damn bed! Once Mr. Hawkins reached the top landing, he carefully took one step. And then another. One step. And then another, until he stood outside his bedroom.

"I tell you, Mr. Boh, that door was wide open, and so were that ho's legs!" recalled Mr. Hawkins. Excuse my language Mr. Boh…but they didn't even see me standing there because they were so engrossed into their fuckin'! I wanted to throw up! I couldn't contain myself any longer! I barged in that damn room like a raging bull!"

❀

What unfolded next was the stuff of movies.

Pushing her lover from atop of her, Anna squealed, "Sweet Daddy!"

"Oh shit!" said her lover, rolling over and looking at Mr. Hawkins.

While trying to explain themselves to Mr. Hawkins, the naked lovers hopped out the bed and scrambled to put their clothes on. Mr. Hawkins headed to his closet and pulled down the shoe box holding his .357 Magnum.

❀

His beer can's unflinching eye looking on, Mr. Hawkins continued to reminisce about the calamitous day.

"I know how this looks Rufus man," said Anna's lover tripping to the floor while trying desperately to step into his pants. "But it ain't like that! It ain't like that at all man!"

Pulling his gun from the shoebox, Mr. Hawkins shouted, "You punk motherfucker! Now I know why that cheatin' heifer knew so much! Not only were you runnin' your mouth, but you were stickin' her too! And in my damn house!"

"Please don't hurt us Sweet Daddy!" begged Anna. "I love you, baby! And I'm so sorry!"

"Don't shoot us Rufus!" pleaded Anna's lover, starting to cry. "Please don't shoot us!"

Anna's lover was none other than Malcolm "Smitty" Green.

❀

Raging mad at catching his 'numbers' man in bed with his girlfriend, Mr. Hawkins pointed his pistol at Mr. Green.

"I see you have been runnin' a number on me!" he bellowed at his longtime friend. "I'm about to put some lead in both of ya'll asses!"

Dressed only in his underwear, Mr. Green ran to the bedroom window, raised it, and jumped out. Clad in just her panties, Anna followed suit.

"Mr. Boh, I rushed over to the window…seeing that they landed on the porch roof. They were scrambling to get up, and I aimed my gun at each of them…having a clear shot at them both! They were sittin' ducks! And I found myself having to make a split-second, life-changing decision. I tell you, Mr. Boh, it was like having an angel sittin' on one shoulder, and a devil on another…the angel yelling 'don't shoot!' and the devil yelling 'shoot!' I was at a crossroads…trying to decide which I would listen to…the angel saying, 'Rufus, you have a young daughter, a nice home, a good job…with benefits…and your freedom! Don't throw all that away by pulling that trigger!' At the same time, the devil was screaming, 'Rufus, ain't you tired of people taking advantage of you?! Look at where helpin' and trustin' people has gotten you! First it was Lila Mae and now it's Anna and Smitty! Enough is enough! Get your revenge! Shoot 'em both!' Now, Mr. Boh, I can't tell you how bad my trigger finger was itchin'! I felt shootin' Anna and Smitty would have given me instant gratification! But then, I thought, 'What about the consequences?' 'What about the afterward?' 'If I shoot them, is the satisfaction I feel in that moment worth it?' Well at that moment Mr. Boh, I stood at that window and lowered the gun, deciding, 'Shooting Anna and Smitty isn't worth throwing my entire life out of the window.' Now I had only been to jail once…and that was after I got locked up after participating in a sit-in during the Civil Rights Movement. But that was for a movement…a cause…a purpose. However, I didn't like jail…and I wasn't about to spend the rest of my life sittin' in some cell with nothin' but time on my hands thinking about what I did. But I tell you this Mr. Boh…I sure got a whooooole lot of satisfaction watching what happened to Anna and Smitty outside on my lawn! That was priceless!"

On the infamous day Anna and Mr. Green – fearing for their lives, jumped off the roof. The two landed in the front yard under the gaze of Mr. Hawkins who stood in the window looking below. Several neighbors including Miss Jenkins were also watching.

"I outta beat both of you with my broom!" Miss Jenkins shouted waving a corn broom at the two. "You ol' nasty man!" she shouted at Mr. Green. "Look at you layin' out here on the ground with your drawers on! And look at you, Adulterous Anna! Layin' out here bare-breasted, showing your titties! Ain't even got a brassiere on! You both ought to be ashamed of yourselves!"

The two jumped off the lawn and ran down the street.

"You better get out of here!" yelled Miss Jenkins, taking a few steps in their direction, and still waving her broom. Some of the neighbors shouted along with her, while others laughed and pointed at Anna and Mr. Green running down the street. Some of the women standing outside used their hands to cover their husbands' and children's eyes. After Anna and Mr. Green were no longer in sight, Mr. Hawkins closed his bedroom window, placed the gun back inside the shoebox, and returned it to the closet shelf. Afterward, he called a locksmith, making arrangements to have all the locks changed. Afterward, he tossed Anna's belongings out on the curb while neighbors looked on, still abuzz as to what they witnessed.

"Rufus, you should burn them durty clothes!" shouted Miss Jenkins, referring to the word dirty.

"You're better than me!" said his neighbor Mr. Brown. "I would have shot their asses!"

"Ned!" said his wife Mrs. Brown. "Watch your mouth!"

"I wonder what in the devil caused Rufus to come home early?" Miss Jenkins innocently asked the group although she was the one who alerted Mr. Hawkins, who walked back to his mail truck and finished his routes for the day.

✺

Chuckling about his longtime neighbor, Mr. Hawkins said: "I tell you, Mr. Boh, that Miss Jenkins is the nosiest woman I know! But sometimes, havin' nosey neighbors is a damn good thing."

Remembering an incident years ago, he described the event to his expressionless beer can.

"Miss Jenkins is the neighborhood town crier. She has this habit of notifying neighbors when she thinks somethin' is gonna happen. Sometimes, she's the one who sparks the mess…and then she stands around like she ain't done nuthin! Anyway, one day back in '96 she went knockin' on doors…including mines to let us neighbors know that police cars were parked on the block. Out of breath she told me, 'Hurry and get your butt outside 'cause something is about to go down at the Thomas house! So I came on outside. It was terrible! We all watched Melvina get locked up…and her children got taken away too. Not to mention she had a house full of drugs! Damn shame how that girl got all messed up on account of them drugs. I guess she's still in jail for what she did to that poor baby."

✺

Decades had gone by since the many events Mr. Hawkins reflected upon – talking to his beer can. To his chagrin and the other neighbors, "Big Mike" moved into the Thomas home. He stayed there for several months before leaving. After he left, squatters took residence there. The neighborhood association acted, and they left. Years later, the house still sat boarded up and empty.

Mr. Green moved out of Baltimore, while Anna eventually took up with another married man.

"I tell you, Mr. Boh," said Rufus. "I don't know why I fooled around with Anna in the first place. You can't make no Queen out of no 'ho."

Mr. Hawkins had long stopped exercising and watching his diet, regaining the weight he lost, and then some. About three years ago, he donated his dust-covered exercise bike, weights, and 'Tae Bo' VHS tapes to the 'Purple Heart'.

"Rufus man, you done let yourself go," he said patting his oversized gut. "Look at this beer belly! These bad children in the neighborhood are even running around here laughin' and callin' you 'Mr. Brown' from them Tyler Perry plays. I don't look like no Mr. Brown!"

The sound of Mr. Hawkins passing gas rippled through the air along with a putrid smell.

"Good googa mooga!" exclaimed Mr. Hawkins, grabbing a can of 'Glade' air freshener sitting nearby and spraying the air. "That was a terrible fart right there! Musta been the blue cheese dip I ate with that pan of buffalo wings earlier! Lila Mae would have had a fit about that one! But sometimes, you just gotta let 'er rip. Ain't that right, Mr. Boh?"

Looking at his feet, Mr. Hawkins said: Lila Mae would have had a fit about these socks too. She was always gettin' on me about my socks and telling me my feet stink! What did she expect?! I got Athlete's Feet! Not to mention my feet sweated in my socks from walkin' mail routes all day! So what if they were a little sour! So what if my socks were dingy! Instead of complain', she should have gone to the store to get me some foot powder! She could have washed my socks or bought me some more! But no! She was too busy complainin' about everything I did!"

Glancing at the barren trees through the windows of his home, Mr. Hawkins reflected on the holiday season.

"Christmas will be here soon," said Mr. Hawkins. "Well, Mr. Boh, it looks like it's just you and me again for the holidays. Next thing you know, another New Year will be ringin' in…and 2018 will be gone…and 2019 will arrive.

"My, my, my, how time flies," said Mr. Hawkins. "I'll be 67 come May."

Mr. Hawkins glanced over at the two, unoccupied recliner seats.

"When I bought these three chairs, I fooled myself into believin' I was buying the other two just in case one of my came over to watch a game. But I wasn't foolin' nobody but myself. In the back of my mind, I bought three in the event Lila Mae and Dancer come back home. We'd be like them three bears in that book I read when I was a little boy," he said, referencing the fairytale 'Goldilocks and The Three Bears.' "'Papa Bear'…that would be me – would sit in the chair I'm sitting in right now. 'Mama Bear'…that's Lila Mae…would be sitting next to me…and 'Baby Bear'…well that's Dancer, would sit in the third. Hell Mr. Boh…I would even let them watch what they wanted to watch on the big screen television…even if the football games were on. I'd be willing to compromise…yep…that's the name of the game…compromise. I guess that's where things went south with our marriage…neither one of us were willin' to compromise. She and I are 'Taurus the Bulls'…her birthday's May 7th…and mines is May 9th. And looking back over our marriage…we were both bullheaded and stubborn."

Mr. Hawkins sat silently for a moment recalling one of the disagreements between him and his ex-wife. Trailing late in a game one Sunday afternoon, the Ravens were called for a costly penalty. Upset, he was screaming at the television when Dr. Hawkins walked through the door from church.

"Rufus!" said Dr. Hawkins. "I could hear you shouting all the way down the street! My goodness! All of that over a football game?! And you are still sitting in the same spot you were sitting in when I left for church! Instead of watching those silly football games every Sunday, why can't you come to church with me?! You should be shouting for the Lord on Sunday!"

Looking at his beer can, Mr. Hawkins replied, "You hear Lila Mae over there blabbin' her mouth Mr. Boh? I wear the pants in this house! Don't no woman tell Rufus Hawkins what to do! Ain't that right Mr. Boh?"

"Keep right on talking to your silly beer cans!' yelled Dr. Hawkins. "One day you may find yourself in this house with no one to talk to but Mr. Boh!"

Picking up his beer can, whilst his ex-wife's words rang in his mind, Mr. Hawkins let out a loud sigh.

"Well Mr. Boh, Lila Mae was right!" he said. "Here I am with nobody to talk to…but you!" Slamming the can back in the cupholder, he hissed, "And I don't know why! You can't answer me! They say silence is golden…but not all the time! Sometimes it does us all a bit of good to have a little noise…even if it's the voice of a pain in the ass wife! Hearing her mouth-off to me was a whole helluva lot better than sitting here talking to myself, or to beer cans that can't talk at all!"

Mr. Hawkins silently wrestled with his thoughts.

I can't help but think things might have turned out differently had Lila Mae and I just compromised. We were supposed to grow old together. But it was hard getting past her calling me 'Blackie'. I guess I could have just forgivin' her and worked harder to keep the marriage together. But it was a lot easier to blame her for everything. I could have also told her the real reason why I stopped going to United in Victory…and maybe attended service on Sunday at another church…they're churches on nearly every corner in Baltimore City. And takin' a class at Coppin might not have been so bad. What harm could it have done? But I was so busy fussin' about her tryin' to tell me what to do, that I didn't think that maybe…just maybe she was just tryin' to make me a better man.

Shifting in his seat, Mr. Hawkins found himself shifting to the 'what ifs?'

What if I would have apologized to Lila Mae first? What if Lila Mae would have apologized to me first? Miss Jenkins' conversation with him years earlier about children not wanting to see their parents separate came to his remembrance. What if Lila Mae and I stayed together…could it have prevented Dancer from turning to drugs? I find myself thinking about that all the time…but I don't know the answer. But one thing I do know is this…short of dyin', ain't nuthin' gonna stop me from attendin' Dancer's graduation.

Once again, Mr. Hawkins stood up and headed to the dented refrigerator - its rusted indentation serving as a timestamp for the day Lila Mae left him.

Dancer's favorite color is purple, so I'll get her a nice NFL Bawl'more Ravens 'Lamar Jackson' jersey, thought Mr. Hawkins. I'll also get her some pretty lilac flowers and purple balloons too. I'll present Dancer with her gifts after the graduation and give her a big hug…she loves hugs…along with her gifts after the graduation ceremony. Then, we'll go to a nice restaurant and eat a steak dinner. We can go to that fancy all-you-can-eat steakhouse down on Pratt Street. I think it's called Fogo Day Chew, he thought referencing 'Fogo de Chão Brazilian Steakhouse.' I'll call them right now to book a reservation for me and Dancer.

Mr. Hawkins picked up his flip phone from a nearby table, and then set it down, opting to find the restaurant's telephone number using his new 'Amazon Echo'.

I remember when we called an operator or used phonebooks like the Yellow Pages and White Pages to find a phone number. Referring to 'Google' and 'Alexa' he added, Now, all you gotta do is ask 'Googaly' or 'Alexis' to get it for you.

After several minutes of fussing with his 'Amazon Echo' about giving him numbers to places he didn't ask for based upon his pronunciation of the restaurant, he was finally connected to Fogo De Chao Brazilian Steakhouse.

"I want to make reservations for Friday, February 8, 2019, at 4 p.m. for two people," he told the maître d'. "It's gonna be a real special occasion. That's the day my Princess is graduating."

CHAPTER TWENTY-SIX

THE JEWELRY BOX

Wednesday, December 5, 2018
Morning

It was a frigid December morning, and icicles hung from tree branches. Inside Serenity House, Sharon laid across her bed staring through her window at nature's popsicles. Earlier, she ate a hearty breakfast prepared by Sister Jackson and was now relaxing until it was time to head downstairs for the start of the group's 9th Serenity Meeting – the group's fifth, sixth, seventh, and eighth meeting having taken place in November.

Prior to Serenity House, Sharon stayed at a recovery house operated by Light of Truth, a residential program in Baltimore for women in addiction founded by Vaile Leonard.

Light of Truth helped save me from myself, recalled Sharon. After staying at Light of Truth for over a year, their holistic approach kept me from relapsing. I really didn't see the need for Serenity House. But Mr. Jenkins felt Serenity House would help keep me grounded and talked me into coming here…and I'm glad he did. This place is beautiful…just like Light of Truth. And like Light of Truth, I feel it's changing me for the better. I'm not perfect…and there's still a lot of room for improvement. But I don't get angry as fast, I don't curse as much, and I'm not so guarded and defensive. And once again, I'm around people who have gone through some of the same struggles I have…just like the ladies, I met at Light of Truth. Now, I even have a 'Bestie.' I never had a best friend until I came to Serenity House and met Dancer.

❧

When Sharon was Born April 10, 1978, her mother, who was a native Baltimorean, was living in The Bronx, New York. Sharon was of mixed heritage. Her late father Fernando Torres was Puerto Rican, and her mother Natalie Johnson was African American.

Like her father, Sharon had long, jet black straight hair, long eyelashes, and thick, connecting eyebrows. Like her father, whose nickname was 'Short Man' Sharon was also small in height. And like her father, who was asthmatic, Sharon had asthma.

On the color palette, her medium-brown complexion was a mixture of her father's light tone and her mother's darker hue. Like her mother, she had dimpled cheeks, relatives always pinched when she was growing up. But as she got older, she developed bad acne and experienced teasing and taunts from her classmates and neighborhood children.

I can still remember being bullied by the other students and kids on my block. They roughed me up, punched me in the stomach, and pulled my hair. They also snatched my lunchbox and took my food.

Sharon's father was shot to death in New York when she was 10. No one was ever arrested in the shooting, but after he died, Sharon and her mother moved to Baltimore. Ms. Johnson found employment in the city as a waitress and moved in with her sister Margot Harris and her daughter Jacqueline – who was now the 'First Lady' of United in Victory. Ms. Johnson stayed with her sister until she saved up enough money to move into an apartment.

I was bullied in New York, and the trend continued when we moved to Baltimore. My hair was so long, it hung down my back. Some of the mean little girls would pull my long pigtails and laugh while I cried. I couldn't seem to fit in…either I was too light to be like other Black children…or too dark to be around the Puerto Rican children. And on top of that…I had bad acne. The kids were always teasing me about my acne and calling me mean names like 'Pizza Face' and 'Pimple Face'. So, I didn't play with the other children…or try to make friends…I stayed to myself. I also walked home from school by myself. But some of the kids would follow me home and pick fights. But all of that changed once 'Uncle Mal' came to stay with us.

Sharon was reminiscing about her uncle Malcolm Johnson, whom she called 'Uncle Mal.' He was the younger brother of Sharon's mother and aunt. One 1991 day, the Newport cigarette smoking former boxer was standing outside the apartment complex drinking a shorty of 'Seagram's Gin' when he saw a group of kids chasing Sharon home the last day of school.

"Leave my niece alone!" Mr. Johnson shouted, walking towards the pack. They ran away, threatening to beat up Sharon when school resumed later that year from the summer vacation break.

"You can't let kids chase you like that!" he told Sharon, taking a long drag off his Newport before plucking it on the ground and snuffing it out beneath his foot. "You from our family and you're from New York! You ain't no damn punk!"

That summer, Mr. Johnson began teaching Sharon how to defend herself.

Uncle Mal made me lift weights, run up and down the stairs of our apartment complex, and jump rope outside near the playground. He showed me how to box and 'stick and move'…in between sipping 'Knottyhead' as he called his Seagram's Gin…out of a brown paper bag. He trained me as if I were a real boxer.

Mr. Johson was a 25-year-old former amateur lightweight boxer with high hopes of becoming a professional boxer. But he became a heavy drinker of gin, and 'Knottyhead' pinned him against the ropes. Unable to escape the bruising punches of drunkenness, Mr. Johnson – whose ring name was 'Mal the Masher' was knocked out the ring by 'Knottyhead.' However, Mr. Johnson's knowledge of the sport never left him. He taught Sharon everything he knew – including intimidation tactics.

"Punch them, grab them, and flip them down to the ground!" Mr. Johnson told her. "Then once you got them down on the ground, punch and kick them a few more times and yell 'Take that Bitch!' Beating and cussing their asses out at the same time makes you even badder! I bet you their punk asses will stop calling you 'Pizza Face' and all those other bullshit names! And for the ones that really mess with you, sneak em' from the back and bust 'em upside their damn heads! I guarantee they won't pick on you again!"

Reflecting on her cousin's training, Sharon thought, Some kids just don't understand the trauma they inflict on other kids when they bully and tease them. But now…I was ready to inflict a little trauma of my own. When I returned to school after the summer break…I was ready for anyone who messed with me.

Sharon's first day back to school began with one of the school's bullies Maggie Diggs slamming her locker closed while Sharon attempted to place her sweater inside. Maggie was among the students who chased Sharon home on the last day of school.

"Where's your protection now?" Maggie teased, referring to Mr. Johnson. "Who's gonna help you now…Pizza Face?" she asked to the laugher of other students in the hallway.

Without saying a word, Sharon turned around and punched Maggie in the face as hard as she could, causing Maggie's mouth to bleed. To the yells of the students who were all shouting, 'Fight! Fight! Fight!' Sharon tripped Maggie and threw her on the hallway floor.

"I'm my own protection!" she yelled at Maggie while beating her up and calling her profane names. "Who's Pizza Face now?" Sharon screamed, slamming Maggie's face to the floor, knocking out one of her front teeth. "I ain't no punk!"

School police rushed to the commotion and pulled Sharon off Maggie. The fight marked the first time Sharon had been suspended from school – but not the last. A long list of suspensions followed with Sharon fighting and beating girls and boys alike. Soon, Sharon became one of the school's most feared students. The quiet introvert other children picked on and called 'Pizza Face' was now known as 'Sharon the Baron.'

The meeting time drawing closer, Sharon got out of the bed. She stopped by Dancer's room, but her door was closed.

That's strange, thought Sharon. Dancer and I usually walk downstairs to the meetings together. Without Dancer to chat with, Sharon resumed thoughts about her fights in school.

I became one of the toughest and loudest-mouth girls in school. Nobody messed with me! I was always fighting and getting suspended and was eventually sent to an alternative school. But I got into fights there too. I used to be a 'scaredy cat', but now I was fearless! I wasn't afraid of nobody! Uncle Mal told me, I wasn't no punk, and that's how I carried it! And it felt good to be feared instead of fearful. But being a loudmouth bad girl came with terrible consequences because there came a time when I should have backed down instead of trying to prove I wasn't no punk…because I took on an opponent that was bigger and badder than I could ever be…Heron.

❦

Before reaching the stairs, Sharon passed by a window and stopped. Backing up a few steps, she peered out its glass panes over at the majestic stained-glass windows of United in Victory.

I want to go to church with the others on Sunday, Sharon thought. But I don't think I can handle seeing my cousin Jacqueline parading around over there in her fancy clothes and hats like she's so perfect! To them, she's First Lady Jacqueline Just…the wife of the pastor…but to me…she's still 'Juicy' from back in the day…the first lady to introduce me to Heron.

❦

I started getting high with Juicy when I was 18…didn't stop until I was 38…and now I'm 40! After Juicy got clean, she had the nerve to act like she didn't even know me! First, Juicy introduces me to heroin, and now she's the First Lady of a church! Go figure!

Sharon continued to stew in her feelings. I wanna go to church, but I don't want to see Juicy sitting up in there like a 'prima donna'! Thanks to her giving me my first hit of Heron, I was 'strung out' for 21 years of my life. 21 loooooooong years! Thanks to good ole Juicy, I went through hell! I damn near died! Actually…I did die! I can't stomach sitting over there in the church looking at her after what she did to me!

Like Sharon, Dancer and Miracle also did not attend Sunday worship services at United in Victory.

Dancer doesn't go to church with Mama Jackson and the others on Sunday because she doesn't wanna embarrass her mother, who's another 'prima donna', thought Sharon. And Miracle…I have no clue as to why that hellcat doesn't go. No, I don't go to church, but I do read my Bible. Snickering, Sharon thought, That's why I know Mama Jackson be messing up those scriptures she's always trying to quote…definitely not her strong suit. I live for the day when she finally gets one right!

❦

Sharon arrived at the Deacon Roy Jackson Room for the day's Serenity Meeting, stopping in her tracks. Appalled, she couldn't believe what Dancer was doing for Willie!

"Dancer!" she yelled. "Stop shining Willie's shoes! Willie can shine his own shoes!"

"Oh Sharon!" said Dancer. "That's why I came downstairs early. Willie asked me if I could shine his shoes for him and of course I said I could and I wanted to h–"

"Help," said Sharon, finishing Dancer's sentence. "I know. But Willie is a grown ass man! He can shine his own shoes! Got the nerve to be sitting in his chair with his head back flipping popcorn in his mouth while you shine his shoes! You're not his personal servant!"

"Mind your business, Sharon!" said Willie. "You always got that big mouth of yours into something!"

"That's right!" snapped Sharon. "Especially when it comes to Dancer! I'm not gonna let you or anybody else around here take advantage of her!"

Meanwhile, the others walked in.

"Hush up you two!" yelled Sister Jackson. "What's going on in here?!"

"Mama Jackson, Willie has Dancer in here shining his shoes!" explained Sharon.

"Sharon's right," said Willie, putting his shoe brush in a bag. "But Dancer agreed to do it."

"Willie's right!" said Dancer. "He asked, and I told him would shine his shoes. I met him down here early to do it."

"Dancer, don't shine Willie's shoes no more!" said Sister Jackson. "And Willie, if I hear of you having Dancer shining your shoes again, I'm gonna see to it that you shine everybody's shoes in Serenity House!"

"No ma'am Mama Jackson!" said Willie. "I don't want to do that! I don't know the first thing about shining shoes."

"Well, you had better learn and start doing your own!" replied Sister Jackson. "You got some nerve up in here havin' someone shining your shoes like they're your slave!" Sister Jackson looked at her watch. "It's ten of ten. We'll be starting our meeting shortly. Everyone have a seat."

Sharon looked over at Willie and at rolled his eyes. Willie flicked a handful of popcorn in his mouth and did the same.

"Girl, you need to pipe down and eat some of this popcorn," he told Sharon, It's light…and you really need to lighten up!"

"I'm about to pop you, Willie!" said Sharon balling up her fist. "Then we'll all be happy! I don't want no popcorn!"

"Poot you then!" said Willie. "There are just some people you can't be nice to!" Looking at the others, he held the bag up and asked, "Does anyone want some of my microwave popcorn?"

"No!" screamed Miracle in bloodcurdlingly fashion. "I hate microwave popcorn!"

"You weren't getting none anyway!" yelled Willie snatching the bag back towards his chest.

"Shut up!" bellowed Miracle.

"Man oh man do we have some crazy, mean women in this place!" declared Willie, drawing laughter from Hank. "How about you Mama Jackson?" he asked. Do you want some of my microwave popcorn?"

"No thank you Willie," said Sister Jackson biting into a cookie. "I got my own snacks. Besides, I don't eat microwave popcorn. As a matter of fact, I don't eat anything cooked in the microwave. It ain't healthy. The Food and Drug Administration says it ain't good for you."

"The FDA said that Mama Jackson?" asked Dancer. "Wow, I've never heard that before."

I don't think Mama Jackson knows what she's talking about, Sharon thought. The way she eats, the last thing

I thought she was concerned about was eating healthy or something cooked in a microwave.

"The Food and Drug Administration has never said that to my knowledge, Mama Jackson," said James.

"I've never heard that either Mama Jackson," said Hank. "I had an uncle who worked for the FDA, and he never told us that."

"When did the word 'healthy' start mattering to you Mama Jackson?" Willie casually asked with a laugh. "'Cause you sure eat everything!"

No Willie didn't just say that to Mama Jackson! Sharon shouted in her mind. I mean…we may have all been thinking that…but I never thought someone would say it!

"Willie! How could you say such a thing to Sister Jackson?" asked Sister Voyant.

"What was that, Willie?!" Sister Jackson bellowed, preparing to get up. "What did you say to me?!"

"Nothing Mama Jackson…nothing," said Willie, cowering in his chair.

Look at Mama Jackson's face! thought Sharon. I have never seen her this mad!

'Knock! Knock! Knock!'

A succession of raps on the front door extinguished the smoldering moment. Her eyes fixated on Willie, Sister Jackson walked over to the door and swung it open. Mr. Jenkins walked in holding a box.

Willie better be glad our social worker knocked on the door when he did! thought Sharon. Mama Jackson looked like she was about to bang Willie in his face!

Mr. Jenkins' quick strides represented his movement throughout the day.

What a busy Hump Day! thought Mr. Jenkins. I have clients to meet throughout the morning, all afternoon, and into the evening. But after finding Miracle's jewelry box in the back of my car, I wanted to get it to her right away. I know Miracle will be very happy to get it back. Especially after the way she behaved when she didn't find it in her bag.

Mr. Jenkins greeted everyone and apologized for interrupting the meeting.

"Here you go, Miracle," he said, handing her the jewelry box. "I found it laying in the back of my car."

Snatching the jewelry box out of his hand, Miracle snarled, "So, you finally decided to bring me back my jewelry box after all these weeks! Thief! I knew you had it!"

That certainly wasn't the reaction I thought I would get, Mr. Jenkins thought. I take time out of my busy day, and this is the thanks I get?

"I guess that meant 'thank you'," he sarcastically said. "Well you're welcome."

"Did you look inside my jewelry box?!" screamed Miracle.

"No, I did not look inside your jewelry box," replied Mr. Jenkins. "Why would I do that?"

"You better not had!" fired back Miracle.

"You're beholden to that jewelry box," said Mr. Jenkins. "I assume it holds something very precious."

"It does," Miracle softly uttered before yelling, "Never mind," while scathingly looking Mr. Jenkins up and down. "You wouldn't understand! You and your educated self! You and your expensive suit...proper diction...and fancy cologne! You would never understand what I've been through!"

"You never know," Mr. Jenkins replied. "We may have more in common than you think."

"You and me ain't got nothing in common Mr. Jenkins! The only thing we share is a client-social worker relationship! Now go on back to your fancy office and leave me alone!"

Mr. Jenkins stared at Miracle silently – pondering whether he should say what was on his heart.

I'm gonna say it, he decided. I typically don't share the story of my childhood publicly, but Miracle's assumptions beg me to do so.

❀

Mr. Jenkins took a few steps closer to Miracle, and began: "Before I leave Miracle, I want to share something with you. You were adopted...and I went through the foster care system…tossed around from foster home to foster home. And I never felt love…never felt wanted. I felt like the only reason I was in a home, was for somebody to collect a check for my being there. That was until God placed me in the home of Pastor Just…or 'Pops' as I call him… and his wife Jacqueline…whom I call 'Moms.'

"Amen! Testify son!" said Sister Jackson gobbling down cookies.

"Hurry up and finish telling your testi-lie!'" demanded Miracle.

"My tests are my testimony!" said Mr. Jenkins. "I know what God did for me."

"Tell it!" urged Sister Jackson.

"Pop and Mom's house was the first place I felt love in years," he said. "They poured so much into me when I stayed with them, that I decided to become a social worker to help others. God placed a special desire in my heart to help foster children...who…like myself, felt rejection because they grew up believing the lie the enemy told them… that they are less than…life's rejects…throwaways…unworthy because the ones who birthed them, didn't want them."

"A lie straight from the pit of Hell!" shouted Sister Jackson emphatically. "Go on Son! Preach!"

"When I was a little boy, the enemy tried to blind me with that lie…so I couldn't see my way out of rejection…that rejection would be my excuse! It would be rejection that I would place the blame upon as to all the reasons why I never would amount to anything! I was nothing! Nobody wanted me…especially my father…and quite frankly, I don't even want to think about what that man put me through! But Pops and Moms taught me about the Love of God…they taught me the words to the song…'Jesus Loves Me'…and every morning they would stand me in front of a tall, oval mirror and make me look at myself, and sing the words to that song!

So, Miracle…I do understand. …I've been there. But in order for me to become what you see standing here today, I had to stop believing the lies! And once I knew the truth...that God loves me…even when I felt nobody else loved me…I was able to move past my feelings of rejection and do the work God destined me to do."

"Amen! Amen! Amen!" cheered Sister Jackson.

"That!" said James, "was mighty powerful!"

"Thanks for sharing that with us Mr. Jenkins!" said Dancer rushing over and giving him a hug.

"You're welcome," said Mr. Jenkins, flustered by Dancer's hug.

"Miracle…it's time for you to stop using what happened in your past as a crux and as an excuse…so you can move forward in your life and follow the path God has just for you," said Mr. Jenkins.

"Get out of here Mr. Jenkins!" Miracle screamed. "You hear me! Get out!"

"I'm very sorry to upset you Miracle," replied Mr. Jenkins.

"Did you hear me?!" Miracle asked. "I said get out!"

"Miracle!" said Sister Jackson.

"No worries, Miss Jackson," said Mr. Jenkin walking to the front door. "I'm leaving. Again, my sincerest apologies everyone for interrupting your meeting. And don't worry about seeing me out Miss Jackson. I'll see my own self out."

Mr. Jenkins turned once more to look at Miracle, who was gazing at her jewelry box crying.

Miracle is always so angry and sad, Mr. Jenkins said silently. I thought that box would finally bring a smile to Miracle's face. I guess I was wrong, he surmised, gently pulling the door shut.

After hearing Mr. Jenkins close the door, Miracle began an internal celebration.

I got my jewelry box back! Miracle silently yelled. I am so relieved! I kept praying I would get it back! I thought it was gone forever! And here it is! The memento inside means everything to me! I'm so happy! But I couldn't let Mr. Jenkins and the others see me happy. I don't trust them. I don't trust anybody!

Meanwhile Sister Jackson walked over to Miracle and tried to put her around her shoulder, prompting Miracle to back her chair further away.

"Miracle baby…tell us what's wrong," said Sister Jackson. "We're here to help."

"That's right Miracle," added Sister Voyant. "We want to help you tear down that wall of mistrust. Everybody isn't bad."

"Oh yeah!" yelled Miracle, no longer able to keep her emotions bottled up inside. "That's easy for you to say! You and 'Fatso' here know what it's like to have a family!"

"Fatso!" shouted Sister Jackson.

"That's right! Fatso!" sneered Miracle. "Both of you know what it's like to have a family! You and your perfect lives! I came into this world drug- addicted! A crack baby nobody wanted! So my addiction goes back! Way back to the time when my mother…whoever she is…carried me in her womb! And passed her crack addiction on to me…and if that weren't enough…she even tried to…she even tried to…"

"Go on my Beloved," said Sister Voyant.

"I will!' she screamed. "Then you will understand. My –"

'Ring! Ring! Ring'

The loud ring of Willie's cell phone rippled through the air.

"Don't think about answering that cell phone Willie!" said Sister Jackson walking over to him and stretching out her hand. "Hand it over!"

"Please Mama Jackson," pleaded Willie. "Not my cell phone!"

"Now!" bellowed Sister Jackson.

Pouting, Willie handed Sister Jackson his cell phone.

"You'll get you phone back after this meeting!" said Sister Jackson. "Sorry for the interruption Miracle. Go on and finish Baby."

"Yes my Beloved," said Sister Voyant, making her way over to them. "Please share the affairs of your young, tender, hurting heart."

"No!' roared Miracle. "I don't want to talk about it anymore! Now get away from me! Both of you!" she yelled, pushing her way past Sister Voyant. The push caused Sister Voyant to stumble and nearly fall. Led by Hank, all the residents began fussing at Miracle who got up to leave.

"Come back here Miracle!" screamed Hank. "You owe Sister Voyant an apology! You almost knocked her down!"

"I'm fine Hank," said Sister Voyant.

"I don't owe her nothing!" Miracle yelled. "I hate you! I hate all of you! And I hate being here!" she screamed, running out of the room.

Still grasping her jewelry box, Miracle slammed her bedroom door and flopped across the bed. After unhinging its brass clasp, Miracle slowly opened the jewelry box. A tune started playing and a tiny ballerina began to twirl.

Gazing at a photograph laying in the jewelry's box's compartment, Miracle whispered to the twirling ballerina, No one can or ever will understand the hell I've been through! Nobody! Sobbing, Miracle sunk her face deep within her pillow, the ballerina continuing to twirl to Tchaikovsky's 'Waltz of the Flowers', the last number in the 'Nutcracker Suite.'

CHAPTER TWENTY-SEVEN

THAT IRRESISTABLE BOY

Monday, December 24, 2018
Early Morning

'Twas the night before Christmas, and all were asleep in the house,
Except for Dancer who was stirring about.

Trying my best to ignore the temptation to use,
But try as I might, I could no longer refuse.

I called my Dealer on his cell phone,
And whispered to him in a hushed tone.

We made plans to meet this wintry morning,
Just hours away from sunset's dawning.

I keep telling myself, 'I know this is wrong!'
But they'll never miss me or know I was gone!

Tiptoeing about my room eyes wide awake,

Thinking long and hard about my daring escape!

Oh! How I long to see my irresistible Boy!
The love of my life! My favorite toy!

You are my weakness…my Kryptonite…my secret sin.
Yet my Lover…I can hardly wait to see you again!

Upon my return I will happily slip back in bed,
Visions of sugar plums dancing in my –

Dancer closed her diary, the pen remaining within the pages of her newly penned poem. She sat the diary on her nightstand next to a clock with large, illuminated numbers and looked at the time.

It's 1:30 in the morning…Christmas eve. I'll finish writing my poem later. Right now, I have to get outside to meet Money. But I have to be really quiet, so I don't wake anyone up. Standing up from her bed and letting out a deep sigh, Dancer thought, I'm know I shouldn't be doing this…but I really need some Boy, she thought referencing Heroin. I am so glad Money answered his phone. After this time, I won't do it again. This will be my last time.

Dancer tip-toed over to her bedroom closet and took out her heavy wool coat and purple 'Ugg' boots, reflecting on she and Sharon's conversations about how comfortable they were. Sharon owned a pair of red ones. There's no need to change out of my pajamas, she thought, putting on her coat. I'll slip out through the front door and leave it unlocked. After I meet Money and get my hit, I'll slip back in and back into my bed as if I had slept there all night. She glanced at the clock again and read the time. It's 1:35 a.m. Money is meeting me outside at 1:45 on the dot. I need to hurry. I don't want to be late. He'll be mad at me if he's standing outside in the cold and I'm not there, she thought, turning off the lamp and quietly heading for the door. She turned around and looked at her room once more and stepped into the hallway.

Passing Sharon's room, Dancer laughed to herself. Sharon is such a snorer. Reminds me of my Mom. She's a loud snorer too. My Mom…boy would she be disappointed if she knew what I was about to do! But she'll never find out.

Dancer got by the rooms without awaking anyone. She crept down the stairs, walking as light as she could possibly walk. Once she was downstairs, her eyes darted left to right and right to left to ensure no one else was downstairs. Dancer halted her steps, stopping to gaze at the Christmas tree.

That Christmas tree sure is pretty, she thought. We sure did a super terrific job assembling and decorating that tree!

Starting from the bottom, her eyes glanced at the gifts she placed under the Christmas tree, then at its twinkling lights, and finally up at the shimmering, fiber optic angel sitting atop holding a harp.

❀

Dancer stood looking at the tree for several seconds until her mind and body reminded her that she needed to hurry outside. 1:38 a.m., she thought, her eyes nervously looking at the time on her cell phone. Money will be outside in seven minutes! Turning completely around she surmised, The coast is clear. Nobody is downstairs but me.

Dancer scampered to the front door, turning its doorknob.

"Dancer!" a voice cried. Startled, Dancer nearly jumped out of her boots.

❀

Dancer stood still, holding the doorknob.

"Do you know what time it is?!" asked Sharon, prompting Dancer to turn around and face her. "Where do you think you're going!"

"Shhhhhh Baby Girl!" said Dancer rushing over to Sharon. "You'll wake everyone up, and I don't want anyone to know I'm leaving."

"Leaving?!" asked Sharon. "What do you mean leaving? Leaving to go where?"

Dancer stared silently at the floor.

"What's going on Dancer?" said Sharon. "You know the rules…you can't just leave…especially this time of night…you'll get kicked out of the program."

Sharon waited for Dancer's response, but Dancer continued to stare blankly at the floor.

"Oh no!' said Sharon. "Dancer, please don't tell me you're going out there to use!"

Tears began to pour down Dancer's face.

"You have come too far to mess up now," said Sharon. "Don't do it Dancer."

"I know you are right Sharon…I have come too far to mess up. And believe me…I'm tired of messing up…really, I am."

"Somebody needs a hug," said Sharon, stretching open her arms. The two shared a long, tight hug, during which time Dancer raised her cell phone to check the time. It's 1:40! And I've only got five minutes to meet Money! If I stay in here any longer, he might leave! And then I won't be able to get my Heroin!

Feeling jittery and nervous about the prospect of missing Money, Dancer freed herself from she and Sharon's tight embrace. Sharon is holding me up! she silently shouted, starting to feel a degree of hostility towards her best friend.

"I have to go Sharon," Dancer said tearfully.

"Please don't go out there, Dancer," pleaded Sharon. "I'm begging you!"

"You know Sharon…I really wish I could wind back the hands of time…back to when I was little girl. Back then, I was a real dancer," she said, reminiscing while gazing at the lights of the Christmas tree. "I danced en pointe in The Nutcracker," the tune of Tchaikovsky's 'Dance of the Sugar Plum Fairy' playing in her mind. "And Sharon…I was good…boy oh boy…was I good!" Dancer smiled, the sound and sights of thunderous applause and packed audiences shouting 'Bravo!' filling her mind. I was a real dancer…that's how I got my name…Dancer…from my mother. She would say 'Look at that fabulous thing! She's going to be a dancer!' And Mom pushed me and pushed me and pushed me to be the best! And I worked hard to live up to her expectations…I really did…and they were extremely high. I just wanted her to be proud of me."

"I'm sure your mother was proud of you Dancer," said Sharon.

"I don't agree with that," said Dancer, the smile fading from her face. "My mom, the great overachiever Dr. Lila Mae Hawkins, never told me she was proud of me. I guess I just wanted to feel appreciated….to be accepted. I wanted to feel special…special in a different kind of way…and different in a special kind of way. You know what I mean?"

"I know exactly what you mean Dancer."

"Becoming a dancer was her dream, not mines. I was living what she wanted to become. Not what I wanted to become. Even my name…Dancer…is a figment of my mom's imagination. I love helping people and wanted to become a nurse – not a dancer. When I was little, my father gave me a pretend children doctor's bag that came with a stethoscope, candy pills, and a plastic needle. I also kept an empty cough medicine bottle in my bag. I would line my doll babies up…Black ones and White ones, along with my Barbie, Ken, Cabbage Patch and Raggedy Ann and Raggedy Andy dolls. They were all my little patients. I would pretend they were sick with colds or the measles. Raggedy Ann and Raggedy Andy had round, red circles on their faces, so of course they were the ones with the measles. I would give them their medicine and shots. Then I would put them in their make-believe hospital beds, which were my twin beds."

"Awww…that's so sweet Dancer," said Sharon.

"Well Sharon, there was something special about making those dolls feel better that I really loved. I dreamed of the day when my patients would be real people. Now, you would think my mom would be happy to see me pretending to be a doctor or a nurse. But she wasn't. Mom didn't like the doctor's bag my dad gave me. Thinking back on it, she never liked anything Dad gave me. Especially if it was fun or make-believe. She didn't want me playing doctor or nurse. All she wanted me to do was practice, practice, practice. She would say, 'Why are you spending time in this room playing doctor when you should be practicing your dance routines? Now put away that silly doctor's bag and put on your ballerina outfit!' I would practice like she told me…but I also kept doctoring and nursing my dolls…until one day," sniffled Dancer, "I came home from school, and they were all gone…every single one. I knew Mom did away with them…although she denied it. I cried and cried until I could cry no more. I was pretty tore-up about it."

"I guess you were," commented Sharon.

"Once Mom told me, 'I gave up my dream of becoming a professional dancer when I married your father. However, Dancer my darling, that doesn't mean you can't become one.' All she wanted me to do was dance…dance…dance! To be the crème de la crème! The best of the best! And I was. By the time I was in my early teens, I was performing in dance recitals all over Maryland and in other states. I would eventually audition for the prestigious Alvin Ailey School in New York and was accepted. But I never made it."

"Wow!" replied Sharon, "Being from New York, I've definitely heard of Alvin Ailey. They are all of that! But why didn't you go?"

"I'll get to that," replied Dancer. "What I want you to understand right now is that all I ever wanted was to do something meaningful and special. And for me…Dancer Angela Hawkins…that was becoming a nurse."

"Wow…'Angela'," said Sharon. "I never knew your middle name was Angela. It fits you Dancer…because you are an angel. You are the kindest…gentlest…sweetest person I have ever met. And as far as doing something meaningful and special…you are always doing meaningful and special things. Everyone here knows and appreciates that…and I'm sure your mother does too. Some people are stoic…they don't show affection or outwardly convey their emotions. I'm sure your mother –"

"Made me feel like I had to do super-duper, unrealistically more in order to meet her standards!" said Dancer. "I've never told anyone this before Sharon, but I have always felt it had a lot to do with my mom wishing that I had been 'light' – like her…as opposed to browner – like my Dad. And she would do over-the-top things that made me feel like she was trying to make me pretty. Like putting the biggest, brightest ribbons and barrettes in my head, perming my hair before I was even old enough to get a perm…things like that. My hair is long like my mom's but not as bone straight as hers.

"You're preaching to the choir," said Sharon. "I've been there."

"And Sharon, she even put bleaching cream on my face…her way of trying to lighten my complexion."

"That's terrible!" said Sharon.

"Tell me about it," said Dancer. "I guess it was her own version of beauty cream. I thought it was regular face cream until I was old enough to read the label on the jar.

"Wow, that's crazy!" replied Sharon.

"I know Sharon…and when I was a little girl, I wrote about it in my diary."

"You kept a diary?" asked Sharon.

"Yes," said Dancer. "Sometimes, I would put my feelings into poems and write them in my little diary book. To this day, I keep a diary…still jotting down poems from time to time."

"I didn't know people still kept diaries," said Sharon.

"Yep," said Dancer. "Some of us do. Just the other day, I wrote something in my diary about the day I flopped across my purple canopy bed to take a nap. I was about nine at the time, and totally exhausted from practicing all afternoon. I was also feeling pretty lousy over the fact that Mom always wanted me to practice – I hardly had time to do little girl things like play, watch cartoons, or even go to the park – unless I was with Dad. Well, on this particular afternoon, Mom came in the room and told me to 'get up and work on my routines.' Well, I never backtalked my mom, but that day, I did. I started crying, while explaining that I was tired of practicing all the time. Well, a few minutes into our heated conversation, Mom blurted 'Dancer, you're not quite as light as the other ballerinas, which means you will have to work even harder to be the best!' I guess that one slipped out…because she apologized right after she said it. But apologies could not take back that comment or the damage it caused to my self-esteem. Because, from that day forward, I had a complex about my complexion.

"I'm so sorry Dancer,' said Sharon. "But I know how you feel. Growing up, either I was too light or too dark…or my hair was too straight…or not straight enough. And, on top of that, I had bad acne. I was an outcast who was picked on all the time... even 'banked' by some of the girls in school. But my Cousin Mal…he's dead now…taught me how to defend myself." Balling up her fist, Sharon said: "Before long, I was giving those mean little bullies a special lunch…'a knuckle sandwich!' – demonstrating by smacking her fist into the other hand.

"Ouch!" said Dancer.

"Ouch is right!" giggled Sharon. "I gave a lot of black eyes, forehead lumps, and sore stomachs. There's a saying, 'Hurt people, hurt people' and I hurt a lot of people. I got in a lot of trouble because my cousin didn't tell me about the consequences of beating people up. But after many hard lessons, I learned to accept that this is how God made me and if someone didn't like it…well too bad! Take it or leave it!" The two laughed. "That's right," said Sharon. God made me, so I am beautiful. And so are you Dancer. When God created us, he made us all different. We are like flowers in His garden. Some light…some dark…some tall…some short…some skinny…some fat…like Mama Jackson –"

"Oh stop!" giggled Dancer.

"Well, you get the picture," said Sharon. "We are all different, but beautiful because God made us. And everything that comes from God is beautiful. The only thing ugly about God's children is the way we act. And Dancer, you are stunningly beautiful – inside and outside. So what, your mother may be a little off her rocker? Well so was mines. People do weird things for their own reasons…but your mother loves you Dancer. She knows you're special."

"She never showed it!" snapped Dancer. "But one night, I did feel special. I was 17, and still in high school. Some of the girls at school invited me to go to a party with them. 'Yah!' I thought…'they want me to go with them!' And so, I did. People at the party were snorting Heroin…and offered me some. I hesitated at first, but then, I thought to myself, 'Well everybody else is doing it…so what the hay…I'll try it'…even though I had been warned about the dangers of drugs. And as the child of Dr. Lila Mae Hawkins…my devout, churchgoing, Bible-toting, Christian mother who always took me to United in Victory Church…I tried it…even though I knew better. It only took that one time…just that one time…and I was hooked. From that moment on, I was chasing that high…and I had to have it…by any means necessary. It made me think I could fly!"

"Fly?!" asked Sharon. "You mean like R. Kelly's song…'I Believe I Can Fly'…like to higher heights…to be the best you can be…to achieve your destiny?"

"I wish," said Dancer. "But no, I thought I could really fly…like a bird. I snorted Heroin before a performance. I was the lead dancer in a routine. At the start of the performance, I took off running…flapping my arms like a bird…jumped off the stage…and landed into the laps of some of the people sitting in the audience."

"Gee Dancer," replied Sharon. "That was one hell of a 'Swan Lake.'

The two laughed.

"I'm sorry," said Sharon. "But that's hilarious!"

"Only you can make me laugh about that performance!" said Dancer, still giggling. "But things only got worse," continued Dancer, her face turning somber. "I dropped out of school…I couldn't concentrate on schoolwork and dance routines…my mind was on two things…and two things only…one…snorting heroin…and two…doing whatever I had to do to get it. The next thing I knew, I was doing another kind of dancing…as a Stripper in a night club down on The Block on Baltimore Street. The spotlights of the stage…now replaced with the strobe lights of the strip club…a ballet barre now replaced with a stripper's pole. And the audiences that delivered standing ovations now replaced with topless bar patrons. I did it for the money…and dancing paid very well. But I spent every dime I made with my supplier. His name is Money and he sure made a lot of money off me. Now Sharon, I didn't like the life I was living…I really didn't. I tried to stop using Heroin…I really did…and my poor mother and father were devastated over the terrible path my life had taken. My father begged me to come stay with him," said Dancer, choking up again. "I refused…not wanting to be a bigger burden. I was already stealing from my parents to support my habit. They didn't want to face the facts…but when Mom caught me red-handed stealing money out of her purse…there was no denying it…and she was heart-broken. 'Dancer! My God!' she cried. 'What are you doing?!" That forced her to come to grips that I was on drugs. She tried everything she could to get me clean…pulling lots of strings to get me into every program you can think of…acupuncture…methadone clinics…hypnosis…residential drug treatment…you name it!"

"I understand that too," said Sharon.

"One time, my Dad and I drove to Deal Island for a weekend fishing trip," said Dancer. "He thought a change of scenery would be good for me. We drove there on a Friday evening and checked into a hotel. But I snuck out in the middle of the night, convinced I couldn't make it through the weekend without Heroin. I will never forget the disappointment in Dad's voice when I finally called him to let him know I was okay. Sharon, I have always snuck out of residential programs…stealing away in the middle of the night…just like I did out at Deal Island. But somehow…someway I managed to make it through the last residential program without running away. But Mom was so afraid I might relapse again, that she pleaded and cried to Pastor Just to allow me to come to Serenity House. Now I know that was hard for my mother to do…extremely hard…because she is a proud woman. She really ate a great deal of Humble Pie."

"Why do you say that?" asked Sharon.

"I remember how Mom complained to Pastor Just about 'those drug people' as she called them…coming into the church for the N.A. meetings. Mom's quite the snoot. She thought they were 'vermin'... 'beneath her'…and 'certainly not worthy of being in her church'. She considered drug addicts and alcoholics 'lowlifes.' She could not wrap her brain around how people could become addicts or alcoholics. Little did she realize one of them would be living right in her home."

A few more seconds went by, the two women sitting silently. Breaking the silence, Dancer said: "Sharon, I will never forget the night when Mom marched up in the strip club where I worked and saw me topless…swinging from the pole! I looked up…and there she was! I thought she would faint on the spot! But she didn't. No siree! She pushed her way up to the stage… even past the bouncers…telling them who she was and who she knew…grabbing me off the pole and telling me to get dressed. She said I was leaving with her and threatened to call the police to come get me if I did not comply. And I believed her…the city's main police station is right there near 'The Block'…and my mother knew some very influential people…including the Police Commissioner. She's retired now…but back then she had a big job with the city's public school system. And she was making such as fuss! So, I did as she asked, also knowing my mother never took 'no' as an answer. I crawled into the back seat of her car…the last thing I wanted to do was sit up front. I didn't want to be anywhere near Mom. I was a bag of mixed emotions…angry at her for pulling me out of the club…which meant she messed up the money I would have made that night to get high…scared of the thought of not being able to buy my heroin…and embarrassed that she saw me dancing topless on that pole. I could have crawled under a rock…it was the lowest moment of my life! As my mother drove…I tell you Sharon, I thought about opening the car door and jumping out. Honestly, I preferred to take my chances tumbling out of the car and rolling out into the street than ride in that car. Mom must have read my mind because she engaged the doors' safety locks so that I couldn't open them. So, I curled myself up in a fetal position on the back seat bawling my eyes out with no clue as to where we were going. When I finally opened my eyes and sat up, we were parked in front of the residential drug treatment facility where I stayed prior to coming to Serenity House. I was 17 when I first tried Heroin…and now I'm 34. And here I am again Sharon…still fighting this monkey on my back!"

"Dancer, you can throw that terrible, ugly, destructive monkey off your back!" said Sharon. "I know it's not easy…but Dancer you can do it!"

"I tried!" cried Dancer. "God knows I tried! I don't want to keep disappointing my parents! I've embarrassed them enough! But Sharon, no matter how hard I try…I keep going back! I just keep going back!"

Sharon gently took Dancer by the hand.

"Dancer, baby…addiction is a powerful spirit…but you can defeat it. But in order to defeat it, you've got to have The Holy Spirit dwelling inside of you to help you fight it. The Holy Spirit leads and guides you to all truth and gives you the supernatural strength you need to resist the temptation. You have to remember what Mama Jackson and Sister Voyant have been telling us since we got here," said Sharon, looking Dancer in the eyes. "We aren't strong enough to fight this thing on our own! This is a supernatural fight, and we have to use our supernatural weapon. And that supernatural weapon is the Holy Spirit."

"I have tried…over and over again Sharon…but I'm just not strong enough."

"Yes you are Dancer. You are strong enough. I know the temptation to use Heron is hard to resist…I was on it too. But I know you Dancer. You can do it. You can beat Heron! I know you can. You ain't no punk!"

"I can't Baby Girl," cried Dancer. "I can't."

"Dancer, listen to me!" said Sharon, grabbing ahold of Dancer's chin. "Don't go back to that nightmare!"

"To tell you the truth Sharon…I don't believe I will ever beat this thing…that I will ever be able to live drug free…but that doesn't mean you can't!"

"But you are living drug-free Dancer! Between the residential treatment program that you were in, and Serenity House, you haven't used in almost a year-and-a-half. Please Dancer…don't give in…don't go out there and use."

Dancer glanced at her cell phone. Oh no! Now it's1:45! I need to leave now! Money is probably standing outside waiting on me. Money is never late.

In a panic, Dancer rushed towards the front door to leave. However, Sharon sprinted in front of her, blocking her path.

"Dancer…please…I'm begging you…don't walk through this doorway," pleaded Sharon, starting to cry.

"I'm sorry Sharon," said Dancer. "I've been fighting this thing all night. I need a fix. I'm hurtin'…you know how it is Sharon."

"You're right Dancer. I do know how it is. I was out there too. And that's why I am determined to keep the door of addiction closed. And armed with the power of the Holy Spirit that we have learned so much about here at

Serenity House, I am going to fight that thing tooth and nail! I'm going to do my part never to allow that door to open back up in my life ever again."

"I have to go Sharon," Dancer said tearfully. "Please don't tell anyone I left out. I'm begging you. Please move out of the way. I'll be back. I promise."

"Dancer, you can't leave. Think about all the people who are depending on you to pull through this! You told me yourself that you called and invited both your parents to our Graduation Ceremony next month. It's only a few weeks away!"

"I can't do it!" said Dancer. "I'm too weak."

"Yes, you can!" said Sharon. "God can help you do it!"

"Just wait right here," said Sharon glancing at the staircase. "I'll call Mama Jackson and Sister Voyant down here and —"

"Shhhhhh!" said Dancer covering Sharon's mouth. "No, no, no, no, no…please no! I'm begging you, Sharon! Don't call them down here!"

Frustrated, sad, and full of angst, Dancer thought, There's no need for me to look at the time again. If I don't get outside, Money is going to leave. Or worse yet, Mama Jackson or one of the others might wake up and come downstairs. I need to get out of here, and Sharon is standing in my way!

"Let's sit down over here and talk," suggested Sharon, looking at two chairs.

"Okay," said Dancer.

The two women walked towards the chairs. But Dancer turned and darted out the front door, rushing out into the frigid winter air to meet Money.

CHAPTER TWENTY-EIGHT

DYING TO HAVE YOU

Monday, December 24, 2018
Early Morning

Despite being inside, Sharon – dressed only in a scant robe and negligee – stood frozen – staring at the front door, hoping somehow…someway, she could 'will' Dancer to come back inside. But behind her stood another Will – one whom she had not heard come down the steps.

"Sharon," said Willie, putting his hand on her shoulder. "What are —

"Willie!" said Sharon, turning around. "You scared the living daylights out of me!"

Looking at Willie bare-chested and dressed in a pair of plaid, blue pajama pants, Sharon thought, Damn! Willie has a nice body!

Sharon tried not to let her eyes have their way, but she couldn't stop them from venturing down Willie's body. They came to a stop after making eye-contact with the large protrusion in his pajama pants. Wow! Now, that's a nice imprint! Oh my gosh! Get it together Sharon! Get your mind out of the gutter!

"I didn't mean to startle you Sharon," said Willie. "And what are you still doing up anyway this time of morning?"

"Up?" asked Sharon, her eyes still locked on Willie's pajama pants. "Up? Oh…up," she giddily giggled, to cover for her wistful moment. "Well, I woke-up and couldn't go back to sleep. So, I came to the kitchen to get a glass of milk…and saw Dancer leave…and I'm worried."

"Dancer's probably outside hugging a tree or something," chuckled Willie.

"In sub-zero degree weather?" said Sharon. "I don't think so. It's so cold, a 'Code Blue Alert' is in effect. That means no one should be outside. But I think we should get dressed and go look for her."

"Stop worrying…Dancer will be back," said Willie, his eyes roving Sharon's sleep attire. "Funny how you and I both couldn't sleep. I was heading to the kitchen to get a glass of water."

"Big coincidence," said Sharon.

"Well Sharon, since we both are down here, may as well make the best of it," Willie said with a grin. "So, come on over here and let ole Willie give you a nice massage while we wait for Dancer."

"You, give me a massage?" Sharon asked sarcastically. "Ha! That's a laugh!"

"What's so funny about that? What you need is a man to calm your butt down…a real man."

"You're right Willie," Sharon said moving around the room looking under chairs, tables, and even a lampshade before heading to the den. Willie followed her into the dark den, where Sharon slid up the dimmer so she could see.

Puzzled, Willie asked, "What are you looking for, Sharon?"

Sharon snickered, proceeding to lift the sofa cushions before putting them back in place. She got down on her hands and knees and peered under the sofa before standing and flopping down on the sofa and laughing at her own antics.

"I was looking for a real man," said Sharon, emphasizing the word 'man.' "Where is he Willie? 'Cause it sure ain't you…little boy! Now go on back to your room!"

Willie's face soured, and he turned to leave, prompting Sharon to think about the story he shared about his family. Now I feel bad…I should not have said that! she thought, chiding herself. I have such a bad habit of running my mouth before thinking first! That's my defense… hurting people with my words…before they hurt me with their own. Not only am I trying to stop that…but now was not a good time to do it. Willie might be an immature womanizer, but he is still a man.

"Willie…don't leave," said Sharon. "I take that back. I didn't mean to say that…I'm sorry."

"Sorry about what?" asked Willie, his face lighting up again. "Playing hard to get? You know you want me," he grinned, making his way over to the couch.

What?! Sharon yelled in her mind. No, Willie didn't just tell me I wanted him! Yes, he did…and shit! I do want him! But I don't want him to know that I want him! And oh my gosh…Willie's coming over here! What am I going to do? Come on Sharon. Get it together! Say something! Looking up at Willie, Sharon whispered, "Don't flatter yourself Willie. I'm sorry about what I said…and all that you've been through…with everything that happened to your parents. I had no idea you had gone through something like that. I can't even imagine dealing with something like that, Willie. "That's a lot."

Sitting next to her on the couch, Willie said, "You're right, Sharon. It was a lot. But I'm hanging in there."

You sure are hanging in there! thought Sharon, quickly glancing at the protrusion of his pajamas. Stop looking between that man's legs, Sharon! Turning to Willie, Sharon again apologized. "Again, I'm so sorry Willie. Sometimes I say things out of my big mouth I should not say."

"You sure do!" laughed Willie. "All the time!"

"Alright Willie," said Sharon, "don't rub it in!"

"I won't," said Willie. "But I didn't realize you had a heart…let alone a soft side."

Willie's words caused Sharon to blush.

"I caught those dimples peek out on your cheeks," he said. "You should smile more often. It becomes you," Willie told Sharon, softly touching her cheek.

This man is sitting here making me blush! thought Sharon. I can't even remember the last time someone made me all slushy! And he just touched my cheek! Ugh! Serenity House might be a place of emotional healing! But right now, Willie is reminding me I could use a little sexual healing!

꩜

The den – its couch, dim lighting, and quiet – accented with the decorum of their scantily clad bodies – was bursting into a flaming hot romantic setting.

Sharon's nostrils began to take in the alluring smell of Willie's cologne.

Damn Willie smells good! she shouted in her mind. Girl! You know this man is a womanizer! Stop it!

Slipping his hands beneath her robe, Willie began to softly massage Sharon's shoulders.

I can't believe I'm sitting here letting Willie do this! thought Sharon. But it feels so good!

"Ooooooh," cooed Willie. "A silk negligee and soft, silky skin. I like that. But your muscles are so tight…just relax."

"You shouldn't be doing this Willie," said Sharon – her mind telling her to pull away from him whilst her body was saying otherwise. Working his hands deeper into the muscles of her shoulders, Willie asked, "Well, do you want me to stop?" Enjoying the deep massage, Sharon whispered "No," and closed her eyes.

꩜

Dancer stood shaking in the dark alley behind Serenity House gazing at the Christmas decorations of neighboring houses to take her mind off the biting cold.

"It's 2:05 a.m. and still no Money," she said, glancing at her cell phone. "I'm freezing! I guess he is not coming. I'm going back inside."

Dancer started back towards Serenity House. But she was halted – grabbed from behind by a shadowy figure who wrapped an arm around her neck. Startled by the grab, Dancer dropped her cell phone. Squirming and wriggling to free herself, Dancer opened her mouth to cry out. The assailant smacked his hand over her mouth, muffling her scream.

꩜

Caressing Sharon's warm shoulders, Willie craftily maneuvered off her robe, unveiling the spaghetti straps of her creme-colored negligee along with her caramel-colored skin.

Sharon is long overdue for a massage, and right now, I am her masseuse, Willie thought. I've been wanting her…and I know she's been wanting me. I've been waiting for this moment a looooooong time.

"Stop!" said Sharon, pulling her robe back onto her shoulders and jumping up from the couch. "I can't let you do this Willie."

"Why? Am I turning you on?" he asked.

"Willie you are nothing but a womanizer!" said Sharon. "You know it and I know it! I am not about to become another one of your hapless victims…falling for your smooth talk and seductive ways."

"Girl…put down your guard."

"Why should I? You use all women! And right now, you are using me to try and get into these panties! Well, I'm not gonna let you, Willie!"

For Willie, who had bragged to Hank he could get Sharon in the bed – which Hank told him he never would – this could prove to become his moment of conquest.

I've got Sharon right where I want her, he thought. But somewhere along the way…Sharon became more than a woman I wanted to get in the bed. I've fallen for Sharon! I don't even know when it happened…it just happened. I've even had wet dreams about making wild, passionate love to Sharon…including this morning. I got tired of laying in bed groping my penis after I woke up. That's why I came downstairs. I thought a cold glass of water might help me clear my head…and wouldn't you know it! There was Sharon!

"Earth to Willie!" said Sharon, snapping her fingers in Willie's face. "Snap out of it!"

"Sorry Sharon," said Willie. "I was just wondering how I could possibly use you? Look at where we are!" he pointed out, glancing around the room. What pray tell, would I be using you to get? Just look around at where we are – a transitional home. You ain't got nothin'! I ain't got nothin'! Add that all together and what have you got?"

"Nothing," the two laughed in unison.

"There are those dimples again," whispered Willie. "I sure would like to see if you have any more."

"Stop it, Willie."

"Sharon, I'm not here to hurt you…just to love you…and right now, I want to make sweet love to you," said Willie who began to softly sing the same song his father would sing to his mother – Lenny Williams' 'Cause I Love You.

Willie's singing would prompt a back-and-forth volleyball match of love Ballard hooks between the two of them.

"Love!" said Sharon doubtfully. "Yeah right Willie! What the hell do you know about love? Oh, I got it. What's love got to do with it?" she asked, singing Tina Turner's 'What's Love Got to Do With It.'

Willie responded with Luther Ingram's 'If Loving You Is Wrong, I Don't Want To Be Right'.

Sharon belted out Rose Royce's 'Love Don't Live Here Anymore.'

Willie stood up from the couch, wrapped his arms around Sharon's waist, and began to sing, Luther Vandross' and Cheryl Lynn's 'If This World Were Mine.'

"But it ain't!" said Sharon, pulling herself singing, Gwen Guthrie's 'Ain't Nothin' Goin' On But The Rent.'

Willie walked behind Sharon. Softly rocking her, he began to sing Freddie Jackson's 'Rock Me Tonight (For Old Times Sake).'

Pulling away from Willie again, Sharon said, "Willie, you're nothing but a player! You know it and I know it! And the last thing I'm gonna do is let you play me like some old record! But I've got just the right song for you Willie!"

"Oh, so you do?" he asked playfully. "Well, let's hear it."

Sharon cleared her throat and began singing Eryka Badu's 'You Better Call Tyrone.' After singing the song's hook, Sharon erupted in laughing, telling Willie, "But you can't use my phone, Willie!" before plopping back down on the couch. "You can't use my phone!"

"Ha…ha," Willie replied sarcastically, sitting next to Sharon. Gently pulling her close to him, he began singing, Teddy Pendergrass' 'Turn Off the Lights.'

"Ooooooh Willie," whined Sharon. "Baby…that's my song," she said, the two engaging in a long French kiss before Willie walked over to the dimmer to slide its switch all the way down. He returned to the couch, the two singing Rick James and Teena Marie's 'Fire and Desire' softly to one another. Willie nuzzled his lips against Sharon's neck, kissing it while laying her back on the couch. Her body going backwards, Sharon began singing Shirley Murdock's 'As We Lay.'

"That's my favorite song of alllllllllllllllll time," said Willie.

"I bet it is!" said Sharon, Willie now stripping her down to her bra and panties and groping her buttocks.

"Can I squeeze the Charmin?" he asked, refencing the toilet paper's popular ad campaign of years past featuring 'Mr. Whipple'.

"Sure, but…where's the beef?" Sharon quipped, alluding to the infamous 1980s 'Wendy's commercial. Sharon began running her hands down Willie chest until they reached the elastic of his pajama pants. She kept going until she felt the warmth of his penis.

"I see somebody is hard," said Sharon, starting to stroke his penis.

"As a brick," added Willie, squeezing her breasts. Willie unhooked Sharon's bra and began to teasingly run his tongue around the nipples of her breasts. Sharon moaned with pleasure, turning him on even more. He began to suck on her breasts, causing Sharon to wildly run her fingers through his curly hair. A few moments later, she gently pushed him backward – flat on his back and began to lick his penis like a lollipop.

"Ooooooh," Willie groaned. "I see you can do more with that mouth than talk trash."

"I sure can," said Sharon, engulfing the top of his penis into her mouth. She began to gently suck, while her fingers twiddled with his scrotum.

Now, she' giving me head and playing with my balls, thought Willie trying not to scream in ecstasy. Moment later, Sharon sat atop Willie, his manhood sliding into her womanhood. His penis deep within the depths of her hot, wet vagina, the two began to make wild passionate love – just like he dreamed.

Outside, Dancer's attacker let her go moments earlier. Still trying to catch her breath, Dancer chastised the familiar figure.

"I can't believe you grabbed me like that Money!" Dancer fussed. "You nearly scared me to death! And you made me drop my phone," she said, stooping down to pick it up."

"If I were a killer, you would have been dead!" laughed Money. "Man o' man that was funny! I scared the shit out of you!"

"Well, you have a warped sense of humor! And look at my phone!" she said, showing him the busted phone.

"It's broke!"

"Fuck that phone Dancer!" he hissed. "Now what's up? It's cold as a shit out here!"

"I know it's cold Money…I literally froze to death waiting for you," said Dancer. "What took you so long?"

"Some new customers held me up. They all wanted this new Boy I got," he said waving a cellophane packet. "And look at you!" he said, stepping back and eyeballing Dancer from head to toe. "Damn Bitch! I see you have put on weight since the last time I last saw you! You look good girl!" Grabbing Dancer, he twirled her around and began to sing, Johnny Gill's 'My, My, My.'

"Why thank you Money," said Dancer. "That's a nice thing to say. You never told me that before."

"That's because you ain't never looked this good before," he replied. You are lookin' phat as shit girl! What you tryin' to do? Get healthy or somethin'?"

"Yes Money," said Dancer. "I've been in rehab."

"Ha, ha, ha," laughed Money. "Rehab. I guess it didn't work, did it? "Ha, Ha, Ha. Once an addict always an addict! My customers always come back," he teased, waving the packet in her face. "And I've got this Boy you love right chere. It's real good…and it's real strong. This some new shit, and everybody's hittin' me up for some!"

"Ooooh! I can't wait to try it!" said Dancer grabbing for the packet.

"Uh, uh, uh…this shit ain't free Dancer!," said Money pulling the packet back. "Where's my fuckin' money?!"

"Money…um…um…I mean…what I'm trying to say is that…gee how can I say this," stammered Dancer. "I…well I don't have any of what your name is…none at all…I don't have any money…Money. You see Money, I've been staying at that nice church house right over there trying to get myself together and I —"

"What the fuck!" Money shouted. "You called me and had me to rush over here in the middle of the night to bring you your shit and you don't have my damn Money! Bitch I should smack the shit out of yo' ass!"

"I'm sorry Money…I'll get you your money. Just one hit! Please Money! I need it! Just one hit!"

Grinning, Money rubbed his hands together. "Come to think of it, there is a way you can pay me," he said, looking Dancer up and down. "Especially since you look so good and all. You need this Boy I got here in my hand," gloated Money, glancing at the packet. "And I need some head! Now get down on your knees and suck this dick!"

"No Money!" exclaimed Dancer. "I…I don't want to do that. I don't do things like that anymore."

"You don't?!" he asked. "Well, I'll go take care of my paying customers! Bye bitch!" he said, walking away. "And don't call my ass again!"

"I need that Boy!" she whispered to herself, her lips shivering from the cold. "I can't let him leave! Waving to get his attention, she called out, Yoo-hoo Money! Come back!"

Money turned around and walked back over to Dancer.

"Okay Money," said Dancer. "I'll do it. Blowing into her hands to warm them up, Dancer thought, My hands feel like they are frostbitten! My, am I cold! Watching Money unzip his pants, she thought, I hate sucking on private parts for drugs or money! I really thought those days were behind me! And here I am…in a cold, dark alley about to do it again. This is the absolute last time I will put myself through this…and that's a promise.

Dancer was now on her hands and knees giving Money oral sex. Listening to his 'ohs' and 'ahs', she thought, I really hope and pray no one from Serenity House walks outside and catches me doing this! I would never be able to look them in the face ever again.

"Stand up!" Money demanded.

Dancer stood up. Money turned her around and yanked her towards his body, causing her back to thump against his chest.

"Gee Money," she said. "You don't have to be so rough."

Like a puppeteer, Money dangled the packet of drugs in her face from his fingers as if she were a puppet on a string.

"Go on and get that hit!" said Money. Dancer snatched the packet out of his hand.

"Damn Ho!" said Money. "You just gonna snatch it like that!"

Her fingers numb from the frigid temperatures, Dancer fumbled to open the packet.

"You go on and get that Boy," said Money. "And this boy, is gonna get some of this ass!" he said, grinding his penis against her buttocks.

"No Money," said Dancer, pulling away from him. "I don't want to do that. It hurts too bad."

"Finally!" she thought, opening the packet. "I didn't think I would ever get this packet open!" Dancer exclaimed, snorting the packets contents.

"Yeah!" said Money, gyrating his hips. "You snatched what you wanted! Now, Money is going to snatch what he wants!" Money grabbed Dancer, holding her place while taking down her pajama pants.

"No money!" pleaded Dancer, trying to free herself. "I don't want to have sex out here...especially that kind of sex. It's freezing out here, and my friends are right over there in the church house."

"What do you think this is!" he shouted. "You got what you wanted! Now Money is going to get what he wants! Fair exchange is no robbery! Some of my assets for some of your ass!"

A few more seconds went by, and Dancer was feeling the effects of the drugs she snorted.

"Wow Money," she said, now feeling more relaxed, and less combative. "You were right. This Boy is strong. I'm feeling good...back in my happy place."

"I told you that shit was good!" said Money, attempting to slide his penis into Dancer's anus.

"But I feel a little weird this time," said Dancer.

"You are feeling good, and right now, I'm about to feel good," said Money, ramming his penis inside Dancer, causing her to scream in pain.

Inside Serenity House, Sharon and Willie were still conducting their lovemaking session on the couch.

"Willie, did you hear that?!"

"Hear what?"

"I thought I heard something," said Sharon. "And it sounded like a scream."

"That's you screaming my name out in your mind," whispered Willie, harmonizing Rick James' 'Give it to me Baby', whilst Sharon rode him like a cowgirl atop a rodeo horse.

Wincing in agony from Money's forceful thrust, Dancer's exposed skin itched terribly against the biting cold. Weathering his repetitive pumps between her buttocks, Dancer thought: Soon, this will be over, and I'll be back inside the warmth of Serenity House. This Boy is good, she thought referencing the Heroin she snorted, but something about it doesn't feel right…and it's scaring me…because I can literally hear my own heartbeat!

Thump-thump, thump-thump, thump-thump, thump-thump…thump-thump…thump-thump…thump-thump…

And not only that, she worried, but my heart seems to be beating irregularly and I'm having trouble breathing! I've never felt like this before! Something's wrong!

Trying to catch her breath, Dancer pulled away from Money, telling him, "Money stop! Was something in that Boy you gave me?" she gasped. "I feel really off-kilter! And it's scaring me!"

Grabbing her back to him, Money replied, "No! I'm almost there! I'm almost ready to come!"

"Just let me catch my breath!" begged Dancer, barely able to keep her balance. "I feel like I'm about to faint!"

Ignoring Dancer's pleas, Money continued to do his business, holding her firmly in place.

Thump…thump…thump…thump…thump…thump.

Dancer could hear her heartbeat slowing, while simultaneously feeling Money's beating faster against her back.

"Ooooooh, yeah, that's it!" said Money, Dancer feeling hot semen gushing into her anus.

Thump…thump…thump…thump…

No longer able to stand, Dancer felt herself going to the ground in slow-motion, a movie reel playing in her mind. That's me…a little ballerina dancing onstage in my tights and tutu….and there's Mom and Dad… Mama Jackson, Sister Voyant, James, Miracle, Hank, Willie, and Sharon…all sitting in the audience and clapping, she thought, smiling. Oh! And there's my late…

Thump! She heard, hitting the cold concrete alley.

Bewildered, Money stared down at Dancer laying in the alley.

"Shit!" said Money, shaking his penis and tucking it back inside his pants.

Dancer!" said Money, stooping down and shaking Dancer. "What's wrong with you? Get up girl!"

Receiving no response, Money pressed his hand against her neck, feeling a slight pulse.

"Don't tell me this Bitch OD'd! Fuck!"

Pacing, Money contemplated what he should do. "I don't want to leave Dancer out here like this! I want to call 911, but what if the call is traced back to my phone? I'm already on probation! I violate that…and I'm looking at 10 to 15 years! I need to get out of here before someone sees me!" decided Money, his heavy breaths materializing into whitish-grey puffs from the wintry air. Maybe someone will find Dancer and get her to the hospital in time," he hoped, dashing up the alley towards his grandmother's house.

❀

Monday, December 24, 2018
Dawn

It was now going on 5 a.m. Lifting her head up from Willie's chest, Sharon sang, "It's morning," referencing words from Shirley Murdock's 'As We Lay.'

"Oh my goodness! It's morning!" she said, looking at a clock. "Willie get your butt up! We fell asleep. We need to get upstairs before somebody catches us down here!"

"You're right," said Willie groggily.

"Somebody's coming!" said Sharon, the sound of footsteps drawing closer.

"Dancer! Dancer! Where are you?" yelled Sister Jackson. "Dancer!"

"It's Mama Jackson!" said Sharon, slipping back into her nightclothes and underwear along with Willie. In their haste to get up, the two rolled off the couch, landing on their knees. Before they could stand, Sister Jackson walked into the den.

❀

Sister Jackson momentarily gazed at Willie and Sharon down on their knees.

"What in the devil are you two doing down here in the den?"

"Who us?" asked Willie.

"Yes, you!" replied Sister Jackson.

"We were praying," replied Sharon.

"Praying!" said Sister Jackson. "Dressed like that?"

"That's right," said Willie. "I came downstairs, and Sharon was down here...visibly upset. I began laying hands on her...like 'Unk' does in church...just trying to give her a little healing," he explained, prompting Sharon to nudge him.

"With hardly no clothes on?" inquired Sister Jackson. "That's not the same kind of laying hands your uncle does in church!"

"I can explain Mama Jackson," said Sharon. "See, we –"

"Never mind that right now," interrupted Sister Jackson. "We'll take this up later! Right now, we're looking for Dancer. Sister Voyant woke up and called out to me, sensing something was wrong. Dancer's not in her room, and we have searched all of upstairs. Now, we are about to check downstairs. Have either of you seen her?"

A terrible feeling enveloping Sharon, she stuttered "I...I...I saw her Mama Jackson."

"You did?" asked Sister Jackson. "Where?"

"I saw Dancer leave," Sharon said. "She left out and I tried to stop here but –"

"What!" shouted Sister Jackson with great alarm. "Dancer left! As cold as it is outside?!"

James rushed into the room leading Sister Voyant, who held tight to his arm. Hank trailed behind them, their faces full of concern.

Stretching an arm towards the front door, Sister Voyant shouted at the contingency, "Dancer's in trouble! I feel it in my spirit! You all have to find her! Please go! Go now!"

Aroused from her sleep by the sounds of Sister Jackson calling out for Dancer, Miracle slipped on her coat and make her way towards the commotion downstairs. Watching them disperse, she thought, They can't find Dancer! I really don't want them to know I'm concerned…or that I even care. But I am concerned about her welfare…and really hope Dancer's okay.

Looking on from the entranceway to the den, Miracle listened and watched…as concern turned into fear…and fear turned into panic.

Just the other day, I promised myself, the next time Dancer offered me a hug, I would accept it, Miracle thought, watching the others frantically searching for Dancer. I pray she's alright.

"We've searched everywhere down here and can't find her!" said James. "Sister Voyant believes she's outside. We need to search out there!"

"We're coming with you!" said Sharon.

"We?" asked Willie. "As cold as it is outside?!"

"Ain't neither one of you going nowhere dressed like that!" said Sister Jackson. "Put on some clothes and meet us outside!"

A short time later, Willie and Sharon returned – fully dressed and wearing coats and boots.

"It's still dark outside," said Willie. "Is there a flashlight anywhere around here Mama Jackson?"

"Yes, I'll get it," said Sister Jackson, rushing to the kitchen and returning with a flashlight. Sister Jackson grabbed her coat from the coatrack and followed Willie, James, Sharon, and Hank out the door.

"Oh! I forgot something," said Sister Jackson, turning around to come back inside.

Look at that greedy lady waddling over to her snack table! thought Miracle shaking her head. And look at her tear open that pack of cookies! Now, she's gobbling them down her throat! That don't make sense for someone to be that greedy! she surmised, watching Sister Jackson race out the door to catch-up with the others.

Miracle quietly made her way to the front door, standing near Sister Voyant, who stood there with both hands stretched outside.

I'm going to stay inside and stand here next to Sister Voyant, thought Miracle. She won't even realize I'm standing here because she can't see. She's as blind as a bat.

"Miracle?" asked Sister Voyant.

"Yes…yes ma'am," stuttered Miracle, stunned that Sister Voyant knew she was standing there.

The two stood at the door, the cold air, now accompanied by a blustery wind, slapping them across the face.

"Brrrrrrr!" said Miracle, pulling the collar of her coat tighter around her neck. "It's really cold outside."

"In the name of Jesus…please…please…please find Dancer," prayed Sister Voyant, oblivious to Miracle's words.

I've been outside in the cold enough times to know a person could freeze to death in temperatures like this, thought Miracle, shivering in the doorway. Extreme conditions make people do desperate things…things they wouldn't normally do…like get in cars with strangers. I hope they find Dancer before someone snatches her up…or worse.

The first one out the door, Sharon's heart was beating so fast, she thought it would jump out of her chest. I can't even remember the last time I was this scared! Sharon thought. Please Lord, let Dancer be okay. I won't be able to live with myself if something happened to her!

"Let's split-up!" suggested James.

"Alright," said Sister Jackson. "But everyone, please be careful!"

"We'll go this way to look for Dancer!" said James, pointing towards the neighborhood. "Maybe she's close by."

Sharon and Willie went the opposite way, jogging towards the rear of the church house.

"Dancer! Dancer!" they cried out in unison.

"I don't see anything," said Willie, shining the flashlight across the yard. "Man, it's cold out here!"

"Maybe we should check over in that alley!" said Sharon, dreading her suggestion.

"I don't want to that alley!" said Willie. "Look at how dark and dank it is over there!"

"Come on 'Fraidy Cat!' said Sharon.

"You're not scared to walk over there?" asked Willie. "What if someone's hiding over there?!"

"No, I'm not scared!" replied Sharon. "I ain't no punk!"

"Well I am!" said Willie. "I'm too good lookin' for something to happen to me out here!"

"Will you come on!" said Sharon, pulling Willie's arm. The two began approaching the alley, Willie pointing the flashlight at the dark area. "I think I see something!" exclaimed Willie, cautiously approaching an unknown shape –

Sharon right behind him.

The two now close enough to see it was someone laying in the alley, Sharon cried, "Please! Please God! Don't let it be Dancer!"

Sharon's heart dropped, seeing purple 'Ugg' boots on the person's feet.

"Oh my God!" Sharon screamed. "It's Dancer!"

"Oh no!" cried Willie.

Screaming and sobbing, Sharon rushed over to Dancer, kneeling by her side, and taking her by the hand. It was cold and stiff.

"Noooooooooooooooo!" screamed Sharon, shaking Dancer. "Dancer! Dancer! Please Wake up! Get up Baby Girl! Please!"

But there was no movement from Dancer. Her eyes were open – her face blue and lifeless.

"Please God, no!" Sharon wailed so loudly, her cries shattered the quiet of the Christmas Eve morning.

Eating cookies, Sister Jackson and the others raced towards the cries.

Lord help her! thought James. How can Sister Jackson eat cookies at a time like this?!

"Hurry! Over here!' shouted Willie, the group running over to him and Sharon.

"Oh my God!" screeched James. "Dancer!"

"She's not breathing!" cried Sharon, cradling Dancer in her arms, slowly rocking back and forth,

"I'm going to grab my phone from the house and call 911!" James yelled frantically, the events evoking thoughts of the night he lost his wife and daughter.

Seeing the empty cellophane bag on the ground, Sister Jackson said, "Dancer may have overdosed on something! Hank go grab the Narcan! Now!"

Cold and out of breath, James and Hank were met at the Serenity House entrance by Sister Voyant and Miracle.

"We found Dancer and she's laying in the alley unresponsive!" James informed them. "I'm going to call 911!"

"And I'm going to grab the Narcan!" Hank added, the two men rushing past them.

"It's too late!" cried Sister Voyant, now standing in the center of the doorway. "Dancer's already gone!"

PART TWO

CHAPTER TWENTY-NINE

IN THE TWINKLING OF AN EYE

Wednesday, January 9, 2019

Over the past several weeks much has happened. The group have held their tenth, eleventh, twelfth, and thirteenth gatherings, with today marking their14th Serenity Meeting. Christmas has come and gone, along with New Year Day's 2019. And four days ago – on Saturday, January 5, 2019, Dancer's funeral was held at United in Victory.

A curtain of sorrow drapes Serenity House. Eyes bloodshot red, Sharon sat listlessly staring at Dancer's empty chair.

"Dancer's funeral was simply beautiful!" said Sister Voyant. "I'm still finding it hard to believe she's gone! And my…my…my…all those wonderful things people said about Dancer and her ballet dancing. All of that talent gone….in the twinkling of an eye."

"What a loss!" said Sister Jackson. "I miss that girl so much! And every time I think about having to call her parents and give them the terrible news! I've known the Hawkins' for years...and that one of the hardest things I've ever had to do in my entire life."

"So much pain and sorrow," said Sister Voyant. "You know, Dancer's mother Dr. Lila Mae Hawkins and I were old classmates at Western High School. We both graduated in 69."

"No, I didn't know that Claire," said Sister Jackson.

"Yes…we are old classmates," said Sister Voyant. "It's a very small world, indeed."

"My best friend is gone!" Sharon cried out, staring at the front door. "I am devastated! I can't stop crying! I should have done more to stop her from leaving! She would still be here!"

"Sharon my Beloved, you've got to let that go," said Sister Voyant. "Stop blaming yourself. You told us that you woke up and came downstairs just as Dancer was about to leave. That's no coincidence, my Beloved. For all we know, God could have been using you to try and save her. God sends us help…but in doing so…He still gives us our own free will to choose."

"But Sister Voyant, Dancer was my best friend!" cried Sharon. "Man o' man, would I do anything to have one of her hugs right now! I miss her so much. Walking down to this meeting without her this morning was so tough…I didn't think I could do it."

"We all miss Dancer," said Sister Jackson, glancing at the Christmas tree. "Perhaps now would be a good time to open the gifts she placed for us under the tree. We've been putting it off, but maybe we should go on and open them."

"I concur," said Sister Voyant. "Dancer may have left those gifts under there never realizing it would be one of her last acts of kindness. Opening them may be difficult…but at the same time healing."

꙼

Dancer's Christmas gifts were all meticulously wrapped in purple Christmas wrapping papers and bows. Dancer placed a gift for everyone under the tree – each person's name written on a gift tag. The group all began unwrapping their gifts, Hank telling them, "I can't even remember the last time somebody gave me something for Christmas."

"The same applies to me too!" said James.

"My ladies always give me Christmas gift!" declared Willie. "And I –".

"And you what?' asked Sharon.

"Ay, yi, yi, yi, yi," stammered Willie, imitating 'Lucy Ricardo' of the 1950s television sitcom, 'I Love Lucy.'

"The last person who gave me something for Christmas was Mama Betty," whispered Miracle, slowly opening her gift.

"Mama Betty?" asked Sister Jackson. "Who's that?"

Miracle continued opening her gift, answering Sister Jackson's question with a silent response.

Sister Jackson went about opening her and Sister Voyant's gifts, everyone tossing wrapping and tissue paper to the floor.

"Dancer would have been rushing to pick that paper up" said Sister Jackson. "Sometimes, we fail to realize the treasure we have…until it's gone."

Simultaneously, the group all pulled their gifts out the boxes, looking with great surprise at one another's gifts. For they all were the same – a stuffed purple bear with open arms wearing a t-shirt that read, 'Here's Your Hug for Today.'

꙼

Overtaken with grief by Dancer's Christmas gift, the entire group began to weep.

"It's not fair!" cried Sharon. "Why did Dancer have to die?! She was one of the good ones! She didn't deserve to die! That should have been me! I overdosed too! Why am I still here?"

"You overdosed?" asked Willie.

"Yes, I overdosed!" sobbed Sharon. "I should be dead and gone! Not Dancer!"

"Oh, my Beloved," said Sister Voyant. "Share what is on your heart."

CHAPTER THIRTY

SHARON'S STORY – CHASIN' THAT HIGH

Wednesday, January 9, 2019

Sharon stood up from her chair, tears streaming down her face, prepared to bare her soul.

"Heron was my universe," said Sharon. "And everything I did, revolved around it. My trip to the outer limits of destruction started out with my cousin 'Juicy.' And Juicy had the streets on lock!"

"With a name like Juicy, I'd like to meet her!" laughed Willie nudging Hank.

"Me too!" said Hank.

"You both already know Juicy," said Sharon.

"We do?" said Willie and Hank turning to look at one another.

"Yep," replied Sharon. "Especially you…Willie. Juicy is none other than your aunt…by marriage of course…and United in Victory's 'First Lady'…Jacqueline Just."

The group all let out a collective gasp of disbelief with Sister Voyant asking, 'First Lady? Oh my…that's Juicy?

"That's right…but you wouldn't know that…because now she's all cleaned up."

"My Lawd!" said Sister Jackson, licking the chocolate icing of a donut. "I can't see 'First Lady' ever being called a name like Juicy!"

"Take it from me Mama Jackson, First Lady Jaqueline Just is juicy from back in the day," said Sharon. "My mother and I stayed with Juicy and her mom…my Aunt Margot… after we relocated to Baltimore from New York. I was about 10 at the time. I didn't hang with Juicy…she was popular…pretty…and petite. Me on the other hand…I was unliked…unaccepted and unpopular. But that all changed once my 'Cousin Mal' taught me how to defend myself," said Sharon balling up her fists and throwing a few jabs. "My mantra became…'I ain't no damn punk!' Anyway, my mother eventually moved out of Aunt Margot's and got her own place. We fell out of touch with them, but one day when I was about 18, I ran into Juicy, and we started hanging out. We went to parties and out clubbing. She was a few years older than me, and my mother thought she was a bad influence. She told me to stop hanging about with Juicy. But I didn't listen. I enjoyed hanging out with my older cousin. She was fun to be around and very spontaneous. One night, we got all dressed up to go to a club called 'Hammerjacks'. I was waiting for Juicy in her room when I watched her shoot up some drugs! I was shocked. 'Jacqueline shoots up drugs?!' I thought. 'I didn't know she got high!' I was shocked. I thought to myself, 'Not Miss Prissy!' I knew she could down some alcohol…but –"

"First Lady drank too?" asked Sister Jackson.

"Oh yeah!" said Sharon. "She could put away some Hennessy! Now of course…you would never know that now! Well, the next thing I know, she was handing me a syringe asking me to try it. 'What is it?' I asked. 'Heroin', she replied. I said, 'No, I had better not. I've heard some really bad things about that stuff…and I don't need no more problems. Besides, I don't like needles.' Then Juicy started taunting me, saying, 'Sharon is a scaredy cat…Sharon is a scaredy cat! Na…na...na…na…na!' I told Juicy, 'Me a scaredy cat?! Never! I'm not afraid of nothing! I ain't no damn punk!' 'Well, try it then!' she dared. And so, I did. That Heron took me to a total state of euphoria! After that first time, I was hooked! And all I wanted was to experience that feeling again…and again…and again."

"I know the feeling," said Hank.

"Before I knew it," continued Sharon. "I was doing anything and everything to support my drug habit! And I didn't give a damn about no consequences! But while I was living in a false world of pleasure, my real world was falling apart. I abused heron…and heron abused me…it was my batterer. I wear long sleeves now just to cover these track marks on my arms," said Sharon, pulling up the sleeves of her shirt. "Each one represents a time I got high…and the beating I was inflicted on myself every time I shot Heron in my body."

Sharon stood silently – momentarily staring at her arms before continuing with her story.

"Like I said earlier," she said, "Jacqueline got 'clean.' Me on the other hand…I got clean too… 21 years later! I spent over decades of my life chasing that high until one day me and my get high buddy 'Felona' who everyone called "Fee-Fee," bought our dope. We were happy too! We laughed and danced all the way back to an abandaminium —

"Abandawhat?" asked Hank.

"Abandaminium," replied Sharon. "Abandaminiums are vacant houses where people live rent-free and get high."

"You mean like 'Trap Houses?'" asked Sister Jackson.

"Yeah, that's right," said Sharon. "What you know about Trap Houses Mama Jackson? You don't know nothing about no streets. All you know about is church.' And food…Sharon thought silently.

"I've been around the block a few times," said Sister Jackson. "I ain't been saved all my life. Now, times a wastin'. Go on and finish your story, Sharon."

"Anyway, after me and Fee-Fee got back to the abandaminium, we shot up our stuff and we were feeling good! But then we got hungry. 'Hey Sis, you want to go get something to eat?' she asked. 'Hell yeah!' I said, 'I'm hungry as a mo-fo!' So, we started walking towards 'Crazy John's' on Baltimore Street...right there on The Block...or 'The Blizzock' as we used to call it to get something to eat...walking past the strip clubs and other places down there," recounted Sharon, imitating their fast pace. "We were walking along when all of a sudden...everything went black!" said Sharon, bringing her words and walk to an abrupt stop.

"Black?" asked Mama Jackson.

"Black," replied Sharon. "That was crazy right? After everything went black, something happened to me...and I have never told anybody this...because I thought people would think I was crazy. But I had an out of body experience! I stepped out of my body and looked at my lifeless self...sprawled out on that sidewalk on Baltimore Street. I had overdosed...and I was dead! 'How can I be standing up here...but laying down there?' I asked myself, said Sharon, staring downward. "Fee-Fee is kneeled down shaking me and screaming, 'Sharon, girl get up! Get up Sharon! Don't die on me Sharon! Get up!' But I wasn't breathing...wasn't moving...nothing," said Sharon, laying herself flat on the floor and staring up at the ceiling to depict the moments. "Unconscious, yet wide awake, I am seeing and hearing everything that is happening...in slow-motion. Fee-Fee yelling at me to get up. People have gathered around to watch...some are nonchalantly walking by as if nothing is happening. Fee-Fee is yelling at them to help. And I'm screaming as loud as I can to wake myself up...to regain consciousness...to get up...to do something...anything...but nothing is working."

"My God!" said James.

"But then," said Sharon, shaking her head, and holding up an index finger. "I could hear the voice of a man shouting, "I'm a physician! Let me through!' Recognizing him, Fee-Fee shouted, 'Please Doc, help my friend Sharon!' Placing two fingers on my wrist, Doc declared, 'She doesn't have a pulse!' Bawling her eyes out, Fee-Fee blurted out, 'She OD'd on Heron! Please do something Doc!' Doc pulled a can out of a bag he was carrying, and squoozed its contents up my nose," Sharon recounted, referring to the word 'squeezed.' I watched my outside body step back into the one on the ground! I was one with myself again!" shouted Sharon, sitting upright. "Gasping for air...but breathing" she coughed. "After asking if I was okay, Doc stated, 'It's a good thing I had that Narcan in my bag.' I would later learn that Doc's name was Dr. Gregory Branch, and that he was the Health Officer for Baltimore County. I met him one day and thanked him for what he did that night. But I didn't deserve it! I shouldn't be here! I should be in a grave...not Dancer."

CHAPTER THIRTY-ONE

AN INFECTION CALLED UNFORGIVENESS

Wednesday, January 16, 2019

Another week went by, and the group were well into their 15th Serenity Meeting. Willie could hear the others talking – but wasn't paying attention. He was too busy thinking about Sharon. While the others slept, he and Sharon had been meeting up late into the night and having sex.

I can't wait to be with Sharon again! he thought. No woman has ever made me feel the way Sharon makes me feel! This must be what it feels like to fall in love…because all I can think about…is her. I can't believe it! I never saw this coming!

Willie could hear Sister Jackson ripping open a bag of Doritos, ceasing his sensual thoughts about Sharon. Everyone turned towards Sister Jackson, including Sister Voyant, who was speaking. Sharon and Willie pulled out their cell phones and began secretly texting one another.

'Look at Sister Jackson eating those Doritos!' Willie texted, including several food emojis. "She eats all the toes…Doritos…Fritos…Tostitos…you name it!'

'LOL!' Sharon texted back, meaning 'Laugh Out Loud!', followed by several emojis crying with laughter. "She sure does!"

'And look at how she's staring down at those Doritos before she puts them in her mouth!' Willie texted. 'Salivating…like she's about to make love to them."

'Just like we will be doing later,' texted Sharon.

'Sitting over here thinking about it now!' Willie texted back. 'Can't wait!'

"Willie!" put that phone away before I take it!" bellowed Sister Jackson, prompting them both to put away their phones.

❀

Accompanied by the sound of Sister Jackson digging in her chip bag and crunching, Sister Voyant she told the group, "My Beloveds, I want to thank each of you who have shared thus far. Pouring out is so powerful...so cleansing...so rrrrrefreshing…so rrrrrejuvenating. The spirit of addiction can only occupy space rent-free in our minds...if we allow it to...it's eviction time!"

"What you just said about eviction time reminds me of a scripture," said Sister Jackson, drawing sighs from the group. "The Bible says in Matthew 8 that Jesus evicted demons out of a possessed woman, and that the demons jumped into pigs, and the pigs jumped clear off a cliff!"

James rushed over to Mama Jackson with his Bible. Mama Jackson rolled her eyes and looked over at James. Willie could tell she was annoyed.

Rushing over to her with his Bible opened, James told her, "Sister Jackson, it says right here in Matthew 8 that Jesus casted the demons out of a possessed man into a large herd of pigs and the whole herd rushed down the steep bank into the lake and died in the water."

"Ain't that what I said?" asked Sister Jackson.

"No, not at all," said James.

"Well, that's exactly what I meant," retorted Sister Jackson.

Walking back to his seat, James mumbled to Willie, "Mama Jackson needs a Picture Bible!"

Now seems to be a good time to ask Mama Jackson what I've been wanting to ask for a long time, thought Willie. Raising his hand, Willie said, "Mama Jackson."

"Yes Willie?" asked Sister Jackson – with Doritos dusting on her lips. "What is it that you want to ask me?"

"Well Mama Jackson, speaking of pigs, I've been meaning to ask you something" said Willie, failing to notice Sharon shaking her head 'no.'

"Please don't take this the wrong way," requested Willie. "I know how sensitive you ladieswomen are when someone says something about your eating."t what you eat....

"Go on Willie!" urged Sister Jackson. "We don't hold nothing back in here! Go on and say it!"

"Well, Mama Jackson, this is all about addictions, and you eat junk food non-stop. Is it possible you might be addicted to junk food? I'm just saying," said Willie, drawing a collective gasp from the group.

❀

Mere seconds went by, but for Willie it seemed like an eternity. Sister Jackson stood peering at him, prompting him to loosen his collar.

Taking a deep gulp, he asked, "Is it something I said?"

He quickly turned to the group, inquiring, "Don't you all agree with me? Doesn't Mama Jackson eat junk food all the time?"

"Beloved, I can't see a thing," replied Sister Voyant looking around the room.

Miracle snickered, while the others acted busy to avoid answering his question.

"What!" roared Sister Jackson. "Me addicted to junk food?! Of course not! Every now and then I might have a little snack…a little somethin'…somethin'…a little Debbie cake every now and then! I ain't hurtin' nobody!"

"Mama Jackson, I'm not trying to be smart, but you eat a whole lot of those little cakes!" said Willie.

"Oh no you didn't!" said Sister Voyant.

"Oh gosh…yes he did," commented Sharon.

"What you trying to say Willie?" shouted Sister Jackson. "That I'm fat?! Fat like a pig?!"

From the walls of The Deacon Roy Jackson room hung several framed photos of famous African Americans – Former President Barack Obama, Blues singer Billie Holiday, abolitionist Frederick Douglass, civil rights leader Dr. Martin Luther King, Jr., entrepreneur Madame C.J. Walker, playwright Lorraine Hansberry and poets Langston Hughes, and poet Maya Angelou. James walked over to the photo of Maya Angelou, and said in his deep voice, "When somebody shows you who they are the first time...believe them," quoting Angelou.

"I wasn't talking to you Mr. Know it All!" screamed Sister Jackson.

Offended, James stood up and said, "Mr. Know It All? I beg your pardon!"

"You heard what I said James!" yelled Sister Jackson. "Now sit down!" Directing her attention back to Willie, she blasted, "I'm waiting Willie! What you got to say! That I'm fat like a pig! Is that what you were insinuating Willie!"

"No, Mama Jackson," replied Willie. "I wasn't saying that at all. I just noticed that you tend to 'pig out' a lot on junk food."

"I know I don't pig out on junk food!" shouted Sister Jackson. Do I?" she asked, looking at the others. "Do you all think I pig out on junk food?!" Everyone began trying to look busy again, while Miracle began laughing.

"Why are we wasting our meeting time talking about me anyway!" shouted Sister Jackson, slamming her Doritos bag down on the table. "This meeting...all of these meetings…are all about you!" she said, pointing her finger at each of them except Sister Voyant. "That's right! This meeting is about all of you! Not about me! Did you all hear me! This meeting is all about you! Not about me!" she yelled.

Sister Voyant stood, while Sister Jackson continued her ranting and raving at the group.

"Our meeting for today has ended my Beloveds," said Sister Voyant. "Same time...same place...next week...I love you all." Turning to Sister Jackson, she asked, "Audrey, would you mind waiting behind with me?"

Heated over the day's meeting, Sister Jackson flatly replied, "Okay, Claire."

The others gathered their belongings and began leaving, staring at Sister Jackson on their way out the door.

"Is everyone gone? Asked Sister Voyant?"

"Yes," replied Sister Jackson.

"Audrey, please come over here to me."

Sister Jackson walked over to Sister Voyant, who took her by the hand.

"Audrey, my Beloved Sister in Christ...tell me…what brought you to this place?"

❋

A few seconds went by, and Sister Jackson stood in silence, wearing a vexed look.

"Audrey my friend," said Sister Voyant, "I know these meetings are tough. Tough on them...and although we do not like to admit it...they are tough on us too. Do you want to pour out to me my Beloved Sister?"

"I ain't got nuthin to pour out about," said Sister Jackson. "Not a thing. Don't you worry about me Claire. I'm just fine."

"Noooooo," said Sister Voyant, shaking her head in disagreement. "You're not fine my Beloved. What took place in today's meeting...that's not like you."

"It's just that sometimes...what's said in these meetings dredges up terrible memories of all I went through," said Sister Jackson.

Turning to look at Sister Jackson's snack table, Sister Voyant said: "Sister Jackson...that junk food you eat...baby that ain't nothing but a weed. It's time for you to get to the rrrrrroot, my Beloved! You battled addiction...and you won. You have been battle-tested and came away with the victory. And now, you are a strong soldier in the Army of the Lord! But Audrey...there's something else you need to conquer...yes...something very deep. Through my spiritual lens, I see an old, open wound that is still hurting...still bleeding...won't heal...can't heal...because it has an infection called unforgiveness! You need to forgive yourself, Sister Jackson! That's the rrrrrroot!"

"Oh Claire," cried Sister Jackson. "You would never understand.

"Ahhhh...Audrey...don't make that assumption," replied Sister Voyant. "You don't know the story behind the oil in my Alabaster Box...and I don't know yours."

"Claire...I did something so unconscionable...I dare not repeat it."

"Sister Jackson, you are infected with 'unforgiveness.' And that infection has been living inside of you for far too long! It's time to fight that thing with a healing, soothing antibiotic called 'forgiveness'. It's time for you to forgive yourself."

"But Sister Voyant," sobbed Sister Jackson, "I did a terrible, terrible thing!"

"God's love is unconditional, Audrey," said Sister Voyant. "When you used drugs...God loved you. When you stopped using drugs...God loved you. He never stops loving us...we just stop loving ourselves. And oft' times, it's because we can't forgive ourselves for something we did."

"That's right where I am," said Sister Jackson. "I will never forgive myself for what I did."

"Audrey, my Beloved. There's not a sin in the world that God... through the shed blood of the Lamb... His son...Jesus Christ...won't forgive us for. And if God ...our Creator...The Alpha and The Omega...The Beginning...and The End...can forgive us...certainly we can find room in our own hearts to forgive ourselves."

"I know you're right, Claire," said Sister Jackson, wiping away tears. "I wish I could forgive myself...but I can't."

"Don't wish my Beloved...pray...because God can hear you. Guilt makes so much noise in our minds, it clouds our ability to hear Him. But He can hear us. And right now, I can hear Him as clear as day. And Audrey, God is telling me to tell you it's time...time for you to face your past. You can't put it off any longer. There's no more time to waste."

"Face my past?" asked Sister Jackson. "I can't face my past, nor do I want to. I'm too afraid of what might happen...if I did."

"Audrey, as Believers, we know that God did not give us the spirit of fear," said Sister Voyant. "You know just as well as I do that the same God who brought you from where you were to where you are now, is the same God who will be with you and give you the strength to do what you can't do for yourself. No, no, no Sister Jackson...you are not alone in this. And whatever it is...whoever it is...that you need to face...face it with unwavering faith and trust that God will be right there with you. God's Word is true! He will never leave your nor forsake you, my Beloved!"

"You're right Claire," replied Sister Jackson. Claire has put this off long enough."

"Thank you, Jesus!" shouted Sister Voyant.

"But I will need to talk to the Pastor about taking off for about a week or so to start the process of straightening things out," said Sister Jackson.

"We will be okay, Sister Jackson," said Sister Voyant. "We'll make out just fine until you get back. Just do what you need to do. And when you get ready to do it, read...not try to recite...Psalms 27:1. Now, let's pray to our Heavenly Father!"

After praying, the two women shared a long, tear-filled hug, Sister Jackson making up her mind to begin to the difficult journey of facing her past.

CHAPTER THIRTY-TWO

A VOICE FROM THE PAST

Saturday, January 19, 2019

It was a cold winter day, and snow covered the streets of Baltimore. Inside the Edmonson Village home of Carl and Caroline Howard, warmth from the oven and its inviting smells filled the air. Dressed in her white, usher uniform, Caroline stirred pots of food, while Carl sat at the kitchen table reading The Baltimore Times newspaper.

"I got my seasoned greens and smoked ham hocks simmering on the stove, homemade macaroni and cheese baking in the oven, and my turkey wings stewing in the slow cooker!" said Caroline, dipping a spoon in the greens and slurping the juice.

"And that food sure smells good!" said Carl.

"That's our dinner for tomorrow after church," said Caroline. "You know I've always cooked Sunday dinner on Saturdays. No cooking or cleaning on Sunday! That's the Lawd's day!" she shouted, doing a praise dance.

"Caroline, why are you cooking in your usher's uniform?" asked Carl.

"Carl, I haven't even had a chance to change my clothes yet," Caroline replied. "I urshered for a funeral this morning and once I got home, I came straight to the kitchen." Glancing at a bag of potatoes and yams sitting on the kitchen table, she declared, "Just look at those bags sittin' over there! I still got to peel them potatoes and yams! I promised the Ursher Board I would fix homemade potato salad and candied sweets for the dinner being served after the Anniversary Service on tomorrow."

"Me and some of the other deacons helped to set-up for the dinner," said Carl.

"I got too much to do!" said Caroline. "I should have never told the Ursher Board I would cook...knowing I got to march too! We have been practicing our special march for the past three weeks! The church is gonna be packed for the Ursher's Anniversary, and we plan to come down the aisles with our best march! And just a few weeks ago, I stood on my feet half the night for the church's New Year's Eve Watch Night Service! I'm a servant of the Lord, but they are workin' this poor servant to death!"

"Maybe you should say 'no' sometimes if it's too much," said Mr. Howard. "They'll understand."

"I can't do that, Carl! They need me to do all those things! You know that! But between all the services and being on hand for funerals too… my bunions hurt!" she said, taking off her white nurse's shoes. "And my feet and back are sore too!"

"There's some 'Bengay' upstairs in the medicine cabinet," said Carl.

"And that's just what I'm gonna be smellin' like too! A durn medicine cabinet!" replied Caroline. "I ain't putting that ointment on my joints! And my Lawd…the artha-ritis in my knees is bothering me too!," she said referring to 'arthritis'. "And it feels like my gout wants to flare up! And just look at my ursher's uniform, Carl!"

Looking over his newspaper, Carl asked, "What's wrong with your uniform, Caroline?"

"You know I keep my uniform pristine white! But hot grease splattered all over it while I was in the kitchen helping to fry chicken for Sister McIlveen's repast after her service today! Now, it's all soiled! Lawd have mercy! Why did Sister McIlveen have to die when she did?! As busy as I am! I tell you, a Saint's work ain't never done!"

"Caroline honey, that cake sitting over there on the counter that you baked for Pastor Payne looks delicious," said Carl.

"Thank you, Carl,," said Caroline. "You know Pastor Payne loves my homemade lemon cake! He requested I bake one just for him. He shouldn't even be eating cake, being diabetical and all."

"You mean with him having diabetes?" asked Carl.

"Whatever you want to call it, he ain't supposed to be eating all that sugar! But I guess Pastor Payne figured he's been eatin' sweets all this time and it ain't killed him!" Caroline commented, walking over to the cake plate and lifting its cover.

Ahhhhhhh," she said, inhaling the cake's sweet aroma. "Jesus Himself would have eaten this cake! What a thing of beauty! Look at those perfect layers! Look at that homemade lemon frosting runnin' down the sides! What a glorious cake!"

Caroline stood looking at the cake momentarily until remembering something else she needed to do.

"Oh Lawd!' she exclaimed.

"What's wrong now?" asked Carl, his eyeglasses peering over the newspaper.

"I promised that heathen brother of mines Michael I would stop past the senior building he lives in and drop him off a plate of food. I got too much on my plate to be droppin' him off a plate!"

"You shouldn't be dropping that snake nothing off," sneered Carl.

"I know, but he's still my bruuuuuuther!" said Caroline. "And I promised him I would do it! I'll tell you this! When Gawd calls me Home, one thing folks can about Caroline Howard is that I was a woman of her word!' Glory be to Gawd! Thank ya Jesus!" she proclaimed, doing a praise dance across the kitchen floor.

Across town, Sister Jackson was riding in an 'Uber' towards her home in Northwest Baltimore.

It sure was nice for Pastor Just to allow me to take the next few days off to get some things in order, she thought. And he insisted that it be paid time off. That was mighty gracious of him too. I cooked, cleaned, washed, and folded the laundry, and other chores. That should hold things over until I get back.

The drive in the 'Uber' took her through familiar neighborhoods – home to pieces of her history. Peering through the car's windows, Sister Jackson's face reflected on its glass while she reflected on her past. Once the driver reached her destination, she thanked him and walked into the house carrying her purse and other belongings. She sat down her things, turned on the lights, and momentarily glanced around.

It's still so hard to coming into this house, she thought. It's full of furniture…but feels so empty since Roy died. She headed for the kitchen, where she began searching through the cabinets.

It ain't a chip in this house! she said. I can't believe I left out and forgot all my snacks! I mistakenly left them all at Serenity House! she lamented, trudging upstairs. Reaching her bedroom, Sister Jackson sat her purse on the bed and headed over to an oak dresser to look for her old phone book.

I used to write down all my contacts' names, addresses and phone numbers in that book, she recalled. But after Roy and some of the youth at the church showed me how to work my cell phone, I began storing my contacts in my phone. Now, everything is so high-tech. So much has changed over the years.

Sister Jackson began digging through the drawer's varied contents, reflecting,

This was always me and Roy's catchall drawer. We dumped all kinds of things in here. Jewelry, old watches that needed batteries, ink pens, church pins, loose change, prescription bottles…long expired that need to be thrown away, and other items. And here…all these things remain.

She sifted through the drawer, picking up several items and reminiscing until reaching her phone book.

"Here you are wedged all the way in the back of the drawer," she said, removing it. "Your cover is coming apart from the spine and you have a few water spills and other stains…but you're still intact. Even my maiden name written on blue ink across the front is still just as legible now as it was years ago. You and I got a little age on us now. But we're still effective."

Flipping through the pages, she came across names and phone numbers of people she had not seen or spoken to in years.

"To my knowledge, some of you are alive and well…some have died, others have moved away, and some of you…well I don't know where you are," she surmised, still talking to her phone book. She continued thumbing through the phone book until reaching the phone number she dreaded calling.

I sure need somethin' sweet right now! she thought. But it ain't a thing in here to eat that's sweet!

Betwixt and between making the call, Sister Jackson stood looking at the number for several minutes.

I don't know if I should do this. After all these years, maybe the phone number has changed. Maybe they moved away. What if she answers? What will I say? What will she say? Maybe I should just wait. My Lawd…my heart feels like it's about to pound through of my chest!

During her internal debate, thoughts of the conversations and events of Serenity House came to her remembrance.

I can still hear Claire telling me there was no time to wait, she recalled. And that God is with me every step of the way…and that fear is not of God. And what about Willie, Sharon, Hank, Miracle, James, and poor Dancer…whose precious life was snatched away because of drugs? Claire and I have spent countless hours preaching to them about overcoming their addictions. Part of that was encouraging them to face their fears. What kind of example am I…if I am scared to death to face mines?

Now sitting on the bed – her Bible and purse beside her, Sister Jackson reached inside her purse. Taking out her cell phone, her hands began trembling. Although it was dead of winter, sweat poured from her forehead and brow. She opened her Bible to Psalms 27:1 – the scripture Sister Voyant instructed her to read. Reciting it aloud, while dialing the number, she said: 'The LORD is my light and my salvation; whom shall I fear? the LORD is the strength of my life; of whom shall I be afraid?'

Gospel music blaring from a radio, Caroline sat at the kitchen table peeling potatoes and yams. In her haste to cut the vegetables, she cut her finger, and was now sporting a bandage. Carl had since left the house to pick up some things she needed from the store.

Ring! Ring! Ring!

"Lawd have mercy! No sooner I started peeling these potatoes and yams again, my phone starts ringing!" fussed Caroline. "Who in the devil could that be calling?" Looking over at the Caller ID with a squinted eye, she declared, "I don't recognize this number! It's probably one of them telemarketers, or robots calling me," she said, referring to 'Robocalls.' I shouldn't even answer it!"

Picking up the phone she pleasantly answered, "Good Afternoon. Praise the Lord!" After waiting for the person on the other end to say something, she again said, "Good Afternoon! Praise the Lord!" Again, there was no response. "I said, Good Afternoon. Praise the Lord!" Once again, there was silence. Clearing her throat, she loudly said, "Listen! I'm over here workin' like Martha back in Jesus' day! I haven't even had a chance to take off my ursher's uniform! Sister McIlveen at the church died, I got chicken grease all on my ursher's uniform, and on top of that, I cut my finger cutting potatoes and yams and almost bled to death! Now, I got too much going on over here to sit on the phone listening to you breathe in my ear! You're about to meet Evangelist Click-up! Now, I'm gonna say this one mo' again! Good afternoon! Praise-The-Lord!" she hollered in the phone.

Finally, the person spoke.

"Hello…Caroline…is that you?" asked the caller.

"Yes, this is Caroline…who is this?!"

"Caroline…this is 'M.'

"What?!" screamed Caroline, nearly dropping the phone.

Shocked, Caroline stared at the phone in disbelief.

"Hello, are you still there?" asked the caller.

"Yes, I'm still here!" shouted Caroline. "You got some nerve calling my house you 'Spawn of Satan!'"

"Just hear me out Caroline," said the caller.

"Why should I hear you out, you sinful heathen you! I was in here minding my own business cooking and listening to gospel on Heaven 600 and here comes the devil herself! Get thee behind me Satan!" she said, pointing the cross hanging from her neck, at the phone.

"Please Caroline, just give me a chance to say what I need to say," said the female voice.

"You ain't got a durn thing to say to me after what you did!" bellowed Caroline. Oh Lawd! I'm about to hang up this phone!"

"No!" exclaimed the caller. "I meant…please Caroline...don't hang up."

"What do you want you wretched woman from the pit of hell!" yelled Caroline. "You have vexed my sperrit!" she said, referring to 'spirit.' "It was a terrible day when they let you out of jail you beast!"

"Please Caroline…I did my time…just let me say a few things."

"You got 30 seconds witch!"

"I'm sorry Caroline…Lord knows I am."

"You should be sorry after what you did! You should have gone straight to hell with gasoline drawers on!"

"You have every right to be angry with me Caroline. But all I want to do is to set things straight with you and Michael. That's why I'm calling. Do you know where he is?"

"Yeah, I know where my bruuuuther is! What's it to you?!"

"I need to talk with him and you Caroline."

"Talk to me and Michael! For what! There's nothing to talk about! And the last time I talked to you, you cursed me out like a dawg! Lucky for you, you're on the phone and not standing here in front of me! Because if you were, I'd sling one of these potatoes over here right between your eyes! Just like David did Goliath!"

"Caroline…so much has changed…I have changed."

"I don't believe that for a moment you sinful heathen! A tiger don't change his stripes! I wish the he–." Caroline stopped, catching herself. "Lawd! You have vexed my spirit so bad, you almost made me cuss!"

"I'm sorry Caroline, but I just want –"

"Go on and spit it out you viper! "You got 10 seconds!"

"It will take longer than 10 seconds Caroline. Can we please meet at our old lunch spot…The Double T Diner on Baltimore National Pike? Just you and me. It'll be my treat."

"Your treat, huh?" said Caroline scratching her chin, weighing the matter.

"That's right."

"I don't know why I'm agreeing to do…but must the Lawd tellin' me to do it…'cause I sure don't want to…but alright. When?!"

"Next Wednesday…Wednesday, January 23 at 10 a.m."

"I'll be there!" replied Caroline. "And if you are one minute late, I'm leavin'! The countdown starts at 10 o'clock!"

"Okay Caroline. I'll see you then."

"And Caroline…"

"What!" yelled Caroline.

"Thank you."

"Yeah! Yeah! Yeah! Whatever!" said Caroline, hanging up the phone, clicking off the caller.

"Wait until Carl gets back, and I tell him who just called me!" said Caroline, resuming her peeling. "There ain't a thing in the world that woman can say for me to forgive her for what she did. Not only to me…but my family."

CHAPTER THIRTY-THREE

THE MEETING AT DOUBLE T

Wednesday, January 23, 2019

Outside, it's a cold Baltimore winter morning. Inside Serenity House, things are sweltering hot. Sharon and Willie are locked in a tight embrace kissing – sneaking in some affection before the others arrive for the group's 16th Serenity Meeting.

"What if someone walks in and catches us?" asked Sharon.

"Who cares?" asked Willie. "You're the one who wants to keep our relationship a secret…not me."

"That's because there should be no hanky-panky going on here at Serenity House," said Sharon.

"I didn't read that in the House Rules," said Willie, prompting the two to giggle. Hearing footsteps, Sharon said, "Here they come!" She and Willie rushed to their seats.

Sister Voyant entered and abruptly stopped. She began motioning her hands slowly in the air and looking around the room. Puzzled, Willie and Sharon looked at one another and shrugged their shoulders.

"Emmmm…I feel love in the air," said Sister Voyant melodiously. Stunned, Willie and Sharon once again turned and looked at one another, their mouths agape.

"Naw Sister Voyant," said Willie, dismissing the claim. "Before you came in, the only ones in here were me and Sharon. And there's definitely no love in the air between us!"

"That's right," said Sharon. "I can't stand Willie's guts! I was about to punch him in the mouth before you came in!"

"Uh-huh," replied Sister Voyant doubtfully. "Tell it to the hand" – she said throwing up her hand – "What my eyes can't see…my spirit can feel."

❧

It was a little before 10 a.m., and everyone was present for the day's meeting. Carrying her jewelry box, Miracle was the last to arrive.

"Where's Mama Jackson?" asked Sharon.

"Yeah, where is Mama Jackson?" Willie asked. "I know she's not coming late! She's a stickler about being on time for these Serenity Meetings! Always talking about 'We ain't got much time.' She probably couldn't find the time to pull herself away from food," he said, imitating stuffing food in his mouth, sending he and Hank howling with laughter.

"That's enough Willie!" said Sister Voyant. "Sister Jackson had some important business to take care of and won't be at this meeting. Now my Beloveds, everyone join hands before we go into our Serenity Prayer. Willie since you got so much to say, now would be a good time for you to lead the Serenity Prayer."

Willie's laughter came to a screeching halt.

"Me?!" he asked sounding like 'Donkey' from the movie, 'Shrek.'

"Yes you Willie," said Sister Voyant. "You've never led the Serenity Prayer before. There comes a time when you have to be comfortable doing things on your own."

"Yeah Willie," teased Sharon. "Go on and lead the Serenity Prayer if you can."

Closing her eyes tightly, she added, "We're waiting."

Willie began, "Now, I lay me down to sleep. I —"

"That's a children's bedtime prayer!" said Sharon opening an eye and peering over at Willie.

"Willie trust yourself and pray from the heart my Beloved," urged Sister Voyant.

"Father God, in the name of Jesus!" said Willie with great authoritativeness. "I ask that you forgive us of all of our sins! And I ask that you look over Mama Jackson…wherever she may be," he said, before going into the Serenity Prayer.

❧

At the Double T Diner, Caroline sat in a booth drinking a mug of coffee and fussing to herself.

"Confarnit that 'M'! Caroline muttered, eyeballing her watch. "The heat stopped working in my car during the drive over here! I nearly froze to death! I was colder than a naked Eskimo in Alaska! That ole 'Bride of Satan' better be here on time! I got here early, and I requested a booth by the entrance so I could see that evil woman the minute she walks in! It is now10' o'clock. Once my watch reads one minute after ten, I'm leaving! She's got about 30 seconds left!"

The restaurant's door swung open.

"Why in the world would someone come in a restaurant eating a cookie?!" Caroline wondered. Ol' glutton!

Caroline watched the woman's eyes scan the restaurant. Their eyes met up and she began making her way towards Caroline.

Why did that big ole woman look at me and start walking over here? I don't know her! Maybe, she got me confused with somebody else, Caroline speculated. People always think I look like somebody they know! I've even been told I look like Benonce', she told herself, referencing Beyoncé. Every time I see her, she's shaking her sinful booty everywhere! Lawd! That fat woman eating that cookie is coming straight over to me! Maybe she knows me from church.

❀

Sister Jackson thought the cookie she was eating would quell her anxiety. It did little from preventing her to want to turn around and head back outside.

I've come too far to turn back now, she thought. Besides, Caroline already sees me. It's been over 25 years but I'm sure that's Carol. She still looks like the Caroline of yesteryear…just older. A lot of people…including me…always thought she looked like a younger version of 'Aunt Esther' from 'Sanford and Son.' She really looks like her now…right on down to the church hat and wig.

Once Sister Jackson reached the booth, she and Caroline stared silently at one another.

"Can I help you?" Caroline finally asked, looking at Sister Jackson with a squinted eye.

"Don't you know who I am?" asked Sister Jackson. "Don't you recognize me?"

"No ma'am!" said Caroline, taking a long sip of coffee. "I don't."

"You can't?"

"No, I can't place your face."

"Caroline," said Sister Jackson. "It's me…'M.'"

"What?!" screamed Caroline, coffee blowing from her mouth. "'M' that's you?! Lawd have mercy! Girl you are big as a house! I didn't even recognize you!"

Caroline's loud reaction prompted waiters, waitresses, and patrons to turn and gaze in their direction.

"What happened to you?!" asked Caroline.

"Do you mind if I have a seat?" Sister Jackson asked.

"Em, em, em, go on and have a seat!" said Caroline, staring at Sister Jackson in utter disbelief. "My Lawd, 'M'! How in the world did you get so big? The last time I saw you 'M', you were as skinny as a rail! If it weren't for your voice, I'd swear it wasn't you!"

❀

Squeezing into the booth, Sister Jackson felt herself about to get defensive.

I hate when people ask me why I picked up so much weight! People don't understand how much it hurts when they say things like that! But I need to hold my tongue and keep my thoughts to myself! I would hate for Caroline and I to get off to a bad start after all this time. I appreciate the fact she even showed up. But Caroline has always been a woman of her word. If she says she's gonna do something…she's gonna do it.

"Lawd have mercy!" cried Caroline. "'M' you done gained so much weight you could hardly fit in the booth! I can't believe you swolled up like this!"

"I know I picked up a few pounds. I —"

"More like a few hundred pounds!" said Caroline. "'M', I swear fore God…you picked up a whooooooooole lot of weight!"

A waitress walked over to their table, asking if they were ready to order.

Thank God she came over here when she did, thought Sister Jackson. I can't take too much more of Caroline goin' on and on about my weight.

"Give us a few minutes," said Caroline. "We haven't looked at the menu yet." After the waitress walked away, Caroline asked, "Lord have mercy 'M', what are you gonna order?!"

"I'm not sure yet, Caroline," said Sister Jackson. "But while I'm deciding, I would like to tell you why I wanted us to meet today. There's some things I need to resolve once and for all, and I need your help."

Back at Serenity House, Miracle sat slouched in her chair staring at her jewelry box.

For some strange reason, I wanted to bring my jewelry box to today's meeting, thought Miracle. I can't explain why. I just felt the need to bring it.

"Praise God my Beloveds!" said Sister Voyant. "And Willie you did an outstanding job leading us into the Serenity Prayer. I am proud of you Willie! I am proud of all of you! The results of all your progress and hard work are about to pay off! Graduation Day is almost here!"

Graduation, thought Miracle. This will be the first Graduation I have ever experienced. Mama Betty homeschooled me until she got sick. And after Mama Betty's died when I was 15, I never stayed in any school long enough to graduate. I was always running away. This is the first time I ever started something and completed it! But I don't have a single person to invite. Not a one…because after Mama Betty died, I no longer had a family. After the graduation, people will be posing with big smiles taking pictures with their family and friends. But me…I will be standing all alone.

Without even realizing it, Miracle opened her jewelry box. Its music began to play.

"What a lovely tune," said Sister Voyant. "That's Tchaikovsky…and I absolutely love Tchaikovsky."

"My Dad loves Tchaikovsky too," said Hank, leaning over and peering inside the jewelry box. "And look at that ballerina spinning. Kind of reminds me of Dancer."

"I know," Miracle whispered softly. "Every time I see her twirling, I think of Dancer."

"Oh my God!" said Sharon. "I can't look! I know I will start crying my eyes out!"

"Miracle, who are those people on those photos inside your jewelry box?" asked Hank, prompting Miracle to slam the jewelry box shut.

Miracle sat quietly for a few moments and began to sob.

"Miracle, my Beloved," said Sister Voyant. "Don't be ashamed of a scar. It is only a mark of your testimony to remind you that you were stronger than whatever or whoever tried to hurt you."

"How did you know I had a scar?!" Miracle screamed. "I never told anybody I had a scar!"

"Miracle, I'm not talking about a physical scar," said Sister Voyant. "Remember, I can't see what's on the outside…only on the inside. I'm talking about the scar that's on your heart."

Miracle stood and placed the jewelry box in her chair. She took off her coat, exposing the hoodie beneath it. She pushed up the sleeve of her hoodie and held out her arm.

"I thought you were talking about this scar!" she cried. "The one on my arm!"

Shocked, James and the others couldn't believe what they were seeing. Staring at the large, raised Mark on Miracle's arm, he thought, Oh my God! That young girl's arm looks like she has been branded!

"What happened to your arm Miracle?" James asked.

"I've had this scar since my mother…since my mother…."

"Since your mother what my Beloved?" asked Sister Voyant.

"I can't say it!" cried Miracle.

"Yes, you can baby," said Sister Voyant. "Please share my Beloved…tell us…who is responsible for not only the scar on your arm…but the scarring on your heart."

CHAPTER THIRTY-FOUR

MIRACLE'S STORY – CLINT'S PLANTATION

Miracle stood gazing at the group trying to determine if she would share the story behind her scars.

All this time, I have tried to cover myself up…and now here I am about to bare it all. Should I do this? Maybe if I do…they will understand me better. They shared their stories…I guess I can share mines too.

Taking a deep breath and exhaling, Miracle began, "I was adopted, and my adoption records are sealed. So what I am about to share for the first time in my life was told to me by my adoptive mother 'Mama Betty' when she gave me this jewelry box on my 15th birthday. That day, she sat me down on her bed and told me the story of how I was born a crack baby because my biological mother was addicted to crack…and that one day, she burned me on the arm with her crack pipe. Rubbing her arm, Miracle said, "That's how I got this scar. And after my biological mother burned me, she put me in the microwave."

"That's terrible!" said James.

"Fortunately, somebody reported her to Child Protective Services, and they, along with the police, came to the house and found me….and my older brother…who she was literally starving to death. They removed us from the home, and we were put in foster care."

"They should have locked her up and thrown away the key!" bellowed Sharon.

"Mama Betty adopted me a short time afterwards…I was still a baby," continued Miracle. "I'm not sure what happened to my brother. Mama Betty told me my biological mother was locked up for what she did to us…and for having a stash house. I believe she's still in jail. As for my biological father, I don't know what happened to him.

Maybe if he had been there, he would have stopped our mother from trying to kill us. The day Mama Betty told me that story was the day I learned she was not my biological mother. She was the only mother I knew. After telling me the story, she gave me the jewelry box," said Miracle, walking over to the chair, and picking it up. "Mama Betty asked me to open the jewelry box. Crying, I opened it, and inside was this photo," said Miracle, taking out the photo and holding it high for everyone to see. "I asked Mama Betty who those people were, and she said, 'Miracle baby…that's your biological family."

❀

Tears streamed down Miracle's face into her jewelry box.

"My God!" said James. "That jewelry box is your Alabaster Box!

"I've cried a lot of tears in this box," said Miracle. "A lot of tears. Anyway, Mama Betty went on to tell me she changed my name to 'Miracle Smith'. Miracle…because she said it was a miracle that I survived being born a crack baby, being burned with a crack pipe, and being put in the microwave...and Smith being her last name. Soon, I began noticing Mama Betty was losing a lot of weight. What I didn't know, was that she was dying of breast cancer. Not long after she told me the story of my past, she died. But not before she gave me a picture of the two of us standing in front of the house. After Mama Betty passed, I was put in a group foster home, but kept running away. I would always be found and taken back. Until I met Clint."

❀

Recalling the freezing cold day, Miracle began walking about the room, rubbing her arms.

"I will never forget the day I met Clint. It was so cold, I thought I would freeze to death. I was walking downtown when I heard someone beeping a car horn. I turned around, and there was this guy driving a fancy Cadillac. 'Need a ride?' he asked, slowing the car, and pulling over to the curb. "I normally wouldn't get in the car with strangers, but it was cold, I was hungry, and I was tired. So, I got in. 'My name is Clint,' he said, "What's yours.' Shivering, I whispered, 'Miracle.' I was 16 at the time, and Clint looked to be about 35…good looking…and was dressed real nice. 'Are you hungry?' he asked. "Yyyyes," I stuttered. So, he took me to an IHOP to get something to eat. I was so thankful for a nice, warm hot meal because I was starving. I normally kept thing to myself, but he seemed nice enough, so I opened up to him about the things that were going on in my life at the time. Clint listened and said he could help. He also promised me a better life. …I thought, 'Anything is better than going back to a group home!' So, I went with him. He put me in a nice place…much nicer than the group home. He also bought me expensive nice things! For the first time since Mama Betty died, someone made me feel beautiful. He took me Rusty Scupper and Phillips Seafood and other fancy restaurants to eat. He purchased nice clothes for me to wear and bought me pricey bags and shoes. No one had ever spent money on me like that!"

"I sure had money spent on me like that…courtesy of the ladies!" said Willie.

"Shut up Willie!" said the group.

"Well Clint told me, 'Babe, you got the prettiest eyes I've ever seen! But I'm going to take you to a friend of mines who will make them even more stunning.' He took me to some lady who arched my eyebrows and did my eyelashes. He also got my hair and nails done! I really felt beautiful then! He got me my very own apartment, furnished it, and paid all the bills! I was so grateful to Clint! Not only that, but I trusted Clint…even opening-up to him about my past. I loved him and would have done anything for him…and I did."

Miracle stood for a moment…mentally visualizing Clint entering her apartment – with two strangers.

"I ran up to Clint and gave him a big hug," said Miracle. "That's when I noticed two seedy looking men standing behind him…undressing me with their eyes. I mean they were literally looking me up and down salivating! One of them said, 'You were right Clint! She is a purdy young thing! And just look at those eyes!' The other one cackled and said, 'She's got a nice body too! I'd sure like to smell her panties!' I thought to myself, These guys are perverts! Why did Clint bring them here?! They made me uncomfortable, so I asked Clint who they were. He took me to the side so we could talk privately. That's when I found out that all the things Clint bought for me weren't free. The place I was in…the clothes…the lavish dinners…the purses…the shoes…all of it…came with a price! And now, it was time to 'pay the piper.'"

Sniffling, Miracle cried, "Right out of the blue, Clint asked me to have sex with those creeps! Can you believe that? The man that I lost my virginity to was asking me to sleep with two complete strangers! 'What?!' I asked. 'You mean you want me to sleep with them?!' I told Clint, pointing at the men who were looking over at us. "Yes, that's what I'm saying, Babe.' I told Clint, 'Hell no!' I'm not doing that! Have you lost your mind!" Well, the two men heard me, and said, 'Clint, we can take our money elsewhere,' and began walking towards the apartment door. 'Wait!' Clint told them. 'Give me a minute.' Turning to me, he whispered, 'Now Babe, I need you to do this for me. You owe me! See, when I found you honey, you were nothing! A throwaway! Trash I picked up off the street! You have all of this', he said, looking around the apartment…because of me! If you love me…you will do what I am asking…no…not asking…telling you to do!' And so, I did what he wanted…I slept with those two dirty, old men…who were probably old enough to be my grandfather!"

"Man," said Sharon. "That ain't right."

"I felt so violated and dirty!" said Miracle. "I figured I did what Clint wanted, and that would be it. No more men. But little did I know, that wasn't the ending…but the beginning. Clint brought more men by my place. He knew I hated sleeping with these men…some who asked me to do things I wouldn't dare repeat… so he started giving me Cocaine to snort…to take my mind off what I was doing. And it did. High as a kite, I became oblivious…numb to the sexual acts. My apartment became nothing more than a sex parlor…until the day he told me, 'Pack your things. I'm taking you somewhere.' I grabbed a few belongings…including my jewelry box…and he drove…what seemed like for hours…making lots and lots of turns. He finally turned onto a dirt road until he reached a big farmhouse sitting alone in a desolate area. I didn't see another house nowhere in sight. I had no clue where we were. We got out the car and went inside. That's when I saw several other girls…who all looked to be about my age…some even younger…some Black…some White…some Asian…all nationalities…sitting on men's laps…being fondled…being kissed…or escorting them into rooms and shutting the door. Them…and now me…all a part of a human sex trafficking ring."

❊

The group sat stunned.

"Poor baby!" said Sister Voyant.

"I've heard about minors being abducted for human sex trafficking," said Sharon. "But Miracle, you're the first girl I ever met that it actually happened to."

"I was a human sex slave," replied Miracle. "All of us were. The things that Clint did for me…that I thought were so wonderful…well all of that was just a set-up…to get me to that terrible…terrible smelly place. Clint operated the sex ring with two other men. And all of us girls…well we were all hand-picked by Clint. But me…I was the most special of them all! He told me, 'Babe, you're my Best Money Maker…my Number One…my Bottom Bitch!'"

❊

Miracle took a long pause. After the moment, she told the group, "I wanted to let that sink in! The fact that I was so brainwashed…so gullible…so naïve…that I really believed the things Clint said, were compliments! That those statements made me better than all the other girls! I even began to lure other runaways into Clint's trap by telling them I knew someone who could give them a better life…and get them off the streets. Once they were in the car, Clint drove them to the place I came to call 'The Hideaway', because I never found out exactly where it was located. So, there I was…on a farmhouse…which was little more than a plantation for sex slaves…existing…but not living."

"That's deep," said James.

"And I was in deep too," replied Miracle. "So deep, that I thought that this was the life I was supposed to be living. That I owed Clint…because after all…he saved me. That was my thinking…until…"

"Until what my Beloved?" asked Sister Voyant.

"Until I finally saw Clint for who he really was!" Miracle hissed. "A master manipulator and a liar who had been using me all that time to make money…lots of money for him and his partners. I'm sure the money he initially spent on me…paled in comparison to the money he made off me! He never loved me! The money he doled out initially was just an investment for a much bigger payday! So many men…or 'Johns' as we called them…young…old…Black, White, Asian, you name it…wanted the services of 'The Girl with the Pretty Eyes'. That was me! I was the one they all wanted! I was Clint's Best Money Maker…his Number One…his Bottom Bitch!' At least I thought I was until I overheard him telling another girl, the same exact thing! I couldn't believe it! I felt hurt, betrayed…all of it! And those feelings of rejection that I had when I met him…well they all came back with a vengeance! I wanted to spit in his face! I wanted to curse him out! I wanted him to hurt him like he hurt me! But I was smart enough to know better than to act out or try to buck Clint! As hard as it was to hold in how I felt…I realized there was another way to skin that cat…to skin him…just like he skinned me! And the way to do that was to hit him in the pocket…to remove myself…'The Girl with the Pretty Eyes'…from his revenue stream! I had to escape from 'The Hideaway.' And I was willing to die…trying."

❈

Miracle again paused…the group captivated…by her story.

"And so, I began plotting how I would get away from there," continued Miracle. "Waiting patiently…for the right opportunity…the right moment…the right time! And it came in the wee hours of the morning…it was still dark outside. Clint and his partners were drunk. They had been up all night celebrating a big money-making weekend. Having just serviced a 'John,' I told Clint I wanted to wash up. 'Okay, but no funny stuff!' he stammered, drinking alcohol straight out the bottle. I got a washcloth and towel, wrapping the towel around me…and slipping my jewelry box beneath it. I headed to the bathroom, locked the door, and took a shower…petrified over what I was about to do…and even more terrified of being caught. But then, I remembered something Mama Betty told me when I was about seven."

❈

Recounting the conversation, Miracle said: "Mama Betty heard me crying in the backyard one day and calling out for her. Looking outside the kitchen window, she saw me cornered by a barking dog. He or she…looked like it would bite me at any moment! Mama Betty ran out of the house with her broom and shooed the dog away. And then she hugged me and told me everything would be alright. And then she said. 'Miracle baby, I won't always be here to rescue you…to help you in times of trouble…you have to learn to pray…you have to learn to call on the name of Jesus in times of trouble.'"

"There's power in the name of Jesus!" exclaimed James.

"And that morning…in that grungy bathroom… located in that shit-hole of a place where they kept us captive…bound…like we were slaves on a slave ship…I did just that…I prayed and called on Jesus. I could hear Clint shout, 'Miracle, what are you doing in there? What's taking you so long! I got another client out here waiting for you!' I yelled, 'Coming Babe…still cleaning up!' I turned the shower back on and ran the faucet to mask the sound of what I was about to do. I tried opening the bathroom window…but I couldn't get it open!' Miracle said, depicting how she strained to raise it. "So, I took a deep breath…and with all the strength I had…I kicked out the bathroom window," said Miracle raising a leg to demonstrate the feat. "After that, I backed up a few steps and hurled myself through the broken shards…still clutching my jewelry box. I jumped from the second floor…but I didn't care how far up I was or the distance below. Like our ancestors who leaped off the ships during their voyage across the Middle Passage…I jumped…preferring to be free in death…rather than alive in captivity."

❈

The group listening in amazement, James said, "Miracle, what you just said was very poignant."

"And then I heard a loud thump!" exclaimed Miracle. "That was the sound of me hitting the ground! I landed on a pile of autumn leaves which helped brace my fall."

"God cushioned your fall with nature," commented Sister Voyant. "How profound!"

Miracle continued, "I opened my eyes and looked around for my jewelry box…and there it was lying next to me…still intact," she said, gazing at her cherished keepsake. 'Thank God, I'm alive!', I thought. But above, stood death…in the form of Clint… staring at me…through the frame of the broken window. I assume Clint must have heard the glass shattering and rushed to the bathroom. 'That crazy Bitch jumped out the fucking window!" he shouted. "We have to go after her! We can't let her get away!' And then he was gone. I knew they were coming after me, so I picked up my jewelry box and started running as fast as I could! I can still hear the rustling sound of my footsteps running through leaves and brush! Running like a slave running for freedom…which in essence…I was. Running towards nowhere…but at the same time running towards somewhere…because I did not know where I was. I kept thinking…'I can't get caught! I can't be taken back to the Plantation! But I kept running because I knew its overseer Clint…and his henchmen were coming after me! And that if I were caught…I would be beaten…maybe even tortured…or perhaps killed. All those things were running through my mind while my legs were running to escape."

Panting to demonstrate how tired she was, Miracle told the group, "I was getting tired, but somehow…someway…I found the strength to keep running…and not look back. Good thing it was fall. Had it been winter, I would have froze to death…because I was completely naked! I came upon a wooded area and ran through that…branches hitting me in the face…thistles cutting my feet! And then I saw something I couldn't believe!"

"What was it?!" asked Hank.

"A road!" replied Miracle.

"Thank God!" said James.

"But then," said Miracle - a petrified look overtaking her face – "I could hear the sound of voices and a dog barking. They were coming after me."

Tears rolling down her face, Miracle cried, "At that very moment, the sound of that dog barking…took me back to the dog barking at me in Mama Betty's backyard. I saw myself as a little girl…wearing a blue dress with white flowers and my hair in two long plaits with white barrettes at the end…Mama Betty having styled my hair earlier that morning. And here I was again…hearing the barks of an angry dog…but this time…running for my life. I could hear Aunt Betty's voice saying, 'Miracle baby, I won't always be here to rescue you…to help you in times of trouble…you have to learn to pray…you have to learn to call on the name of Jesus in times of trouble.' I called on Jesus the same way I did in the bathroom…but this time…I called it out loud…'Jesus!'… the sound of barking and voices drawing closer and closer. I kept running towards the road…the sunshine above it…light in the midst of my darkness. 'Keep running towards the light!' I kept telling myself! 'Keep running towards the light!' I finally reached the road…and saw no houses…no cars…nothing. But I started running down that road calling out to 'Jesus' to help me. That's when I heard the sound of a car."

"A miracle!" exclaimed Sister Voyant. "Just like your name."

"I was totally exhausted…running on fumes…wanting to turn around and look…but afraid to do so. I saw an old, beat-up station wagon…being driver by an old White lady…chug past me. It was loaded with all kinds of junk…clothes…antiques…you name it. She honked the horn, slowed down, and pulled over. 'Come on Dearie!' she yelled out the window. "'Hop in!'" And I did…bloodied…bare…and beaten. I slid down in the front seat…while peering out the dusty sideview mirror. In it…I could see Clint and his boys…they had reached the road. 'Please pull off!' I begged. She pulled off and I could hear what sounded like her car backfiring. It could have been Clint shooting at us. I don't know which it was! All I know is that she was my angel! I don't even want to think what Clint would have done he had gotten to me before she did. That was the last time I ever saw Clint."

Stopping momentarily…taking in the breadth of what she shared, Miracle stared back into the faces of the group – her mind still on the stranger who plucked her up from the side of the road.

"My name's Susan…what's yours?" the woman said, peering up at her rearview mirror. 'Those men who were chasing you…who were they? And where are your clothes?' she asked glancing over at me while she drove along. And what's that you're clasping so tightly in your hands" she wanted to know, looking at my jewelry box. I was trying to answer her questions, but I was so traumatized by my ordeal that my mouth was moving…but no words were coming out. She turned onto another road, constantly checking her review mirror to make sure no one was following us. I was huddled in the passenger seat…shivering from fright and fear. After riding along for a while, she looked in her rear-view mirror once more and pulled over to the side of the road, opening the hatch of her station wagon. She returned carrying a jacket and some clothes in her hand and told me to put them on. Then we pulled off…and it didn't come soon enough for me. I was afraid Clint and his boys would catch up with us and kill us both."

Remembering the events like they happened on yesterday, Miracle began to describe 'Susan.'

"Susan looked like an old Hippie," said Miracle. "She was skinny and had on a paisley top and blue jeans. She had long, stringy grey hair that was parted down the middle, and wore a band around her head with a peace emblem on it. She even had on round glasses like the ones John Lennon would wear."

"You know about John Lennon?" asked Hank.

"A little," said Miracle. "I've been around all kinds of people…which exposed me to all kinds of music. Anyway, Susan told me she bought the station wagon to drive to something called Woodstock back in the 1970s."

"Wow Woodstock!" said Hank. "I remember hearing my grandparents talk about Woodstock and how they drove to New York to attend. They always said attending that music festival was one of the best experiences of their lives."

"I was at Woodstock too," said Sister Voyant.

"You were at Woodstock?!" asked Sharon.

Sister Voyant replied, "I certainly was! It was such a beautiful event…people of all hues coming together and enjoying music…peace…and one another! What a beautiful time in our history! As you can tell from my attire," chuckled Sister Voyant, the style of the day stuck with me. Now go on my Beloved…finish your story."

"I put on the clothes and jacket Susan gave me…and she had the heat in the car turned all the way up… but I couldn't stop shaking," recalled Miracle. "Susan pulled over again, opened her hatchback and started digging through all the things jumbled up back there. A short time later, she returned with a blanket. She wrapped it around me and said, 'I hope this helps to warm you up Dearie', and we drove off. I managed a raspy, 'thank you,' completely astonished that a stranger could be so kind."

Once again, Miracle began to cry, her voice breaking. "Susan said to me, 'I was on my way into town when I saw you naked as a jaybird running down the road. And to be perfectly honest Dearie…I hadn't planned on leaving so early. But the good Lord hastened me out of the bed early this morning before the rooster crowed. And when you get to be my age…if the Lord hastens you out of the bed, it's best you listen. And Dearie…take it from me…I normally don't take that road because too many deer and possum run across there…and I would hate to one or run one over. But something told me to take that road…and that's when I saw you running down the road naked as a newborn baby.' She stopped by a convenience store and got me a cup of hot tea to drink…and a warm sandwich. That, along with the blanket finally helped me to stop shivering. Barely able to speak about a whisper, I thanked Susan and asked, 'What year is this?' 'Why Dearie, it's 2017', she replied. Using my fingers, I began to count the years since Clint took me from my apartment. I was 16 when I was taken in 2014…and now I was 19. I had been a human sex slave for three years."

"That's unbelievable!" said Sharon.

"I know," replied. Miracle. "But that's what happened to me. Susan told me she knew of a place in town that could help me. She took me to a shelter…prayed for me…and dropped me off. I never saw her after that. The shelter took me in…and asked what happened to me. I was so ashamed…I didn't tell them. I never told anyone what had happened to me…until now. So, there you have it," said Miracle. "That's my story." Picking up her jewelry box, she opened it, and removed one of the photos. To the sound of the jewelry box's melody, Miracle displayed the photo. "This is me the photo Mama Betty gave me," said Miracle. "I guess I was about six at the time. This other photo…well that's me when I was a baby and the biological family I never had. That woman holding me…that's my real mother! And if it weren't for her…I wouldn't have gone through the hell I went through! Everything that happened to me was all her fault! Thanks to her, I came into this world crack addicted and she tried to kill me in the microwave! Looking at her arm, Miracle shouted, "Just look at what she did to me! She scarred me for life! I hate my mother for what she did to me! I hate her! If I ever laid eyes on her…I don't know what I would do! I will never forgive her for what she did to me! Never!"

Sister Voyant now stood next to Miracle. She placed her hand on Miracle's shoulder, and for the first time,

Miracle didn't shun away.

"Miracle baby…I know how you feel…but you have to forgive," said Sister Voyant. "You have to forgive your mother for what she did…in order to heal…in order to move forward…in order to let go of the anchor that has you stuck. Until then, you will continue to be a lonely passenger… floating aboard a boat…unable to move in any direction…with no paddle…no sail…floating amidst the ugly, dark sea of unforgiveness.

"Did you hear anything I just said"!" yelled Miracle. "Anything!"

"Alright everybody," Sister Voyant told the rest of the group, "I am going to need you all to leave us alone. I am now adjourning today's meeting. We will meet again here next week."

On their way out the door, the others gave Miracle words of encouragement.

"I'll be praying for you Miracle," said James. "You're going to be alright."

"Hang in there, Miracle," said Hank.

"I know it took a lot for you to share your story," said Sharon. "That was a very brave thing to do."

"Kiddo, Big Willie's proud of you!" smiled Willie.

"Thank you," said Miracle, mustering a smile. "Thank you all."

"Is everyone gone?" asked Sister Voyant.

"Yes, they're all gone," replied Miracle.

Taking Miracle by the hand, Sister Voyant told her: "Now Miracle, I heard everything you said. But if I can forgive my husband for what he did to me…I know you can forgive your mother."

Sister Jackson and Caroline spent the last hour and a-half eating and catching each other up on what had transpired in their lives over the years.

"I'm so sorry about you losing your husband and all," said Caroline. "I can't even count the number of funerals I've attended at March Funeral Home – East…and West and Carlton Douglass Funeral Home! But like I told you earlier, Carl is still alive and kickin'! Me and that man have now been married for almost 30 years."

"I remember when you too got married," said Sister Jackon. "My how time flies!"

"Speaking of time flying, I got to get ready to fly home," said Caroline. "My calendar is chock full of things to do! And before I even do that, I got to take my car someone to get looked at! My heat completely stopped working on my way over here to meet you!"

"My Lawd!" said Sister Jackson. "As cold as it is?"

"Yep," replied Caroline. "No warning or nuthin! I was colder than a popsicle!"

"Well thank God for agreeing to meet with me Caroline," said Sister Jackson.

"You're welcome, 'M', said Caroline, looking around the restaurant. "I haven't been to Double T since you and I would come here for lunch years ago."

"Still looks the same," said Sister Jackson.

"It sure does," said Caroline.

Sister Jackson picked the check up from the table and signaled to the waiter she was ready to pay. After paying for their lunch, Sister Jackson reached into her purse and handed Caroline $40.

"M, you ain't got to worry about payin' me that money back," said Caroline, trying to return the money.

"I owe you that money," said Sister Jackson. "Please keep it."

"Well since you insist," said Caroline, stuffing the money inside her bra. "After all, you did take it out my pockabook."

"Still the same ole Caroline," smiled Sister Jackson.

"I ain't changed a bit!" said Caroline.

"I have," said Sister Jackson. "Thank Gawd for that! Every time I hear that gospel song 'I Know I've Been Changed' by LaShun Pace I feel she's singing about me."

"Praise Him!" shouted Caroline, stepping from the booth and shouting in the aisle.

Once Caroline sat down, she and chatted for a few more minutes and prepared to leave.

This wasn't so bad after all, Sister Jackson thought. And it was so nice to see Caroline after all these years.

"Thanks again for the lunch 'M', said Caroline. "Like I said earlier, I will do my best to get my bruuuuthcr at that Graduation. He's very sickly, but he's still as mean as a rattlesnake! I can't promise I can get him to come."

"Thank you, Caroline," replied Sister Jackson. "I appreciate you even tryin. Oohh, my Uber is outside now," she said, seeing a car pull up outside.

"You never got your Driver's License?" Caroline asked.

"No," replied Sister Jackson. "I kept saying I would get it…but never did."

"Have you seen Miss Moonie?" asked Caroline.

"No, I haven't seen here in a long time. But I plan on inviting her too."

Caroline slid out from the booth. Sister Jackson followed suit but was having difficulty.

"Lawd 'M'," said Caroline. "Your belly done swolled up even bigger since you ate all that food! My Lawd! Can you make it out?"

"Yes Caroline," said Sister Jackson, agitated over Caroline's comment. "Just give me a second. I can make it out."

While Sister Jackon made her way out of the booth, a young man walked over to Caroline and tapped her on the shoulder.

"Excuse me ma'am," he said. "Aren't you Aunt Esther from Sanford and Son? Can I get your autograph?"

"What!" shouted Caroline, looking at him with a squinted eye. "The devil is a liar! Boy I outta go upside your head with my pockabook! I don't look like no Aunt Esther! Maybe Halle Berries," she said referring to Halle Barre. "But not Aunt Esther! Now get on away from here!"

The young man apologized and scampered away. Meanwhile Sister Jackson finally stood up from the booth, still laughing at his exchange with Caroline.

"The nerve!" said Caroline. "I don't know what's wrong with these young peoples today!"

"That wasn't funny 'M'," said Caroline.

"Awww Caroline, chile…give me a hug!"

The two shared a long hug. Before they walked out the door, Caroline said, "Lord willin', I will be at that

Graduation. Hopefully, that heathen bruuuuther of mines will come too."

Back at Serenity House, Sister Voyant finally managed to calm Miracle down. She was now holding Miracle in her arms and rocking her softly. With my many years of counseling and therapy experience, I believe the residents need psychiatric services, intense mental counseling, and therapy to deal with their trauma, she thought. But Miracle is so much younger and fragile than all the others. She is broken. Her spirit is broken...her heart is broken...and her ability to trust is broken — all byproducts of being deeply hurt. I know how Miracle feels. I have walked in those same painful shoes. I understand how it feels to be hurt deeply...to be betrayed by someone you love and trust. I must share my own personal story with Miracle... about what Billy did to me.

CHAPTER THIRTY-FIVE

BLINDED BY JEALOUSY

Like Miracle, Sister Voyant would be sharing her story for the first time. But to tell its harrowing ending, she would have to rewind to its harmonic beginning.

"Miracle...my Beloved, you might think I was born blind, but that was not the case," Sister Voyant divulged. "There was a time I could see just like you."

"Really?" asked Miracle looking up at Sister Voyant, who was still holding her.

"Yes, Miracle. I wasn't always blind," replied Sister Voyant. "I was born and raised in Baltimore...growing up on Powhaten Avenue in Ashburton. An area where many influential African Americans live. My parents lived in a beautiful Victorian mansion. At that time, many influential black doctors, pastors, lawyers, politicians, and others lived in the area and still do. Father was a doctor at Garwyn Medical Center, a pioneering medical building owned and founded by African American doctors who served many in the Black community. I believe it was one of the first Black-owned HMOs in the country at the time."

"Mama Betty would take me there for my shots," said Miracle. "It's on Garrison Boulevard."

"That's right," said Sister Voyant. "Mother was an Art teacher in the city's public school system. Father and Mother both loved the arts. Needless to say, I was exposed to visual and Performing Arts at an early age. Plays, concerts, exhibits, symposiums, you name it. If it had something to do with the Arts, my parents were there. By the time I was five, I was playing the violin, acting in plays, and singing Opera. I was a gifted, highly-intellectual child. Throughout my elementary, junior high, and high school years, I excelled academically. I also participated in and won numerous oratorical contests. In 1969, I graduated from Western High School, and from there I attended The Juilliard School in New York, receiving a full scholarship. There, I received my Classical Music training. While living in New York, I attended the Woodstock festival we talked about earlier. After completing my studies at

Juilliard in 1973, I worked as an actress and singer in New York. I was doing quite well, but Father's health began to fail. I decided to move back to Baltimore to help Mother take care of him. Once I arrived back in Baltimore, I was hired at Social Security on Woodlawn Drive. A lover of knowledge, I decided to enroll at John Hopkins University, graduating in 1975 with a Master's Degree in Public Health. I was 24 at the time. Not long after I graduated, father passed. I – "

"I wish I had the opportunity to meet my father," said Miracle with a dejected look. "I don't know if he's dead or alive. I doubt if I will ever know."

"Never give up Miracle," said Sister Voyant. "God has a special way of revealing things to us when we least expect it."

"I'm sorry to interrupt Sister Voyant," said Miracle, wiping tears from her eyes. "Please go on."

Sister Voyant continued, "I began working part-time job as a counselor with an addiction recovery program. I also earned a second master's degree in 1977, this one in Social Work from the University of Maryland."

"That's pretty impressive," said Miracle. "Graduating from all those schools. I have never graduated from a school. The Serenity House commencement will be my first-ever graduation."

"That's pretty impressive too," said Sister Voyant. "Keep in mind Miracle…you're still very young and have your whole life in front of you. There can be more graduations for you…if that's what you want. Once a person puts their mind to something…there's nothing they can't do."

"Thank you, Sister Voyant," Miracle smiled. "Maybe I will go back to school…just like…Mama Jackson. She told us one day that she dropped out of school, but decided to earn her G.E.D. I think I may do the same…and then go to college."

"That would be wonderful my Beloved!" said Sister Voyant. "Simply wonderful!"

"Go on and finish your story, Sister Voyant," urged Miracle. "I would like to hear the rest."

"Well, my Beloved, I was 26 when I began working with the addiction recovery program. A position as a Clinical Social Worker opened, and I was offered the job. I accepted, with plans to also pursue a doctorate in Public Health from Johns Hopkins. Life was delightful! Aside from losing Father, I never really experienced a major loss or setback. All was going so well for me until…"

"Until what?" asked Miracle. "Please tell me…you can say it."

"Oh, my Beloved," said Sister Voyant with a smile. "You sound like me now…encouraging you all to share your stories. My, my, my…such a hard thing to do. But my Beloved there comes a time when the teachers become the students…and the students become the teachers and we can learn from those we have taught. One is never too old to learn…or too young. I learned a lot from each of you."

"Wow," said Miracle. "That's really nice. I never thought anybody could learn anything from me."

"Well among many things we learned from you story Miracle…was the power of human resiliency."

Smiling, Miracle said, "That's nice to know."

"And one day Miracle," said Sister Voyant. "You will be able to share your story with someone else…another young girl…or even boy…that could save them from the snares of human sex trafficking. And for me Miracle…my snare was Dr. Billy Voyant."

❧

Sister Voyant momentarily sat quietly - slipping into deep thought about her former husband – Billy Voyant.

"I met my ex-husband in 1978 at a gas station," recalled Sister Voyant. "I lifted the gas nozzle to put fuel in my car when a handsome stranger walked over and offered to pump my gas. Well of course I took him up on his offer! He told me his name was 'Billy' and asked me to give him a call, handing me his phone number. 'Maybe we can go out for dinner sometime,' he said. Having been immersed in education, the Arts, and work just about my entire life, I really had not spent a lot of time dating or anything of the sort. But he was so kind and handsome, I thought, 'Why not, Claire? You're 27 now. Take a break…have a little fun. Going out on a date might be nice.' So I called Billy. Now Miracle, not only was Billy 'Eye Candy' as the young folks say, but the man was brilliant! He was a chemist, having earned a PhD in Chemistry."

"He was smart!" said Miracle.

"That's right my Beloved," said Sister Voyant. "However…from the moment Mother laid her eyes on him…she didn't like Billy. She would look at him side-eyed. When we were alone, she would say to me, 'Claire…Sweetheart, there's something about him I just don't like'," said Sister Voyant, imitating her late mother's voice. 'He's not right for you Claire. I don't trust him.' Well Miracle, I couldn't understand why Mother felt that way about Billy. 'Why Mother?' I asked. "Billy's never done anything to you. Why don't you like him?' Mother looked at me with a serious look on her face and replied, 'Call it mother's intuition' Claire…remember this…there's more to a man than looks and intelligence. That's what you're looking at. You can be the smartest man in the world with looks to boot and still be evil. Something about that man isn't right.' I replied, 'Okay Mother'…my mind already made-up to disregard anything she said against Billy. 'What does Mother know?' I thought to myself. 'Now that Father's passed on, I guess she wants me to be all alone…like she is…refusing to date or see another man! Well, I'm not doing that.' So Miracle, I continued dating Billy. I so enjoyed being with him! He was a huge lover of Opera, so we attended many shows together. We traveled to New York to see Broadway shows, and even to the Grand Ole Opera in Nashville. He loved Country Music! He even taught me how to Square Dance! My goodness, we had so much fun! He even proposed to me at a Country Music concert?! Oh my, I will never forget him getting down on his hands and knees on his cowboy attire and asking in deep Southern vernacular, 'Howdy ma'am…do you care to marry me?' I happily shouted, 'Yes! Yes, Billy, I will marry you!' I waited as long as I could to break the news to Mother…and when I did…she was very upset."

"What did she say?" asked Miracle.

"Mother asked, 'What?!' she asked. 'Please tell me you're not serious! You're actually going to marry him?' 'Yes, Mother', I replied. 'What about plans to earn your doctorate?' Mother inquired. 'I haven't heard you say a thing about that lately!' 'Don't worry Mother', I assured her. 'I still plan on attending Johns Hopkins to earn my doctorate.' Mother did all she could to talk me out of marrying Billy. Despite her objections, I married him. It was an unceremonious ceremony…we simply went down to the courthouse and tied the knot. I was so afraid that if we got married in church, my mother would stand and publicly object! So we married in 1979…about a year after we met. I was 28 and Billy was 31. Before long, I noticed things that made me think…'Maybe there is something to what Mother was trying to tell me."

❀

Cupping her hands over her mouth, Sister Voyant looked upward and whispered, "God…please give me the strength to finish my story." Second later, she said, "Thank you, Father," and proceeded.

"Miracle, what I didn't know before I married Billy was that he was as delusional as he was intelligent," said Sister Voyant. "I realized he was suffering from Mental Illness. I married him for better or worse…and I was prepared to honor my vows. With my background and experience, I knew that with help and treatment, Billy could get better. But he was never willing to admit he had a problem. 'How could I earn a Ph.D. in Chemistry, finish in the top 1 percentile of my class, and have one of highest SAT's ever recorded at my high school if I were crazy?' he asked. I said to Billy, 'Honey, I'm not saying you are crazy. All I'm saying is that you need treatment. There are times you are doing and saying things that just aren't normal.' 'Like what?!' he demanded to know. "Well Billy…Honey…like being so paranoid all the time. Accusing me and other people of doing things we're not doing. Things that make me think you may possibly be suffering from 'High Functioning Autism' or Paranoid Schizophrenia.' 'Oh, so now you are calling me a 'Schizo!' he roared. 'Well, how do you like that?' He totally disagreed with that, making it a point to always note how intelligent he was, and that he worked as a chemist. Somewhere along the way, he began to drink heavily, and that only made things worse."

"Really?" asked Miracle. "Why?"

"Well because, alcohol only exasperated his paranoia," replied Sister Voyant. "He became increasingly jealous, controlling, and insecure. Billy was always accusing me of fooling around on him. I was faithful to him. But I couldn't tell him and his delusional mind that. I tried everything I could to hold our marriage together. I'd be lying if I sat here and said I didn't think about leaving my husband…because I did think about it. But I stayed because I loved him…and I really wanted our marriage to work. But no matter how hard I tried, things continued to get worse…eventually escalating to emotional and verbal abuse."

"Did your mother know what was going on?" Miracle asked.

"Miracle, my Beloved, I did everything I could think of to keep what was happening with me and Billy from my mother. The last thing I wanted to hear was 'I told you so.' Finally, in 1984, after years of putting off working toward a doctorate, I finally decided to enroll at Hopkins. My mother was happy about it…but Billy was not. When I told him what I was going to do, he cursed something terrible! 'Rrrrrrrreally?!' I said to him. 'Why are you mad? Why are you upset? You should be happy for me!' He grumbled something and stumbled upstairs to the bedroom. By that time, he no longer worked, having been fired from his job. That meant he was home all the time. Nevertheless, my mind was made up, and at age 33, I began my doctoral coursework at Hopkins. I would come home from work and find him sprawled out on the couch in a drunken stupor with an empty liquor bottle at his feet. Other times, I wouldn't see him at all. He would be downstairs in the back of the basement. That was his little laboratory area. Talk about a real-life Dr. Jekyll and Mr. Hyde — that was Dr. Billy Voyant. And he was becoming more and more like Mr. Hyde."

A wide variety of images coming to mind, Sister Voyant recalled her ex-husband's basement laboratory.

"Billy had all kinds of things in his laboratory area…flasks, pipettes, scales, Bunsen burners, freezers, hot plates, incubators, coolers, stirrers…you name it," recalled Sister Voyant. "I tried not to go anywhere near it…and for the most part…I didn't. My trips to the basement were primarily to the front area. Billy outfitted the basement so that the washing machine and dryer were in the front area of the basement along a few other things. To tell you the truth, I was more concerned that he would mix some concoction in his drunkenness and blow the house up. If he wasn't knocked-out drunk on the sofa or in his basement laboratory, he would be sitting somewhere near the front door waiting for me to arrive home. No sooner than I walked through the door, there he was ready to pick an argument. To avoid violent confrontations with him, I worked longer hours at work and took the heaviest caseload of classes I could take at Hopkins.

For me, longer school and work meant longer hours away from the house. For him, that equated to me spending time with another man. The emotional and verbal abuse now included physical abuse. I remember coming through the door one night and him slapping me across the face. That was the first time he put his hands on me…but not the last. But I took the abuse because I loved him."

"I understand that," Miracle replied.

"Now Miracle, despite all the physical, mental and emotional abuse I was taking — me of all people — a clinical social worker – I still managed to balance school and work around my life of hell at home. After Billy started beating on me, I could no longer hide what was going on from my mother. One day, Mother noticed a bruise on my face. I thought I did an outstanding job of concealing it with make-up. But Mother was not fooled. Never once saying, 'I told you so,' Mother angrily pleaded with me to leave Billy. I told her I would, but never did. I still was holding onto the hope that once Billy got help, we could save our marriage. But in 1985…one year into working on my doctorate, Billy did the unthinkable…a terrible premonition I had about him hurting me…would come to pass."

No longer able to hold back tears, they began rolling down Sister Voyant's face beneath her dark glasses.

"It was Monday, July 1, 1985," recalled Sister Voyant. "Me and a few co-workers had just gotten off work and were walking across the parking lot talking about our plans for the Fourth of July holiday. We all went our separate ways and headed to our cars. Suddenly, out of nowhere, out jumped Billy….all drunk…eyes fireball red… ranting and raving…with a liquor bottle in his hand. He opened the bottle and flung its contents in my eyes. I threw up my hands to protect my face…but it was too late. 'You won't look at another man again Claire!' he hollered. 'And no man will look at you either!' Well Miracle, the bottle did not contain alcohol…but some kind of agent…I'm assuming he mixed in the basement. My eyes began to burn and the light of day I saw just second earlier…was fading to darkness. Screaming for help, I fell to the group. Some of my co-workers hadn't reached their cars and heard me screaming. Seeing them coming to help, Billy ran off. I was rushed to the hospital…but the damage was done. I was permanently blinded."

For several seconds, Miracle and Sister Voyant sat in silence.

"My Beloved…at 34 years of age, I could no longer see. Miracle, my whole life changed. I couldn't work…couldn't drive…couldn't do anything. I moved back home with Mother trying to adjust to my new norm. And Miracle…I hated my husband for what he did! He was sent to jail and is still serving a lengthy prison sentence. But his punishment was little solace for me. I loved that man — gave him every part of me, and he took away my eyesight."

"That's terrible," said Miracle. "I know how it feels to be betrayed…by the one you love."

"That's how I felt," said Sister Voyant. "Soon, I found myself weighted down in hatred for him, self-pity for myself, and anger for the world. I asked myself over and over, 'Why me?' 'I didn't deserve this! I did it right! I waited until I was married to lose my virginity…I obeyed my parents…I went to school…I worked hard…I got good grades! This wasn't supposed to happen to me!' And Miracle, the more I dwelled on all the reasons why I didn't deserve to lose my eyesight…the angrier I became…the more I felt sorry for myself, the more reclusive I became…and the more I detested Billy. And Miracle, my Beloved, I could have stayed stuck in that muck of hatred, self-pity, and rage…but I didn't. You see Miracle, so often we're stuck at the moment in which the trauma occurred in our lives. But Miracle, I was in pain being stuck…in pain being angry…in pain feeling sorry for myself. And to be perfectly honest Miracle…I had never hurt a fly. But I wanted to kill my husband for what he did to me!"

"I can't see you ever wanting to kill anybody Sister Voyant," said Miracle.

"You see me where I am now, Miracle," replied Sister Voyant. "But that's where I was back then. Things like hatred…jealously…and anger…drives people to do all kinds of things they never thought they would do. Stewing in my abhorrence for him, I would think, 'Jail is too good for Billy Voyant! He can still see! But me…he put me in a place where I can no longer do the things I used to do! I said things to myself like, 'I wish he had just killed me! What good am I?'"

"Gee," said Miracle. "I used to feel like that…to be honest…sometimes I still feel that way. What made you change?"

"Miracle, my Beloved, I dug deep…real deep…and from the deepest bowels of my soul …I tearfully cried out to God… 'Lord, help me! I don't want to be like this! Help me! Please God! Help me!' And Miracle, God reminded me of Romans 8:26, which tell us… 'Likewise the Spirit also helpeth our infirmities: for we know not what we should pray for as we ought: but the Spirit itself maketh intercession for us with groanings which cannot be uttered.' Miracle, God can take the prayers of our hearts and perfect them in His own flawless way. And His way is always best…even though we may not understand. And do you know what the Lord said to me, Miracle?"

"No, I don't," replied Miracle.

"God said to me, 'You are going to have to forgive your husband.' I said, 'Forgive my husband? After what he did to me? I don't understand. Why should I forgive him?' But I wanted to move forward, so I stopped questioning God, and asked Him to help me…and He did. Now, it was a process…yes Lord…it was a process! It took some time…but I forgave Billy for what he did to me. Miracle, for six long years I walked around mad with everybody…and sometimes…it's still a struggle. I was 34 when Billy blinded me, and 40 when I finally forgave him…40…a number with such spiritual significance in The Bible. And Miracle, once I forgave Billy, doors of opportunity began to open."

Smiling, Sister Voyant began reflecting on a call she received.

"Miracle, I wasn't even looking for a job. But one day…totally out of the blue…one of my former co-workers called and told me about a counseling opportunity at a behavioral health services agency. I applied for the job and was hired. They eventually offered me a position there as a Clinical Social Worker. I took the position, working there for 27 years – from 1991 until 2018. I probably would have still been there had it not been for my former Western High School classmate Dr. Lila Mae Hawkins –"

"Dancer's mother?" asked Miracle. "I remember hearing her speak at Dancer's funeral."

"Yes, Dancer's mother," replied Sister Voyant. "We are Western High School alums…both graduating with the Class of 1969. She came to the agency where I was working desperately seeking resources to help Dancer. Well Lila Mae and I had not been in touch for years, so when she walked in and told me who she was, I was quite surprised. We chatted about things that happened since we graduated, during which time I told her I lost my eyesight. She told me she and her husband had a daughter…Dancer…and that she kept relapsing. I gave Lila Mae some information I thought might help. She bid me goodbye, and got up to leave and said, 'Oh Claire, I just remembered something. My pastor is opening a transitional house for men and women struggling with addiction. I am praying that Dancer gets into the program. At any rate, I saw a posting on the church bulletin board. He is looking to hire a clinical social worker for the program. Perhaps, it might be of interest. I jotted the information down just in case I ran into someone who would be qualified. Judging from what you are doing here…and all of your credentials…you would be a good fit,' she said, reaching into her purse and handing me the information. 'Why thank you Lila Mae,' I said. 'I love what I'm doing here…but I never know where God is going to take me.' I have to say…there was something exciting about the program being run by a church that excited me. I prayed about it and called the next day. I went through the application process, which included an interview with Pastor Just…and here I am."

"After all you went through, it's nice to hear that something good really came out of your life," said Miracle. "But it's hard to believe anything good will ever come out of mines. I was born a crack baby…and according to Mama Betty… I spent the first few months of my life struggling to survive in a hospital before my mother brought me home. She should have left me in the hospital."

"I know how you feel Miracle," replied Sister Voyant. "So many times, I wished Billy left me right there at that gas pump without ever saying a word to me. So many times, I wished I hadn't stopped at that gas station to put gas in my car…or that I simply refused his offer to pump my gas. But what was done…was done. I couldn't keep looking back…I had to look forward. And that brings me to why I wanted to share my story with you, Miracle. Once my outlook on life changed, I began to see that God had given me a special gift! Like Joseph in The Bible…I was always a dreamer…seeing things, but now I could see things I could never see before…even before I lost my sight! Once I got rid of all that anger and unforgiveness about Billy, The Holy Spirit could dwell inside of me! And Miracle, once that happened, guided by power of The Holy Spirit inside of me, I began to see inside the hearts of people! Miracle, I lost my eyesight, but God gave me insight! And Miracle my Beloved…when I look at you through the eyes of my spiritual gift, I see a void that yearns to be filled. And God wants to fill that space…yes, He does…and He wants to mend your broken heart. He has something wonderful in store for you Miracle. But first, you must let go of hate and unforgiveness. They're poison…toxic things…that kill us on the inside…if we let them. How can The Holy Spirit take residence in a place like that? It's time Miracle…time for you to move forward and became what God has called you to be. You have purpose and you're special! Why do you think you survived Cocaine…being born addicted to it and then re-addicted through your sex trafficker? Why do you think you survived being burned? Why do you think you survived jumping out a second-floor window? Miracle you are a miracle, and you have a great destiny! But the only way you're going to reach it is to forgive your mother."

Miracle jumped up, staring at Sister Voyant in disbelief.

"Forgive my mother? Why should I forgive her? I can't forgive my mother!" Miracle cried. "She ruined my life! I can't believe you feel I should forgive my mother after hearing all I went through!"

"Miracle, the words you just said are nearly identical to what I said to God when He told me I had to forgive my ex-husband," replied Sister Voyant. "Now Miracle…my mother passed away. You still have yours. Now, I don't know where she is my Beloved. But The Holy Spirit is telling me she's out there somewhere. I'm almost 68-years-old Miracle…and one thing I've learned in my years on this earth is that there are always two sides to every story. Now, I don't know who your mother is, or where she could be, but you haven't heard her side yet…just what people have told you. I'm a living witness that God can reveal things when we stop allowing ourselves to be blinded by our own thoughts…insinuations…judgements…and here say. I know it's hard…with all the hurt, disappointment, and pain you've been through. But Miracle, if you can find it in your heart to forgive your mother…then all that I went through would not have been in vain. My story would have helped somebody. I pray that somebody will be you."

CHAPTER THIRTY-SIX

GRADUATION DAY

Friday, February 8, 2019
7 a.m.

Two weeks zipped by flurrying with activity. Sister Jackson returned, the 17th and 18th Serenity Meetings along with rehearsals for graduation took place, and the residents decorated the Deacon Roy Jackson Room for their closing exercises.

High above Serenity House, the sun – marigold in color shined brightly, and birds soared against a backdrop of azure blue skies. Inside Serenity house this beautiful Friday morning, excitement filled the air. It's Graduation Day!

Earlier, Sister Jackson prepared omelets, bacon, sausage, grits, fried apples, Belgian waffles, home fries, and Jiffy Cornbread with corn, crackling and other secret ingredients, along with her special mix 'Sweet Tea' laden with sugar.

That breakfast Mama Jackson prepared, was soooooooooo good! thought Miracle, rubbing her stomach. I've never told her this, but her food always is delicious. But today, it was extra delicious! The tea was good too…but it was like drinking candy!

Knock! Knock! Knock!

I wonder who's at my door? Miracle wondered, walking to her bedroom door.

"Hi Sharon," said Miracle, opening the door, surprised to see Sharon standing on the other side.

"Hey, Miracle," said Sharon. "Do you mind if I come in?"

After a short hesitation, Miracle said, "Okay."

"I know you normally don't allow people in your room," said Sharon. "Sorry for barging in like this…but I was checking to see what you were planning to wear for today's Graduation."

"Hoodie…jeans…the usual," said Miracle. "I don't have any dressy clothes to wear. Why do you ask?"

"Just wondering," chorused Sharon. "I'll be right back," she said, leaving the room.

Hmmmm, thought Miracle. That was strange. Why was Sharon inquiring about what I was going to wear today? I'm pretty excited about graduating today…but I didn't see the need to get dressed up. I don't have anyone coming…besides, I have no dresses or fancy things to wear. I haven't dressed-up since Clint.

Knock! Knock! Knock!

"Come on in," said Miracle. "The door's unlocked."

Sharon walked in toting a large plastic bag and a garment bag draped over her arm.

"Miracle, these things are for you," said Sharon, handing her the items.

"For me?" Miracle asked.

"Yes, for you Miracle," said Sharon with a smile. "Go on! Open them up! Mind if I sit down?"

"Sure, you can sit down," said Miracle, looking at the bags in her hand.

"Whoa, you don't have any booby traps in this chair, do you?" joked Sharon.

"No," said Miracle giggling. "Of course not!"

"Okay," replied Sharon. "Just checking."

Miracle continued gazing at the garment bag and plastic bag.

"Well open them up already!" cried Sharon.

"Okay!" agreed Miracle with giddy excitement.

Miracle began unzipping the garment bag but stopped. "Is there anything you want from me…you know…taking these things?" she asked. "Nobody just gives me anything."

"No strings attached," said Sharon. "While there are those who give always expecting something in return…there are those who give expecting nothing in return…except to brighten someone's day."

Miracle completely unzipped the garment bag, taking out a fashionable short-sleeved white chiffon dress.

"It's beautiful!" cried Miracle, sizing the dress against her body.

"I'm glad you like it," replied Sharon. "Once you took off your big coat the other day, I realized we were about the same size. I wear a size five. Go ahead! Try it on! I'll be right back."

A few minutes later, Sharon returned, her face lighting up.

"That dress fits you perfectly Miracle!" exclaimed Sharon, gazing at Miracle. "It looks great on you! I have a couple of dresses in the closet, so I figured why not give one to you? Look at yourself in the mirror."

Gazing into a standing mirror, Miracle said, "Wow! Look at me! Oh, thank you Sharon!"

"You're welcome," Sharon replied. "Now open the other bag."

Miracle opened the bag, pulling out a shoe box.

"I hope you can fit those," said Sharon. "I wear a size six."

"Me too!' said Miracle, tearing the top off the box and taking out a pair of white heels. Trying them on, she declared, "Sharon, they fit!"

"Great!" said Sharon. "I was hoping they would. Miracle, I'll be back in about 30 minutes to do your make-up and hair."

"Oh, my goodness, really?" asked Miracle. "I didn't even know you did make-up and hair."

"Yeah, I dabbled in it before I was out there…you know…in addiction," said Sharon. "I was planning to go to cosmetology school before… well you know the story."

"I know," said Miracle. "We all have our stories."

"But we made it Miracle!" declared Sharon. "You…me…Willie, James, and Hank. Sniffling, Sharon said, "Dancer isn't physically graduating with us…but I know she's okay. I had a dream about her the other night. She was dressed in all-white dance attire and had these large angel wings, 'Sharon!' she said, barely above a whisper, 'Stop crying! Stop blaming yourself for what happened to me! I believed I could fly…and now I really am!' And she soared upwards…towards Heaven.'"

9 a.m.

Having done Miracle's hair, make-up, eyelashes and brows, Sharon returned to her own room to get ready for the Graduation. Miracle stood staring at herself in the mirror.

"I can't believe you're me!" she told her reflection – also donning dangling earrings, stockings, and a purse – all given to her by Sharon. "Ever since my sex trafficking experience, I have gone out of my way to look unattractive…all the way down to my eyes. I had been touched by so many men…and I hated it! That's why I couldn't stand for anyone to come close to me…let alone lay a finger anywhere on my body. I also made sure I kept this scar on my arm covered…and here I am in a sleeveless dress. But Sharon gave me that shawl on the bed," she said glancing at it, "In case I wanted to cover my arms or got chilly. But this dress…and me…are too pretty today…to cover up."

For the past several minutes, Miracle stood gazing at the beautiful reflection staring back. Talking to the reflection, she said, "Well Miracle, I have to say that since Sister Voyant talked to you about prayer and forgiveness you've had a lot to think about. Afterwards, you prayed and asked God to help you forgive your mother. And things have shifted. You aren't as upset and angry…you're getting along with the others much better now…and Sharon even gave you this make-over! I feel like 'Cinderella' or somebody!" she said spinning around.

The sound of Sister Jackson's voice in the hallway interrupted Miracle's fairytale moment.

"Alright everyone!" announced Sister Jackson. "It's almost time to head downstairs! The Graduation Ceremony will be starting soon!"

"The big moment's almost here!" exclaimed Miracle, walking over to her jewelry box, balancing herself on her heels. "It's been so long since I've had on pumps, I feel like a baby trying to walk!" she laughed. Miracle opened her jewelry box and took out the photos of Mama Betty and her biological family. "My way of having all of you with me when I graduate today," said Miracle, dropping the photos in her purse. "Coming Mama Jackson!" she yelled.

Downstairs, people are beginning to arrive for the 10 a.m. closing exercises. Attendees include family members and friends of the graduates, Mr. Jenkins, and several members of United in Victory Church.

I wouldn't miss this program for the world! thought the church's self-appointed historian Gertrude 'Gertie' Green whom the church members called 'Usher Gossippin' Gertrude.' I need to be here just in case some drama goes down! Not only to witness it…but to record it! And my cell phone is fully charged and ready to go! she said, peering inside her purse at her cell phone. After all, I am the Church Historian!

Usher Green flashed angry looks over at two of the church's other ushers – Usher Annette Gilkesson and Usher Laverne Gilmore, who were standing at the door in usher attire greeting attendees, handing out programs, escorting people to their seats, and giving them fans.

Usher Green silently fumed, I'm still upset with Pastor Just for not allowing me to usher today! Certainly, it had to be an egregious oversight on his part! It must have slipped his mind! Look at Usher Gilkesson and Gilmore standing over there! I should be over there too! Maybe they can tell me what happened! Usher Green marched towards them. Seeing her coming, both ushers held up their hands, gesturing her to 'stop.'

"We don't know why the pastor didn't ask you to usher, so don't ask," said Usher GIlkesson.

"That's right," Usher Gilmore chimed in. "And we don't have time for any of your gossip! We're over here working!"

"That's not even what I was coming over here for!" she told them, doing a turnabout.

For the past several minutes, Usher Green asked several congregants including Mother Pearl Carter, Miss Jenkins, Mrs. Brown, and Deacon Larry Williams, whom they called 'Deacon Lastchurch' why the pastor had not asked her to usher for the day's event. She also posed the same question to Hattie Hatfield, who wore large, expensive hats. None of them know a thing! thought Usher Green! What a waste of my time! She skedaddled over to 'Weepin' Wanda Williams', so named by church members because she cried all the time. In walking over to Mrs. Willams, Usher Green thought, Maybe that crybaby knows something! She also asked, Paula Stepney, nicknamed 'Praiseful Paula' because she loved to shout for the Lord, and nun Sister Wilhelminia Velencia, who came dressed in her habit. They didn't have any answers either. Despite fishing around trying to find out why Pastor Just did not ask her to usher, Usher Green did not reel in any answers.

Out of options, she turned to Deacon Brian Mayberry, nicknamed "Deacon Mumbles" because of his tendency to mumble incoherently. His best friend Deacon Willie Samuels, who was his interpreter of sorts, stood next to him.

Deacon Mumbles works closely with the Pastor and does his biding. Certainly, he knows something! assumed Usher Green. He's my last resort, but I hate to ask him anything! I can't understand a thing he says!

"Do you have any idea why the pastor forgot to ask me to usher today?" she asked Deacon Mayberry. After listening to his rambling, unintelligible response, she turned to Deacon Samuels and asked, "What did he say?"

Deacon Samuels replied, "Deacon Mayberry said,' Pastor didn't tell me why. But if I had to guess, I reckon it's because you do more gossiping than ushering!'" said Deacon Samuels.

"What!" roared Usher Green. "He doesn't know what he's talking about!" said Usher Gertrude marching off in huff. "I don't know why I asked him anyway!" she grumbled under her breath. "I can't understand a mumbling word he says!"

Sister Jenkins who stood a few feet away from the ushers, waved Usher Green over to her.

"Stop running around here stirring up trouble," said Sister Jenkins.

"Stirring up trouble?" asked Usher Green.

"That's right, stirring up trouble," replied Sister Jenkins. "Stand over here with me near the door. I'm watching the peoples as they come in."

"You are such a nosy busybody," laughed Usher Green.

"I'm not a nosy busybody," replied Miss Jenkins. "I just keep my eyes open and my ears to the ground. Besides, I'm President of the Welcome Ministry."

"Welcome Ministry?!' asked Usher Green. "United in Victory doesn't have a Welcome Ministry!"

"Now we do," said Sister Jenkins. "Now smile and greet the peoples."

After exhaling, Usher Gertrude stood next to Sister Jenkins, who vented to her about Mother Carter sitting in a special seat on the front row. "Look at that ole phony Mother Pearl sittin' up there!' complained Sister Jenkins. "I should be sittin' up there! Not her! I'm the rightful Mother of the church! Not her!"

"Please don't start on that again!" commented Usher Green.

"Oh look!" said Miss Jenkins, "There's radio personality Ernestine Jones of WEAA 88.9 FM!"

"Hey Ernestine!" cried Miss Jenkins, waving. "Chile, I listen to you every Sunday morning on 'Gospel Grace.'"

"That's wonderful!" said Mrs. Jones. "We love our listeners!"

"And there's more celebrities from the radio…Doresa Harvey and Marva Williams!" cried Miss Jenkins. "And look…Comedienne Miss Maybelle!"

"Coming in behind them are Rev. Lee Michaels and John Carrington of Heaven 600!" said Usher Green, waving at the two men. "I tell you everybody is here!"

Noticing two people they did not recognize coming through the door, Usher Green asked, "Do you know them?"

"Naw, can't say that I do," said Miss Jenkins, pulling her cat-eyed style prescription glasses up to her eyes, while chewing on Spearmint gum.

"Take that gum out of your mouth in church!," said Usher Green.

"We're not in church! We're in the church house! But since you want to make such a big fuss about it…here, take it!" said Sister Jenkins, folding the wad in a napkin, and handing it to Usher Green.

"Ewwww!" said Usher Green looking at the folded glob. "Why did you hand this to me?!" Rushing to a trash can to dispose of it, she immediately returned stating, "The woman pushing the man in the wheelchair has on an usher's uniform…but I've never seen her before."

❀

For the next several seconds, Usher Green and Miss Jenkins stood looking at Caroline, and her brother Michael "Big Mike" Adams.

"If I didn't know any better, I'd swear that woman pushing that mean-looking man was 'Aunt Esther'," whispered Miss Jenkins.

"She sure does!" replied Usher Green. "From 'Sanford and Son!' And he's a dead-ringer for 'Grady' from the same television show! The only difference is that man's eyes are much lighter!"

"He sure is an evil, ornery lookin' man!" Miss Jenkins observed. "Look at him sittin' in that wheelchair with his face all twisted up!"

"You're right," said Usher Green. "He looks like a real sour puss! And she doesn't look too friendly either…with her eye squinted up. And it looks like they're fussing at one another."

Continuing to gaze at Caroline and Michael, Miss Jenkins said, "Studyin' those two a little closer…I believe I have seen them before…but I can't place where. Now hush-up Gertie and let's get to our seats! The program is about the start!"

"Let's sit back here," suggested Usher Green, pointing to two seats.

"Why not closer to the front near that phony Mother Carter?!" asked Miss Jenkins.

"Because we can see everything from back here," explained Usher Green.

"You've got a point there," agreed Miss Jenkins, the two women scurrying to the seats. "Just as long as it isn't behind Sister Hatfield. We won't be able to see a thing behind that big trapezoid hat of hers!"

CHAPTER
THIRTY-SEVEN

PURGING THE WOUND

Friday, February 5, 2019
11 a.m.

The Deacon Roy Jackson room filled to capacity, the graduates entered in single file procession to cheers and applause. The program now reaching its halfway point, the atmosphere was one of a foot-stomping church service from the very start.

Sister Voyant eloquently delivered "The Welcome" and "The Occasion." Dynamic Gospel trio 'Serenity' – Vonnie, Byrd, and Pam – led by Sister Jackson, sang Will Green's 'Setback for a Comeback', and musician Howard "Buddy" Lakins played the organ.

Sitting on the front row next to his wife Jacqueline, Pastor Just whispered, "Honey, just look at the graduates sitting up front along with Sister Jackson and Sister Voyant shoulder to shoulder facing us all! I am so proud of them!"

"You should be!" replied Mrs. Just. "And they all look so nice! And that young lady Miracle…she looks stunning!"

"Yes, she does," said Pastor Just. "This is the first time I've actually seen her without a coat on and a hoodie pulled over her head."

"To think…she was covering up such beauty!" said Mrs. Just.

"You're right," agreed Pastor Just, turning around to glance at the packed room. "I didn't anticipate so many people being here."

"Yes, it is packed," said Mrs. Just. "And oh my…look at that empty chair draped in purple in loving memory of Dancer! How sad!"

"They are all seated in the same chairs they sat in throughout the Serenity Meetings and in the same seating order," Pastor Just explained. "That chair…was Dancer's chair. It breaks my heart to see that chair there…without her in it."

※

James walked up to the podium, opened his Bible, and read a Scripture.

"'Therefore, if any man be in Christ, he is a new creature: old things are passed away; behold, all things are become new.'" said James. "I have just read 2 Corinthians 5:17."

Making his way back to his chair, Sister Jackson headed to the podium.

"Thank you, James," said Sister Jackson, "And with that, we will move to the highlight of today's program. The awarding of 'Certificates of Completion' to our graduates!"

※

By now, the graduates had all been awarded their Certificates, drawing a standing ovation. Pastor Just now stood at the podium holding a plaque in his hand.

"At this time," said Pastor Just, "We will honor Dancer's memory by presenting her father…Rufus Hawkins…and her mother…our very own Dr. Lila Mae Hawkins…who saw to it that Dancer got in this program…with a plaque in her memory."

Mrs. Williams, whom some of the members called "Weepin' Wanda' ran over to Dr. Hawkins crying, prompting the ushers to rush over to console them.

※

"Look at 'Weepin' Wanda up there boohooing and makin' all that ruckus!" Sister Jenkins whispered to Usher Green.

"I know!" said Usher Green. "Is this a funeral or a graduation ceremony? I can't tell the difference! Weepin' Wanda is up there carrying on like it was her daughter. But I've seen her cry like that at funerals for people she didn't even know."

"Some people will do anything for attention!" declared Miss Jenkins.

"The man walking up with Dr. Hawkins…," said Usher Green. "Isn't that her ex-husband?"

"Yep," replied Miss Jenkins. "That's ole Rufus. We're neighbors you know. Him and Lila Mae not only walked in together, but they sat next to each other. Maybe they might be able to work things out."

"I don't think so!" said Usher Green. "Not after all these years."

"Gertie don't be so quick to make such assumptions," said Miss Jenkins. "I'm 83 years old going on 84 now. I've been around long enough to know that death has a way of bringing people back to church and families back together."

"That may be true," said Usher Green. "But death can do the opposite too. It can cause people to leave the church and tear families apart over things like money…funeral arrangements…even obituaries. Leave a name off an obituary, and you might have a fight on your hands…right in the church…during the funeral. I've seen it happen."

There was hardly a dry eye in the house, Pastor Just having presented the plaque to her parents, and Sister Jackson, Sister Voyant, and Sharon all sharing memories of Dancer. Dr. Hawkins now stood at the podium staring at the plaque Pastor Just presented to her and Mr. Hawkins.

"More than a month has passed since our Dancer died," Dr. Hawkins told the crowd, tearfully looking at Dr. Hawkins. "But time has yet to mend our broken hearts! We were devastated…and we still are. "To be perfectly honest, I have little to no appetite, cry all the time, and am currently going to 'Roberta's House' on North Avenue to help me cope with my unbearable grief. I also got involved with A Mother's Cry, an organization founded and run by named Millie Brown. The group helps women who have tragically lost their children. Now, I will have you all to know that when my dear Dancer called and invited me to this Graduation a few months ago, I never thought in a million years she would not live to see it."

"We are so sorry for your loss," said Pastor Just. "We are hopeful that this plaque in Dancer's memory will serve as some consolation as you and your husband mourn the loss of a wonderful young woman who was loved and endeared by so many."

"Thank you Pastor Just…thank all of you," said Dr. Hawkins, struggling to speak.   "This means so much to me. And the chair draped in purple cloth is so touching…purple was Dancer's favorite color. She always thought purple was so regal…so majestic. You know when Dancer was quite young, I would say…'look at that fabulous thing! She's going to be a dancer!' I only wish I told Dancer how much I loved her…how proud I was of her…how special she was. Perhaps my Dancer would be here today," she sobbed. "I implore every parent here today to let your children know how much you love them…how special they are…and how proud you are of them…because tomorrow is not promised! Dancer might be gone…but our loving memories of her…are very much alive...my God, we miss her…but she continues to dance on in our hearts." Looking up, Dr. Hawkins said, "I love you Dancer. Mother is so very proud of you!"

Consoling Dr. Hawkins, Mr. Hawkins added, "And so is Daddy my Princess...so is Daddy."

The Hawkins having taken their seats, Sister Jackson now stood at the podium.

"We will now move to the next part of today's Commencement Program," said Sister Jackson. "'Purging the Wound'." Nervous, Sister Jackson craved for something sweet to eat. You can't eat nothin' right now Audrey! she internally screamed at herself. You're standing in front of all these people! No, you can't do that! Not right now!

Her hands shaking, Sister Jackson lifted the mic from the podium. "'Purging the Wound' was totally optional," she explained to the crowd. "Our graduates could invite someone here they felt they hurt the most…and apologize to them. Although painful, they felt it was a necessary step to help make amends and find closure in their recovery. As House Mother of Serenity House, I wanted to lead by example and go first."

"Good job Sister Jackson," Sister Voyant said softly.

Demonstrating something being sifted, Sister Jackson said, "For The Bible tells us that, Simon Sez…Satan desires to have you so that he may sift you as Crème of Wheat! And when you are done finished eating, feed your brethren! Now that's what The Bible says! I know that one by heart!"

Looking at James rushing over to her, Sister Jackson thought, Here comes James! Don't tell me he's coming over to correct me in front of all these people!

"That's not what The Bible says Mama Jackson!" said James. "Luke 22:31-32 says, 'And the Lord said, Simon, Simon behold, Satan hath desired to have you, that he may sift you as wheat: But I have prayed for thee, that thy faith fail not: and when thou art converted, strengthen thy brethren.' Now that's what The Bible says!"

"Ain't that what I said?" asked Sister Jackson, staring out at the crowd feeling embarrassed.

"No!" said James.

"Well, that's exactly what I meant!" she responded, the urge to eat something sweet growing stronger.

Sister Jackson's eyes swept across the audience, the unflinching eyes of the audience – pairs and pairs of them – staring back. I want to run from this podium! she thought. But I can't turn back now! What I have wanted to say for over 20 years has to be said today.

No longer able to resist her emergency stash of sweets, she told the audience, "Excuse me for a second," turning her back to them, to prevent them from seeing what she was about to do. She reached down into her bosom and pulled out a pack of cookies. After tearing open the package, she began nibbling on them.

Sister Jenkins stretched her neck to see what Sister Jackson was doing and then stood up.

"What's Sister Jackson doing up there?" asked Miss Jenkins.

"It looks like she's standing up there eating," said Usher Green. "How greed can you get?!"

"Em…em…em…standing up there eating in front of all these peoples?" asked Miss Jenkins. My Lawd, what a glutton!"

"Maybe she's nervous," said Usher Green. "Before Sister Jackson turned around, she kept looking over at the mean-looking, green-eyed man in the wheelchair who came in with the 'Aunt Esther-looking' usher."

"Have a seat Usher Green," said Usher Gilkesson. "You can't stand like that during the program."

Rolling her eyes, Usher Green took her seat.

To the sound of chatter, Sister Jackson wiped crumbs from her mouth and turned around. I can't believe I just did that! she thought. But I just couldn't help myself! The crowd now hushed, Sister Jackson sheepishly said,

"Sorry everyone, but I was having a little snack attack."

Sister Williams stood up and began to sob.

"A heart attack! Oh Lord no!" she cried.

"No Sister Williams," said Sister Jackson. "I said a snack attack…not a heart attack!"

"Oh," said Weepin' Wanda, who immediately stopped crying and sat down.

I didn't have a heart attack, but my heart sure is racing! thought Sister Jackson, glancing at Michael, who sat peering at her from his wheelchair, parked against a side wall. Directing her attention back to the audience, she said, "While I am not in the Serenity House program…but a part of it, I want to apologize to someone I invited here that I deeply hurt many years ago," said Sister Jackson. "Mike and Caroline…please come up."

The buzz of chatter again filled the room – many turning to look at Caroline push Michael to the front. While Caroline was dressed in her uniform, Michael was dressed in a crumpled brown suit that was far too big, a dingy white shirt, a tie adorned with food stains, scuffed white leather shoes, and a brown fedora hat.

Look at Big Mike! thought Sister Jackson. I hardly recognize him! He's so frail looking! He has aged considerably! And look at the way he is dressed! That's a big contrast to the Big Mike I remember…always dressed in Adidas sweat suits and color-coordinatin' down to his socks and shoes! The only thing that hasn't changed are his piercin' green eyes!

Standing just a few feet from her 'green-eyed monster of her past', Sister Jackson gulped spit and walked closer to him. Taking him by the hand, Sister Jackson said: "Mike, I asked Caroline to bring you here…so I could apologize. I am very sorry for what I did years ago. Because of my addiction our children were taken away. I love my children…Gawd knows I do! But I don't even know where the children are now...not even my oldest daughter Earlene. Once I got out of jail, I tried to find our children…I really did…but their adoption records were sealed…and their names were changed. But through Caroline, I was able to invite you to this ceremony today. I wanted to apologize…to tell you I am truly and deeply sorry for what I did. Mike...would you please…please forgive me?"

Sister Jackson stood waiting with baited breath for his response, the entire place also waiting in complete silence. Michael's scowl softened and he smiled, prompting James to yell, "That's right man…do the right thing! Forgive her!" Others yelled out similar things, anticipating Mike would accept Sister Jackson's apology.

"Hell no!" hollered Michael, violently snatching away his hand, and to the sound of a collective gasp in the room. "I don't accept your sorry ass apology! You had my sister to get me all dressed up, put my damn dentures in, and bring me here for this purging shit! And just like that…you think I am supposed to forgive you! Hell naw! I don't forgive you! If I had my way, your ass would still be in jail after what you did to my daughter and my son! You crackhead! You got some nerve! I outta knock the sh–"

"Michael!" cried Caroline. "You promised me you would behave yourself! And here you are actin' like a heathen! I swear fo' Gawd, I would never have brought you here if I knew you would embarrass me like this! Now, I know 'M' did some sinful, vile, Gawd-awful things, but you need to watch your mouth! We are in a church house…among the Lord's people!"

"You think I care about that Caroline?!" Michael shouted, spit flying from his mouth. "Well, I don't!"

Walking to the front, Pastor Just said, "Order up in here! Now this may not be the courthouse, but it's the church house, and you will respect it! Now I know you were invited here by Sister Jackson, but you will show respect up in here!"

"I ain't got to do a damn thing!" roared Michael. "She asked me to come here! I didn't ask her to come here!"

Dejected, Sister Jackson thought, Not only am I embarrassed, but I feel terrible! This was the worst possible outcome...and this rejection I am feeling right now...it is what I dreaded...and feared the most!

CHAPTER
THIRTY-EIGHT

JUICY AND THE FIRST LADY

Pastor Just and the ushers consoled Sister Jackson who was overcome with emotion and helped her back to her seat.

"Don't let him upset you, Sister Jackson," said Pastor Just. "Some people just don't understand the beauty of forgiveness. They would rather stay stuck in their unforgiving, stubborn ways."

"That's right!" said Mrs. Just. "You should learn to forgive," she told Michael.

"Aw shut up 'Juicy!'" Michael roared. "You might be bouchée now, but I remember you standing in my homeboy's line waitin' to be served back in the day! I also know the reason why they all called you Juiccccyyyyyyyyy," he taunted.

A universal gasp again sounding in the room, Pastor Just felt his innards about to burst in anger.

This man just disrespected my wife! thought Pastor Just. I know Jacqueline's past challenges with addiction…and she's done so much to put that life behind her! And here is this man not only referencing her past but calling Jacqueline by her old street name…'Juicy!'

Before he knew it, Pastor Just was sprinting towards Michael.

"Listen here, I don't care who you are, but you are going to respect my wife!" shouted Pastor Just. "I ain't been saved all my life! Talk to my wife like that again, and I'll put you down on that floor so fast, you won't know what hit you!"

"I wish you would!" Michael dared.

"Punch him Pastor!' someone yelled.

Looking at the shocked attendees, and now flanked by ushers and deacons on each side along with Mrs. Just, Pastor Just quickly gathered himself. Just that quick, I lost control of my emotions! I'm the Shepherd of United in

Victory and many of my sheep are in attendance. I'm supposed to lead by example, and this isn't a good one! Galatians 5:22 tells us …'But the fruit of the Spirit is love, joy, peace, forbearance, kindness, goodness, faithfulness, gentleness and self-control.' As a preacher of the Gospel, I also must live by it! Walking away from Michael's wheelchair, Pastor Just told Michael, "I'm going to pray for you brother!" Directing his attention to his nephew, Pastor Just said, "Willie, I understand you are coming up next for 'Purging the Wound.' Please make your way up to the podium."

Willie began making his way up to the podium, while Caroline pushed Michael back to the area where they sat.

"I'm so sorry for my bruuuuuuther's behavior everyone," Caroline told the crowd.

"Take me home!" Michael demanded. "I knew I shouldn't have come here!"

"I'm not ready to go yet!" Caroline shouted. "I told 'M' I was going to bring you here for this program, and we're going to stay until it's over! Now unless you plan to wheel your way back to the senior building in that wheelchair, you're gonna stay put Michael!"

Willie stood at the podium wondering, 'Who is M?' while Michael continued to swear under his breath and Caroline parked his wheelchair, sitting in the chair next to him.

"Would all the ladies I invited here today please stand," said Willie.

Several women stood, each of them looking at one another with great surprise.

I invited these ladies here today because I owe them an apology for using them, thought Willie. But I had no idea all of them would show up! Let me get this over with, he decided, looking at their angry stares. Willie started, "I invited you all here today for a reason," he said. "The truth of the matter is that I lied and used each of you to get what I wanted. It wasn't right, so at this time, I am apologizing. I am sorry."

"You're sorry alright!" screamed Demetria Jones. "You owe me more than an apology! Singing in my ear talking about some 'Me and Mrs. Jones!' I thought I was the one! I thought you loved me! That's what you told me Willie!"

"He told me the same thing," yelled another woman.

"Me too!" shrieked another.

"I asked my husband for a divorce to be with you!" continued Mrs. Jones. "You also told me you were on vacation…and this" – she said looking around – "Is where you were staying the entire time!" prompting all the women who stood, to all begin fussing at Willie.

"Ladies…ladies…ladies," said Willie standing up from his chair. "I know you're hurt and angry with me…and I admit here today…in front of all these people…that I am sorry. Do you all accept my apology?"

"No!" the women screamed in tandem.

"I know I did all of you wrong," said Willie apologetically. "And all of you deserve to be mad at me for doing what I did for my own selfish gain.

And that's why I invited all of you here today…to tell you I'm truly sorry. I know you all don't believe me…and I don't blame you. But the truth is…I stand here today as a changed man…changed by God…changed by my stay here at Serenity House…and changed by now understanding what love is all about. It's not about using someone to get what you can get…that's not the type of love God wants us to have. It's about unconditional love...the same kind of love that God has for us. Someone loving me despite my past…and despite my faults…and me loving them despite their past…and despite their faults…that's what real love is all about. Some ask…what's love got to do with it? My answer is…love has got everything to do with it! I realize that now thanks to a special lady here who has stolen my heart."

Believing Willie is talking about her, all the women standing, smile and blush.

"She is beautiful on the outside and beautiful on the inside," said Willie. "She is the icing on my cake…she is the dew on my dewdrop...she is the woman that God created especially for me…Sharon come on up here girl."

"Sharon!" the women all shouted with disbelief.

"I knew Sharon had something going on!" said Sister Voyant. "My spirit never lies!"

Blushing herself, Sharon walked over to Willie under the stabbing glares of the other women, some who left.

"Sharon, like a thief in the night, you stole my heart," said Willie, taking ahold of Sharon's hand, prompting some of the women to suck their teeth and roll their eyes. "We started an incredible journey here together at Serenity House…and I want to continue to walk this path with you…and only you…and I promise to be faithful. You're all the woman I need."

"Okay Willie, but you have to get a job," said Sharon, who began singing the hook from Gwen Guthrie's 'Ain't Nothin' Goin' on but the Rent', which led many women in attendance to chorus along.

Standing, Pastor Just said, "You know Willie, we do need to hire someone to clean the church."

"Me?! Clean?! As clean as I am?" said Willie, primping. "I don't think so."

Folding her arms, Sharon said, "I plan to get a job…and you need to do the same. Take the job Willie!"

"That's right!" someone in the audience yelled. "You got the lady! Now keep her! Take the job, man!"

Exhaling, Willie said, "I'll take the job Uncle Just. I guess we all have to start somewhere." Picking Sharon up and doing a 360-degree turn, Willie said, "I thank God for giving me just what I needed…and it wasn't alcohol."

"And I thank God for giving me just what I need…and it wasn't Heron," said Sharon. "Having said that, this is the perfect 'Purging the Wound' moment for me. Willie lowered Sharon down to her feet, and she walked to the podium.

Sharon stood at the podium, staring out at the crowd. 'How can I say what I need to say in front of all these people?' she asked herself. Right now, I want to run back into Willie's warm, comforting arms, she wished, glancing at him. But I gotta do this…and I will…'cause Sharon Torres ain't no damn punk!

Turning to look at Sister Jackson, Sister Voyant, Willie, and then back to the audience, Sharon said, "I didn't invite anyone here today," she told them. "I didn't have anyone to invite…but there is someone I owe a big apology to…someone who I have beat up mentally and physically. That person is myself. And I stand forgiven."

SERENITY was now singing Judson W. Van DeVenter's old hymn, 'I Surrender All'. Mrs. Just sat in her chair with her eyes tightly closed taking self-inventory.

I feel convicted! thought Mrs. Just. I feel ashamed! To think Sharon…my own cousin feels she didn't have anyone to invite…although me…her cousin…is sitting right here! But who can blame her? After the way I treated her? I introduced Sharon to Heroin, and after I got clean, I turned a blind eye. By God's Grace, I was able to stop using. I should have tried to help Sharon.

One by one, Mrs. Just looked into the faces of the graduates. I don't know their stories, she said to herself. But I know my own. There was a time when I sat on the filthy floors of shooting galleries, stash houses, and dope houses amongst the rats and other vermin while they scurried all around me! I cringe now, but back when I was getting my fix, I didn't care! Opening her eyes to glance over at her husband, who smiled, she thought, Thank God for Al! He risked his own safety to come into some of the city's most dangerous areas to pull me out of those places. I put that man through so much! But he stood by me through it all…even when I relapsed! He never gave up on me! And now that I'm cleaned-up and 'churchified' I act as if those things never happened! Listening to Sharon…followed by that trio…those beautiful songbirds SERENITY singing that song…I Surrender All…has me sitting here feeling like all this time…me…the Pastor's wife…has walked around with a haughty eye…which the Bible clearly tells us in Proverbs 21:4…is an unplowed field of the wicked and produces sin.

Continuing to examine herself, Mrs. Just turned and looked at Michael, sitting in his wheelchair fuming. The Bible says what's done is the dark comes out in the light, and for me…that was earlier at this program! How embarrassing it was for that evil man to show up here today and call me Juicy! I never wanted anyone to call me that name again! Men I met on the streets years ago, nicknamed me Juicy because they said I had the juiciest lips around! But I put that life behind me…and that's where I wanted it to stay. The last thing I wanted was a reminder, and that green-eyed man came here today and broadcasted it for everyone to hear! Sharon could have stooped low to do the same thing…but she didn't! She apologized to herself…but I'm the one who owes her an apology, concluded Mrs. Just. As soon as SERENITY finishes their selection, I'm going up to the podium to give her one…it's long overdue.

Sharon looked at Mrs. Just whisper something in Sister Jackson's ear. Sister Jackson nodded and Mrs. Just walked up to the podium. Why did Juicy walk up to the podium? wondered Sharon. She's not on the program.

"Hello everyone," said Mrs. Just. "I was not on the program to speak today but asked that I be allowed to say a few things. Thank you, Sister Jackson. Taking a deep breath, Mrs. Just said, "I never thought I would ever find the courage to stand publicly before my husband…before my church family…and before God… and admit my past…but here I am. For nine years of my life, I used Heroin on and off."

Sharon's mouth dropped open in tandem with the gasps of the crowd. I can't believe Juicy just admitted that!

she shouted in her mind.

"And not only did I use Heroin," admitted Mrs. Just tearfully, "but I introduced my younger cousin Sharon who spoke earlier, to Heroin. And for that, I am so sorry Sharon. I hope you can forgive me."

Sharon walked over to Mrs. Just and gave her a hug. "All is forgiven," said Sharon. "And I accept your apology. What happened took place a long time ago…you got on the wrong track…I got on the wrong track…but thank God for U-turns!"

"Thank you, Sharon," said Mrs. Just. "Before I take my seat, I would also like to thank my wonderful husband…the fine pastor of this church…Rev. Al. B. Wright, Just, Jr! He never threw in the towel! He prayed for me…prayed with me…and never gave up on me when I was in addiction! He pulled me out of some of the dirtiest, darkest, most dangerous places in this city. And Honey, I want to say…with all of these people here as my witnesses…that I am sorry to have put you through all of that."

Walking to join her at the podium, Pastor Just said, "I love you Jacqueline…and when I said, 'I do' during our wedding vows which included 'for better or worse' I meant it. Even with all the trials and tribulation we went through, I was determined to stick with my wife. God never gave up on me…and I never gave up on you. Prayer changes things!"

The two shared a long hug, the entire room erupting in applause along with 'Hallelujahs! and 'Amens!'

"Thank you honey," said Mrs. Just. "Now there's one more thing I would like to say before I take my seat. To the graduates…and all of those here who have struggled with addiction…I want to share something with you. I may be the First Lady of United in Victory…and I might not look like what I've been through…or what I came out of…but that man sitting back there in that wheelchair was right…I was Juicy," she said, pointing at Michael. "Sometimes, we tend to forget where we came from…but for me, my reminder came today. To him…and all of those like him who find fulfillment in bringing up mistakes of the past…I say this…thank you for bringing up my past…because it reminds me of where I was…and from where God brought me."

The Justs were back in their seats, and Hank now stood at the podium, but the crowd were still rejoicing over Mrs. Just's words.

After seeing that dude in the wheelchair totally embarrass Mama Jackson, I'm glad my parents didn't come," thought Hank. That grumpy old man hates Mama Jackson for whatever she did…just like Dad and Mom hate me for what I did. I'm glad they didn't respond to the letter I mailed inviting them to my Graduation. If given the opportunity, Dad would probably talk to me the same way that man talked to Mama Jackson.

Hank cleared his throat in the podium microphone, prompting the crowd to quiet. "I invited my parents to be here today…but they didn't show up," Hank said, his voice quivering. "But if they were here…I would tell them both how truly sorry I am for my actions…and for the part I played in the loss of an irreplaceable family jewel…my beloved Grandma Emma." Feeling his knees buckling under the weight of emotion, Hank tried to remain upright, but fell to his knees and began to sob. Oh no! Hank thought. I didn't mean to breakdown like this! Especially in front of all these people!

Willie, James, and Sharon rushed over, helping Hank to his feet.

"I'm okay guys…thank you," said Hank. "Anyway, I don't blame my Dad and Mom for not showing up today. But I pray they will understand how sorry I am for hurting not only them…but our entire family…and can find it in their hearts to forgive me." Turning to walk away from the podium, Hank heard a familiar voice say, "Hanky…I forgive you." It was his mother, Chelsea.

❧

Stunned, Hank watched his mother walking up to him. "Mom!" he cried. "Oh my God! Mom, you came! I didn't even know you were here!"

Mrs. Riley stroked Hank's face and told him, "I know son. I wanted it to be a surprise. I sat far in the back so you couldn't see me…and heard everything you said. And I mean what I said Hanky…I forgive you son. I mean that from the bottom of my heart. What happened was a terrible accident…I know you Hanky…and I know you never meant to hurt your grandmother."

"Mom, it feels so nice to feel your touch…a mother's touch again," said Hank. "And to hear you say you forgive me…Mom…you will never know how much hearing those words mean to me…thank you."

"I love you son and I will love you until the day I die," said Mrs. Riley, tears streaming down her face. "But Hank, it's the love of God that transcends even my love. Because it's His love that has the power to change your father's heart and close the gaping wound in yours…if you allow Him to. And as much as I love you Hanky…even I don't have the power to do that. But Hanky…what I can do is love and support you in this process in every way I can…and I plan to do that."

"Thank you, Mom," said Hank. "I missed you so much!"

"You're welcome Hanky and I missed you too," replied Mrs. Riley. "Your father didn't come with me today Hanky, but he still loves you…and he misses you too. But he's still hurt over what happened. But Hanky…we're going to pray until we see a change come."

❧

Hank and Mrs. Riley took their seats, the crowd erupting in jubilation at their tearful reunion. James now stood at the podium for 'Purging the Wound' to offer his apology.

"First and foremost, I would first like to thank God for today's program and this opportunity," said James. "At this time, I would like to apologize to my late wife Pauline….and my late daughter Tiffany…for my prideful spirit," said James looking upwards. "You've both earned your heavenly wings…but Pauline and Tiffany…I want you to know that I love and miss you…and ask for your forgiveness in the name of the Father…the son…and the Holy Ghost. Amen."

Walking back to his seat from the podium to rousing applause, James saw something that took him by surprise. Miracle is walking up to the podium! James silently shouted. I can't believe it! She was adamant about not inviting someone! Maybe she changed her mind! I wonder what Miracle is going to say?

CHAPTER THIRTY-NINE

I ROSE ABOVE IT ALL

Miracle stood at the podium gazing at the audience. I am so nervous! she thought. I got so antsy before I came up here that I got goosebumps on my arms…and had to put on the shawl Sharon gave me! I can't believe I'm standing up here in front of all these people! I have never spoken at a public event like this in my life! And this podium is almost as tall as me! But if I made it through all the terrible things I have endured, I can stand up here today and say what I need to say.

"Up until a few weeks ago, I had no plans to participate in 'Purging the Wound'," said Miracle. "I felt my not wanting to participate was justified. This part of the program is all about apologizing to those you hurt the most. I didn't feel like I hurt anyone. I was the one who had been hurt time and time again. The world had molded me into an angry, distrustful, anti-social young woman…and I felt the world owed me an apology. I didn't owe it an apology…or anyone in it. But Sister Voyant opened my eyes to see…my view was totally wrong," said Miracle, turning to look at Sister Voyant, who smiled. Before I came to Serenity House, I didn't see the value in myself. But being here has helped me to realize I was born with all the value I need because Jesus loves me."

"Praise God!' said Sister Voyant.

Miracle stood tippy toed to see Michael over the podium. Pointing at him, she said, "When I saw that sad, pathetic, mean old man sitting back there yelling at Mama Jackson…and Mrs. Just…I saw myself. And I didn't like what I saw! His behavior only reaffirmed that I needed to do what I am about to do now…and that's apologize. I have been through a lot. But it doesn't give me the right to treat people the way I have treated them. I am sorry, and I apologize to everyone I hurt for my behavior." Looking at Mr. Jenkins, Miracle added, "Especially my caseworker," she said. "Mr. Jenkins, I am so sorry for treating you so mean."

Mr. Jenkins stood and began to make his way over to Miracle, toting a large gift bag.

"Apology accepted," said Mr. Jenkins. "I have seen your transformation, and I am very proud of you Miracle. I have something for you…it's your graduation gift," he said handing her the gift bag.

"A gift?! For me?!" she asked ecstatically, pulling out a large pink and beige duffle bag.

"Ooooh! It's beautiful!" Miracle cried. "Wow, and it's Coach!"

"Yes, it's a Coach," chuckled Mr. Jenkins. "…Yyou needed a new duffle bag with that broken zipper on the one you have. So I brought you a new one. Now, you don't have to worry about your things falling out."

"Oh my goodness!" said Miracle. "Thank you, Mr. Jenkins! That was so thoughtful!"

Feeling the weight of something else in the bag, Miracle unzipped it and peered inside.

"There's something else in here," she said.

"There is," said Mr. Jenkins. "Go on and take it out."

Reaching inside the duffle bag, Miracle pulled out a book. "I Rose ABOVE it all by Ursula V. Battle," said Miracle, opening the book and flipping through the pages.

"That book is very special to me Miracle…but you're special," said Mr. Jenkins.

"I know life hasn't been easy for you…but despite all that you have gone through…look at you today! You rose above it all! That book helped me to get through some really tough times in my life. That's why I wanted you to have it. To encourage you…just like it encouraged me. To keep rising…no matter what. It was my mother's 'favor-ite' book".

Sister Jackson was still feeling glum about what transpired between her and Michael. But what she heard Mr. Jenkins tell Miracle immediately got her attention.

Hoisting herself up from the chair, she walked over to Mr. Jenkins and asked, "What did you just say?"

"I said, it was my mother's favor-ite book," said Mr. Jenkins imitating his mother's mispronunciation. "That's how she pronounced the word favorite."

Dumbfounded, Sister Jackson told Mr. Jenkins, "I Rose ABOVE it all was…and still is my 'favor-ite book'. Mr. Jenkins…if you don't mind me asking…where did you get that book?"

"My biological mother gave it to me," replied Mr. Jenkins. "When I was a little boy…for Christmas."

"How old were you?" asked Sister Jackson.

"About seven or so," answered Mr. Jenkins. "Why?"

"Do you happen to know your biological mother's name?" Sister Jackson inquired.

"Thomas…Melvina A. Thomas," said Mr. Jenkins using his finger to cursively write the name in the air. Mr. Jenkins' motions immediately made Sister Jackson recall how she would demonstrate writing her name in the air in front of her own child.

"Look!" said Miracle pointing to a handwritten name on the inside cover of the book. "That's the same name written here in child's handwriting…Melvina A. Thomas!"

"Oh my God! Yes!" screamed Sister Jackson.

"What's wrong Mama Jackson?" Miracle asked. "Why are you so emotional?"

Hardly able to get her words out, Sister Jackson said, "My name was Melvina A. Thomas. My first name is

Melvina...my middle name is Audrey...the name I now go by...and my maiden name was Thomas before I married my late husband Roy Jackson!"

Sister Jackson could hardly contain herself! Looking upward to God she asked, "Lawd...is it possible" – glancing at Mr. Jenkins – "that this is my son?!"

There was a collective gasp in the room and then complete silence, save for the whizzing sound of Michael wheeling himself towards Sister Jackson, Mr. Jenkins, and Miracle.

❀

Sister Jackson watched Michael speeding in her direction, hastily turning the wheels of his wheelchair, nearly running over anyone or anything that stood in his way.

"Michael!" shouted Caroline, hot on his trail. "You had me pushin' you in your wheelchair with my bad knees and gout when you could wheel yourself all along?!"

"Shut up Caroline!" Mike hollered back. "And quit runnin' behind me!"

"Get thee behind me Satan!" she shouted. "I ain't finna to go nowhere! It sounds like 'M' is trying to say that young man standing up might be her son. And if that's 'M's son, that would make him...oh my Lawd...I'm about to fall out on this floor! I can't believe it!"

❀

Sister Jackson stood looking at Mr. Jenkins in amazement – digging decades into her mind excavating memories long buried away.

"I gave my son that book...as a Christmas present," recalled Sister Jackson, uncovering a memory from 1997. "I ain't have no money to buy gifts...but that book was priceless to me. And on the day my children were taken away, my son was trying to recite that poem.

Speaking the words as they came to her remembrance, Sister Jackson whispered, "'Not now baby...Mama's tired...recite it to your father...'" she said, slowly turning to Michael - his green pupils and black iris' sitting in the corners of his eyes fixated on her. Pointing at him and said, "'He's here...'"

Mr. Jenkins ran over to Michael, aguishly crying out, "'Writing in the annals of your twisted mind...I will never escape the lies of your binds!" He shouted, "Oh my God...it was you!"

"Me what?!" shouted Michael, his eyes now following Mr. Jenkins circling around his wheelchair. "I don't know you!"

"I know you!" screamed Mr. Jenkins. "And it was you!"

"What's he talking about Michael?!" asked Caroline "What did you do?!"

"I ain't do a damn thing!" yelled Michael. "And I don't know what the hell that boy is talkin' about! I knew I shouldn't have come here! Take me back to my damn building Caroline!"

"What I tell you about that filthy mouth of yours Michael!" cried Caroline. "Now I told you that I —"

"You look much different now," interrupted Mr. Jenkins, gazing at Michael. "But I recognize you and those scary eyes! And I can see those burn marks beneath the cuffs of your shirt on your arms! The ones you threatened to put on me!"

"Boy, I don't know what in the Sam Hill your ass is talking about, but I ain't threaten to do a damn thing to you!"

"I swear 'fore Gawd, you better watch that dirty mouth of yours Michael!" yelled Caroline. "You might be my bruuuuuther, but you ain't too old for me to wash that cesspool of filth you call a mouth, out with soap!"

Standing directly in front of Michael – his chest heaving up and down, Mr. Jenkins cried, "Oh my God…it was you who put my baby sister in the microwave!"

❈

To the horrified gasps of the audience – and Usher Green – filming what was unfolding with her cell phone – Miracle rushed over to Mr. Jenkins.

"What?!" she asked. "That's the same thing that happened to me! When I was a baby, my mother put me in the microwave!"

"I ain't put nobody in no damn microwave!" bellowed Michael.

"I know what I saw!" Mr. Jenkins fired back. "Mama asked me to get the baby's bottle out the microwave…and just as I was about to walk in the kitchen…I saw you open the microwave…take my food and my baby sister's bottle out…and throw it in the trash can! And then you put my little sister in the microwave! But you didn't see me because your back was turned!"

"Jesus! Jesus! Jesus! Jesus! Jeeeeeeeeeeesus!" shouted Caroline. "I'm having heart pal-la-put-tations!" she declared, referencing palpitations. "'Michael, you said 'M' put that baby in the microwave! You mean to tell me you did it?!"

"'M'?! asked Michael. "I don't know a damn person named 'M'!"

"Don't get 'selective Dementia' on me now, you devil you!" screamed Caroline. Pointing at Sister Jackson who stood near them with her mouth agape, Caroline yelled, "Michael, you know good and well I used to call Melvina…who's standing right here…'M' for short!"

"You put my baby sister in the microwave!" Mr. Jenkins again asserted. "I saw what you did!"

"Don't listen to him!" Mike screamed. "Like I said, I ain't put nobody in no damn microwave! He's lyin'!"

"What!" roared Mr. Jenkins. "No I'm not! I know what I saw! And I kept trying to tell Mama…but before I could…the police came and locked her up and two ladies took me and Angel away."

"Mr. Jenkins, did you say Angel?!" Miracle asked with a bewildered look.

"Yes Miracle…I did," replied Mr. Jenkins. "Angel was my baby sister's name."

"That's unbelievable!" cried Miracle. "Angel was my birth name. What a coincidence!"

With her hands clasped together, Sister Voyant rose from her chair and shouted, "Oh my God…Jesus! Lord, is it possible…that you have sent Sister Jackson…her son…and her daughter?!"

❈

Miracle was frazzled and confused by all she was hearing.

444

"Mama Jackson you definitely aren't my biological mother!," said Miracle. "It's impossible, and I have proof! I have a picture of her!"

With great haste, Miracle rushed over to her purse and took out one of the photos she dropped inside earlier.

"See," said Miracle, holding the photo in front of Sister Jackson. "That's my biological mother on this photo. She was a petite, small lady. And you don't look anything like her at all."

Sister Jackson let out a piercing scream. "Thank you, Jesus!" she jubilantly cried.

"Miracle! That's a photo I took years ago with my children at Mondawmin Mall! Back then, I was skinny as a rail from being on that stuff! They were itty-bitty little things back then! This is me with my sonme...Lil' Mike –"

"Lil' Mike?!" Mr. Jenkins asked incredulously. "That's the same name my parents called me! They, along with my Aunt Caroline!" he recalled, looking at Caroline. "Nobody has called me that name since I was a little boy!"

"Nephew!" cried Caroline. "Jeeeeeeeesus!"

"The last time I saw you son, you were yay high," said Sister Jackson, holding one of her hands a few feet above the floor. "My little, big man...Lil' Mike. My adorable, caring son who always helped me with the precious baby I'm holding in my arms on that photo." Sister Jackson, along with the others...including those who sat in the crowd...all turned and looked at Miracle.

Stunned, Miracle could not believe what she was hearing! Turning to Mr. Jenkins, she asked, "You're my brother?!"

"And you're my sister?!" he said, responding to Miracle's question with one of his own.

Mr. Jenkins and Miracle turned to Sister Jackson, and simultaneously asked, "And you're our biological mother?!"

"Oh my Gawd...my babies!" Sister Jackson cried. "I believe that I am!"

"Good Gawd Almighty in Heaven!" shouted Caroline. "For years, I've been prayin' that I would live to see my niece and nephew again! I believe God has answered that prayer! You two," she said staring wide-eyed at Mr. Jenkins and Miracle, are "Michael and M's children!"

Dizzied by so many revelations, Miracle looked at Sister Jackson, Mr. Jenkins, and Caroline, stating, "So you're my mother...you're my brother...and you're my aunt?!" Turning to Michael, she screamed, "And you're my father! You are the one who...who...who put me in the microwave?!"

"I ain't put you in no damn microwave!" roared Michael. "Take me back to my buildin' Caroline! I ain't gonna sit up in here bein' accused of doin' things I know good and damn well I didn't do!"

Snatching off her shawl and pointing at the scar on her arm, Miracle hysterically cried, "It was you who did this to my arm?! You were the one who burned me with a crack pipe! You did this to me?!"

"Michael!" screamed Caroline. "You didn't?! Please tell me this isn't true!"

"It ain't true!" yelled Michael. Turning his wheelchair to face Miracle, he hissed, "You listen…and you listen good…Miracle…Angel…or whatever the hell your name is! I ain't burn you and I sure as hell didn't put you in no damn microwave!"

"You did put her in the microwave!" bellowed Mr. Jenkins.

"I did not!" said Michael. "You're blamin' the wrong one!" Turning his wheelchair to face Sister Jackson, he pointed at her and shouted, "Your mother standing over there did it! Not me! She was so high on Crack she ain't know what she was doing!"

"How dare you!" said Mr. Jenkins. "It was you…not her!" he roared, turning to look at Sister Jackson. Shaking his head, he turned back to Michael and told him, "You have the nerve…the unmitigated gall…to sit in here and listen to her heartfelt apology earlier…and not accept it…all the while knowing you were the one who had done all of this!"

"Michael!" shouted Caroline. "You mean to tell me that you were the one who burned my poor little niece and put her in the microwave? And threw my poor little nephew's food away…but told us he was starvin'! You mean to tell me all these years me and the rest of our family were mad at 'M' and harbored hate in our hearts over what we believed she had done…and it was all a lie?!"

"I'm telling the truth!" Michael yelled. "Now I be damned if I'm gonna sit up in here and listen to these people lie on me! Take me home!"

"Why you vile, fork-tongued, double-talkin', unhinged, sinful, hateful, lyin' beast!" said Caroline. "I should have known you weren't tellin' the truth. Carl tried to tell me you were lyin' But I didn't listen on account you were my bruuuuuther! I gave you the benefit of the doubt…and you made fools out of us all!

Turning to Look at Sister Jackson, Caroline said, "Oh Lawd 'M' I am so sorry for believing that heathen!"

"Caroline why are you apologizing to that 'Crackhead!' hissed Michael. "And that boy over there in those fancy duds is lyin' through his teeth!"

"I'm telling the truth!" cried Mr. Jenkins. "I know what I saw!"

"Well if you saw so much boy, then why would you wait so long to say something! Just like them women did Bill Cosby, Clarence Thomas, Donald Trump, and Harvey Weinstein! I know why! Because you're making it all up! Liar!"

"I'm not lying! And as far as I'm concerned…those women…those victims…weren't lyin' either! Mr. Jenkins fired back. "And in your case…it was more like Kevin Spacey!"

"Shut up!" roared Michael, leaning towards Mr. Jenkins, nearly falling out of his wheelchair.

The missing pieces to the puzzle of my life are coming together! thought Miracle.

Reflecting on his social worker experience, Mr. Jenkins thought, Nothing prepared me for this! I have helped many clients who have been traumatized…but here I am…face-to-face with the man who traumatized me!

Walking closer to Michael, he yelled, "You have no idea how much guilt I have carried around all these years! I blamed myself…because I thought Mama was taken away because I did something wrong! So I buried what I saw you do way in the back of my mind…I suppressed it…I didn't tell nobody! But I know what I saw…and everything I've said…is true."

"Ye shall know the truth and the truth shall set you free!" declared Sister Jackson, jubilantly raising her hands in the air.

Jumping up from his chair, James said, "John 8:32 says 'Ye shall know the truth and the truth shall set you free!'"

"Ain't that what I said?!" asked Sister Jackson.

"Yes!" exclaimed James.

"Well that's exactly what I meant!" Sister Jackson exclaimed, to the sound of the crowd standing to their feet shouting and delivering thunderous applause.

Sister Jackson grabbed and hugged Mr. Jenkins and Miracle, holding them close to her bosom.

"The last time you hugged me Mama…I was eight," sobbed Mr. Jenkins. "Now, I am 28. How good it feels to be in your loving arms once again!"

Usher Green happily showed Miss Jenkins some of the footage she captured with her cell phone camera.

"I don't want to see that!" said Miss Jenkins, pushing away the phone. "Why do I need to look at that when I'm sitting here watching everything unfold live and in living color! I can't believe you are running around here videotaping at a time like this! I can't stop crying!"

"Somebody has to capture all of this live footage as part of United in Victory's archives!" said Usher Green. "After all, I am the Church Historian!"

"You're Usher Gossippin' Gertrude!" said Miss Jenkins. "That's who you are! Everyone calls you that!"

"Call me what you want Sister Two-Faced!" laughed Usher Green. "That's what everybody calls you…Sister Two-Faced!"

"And they're bald-faced liars too!" grimaced Sister Jenkins. "Just like that lyin' fake Mother Carter skinnin' and grinnin' up there on the front row!"

"Paaaaaleeeeasssse don't start on that again!" stressed Usher Green. "Everybody…including me…knows Mother Carter is the rightful mother of this church!"

"Phooey!" said Miss Jenkins.

"Listen," said Usher Green. "Since Pastor clearly forgot to ask me to usher, I figured I would record today's events for archival purposes."

"If it's one thing I know about Pastor…just like me…he don't forget nothin'!" said Sister Jenkins. "I don't bite my tongue either! I tell it like it is! Now if you want to know the real reason…in my own opinion why he didn't ask you to usher today?"

"Yes, tell me!" replied Usher Green.

"Well, since you begged me, I'll tell you," said Miss Jenkins. "My guess is that Pastor didn't ask you to usher today because of your gossipin' ways! Instead of spreading the 'Good News of the Gospel'…you like spreading the 'Good News of The Gossip!'"

Usher Green retorted, "I don't be –"

Seeing Sister Jackson motioning to the crowd, Miss Jenkins told Usher Green, "Hush up and sit down Gertie! Sister Jackson wants everyone to quiet down! She's about to say somethin!" Before today, the last time I saw Sister Jackson and them two kids together was the day she was locked up and them two chil'ren were taken away."

"You ought to know!" said Usher Green. "I heard through the grapevine that you were the one who called DSS on them!"

"Another bald-faced lie!" Miss Jenkins replied. "Lyin' just like that Mother Carter sittin' up there like she's some angel!"

"Don't start that up again!" said Usher Green, pushing record on her phone, aiming its lens towards Sister Jackson.

CHAPTER FORTY

DELIVERANCE

It felt so good holding her children after so many years, Sister Jackson did not want to let them go.

"I have yearned for this moment for so long!" she cried. "God has answered my prayers. I just can't stop cryin'! What a glorious day this is!"

"I'm about to puke!" yelled Michael, sneering at the three. "Between all the lies and mushy moments...I feel like I'm about to throw-up any moment!"

"Wait a minute, babies," said Sister Jackson, releasing her tight embrace around Mr. Jenkins and Miracle. "I'll be right back," she told them, making her way over to Michael.

Hissing, Michael told Sister Jackson, "Don't wobble your fat ass over here! I ain't got nuthin' to say to you!"

"Michael!" shouted Caroline. "You –"

"I got this Caroline," declared Sister Jackson. Reaching Michael's wheelchair, Sister Jackson told him, "Keep throwin' your fiery darts at me from that pit you call a mouth! Despite all the names you have ever called me...as you can see, I am still standing!" Peering down at him, she said, "Big Mike, I loved you...I fathered your children! But because of you Michael Adams, Sr., I spent 15 years of my life in jail! Because of you... I was introduced to crack... lost my children...lost my house...lost my dignity...lost my self-worth...and because of you...I ate my ass off..."

The crowd gasped at Audrey's expletive.

"Mama Jackson broke her own rule!" Willie shouted.

"Shut up Willie!" the Serenity House residents yelled at him.

"Forgive me Father," said Sister Jackson, looking upward to God. "I ain't cussed in years but I'm mad right now and that one got past me." Sister Jackson continued gazing at Michael, who sat in his wheelchair as if his mouth were wired shut. Not saying a word, he turned his wheelchair, so that his back was facing Sister Jackson.

"No!" yelled Sister Jackson, turning the wheelchair back around so that it was facing her once again.

"Take your paws of my wheelchair!" Michael screamed, turning the wheelchair away from her again. With that, Usher Gilkesson and Usher Gilmore rushed up front and stood on each side of his wheelchair.

"Go on and say what you need to say Sister Jackson," said Usher Gilkesson. "I guarantee if he tries to turn it, he won't be able to do it with us standing here."

"That's right!" said Usher Gilmore.

"Go on and say what you got to say!" Michael lashed out. "Now that you got your wardens here! You know a thing or two about wardens...don't you Melvina!"

"I got one question for you Big Mike," said Sister Jackson. "Why? Why did you do all of this? All these years, I've been walkin' around drownin' in guilt and beating myself up over what I thought I had done to my children! Now, come to find out you did it! Why did you do it! Tell me! Why!" she screamed.

Michael kept his silence, while Sister Jackson pressed him for answers.

"Tell me Mike!" beseeched Sister Jackson. "It's the least you can do!" You owe me that...and you owe our children that! Why did you do it! Why?!"

"Damnit!" bellowed Michael. "Alright! I'll tell you why I did it! What I got to losc! I'm about to dic anyway! I did it because I ain't want no damn children! I told you I ain't want no children before you had them! I went through hell as a child and I ain't want to bring no children of my own into the world! Sure, we messed around a few times...yeah we used to kick it a little...but I sure as hell didn't love you...and damn sure ain't want none of your children!"

"'M', I tried to warn you about my bruuuuther," cried Caroline. "But you wouldn't listen! I told you he was mean as a snake and –"

"Shut up Caroline!" snapped Michael. "Melvina asked questions, so shut your trap so I can answer them!"

"Tell me to shut up again you heathen, and I'll slap you across your lips with my Bible!" threatened Caroline. "Go on and answer 'M'! She's waiting...we're all waiting!"

Staring at the woman he came to loathe, Michael began, "Melvina, you were trying to trap me and –"

"Trap you?!" asked Sister Jackson.

"That's right!" replied Michael. "Trap me by having those two kids standing over there!" – he said gazing at Mr. Jenkins and Miracle. "You were trying to trap me, and you know it! When I met you at Caroline and Carl's house, I just got out of jail! I was also put on probation for drug possession! I ain't wanna go back to jail. So I figured I'd get me a job and make an honest livin'! I filled out dozens and dozens of job applications. But nobody would hire me because I had a background. I finally realized that the only way I could get a job was to lie on my job application...and that's what I did. Instead of being honest and checking 'yes' in the box on the job application that asked if the applicant had a criminal background, I started checking 'no'. After a few times of doing that, I finally got a job as driver. And then after all of that, here you come talkin' about havin' some children! Imitating Sister Jackson's younger voice, Michael said, 'Big Mike, I can't wait to have your baby!' you said. 'Big Mike, our baby is gonna have green eyes just like yours!' you said. 'Big Mike, our baby is gonna be beautiful!' you said. 'Big

Mike we gonna dress the baby in cute, little outfits', you said. "I told you then I didn't want no baby! But did you listen? No! You also told me you were on birth control! But we know that wasn't true! Now don't we! And you got pregnant not once, but twice! Did you think that havin' those kids would make me love you, Melvina? Huh? Did you? Did you think that having those kids would somehow make me finally realize that I wanted to marry you? Huh, Melvina? Did you think that once you had those children, I wouldn't want any other woman but you? Huh, Melvina?!"

Sister Jackson began to cry. Grinning, Michael continued, "I know that's what you thought, but you were wrong Melvina! Dead wrong! Because all it did was make me madder because I knew what you were trying to do! Make me love you! Somewhere along the way, you finally got it through that crackhead of yours that you were nothin' more than a booty call to me...that I didn't want what you wanted! And after you realized your dream of us being this perfect family wasn't gonna happen, then you decided to take me downtown to pay child support for two kids I never asked for or wanted! Put yourself in my shoes! There I was, faced with the prospect of surviving off what little pay I had left once my paycheck was garnished for child support payments! My paycheck was only $300 a week, and they wanted to take $200 out of every pay for child support! How could I survive off $100 dollars a week, Melvina, did you think about that? After finally getting' my own place...how could I pay rent? Put gas in my car? Be productive? Tell me that Melvina?! How?! And then on top of that, my Driver's License would be suspended if I failed to pay Child Support! How could I keep my job as a driver without a Driver's License, Melvina! Huh? Tell me that?! And we both know that you didn't take me downtown for child support because you needed the money for them kids! All you would have done with my hard-earned money had you gotten your grubby hands on it...was smoke it up! All you wanted to do was get high and lay on that pissy sofa! You wouldn't even wash your nasty butt...and that's putting it mildly!"

"Don't talk to my mother like that!" Michael yelled.

"No son," said Sister Jackson. "Let him finish. I wanna hear the rest of what he got to say."

"You laid on that dirty filthy sofa drinkin' forties...pissing on yourself and high off Crack!" said Michael. "You lost your job, and you damn sure wasn't about to make me lose mines! It was too hard to get! I wasn't about to let you mess that up for me! You wanted to hurt me because I didn't want a relationship with you! So, you can stand there all innocent if you want, but you played your part in this too! I don't hear you sayin' nothin' now!"

"Go on and finish Mike!" yelled Sister Jackson.

"Well on the day in question, you were waiting for me to bring you some Crack!" said Michael. "Ain't that right!"

"That's right," admitted Sister Jackson.

Grinning, Michael said, "And I told you I would take care of you before I went to work...and I did. I got you good and high on that Crack you loved so much...planted drugs in the drawer...and burned Angel with your crack pipe, which was still hot...burned her on her arm...just like my grandpa did to me with his cigarettes butts every time I threatened to tell what he was doing to me."

"What?!" shouted Caroline. "Grandpa was burning you?!"

"You damn right he was burnin' me!" replied Michael. "Burnin' me like he was brandin' one of those pigs on our farm!"

"My Lawd!" cried Caroline.

"Well once I burned Angel, I put her inside the microwave just like that boy said earlier," admitted Michael, glancing at Dr. Jennings. "After that, I placed an anonymous call to the police, gave them your address, and told them the place was a stash house! I also told them two children who were being abused and neglected were living there with their mother who was a Crack addict!' Re-enacting some of what he said during his call, Michael said, "Please! Please! Get there right away! I saw her put her baby in the microwave before, and I'm scared she might do it again! She's high again! Please hurry! I'm afraid for those children!' Cackling, Michael added, "I should have an EGOT…because I sure as hell deserved an Emmy, Grammy Oscar and Tony Award for that performance! So, there you have it Melvina! As I see it, we both were setting each other up! You were trying to set me up…and all the while, I was setting your ass up! Now leave me the hell alone!"

Michael began wheeling himself away, the people in attendance taking his photo and shouting at him. Usher Green walked alongside his wheelchair, filming him. Shouting back to the attendees and sticking up his middle finger at them, Sister Jackson shouted, "Michael! You really think you set me up don't you!"

Michael brought his wheelchair to a screeching halt.

Sister Jackson watched Michael spin the wheels of his wheelchair as fast as he could, thinking, *I have been on a topsy-turvy ride of emotions today… joy, pain, happiness, sadness, surprise, fear, anger, regret, embarrassment…the list goes on and on. I never thought I could take the things Michael said to me today, but I am still holding on to Gawd's unchanging Hand! I know He is with me!*

His wheelchair parked in front of Sister Jackson once again, Michael shouted, "Do I think I set you up?! What kind of question is that! Damn right I set you up!"

"You might think you set me up Michael," said Sister Jackson. "But no man…do you hear me…no man…could ever set me up like Gawd set me up! Now as hard as it is for me to stand up here and admit it, all those things you said about me were true. I was on Crack, and I was a mess! I had to go through everything I went through…losing my house…losing my freedom… and losing my children…to clean myself up! To make me the mother I needed to be for my children! And for me to get away from you to clear the way for God to send me Deacon Roy A. Jackson! A man who loved me and accepted me with all my issues and all my faults! God made a way for me to become the House Mother of Serenity House despite my record, so that I could help somebody else! He united me with my children and my best friend Caroline!"

"Praise Him!" shouted Caroline, doing a Praise Dance.

 "And not only did God do all of that," continued Sister Jackson. "But He also set me free from the bondage of guilt by allowing the truth to come out despite the lies that you told! And He used this event to do it! And I know without a shadow of a doubt Michael, that had God not given me the courage to bring you here, you would have taken your horrible lie straight to the grave! So you see Michael, God set me up, not you."

Leaning forward in his wheelchair, Michael bellowed, "Shut your mouth, Melvina!"

"No Michael, you don't control me anymore! I'm not the same Melvina you abused, used, and introduced to Crack! No! That's not me! I'm Melvina Audrey Jackson! A woman God set up in a way no man can! That includes you! And Michael, not only did God set me up, but He also set you up too! Not only to expose you for the liar that you are, but to use this situation as an example to the world! To show that He can use a demonic thing…that's you," she said, pointing at Michael. "To turn it around for His glory…that's Him, she said, pointing upwards, "And our good…that's me" she said, pointing to herself. "And if that's not a set-up, then I don't know what is!"

❀

Miracle silently listened to the exchange between two people who appeared to be her biological parents. No longer able to contain her emotions, in tears, she blurted out at Michael, "You mean to tell me…you did this to us over child support?! You have no idea of the hell you put me through…us through…and all over child support?"

"Listen here little lady!" Michael exclaimed. "How the hell do I know you really are my daughter! Turning to Mr. Jenkins, he added, "Or if that boy standing over there in that fancy getup is my son! I want a DNA test!" Wheeling closer to Miracle, Michael seethed, "I know for a fact you ain't my baby girl! You know how I know? Because she had green eyes!" he hollered, pointing at his eyes. "Green eyes! Just like mines! And Miss Lady you ain't got no green eyes! Hell, your eyes ain't even light!"

"The hell they ain't!" cried Miracle. Reaching into her eyes, she removed her dark-colored contact lenses, revealing glistening, green eyes.

❀

Several seconds of silence went by, the crowd looking on in astonishment.

"Your eyes are the same color as my bruuuuuther's," said Caroline, breaking the silence.

"These eyes!" cried Miracle. "Are your eyes! I inherited them from you!" she yelled at Michael. "You have no idea what I've seen through these eyes! Through these eyes, I saw the inhumanness, filth, and deprivation of human sex trafficking! You know how I saw it! I was in it! And so many men wanted 'The Girl with the Pretty Eyes!' After I escaped from that hell, I wanted to cover-up anything that made me look good to anyone…especially my eyes! And, to reach this pinnacle of my life today…where I felt I finally accomplished something…where I experienced my first graduation… where I finally felt happy…only to hear how you…my biological father nearly destroyed the lives of me, my brother and our mother…over child support?!"

❀

Miracle lunged towards Michael but was held back by Mr. Jenkins.

"No Miracle, I'll handle this," said Mr. Jenkins. "And Miracle…or Angel as I called you back then…those emerald eyes of yours are still just as pretty as they were when they looked up at me when I fed you your bottle."

"That's right," said Sister Jackson, giving Miracle a hug. "My little Angel."

"And my little cat-eyed niece," said Caroline, also wrapping her arms around Miracle.

Michael looked at the three intwined in a hug and turned his face away from them.

❀

Mr. Jenkins stooped low enough to reach Michael' face. Their faces were so close, their noses touched.

"Get out of my face, boy!," said Michael pushing him away.

"Coward!' shouted Michael. "Tell the truth! This is bigger than just child support money! Isn't it!"

Mr. Jenkins again got in Michael's face, prompting him to turn the other way.

"Look at me!" demanded Mr. Jenkins. "There's more to why you did all this? Isn't it?!"

Receiving no response from Michael, Mr. Jenkins grabbed him by the collar, and yelled, "Answer me! This is bigger than child support! Isn't it! Answer me!"

"Get…your…damn…hands…off… of…me boy!" hissed Michael, grabbing Mr. Jenkins hand and ripping it away from his collar.

Walking over to him, Sister Jackson asked, "Son…what are you saying?"

"What I'm saying Mama…is that this man…my ffffffather…" stuttered Mr. Jenkins.

"Your father what son?" inquired Sister Jackson. "Say what you need to say, baby…Mama is right here."

"He…he…raped me!" cried Mr. Jenkins, his admission causing Caroline to faint.

"You're lyin'!" said Michael, standing up from his wheelchair. Sister Jackson slapped him so hard, it sent him sprawling backwards to the floor, his dentures falling out of his mouth. The ushers and deacons rushed Caroline to the back, while Sister Jackson screamed, "Michael, remember those days when you slapped me to the floor! Now it's my turn!" Watching him pull himself back up onto the seat of his wheelchair, putting his dentures back into his mouth, she yelled, "You bastard! How dare you sodomize my son!? How could you Michael?!"

Splash!

Caroline felt the sting of something ice cold hitting her face.

"What the hell!!?" Caroline shouted, opening her eyes. She was laying on a couch flat on her back. With a squinted eye, Caroline looked up at Deacon Samuel, Deacon Mayberry, and Usher Gilkesson, who stood above her looking down into her face.

"Where am I at?" asked Caroline. "What happened?"

"You fainted," said Deacon Samuels. "So, we picked you up and brought you back to this room and laid you on the couch.

Sitting up, Caroline asked, "What in the devil did you throw in my face!"

"A pitcher of ice water," said Usher Gillkesson. "To bring you to. You were out cold."

"Just because I was out cold didn't mean you had to throw cold water in my durn face!"

Deacon Mayberry mumbled something unintelligible.

"What did he just say?" Caroline asked.

"He asked how you could cuss after getting on your brother out there about cussing," said Deacon Samuel.

"He'd be cussing too if someone threw some freezing water in his face!" said Caroline. "And look at how you all wet up my ursher's uniform! You might have thrown cold water on me, but right now I'm pipin' hot! I should throw ice water in all ya'll faces! Now git me some towels so I can dry my uniform and wipe my face!"

The three rushed off to get Caroline some towels. She eased her head back on the couch, reflecting on the things she heard during the Graduation. Sighing, she thought, Our incestuous family secret has reared its ugly, sinful head again.

Meanwhile, a few feet away in the Deacon Roy Jackson Room, Mr. Jenkins' shocking revelation caused mass pandemonium to erupt. Restrained by deacons, Usher Gilmore, and other members of the church, Pastor Just yelled at Michael, "How could you do such a terrible thing to my son?!"

"Your son?!" Michael fired back. "That boy is my son! So they say!"

"You were nothing but the sperm donor!" shouted Pastor Just. "When he first came to me and Jacqueline, he was a hurt, fragile little boy! Where were you when he needed help with his schoolwork?! Where were you when he couldn't sleep at night?! Where were you when we took him to counseling?! Where were you Mr. Father?! Where were you when he would wake up in the middle of the night yelling out when he had nightmares?! We were there! Not you!"

"Well thanks for nothing!" growled Michael, peering at Mr. Jenkins.

"Nothing! That's a laugh coming from you!" shouted Mr. Jenkins. "And nothing you say will ever justify what you did to us! Turning to Sister Jackson with tears running down his face, Mr. Jenkins said, "Mama, on the day we were taken away…I told my father that I was going to tell you what he was doing to me. And he took me to KB Toys in Mondawmin Mall …and brought me a truck…a red truck…and said he would never do it again. Mama…he did all of this…because he was afraid that I would tell."

Having opened the vault of this terrible secret for the first time in his life, Mr. Jenkins exposed more.

"I am 28 years old now!" he sobbed. "I was eight when Mama was torn away from us! Eight! I was just a little boy! A child carrying around so much guilt about what happened to his mother and what he should have done to stop it! A minor who became a man still burdened down with those feelings! Right along with being embarrassed and confused about what you did to me! And it's not just about what you did to me! It's about what you did to us!" he said, glancing at Sister Jackson, Miracle, and Caroline. "You took things away from all of us that we will never get back! That includes the years we lost being together as a family!" he yelled, embracing Miracle, Sister Jackson, and Caroline.

"Family!" yelled Michael, his voice breaking. "You wanna talk about family?! My grandfather burned me…molested me…threatened me…and who helped me?! Nobody! And then on top of that…I was the one who found my mother after she hung herself! Can you imagine what that was like! But did anyone help me? No! And you all are all locked in each other's arms slobbering on one another like you are the victims in this! If anybody was the victim, it was me!"

"You?!" everyone in the place said in unison.

"You think I was born like this!?" asked Michael. "That outta the blue I just woke up one day and decided I was going to have sex with my own son! No! My Grandpa did the same thing to me! And every time I told him I was going to tell my Mama what he was doing, he burned me with his hot cigarette butts! Grandma knew what he was doing! You know how I know? Because one day, she walked in and caught him gettin' at me! But all she did was turn a blind eye! Ain't that right Caroline! 'Cause you and I both know that Grandpa got after you too! And he got you good and pregnant! But Grandma took care of that! Ain't that right Caroline?! She used that metal clothes hanger on you, didn't she! Grandma gave you an old-fashioned abortion! Ain't that why you couldn't never have no babies! You got the hanger!" he cackled.

"Shut up Michael!" screamed Caroline bursting into tears. "This ain't about me! It's about you and what you did! You might be my bruuuuuther, but I have no pity for you! I mightta gone through some terrible things in my life, but I turned to God. You on the other hand…chose another path!"

"Aunt Caroline's right!" Mr. Jenkins hollered at Michael. "And I know I should despise you for what you have done…to me…and to our family! I should hate your guts! But I don't! You want to know why?"

"No!" Michael bellowed.

"Well, I'm going to tell you why!" said Mr. Jenkins. "Instead of having hatred in my heart for you…I have compassion! I feel sorry for you because you are a sad, pathetic human-being! The things you went through were traumatic and devastating! I understand that all too well! But you used those things as justification for what you did to us! Instead, of using what the devil meant for evil…and turning it around for your good! Like I did…like Miracle did…like Mama did, like Aunt Caroline did!" said Mr. Jenkins, looking at the others in that order. You could have chosen another path! But you didn't!"

"Shut your damn mouth boy!" said Michael. "Before I –"

"Before you what?!" asked Mr. Jenkins. "Burn me with your cigarette butts?! In case you didn't notice, I'm not that scared little boy you abused and threatened anymore! I'm a grown man now, and I'm not afraid of you! Did you think that I would stay that timid, frightened little boy who trembled every time he saw you for the rest of my life?! Well, you were wrong! And you know something else? I forgive you! I forgive you because it's the right thing to do. You don't need hate and unforgiveness...no that's not it! As a social worker, I know you need help…lots of mental help and counseling…to deal with those issues in your mind which have never been dealt with or addressed. I see many angry, sad, traumatized, abused children and young adults on a daily basis! And my job is to make sure they don't turn out like you! Michael Adams, Sr., you are the main reason why I decided to become a social worker! Oh…and one more thing," said Mr. Jenkins, stooping while looking at his father, "Writing in the annals of your twisted mind; I would never escape from the lies of your binds. That I'd never make it because of what you took; But there's another ending to the story of my book! Despite all you did to cause me to stumble and fall, I'm here to tell you, I rose! I rose! I rose…above it all!" he shouted, standing to his feet peering down at Michael.

The audience all stood, delivering rousing applause.

After a standing ovation that spanned several minutes, Sister Jackson signaled to the crowd to quiet.

"As we move towards the conclusion of today's program, I would like to say this," announced Sister Jackson. "I never thought in a million years so many things would come out of today's program…especially, 'Purging the

Wound'…which required us to invite those we hurt the most. I'm not gonna stand here and lie…I was scared to death to do what was required to bring Michael here today! But along with words of encouragement…Sister Voyant gave me Psalm 27:1…and I didn't just try to recite that Scripture," said Sister Jackson, smiling at Sister Voyant, "but I took the time to really read and meditate on it. And that scripture, encouraged me not to be afraid…and to trust God…and I did. And God reunited me with my children and best friend. I was also set free from the bondage of guilt and unforgiveness I felt towards myself. I believe all of us," she said, looking at Mr. Jenkins, Miracle, Sister Voyant, and the graduates – have all been purged of something. As for you Michael," she said, turning to him, "Like our son…I forgive you. As justified as I feel not to forgive you, I know that forgiveness is the right thing to do…the Godly thing to do. And you need God…we all do. And I am going to pray hard that one day, …one day… the coldness of your selfish, evil heart will melt away…and that it's replaced with the true warmth, joy, and love that comes only with truly knowing God. Until then, you will continue to be the miserable, lonely man you have become…and you will die that way. Until you decide to change…until your tests…become your testimony…and not your excuse."

"Mama…I'm so sorry!" cried Miracle. "I blamed you for everything that happened to me…and it wasn't even you!"

"You ain't got nothin' to be sorry about my little Angel," said Sister Jackson, cupping her hands directly around Miracle's cheeks, and looking her straight in the eyes. "None of this was your fault. And I ain't got a bitter bone in my body! Lawd knows…I am grateful! Gawd can use anything or anybody…even an event like this…to bring families back together! So that His Will…not our will…will be done! And everyone in attendance," she said gazing out at the crowd, can go out into the world and share the miraculous things they witnessed today! God gets the Glory! Hallelujah!"

Grabbing her children and hugging them Sister Jackson shouted, "The last time we were together was in a crack house. But today…this glorious day…God brought us all back together in the church house! Only God could have brought me From Addiction to Deliverance."

THE END

EPILOGUE

Saturday, May 18, 2019
Three Months Later

    It was a sunny Saturday afternoon, and a little over three months have gone by since the Graduation. This day was one of significance for Baltimore. It marked the running of the Preakness Stakes at Pimlico Racetrack, and there was the usual fanfare around the famous race. Trainers talked about their horses, women wore eloquent hats and sipped on Mint Julips, and thousands of spectators were excitedly making their way inside the storied track. Across town at United in Victory, the mood was quite the opposite. Somberness draped the air, for this day marked a sad occasion in the church's history. Today, the church's longtime musician Dr. Malachi Madison would be funeralized. A week ago, Dr. Madison suffered a fatal heart attack during morning Worship Service. To the shock of Pastor Just and his congregation, Dr. Madison was playing the church's majestic Hammond B-3 when he hit the keys – face-first. The deacons rushed up the organ loft along with members of the church to assist the famed 82-year year-old musician, who was slumped over the grand instrument. Those who sped up the loft included members of the Nurse's Auxiliary. But to everyone's great surprise, not one of them was a nurse. Usher Gilkesson, who was a RN, cleared them all out the way and administered CPR. The paramedics arrived minutes later, rushing Dr. Madison to Johns Hopkins Hospital, but he passed away.

    Sitting in his study, Pastor Just found himself struggling to finish the Eulogy he would soon be delivering for Dr. Madison.

    This Eulogy should be done, he thought, glancing at the few lines he scribbled down on a notepad. *I've had more than a week to write this Eulogy. It shouldn't be this hard for me to assemble a message for a man who has led this church's music ministry for nearly 60 years. Despite Dr. Madison's incomparable musical talent, it's still extremely difficult for me to stand in the pulpit and say anything good about him. Dad protected Dr. Madison…covering up his dirty laundry…something I stumbled upon by happenstance. He went to great lengths to protect Dr. Madison's sordid secrets. I'll never understand why. But knowing what I know has always troubled my heart.*

    Years earlier, Pastor Just learned of an elaborate cover-up concerning Dr. Madison to avert a church scandal. It involved Dr. Madison, Sister Jackson, her oldest daughter Earlene, Mother Pearl Carter, his father Bishop Just and other longtime members.

    Finding out that tidbit of information made me wonder about a lot of things…including what happened to my mother Amanda…who went missing when I was just a boy…and has never been found. No one just vanishes. And this church has spent a mint taking care of Mother Carter all these years. My father made sure of that and even made me promise I would so the same. And that Sunday he cursed at Mother Carter and accused her of blackmailing him… not only turned the rumor mill even more…but it added more burning questions to the ones I already had in my mind. "Oh, stop it, Al!" said Pastor Just chastising himself. "Don't start those meritless innuendoes up in your mind again! Get your mind back on this Eulogy you must deliver today," he sighed glancing down at his watch. "The deacons are picking Dad up from Bicentennial Towers and will be arriving within the hour," he estimated, looking at his watch. "Dad and Dr. Madison had such a longstanding friendship...one that stretches all the way back to their days at Morehouse College. It was only fitting that Dad attend his funeral. Despite Dad's dementia, he has been doing well...even ministering to the residents of Bicentennial Towers. He even wanted to sing today. Despite his age, Dad still has a powerful singing voice! But I was too fearful of what might come out of his mouth, so I decided against letting him sing today. But I can't help but feel a little antsy. Hopefully, he will not have one of his outbursts."

Over in Serenity House, Sister Voyant, Miracle, Willie, Sharon, and James, just finished eating a hearty breakfast prepared by Sister Jackson, who also sat at the kitchen table. The group were sharing memories about their unforgettable graduation. The remarkable event has since been dubbed, "The Miracle at Serenity House." Hank returned to Clarksville and was not present. James, Willie, Sharon, and Miracle were now living elsewhere. Sister Jackson and Sister Voyant requested they all come today to welcome the incoming residents, who would be arriving soon. "That graduation was such a glorious day!" said Sister Voyant. "My Beloveds, we have been sitting here half the morning talking about that ceremony, and we are still talking about it!"

"Ain't that the truth!" exclaimed Sister Jackson. "But I ain't got much more time to spare. This is a very busy day. The new residents will arrive any moment, and I've also got to attend Dr. Madison's funeral."

"Are you singing during the services Mama Jackson?" asked James.

"No, I'm not singing at that man's funeral," said Sister Jackson, feeling an adrenaline of old emotions.

"You said that quite tersely," said James. "Dr. Madison was certainly beloved, well-known, and highly-talented. I enjoyed hearing him play...and will also be attending his funeral. Mama Jackson, did you have an issue with Dr. Madison?"

"I'll just say that I plan on paying my respects," said Sister Jackson. "I'll leave it at that."

"I saw the hearse parked out front," said Sharon. "I thought the undertaker and his staff would never stop bringing in flowers."

"The undertaker was Carlton Douglass," said Sister Jackson. "He handled the final arrangements for my husband, Roy."

"Speaking of your husband Roy," said James, "I've always wondered...how did you two meet?"

"Well James, I ain't got time to tell the whole story, but when I was incarcerated, Roy came to the jail with other members of United in Victory's Prison Ministry. "During one of those visits, he heard me sing. Afterwards, he came over and complimented me on my singing ability. We struck up a conversation and he began coming to the jail to personally minister to me. I began writing Roy every opportunity I got. We exercised every means we could to communicate, and he encouraged me during a very difficult time of my life. Eventually, we tied the knot."

"You got married in jail?" asked James.

"Yep," said Sister Jackson. "Pastor Just married us."

"Well, if Willie can keep his job here at the church, maybe one day we might do the same," smiled Sharon.

"And be faithful," James added.

"Maybe I will," said Willie, kissing Sharon on the forehead.

"What do you mean, maybe?" asked Sharon, elbowing Willie.

"Just kidding," said Willie, crossing his fingers behind his back.

"Has anyone spoken to Hank recently?" asked Miracle.

"I spoke to him a few days ago," said Willie. "He said moving back home with his parents was an adjustment, and that his father still isn't speaking to him. But on a brighter note, he told me he was enrolling in college. He was pretty excited about that."

"Some things take a little more time than others," said Sister Voyant. "I will keep Hank and his family in prayer. But it is a blessing to hear Hank plans to go to school. He often talked about wanting to attend college like he planned before his injury. I'm ecstatic to hear that he decided to do it!"

"And I'm going to cosmetology school to get my license!" said Sharon dancing.

"That's wonderful, my Beloved!" exclaimed Sister Voyant. "And Miracle…you look so vibrant and lovely. What are you doing these days?"

Smiling and looking at Sister Jackson, Miracle said, "I'm living with Mama Jackson…um…well my real mother. I'm also working with Mr. Jenkins…well…my new big brother to enroll at Coppin to become a social worker like him…to help people. He is also setting things up for me to speak to groups of young men and women…who like me…fell victim to human sex trafficking. Maybe one day…I'll even start a non-profit organization to help lots of people."

"That's my baby!" exclaimed Sister Jackson. "And you're gonna do it too sugar! Your testimony will help many! And Miracle, me, and Anthony are catching up on years of lost time…my Lil' Mike and Angel," she said jubilantly gazing at Miracle. "I know my Roy is smiling down from Heaven!"

"Indeed!" said Sister Voyant. "Indeed!"

"And as you all know," said James standing proudly. "I joined United in Victory, and now serve as a deacon!"

"That's right James!" said Sister Jackson. "Not to mention you joined the choir and teach Bible Study!"

"Praise the Lord!" said James. "Singing and teaching with more power and anointing than ever!"

"Amen! my Beloved!" said Sister Voyant. "And you are helping the church and Serenity House with ensuring all of its paperwork is in order."

"I am," proclaimed James. "No use letting all this legal expertise go to waste. Might as well use it."

"I am proud of you James," said Sister Voyant. "I am proud of all of you, my Beloveds."

"Sister Voyant, I am the happiest I have been in a long time!" announced James. "I thank God for what He is doing in all of our lives," he declared, looking around at the group. "He has brought us all a mighty long way and I am grateful! I will serve Him until the day I die!"

Knock! Knock! Knock!

"That's Mr. Jenkins and the new residents," said Sister Jackson. "Time to go and welcome them to Serenity House! I'm so happy you all agreed to be here today to share your Serenity House experience with them and provide encouragement. Now Willie and Sharon, I'm gonna need you two to clean the dishes. I won't have time. After we welcome the residents and help get them settled, I have to get dressed and over to the church for the funeral."

"Yes, Mama Jackson," said Sharon.

"Do they look like dishpan hands to you Mama Jackson?" asked Willie holding up his hands.

"Shut up Willie!" said the group, exiting the kitchen to meet the incoming residents, he and Sharon playfully sharing love taps.

Knock! Knock! Knock!

"Coming!" yelled Sister Jackson, the group now reaching the living room.

"I'll get the door," said James, sipping coffee from a mug.

"Why thank you James," said Sister Jackson.

Smiling, James opened the door, greeting the incoming residents.

"Welcome to –," said James, stopping abruptly in midsentence, after making eye contact with one of the people in the group. His mug fell from his hands, hitting the floor and breaking. Coffee splattered all over the floor.

"What's wrong James?!" asked Sister Jackson.

"It's…it's…it's…" stuttered James.

"It's who my Beloved?" asked Sister Voyant.

"J…J…J…Jack Reynolds!" James stammered, gazing at Mr. Reynolds, who was returning a petrified look. "The drunk driver who took the lives of my Pauline and Tiffany…"

Later that same morning

Over in the sanctuary, Dr. Madison's service was now at the midway point. A police motorcade awaited outside the church to escort the hundreds of mourners to King Memorial Park. While United in Victory could hold a thousand people, the sanctuary was packed to capacity. Usher Green who was busily moving about handing out fans and Kleenex, squeezed between Miss Jenkins and Sister Hatfield, drawing a nasty stare from Sister Hatfield.

"Don't come over here bothering me while Dr. Madison's service is going on Gertie," whispered Sister Jenkins.

"I just had to come over here and ask you about the Sunday all of this went down," said Usher Green. "How is it the church has a Nurse's Auxiliary and ain't one of them know CPR? What kind of mess is that? If I fall out in here like Dr. Madison did, please don't ask them to help!"

"Quiet Gertie," said Miss Jenkins, chewing her Spearmint gum and looking over her cat eye-style glasses. "When it's your time to go…it's your time to go. His time just came while he was up there playing those keys."

"I guess you're right," agreed Usher Green. "But why did they have Dr. Madison cremated?"

"I don't know," said Miss Jenkins. "I ain't used to attending services and not seeing a body." Looking around, she commented, "Just look at all of these peoples in here. I ain't seen some of them in many a year. And just look at that fake Mother Carter sitting up on the front pew smiling and showing her fake teeth! Fake! Just like she is!"

"Pleeeeeeeze don't start on that again!" said Usher Green. "We all know that Mother Carter joined this church before you did! Now let it go!"

"That's because you all went on Bishop' memory," said Miss Jenkins. "He knows just as well as I do that I joined this church before that lyin' Mother Carter!"

"Shhhhh!" said Usher Gilmore, walking over to them. "Stop all that talkin' over here during the service!"

"Look at Bishop sitting up there in the pulpit looking all around," said Miss Jenkins, lowering her tone. "He looks like he doesn't know what's going on! I tell you what! I hope he don't start cussin' and carryin' on and talkin' all that Michael Jackson mess up in here today!"

"I hope not either!" said Usher Green. "But if he does, you know I got my phone camera ready! Because as you know, I am the –"

"Yeah, yeah, the church historian," said Sister Jenkins. "Yeah right! You're Gossippin' Gertrude! That's who you are!"

"Whatever you say, Sister Two-Faced," laughed Usher Green. "Now I wonder who our new musician is going to be?"

"Quiet Gertie," said Miss Jenkins. "Pastor Just is walking back up to the pulpit. I tell you, he is doing a fine job officiating this service."

"We will now have Words of Comfort," said Pastor Just. "We have fifteen people scheduled to give Words of Comfort."

"Fifteen people!" Usher Green whispered to Miss Jenkins. "We'll be here all day!"

"This funeral is gonna be longer than Aretha Franklin's funeral!" replied Sister Jenkins.

"And that was about seven hours!"

"Quiet over here!" said Usher Gilmore.

"I'm going to ask all of those who are scheduled to give Words of Comfort to limit them to two minutes," said Pastor Just. "If you go over two-minutes, we will kindly ring the bell," said Pastor Just. "Show them the bell, Deacon Mayberry." Deacon Mayberry mumbled a few words and shook a small bell. "Now I don't want to ring the bell on anyone," continued Pastor Just, "So please limit your Words of Comfort to two minutes. With that, I call up our first speaker the Rev. Dr. –"

"I'm not on the program to speak, but I came a long way to get here, and I'm going to say what I came here to say!" said a loud voice from the rear of the church, prompting everyone to turn and look.

Miss Jenkins' mouth dropping open, the elder woman turned and looked at Usher Green. "Oh my God!" said Miss Jenkins. "I don't believe it! That's Sister Jackson's oldest daughter Earlene!"

"Something's about to go down!" said Usher Green, pulling out her cellphone.

Miss Jenkins peered over her glasses at Sister Jackson, who wore a look of great shock and surprise. Now stretching her neck to look at Earlene Jones, who was making her way up front, Miss Jenkins said, "It looks like the chickens have come home to roost."

From the Annals of United in Victory Church, would come its next saga — ***DisChord in The Choir: Pitch Please!***

I Rose ABOVE it all

By Ursula V. Battle

With the arrows of your words, you've shot me again
Piercing a piece of my heart so hard to mend,

You say success is something I'll never taste
Feasting on the sadness that besets my face,

You delight in seeing me in my lowest place
Pain and hurt you love to paste,

As if life were a piece of paper and you the glue
Affixing shapes of bitterness in all you do,

You say things to hurt me all the time
To dampen my spirit and poison my mind,

You seek to implode my confidence and esteem
As if I were a building toppling down from its beams,

Why do you look at me with malice in your eyes?
Hating that I dance with such soul in my thighs,

Why does it bother you that I jaunt with joy?
A stride full of confidence you seek to destroy,

But like the sun climbing towards its horizon
And an eagle soaring high
I too, will rise!

Like ocean water gushing in during morning tide
Upon a wave of hope I will continue to ride,

You seek to crush my spirit with your ploys and acts
Your words, your actions, your relentless attacks,

You swing words like an ax to chop me down
You the lumberjack, me…the tree hitting the ground,

You tell me I have nothing to offer at all,
Saying what you can to make me feel small,

With the words from your lips
You whip me with your lashes,

And with the lighter of your tongue
You burn me to ashes,

Despite your venomous spew
I hold my head up high!
Determined not to believe nar' one of your lies,

I have goals and dreams, inner treasures so rich!
But you seek to bury them all deep down in a ditch,

Aspirations you hope I never discover,
You throw me in a pit like Joseph's brothers,

Out of the cistern of your words, I will climb
It may seem unlikely, but give it some time,

You pummel me with your words to bring me
down in defeat,
But the Lord gives me strength to get back on my feet!

For my faith is in Him and not in you!
God is the One who will bring me through!

Like the song of the birds high up in the trees
I too will sing a melody as free as can be,

You foolishly believe I am ink, and you are the pen!
The author of my story 'til the very end,

Writing in the annals of your twisted mind
I will never escape from the lies of your binds,

That I'd never make it because of what you took,
But there's another ending to the story of my book!

Despite all you did to cause me to stumble and fall,
I'm here to tell you,
I rose…
I rose…
I rose…
ABOVE it all!

About the Author

Ursula V. Battle is an award-winning playwright, journalist, and entrepreneur. The CEO of Battle Stage Plays, LLC, the goals of her stage play productions are to uplift, inspire, educate, and encourage through sidesplitting comedy, unforgettable storylines, riveting drama, soul-stirring singing, and powerful ministry. The many stage plays she has penned include the highly acclaimed *Serenity House: From Addiction to Deliverance*, *My Big Phat Ghetto FABULE$$ Wedding*, *DisChord in The Choir: Pitch Please!*, *The Teachers' Lounge*, and *FOR BETTER OR WOR$E*. Her pieces are regularly performed at the prestigious Johns Hopkins University.

The native Baltimorean is a Magna Cum Laude graduate of Coppin State University, where she earned her bachelor's degree in English and a Minor in Journalism. Ursula received her master's degree from the University of Baltimore. She is also a graduate of the Broadcasting Institute of Maryland and Walbrook High School. The author is a Staff Writer for The Baltimore Times Newspaper and a former reporter for the Baltimore AFRO-American Newspaper. She has written extensively about addiction, and has covered Crime, Politics, Human Interest, and other areas. Ursula has been featured in several newspapers and magazines, and interviewed on radio, internet broadcasts, and other media.

Ursula is the recipient of numerous journalistic and creative writing awards including her selection as a Patapsco River (MD) Chapter of the Links Women in the Arts 2021: "Valiant Women of Freedom" and a "Leah's Book Club" Honoree. Other honors include the Maryland, DC Press Association and Society of Professional Journalist Award, The NAACP's "Thurgood Marshall Community Leadership" Award, Aunt Hattie's Place 'Hearts of Love' Award, Newsome Awards' "Playwright of the Year" Award, and induction into the Broadcasting Institute of Maryland's Hall of Fame.

She is the mother of three children and has two grandchildren. Her favorite scripture is **"For walk by faith, not by sight."** (2 Corinthians 5:7 KJV).

Website: www.battlestageplay.com. Twitter, and Instagram: @battlestageplays.
Facebook.com/SerenityHouseFromAddictiontoDeliveranceTheNovel.

Made in the USA
Columbia, SC
10 February 2024

555919ef-4b7c-4ff1-8ffe-cf067e1b6f46R01